The American Century
COOKBOOK

The American Century COOKBOOK ❖

THE MOST POPULAR RECIPES
OF THE 20TH CENTURY

JEAN ANDERSON

GRAMERCY BOOKS
NEW YORK

The publisher gratefully acknowledges the assistance of Barbara Kuck,
Director of the Culinary Archives and Museum at Johnson & Wales University.

Permissions appear on page 516.

This 2005 edition is published by Gramercy Books, an imprint of Random House Value Publishing,
by arrangement with Clarkson N. Potter/Publishers, a member of the Crown Publishing Group,
divisions of Random House, Inc., New York.

Gramercy is a registered trademark and the colophon is a trademark of Random House, Inc.

Random House
New York · Toronto · London · Sydney · Auckland
www.randomhouse.com

Interior book design by Jill Armus

Printed and bound in the United States.

Library of Congress Cataloging-in-Publication Data

Anderson, Jean, 1929-
The American century cookbook : the most popular recipes of the 20th century / Jean Anderson.
p. cm.
Includes bibliographical references and index.
ISBN 0-517-22598-0
1. Cookery, American. 2. Cookery—United States—History. 3. Food habits—
United States—History. I. Title.

TX715.A56642 2005
641.5973—dc22

2005040207

10 9 8 7 6 5 4 3 2 1

CONTENTS

SHELL FISH.

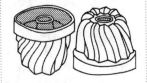

ACKNOWLEDGMENTS

THIS BOOK WOULD never have seen the light of day without the generous cooperation of archivists, home economists, and media people at the major food companies and manufacturers of appliances large and small. To list them all would require a book all its own. So I hope they will forgive me if I offer a blanket "thank you" to each and every one—you know who you are.

I am indebted, in addition, to these editors, food editors, and publicists, past and present, who gave me access to their back issues and who kept the tearsheets coming: Elizabeth Alston, *Woman's Day;* Myrna Blythe, *The Ladies' Home Journal;* Dale Brown, formerly *Time-Life Books;* Nancy Byal, *Better Homes and Gardens;* Tim Clark, *Yankee;* Dana Cowin, *Food & Wine;* Jerry Di Vecchio, *Sunset;* Malachy Duffy, formerly *Food & Wine;* Barbara Fairchild, *Bon Appétit;* William J. Garry, *Bon Appétit;* Mary Gunderson, *Farm Journal;* Judson D. Hale, Sr., *Yankee;* Lou Rena Hammond, Lou Hammond & Associates; Zack Hanle, *Bon Appétit;* Margaret Happel, formerly *Redbook;* Karen Haram, San Antonio *Express-News;* Joanne Lamb Hayes, *Country Living;* Jan Turner Hazard, *The Ladies' Home Journal;* Jean Hewitt, formerly *Family Circle,* and her capable assistant, Sheena Devine Gonzales; Sue B. Huffman, formerly The Food Network; Barbara Hunter, Hunter MacKenzie, Inc.; Peggy Katalinich, formerly *New York Newsday* and now *Family Circle;* Carole Lalli, formerly *Food & Wine;* Marcy MacDonald, *Bon Appétit;* Louis Mahoney, *Richmond Times-Dispatch;* Suzanne Martinson, *Pittsburgh Post-Gazette;* Helen Moore, columnist, *The Charlotte Observer* and Raleigh *News & Observer;* Debbie Moose, the Raleigh *News & Observer;* Sara Moulton, *Gourmet;* Georgia Orcutt, *The Old Farmer's Almanac Hearth & Home Companion* and *Good Cook's Companion;* Mardee Haidin Regan, formerly *Food & Wine;* Geraldine Rhoads, formerly *Woman's Day;* Bill Rice, *Chicago Tribune;* William P. Roenigk, National Broiler Council; Irene Sax, formerly *New York Newsday* and now Disney Online; Arthur Schwartz, formerly *Daily News* and now host, "Food Talk," WOR radio, New York; Bill Sertl, *Saveur;* Gloria Spitz, Burson-Marsteller; Ila Stanger, formerly *Food & Wine;* Zanne Early Stewart, *Gourmet;* Dot Tringali, formerly Newman Saylor & Gregory for the National Broiler Council; Tina Ujlaki, *Food & Wine;* Jeanne Voltz, formerly *Woman's Day;* Susan Sarao Westmoreland, *Good Housekeeping;* Jerry Wright, formerly Corning Glass Works; Gail Zweigenthal, *Gourmet.*

Special thanks go, too, to these relatives, friends, and colleagues who agreed to lend me rare early cookbooks from their private collections: Anne Lewis Anderson, James and Sharen Benenson, Catherine

Bigwood, Ruth Buchan, Narcisse Chamberlain, Marion Gorman, Joanne Lamb Hayes, Jeanne Lesem, Mary Lyons, Jack MacBean, Anne S. Mead, Neal O'Donnell (who shipped two weighty boxes to me from Corning, New York), and Ruth Stewart.

I would be remiss if I did not also thank food historians/writers Meryle Evans, Jim Fobel, Leslie Land, Anne Mendelson, Russ Parsons, and James Villas for dozens of valuable assists; colleagues Anne S. Anderson, Sandy Gluck, Maureen Luchejko, Karen Pickus, and Tracey Seaman for sharing their knowledge of food and/or recipes; Barbara Deskins for putting me in touch with key food people in Pittsburgh; my cousin William G. Anderson, formerly of Sunkist, for lugging a ton of company recipe booklets from Los Angeles to New York; Betty Buchan and York Kiker, for probing their memories of their early years at Ocean Spray Cranberries, and the North Carolina Department of Agriculture, respectively.

I owe Ella Elvin, formerly food editor of New York's *Daily News,* and Jean Todd Freeman, formerly asso-

ciate editor at *The Ladies' Home Journal,* more than I can say for endless hours of research and editorial advice. Deep gratitude goes, too, to Barbara Kuck, Director of the Culinary Archives and Museum at Johnson & Wales University, Providence, R.I., Barbara Haber, Curator of Books, The Schlesinger Library at Radcliffe College, and Alison Ryley, bibliographer for Cookery and Culinary History, New York Public Library, for going the extra mile. Also to Nach Waxman of Kitchen Arts & Letters, who answered every call, dug up the dozens of archival cookbooks I needed, and lent support almost from Day One. And to Margaret Gorenstein, who chased down every right, every permission.

Finally, I have been blessed with three of the most patient editors on earth—Barbara Greenman and Karen Murgolo of GuildAmerica Books and Roy Finamore of Clarkson Potter, who nudged but did not push. Blessed, too, with the most supportive literary agent, Barney Karpfinger. Thank you one and all. If I have forgotten anyone—and I pray not—a thousand apologies.

INTRODUCTION

FOR THE PAST TEN YEARS, I have been traveling backward in time. Back across the decades to 1900 and beyond. My quest: To trace this century's role in our culinary coming of age. To track the recipes, foods, food trends, food people, appliances, and gadgets that have had an impact on our lives from 1900 onward.

For starters, there were plenty of surprises. Many of the recipes I'd considered twentieth-century creations actually surfaced last century: Angel Food Cake, Baked Alaska, Eggs Benedict, Lobster Newburg, Potato Chips, Salisbury Steak, and Waldorf Salad to name a few.

Baking powder belongs to the nineteenth century as do graham (whole-wheat) and self-rising flours, margarine, Tabasco Sauce, saccharin, sweetened condensed milk, compressed yeast, canned deviled ham, even Jell-O and peanut butter, although these last two certainly did not become popular until after the turn of the century. Indeed, Jell-O barely survived the 1890s.

Has any century done more to revolutionize the way we cook, the way we eat, than the twentieth? I doubt it.

Take the home kitchen. At the beginning of this century, women were still cooking on stoves fueled by wood, coal, or petroleum, cantankerous behemoths that demanded constant stoking, cleaning, prodding, and pleading.

Fast-forward to 1939 and the New York World's Fair. Women were dazzled by General Electric's "kitchen of tomorrow." A G.E. Fair booklet ad read:

With a dishwasher so very fast and sanitary
She'd never break another dish—'twas plain
And the work she most despised was completely
*   modernized*
When the garbage went like magic—down the drain.

Only in this century did home kitchens go gas and/or electric. That meant electric refrigerators instead of iceboxes (for a while there were also "silent" gas refrigerators). It meant trim, easy-to-clean electric ranges or gas ranges with automatic electric ignition. It meant electric dishwashers and garbage disposals . . . microwave and convection ovens . . . food processors, electric mixers, and blenders . . . electric slow cookers, skillets, and woks . . . electric toasters, griddles, and waffle irons . . . electric coffeemakers, hot trays, can openers, knife sharpeners, even electric carving knives. Toward the end of the century it also meant electric fruit and vegetable juicers, automatic pasta, bread, and ice cream machines. What would great-grandmother have thought?

In the 1960s, kitchens began to go glamorous, to become the status symbol of ambitious cooks and hostesses. Designers went all out creating the chic look of "country French, Italian, or Scandinavian."

In the '70s and '80s, state-of-the-art stainless steel institutional equipment topped the list of must-haves, brick ovens returned to the kitchen, charcoal grills arrived along with wine storage coolers, boiling water taps, and refrigerators that dispensed ice cubes and ice water through the door.

The twentieth century also gave us the pressure cooker, aluminum foil, plastic wrap, national cook-offs (from chicken and chili to cakes and cookies), food magazines, the TV chef, and not least, the twenty-four-hour television Food Network.

Food advances were no less revolutionary. Ice cream cones, "hot dogs and hamburgers all the way" entered our lives as did salad and sushi bars, fast-food chains, frozen and freeze-dried foods, and TV dinners—to say nothing of instants and mixes galore. There was a proliferation, too, of the kinds of food put into cans, of herbs, spices, herb and spice blends, of ersatz salts and powders.

But most of all, the twentieth century was the era when the average American began to appreciate the foreign cuisines once enjoyed only by those who could afford to travel or buy imported delicacies from France, Italy, and elsewhere. By the 1960s, jet travel had put the world within easy reach at prices nearly everyone could afford.

Until this century what most of us ate was the bland, boring stuff of our British forebears. "My mother never allowed onions in her kitchen, let alone *garlic*," a Waspy New England friend told me recently. She—the friend, not the mother—now adores both.

The colorful fare of Italy and Middle and Eastern Europe, originally confined to big-city immigrant enclaves, began to "go national" during the early decades of this century, then after World War II, reached "Our Towns" across the country. Who knew pizza before the 1940s and 1950s? Who knew the satiny Jewish-style cheesecake? Who knew borscht? For that matter, who knew quiche Lorraine, croissants, or Danish pastry?

Not that we lived in a gastronomic void before the twentieth century. Far from it. But for most Americans, cooking was more necessity than hobby. The rich not only employed live-in cooks but also dined lavishly at the nation's finest hotels and restaurants —Delmonico's in New York, Antoine's in New Orleans, the Tremont House in Boston, the Palmer House in Chicago, the Brown Palace in Denver, the Palace Hotel in San Francisco. They roamed the Continent, too, pigging out in London, Paris, Rome, Vienna, and elsewhere. For the middle and lower classes, however, putting three "squares" on the table every day, often for whopping families, was a chore.

Around the turn of the century, as domestics began leaving home service for better-paying jobs in factories, upper-class women found it necessary to learn to cook, too. There to guide them was Fannie Merritt Farmer of the Boston Cooking School.

Often called "the mother of modern measurements" because she banished such quaint (and imprecise) phraseology as "butter the size of an egg," Fannie Farmer produced the book that eased the cook's entry into the "more scientific" twentieth-century kitchen. In truth, Fannie Farmer's *Boston Cooking-School Cook Book* (1896) was an outgrowth of *Mrs. Lincoln's Boston Cook Book* (1883) by Mary J. Lincoln, who preceded Miss Farmer at the Boston Cooking School. By 1902, Fannie Farmer had opened her own cooking school in Boston, and by 1905 she had become food editor of *Woman's Home Companion*.

Almost as visible was her contemporary, Sarah Tyson Rorer, principal of the Philadelphia Cooking School and to my mind, a more imaginative cook than Fannie Farmer. For a time Mrs. Rorer was the food editor of the Philadelphia-based *Ladies' Home Journal* and, like Fannie Farmer, was quick to endorse products she liked—Knox Gelatine and Pyrex glass baking dishes, to name two.

Fannie Farmer died in 1915, but Ida Bailey Allen, a Chatauqua lecturer, took the stage, and throughout the teens, '20s, '30s, and '40s churned out cookbooks, lectured, wrote newspaper and magazine columns, endorsed products, and generally kept her name before the public.

Many of the recipes our mothers and grandmothers loved were product-driven: canned-soup casseroles, molded salads, mayonnaise cakes, graham cracker crusts, even chocolate chip cookies. We may scoff at the hokier of these today, but they belong to this century's culinary history and cannot be ignored. Moreover, as a riffle through any regional cookbook quickly proves, they remain popular over much of the country.

In the 1930s (despite the Depression) and continuing into the 1940s (despite World War II), new voices began to be heard. First there was Irma S. Rombauer, an engaging St. Louis widow of genteel German stock, who gathered up the recipes of family, friends, and acquaintances and paid to have them published in book form in 1931. *The Joy of Cooking,* she called the collection. In 1936, the Bobbs-Merrill Company of Indianapolis brought out a commercial edition of *Joy,* introducing thousands of Americans to a culinary free spirit who made cooking seem less scientific and more fun. Much of this had to do with Rombauer's innovative recipe style, which interwove directions and ingredients. Rombauer might begin:

Split and remove the bones from:
  A 4 pound white fish,

  Then,

Flatten it out. Rub it inside and out with:
  Salt,
  Paprika,
  Butter . . .

In this way, Irma Rombauer took her readers by the hand and led them through each step of a recipe. This easy style plus the author's considerable charm made the 1943 edition of *Joy* a national best-seller.

But more sophisticated voices were beginning to be heard, too, the voices of well-educated, well-traveled men and women, many of whom had lived abroad.

There were James Beard, Lucius Beebe *(Town & Country),* Samuel Chamberlain (aka Phineas Beck, *Gourmet*), Pearl Metzelthin (*Gourmet's* first editor), and John MacPherson (radio's "Mystery Chef"). There were Sheila Hibben *(The New Yorker),* June Platt *(House & Garden),* Ann Batchelder *(The Ladies' Home Journal),* M.F.K. Fisher *(The New Yorker),* Clementine Paddleford *(The New York Herald Tribune),* Jeanne Owen (the International Wine & Food Society), and Mary Grosvenor Ellsworth *(House Beautiful),* to recognize a few.

Early in the 1950s—in some quarters at least—it became chic *not* to cook. I remember my Raleigh, North Carolina, school chums bragging that they "couldn't boil water." The suggestion being that they had cooks to do the job. In fact many did. The '50s anticooking vogue produced Poppy Cannon's *Can-Opener Cook Book* (1951) and spilled over into the 1960s with Peg Bracken's best-seller, *The I Hate To Cook Book* (1960).

But this was soon to change. Craig Claiborne, once firmly ensconced as food news editor at *The New York Times,* shook up the old order of food reporting. For years many magazine food editors, and to a lesser extent their newspaper counterparts, had bowed ever so discreetly to the demands of advertisers. Their recipes would showcase new prepared foods, new seasonings, new pans, new appliances. Never by brand names. But "generics" were permissible.

Claiborne's voice, on the other hand, was international, authoritative. He loaded the *Times* with an ethnic sampler and set the recipes down so simply they seemed doable to all but the worst klutz. In 1961, *The New York Times Cook Book,* edited by Claiborne, came off the press. Unlike the cookbooks we knew, it was global in scope, a compilation not only of recipes published during his own hitch at the paper but also during those of his predecessors: Food news editor Jane

Nickerson, home economist Ruth P. Casa-Emellos, food news reporters June Owen, Nan Ickeringill, and Anne-Marie Schiro. More than one reviewer praised the book to the skies and in print.

Then along came Julia Child. In 1962 "The French Chef" PBS television series began airing. At first, many of us found comic relief watching the accident-prone cook with the high-pitched voice. Then we fell in love with Julia and began to take her seriously. She had much to teach us, we were eager acolytes, and we soon added *Mastering the Art of French Cooking,* Volumes I and II, to our kitchen libraries. Although James Beard had already had a television series, it was Julia Child who won our hearts and set the style of cooking shows to follow.

From the mid-'60s well into the '70s, the counter-culture flourished, vegetarianism became a major movement and before long, tofu and granola, brown rice, and sprouted grains landed at the corner supermarket. So did organic fruits and vegetables. The '70s also saw the ascent of peppery Szechuan and Hunan cooking, which for a time eclipsed the delicate Cantonese, the only Chinese cuisine most Americans knew. More important, this decade launched a new wave of young American chefs pledged to the simple preparation of garden-fresh produce, among them Alice Waters whose Chez Panisse restaurant—opened in 1971 in Berkeley, California—helped redefine American cooking.

The '80s brought conspicuous consumption, show-off chefs, glitz-and-flash restaurants, and a passion for nearly everything Italian (including the cookbooks of Marcella Hazan and Giuliano Bugialli). But Tex-Mex was gaining ground.

By the '90s, our love of things Italian had broadened to include the whole of the Mediterranean Basin. Thai food was grabbing our attention, too, as well as "fusion" (Franco/Asian) and something called Pacific Rim (the marriage of Asian spice and fresh Hawaii/California flavors).

Concurrently, nutritionists told us to "hold the fat,"

"hold the cholesterol," "cut down on calories." There were diets *du jour,* dozens of them, but none worked over the long haul. And inevitably, there was a ballooning of spas and health and fitness clubs.

Now we're on a nostalgia kick, returning—part time, at least—to our roots and the comfort of Grandma's rib-sticking best.

Any culinary history of the twentieth century must, by its very nature, be an anthology of sorts. I did not personally create every one of the recipes that came into our kitchens from 1900 onward. So what you will find in these pages are many "old friends"— recipes from the cookbooks, magazines, newspaper food sections, chefs, cooking-school teachers, television chefs, and, yes, food companies—that were (and in many cases, still are) major players.

However, you will also find scores of my own recipes here plus scores more from my mother, grandmothers, and aunts—inventive cooks, all—who passed their yellowing, well-thumbed, handwritten file cards on to me (it's easy to tell the family favorites—they're splattered with grease or chocolate). Many of these family recipes date back to the opening years of this century, proceed right through the '60s, and when reviewed as a group, constitute a culinary timeline all their own.

What does the twenty-first century promise? Perhaps more light will be shed on the cooking of Africa, in particular on that of Egypt, Angola, and South Africa. Perhaps there will be an upsurge of interest in the cuisines of Argentina, Brazil, Chile, Colombia, and Venezuela. Perhaps robots will be running our kitchens. Perhaps printed cookbooks will go the way of the wood stove and our recipes will have to be downloaded from cyberspace. Perhaps fat pills or gene-splicing will make us all our old sylphs again. I'm no culinary Cassandra, so it's hard to tell.

But unless we begin gardening on the moon, we're not likely to top the culinary ride that began in 1900.

JEAN ANDERSON
New York, New York

HOW TO USE THIS BOOK

✳ Unless otherwise specified, flour is all-purpose flour, sifted *before* measuring, scooped *lightly* into a cup for measuring dry ingredients (no tamping), and leveled off with the edge of a thin-blade spatula or knife.

✳ Sugar, unless otherwise specified, is granulated sugar. If more than one kind of sugar is used in a recipe, both types will be specified. For example: 1 cup granulated sugar; ¼ cup confectioners' sugar.

✳ If a recipe says "brown sugar," use light or dark. If one or the other is preferable, recipes will specify. Always pack the sugar into the measuring cup and level off with the edge of a spatula.

✳ Do not substitute margarine or vegetable shortening for butter unless a recipe offers them as alternate ingredients. Both have greater shortening power (and usually less flavor) than butter and may, in some instances, produce a less-than-perfect product. Whenever a recipe does specify shortening, pack it into the measuring cup, then level the top with the edge of a spatula.

NOTE: *As for salted butter vs. unsalted, our mothers and grandmothers were more likely to have used the salted because it kept longer and was more widely available. But choose whichever one you prefer. The salt—or lack of it—will not sabotage a recipe.*

✳ Lard is rendered pork fat, not vegetable shortening.

✳ All eggs are extra-large.

CAUTION: *Cold gelatin mousses, chiffon pies, and Caesar Salad all use raw eggs. I have not altered the original recipes but do warn you about the possibility of salmonella contamination of some eggs and urge you to know that your eggs are safe before trying such recipes. There are two ways to make "safe" egg-white chiffon pies and gelatin mousses: (1) Fold in a Swiss (cooked) meringue (recipes appear in many basic cookbooks and most comprehensive dessert or baking books) instead of a raw meringue. Or (2) use dehydrated egg whites or meringue powder according to package directions. Bakery supply houses sell both as do some specialty food shops and upscale supermarkets.*

✳ Baking powder is double-acting.

✳ Black pepper should be freshly ground. If a recipe calls for white pepper, the commercially ground is acceptable.

✳ Lemon, orange, and lime juice should be freshly squeezed.

✳ Unless noted, all garlic cloves are medium-size.

NOTE: *Many '40s, '50s, and even '60s recipes call for garlic salt or powder, but you may prefer to use fresh garlic. For the record: 1/4 teaspoon garlic powder = 1 clove garlic, peeled and minced or crushed; 1/4 teaspoon garlic salt = 1 clove garlic, peeled and minced or crushed + 1/4 teaspoon salt; 1/2 teaspoon bottled minced garlic = 1 clove.*

✳ Do not make recipe ingredient substitutions unless alternates are suggested.

✳ Always use the pan, casserole, or mold size and shape specified. They are critical to the recipe's success.

✳ Preheat the oven fifteen full minutes before baking or roasting.

✳ Preheat the broiler ten full minutes before broiling.

✳ "Cool" means to bring something hot to room temperature.

✳ "Chill" means to refrigerate something or to set in an ice bath until uniformly cold.

APPETIZERS
SNACKS

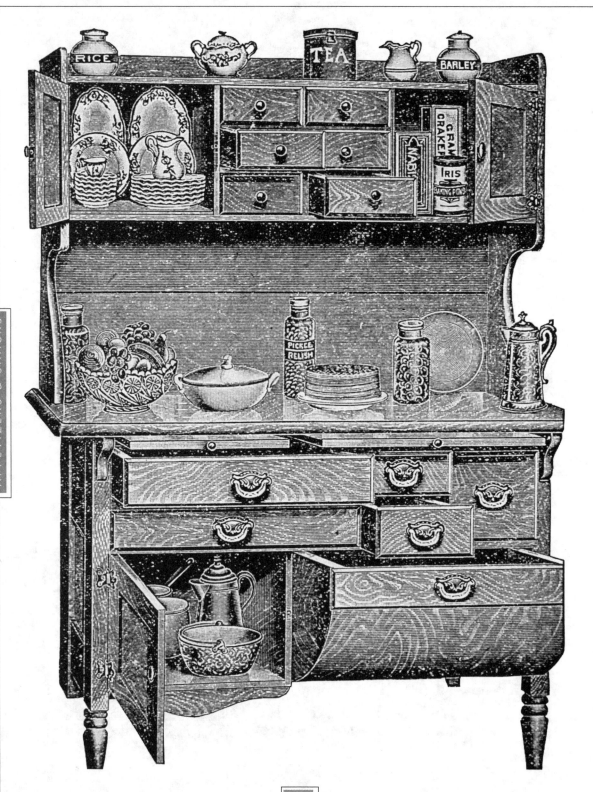

BITE-SIZE PARTY morsels appear to be a twentieth-century phenomenon. Not that American hostesses of the nineteenth century and earlier didn't serve appetizers. They did. But these consisted mostly of soups, oysters on the half shell, or canapés (usually dainty open-face sandwiches), served mainly at table.

Here's Fannie Farmer on the subject (*Boston Cooking-School Cook Book,* 1896): "Canapés are served hot or cold and used in place of oysters at dinner or luncheon. At a gentleman's dinner, they are served with a glass of sherry before entering the dining room."

Fannie's roster of canapés is both small and lackluster: Toast strewn with grated cheese and cayenne, then baked; toast spread with sardine paste, anchovy butter, or a Lorenzo (crab) salad.

Still, I find no early-twentieth-century cookbook with a larger collection of appetizers—until the 1906 edition of *Fannie,* which adds a few new flavored butters and spreads.

APPETIZERS & SNACKS

Indeed, many cookbooks of the period avoided the subject altogether.

By the teens and 1920s, hostesses were making "marbles" of seasoned, mashed, canned tuna and rolling them in minced parsley. They were also stuffing celery. Ida C. Bailey Allen tells her fans (*Mrs. Allen's Cook Book,* 1917) to "Select tender celery, trim the ends square, and fill the grooves with sardine paste made according to the proportions given for making tuna fish balls. . . . Chill and cut in two-inch strips." By the time she wrote *Vital Vegetables,* ten years later, Mrs. Allen recommends stuffing celery with cream cheese flavored with everything from Roquefort to chopped salted nuts to minced pimiento to green bell pepper. She has also become an advocate of cream cheese balls.

In *Hors d'Oeuvre and Canapés* (1940), James Beard suggests that American cocktail appetizers evolved from the free nibbles set out on bars and further suggests Cal-

ifornia as a probable source. On the other hand, John Mariani (*The Dictionary of American Food and Drink,* Revised Edition, 1994), points to Prohibition, which, he says, gave rise to the home cocktail party. The Eighteenth ("prohibition") Amendment to the Constitution, passed in 1919, went into effect in 1920.

Anne Mendelson, a food historian and writer for whom I have enormous respect, agrees that Prohibition launched cocktail finger foods. In *Stand Facing the Stove* (1996), her engrossing biography of Irma S. Rombauer and Marion Rombauer Becker, the mother-and-daughter team who gave us *The Joy of Cooking,* she writes that Prohibition "cemented a new relationship between eating and drinking, driving hard liquor from the male bastion of the saloon into the home and creating an urgent need for handy, smart foods to soak up booze—preferably filling foods with assertive flavors."

She adds that this proliferation of nibbles led to a general confusion about the difference between appetizers, hors d'oeuvre, and canapés, a befuddlement obvious in the original *Joy of Cooking.*

"The new popularity of cocktail parties," Mendelson continues, "whether powered by good bootleg liquor or bathtub swill, further boosted the popularity of cocktail tidbits and spurred the invention of easier spinoffs on the old canapé idea."

Though Prohibition ended in 1933, the cocktail party —and thus bite-size nibbles—were slow to reach Grass Roots America, perhaps because many Christian denominations continued to damn alcohol, particularly in the "Bible Belt" of the South. Whatever the reason, finger foods seem not to have come of age until after the first third of this century. There's a dearth of recipes for them in women's magazines and cookbooks right through the 1930s. I'm not talking tea sandwiches, cream cheese balls, and stuffed celery, for which there were recipes aplenty; I'm talking *serious,* grown-up cocktail fare.

Then, as now, food trends radiated from sophisticated metropolitan areas outward into the heartland. That's the case, certainly, with bite-size appetizers and snacks. I believe that the big change began, albeit on a small scale, in New York City in the late 1930s when at the suggestion of *bon vivant* Lucius Beebe, James Beard and Bill and Irma Rhode opened a catering shop devoted exclusively to buffet and cocktail food.

Beard's breakthrough cookbook, *Hors d'Oeuvre and Canapés,* was published in 1940, and the fact that it is still in print more than half a century later says something about our commitment to party food. Because not every American knew what an hors d'oeuvre was, Beard began his book with this explanation: "The hors d'oeuvre is a rite rather than a course and its duty is to enchant the eye, please the palate, and excite the flow of gastric juices. . . ."

Today, cookbooks, food magazines, and women's magazines, to say nothing of food-company brochures and newspaper food sections of substance, offer dozens of recipes for hors d'oeuvre, appetizers, and snacks. The list is long—and lengthening. What follow are some of the best that surfaced this century.

Oysters Bienville

Makes 6 Servings

❋

UNLIKE OYSTERS ROCKEFELLER (right), an earlier American classic created at Antoine's in New Orleans, this recipe is no longer secret. According to Antoine's present proprietor, Roy F. Guste, Jr., Oysters Bienville was created about 1940 by his grandfather Roy Alciatore and his chef of many years, Pete Michel. Guste adds that the dish was named for Jean Baptiste LeMoyne, Sieur de Bienville, who in 1718 "with the help of eighty French exiles, cleared some wilderness near the mouth of the river [Mississippi] and established La Nouvelle Orleans." The recipe here is adapted from Guste's *Antoine's Restaurant Since 1840 Cookbook* (1980).

BÉCHAMEL SAUCE
3 tablespoons butter
3 tablespoons flour
2 cups warm scalded milk
½ teaspoon salt (or to taste)
⅛ teaspoon white pepper (or to taste)

BIENVILLE SAUCE
¼ cup (½ stick) butter
1½ cups minced green bell pepper (about 2 medium)
1 cup minced scallions (10 to 12 large scallions)
2 cloves garlic, peeled and minced
½ cup dry white wine
½ cup chopped pimiento
Béchamel Sauce (above)
⅔ cup shredded American cheese
½ cup fine soft bread crumbs
½ teaspoon salt (or to taste)
⅛ teaspoon white pepper (or to taste)

OYSTERS
3 dozen raw oysters on the half shell
6 (9-inch) pie pans filled with rock salt
Bienville Sauce (above)

1. BÉCHAMEL SAUCE: Melt butter in small heavy saucepan over moderate heat. Blend in flour and cook, stirring, until foamy—1 to 2 minutes. Whisk in milk and cook, stirring constantly, until thickened and smooth—3 to 5 minutes. Season to taste with salt and pepper, cover, and keep warm.

2. BIENVILLE SAUCE: Melt butter in large heavy saucepan over moderate heat. Add green pepper, scallions, and garlic and sauté until glassy—2 to 3 minutes. Add wine and bring to boiling. Add pimiento, Béchamel, cheese, bread crumbs, salt, and pepper to taste and simmer slowly, stirring often, until very thick —about 15 minutes.

3. OYSTERS: Preheat oven to 400° F. Bed 6 oysters in each pan of rock salt. Cover each oyster with Bienville Sauce and bake, uncovered, until bubbly and tipped with brown —about 10 minutes. Serve at once at the start of an elegant meal.

OYSTERS ROCKEFELLER

ALTHOUGH JULES ALCIATORE of Antoine's Restaurant in New Orleans concocted them in 1899, these oysters on the half shell baked under a puree of greens really belong to the twentieth century because only then did word of them spread beyond the Louisiana parishes to become a "household name."

Even today, the recipe remains a mystery, although chefs have tried for years to "crack" it. Most make Oysters Rockefeller with spinach, which according to Roy F. Guste, Jr., Alciatore's great-grandson, is dead wrong.

Guste does not include a recipe for *Huîtres en Coquille à la Rockefeller* in *Antoine's Restaurant Since 1840 Cookbook* (1980), but he does have this to say about it:

Oysters Rockefeller was created in 1899 by my great-grandfather Jules Alciatore. At that time there was a shortage of snails coming in from Europe to the United States and Jules was looking for a replacement. He wanted this replacement to be local in order to avoid any difficulty in procuring the product. He chose oysters.

Jules was a pioneer in the art of cooked oysters, as they were rarely cooked before this time. He created a sauce with available green vegetable products, producing such a richness that he named it after one of the wealthiest men in the United States, John D. Rockefeller.

The original recipe is still a secret that I will not divulge. As many times as I have seen recipes printed in books and articles, I can honestly say that I have never found the original outside Antoine's. If you care to concoct your version, I would tell you only that the sauce is basically a puree of a number of green vegetables other than spinach.

Bonne Chance!

1900–10

Jell-O goes mainstream.

1900

Sugar is spun into cotton candy.

Hershey manufactures a milk chocolate bar.

1901

At the New York Polo Grounds, a frankfurter served in a heated bun with assorted condiments starts an American passion.

First edition of *The Settlement Cook Book,* a slender, 174-page fund-raiser edited by Mrs. Simon Kander and called *The Way to a Man's Heart,* is published in Milwaukee.

1902

Fannie Farmer establishes her own cooking school in Boston.

OYSTERS KIRKPATRICK

....

NEW ORLEANS may have its Oysters Rockefeller and Bienville, but San Francisco can point with pride to Oysters Kirkpatrick. According to Helen Evans Brown (*Helen Brown's West Coast Cook Book,* 1952), this Palace Hotel creation is named for John C. Kirkpatrick, who managed the hotel in the early 1900s. There are many variations on the theme, but the original, which the hotel sent to Brown, goes like this:

Open oysters on deep shell, put in oven for about 3 or 4 minutes until oysters shrink. Pour off the liquor, then add a small strip of bacon and cover with catsup and place in very hot oven for about 5 to 6 minutes (according to oven) until glazed to a nice golden brown.

Many chefs now prefer to bed raw oysters on the half shell in pie pans of rock salt (see Oysters Bienville). They may also mix a little finely diced green bell pepper with the ketchup, perhaps a bit of scallion, too, and spoon this mixture on the oysters before adding the bacon (partially cooked) and, sometimes, a few shreds of cheese and a dot or two of butter. Then it's into a 450°F oven until browned and bubbling.

SHELL FISH.

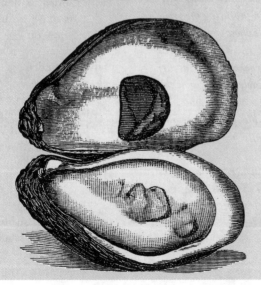

Clams Casino

Makes 4 Servings

✳

A NEW YORK restaurant recipe, specifically one dreamed up at the Casino at Narragansett Pier in 1917 for a luncheon society mover-and-shaker Mrs. Paran Stevens was giving. She had asked Maître d'Hôtel Julius Keller to create a special dish for her party. His inspiration: Clams on the half shell baked with bacon, shallots, green bell pepper, lemon juice, and assorted other seasonings. "What do you call it?" Mrs. Stevens asked. To which Keller replied, "I shall call it Clams Casino in honor of this restaurant." The version here is adapted from one Elaine Hanna and I developed for *The Doubleday Cookbook* (1975).

> 4 (9-inch) pie pans filled with rock salt
> 2 dozen raw cherrystone clams on the half shell
> ¼ cup (½ stick) butter or margarine, at room temperature
> 1 teaspoon anchovy paste
> 1 tablespoon fresh lemon juice
> ¼ cup minced green bell pepper
> 2 tablespoons minced shallots
> 2 tablespoons minced pimiento
> 6 slices bacon, each cut crosswise into 4 equal pieces, partially cooked, and drained

1. Dampen rock salt with water, set pans in oven, and preheat to 450°F.

2. Bed six clams in salt in each pan. Quickly blend butter, anchovy paste, and lemon juice until smooth and slip ½ teaspoon under each clam. Mix green pepper, shallots, and pimiento and sprinkle evenly over clams. Top with bacon.

3. Bake uncovered until bacon is crisp and nicely browned—6 to 7 minutes. Serve at once.

Crabmeat Remick

Makes 6 to 8 Servings

❋

IN 1940, on the fiftieth anniversary of the opening of the Plaza, *New York Times* food news reporter June Owen profiled the luxury hotel for her paper. Her article included the recipe for this Plaza classic, created in 1920 by Chef Albert Leopold Lattard to honor William H. Remick, then president of the New York Stock Exchange. The recipe here is liberally adapted from *The New York Times Cook Book* (1961), edited by Craig Claiborne.

6 slices bacon
1 pound lump or backfin crabmeat, bits of shell and cartilage removed
1⅔ cups mayonnaise
½ cup chili sauce or ketchup
2 teaspoons tarragon vinegar
1 teaspoon dry mustard
¾ teaspoon paprika
½ teaspoon celery salt
¼ teaspoon hot red pepper sauce
Pinch dried leaf tarragon, crumbled

1. Preheat oven to 375° F. Butter 6 to 8 crab or scallop shells or shallow individual ramekins and set aside.

2. Fry bacon in medium heavy skillet over moderate heat until crisp and brown—3 to 5 minutes. Drain on paper towels, crumble, and set aside.

3. Divide crab evenly among shells, set on large baking sheet and top with crumbled bacon, again dividing evenly. Bake uncovered just until warmed through—about 10 minutes.

4. Meanwhile, whisk together mayonnaise, chili sauce, vinegar, dry mustard, paprika, celery salt, red pepper sauce, and tarragon.

5. Remove crab from oven and preheat broiler. Quickly cover crab with mayonnaise mixture.

6. Broil 5 to 6 inches from heat just until bubbly and tipped with brown —2 to 3 minutes. Serve at once.

Marinated Shrimp

Makes 8 Servings

❋

IN THE early '60s, marinated shrimp were on every cocktail table, it seemed. The simplest version was nothing more than cooked shelled and deveined shrimp marinated in a good bottled Italian dressing with, perhaps, the garlic souped up a bit. I prefer this recipe of Anne Anderson's (no relation), whose husband was editor-in-chief of three magazines where I worked in the '60s and '70s (*The Ladies' Home Journal, Venture,* and *Diversion*). Anne, too, was an editor, working at different times for *Better Homes & Gardens, Woman's Day,* and *House Beautiful.* She says that the beauty of this appetizer is that it can be made with frozen shrimp and rustled up for "emergency guests."

1 tablespoon minced fresh ginger
1 teaspoon light brown sugar
½ cup Japanese soy sauce
¼ cup dry sherry
2 tablespoons vegetable oil
2 large cloves garlic, peeled and minced
1½ pounds shelled and deveined raw shrimp or 2 (12-ounce) packages frozen shelled and deveined raw shrimp

1. Mix ginger and sugar in medium mixing bowl. Slowly whisk in soy sauce, sherry, and oil, then stir in garlic.

2. Add shrimp and turn to coat all over with marinade. Cover and marinate in refrigerate for at least 1 hour but better yet, overnight.

3. Heat large heavy nonstick skillet over moderately high heat 1 minute. Add shrimp and marinade to skillet all at once and stir-fry just until shrimp are pink—3 to 4 minutes.

4. Serve shrimp hot, topped with a little of the marinade. Put out toothpicks so everyone can help himself.

Chef Paul Prudhomme's Cajun Popcorn with Sherry Wine Sauce

Makes 12 Servings

＊

FEW YOUNG American chefs exploded onto the '70s scene with greater impact than Cajun Paul Prudhomme, who cooked his way around the U.S., then returned to New Orleans to work as corporate chef for the Brennan family (Brennan's, Commander's Palace, etc.). In 1979, Chef Paul opened his own place, K-Paul's Louisiana Kitchen, and in no time crowds were lined up on the sidewalk waiting to get in. Among his signature dishes are these crispy-fried crawfish, which he calls "Cajun popcorn." Chef Paul serves them with a sherry dipping sauce, but many people prefer to gobble them *sans* sauce. Suit yourself. This recipe is adapted from *Chef Paul Prudhomme's Louisiana Kitchen* (1984).

CAJUN POPCORN

2 eggs, well beaten
1¼ cups milk
½ cup corn flour
½ cup all-purpose flour
1 teaspoon sugar
1 teaspoon salt
½ teaspoon onion powder
½ teaspoon garlic powder
½ teaspoon white pepper
½ teaspoon ground hot red pepper (cayenne)
¼ teaspoon dried leaf thyme, crumbled
⅛ teaspoon dried leaf basil, crumbled
⅛ teaspoon black pepper
Vegetable oil for deep frying
2 pounds peeled crawfish tails, small shrimp, or lump crab, picked over

NOTE: Corn flour is available in specialty groceries and health food stores. Pale gold in color, it is as fine and feathery as regular flour; do not substitute cornmeal.

SHERRY WINE SAUCE

1 egg yolk
¼ cup ketchup
3 tablespoons minced scallions
2 tablespoons dry sherry
1 teaspoon Creole or brown mustard
¼ teaspoon salt
¼ teaspoon white pepper
¼ teaspoon hot red pepper sauce
½ cup vegetable oil

1. CAJUN POPCORN: Mix eggs and milk in small bowl. Mix corn flour, flour, sugar, and all seasonings in large bowl. Whisk in half of egg mixture, then whisk in balance. Let stand at room temperature 1 hour.

2. Pour oil to a depth of 1 inch in large heavy skillet and heat to 370° F. Coat seafood with batter and fry in batches until crisply golden on both sides—about 2 minutes total. Do not crowd skillet. Drain on paper towels.

CAUTION: The sauce contains raw egg yolk, so be sure to use eggs you know to be safe.

3. SHERRY WINE SAUCE: Place all ingredients except oil in electric blender cup or food processor fitted with metal chopping blade and churn until smooth—about 30 seconds. With motor running, add oil in thin, steady stream, then continue churning 1 minute more until fluffy.

4. To serve, put out bowl of "popcorn" and second small bowl of sauce for dipping.

Buffalo Chicken Wings

Makes 4 to 6 Servings

✳

Few twentieth-century appetizers caught fire like this one, versions of which began appearing in cookbooks in the 1970s. The original, it's said, comes from the Anchor Bar in Buffalo, New York, and was first served in 1964. Yet Janice Okun, food editor of the *Buffalo News,* attributes Buffalo Chicken Wings to no one in particular in *Food Editors' Hometown Favorites Cookbook* (1984): "They are served in all bars and corner taverns, as well as in 'fancy' restaurants and pizza joints. Naturally, no restaurateur is about to divulge his recipe, so we set out to make our own—spying and tasting like mad. After many, many tries, we came up with a recipe with fourteen different ingredients . . . we printed it and the recipe was a fair success." Okun then goes on to say that two years later, a reader submitted this recipe. "What do you know? An exact duplicate of restaurant chicken wings. Simplicity and perfection combined." In closing, Okun writes that in Buffalo, "chicken wings are always served with celery sticks and Blue Cheese Dressing. No one knows why, but it is part of the ritual. Use the dressing recipe given, or a commercial blue cheese dressing." Here, then, is an adaptation of the *Buffalo News* recipe, which was reprinted in *Food Editors' Hometown Favorites Cookbook.*

BLUE CHEESE DRESSING

2 tablespoons minced yellow onion
1 clove garlic, peeled and minced
¼ cup minced parsley
1 cup mayonnaise
½ cup sour cream
1 tablespoon fresh lemon juice
1 tablespoon white vinegar
¼ to ⅓ cup crumbled blue cheese
Salt to taste
Black pepper to taste
Ground hot red pepper (cayenne) to taste

CHICKEN WINGS

20 to 25 chicken wings
Vegetable oil for deep frying
¼ cup (½ stick) butter or margarine
½ to 1 (2-ounce) bottle Louisiana hot sauce
12 to 18 celery sticks

1. Dressing: Mix all ingredients in medium bowl, cover, and chill 1 hour or longer.

2. Chicken Wings: Halve wings at "elbow" and discard tips. Do not dredge, crumb, or batter wings. Deep-fry in 2½ to 3 inches 375° F vegetable oil in a sauté pan or deep fat fryer until crisp and golden brown on all sides—8 to 10 minutes. Drain well on paper towels.

3. Melt butter in small saucepan and blend in ½ to 1 bottle hot sauce, depending on how "hot" you like things.

4. Place chicken wings in large bowl; pour hot butter sauce over wings and mix well.

5. Arrange wings on deep platter and serve warm with celery sticks and Blue Cheese Dressing for dipping. Don't forget to put out plenty of napkins—Buffalo Chicken Wings are deliciously messy!

Sweet 'n' Sour Meatballs

Makes 40

✳

I REMEMBER these becoming popular in the late '50s. Often—but not always—they were served from chafing dishes with plenty of toothpicks and napkins placed nearby. This recipe, sent to me by Marilyn Brown, manager of the Consumer Test Kitchens at H.J. Heinz in Pittsburgh, is both easy and classic.

1 pound lean ground beef
1 cup soft white bread
* crumbs*
1 egg, slightly beaten
2 tablespoons milk
2 tablespoons minced
* yellow onion*
1 clove garlic, peeled and
* minced*
½ teaspoon salt
⅛ teaspoon black pepper
1 tablespoon vegetable oil
⅔ cup chili sauce or ketchup
⅔ cup grape or red currant jelly

1. Mix beef, bread crumbs, egg, milk, onion, garlic, salt, and pepper and shape into 40 bite-size balls.

2. Heat oil in large, heavy nonstick skillet over moderately high heat, add meatballs, and brown lightly on all sides—2 to 3 minutes. Reduce heat to low, cover, and cook 5 minutes; drain off excess drippings.

3. Mix chili sauce and jelly, pour over meatballs and heat, stirring occasionally, until jelly melts. Simmer uncovered, stirring and basting occasionally, until sauce thickens and meatballs are nicely glazed—10 to 12 minutes.

4. Serve hot with toothpicks.

Sausage-Cheese Cocktail Balls

Makes 5 to 5½ Dozen

✳

THESE NIPPY hors d'oeuvre contain only three ingredients: General Mills's all-purpose baking mix (Bisquick), pork sausage, and sharp Cheddar cheese. In the '60s, no party would have been complete without them. The variation below (adapted from a Pillsbury recipe) uses pancake mix as the foundation, halves the amount of sausage, and rounds out the flavor with dry onion soup mix and cayenne.

1 pound bulk pork sausage
½ pound sharp Cheddar
* cheese, finely grated*
3 cups all-purpose baking mix

1. Preheat oven to 375°F. Lightly coat two baking sheets with cooking spray and set aside.

2. With hands, mix all ingredients thoroughly in large bowl to make smooth dough. Pinch off bits of dough and roll into 1-inch balls.

3. Space 1½ inches apart on baking sheets and bake 15 to 18 minutes until richly brown, turning the balls over at halftime. Transfer at once to wire racks to cool slightly. Serve warm.

——— **VARIATION** ———

SAUSAGE BALLS: Mix ½ pound bulk pork sausage, 2 cups shredded sharp Cheddar cheese, ¼ cup milk, and 1 egg thoroughly in large bowl. Add 1½ cups buttermilk complete pancake and waffle mix (Hungry Jack), 2 tablespoons dry onion soup mix, and ⅛ to ¼ teaspoon ground hot red pepper (cayenne). Blend well. Pinch off bits of dough and shape into 1-inch balls. Place on lightly greased baking sheets, spacing 1½ inches apart, and sprinkle lightly with paprika. Bake 10 to 15 minutes at 375°F until deep golden brown, turning the balls over at halftime. Remove from baking sheets at once and serve. Makes 5 to 5½ dozen.

Marinated Mushrooms

Makes about 3½ Cups

✻

THESE HAVE remained popular right through the last half of the twentieth century. This particular recipe is adapted from one developed by the Consumer Test Kitchens at H.J. Heinz in Pittsburgh.

¾ cup vegetable oil or fruity olive oil
½ cup Tarragon-Chive Vinegar (page 298)
1½ teaspoons salt
1 teaspoon sugar
½ teaspoon dried leaf basil, crumbled
¼ teaspoon ground thyme
6 peppercorns
1 clove garlic, peeled and split
1 whole bay leaf
1½ pounds fresh small mushrooms of uniform size, stemmed and rinsed

1. Mix oil, vinegar, salt, sugar, basil, thyme, peppercorns, garlic, and bay leaf in large saucepan. Set over moderate heat, cover, and simmer 10 minutes.

2. Add mushrooms and simmer, uncovered, 3 minutes. Pour all into heat-proof ceramic bowl, cover, and chill several hours or overnight, stirring occasionally.

3. Drain mushrooms, discard bay leaf, and serve with toothpicks as a cocktail appetizer.

BITE-SIZE STUFFED VEGETABLES

·······················

AMERICANS, IT seems, have long liked to stuff vegetables, but nearly always as accompaniments to the main dish. In her solidly researched, wryly written *Perfection Salad* (1986), Laura Shapiro mentions stuffed pimientos as part of "a Boston Cooking School dinner-menu demonstration held in March 1898" in which "every dish except the introductory bowl of soup showed the effort to disguise food, reduce its volatility, and keep it within visible borders." And in the chapter devoted to Fannie Merritt Farmer, she writes of Thorndike Potatoes, "which were potatoes and bananas mashed together, stuffed into banana skins, sprinkled with Parmesan, and broiled."

The bite-size, stuffed-vegetable hors d'oeuvre, however, appears to belong to the twentieth century, boosted I believe, by the cocktail party, which, says John Mariani (*The Dictionary of American Food and Drink,* Revised Edition, 1994) was born of "Prohibition when alcoholic drinks were hard to find outside the home except illegally." Here, where guests were forced to circulate, juggling drinks, cigarettes, napkins, and nibbles, the most accommodating hors d'oeuvre was the morsel small enough to be popped into the mouth whole. The best of them teamed something crunchy with something smooth and creamy.

In *Mrs. Allen's Cook Book* (1917), I find chunks of celery stuffed with sardine paste, and in *Good Housekeeping's Book of Menus, Recipes and Household Discoveries* (1922), celery sticks stuffed with Roquefort. But it is James Beard's *Hors d'Oeuvre and Canapés* (1940) that opens up a world of possibilities: raw mushroom caps stuffed with Roquefort, fourteen ways to stuff hard-cooked eggs, plus stuffed artichoke buds, stuffed cucumber rings, stuffed tomatoes, even stuffed dill pickles.

James Beard's Mushroom Caps Filled with Roquefort

Makes about 1½ Dozen

✱

IN 1940 when these stuffed raw mushrooms appeared in James Beard's first cookbook, *Hors d'Oeuvre and Canapés,* they were considered exotic. In those days, almost no one ate raw mushrooms. Indeed, until the early '60s in much of the land, even cultivated mushrooms were something you had to ask your grocer to order especially for you. The recipe here is adapted from the James Beard original, of which he writes, "The raw mushroom flavor has a peculiar sympathy of flavor with the Roquefort." Quite so.

ROQUEFORT STUFFING
*4 ounces Roquefort cheese, at
    room temperature*
*½ cup (1 stick) butter,
    softened*
½ teaspoon dry mustard

MUSHROOMS
*12 perfectly shaped, medium
    mushroom caps*
Roquefort Stuffing (above)
*¼ cup minced ripe or green
    olives*

1. STUFFING: Cream Roquefort, butter, and dry mustard until smooth; set aside.

2. MUSHROOMS: Peel mushrooms carefully, fill with Roquefort mixture, and sprinkle with minced olives.

3. Serve as a cocktail hors d'oeuvre.

Stuffed Snow Pea Pods

Makes 50

✱

I ALWAYS thought that Martha Stewart, "The Princess of Pretty," taught us to stuff snow peas. She talks of them, showing dainty pictures of them in her lavishly illustrated first book, *Entertaining* (1982). Yet nearly twenty years earlier, *Gourmet's Menu Cookbook* (1963) offers a recipe. I've adapted that recipe here.

*50 fresh snow pea pods no more
    than 1½ inches long*
*2¼ (8-ounce) packages cream
    cheese, softened*
*6 tablespoons fresh tomato
    puree (about 1 small ripe
    tomato, peeled, cored, seeded,
    and pureed)*
2 tablespoons mayonnaise
½ teaspoon dry mustard
*¼ teaspoon ground
    coriander*
½ teaspoon salt (or to taste)
*¼ teaspoon white pepper
    (or to taste)*

1. Blanch snow pea pods 1 minute in boiling salted water; drain well and pat dry on paper towels. While pods are warm, carefully make ¼-inch, horizontal slit on flat side of each. Cool pods.

2. Blend cream cheese, tomato puree, mayonnaise, dry mustard, coriander, salt, and pepper until smooth; taste for salt and pepper and adjust as needed.

3. Fit pastry bag with plain tip and pipe cheese mixture through slits into pea pods.

4. Chill at least 1 hour, then serve as a cocktail hors d'oeuvre.

New Potatoes with Black Caviar

Makes 1 Dozen

✱

IN THE summer of '77, a tiny take-out shop opened on Manhattan's Upper West Side and had a huge effect on the way Yuppies ate. The Silver Palate, it was called, and the two dynamos behind it were Sheila Lukins and Julee Rosso. With the publication of *The Silver Palate Cookbook* in 1979, thousands of upwardly mobile young Americans across the country began eating and entertaining the Silver Palate way. A particular party favorite: These bite-size potatoes crowned with sour cream and caviar. The recipe here is adapted from one in *The Silver Palate Cookbook.*

APPETIZERS & SNACKS

*12 tiny new potatoes of
    uniform size (about 1
    pound)*
Vegetable oil for deep frying
½ cup sour cream
*1 (3½- to 4-ounce) jar black or
    golden caviar*

1. Preheat oven to 450° F.

2. Arrange potatoes one layer deep in 8- or 9-inch pie pan and bake, uncovered, 30 to 35 minutes until tender.

3. Halve potatoes, then with melon baller scoop out flesh, leaving shells about ¼-inch thick. Mash potato pulp in small bowl and keep warm.

4. Fry potato shells in about 2 inches of vegetable oil at 375° F in a deep skillet until crisply golden—2 to 3 minutes; drain on paper towels.

5. Fill potato shells with mashed potato, top each with a generous teaspoon sour cream, then one of caviar. Serve warm.

Broiled Potato Skins

Makes 4 Dozen

✳

"SURE, I remember these," said Sara Moulton, executive chef at *Gourmet* magazine, when I asked her about these nibbles. "We used to get them at T.G.I. Friday's in Boston in the late '70s. It was one of the cool things we used to do . . . go into the bar and order up a plate of potato skins. They were sort of like nachos only they were made with baked potato skins instead of tortilla chips." Of course, they were served elsewhere, too. I remember them in New York at about the same time. By 1986, they were so widely known they'd made it into *Betty Crocker's Cookbook,* from which this recipe is adapted.

4 large Idaho potatoes
*2 tablespoons butter or
    margarine, at room
    temperature*
½ teaspoon salt
¼ teaspoon black pepper
*1 cup finely shredded Monterey
    Jack with jalapeño peppers
    (about ¼ pound)*
*4 slices bacon, crisply cooked
    and finely crumbled
    (optional)*

1. Preheat oven to 425° F.

2. Prick potatoes and bake until fork pierces them easily—about 1 hour.

3. Halve potatoes lengthwise and scoop out flesh leaving shells ⅜-inch thick (save flesh for soup or mashed potatoes). Spread inside of shells with butter, sprinkle with salt and pepper, then cut each into 6 pieces of equal size.

4. Arrange potato skins buttered-side-up on broiler pan and sprinkle evenly with cheese and, if desired, bacon.

5. Broil 5 inches from heat just until cheese melts—about 2 minutes. Serve at once.

TIMELINE

1902

Horn & Hardart opens an Automat (in Philadelphia).

Karo corn syrup goes on sale.

Animal Crackers debut.

Chili powder is packaged and sold in Texas.

1903

A new, larger edition of *The Settlement Cook Book* is published.

The Boston Cooking School closes.

Tuna is put into cans.

A machine for making peanut butter is patented by Ambrose W. Straub.

1904

Tea merchant Thomas Sullivan invents the tea bag.

FANNIE FARMER

She's not hip. She's not hot. She's not Martha. But she's ours, and when it comes to cooking, she wrote the book . . . —Yankee, *April 1996*

THIS COVER line on *Yankee* magazine's "100 Years with Fannie Farmer" issue wraps around a colorized photograph of Miss Farmer. How starchy she looks—graying red hair tightly knotted atop her head, *pince-nez* clamped into place, gaze piercing, lips pursed.

No beauty, Fannie Farmer was lucky to have her *Boston Cooking-School Cook Book* hit the bookstores before the age of television when "image" became "everything." In 1896, however, Fannie Farmer was a force, the most famous cookbook author of her day, an enthusiastic crusader not only for precise kitchen measurements but also for putting heart and soul into cookery.

She came to cooking late. Born in Boston in 1857 to a bookish Unitarian family, she grew up in Medford, Massachusetts. Considered the brainiest of the four Farmer girls (a fifth had died as a baby), Fannie was college-bound until felled by a mysterious illness—probably polio. For months she was paralyzed and for years, invalided. Job prospects were slim and marriage prospects slimmer still.

In time, Fannie Farmer learned to walk again but she limped as long as she lived. In her late twenties, she found housework in Cambridge, then in 1888 at the age of thirty-one, she enrolled in The Boston Cooking School. A star pupil, she was asked to assist at the school and within five years she had become its principal.

Three years later, Fannie Farmer donned her prettiest dress and headed for the offices of Little, Brown. Her mission: To have the venerable Boston publishing house print her "scientific" revision of *Mrs. Lincoln's Boston Cook Book,* since 1884 the Boston Cooking School text.

Little, Brown didn't see a cookbook as a blockbuster, but they made a deal with Fannie Farmer. If she'd pay the publishing costs, they'd print and distribute the book. The 3,000-copy first edition sold out and by 1897, the book had made two trips back to press. There were reprintings every year between 1898 and 1906, when a substantially revised edition appeared. Its first printing: 20,000 copies, nearly seven times that of the original.

Accounting for the book's success was Fannie Farmer's use of *level measurements,* also of the measuring cups and spoons that had begun to appear in the mid-1880s and were standard equipment at The Boston Cooking School.

In 1902, Fannie Farmer left the Boston Cooking School to open Miss Farmer's School of Cookery, a move that would shut the older establishment down within the year.

By 1905, Fannie Farmer was writing a monthly food column for *The Woman's Home Companion* and lecturing across the country, nearly always to packed houses. She also wrote five other cookbooks, now long forgotten, among them *Food and Cookery for the Sick and Convalescent* (1904), *Catering for Special Occasions* (1911), and *A New Book of Cookery* (1912).

For the last two years of her life, Fannie Farmer was confined to a wheelchair. Still, she continued to travel, to lecture, and to write until her final illness. According to Laura Shapiro (*Perfection Salad,* 1986), she "was taken to the hospital" a week before she was to give a lecture "on one of her favorite subjects—cake and frosting."

Fannie Farmer died on January 15, 1915, leaving an estate of nearly $200,000. *The Boston Cooking-School Cook Book,* according to Shapiro, had just "been revised to incorporate *A New Book of Cookery,* so the lavish culinary style that made her distinctive was at last fully represented in the plain-spoken book that made her famous."

The Boston Cooking-School Cook Book lived on through many editions with Wilma Lord Perkins, Fannie Farmer's nephew's wife, assuming the role of reviser and updater. Over time the book's name changed—to *Fannie Farmer's Boston Cooking-School Cook Book,* then simply to *The Fannie Farmer Cookbook.*

The latest editions, complete overhauls that Fannie Farmer would scarcely recognize, were done by Californian Marion Cunningham, a gifted protégée of James Beard. Even the book's publisher has changed—from Boston's Little, Brown to the prestigious New York firm of Alfred A. Knopf

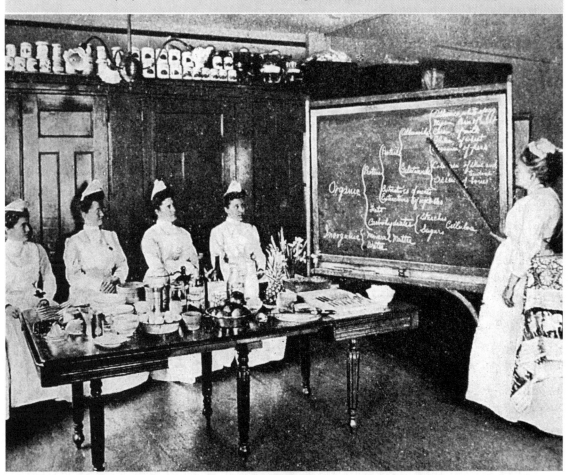

Artichoke Nibbles

Makes 64

✳

FEATURED IN *Sunset All-Time Favorite Recipes* (Sunset Publishing, 1993), these unusual hors d'oeuvre, which *Sunset* calls a "western classic," had by the 1980s become an all-American party mainstay. They're also a staple of many trendy take-out shops and the recipe appears in dozens of community cookbooks. *Sunset* doesn't say when it first published Artichoke Nibbles, but on the page facing the recipe, a box on entertaining says: "In 1969, we presented a 'Nothing-to-it Party' for 36 guests." The timing sounds about right.

2 (6-ounce) jars marinated artichoke hearts
1 small yellow onion, peeled and finely chopped
1 clove garlic, peeled and minced
4 eggs, lightly beaten
¼ cup fine dry bread crumbs
¼ teaspoon salt
⅛ teaspoon black pepper
⅛ teaspoon dried leaf oregano, crumbled
⅛ teaspoon hot red pepper sauce
2 cups coarsely shredded sharp Cheddar cheese (about ½ pound)
2 tablespoons minced parsley

1. Preheat oven to 325° F. Grease 8 × 8 × 2-inch baking pan; set aside.

2. Drain marinade from 1 jar artichokes into small skillet; discard marinade from second jar. Coarsely chop artichokes and set aside.

3. Add onion and garlic to skillet, set over moderate heat, and stir-fry until glassy—3 to 5 minutes. Cool 5 minutes.

4. Transfer to large bowl, add eggs, bread crumbs, salt, pepper, oregano, hot pepper sauce, cheese, chopped artichokes, and parsley and mix well.

5. Pour into pan and bake, uncovered, until set like custard, about 30 minutes. Cool slightly, cut into 1-inch squares, and serve warm or at room temperature.

Impossible Green Chili-Cheese Pie

Makes 8 Servings

✳

A JIFFY first course developed in the Betty Crocker test kitchens as a way to use Bisquick Original baking mix.

It quickly became one of the company's most popular recipes and is used here courtesy of the Betty Crocker Kitchens.

NOTE: If you divide the wedges into bite-size pieces, these make good cocktail finger food.

2 (4-ounce) cans chopped green chilies, well drained
4 cups coarsely shredded sharp Cheddar cheese (about 1 pound)
2 cups milk
4 eggs
1 cup biscuit mix

1. Preheat oven to 425° F. Grease 10½-inch pie plate.

2. Sprinkle chilies and cheese over bottom of prepared pie plate and set aside.

3. Blend milk, eggs, and biscuit mix in electric blender at high speed until smooth—about 15 seconds. Or beat in large electric mixer bowl at high speed 1 minute. Pour into pie plate.

4. Bake, uncovered, until knife inserted in center of pie comes out clean—25 to 30 minutes.

5. Cool on wire rack 10 minutes, cut into wedges, and serve.

Garlicked Olives

Makes about 2 Cups

✳

IN THE '50s, before a dozen different varieties of brined, herbed, or spiced olives could be had at the nearest specialty food shop, hostesses would take the curse off the canned variety by marinating them with garlic, hot peppers, and herbs. I still think these are good.

> 2 (8- to 9-ounce) jars or cans unpitted green or ripe olives with their liquid
> 4 large cloves garlic, peeled and slivered
> 6 small dried chili pequins
> 6 black peppercorns
> 1/4 cup red wine vinegar
> 4 sprigs fresh thyme or oregano, washed well and patted dry

1. Drain olive liquid into small saucepan. Add garlic, chilies, and peppercorns. Cover and simmer 5 minutes. Add vinegar.

2. Place olives in 1-pint preserving jar, tuck in thyme sprigs, then pour in saucepan mixture.

3. Cover tight and marinate at least a week in refrigerator before serving, inverting jar from time to time.

DIPS, DUNKS & SPREADS

IT'S BEEN said that dips originated in the 1950s with that gloppy blend of sour cream and dry onion soup mix known as California Dip. Not so.

Barbara Kuck, Director of the Culinary Archives and Museum at Johnson & Wales University in Providence, Rhode Island, presides over what she calls "The First Stomach" collection, presidential culinary memorabilia amassed by her father, the late chef Louis Szathmary of Chicago. Among these papers is a recipe for a clam and cream cheese dip penciled on a 3 × 5-inch file card by Mrs. Woodrow Wilson. It is said to have been one of the President's favorites. That would push the advent of dips back to the second decade of this century. And perhaps even further.

Still, dips did not come into vogue until twenty or twenty-five years later. And the man who popularized them, I'm convinced, was James Beard. In his very first cookbook (*Hors d'Oeuvre and Canapés*, 1940), Beard wrote:

I think it delightful to have large bowls of cheese mixtures which are of a consistency that permits "dunking." Cream cheese mixed with chopped chives and sour cream, and perhaps a little green pepper and a great deal of parsley, is always welcome. Roquefort cheese or Gorgonzola mixed with cream cheese or sour cream, with a flavoring of chopped chives and chopped raw mushrooms, is another good dunker. Cream cheese, sour cream, and grated fresh horseradish and a few chopped chives is another delightful addition to this family. You may have your choice of dunkers—potato chips, pretzels, crackers, Italian bread sticks—any of them.

Dips gained in popularity during the 1940s, at least in some parts of the country. In Raleigh, North Carolina, where I grew up, club women loved to dream up new dips. And none more so than my mother, whose recipe box contains more than two dozen of them, dated from 1942 to 1960.

The collection of dips and spreads that follows concentrates on the very best of them, those time-honored recipes that appear in community cookbooks decade after decade.

California Dip

Makes about 2 Cups

✳

THIS MAY not be "the mother of all dips," but it is surely America's most beloved. The Lipton Company, whose dry onion soup mix is the basis of California Dip, doesn't claim to have invented it. That distinction belongs to an anonymous California cook, who blended sour cream with the soup mix back in 1954—two years after it hit the market. Word of the new dip spread through Los Angeles faster than a canyon fire, newspapers printed the recipe, onion soup mix sales soared, and Lipton executives, a continent away in New Jersey, were ecstatic. They tracked down the recipe, perfected it, and beginning in 1958, printed it on every box of Lipton Recipe Secrets Onion Soup Mix (it's still there). In a December 1995 *New York Times* article, Suzanne Hamlin quotes a Lipton public relations spokesperson as saying that "some 220,000 envelopes of the mix are used across the nation every day" with sales peaking "between mid-November through Super Bowl Sunday." According to Jane and Michael Stern (*Square Meals,* 1984), there are two ways to mix California Dip. "The safe way," they say, is to combine "the soup and sour cream an hour before serving, giving the onions time to soften and all the enhancers time to spread their savor evenly through the sour cream." Then there's the "punkier approach"—*barely* mixing the dip

just before serving. "The onions," the Sterns write, "will retain a dehydrated crunch . . . and the sour cream will be streaked with veins of zest, little nuggets radiating a raunchy salt sting."

NOTE: To reduce fat and calories, use yogurt or low- or no-fat sour cream.

>   1 envelope dry onion soup mix
>   2 cups sour cream

Mix ingredients and serve with potato chips, crackers, or bite-size chunks of raw vegetables (celery, carrots, broccoli, cauliflower).

Hot Crab Dip

Makes about 3¾ Cups

✳

A 1950S dip from the Baltimore test kitchens of McCormick & Company, which appeared in *100 Best Recipes for 100 Years from McCormick* (1988). The headnote describes the recipe as "a delicious new version of an old Maryland specialty." It also says that it's "best made with the backfin meat of the blue crab."

>   1 pound backfin or lump
>   crabmeat
>   1 cup sour cream
>   1 cup mayonnaise
>   1 teaspoon instant minced
>   onion
>   ¼ teaspoon curry powder
>   ½ teaspoon dillweed
>   ½ teaspoon Bon Appétit
>   seasoning
>   ½ cup shaved or slivered
>   almonds

1. Preheat oven to 350°F. Butter 1-quart *au gratin* dish or shallow casserole and set aside.

2. Pick over crabmeat, discarding bits of shell and cartilage; place in in medium bowl; set aside.

3. Blend sour cream, mayonnaise, onion, curry powder, dillweed, and Bon Appétit seasoning in small bowl. Add to crab and mix well.

4. Transfer to *au gratin* dish and scatter almonds evenly on top.

5. Bake, uncovered, until bubbling—about 20 minutes. Serve as a dip for melba toast, potato chips, or crackers.

——— VARIATION ———

QUICK MICROWAVE CRAB DIP: Prepare crab mixture as directed, place in microwave-safe 10-inch pie plate, cover, and microwave on MEDIUM (50 percent power) 6 minutes, stirring and rotating twice. Top with almonds and microwave, uncovered, on LOW (25 percent power) 3 minutes. Makes about 3¾ cups.

Clam Dip

Makes about 1½ Cups

✳

WHEN AND where did clam dip originate? I was unable to track it any further back than 1939. In fact, the recipe published that year in Irma S. Rombauer's little-known *Streamlined Cooking* is titled Clam Canapé, not clam dip, although the two are practically identical. Rombauer calls for mixing a drained 7-ounce can of minced clams with 3 ounces of softened cream cheese, a tablespoon of Worcestershire, a pinch of dry mustard, and a tablespoon "more or less" of onion juice. And even though she directs the reader to spread the mixture on crackers or toast, I felt that this must surely be the "original" clam dip. Not true.

On the eve of President Clinton's second inauguration, along comes *The New York Times* (January 15, 1997) with a front-page Living Section feature by James Barron titled "Feasts and Follies of Inauguration Day." To my astonishment, one of the featured recipes was Woodrow Wilson's Clam Cream Cheese Dip, which had been adapted from a recipe in *The Old Farmer's Almanac Hearth & Home Companion for 1994.*

I must admit that I was hugely skeptical that our twenty-eighth president was partial to anything as simple as clam dip or as laden with processed foods. And clearly the *Times/Hearth & Home Companion* recipe was a modern one, calling as it did for an 8-ounce package of cream cheese—not available in Woodrow Wilson's day.

I next chased down *Hearth & Home Companion* editor Georgia Orcutt in Cambridge, Massachusetts, who sent me the "clam dip" issue. The Woodrow Wilson recipe, she said, had come from Barbara Kuck, Director of the Culinary Archives and Museum at Johnson & Wales University in Providence, Rhode Island, an institution known for its presidential culinary memorabilia (see Dips, Dunks, & Spreads, page 23). I then called Kuck, who faxed me the recipe just as Edith Bolling Galt Wilson (the second Mrs. Wilson) had scribbled it sometime between 1915 and 1921 (where she got it, she doesn't say). Anyhow, here it is verbatim:

> *1 Can Clams Small*
> *1 part Cream Cheese*
> *drain off Juice*
> *add onions grated*
> *& Salt – pepper*

So when and how did clam dip enter the American mainstream? According to Sylvia Lovegren (*Fashionable Food*, 1995), the recipe was

featured in the early 1950s on TV's *Kraft Music Hall*. Jane and Michael Stern are even more specific in *Square Meals* (1984). "This recipe," they write, "comes from a 1951 booklet called *Food Favorites from the KRAFT Television Theater . . . Selected by Popular Request.*" The version here was my mother's.

> 1 clove garlic, peeled and
>   halved
> 1 (8-ounce) package cream
>   cheese, at room temperature
> 2 teaspoons fresh lemon juice
> 1½ teaspoons Worcestershire
>   sauce
> ½ teaspoon salt
> Pinch black pepper
> 1 (7-ounce) can minced clams,
>   drained, juice reserved

1. Rub small bowl well with garlic; discard garlic.

2. Add cheese to bowl and cream until smooth. Mix in lemon juice, Worcestershire sauce, salt, pepper, clams, and, one by one, 4 tablespoons reserved clam juice. For a looser dip, add a little more clam juice.

3. Mound dip in small serving bowl and surround with potato chips, crackers, or bite-size chunks of carrot, celery, zucchini, broccoli, and cauliflower.

KOOL-AID

I N 1930, during the early days of the Depression, juvenile entrepreneurship underwent a radical change as all across America neighborhood lemonade stands were replaced by stands selling a new, cheap, lollipop-bright and wildly popular kids' drink—Kool-Aid. This was hardly surprising, since Edwin E. Perkins, the inventor of Kool-Aid, had begun his own career at eleven, stirring up patent medicines and perfumes in the kitchen sink. Perkins went on to market flavorings, spices, cleaning products and "Nix-O-Tine," a very early quit-smoking kit containing herbal tablets, herbal laxatives, and silver nitrate mouthwash. Nix-O-Tine, aimed at World War I vets who had picked up the habit abroad, was sold, like Perkins's other products, both door-to-door and by direct mail.

Kool-Aid, reincarnated from an earlier liquid fruit concentrate Perkins had sold as "Fruit Smack," first appeared in 1927 and was an instant hit. It was cheap, easy to store, simple to mix in quantities large or small. Best of all, children loved it. By 1929, the demand for Kool-Aid was so great Perkins had to abandon all his other products; in 1931 net sales reached $383,000; in 1936, ten times that. Children from four to twelve still make Kool-Aid their soft drink of choice. Favorite flavors? Cherry, lemonade, grape, and tropical punch.

Texas Caviar

Makes 5 Cups

✳

I AM indebted to Karen Haram, food editor of the San Antonio *Express-News,* for sending me this recipe, which, she says, "is as popular as you have heard it is." Strangely, it's a black-eyed pea salad that's served as a dip for tortilla chips. Haram adds that Helen Corbitt, often called "the mother of modern Texas cooking," is credited with creating Texas Caviar. And indeed a recipe for it appears in *The Helen Corbitt Collection* (1981). The Texas Caviar below is an evolved recipe and, adds Haram, is the way many Texans prepare it today.

> *3 (15½-ounce) cans black-eyed peas, rinsed and drained*
> *½ cup bottled Italian dressing (about)*
> *½ cup chopped green bell pepper*
> *2 to 3 teaspoons minced, drained, and seeded canned jalapeño pepper*
> *½ cup chopped Vidalia or other sweet onion*
> *1 clove garlic, peeled and minced*
> *¼ teaspoon salt (or to taste)*
> *¼ teaspoon coarsely ground black pepper (or to taste)*

1. Mix all ingredients in large bowl, cover, and refrigerate at least two hours, but better yet, two days.

2. Let stand at room temperature 30 to 40 minutes, taste for salt and pepper, and adjust as needed. Also, if mixture seems dry, add a little additional Italian dressing.

3. Serve as a dip for round tortilla chips.

Beer Cheese Dip or Spread

Makes about 5½ Cups

✳

IN HER *Southern Cook Book* (1951), Marion Brown includes a recipe for Beer Cheese, which, she writes, was shared with her by Marion Flexner, author of *Out of Kentucky Kitchens* (1949), together with this bit of background: "In the days when free lunches were served in Kentucky saloons with every 5-cent glass of beer, we were told of a wonderful Beer Cheese that decked every bar. Finally we found someone who had eaten it and who told us vaguely how to prepare it." The recipe here is my mother's improv on the Beer Cheese in the *Southern Cook Book* (Mother had that book but not Flexner's). She added onion to the mix, reduced the garlic from three cloves to one and the Worcestershire from three tablespoons to one. She also substituted Dijon mustard for the dry and mellowed the lot with ketchup, an ingredient not in the original. By increasing or decreasing the amount of beer, Mother could make her Beer Cheese a dip or a spread. She passed her recipe along to scores of friends and relatives, and I've seen it published in local fund-raiser cookbooks thousands of miles from Raleigh, North Carolina, where we lived.

1 pound sharp Cheddar cheese, finely shredded, at room temperature
1 pound mild Cheddar cheese, finely shredded, at room temperature
3 tablespoons ketchup
1 tablespoon Dijon mustard
1 tablespoon Worcestershire sauce
2 large scallions, trimmed and finely minced (white part only)
1 clove garlic, peeled and minced
¼ teaspoon hot red pepper sauce
1½ to 2 cups flat beer (about)

NOTE: For better flavor, refrigerate the Beer Cheese several days, then bring to room temperature before serving.

1. Blend all ingredients except beer until smooth in electric mixer at high speed or in food processor fitted with metal chopping blade.

2. With motor running, add beer in slow steady stream until mixture is as thick or thin as you like.

3. Pack into 1-quart container, cover tight, and refrigerate several days to mellow flavors.

4. Bring to room temperature, then serve as a spread for crackers or a dip for potato or corn chips or bite-size broccoli or cauliflower florets.

Curry Dip

Makes about 2 Cups

✳

THERE ARE curry dips and curry dips but this one is a particular favorite, not only because it was my mother's invention but also because it's been a huge hit whenever she or I served it. Like California Dip (page 24), this one begins with an envelope of Lipton Recipe Secrets Onion Soup Mix.

1 envelope dry onion soup mix
1 (8-ounce) package cream cheese, at room temperature
2 tablespoons curry powder
¼ cup chopped chutney
1½ cups sour cream

1. Using a fork, blend all ingredients well in small bowl.

2. Cover and refrigerate several hours.

3. Before serving, let stand at room temperature 30 to 45 minutes. If too thick, thin with a little milk.

4. Mound in small serving bowl and surround with potato or corn chips, crackers, cherry tomatoes, or bite-size chunks of carrot, celery, zucchini, broccoli, and cauliflower.

Mushroom Caviar

Makes about 1 Cup

✳

THIS GORGEOUS dip/spread, also known as "poor man's caviar," is my variation of a recipe that appeared in *House & Garden's New Cook Book* (1967). If you processor-chop the scallions and mushrooms as I do, the recipe's a snap.

- 1 cup moderately coarsely chopped scallions, with some green tops (10 to 12 large scallions)
- ¼ cup (½ stick) butter or margarine
- 2 cups moderately coarsely chopped mushrooms (about ½ pound)
- 1 tablespoon fresh lemon juice
- ½ teaspoon salt (or to taste)
- ¼ teaspoon black pepper (or to taste)
- ¼ teaspoon ground hot red pepper (cayenne)
- ¼ cup snipped fresh dill
- ⅔ cup sour cream (about)

1. Sauté scallions in butter in large heavy skillet over moderate heat until glassy—1 to 2 minutes.

2. Add mushrooms, lemon juice, salt, black pepper, and cayenne and stir-fry 5 to 6 minutes, until mushrooms release their juices and these evaporate.

3. Off heat, mix in dill and sour cream. Taste for salt and pepper and adjust as needed. If to be served as a dip and mixture seems too thick, blend in a little extra sour cream.

4. Spread on freshly made melbas or serve as a dip for potato chips, cherry tomatoes, or bite-size chunks of raw zucchini, broccoli, or cauliflower.

Tex-Mex (or Layered) Dip

Makes about 16 Servings

✳

ACCORDING TO Karen Haram, food editor of the San Antonio *Express-News*, "This dip is served at NEARLY every party in Texas. I don't know the origin of it," she says, "but it started becoming very popular in the very early '80s, helped in large part by Jo Anne Vachule. She was food editor at the *Fort Worth Star-Telegram,* and the recipe ran in one of the big women's magazines [*Family Circle,* February 3, 1981] as her favorite recipe in a story on food editors' favorites. The recipe was around before then, but it really took off at that time." Haram adds that when making the dip, "make sure that you cover the avocado layer completely with the sour cream layer; if you do, the avocado doesn't darken, even if made the day before." *Family Circle* editors thought so highly of Tex-Mex Dip, they included it in their anthology, *Recipes America Loves Best* (1982).

- 3 medium ripe Haas avocados (about 1½ pounds)
- 2 tablespoons fresh lemon juice
- ½ teaspoon salt
- ¼ teaspoon black pepper
- 1 cup sour cream
- ½ cup mayonnaise
- 1 (1¼-ounce) package taco seasoning mix
- 2 (10½-ounce) cans plain bean or jalapeño bean dip
- 1 cup chopped scallions (include tops)
- 2 cups coarsely chopped, cored, and seeded tomatoes (about 3 medium)
- 2 (3½-ounce) cans pitted black olives, drained and coarsely chopped
- 2 cups shredded sharp Cheddar cheese (about ½ pound)

1. Peel, pit, and mash avocados in medium bowl with lemon juice, salt, and pepper.

2. Blend sour cream, mayonnaise, and taco seasoning mix in separate bowl.

3. Spread bean dip on large shallow serving platter, top with avocado mixture, then sour cream mixture.

4. Sprinkle with chopped scallions, tomatoes, and olives; cover with shredded cheese.

5. Serve chilled or at room temperature with round tortilla chips.

COCA-COLA: THE REAL THING

AMERICA'S BEST-SELLING soft drink was created by pharmacist John Styth Pemberton, who is said to have stirred it up with an oar in a big black kettle in his backyard in Atlanta. It's unclear whether Pemberton was aiming for a palatable soft drink or a patent medicine, probably the latter because the syrupy concentrate, first sold in Jacob's drugstore in 1886, mixed with plain water and dispensed at the soda fountain, was advertised as an "esteemed Brain Tonic and Intellectual Beverage."

When early soda jerks discovered it tasted better mixed with carbonated water, fizz was added to the formula. This formula, locked in a bank vault and passed on in whispers from retiring to incumbent company president, has been kept secret for more than a century.

That Coca-Cola contained flavorings from coca leaves and the kola nut we know by its name, but persistent rumors that it can produce a cocaine high are without foundation (in fact, the coca was deleted long ago). In the beginning and in the South, Cokes were also called "dopes," and whenever thirst struck, people would sidle up to the soda fountain and say, "Gimme a dope." In some isolated communities, they still do.

Whatever its contents, Coca-Cola caught the public's fancy quickly: By the early days of this century it was being sold in every state in the union, and its colorful ads decorated serving trays, wall mirrors, paper fans, and the sides of barns across the country.

In 1916, ownership of Coca-Cola, by then bottled in the familiar wasp-waisted green glass, went for $25 million to a group of investors led by Ernest Woodruff. On the eve of World War II, Woodruff's son Robert vowed publicly to make sure American soldiers could get nickel Cokes wherever they might be—a pledge both patriotic and clever, since an appreciative General Eisenhower saw to it that Coca-Cola bottling plants were placed near major battle fronts.

This encouraged soldiers to develop a taste for Coke during the war. Afterward, the bottling plants fit in with company plans for worldwide distribution. Today Coca-Cola is so well known that "Coke" is said to be the first American word many non-Americans learn to speak. Coca-Cola is used in recipes for chocolate cake, baked ham, and pot roast, for reviving wilted bouquets, and for settling upset stomachs. A specially made can of Coke was carried aboard the space shuttle in 1985 and is now in the "World of Coca-Cola" museum in Atlanta, along with a jukebox that plays "When the Dodo Bird is Singing in the Coca-Cola Tree."

The Famous Texas Cheese Dip

Makes about 3½ Cups

❋

EXCEPT FOR Texans, few Americans had ever heard of Ro-Tel canned tomatoes and green chilies until President Lyndon B. Johnson put them on the culinary map by releasing his Pedernales River Chili recipe. It specified Ro-Tel, a fiery brand of canned tomatoes put up in the little Texas town of Elsa. Now that Ro-Tel belongs to International Home Foods, cooks across the country are learning to punch up the flavor of soups, sauces, casseroles, and chilis by substituting these zippy canned tomatoes for more tepid varieties. Johnson's chili aside, the most famous Ro-Tel recipe is this party dip, an absurdly easy two-ingredient affair that can be made in 15 minutes (5 by microwave). It's printed on every can of Ro-Tel Whole Tomatoes and Green Chilies (to save the trouble of chopping, I now use Ro-Tel diced tomatoes and chilies). This tomato/green chili combo is "an original, secret old family recipe," the label declares, that will "make ordinary recipes come *alive* . . . and jump start y'er heart."

> 1 (1-pound) package
> pasteurized process cheese
> spread, cubed (1½ packages
> for a thicker dip)
> 1 (10-ounce) can diced
> tomatoes and green chilies,
> with their liquid

NOTE: I find this dip soupy. For a thicker dipping consistency, add an extra ½ pound cheese.

1. Place cheese, tomatoes, and jalapeños and their liquid in small heavy saucepan.

2. Set over low heat and cook, stirring often, about 15 minutes until

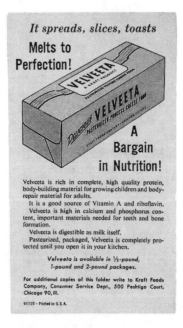

It spreads, slices, toasts

Melts to Perfection!

A Bargain in Nutrition!

Velveeta is rich in complete, high quality protein, body-building material for growing children and body-repair material for adults.
It is a good source of Vitamin A and riboflavin. Velveeta is high in calcium and phosphorus content, important materials needed for teeth and bone formation.
Velveeta is digestible as milk itself.
Pasteurized, packaged, Velveeta is completely protected until you open it in your kitchen.

Velveeta is available in ½-pound, 1-pound and 2-pound packages.

For additional copies of this folder write to Kraft Foods Company, Consumer Service Dept., 500 Peshtigo Court, Chicago 90, Ill.

511123 - Printed in U.S.A.

cheese melts and mixture is smooth, or microwave 5 minutes on HIGH (100 percent power) in covered, microwave-safe casserole, stirring once at halftime.

3. Serve warm with corn chips or bite-size broccoli or cauliflower florets, celery, carrot, or zucchini sticks.

──── **VARIATIONS** ────

VELVEETA SALSA DIP: It's not surprising that Kraft would come up with its own version of a dip that already uses one of its best-selling products, then print the recipe on the cheese carton. Cube 1 (1-pound) package pasteurized process cheese spread; heat with 1 (8-ounce) jar salsa in small heavy saucepan over low heat, stirring often. If desired, stir in 2 tablespoons freshly chopped cilantro. Serve hot with tortilla chips. Makes 3 cups.

NOTE: In the *Food Editors' Hometown Favorites Cookbook,* Kitty Krider of the *Austin American-Statesman* says that to the Ro-Tel recipe, Texans often add an extra pound of cheese (bringing the total to 2 pounds) and also mix in 1 pound cooked, crumbled pork sausage. Or to the original recipe they might add 1 pound each browned, crumbled ground beef and cooked, crumbled pork sausage. Both variations, she says, are "very popular."

Black Bean Bonanza Dip

Makes about 4 Cups

✳

CREATED BY Pace Foods of San Antonio, Texas, to feature Pace Picante Sauce, this black bean dip is plenty spicy. It contains just 14 calories per tablespoon and is therefore lower in fat and calories than most bean dips.

> 2 (15-ounce) cans black beans, rinsed and drained
> 1¼ cups picante sauce
> 1 cup finely chopped yellow onion (about 1 medium)
> 1 cup finely chopped red bell pepper (about 1 medium)
> 3 cloves garlic, peeled and minced
> 2 tablespoons vegetable oil
> 2 teaspoons ground cumin
> ¾ teaspoon salt
> ¼ cup chopped fresh coriander (cilantro)
> 2 ounces reduced-fat Cheddar cheese, coarsely shredded
> ½ cup diced, cored, and seeded tomato (about 1 small)
> ⅓ cup light sour cream (optional)

1. Puree half of beans and ¼ cup picante sauce in food processor fitted with metal chopping blade; set aside.

2. Stir-fry onion, bell pepper, and garlic in oil in large heavy nonstick skillet over moderate heat until limp but not brown—3 to 5 minutes.

3. Add pureed mixture, whole beans, remaining picante sauce, cumin, and salt and mix well. Bring to simmer and cook, stirring frequently, 5 minutes. Mix in 2 tablespoons coriander.

4. Transfer dip to shallow serving bowl or 9-inch pie plate, sprinkle with cheese, then garnish with tomato, remaining coriander and, if desired, drift with sour cream. Serve with corn chips, cherry tomatoes, or bite-size chunks of carrot, celery, zucchini, red, green, or yellow bell pepper.

Refried Bean Dip

Makes about 5 Cups

✳

SOME BEAN dips are bland, but not this one, adapted from *The Los Angeles Times California Cookbook* (1981).

> 2 (16-ounce) cans refried beans
> 1 (4-ounce) can chopped ripe olives
> 1 small yellow onion, peeled and minced
> ¼ cup bottled taco sauce
> 1 teaspoon garlic salt
> 1¼ cups coarsely shredded sharp Cheddar cheese

NOTE: Don't drain the beans or olives; their liquid gives the dip its "dunking" consistency.

1. Preheat oven to 350° F. Grease 1-quart casserole and set aside.

2. Mix beans, olives, onion, taco sauce, garlic salt, and 1 cup cheese; spoon into casserole and scatter remaining ¼ cup cheese on top.

3. Bake uncovered for 30 minutes. Serve hot with tortilla chips.

Deviled Ham Dip

Makes about 1½ Cups

✳

I REMEMBER my mother serving this dip at her book club in the late 1940s. In fact, it was my job to pass the dips and chips.

> 1 (4½-ounce) can deviled ham
> 1 (3-ounce) package cream cheese, at room temperature
> 2 tablespoons minced yellow onion
> 1 tablespoon Dijon mustard
> 1 tablespoon India relish
> ½ cup sour cream

1. Mix all ingredients until smooth.

2. Cover and refrigerate several hours.

3. Before serving, let stand at room temperature 30 to 45 minutes.

4. Mound in small serving bowl and surround with potato or corn chips, crackers, cherry tomatoes, or bite-size chunks of carrot, celery, zucchini, broccoli, and cauliflower.

RITZY CRACKERS

ALMOST EVERYONE has sampled—or at least heard of—Ritz Mock Apple Pie (page 387). As the name suggests, it's made with Ritz Crackers but tastes like apples. Few people, however, know that the recipe grew out of the Depression when soda crackers were handed out free at soup kitchens while costlier apples were sold on street corners by unemployed Wall Street bankers. Or so the story goes. It was during these gloomy days that Nabisco cheered everyone up with a round, buttery, crunchy cracker it called Ritz, hoping to conjure up images of Manhattan's posh Ritz-Carlton Hotel. Like the hotel, the Ritz Cracker was a luxury, but at 19 cents a box most people could afford it and soon made it the best-selling cracker in the world. Nabisco, realizing recently that there was no longer any reason for anyone to make Ritz Mock Apple Pie, since apples had long been cheaper than Ritz Crackers, took the recipe off the box—only to reinstate it by popular demand. How much of the $150 million spent annually on Ritz Crackers goes into pies and how much into nibbling, only Nabisco knows.

Almost overnight

America's most popular cracker

RITZ

NATIONAL BISCUIT COMPANY

A flavor so tantalizingly good that in a few short months it has conquered America! That is the dramatic story of Ritz.

Here is a cracker that it is almost impossible to resist. Eat one—just by itself—and you want to keep on eating them! What's more, Ritz improve the taste of everything you serve with them.

Let your family enjoy this cracker sensation. Get a 1 lb. or ½ lb. package of Ritz from your grocer. Serve them alone or with cheese, soup, salads, spreads or beverages. They're sure to like them!

A Product of NATIONAL BISCUIT COMPANY
makers of **Uneeda Biscuit** *and hundreds of other favorite varieties*

Hot Broccoli Dip in Sourdough Loaf

Makes 6 to 8 Servings

✳

THE HARDEST part of this showy late twentieth-century recipe is hollowing out the bread to make a "bowl" for the dip. The dip itself contains frozen chopped broccoli, assorted seasonings, and a full pound of Velveeta Pasteurized Process Cheese Spread. The recipe—surprise—was developed at The Kraft Kitchens in Glenview, Illinois.

1 (1½-pound) round
    sourdough loaf
2 tablespoons margarine
½ cup finely diced celery
½ cup finely diced red bell
    pepper
¼ cup finely chopped yellow
    onion
1 pound pasteurized process
    cheese spread, cubed
1 (10-ounce) package frozen
    chopped broccoli, thawed
    and drained very dry
¼ teaspoon dried leaf rosemary,
    crumbled

1. Preheat oven to 350° F.

2. Slice top off loaf of bread, then scoop out center leaving "bowl" with 1-inch-thick sides. Cut removed bread in bite-size cubes. Set top of loaf back in place, place bread on ungreased baking sheet, and surround with bread cubes. Set in oven and toast until lightly browned—about 15 minutes.

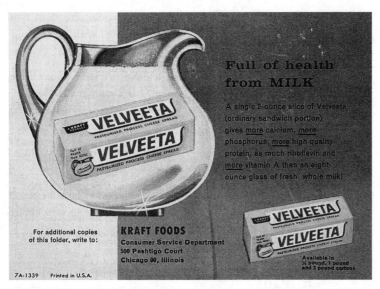

3. Meanwhile, melt margarine in large heavy skillet over moderate heat. Add celery, bell pepper, and onion and stir-fry until limp, 2 to 3 minutes. Reduce heat to low. Add cheese, broccoli, and rosemary and heat, stirring constantly, until cheese melts.

4. Set toasted sourdough "bowl" on large platter, fill with broccoli-cheese mixture and set sourdough "lid" on askew. Wreathe with bread cubes and serve at once.

Spinach and Artichoke Dip

Makes about 3 Cups

✳

A NUMBER of artichoke dips surfaced in the '70s and '80s but none better than this cold one and the hot one that follows on page 34. The cold one is adapted from Phyllis Méras's *New Carry-Out Cuisine* (1986). It comes from a Providence, Rhode Island, take-out shop called Culinary Capers that's run by Rosalind Rustigian. In her recipe headnote, Méras writes, "This spinach and artichoke dip is popular at faculty cocktail parties at nearby Brown University and the Rhode Island School of Design."

1 (10-ounce) package frozen
chopped spinach, thawed in
a large, fine sieve, then
pressed as dry as possible
1 (14-ounce) can artichoke
hearts, drained
1 cup mayonnaise
1 teaspoon snipped fresh dill
1 clove garlic, peeled and
minced
1 tablespoon fresh lemon juice
½ teaspoon salt (or to taste)
¼ teaspoon black pepper (or to
taste)

1. Pulse spinach and artichokes 6 to 8 times in food processor fitted with metal chopping blade until coarsely chopped.

2. Add remaining ingredients and churn until smooth. Taste and adjust salt and pepper as needed.

3. Mound into colorful serving bowl and accompany with bite-size chunks of carrot, celery, zucchini, broccoli, or cauliflower. Good, too, with cherry tomatoes.

Green Onion Dip

Makes about 2 Cups

✳

A BLENDER or food processor party dip developed by the Best Foods Creative Kitchens to promote one of its most important products—Hellmann's and Best Foods mayonnaise. It can be made with "real mayonnaise" (the original Hellmann's) or Best Foods Real Mayonnaise or Light or Low Fat Mayonnaise Dressing.

1 cup mayonnaise
½ cup sour cream
½ cup thinly sliced scallions
1 cup loosely packed parsley
sprigs
1 teaspoon Dijon mustard
1 clove garlic, peeled and halved
½ teaspoon salt

1. Puree all ingredients in electric blender at high speed or in food processor fitted with metal chopping blade.

2. Scoop into small bowl, cover with plastic wrap, and chill several hours.

3. Serve with crisp vegetables, cut in bite-size chunks, or with chips or crackers.

Hot Artichoke Dip

Makes about 2 Cups

❈

THIS DIP is a great club woman's favorite and appears in dozens of fund-raiser cookbooks. It was developed by Best Foods as a way to use Hellmann's and Best Foods Real mayonnaise. It can also be made with Hellmann's or Best Foods Light or Low Fat Mayonnaise Dressing. And it can be made by microwave (see Variation).

½ cup mayonnaise
½ cup sour cream
1 (14-ounce) can artichoke hearts, drained and chopped
¼ cup freshly grated Parmesan cheese
⅛ teaspoon hot red pepper sauce

1. Preheat oven to 350° F.

2. Mix all ingredients and spoon into lightly greased 2½- to 3-cup ovenproof dish.

3. Bake, uncovered, until bubbly, about 30 minutes.

4. Serve as a dip for potato or corn chips, crackers, melbas, or freshly toasted pita triangles.

———— VARIATION ————

MICROWAVE HOT ARTICHOKE DIP: Mix all ingredients in microwave-safe 1-quart bowl and microwave uncovered on HIGH (100 percent power) 3½ to 4 minutes until bubbly, stirring once at halftime. Makes about 2 cups.

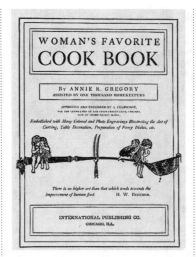

WOMAN'S FAVORITE
COOK BOOK

BY ANNIE R. GREGORY
ASSISTED BY ONE THOUSAND HOMEKEEPERS

INTERNATIONAL PUBLISHING CO.
CHICAGO, ILL.

Holiday Cheese Ball

Makes about 3 Cups

❈

FOR ITS December 1988 issue, *The Ladies' Home Journal* queried America's newspaper food editors for their most requested holiday recipes. Among those printed was this cheese ball, which *Dallas Morning News* Food Editor Dotty Griffith says she gets scores of requests for each Christmas.

10 ounces mild Cheddar cheese, at room temperature, cubed
1½ (8-ounce) packages cream cheese, at room temperature
6 ounces blue cheese, at room temperature
2 tablespoons grated yellow onion
1 teaspoon Worcestershire sauce
1 cup finely ground pecans
½ cup minced parsley

1. Pulse Cheddar cheese in food processor fitted with metal chopping blade until crumbly.

2. Add cream cheese, blue cheese, onion, and Worcestershire sauce and churn until smooth.

3. Add ½ cup pecans and ¼ cup parsley and process until well blended.

4. Place in bowl lined with plastic wrap, cover, and refrigerate 4 hours or overnight.

5. When ready to serve, mix remaining ½ cup pecans and ¼ cup parsley in pie plate. Shape cheese into ball and roll in pecan-parsley mixture until evenly coated.

BURNING BUSH

ACCORDING TO Sylvia Lovegren (*Fashionable Food*, 1995) this novelty hors d'oeuvre belongs to the 1930s. Despite its catchy name, it is nothing more than bite-size balls of cream cheese dredged in finely minced dried chipped beef. These, explains Lovegren, were then toothpicked onto "a polished eggplant to resemble a bush in autumn foliage." Crackers were put out, too, so guests could plop or spread the balls of cheese onto them before popping them into their mouths.

6. Center cheese ball on colorful serving plate and surround with crackers or freshly made melbas.

Almond Cheddar Pinecone

Makes about 25 Servings

✳

ANOTHER LONG-POPULAR cheese ball is this one from the Blue Diamond kitchens. It is included in an undated booklet, *Classic Almond Recipes,* printed by Blue Diamond, together with the blue cheese variation.

    2 (8-ounce) packages cream
        cheese, at room temperature
    ½ pound sharp Cheddar
        cheese, finely shredded, at
        room temperature
    6 tablespoons dry port wine
    ⅛ teaspoon ground hot red
        pepper (cayenne)
    ¼ cup finely sliced scallions
    2 cups unblanched whole
        almonds or lightly toasted,
        blanched whole almonds

1. Beat cream cheese, Cheddar, port, and pepper until smooth; mix in scallions. Cover and refrigerate 1 hour.

TANG: ASTRONAUT O.J.

....

IN 1955, General Foods decided to create an instant orange juice to go with its instant (Maxwell House) coffee. This revolutionary breakfast drink would have all the nutrients of natural orange juice, would be in powder form, would keep indefinitely, and would mix instantly with water. Ten years after the idea was conceived, General Foods chemists came up with just the right formula: a complex mix of sugar, citric acid, gum arabic, natural orange flavor, sodium carboxymethylcellulose, calcium phosphate (to prevent caking), sodium citrate, vitamin C, hydrogenated vegetable oil, vitamin A, artificial color (because people prefer orange "orange juice"), and BHA, a preservative. The original Tang contained none of the real orange juice solids it has today. How on earth could General Foods persuade the public to drink this chemical cocktail? The answer was not on Earth, but maybe in space.

In March 1965, just three months after Tang hit the market, NASA chose it as the official breakfast drink for the Gemini astronauts and for later space missions through the first moon landing in 1969. Space-mad kids couldn't wait to try what the astronauts drank nor could their parents, a few of whom went so far as to use Tang for vodka screwdrivers. It took ten years for consumers to accept instant coffee. Thanks to the astronauts, they embraced Tang in just over ten weeks.

2. Shape mixture into a large pinecone and center on serving plate. Beginning at pointed end of cone, press rounded ends of almonds ¼-inch deep into cheese mixture in neat rows so pointed ends angle upward slightly; also overlap rows slightly, simulating the look of a real pinecone.

3. Garnish, if desired, with fresh pine sprigs and serve as a spread for crackers or freshly made melbas.

——— VARIATION ———

ALMOND BLUE CHEESE PINECONE: Cream until smooth 2 (8-ounce) packages softened cream cheese, ¼ pound each crumbled blue cheese and shredded Swiss cheese, ¼ cup brandy, 1 minced clove garlic, and ¼ teaspoon white pepper. Chill, shape, and stud with almonds. Makes about 25 servings.

Easy Chicken Liver Pâté

Makes 6 to 8 Servings

✳

IF MEMORY serves, Helen Mc-Cully, food editor of *House Beautiful* in the '60s and '70s, originated this recipe. And if not its creator, she was certainly its popularizer. I remember her bringing a crock of it to her good friend Louella G. Shouer, food editor of *The Ladies' Home Journal,* who urged it on each member of her food staff. That was in the early '60s. The recipe here is a variation of one Elaine Hanna and I developed for our *Doubleday Cookbook* (1975).

PÂTÉ

1 pound chicken livers, halved
2 tablespoons butter
1 (8-ounce) package cream
   cheese, at room temperature
⅓ cup brandy
1 teaspoon salt (or to taste)
¼ teaspoon black pepper
⅛ teaspoon freshly grated
   nutmeg
⅛ teaspoon ground cinnamon
1 tablespoon finely grated
   yellow onion

GLAZE

1 (10½-ounce) can madrilène
   or beef consommé
1 teaspoon unflavored gelatin
Pimiento or truffle cut-outs
   (optional)

1. PÂTÉ: Brown chicken livers in butter in medium heavy skillet over moderately high heat 4 to 5 min-

utes, until no longer pink inside. Puree in electric blender at high speed or in food processor fitted with metal chopping blade.

2. Add remaining pâté ingredients and churn until smooth. Taste for salt and adjust as needed.

3. Spoon into 2½- to 3-cup serving bowl and chill until firm—3 to 4 hours.

4. GLAZE: Heat madrilène and gelatin in small saucepan over low heat, stirring often, until gelatin dissolves, 3 to 4 minutes; chill until consistency of unbeaten egg white. Spoon thin layer over pâté and, if desired, decorate with pimiento and/or truffle cut-outs. Seal with remaining glaze and chill until set. If not adding optional decoration, simply spoon all of madrilène over pâté and chill until set.

5. Serve pâté with freshly made melba rounds.

Granola

Makes about 4½ Cups

✳

IT MAY have begun as a hippie health snack in the '60s, but granola is now both mainstream and big time. There is no "correct" recipe. But the basic formula here, adapted from *The Woman's Day Cookbook* (1995), is a good one upon which to improvise. To it you can add or substitute almost anything in the dried fruit, nut, and/or seed department: Coarsely chopped dried

apples, apricots, or pears . . . toasted pumpkin or sunflower seeds . . . toasted chopped pecans or hazelnuts, even peanuts or cashews. Some people like to add toasted shaved coconut—a no-no because it's high in saturated fat. Stored in an airtight container at room temperature, granola will keep for about 2 weeks.

⅓ cup vegetable oil
⅓ cup honey
4 cups old-fashioned rolled oats
¼ cup wheat germ
⅓ cup sliced almonds
¾ cup seedless raisins

1. Preheat oven to 300° F. Line a 15½ × 10½ × 1-inch jelly roll pan with foil; set aside.

2. Blend oil and honey in large bowl. Add oats, wheat germ, and almonds and mix well to coat.

3. Spread mixture evenly in pan and bake uncovered, stirring occasionally, until golden brown, about 25 minutes.

4. Remove from oven, stir in raisins, and cool to room temperature.

5. Serve as a between-meals snack or TV nibble.

Traditional Chex Brand Party Mix

Makes about 9 Cups

✳

THIS CRUNCHY nibble hit the party circuit in 1955. In St. Louis. There's good reason for this. The recipe was dreamed up by the savvy folks at Ralston Purina—a St. Louis company—as a way to push its Chex Brand cereals (wheat, corn, and rice). Today, it's a staple in millions of homes from Maine to Monterey. Some cooks fiddle with the classic recipe, loading it with a favorite nut, perhaps. Or using garlic butter instead of plain. But most TV and cocktail scarfers are happy with this original.

¼ cup (½ stick) butter or
margarine
1¼ teaspoons seasoned salt
4½ teaspoons Worcestershire
sauce
1 cup mixed salted nuts
1 cup thin pretzel sticks
8 cups crisp, bite-size
checkerboard cereal (corn
and/or wheat and/or rice)

1. Preheat oven to 250° F.

2. Melt butter in large, shallow roasting pan in oven. Mix in seasoned salt and Worcestershire sauce.

3. Add nuts, pretzel sticks, and cereal gradually, stirring as you go to coat all well with butter mixture.

4. Bake, uncovered, 1 hour, stirring every 15 minutes.

5. Spread on several thicknesses of paper towels and cool to room temperature.

6. Store in airtight container and serve as a snack or a TV or cocktail nibble.

CAVIAR PIE

A STRUT-YOUR-STUFF appetizer that swept the South in the '70s. Where it came from, I know not. Nor have I been able to learn, for none of the recipes in my community cookbooks gives a clue as to origin. Obviously, the success of the dish depends upon the amount— and quality—of the caviar you use. Beluga isn't necessary. Or sevruga or osetra. But these clearly make better pies than gritty lumpfish caviar. If you can't afford good black caviar, go for red salmon caviar.

Here, more or less, is how to make caviar pie. Line a well-buttered 8- or 9-inch pie pan with finely minced hard-cooked eggs blended with just enough mayonnaise to bind them (6 to 8 eggs and 2 to 3 tablespoons mayo is about right), pressing firmly over the bottom and up the sides to form the "crust." Scatter ½ cup finely minced scallions or yellow onion over the "crust," then spread with 1 to 1½ cups caviar. Frost with 1 to 1½ cups sour cream and refrigerate until ready to serve. Set the caviar pie on a cocktail table with crackers or freshly made melbas, which can be dipped or spread.

APPETIZERS & SNACKS

that Entered the American Mainstream
During the Twentieth Century with Their Source

....

(*Recipe Included)

FRANCE
*Aïoli, *Brandade de Morue
Crudités, Pâtés, Steak Tartare, *Tapenade

❋

ITALY
Antipasto, *Bagna Cauda
*Caponata (see Breads & Sandwiches)
*Olivada

❋

EASTERN MEDITERRANEAN (GREECE, TURKEY, MIDDLE EAST)
*Baba Ganouj, *Hummus, *Skordalia
*Dolma, Taramasalata

❋

RUSSIA/MIDDLE EUROPE
*Liptauer Cheese
Cheese Boreks, Pirozhki

❋

SPAIN & PORTUGAL
Empanaditas
*Bolinhos de Bacalhau (Fried Codfish Balls)
Tapas

❋

ASIA/HAWAII/SOUTH PACIFIC
*Rumaki, Satay, Teriyaki, Yakitori

❋

CARIBBEAN/MEXICO/ LATIN AMERICA
Ceviche, Escabeche, *Guacamole
*Nachos, Quesadillas

Bolinhos de Bacalhau (Portuguese Fried Codfish Balls)

Makes about 2 Dozen

❋

THOUGH A staple in such Portuguese enclaves as New Bedford, Massachusetts, and Newark, New Jersey, these bite-size morsels gained few fans elsewhere until recently. Now many good bars and restaurants —and not all of them Portuguese— set them out as cocktail nibbles. I like to serve them, myself. The secret of truly light codfish balls is ridding the fish of as much salt as possible, then rubbing it in a clean dry towel until as fine and fluffy as cotton.

> 1/3 cup finely minced yellow onion
> 2 tablespoons fruity olive oil
> 10 ounces boned and skinned dried salt cod
> 1 quart boiling water
> 1 large baking potato (1/2 pound)
> 1 quart scalding hot milk
> 2 tablespoons finely minced flat-leaf parsley
> 1/4 teaspoon black pepper
> 2 eggs
> 5 cups vegetable oil for deep frying

1. Mix onion and olive oil and let stand while you proceed.

2. Rinse cod in several changes cold water, cut in 2-inch chunks and place in large heatproof bowl. Pour in boiling water and let stand 30 minutes.

3. Meanwhile, boil unpeeled potato in small saucepan of water.

4. Drain cod, place in large fine sieve, rinse well in cool water, and return to bowl. Pour in hot milk and let stand 30 minutes.

5. When potato is tender, drain and cool until easy to handle. Peel, break into small chunks, spread on paper towels to blot up excess moisture.

6. Drain cod, discarding milk, place in a large fine sieve, rinse well again in cool water, then spread on clean dry towel. Place one-fourth of cod on second clean dry towel and rub briskly until cottony. Transfer to mixing bowl. Rub remaining cod the same way, in three batches, and add to bowl.

7. With potato masher, mash potato on paper towels. Add to cod along with onion mixture, parsley, and pepper; beat hard to blend. Add eggs, one by one, beating well after each addition. Mixture should be smooth and light; set aside.

8. Heat vegetable oil to 375° F in a medium deep skillet over high heat. Meanwhile, set out glass of cold water and stand two teaspoons in it.

9. As soon as oil reaches 375° F, take up heaping teaspoon of cod mixture, then with second wet teaspoon, shape into a little oval and ease into oil. Shape four more balls the same way and ease into oil.

10. Keeping temperature of oil as near to 375° F as possible, fry codfish balls in batches until richly browned—about 2 to 3 minutes per batch.

11. Drain on paper towels and serve hot or at room temperature as an hors d'oeuvre.

TIMELINE

1904

The St. Louis World's Fair introduces:
Puffed rice
Popcorn
Burgers on buns
Iced tea
Ice cream cones
A new "health food" called peanut butter

A load of California artichokes is shipped cross country to New York and New England.

Campbell's cans Pork & Beans.

The "Campbell Kids" debut in Philadelphia streetcar ads.

Jell-O publishes its first recipe booklet, which features such "dainties" as Jell-O Marshmallow Dessert, Minty Velvet, Paradise Pudding, and Raspberries Supreme.

1905

America's first pizzeria opens in New York's "Little Italy."

Dolma (Stuffed Grape Leaves)

Makes 2 Dozen

✳

ALTHOUGH POPULAR in Greek communities by the turn of the century (in *A History of Food and Drink in America* [1981], Richard J. Hooker writes that from 1895 onward, Greek immigrants began opening groceries in New York, Chicago, and other big northern cities that stocked Greek foods), dolma were unknown beyond these enclaves until after World War II when Americans began traveling to Greece. I found this recipe in Athens in 1963.

DOLMA

  1 large yellow onion, peeled and finely chopped
  2 cloves garlic, peeled and minced
  3 tablespoons fruity olive oil
  ⅔ cup raw converted rice
  ⅓ cup coarsely chopped pine nuts
  2 tablespoons dried currants
  2 tablespoons minced flat-leaf parsley
  1 tablespoon snipped fresh dill
  Pinch ground cinnamon
  ¾ teaspoon salt (or to taste)
  ¼ teaspoon black pepper (or to taste)
  1¼ cups cold water
  3 tablespoons fresh lemon juice
  ½ pound brined grape leaves

COOKING LIQUID

  ¾ cup water
  2 tablespoons fruity olive oil
  ¼ cup fresh lemon juice

1. DOLMA: Stir-fry onion and garlic in olive oil in large heavy saucepan over moderate heat 3 to 5 minutes until glassy; do not brown.

2. Add rice and pine nuts and stir-fry 2 to 3 minutes. Stir in currants, parsley, dill, cinnamon, salt, pepper, and water and bring to boiling.

3. Adjust heat so water bubbles gently, cover, and cook 10 to 15 minutes until all liquid is absorbed.

4. Mix in lemon juice, taste for salt and pepper and adjust as needed. Fluff mixture with fork.

5. TO FILL AND ROLL DOLMA: Select 24 young and tender grape leaves and blanch 1 minute in boiling water. Pat dry on paper towels. Place a leaf shiny-side-down on counter and snip off coarse stem. Place mounded teaspoon of rice mixture near stem end of leaf, fold sides in to enclose filling, then roll up jelly-roll style. Repeat until all 24 leaves have been rolled.

6. TO COOK DOLMA: Make bed of remaining grape leaves in bottom of very large, heavy skillet (not iron). Arrange dolma on top as close together as possible but no more than one layer deep. Add water, sprinkle dolma with olive oil and lemon juice. Cover and simmer slowly 45 minutes, checking skillet from time to time and adding more water if it threatens to boil dry. When dolma are done, drain at once.

7. Transfer dolma to 9 × 9 × 2-inch baking dish, again arranging one layer deep. Cover and chill several hours or overnight.

8. Let stand at room temperature at least 30 minutes before serving. Put out toothpicks and, if desired, fresh lemon wedges so guests can add a squeeze of juice.

Nachos

Makes about 2 Dozen

✳

THIS RECIPE is adapted from one Elaine Hanna and I developed for *The New Doubleday Cookbook* (1985).

  24 (2½-inch) round tortilla chips
  2 cups coarsely shredded sharp Cheddar or Montery Jack cheese (about ½ pound)
  1 (4-ounce) can peeled jalapeños, drained well and finely chopped

1. Preheat broiler.

2. Spread tortilla chips over bottom of large, ungreased baking sheet, sprinkle each with cheese, dividing amount evenly, then top with about ½ teaspoon jalapeños.

3. Set 6 inches from heat and broil just until cheese melts—1 to 2 minutes. Serve hot.

NACHOS

I IT WAS KAREN HARAM, food editor of the San Antonio *Express-News*, who told me the story of nachos, and who later sent me the story she'd written about them for her paper in 1986. Here it is, just as she wrote it:

LEGEND OF FIRST NACHO LEADS TO PIEDRAS NEGRAS

Although there is some disagreement about who prepared the first nacho, Jean Andrews of Austin, author of "Peppers: The Domesticated Capsicums," believes the credit goes to a Mexican chef named Ignacio "Nacho" Anaya at the Victory Club in Piedras Negras, Mexico.

Groups of women from such Texas cities as San Antonio, Abilene, and San Angelo traveled to Piedras Negras for a day of shopping and lunch, just as they do now, Andrews said in a telephone interview.

"The story I heard and believe to be true is that one day a group went to the Victory Club and ordered something to eat. Because the restaurant was out of things, Ignacio, whose nickname was Nacho, just kind of threw together something for the group to have with their drinks before lunch," she says.

"He put cheese on toasted tortillas with a jalapeño slice on top. It was just one of those things that happen."

The Victory Club no longer exists today, and Andrews has been unable to track down Anaya.

However, an article by Dotty Griffith, food editor of the Dallas Morning News, *adds substance to Andrews's theory.*

She says a reader, Eleanor H. Magnuson, sent her a copy of St. Anne's Cookbook, published in 1954 by the Church of the Redeemer in Eagle Pass, just across the border from Piedras Negras.

The book contains an advertisement for the Victory Club, which called itself the birthplace of "Nacho Specials."

Nacho Anaya, head chef, was credited with the discovery in the cookbook's ad.

Griffith says another reader told her about Audrey Colley of Crystal City, who may have been the first person to taste a nacho.

In a telephone interview with Colley, the 82-year-old South Texan couldn't remember the first time she had the now-famous Mexican snack, although she admits she may be the person for whom Anaya made the first nacho.

"It might have been in the '40s or '50s. I can't remember when. We'd go to Piedras Niegras three or four times a week," she says.

"I probably said the waiter's name and told him to bring us something to nibble on. I just remember he brought out nachos."

Asked if she enjoyed the snack, Colley says, "Of course, I did. Don't you?"—KAREN HARAM

POSTSCRIPT: Karen Haram tells me that shortly after her article ran in the San Antonio *Express-News* in 1986, she received a letter from Nacho's son, also named Ignacio, who was then a banker in Eagle Pass, Texas. "He told me the story was correct," Haram continues, "that his father did originate the nacho, and that as many as have been sold throughout the world, his father never made any money from them except for what he sold in his restaurant."

GUACAMOLE

IN *THE Dictionary of American Food and Drink* (Revised Edition, 1994), food writer John Mariani pinpoints 1920 as the date of the first American (English-language) reference to this avocado dip. My own research has turned up nothing earlier than 1942. Even Artemis Ward's exhaustive *Encyclopedia of Food* (1923) makes no mention of guacamole despite two pages on the avocado. This is, he says, "primarily a salad fruit to be served in halves or sections to be eaten with salt (and pepper and vinegar if desired), or with a little lime, or lemon juice and sugar. . . . It is also combined in soups and cooked as a vegetable."

A starchy man, Ward goes on to say that "the title 'alligator pear' is deservedly losing ground. It is, under present conditions, a misleading misnomer and should be consigned to oblivion. The smooth skin of the fruit conveys no suggestion of an alligator or its skin." Clearly the leathery, black-skinned Haas and Fuerte avocados of California were unknown to Ward; he wrote only of the giant, smooth, green-skinned Florida variety, which had been introduced in the 1830s. Ward further says that "the word 'avocado' is . . . merely a development of a phonetic substitute for *'ahuacatl,'* the Aztec name for the fruit." Most etymologists agree. They also agree that *guacamole* descends from *abuacamolli,* the Indian name for "avocado sauce."

The first mention (and recipe) for guacamole I've located after digging through scores of late-nineteenth- and early-twentieth-century cookbooks appears in *The Good Housekeeping Cook Book* (1942). The next year, Irma Rombauer included "Avocado Spread (Guacamole)" in *The Joy of Cooking.* But her recipe would hardly pass for *guacamole* today. It directs the cook to mash the pulp of one or two avocados, to mix with onion juice, lemon juice, and salt (no quantities given), then to "heap on small crackers or toast" and "garnish with paprika and parsley." Irma goes on to say that "a good holiday touch is a bit of pimiento or a slice of stuffed olive."

That same year *Sunset* magazine's "Kitchen Cabinet" column ran a recipe for a spicier "Huacamole" made with chopped tomato, onion, and garlic plus mayonnaise, salad oil, sugar, and "2 teaspoons (or more) chili powder."

Helen Evans Brown (*West Coast Cook Book,* 1952) also dishes up an unorthodox guacamole:

You'll want very ripe avocados for this—never mind the blemishes; they are easily cut out. Mash a large one in a bowl that has been rubbed with garlic, and season it with ¼ teaspoon each of salt and chili powder, and a teaspoon of lemon juice. Add 2 teaspoons of very finely minced onion. Now taste it and add more salt if need be, and a little more chili powder, if that's the way you like it. The flesh part of ripe tomatoes, cut in dice, may be added, or small pieces of canned green chilis, or sliced ripe olives, or crisp and crumbled bacon. Mix well and put in a bowl, covering the top with a thin layer of mayonnaise—this to keep the mixture from blackening.

In *Elena's Secrets of Mexican Cooking* (1958), Elena Zelayeta, who for years ran a successful San Francisco restaurant, is the first cookbook author I've found to suggest chopped fresh coriander (cilantro) as a seasoning—a thoroughly Mexican touch. And why not? Elena was born in Mexico, the daughter of innkeepers. Most 1990s cooks, now aiming for authenticity, do add cilantro to their guacamole along with chopped jalapeños. And many prefer lime juice to lemon.

In big-city restaurants, the making of guacamole has been elevated to high art. Take New York City's Rosa Mexicano, for example. Here, all ingredients are trundled to your table, then the guacamole is ceremoniously prepared before your eyes in stone *metates*—tailored, you might say, to your own taste.

"More garlic?" . . . "More onion?". . . . "More jalapeño?" . . . "More cilantro?" You've only to speak up.

Bagna Cauda

Makes about 2 Cups

✳

THE HEADNOTE for this recipe in *Sunset All-Time Favorite Recipes* (1993) states that this Italian "hot bath" (pot of bubbling garlic-and-anchovy-spiked butter and olive oil into which bite-size chunks of raw vegetable are dunked) is one of the readers' three favorite dips. The other two? Guacamole and caponata.

1 cup (2 sticks) butter or margarine
½ cup fruity olive oil
5 large cloves garlic, peeled and minced
2 tablespoons fresh lemon juice
1½ teaspoons black pepper
2 (2-ounce) tins flat anchovy fillets with their oil
Crisp raw vegetables, cut into bite-size chunks
Thinly sliced crusty French or Italian bread

1. Heat butter, olive oil, garlic, lemon juice, and pepper in 3- to 4-cup chafing dish over moderate heat, stirring often, until butter melts.

2. Drain anchovy oil into chafing dish, then finely chop anchovies and add, stirring well to blend.

3. To serve, set chafing dish over candle or low alcohol flame and keep *bagna cauda* at a "tremble." Dunk vegetables—broccoli or cauliflower florets, chunks of zucchini or finocchio—into hot mixture, holding a slice of bread under each to catch drips as you eat.

Guacamole

Makes about 1 Quart

✳

NOT EVERY avocado makes good guacamole. I insist on the black, warty Haas avocados from California. They are small in size but big in flavor. This recipe is my own, one that evolved from my first crude attempts at guacamole making in the 1950s. My early guacamoles were full of mayo and chili powder. And they were smooth as silk. Today I prefer lumpy guacamole. I also like it well seasoned with chopped fresh coriander (cilantro), and lime and onion (I use scallions instead of yellow onion because they're more biting and less watery). Because avocados and tomatoes are rarely at their peak of flavor at the same time, I use canned tomatoes—a diced tomato/diced jalapeño combo with a medium degree of heat.

5 small ripe Haas avocados, pitted, peeled, and cubed (about 2½ pounds)
¼ cup fresh lime juice
5 large scallions, trimmed and chopped (include some green tops)
1 clove garlic, peeled and minced
⅓ cup coarsely chopped fresh coriander (cilantro)
1 (10-ounce) can diced tomatoes and jalapeños, very well drained
½ teaspoon salt (or to taste)

1. Place avocados and lime juice in large bowl and toss well; using potato masher, mash lightly leaving plenty of lumps.

2. Add remaining ingredients, mix well, spoon into 1-quart container, place plastic wrap flat on surface, cover, and refrigerate several hours.

3. Serve as a dip with tortilla chips or mound on shredded lettuce and serve as a first course or salad.

Rumaki

Makes about 2 Dozen

✳

THESE CRISP bacon-wrapped chicken livers are one of the bite-size nibbles on the standard *pupu* (hors d'oeuvre) platters of Hawaii. According to Doris Muscatine (*A Cook's Tour of San Francisco,* 1963), they were popularized in the U.S. by Vic Bergeron, who opened his first Trader Vic's restaurant in Oakland in 1934. His second—a bigger, fancier place—came to San Francisco in 1951 and served rumaki straight from the deep-fat fryer. Word of these sizzling hors d'oeuvre spread across America during the '50s and reached the New York test kitchens of *The Ladies' Home Journal.* Soon we were serving rumaki to visiting VIPs. Ours were baked, not deep-fat-fried, and remain my personal favorite.

> 6 chicken livers, quartered
> 12 slices bacon, halved
>   crosswise
> 2 cups soy sauce
> 12 water chestnuts, sliced thin
>   (preferably fresh)
> 1 cup loosely packed light
>   brown sugar

NOTE: Although the *Journal* recipe doesn't call for it, I like to add a tablespoon of minced fresh ginger to the soy marinade.

1. Marinate chicken livers and bacon in soy sauce 4 hours in refrigerator. Toward end of marinating period, preheat oven to 400° F.

2. Make slits in each chicken liver piece and insert water chestnut slice. Dip in brown sugar, wrap in bacon, and fasten with toothpicks; again dip in brown sugar.

3. Arrange rumaki on wire rack over shallow roasting pan and bake about 30 minutes, turning occasionally, until bacon is crisp. Serve at once.

Brandade de Morue

Makes about 6 Cups

✳

ACCORDING TO Craig Claiborne, for many years food editor of *The New York Times,* this French spread made of dried salt cod is "one of the finest of all appetizers, served frequently in my home as a part of a New Year's Eve buffet." He does not give a recipe for it in *The New York Times Cook Book* (1961) or *The New York Times Menu Cook Book* (1966), but it does appear in *Craig Claiborne's Favorites from The New York Times, Volume 3* (1977), also in the Revised Edition of *The New York Times Cook Book* (1990), which builds a bit of a timeline. For what the *Times* lauded, America's cooks rushed to try. This recipe is adapted from the Revised Edition of *The New York Times Cook Book.*

> 1½ pounds boneless dried salt
>   cod
> 1 pound baking potatoes
> 2 cups milk
> 1 whole bay leaf
> 1 small yellow onion, peeled
>   and thinly sliced
> 2 whole cloves
> 1½ tablespoons minced garlic
>   (about 2 large cloves)
> ½ teaspoon salt (or to taste)
> ¼ teaspoon black pepper (or to
>   taste)
> Pinch freshly grated nutmeg
> Pinch ground hot red pepper
>   (cayenne)
> 1 cup fruity olive oil
> 1½ cups light or heavy cream

1. Soak cod overnight in several changes cold water.

2. Preheat oven to 425° F and bake potatoes until tender, about 1 hour.

3. Meanwhile, drain cod and place in large heavy saucepan. Add enough cold water barely to cover, add milk, bay leaf, onion, and cloves. Bring to boiling, then simmer just until cod flakes—4 to 5 minutes.

4. Drain cod well, discarding cooking liquid, bay leaf, onion, and cloves. Pick through cod, removing bits of skin, bone, and dark flesh.

5. Transfer cod to food processor fitted with metal chopping blade and pulse quickly to flake. Scoop flesh from baked ptatoes and add to cod along with garlic, salt, pepper, nutmeg, and cayenne. Pulse quickly to incorporate.

6. With motor running, add oil alternately with cream, then continue churning until fluffy. Taste for salt and pepper and adjust as needed.

7. Serve as a spread for freshly made melbas or thinly sliced French bread.

FRITOS

....

AN ICE cream salesman named Elmer Doolin, traveling through Texas in 1932, stopped for lunch at a San Antonio sandwich shop and bought a nickel bag of fried corn chips that would forever change his life. Doolin, bored anyway with the ice cream business, found the crisp chips (made with Mexican corn *masa*) unusual, flavorful, and irresistible. He tracked down the man who had made the chips and as luck would have it, he was a homesick Mexican eager to return home. For $100, he told Doolin, he'd sell his recipe, the Fritos name,

nineteen store accounts, and the hand-operated potato ricer that served as a chip-maker. But where on earth could Doolin raise that kind of cash in the depths of the Depression? His mother came to his rescue by hocking her wedding ring.

It was $100 well spent. Starting out modestly, selling Fritos out of the back of his Model T and making about $2 a day, Doolin slowly expanded his original territory. Then one day he met potato chip mogul Herman W. Lay, who agreed to distribute Fritos. And before long Americans from East Coast to West were discovering what fun it was to "muncha buncha Fritos."

3. Add 3 tablespoons cream and pulse several times to incorporate. If mixture seems thick, add remaining 1 tablespoon cream and churn 5 seconds.

4. Serve as a dip for bite-size pieces of zucchini, carrot, celery, broccoli, or cauliflower.

Aïoli (Provençal Garlic Mayonnaise)

Makes about 1½ Cups

✳

I THINK it must have been Julia Child who introduced mass America to *aïoli* in the '60s during her "French Chef" PBS television series. Certainly the recipe appears in *Mastering the Art of French Cooking*, Volume I (1961), which Child co-authored with Simone Beck and Louisette Bertholle and which formed the basis of the TV series. The version here is my own, one developed especially for the food processor, which makes short shrift of it.

NOTE: This recipe contains raw egg, so you must be sure of your source. Otherwise, you risk salmonella food poisoning.

1 slice firm-textured white bread, trimmed of crusts and torn into small pieces
5 cloves garlic, peeled
2 egg yolks
Juice of ½ medium lemon
¼ teaspoon salt
⅛ teaspoon white pepper
1 cup fruity olive oil
3 to 4 tablespoons light cream

1. Churn bread, garlic, egg yolks, lemon juice, salt, and pepper in food processor fitted with metal chopping blade 10 seconds nonstop. Scrape down work bowl sides, recover, and churn 5 seconds longer until smooth.

2. With motor running, drizzle olive oil down feed tube in finest of streams. Once all oil is in, continue churning until thick and fluffy, about 5 seconds longer.

Tapenade (Provençal Olive and Caper Dip)

Makes about 1½ Cups

✳

NOT LONG after *aïoli* made its way into our consciousness in the '60s, along came *tapenade,* a salty Provençal mayonnaise compounded of anchovies, black olives, and capers (its name comes from *tapeno,* the Provençal word for *caper*). Like *aïoli, tapenade* makes a splendid dip for crisp raw vegetables—especially finocchio, zucchini, broccoli, and cauliflower. This recipe is my own, a modern variation you can buzz up in a food processor.

NOTE: This recipe contains raw egg so there is a danger of salmonella food poisoning unless you know your egg supply to be safe.

¼ cup loosely packed parsley sprigs
5 flat anchovy fillets, rinsed well and patted dry on paper towels

6 pitted ripe olives, preferably
   large Provençal or Greek olives
1 clove garlic, peeled
2 tablespoons drained small
   capers
Juice of ½ medium lemon
1 slice firm-textured white
   bread, torn into small pieces
¼ teaspoon black pepper
1 egg
1 cup fruity olive oil

1. Churn parsley, anchovies, olives, garlic, capers, lemon juice, bread, and pepper in food processor fitted with metal chopping blade for 10 seconds. Scrape down work bowl sides, re-cover, and churn 5 seconds longer until smooth.

2. Break egg into work bowl and pulse 3 to 5 seconds to incorporate.

3. With motor running, drizzle oil down feed tube in very fine stream, then continue churning 10 seconds until mixture is fluffy.

4. Spoon *tapenade* into bowl, cover, and store in refrigerator.

5. Let stand at room temperature 30 minutes, spoon into serving bowl, and wreathe with bite-size pieces of raw vegetables.

Olivada (Italian Black Olive Spread)

Makes about 1 Cup

✳

BY THE early '80s, serious students of food had discovered that Italian ripe olive mash called *olivada,* among

them John Thorne, the American food essayist who deserves to inherit M.F.K. Fisher's mantle as our poet laureate of all things culinary. In *Simple Cooking* (1987), Thorne describes his introduction to *olivada:* "The first time I ever saw it I knew exactly what it really was—olive jam—and my ecstatic appetite wanted it so badly, I had the cap loose hardly out of the store and I hunkered down on a stoop just around the corner to devour the whole of it, a French loaf as knife, plate, and napkin. I went back and bought a second jar 'for home.'" Thorne goes on to say that *olivada* is the perfect foil for starch —any starch—bread, toast, baked potato, pasta, polenta, even pizza. He then offers three *olivada* recipes, including this ambrosial one made with fresh basil. I've adapted the recipe here, but only the language.

1 cup firm, brine-cured black
   olives, pitted
2 cups firmly packed fresh basil
   leaves
1 small clove garlic, peeled and
   crushed
¼ cup fruity olive oil

1. Churn olives, basil, and garlic to paste in electric blender or food processor fitted with metal chopping blade—20 to 30 seconds.

2. With motor running, drizzle in olive oil in fine stream and continue churning until smooth—10 to 15 seconds.

3. Serve as a spread for bite-size chunks of French or Italian bread or freshly made melbas.

TIMELINE

1905

A Pennsylvania woman enters her "congealed" (gelatin) salad in a national salad contest, places third, and begins a fad that continues to this day. Perfection Salad, she called it.

Galatoire's opens in New Orleans.

1906

U.S. Pure Food and Drug Act passes.

First revision of *The Boston Cooking-School Cook Book* by Fannie Merritt Farmer is printed (first edition, 1896).

Annual sales of Jell-O approach the $1,000,000 mark.

The hot fudge sundae is created at C.C. Brown's, a brand-new ice cream parlor on Hollywood Boulevard in Los Angeles.

Novelist Owen Wister popularizes Lady Baltimore Cake.

Liptauer Cheese

Makes about 2 Cups

✻

ASSOCIATED PRIMARILY with Hungary, liptauer is nonetheless a staple in Austria, Germany, and, after World War II, across much of America, too, thanks to a new wave of Hungarian immigrants and to returning GIs who'd developed a fondness for it. There are dozens of variations on the theme but this one is my own, my processor improv on the liptauer recipe my mother brought back from Austria where she and my father had lived in the late 1920s before I was born.

> *1½ (8-ounce) packages cream cheese, at room temperature*
> *½ cup (1 stick) unsalted butter, cut into 1-inch chunks*
> *2 teaspoons freshly crushed caraway seeds*
> *2 tablespoons snipped fresh chives*
> *1 tablespoon drained capers*
> *1 tablespoon Dijon mustard*
> *1 tablespoon Hungarian sweet rose paprika*
> *1 teaspoon anchovy paste*

NOTE: For this recipe, you should use unsalted butter. To trim fat and calories, use light cream cheese (Neufchâtel), or low- or no-fat cottage cheese. If you have no food processor, use an electric mixer.

1. Churn all ingredients in food processor fitted with metal chopping blade 15 seconds. Scrape down work bowl sides and churn 15 to 20 seconds longer, until smooth and fluffy.

2. Pack into 1-pint container, cover, and let "season" in refrigerator several hours.

3. Serve as a spread with freshly made melbas or crackers.

Skordalia (Garlic-Potato Puree)

Makes about 1½ to 2 Cups

✻

IN THE '20s and '30s when Greek immigrants moved beyond the big metropolitan areas and began opening restaurants across America, they cooked what they thought the locals wanted instead of serving the splendid dishes of their own country. They fared badly and in much of the land, their restaurants were known as "greasy spoons." Only after World War II did Americans begin to explore Greece in any numbers. And only then did they learn to appreciate Greek food. As a result, upscale Greek restaurants began to appear in big U.S. cities in the early '80s and within ten years the "hot" spread among cutting-edge hostesses was *skordalia,* an intensely garlicky puree of potatoes (or bread or dried limas). This one is adapted from *The Food and Wine of Greece* (1990) by Diane Kochilas, to my mind the best Greek cookbook now available. She adds walnuts to the mix—a Macedonian touch—which makes the *skordalia* gritty. I make the nuts optional. Kochilas says that in Greek tavernas *skordalia* is served as an accompaniment to deep-fried cod, shark fritters, wild greens, or beets. At Periyali, a superb Greek restaurant in Manhattan's Chelsea-Flatiron district, it's brought forth with marinated white beans.

NOTE: The temptation is to make *skordalia* by food processor but it can turn the potatoes gluey. Use a good potato masher or ricer and plenty of elbow grease.

> *2 medium to large potatoes (about 1 pound), boiled, peeled and mashed*
> *4 to 8 cloves garlic, peeled and crushed*
> *1 cup finely ground walnuts (optional)*
> *¾ teaspoon salt (or to taste)*
> *2 tablespoons fresh lemon juice*
> *½ cup fruity olive oil*
> *¼ cup red wine vinegar*

1. By hand, beat potatoes, garlic (your fondness for garlic determining the number of cloves), walnuts, if desired, and salt until smooth and fluffy.

2. Alternately drizzle in lemon juice, olive oil, and vinegar, beating hard after each addition. Continue beating until smooth. Taste for salt and adjust as needed.

NOTE: You can at this point use a hand electric mixer without turning the potatoes to glue.

3. Serve as a spread for crackers or freshly made melbas, or as a dip for bite-size chunks of cucumber, zucchini, or yellow squash.

Hummus (Middle Eastern Sesame-Chick-Pea Spread)

Makes about 2¼ Cups

✳

IN THE Eastern Mediterranean, hummus is one of the components of the classic *meze,* that nonstop parade of hors d'oeuvre that begins a meal (in Turkey, I was once served a thirty-dish *meze* and in Lebanon, a forty-dish one!). Only in the '70s —spurred perhaps by the vegetarian movement or perhaps by our discovery of travel destinations beyond Europe—did this mellow dip begin to show up at stylish American cocktail parties. In addition to making a memorable cocktail dip (with triangles of pita bread or crisp cucumber, zucchini or carrot sticks, broccoli or cauliflower florets), hummus is the "sauce" drizzled over felafel in pita pockets. It's good, too, substituted for butter or mayonnaise in many American sandwiches— peanut butter, club, BLT, and such.

> *2 cups drained, canned chick-peas*
> *⅔ cup sesame seed paste (tahini)*
> *2 large cloves garlic, peeled*
> *6 tablespoons fresh lemon juice*
> *1 teaspoon salt (or to taste)*

NOTE: I find that canned chick-peas make a creamier dip than dried ones because these never soften enough to puree smoothly.

1. Churn all ingredients 30 to 40 seconds in food processor fitted with metal chopping blade or in electric blender at high speed. Scrape work bowl sides down and churn 30 to 40 seconds more, until smooth.

2. Spoon into small bowl, cover, and refrigerate several hours.

3. Let stand at room temperature about 1 hour, stir well, and serve as a spread for bread or crackers or as a sauce for food served in pita pockets.

NOTE: In Turkey, a depression is made in the middle of the bowl of hummus and 1 to 2 tablespoons fruity olive oil spooned in. A nice touch but it ups the fat and calorie content. Suit yourself.

Baba Ganouj (Middle Eastern Eggplant Dip/Spread)

Makes about 3 Cups

✳

SOMETIMES CALLED "eggplant caviar," baba ganouj, like hummus, which precedes, became a trendy cocktail dip in the '70s. This recipe was given to me by a Lebanese friend.

NOTE: For smokier flavor, grill the eggplant quickly until brown instead of baking it.

> *2 large eggplants (1½ to 2 pounds), halved lengthwise but not peeled*
> *4 tablespoons dark roasted sesame oil*
> *2 tablespoons fruity olive oil*
> *2 tablespoons fresh lemon juice*
> *2 cloves garlic, peeled and crushed*
> *1½ teaspoons salt (or to taste)*
> *¼ teaspoon black pepper (or to taste)*
> *2 tablespoons coarsely chopped flat-leaf parsley*

1. Preheat oven to 425°F.

2. Brush cut surface of each eggplant half with 1 tablespoon sesame oil; arrange oiled-sides up on baking sheet and bake, uncovered, 45 to 50 minutes until well browned and soft. Cool until easy to handle.

3. Scrape eggplant flesh into large bowl; discard skins. Roughly mash eggplant (it should be lumpy), then mix in remaining ingredients.

4. Transfer to 1-quart container, cover, and chill several hours.

5. Before serving, let stand at room temperature 30 minutes. For dipping, put out small triangles of toasted pita bread.

SOUPS

SOUP'S ON!

Heinz Home-style Soups Are Being Served At Lunch Counters Everywhere!

HEINZ *Homestyle* SOUPS

...IONED BEAN
...OF TOMATO
... CHOWDER
CREAM OF PEA
VEGETABLE BEEF

CREAM OF MUSHROOM

LARGE B...

Copr. 1938, H. J. Heinz Co.

RESTAURANTS, drug-store luncheonettes, and tea rooms all over the United States are now serving home-tasting soups by *Heinz!* In less than a year the new Heinz Electric Soup Kitchen has taken the country by storm! Wherever you go, you can now enjoy the same delicious Heinz Soups you get at home.

Millions thrill to that "brewed-in" goodness!

With the Heinz Electric Soup Kitchen you wait only *two minutes* for your order! The soup is heated in an electric cup—in full view. Every spoonful is fresh and delicious—full of that luscious, "brewed-in" goodness

that has given Heinz Soups their wide-spread reputation for distinctive, *home-made* flavor! You'll find any of Heinz 22 Soups—such as the rich cream soups, thick vegetable soups, chicken soups—are perfect for cold-weather lunches! If there isn't a Heinz Electric Soup Kitchen where you eat, suggest that the proprietor investigate this new time-saving device.

Serve Heinz Soups in your home, too

Remember to order from your grocer a supply of fully prepared Heinz Soups for your pantry so that you may enjoy their hearty goodness at home as well as abroad!

RESTAURANT AND FOUNTAIN LUNCH OWNERS—CLIP THIS COUPON TODAY!

H. J. HEINZ CO., DEPT. 133, PITTSBURGH, PA.

Please rush me details about the Heinz Electric Soup Kitchen—and enclose descriptive material about Heinz Two-Minute Soup Service for my customers!

Name

Street

City _____ State

Kind of Business Operated

HEINZ *home style* SOUPS

GREAT-GRANDMA had a farm, grandma had a garden, mother had a can-opener.

When it comes to soup, that pretty much sums up this century.

Apart from Senate Bean Soup, Vichyssoise, Boula-Boula, and a few other classics, the twentieth century has been The Age of Campbell's. And Heinz. And Lipton. Indeed, the age of all manufacturers of prepared soups—the canned, the frozen, the dried and freeze-dried.

In ethnic enclaves, however—in the "Little Italy"s, the Chinatowns, the Greek, German, Jewish, Portuguese, and Scandinavian communities scattered from East Coast to West—cooks were slow to embrace convenience foods. Old ways persisted and in some quarters, still do. A good thing, too, because here soups continue to be made the time-honored way according to word-of-mouth or handwritten recipes that have been lovingly passed along from one generation to the next.

Interestingly enough, some of these so-called immigrant recipes—sweet-sour cabbage soup, green split-pea soup, chicken noodle soup with dumplings, leek and potato soup—are now frozen on a commercial scale and can be picked up at the nearest supermarket. Many of them are first-rate with no stinting on top-quality vegetables or fresh herbs.

From the '60s on—you might say from Julia on—there was a return to the homemade. We graduated from canned-soup combos, even from French Onion Soup Gratinée, and began to try long-winded French classics.

Then as jets put the farthest corners of the globe within easy reach, as well-traveled chefs took up the tasting spoons in restaurants across the country, as television cooking shows proliferated, we discovered the beauties of the Italian and Thai soup kettles, not to mention those of a half dozen other ethnicities.

Cold soups came of age this century, too—earlier than one might think. The 1906 edition of *The Boston Cooking-School Cook Book,* for example, offers recipes for Clam and Chicken Frappé and Iced Bouillon.

And Campbell's, perhaps following Fannie Farmer's lead, suggests in its 1910 *Menu Book* that its consommé, "made with prime beef and daintily flavored with selected vegetables, herbs, and spices" is equally good hot or cold.

"For cold consommé," it instructs the cook, "add ice water, mix thoroughly, pour into cups, and set in refrigerator. After four hours it will be found jellied and of just the proper consistency."

However, it was probably the creation of Vichyssoise in 1917 by New York chef Louis Diat—not to mention the arrival, a few years later, of the electric refrigerator in the average home kitchen— that officially launched "iced" soups. Today they are as popular as hot soups, and inventive modern chefs keep busy inventing new ones, often two-soup combos of contrasting colors that can be marbleized in the bowl for showy presentations.

SOUPS

It may seem that I have devoted too much attention in this chapter to canned soups and "instants." Well, like it or not, heat-and-eat soups have revolutionized our lives this century, and mass America still depends on them, as a thumb through any community cookbook or trundle down any supermarket aisle quickly proves.

Canned soups, frozen soups, and dry soup mixes cannot be omitted from a chapter on twentieth-century soups.

Fortunately, there are plenty of from-scratch soups here, too, ones that have made their mark during the last hundred years.

There isn't space, alas, to include them all, so I've exercised my editorial prerogative and picked what for me is a representative group.

Senate Bean Soup

Makes 10 to 12 Servings

✳

IN 1952, the Indiana University Press published *Coast to Coast Cookery*, a collection of regional American recipes gathered by newspaper food editors. It's a fascinating book, given new life in 1976 when Dover issued a paperback edition. Among the entries is "The Senate's Bean Soup," submitted by Lucia Brown, then food editor of *The Washington Post*. I've adapted the recipe but left Brown's headnote untouched:

Bean soup is one dish that appears every day on the menus of the Senate and House restaurants on Capitol Hill. It's a tradition of more than forty years' standing [Brown wrote this in 1952].

The late Senator Knute Nelson, Minnesota Republican, started the custom back in 1907. A bean-soup fancier, he was also chairman of the Senate Committee on Rules. He decreed that the soup should be served daily in the Senate dining rooms. It was, and became so popular that it's never left the menu since. The Hon. Joseph ("Uncle Joe") Cannon, Speaker of the House from 1903 to 1911, who was irate because only the senators were being stoked to daily feats of eloquence with this hearty dish, issued a similar order for the House.

Brown goes on to say that the recipe was given to her by Paul C. Johnson, the man in charge of service in the Senate dining rooms. Also that the soup is "made in a big brass kettle, but Mr. Johnson says other utensils can be used." Quite so. I find an enameled cast-iron kettle works well.

Note that the dried beans are not soaked, only rinsed in hot water, then simmered very slowly with ham hocks until soft. You can hurry the recipe by soaking the beans overnight. However, long, slow cooking—with the water never at an active boil—is what gives this soup its character.

1½ pounds dried navy or pea beans, washed and sorted
4 quarts hot water
¾ pound smoked ham hocks (or for smokier flavor, 1 pound)
2 cups coarsely chopped yellow onion (about 1 extra-large)

2 tablespoons butter
1 tablespoon salt (or to taste)
½ teaspoon black pepper (or to taste)

1. Place beans in colander and let hot tap water run over them 1 minute.

2. Dump beans into large heavy kettle, add hot water and ham hocks, and bring to boiling. Adjust heat so water barely bubbles, cover, and simmer very slowly until beans are mushy and meat falls from bones—2½ to 3 hours. Check and stir beans from time to time, and if needed to keep water just below boiling, slide flame-tamer under kettle.

3. Remove ham from bones and cut into bite-size pieces; discard bones. With potato masher, roughly mash beans in kettle (or use immersion blender—soup should be lumpy). Return ham to kettle. If soup seems thin, boil, uncovered, stirring frequently, about 10 minutes to thicken slightly.

4. Sauté onion in large heavy skillet in butter over moderate heat, stirring often, until richly browned—8 to 10 minutes.

5. Add browned onion to soup and cook, uncovered, stirring often, 10 to 15 minutes longer. Season to taste with salt and pepper.

6. Ladle into heated soup bowls and serve.

The Origin of Vichyssoise

FEW WOULD deny that this is America's most famous twentieth-century soup. It was created in the early 1900s (some say 1910, others 1917) by Chef Louis Diat of New York's Ritz-Carlton Hotel. As Diat explains in *Cooking à la Ritz* (1941), vichyssoise had its origin in France in his mother's kitchen: "She used to make a hot soup of leeks and potatoes which was liked very much by her children. But in the summer when the soup seemed to be too hot, we asked her for milk with which to cool it. Many years later, it was this memory which gave me the inspiration to make the soup which I have named Crème Vichyssoise."

The fact that the Ritz-Carlton opened in December 1910 (with Diat newly arrived from the London Ritz) makes it highly unlikely that this cold summer soup was created that year. Quoting an early *Vanity Fair* article, Craig Claiborne notes (in *The New York Times Food Encyclopedia*, 1985) that vichyssoise dates to the June 1917 opening of the Ritz-Carlton's rooftop restaurant. English food writer Elizabeth David concurs. At least about the date. In *French Provincial Cooking* (1960), she writes: "*Crème vichyssoise* is, as is well known, an American soup. But it was evolved by a Frenchman, Louis Diat, for forty-one years *chef des cuisines* at the Ritz-Carlton in New York." After explaining that the soup is based on *potage bonne femme*, "the leek and potato soup known to every French housewife," David goes on to say that "iced *vichyssoise* was served for the first time by Louis Diat at the Ritz-Carlton in the summer of 1917, and has since become famous all over the United States."

In a chapter devoted to luncheons toward the end of *Cooking à la Ritz*, Diat himself says, "This soup was introduced by me at the Roof Garden of the Ritz-Carlton about twenty years ago." With *Cooking à la Ritz* published in 1941, that would put the date around 1920, but perhaps Diat was rounding off the numbers. He goes on to say: "I decided on the name Vichyssoise because the town where I was born is near Vichy, world famous for its spring water."

According to Evan Jones (*American Food: The Gastronomic Story*, 1975), vichyssoise "just missed entering history as '*crème gauloise*' in 1941 when a group of chefs in America voted to change the name because they were offended by the wartime Vichy government." That name never took because too many Americans already knew and loved the soup called *vichyssoise*.

Here, then, "the original and genuine *Cream Vichyssoise Glacée*," just as it appears in *Cooking à la Ritz*.

CREAM VICHYSSOISE GLACÉE

Serves eight

4 leeks, white part	5 medium potatoes	2 cups milk
1 medium onion	1 quart water or chicken broth	2 cups medium cream
2 ounces sweet butter	1 tablespoon salt	1 cup heavy cream

Finely slice the white part of the leeks and the onion, and brown very lightly in the sweet butter, then add the potatoes, also sliced finely. Add water or broth and salt. Boil from 35 to 40 minutes. Crush and rub through a fine strainer. Return to fire and add 2 cups of milk and 2 cups of medium cream. Season to taste and bring to a boil. Cool and then rub through a very fine strainer. When soup is cold, add the heavy cream.

Chill thoroughly before serving. Finely chopped chives may be added before serving.

It's interesting to note that Diat, himself, gives two variations: Cream Glacée à la Ritz, in which 1 cup tomato juice is blended with 3 cups vichyssoise, and Cream Glacée Sorrel, in which 2 tablespoons chopped, butter-sautéed sorrel is blended with 4 cups vichyssoise. Both variations are served cold. J.A.

A Modern Vichyssoise

Makes 6 Servings

✳

AN EASY vichyssoise that I developed especially for the food processor. Use only "Idahos" or baking potatoes (Russet Burbanks). Their flavor is superior, and because they lack the glutinous quality of new or all-purpose potatoes, they can be processor-pureed with a little liquid without turning into library paste.

2 large baking potatoes, peeled and halved lengthwise
4 large leeks, trimmed, washed, and chunked
1 medium celery rib, trimmed, washed, and chunked
3 cups chicken broth
2 cups half-and-half
1 teaspoon salt (or to taste)
¼ teaspoon white pepper (or to taste)
1 cup heavy cream or sour cream
2 tablespoons snipped fresh chives

1. Thin-slice potatoes in food processor, then leeks and celery (no need to empty work bowl until all are sliced).

2. Transfer sliced vegetables to large heavy saucepan, add broth, cover, and cook until vegetables are mushy —20 to 25 minutes.

3. With small strainer, scoop vegetables from broth into clean processor work bowl equipped with metal chopping blade. Add ½ cup hot broth and puree by pulsing quickly until smooth.

4. Stir back into pan, add half-and-half, salt, and pepper, and bring just to simmering. Cool to room temperature, then smooth in heavy cream.

5. Cover and chill several hours or overnight. Taste for salt and pepper and adjust as needed.

6. Ladle into small soup bowls and top with snipped chives.

Michael McLaughlin's Basil Vichyssoise with Garden Tomatoes and Roasted Sweet Peppers

Makes 6 to 8 Servings

❋

ONE OF the "new American chefs" who surfaced in the late '70s and early '80s, Michael McLaughlin, formerly of The Silver Palate and The Manhattan Chili Co., puts a colorful new spin on Louis Diat's classic. This recipe is adapted from McLaughlin's *The New American Kitchen* (1990).

>   3 tablespoons butter
>   5 medium leeks (white part only), well cleaned and sliced
>   2 cloves garlic, peeled and minced
>   6 cups chicken broth, canned or homemade
>   1 pound baking potatoes, peeled and chunked
>   1 teaspoon salt (or to taste)
>   2 cups loosely packed fresh basil leaves
>   ½ cup heavy cream
>   1 medium sweet yellow or orange bell pepper
>   1 large, vine-ripe beefsteak tomato
>   6 to 8 small sprigs fresh basil

1. Melt butter in large heavy saucepan over moderate heat. Add leeks and garlic, reduce heat to low, cover, and cook, stirring once or twice, until leeks are tender—about 15 minutes.

2. Add broth, potatoes, and salt and bring to boiling. Adjust heat so broth bubbles gently, set lid on askew, and boil until potatoes are mushy—35 to 40 minutes.

3. Mix in basil leaves, set soup off heat, and let stand, covered, until cool. Pour soup through strainer set over large bowl.

4. Transfer solids to food processor equipped with metal chopping blade and add 1 cup soup liquid. Puree until smooth.

5. Stir puree back into soup liquid, blend in cream, cover, and chill several hours or overnight.

6. In open flame of gas burner or in preheated broiler, roast pepper, turning often, until evenly charred. Cool pepper in sealed paper bag or covered bowl, then rub away charred skin. Stem and core pepper, pat dry on paper towels, and cut into ½-inch dice.

7. Halve tomato crosswise, squeeze out seeds and juice, then cut tomato into ½-inch dice.

8. Taste soup for salt and adjust as needed. Ladle into chilled bowls and garnish with sprinklings of roasted pepper and tomato. Top with fresh basil sprigs and serve.

TIMELINE

1906

Mama Leone's Restaurant opens behind the Metropolitan Opera House in New York City.

Frankfurters are nicknamed "hot dogs" after Hearst cartoonist Tad Dorgan begins depicting Germans as dachshunds.

Kellogg's Corn Flakes go on sale.

1907

Hershey's Kisses introduced.

1908

The first Dixie Cup.

1910

Gas ranges begin to phase out coal, wood, and petroleum stoves.

PUREE MONGOLE, CRÈME MONGOLE, OR MONGOLE SOUP

DID LOUIS DIAT also create this half-and-half combo of tomato and green pea soups? I'd always assumed it was a Campbell's concoction dating back to the 1930s, but Campbell's archivists say no. In *Cooking à la Ritz* (1941), Louis Diat includes *Mongole Soup (Potage Mongol)* as a variation of *Potage Saint Germain* (cream of green pea soup). It calls for equal parts green pea and cream of tomato soups—both made "from scratch."

I find an altogether different recipe for *Puree Mongole* in Henri Charpentier's *Those Rich and Great Ones* (1935), which combines three bean purees (green, lima, and navy) with pureed green peas, onion, celery, and tomatoes, then blends in milk, beef or chicken consommé, and heavy cream. Charpentier, who worked at New York's Knickerbocker Hotel, served as assistant head waiter at Cafe Martin at the Hotel Plaza, then opened his own restaurant in Lynbrook, Long Island, in 1910, where *Puree Mongole* became a signature dish.

In *Streamlined Cooking* (1939) and in the 1943 and 1946 editions of her best-selling *The Joy of Cooking*, Irma Rombauer gives two recipes for Mongole Soup, a two-ingredient one in her "Soup Merger" chart (see page 61) and a fancier version, in which she gussies up the canned pea and tomato soups with 2 cups top milk (the cream that rose to the top of the bottle before milk was homogenized) and an optional ¼ cup sherry plus a blush of paprika and scattering of grated cheese. This one she introduces with flowery prose, both in *Streamlined Cooking* and the early *Joys*):

I should like to sing a paean of praise about this and the following soups made with a basis of pea and tomato. If there is anything better in the hurry-up culinary art

I don't know what it is. Rich? Yes, but you may plan to serve simple food afterward. This is worth adding a fraction of a pound to your avoirdupois, only don't fall in love with it and serve it too often.

John and Karen Hess (*The Taste of America*, 1977) deplore America's abandonment of the soup kettle in favor of canned soups and damn, in particular, the eight pages Rombauer devotes to such "canned-soup combinations" as Mongole Soup in the 1943 *Joy of Cooking* (much of this material had been recycled, word for word, from Rombauer's *Streamlined Cooking*, 1939). To the Hesses, Mongole Soup epitomizes America's new dependency on canned soups. After bemoaning its inclusion in the 1943 *Joy of Cooking*, they point out that "This recipe does not appear in the 1975 edition but a variation does: Quick Crab or Lobster Mongole." This is merely Mongole Soup with a cup of canned crab or lobster tossed in and dry white wine substituted for sherry.

"Nothing," the Hesses complain, "could be more 'gourmet' than this undiscriminating use of 'dry white wine,' and no recipe could better illustrate the lack of understanding of basic culinary principles and of plain good taste that prevail in American fancy cooking today."

Strangely, Mongole Soup appears in no edition I have of Fannie Farmer—1896, 1906, 1918, and right through the 1920s, 1930s, 1940s up to the completely revised Marion Cunningham editions. In fact, *The Boston Cooking-School Cook Book* makes far less use of canned soups than *Joy*.

So when, where did Irma Rombauer discover Mongole Soup? Did she taste Diat's Mongole on a trip to New York, then turn to canned soups as a way to short-cut a long process? Or, as seems more plausible, did some soup-company home economist do this? All leads I've pursued as to the origin of Mongole Soup have come to naught. If Diat did concoct it, his inspiration, unlike that for vichyssoise, was apparently not French. None of the several dozen French cookbooks and culinary dictionaries I consulted makes any mention of *Puree* or *Potage Mongol.*

What I do know is that Mongole Soup was popular from the 1930s right into the 1960s. Then it fell from favor. According to Sylvia Lovegren (*Fashionable Food,* 1995), the creamy Mongole served at New York's "21" Club contained "fresh peas, shoestring carrots, and a little onion juice." She adds that John MacPherson (radio's Mystery Chef) developed a

creamless Mongole and dubbed it "Mystery Chef Soup"—all of this in her 1930s chapter.

According to Poppy Cannon and Patricia Brooks (*The Presidents' Cookbook,* 1968), "For some reason, Mongole Soup was an inaugural-day favorite during the Roosevelt administration [FDR, not Teddy]. A number of these occasions were rainy as well as cold, and the hordes who showed up for lunch found this a satisfying and warming addition to the standard cold cuts, salads, and rolls. It also made a hearty midnight snack for Roosevelt guests who were often a little peckish in the late hours."

THIS RECIPE is adapted from one in Volume 11 of the *Woman's Day Encyclopedia of Cookery* (1966) edited by Nika Hazelton, one of America's more reliable food writers and historians. It is typical of the quick Mongole Soup recipes that proliferated in the late '30s, '40s, and '50s.

PUREE MONGOLE, CRÈME MONGOLE, OR MONGOLE SOUP

Makes 4 Servings

1 (10½-ounce) can green
   pea soup
1 (10-ounce) can cream of
   tomato soup
¾ cup water

1 cup light cream
2 teaspoons Worcestershire
   sauce
¼ cup dry sherry

1. Mix pea and tomato soups, water, cream, and Worcestershire sauce in medium heavy saucepan. Set over moderate heat and bring just to serving temperature, stirring often.

2. Off heat, blend in sherry.

3. Ladle into soup bowls and serve.

Chilled Avocado and Green Chili Soup

Makes 8 Servings

❋

I'LL NEVER forget the first time I tasted avocado soup. It was the spring of 1959, I'd been sent by *The Ladies' Home Journal* to Los Angeles to interview actress Joan Fontaine, and she had me up to her house on Mulholland Drive to sample the recipes we'd be using in the magazine. Among them was a stellar curried avocado soup, served ice cold (I've subsequently traced pureed avocado soup—minus the curry—

to a 1943 issue of *Sunset*). For years I served Fontaine's avocado soup to raves. In recent years, I've tasted many variations and my new favorite comes from Cafe Pasqual's

in Santa Fe. Owner Katharine Kagel is one of the most creative cooks I've ever known. This recipe, adapted from *Cafe Pasqual's Cookbook* (1993), deliciously proves the point.

NOTE: If you prefer, you can substitute ¾ to 1 cup well-drained, chopped green chilies for the fresh. I also like to add a couple of squeezes of fresh lime to the soup just before I chill it so that it is less likely to turn brown.

1 cup coarsely chopped, peeled,
   seeded, roasted green chilies,
   preferably New Mexico green
   chilies (about ¾ pound)
6 medium ripe Haas avocados,
   peeled, pitted, and cubed
½ teaspoon curry powder
¼ to ½ teaspoon ground hot
   red pepper (cayenne)
4 to 6 cups milk
1 tablespoon salt (or to taste)
2 tablespoons finely minced
   red onion

1. Puree chilies and avocados in 2 to 3 batches with curry powder, cayenne, 4 cups milk, and salt in electric blender at high speed or in food processor fitted with metal chopping blade. Add as much of remaining 2 cups milk as needed for good consistency; churn until smooth.

2. Transfer soup to large bowl, cover, and chill 4 to 6 hours—but no longer because the soup will turn brown. Taste for salt and adjust as needed.

3. Ladle into bowls and garnish each portion with a little minced red onion.

MIXING CANNED SOUP FLAVORS

"*A finer product than canned soup was never produced and anything I might say in its praise would prove to be an understatement. In addition, it is an ideal time-saver. Canned soups are good as they come from the can but they may be varied in endless ways.*"—Irma Rombauer, *Streamlined Cooking* (1939)

AFTER LISTING forty-six flavors of canned soup then available (the Heinz line plus many others, including borscht, crawfish bisque, vermicelli, and vegetarian), Rombauer offers a "Soup Merger" chart. This same chart appears in the 1940s editions of *The Joy of Cooking*.

Cream of Spinach Soup	+	Cream of Mushroom Soup	=	St. Patrick's Soup
Clam Chowder	+	Chicken Gumbo (Creole)	=	Clamole Soup
Vegetable Soup	+	Cream of Tomato Soup	=	Cooperstown Soup
Cream of Mushroom Soup	+	Chicken Noodle Soup	=	Old-Fashioned Velvet Soup
Cream of Oyster Soup	+	Cream of Tomato Soup	=	Oyster Soup Louisiane
Pepper Pot Soup	+	Vegetable Soup	=	Pittsburgh Pepper Pot
Cream of Celery Soup	+	Chicken Noodle Soup	=	Aunt Ellen's Soup
Chicken Gumbo (Creole)	+	Vegetable Soup	=	Soup Paysanne
Cream of Tomato Soup	+	Cream of Green Pea Soup	=	Puree Mongole
Corn Chowder	+	Onion Soup	=	Indian Chowder
Cream of Mushroom Soup	+	Cream of Oyster Soup	=	Soupe St. Martin
Onion Soup	+	Chicken Gumbo (Creole)	=	Onion Soup Creole
Cream of Tomato Soup	+	Cream of Celery Soup	=	Traymore Soup
Consommé	+	Chicken Noodle Soup	=	Dutch Consommé
Corn Chowder	+	Cream of Tomato Soup	=	Berkshire Soup

Note: The only one to attain any permanence is the cream of tomato/green pea blend—Puree Mongole, or as it's now better known, Mongole Soup.—J.A.

Cold Senegalese Soup

Makes 6 Servings

✳

THIS RECIPE is adapted from one that appears in the *Waldorf-Astoria Cookbook,* Golden Anniversary Edition (1981) by Ted James and Rosalind Cole.

NOTE: The "21" Traditional Senegalese Soup is livelier. For 4 to 6 servings, it adds an onion and a garlic clove, 3 chopped apples, 2 chopped carrots, ¼ cup raisins, 1 tablespoon tomato puree, and 3 tablespoons curry powder. Moreover, it is thickened with flour instead of egg yolks, which significantly lowers the cholesterol count.

3½ cups clear chicken stock or
    broth, canned or homemade
1 cup finely chopped cooked
    chicken
1½ to 2 teaspoons curry
    powder
4 egg yolks, lightly beaten
2 cups light cream
½ teaspoon salt (or to taste)
⅛ teaspoon white pepper (or to
    taste)
6 tablespoons cooked shredded
    chicken, white meat
    preferably

1. Bring stock, chopped chicken, and curry powder to boiling in medium heavy saucepan. Reduce heat to lowest point and simmer, uncovered, about 5 minutes to blend flavors.

2. Quickly whisk ¼ cup hot stock into egg yolks, mix in cream, then stir back into pan. Cook and stir constantly over low heat until soup thickens slightly, about 5 minutes; do not allow to boil. Season to taste with salt and pepper.

3. Transfer to large bowl, cover, and chill several hours or overnight. Taste for salt and pepper and adjust as needed.

4. Ladle into soup bowls and garnish each portion with 1 tablespoon shredded chicken.

Senegalese Soup with Coriander

Makes 4 Servings

✳

A SNAPPY modern Senegalese adapted from *The Best of Gourmet* (1989).

1 quart canned chicken broth
1 whole skinless chicken breast
    (about 10 ounces), halved
2 medium yellow onions, peeled
    and chopped
1½ cups finely diced celery
3 tablespoons vegetable oil
2 tablespoons curry powder
1 teaspoon ground turmeric
¼ teaspoon ground hot red
    pepper (cayenne)
¼ cup chopped mango chutney
¼ cup minced fresh coriander
    (cilantro)
4 sprigs fresh coriander

1. Bring broth to boiling in medium heavy saucepan over moderate heat. Add chicken, adjust heat so broth bubbles gently, cover, and poach just until cooked through—10 to 15 minutes.

2. Meanwhile, stir-fry onions and celery in oil in large heavy skillet over moderately low heat until limp—3 to 5 minutes. Blend in curry powder, turmeric, and cayenne and cook, stirring, 2 minutes to mellow flavors. Lift chicken from broth and set aside. Pour broth into skillet and cook, stirring occasionally, 5 minutes.

3. Meanwhile, coarsely chop chicken breast and add half to electric blender cup or food processor fitted with metal chopping blade. Add skillet mixture and chutney and puree until smooth.

4. Quick-chill pureed soup mixture in ice bath or freezer, then stir in remaining chopped chicken and minced coriander.

5. Ladle into soup bowls and garnish with coriander sprigs.

SENEGALESE SOUP

ERE'S ANOTHER easy soup that became popular this century. There's no obvious source—and negligible leads. Few food historians have anything to say about this cold, delicately curried cream of chicken soup. One who does is Norman Odya Krohn, a Swiss-trained hotelier/restaurateur who once served as maître d'hôtel at New York's fashionable Four Seasons Restaurant. In *Menu Mystique: The Diner's Guide to Fine Food & Drink* (1983), he writes: "Since curry is rarely, if ever, used in Senegal (formerly part of French West Africa), one might logically conclude that the soup was born in Ceylon, which is today Sri Lanka."

He might be onto something. Craig Claiborne (*The New York Times Food Encyclopedia*, 1985) says that a "highly informative letter from a Jersey City gentleman" also suggested Sri Lanka as the soup's likely source, then goes on to quote that letter: "There are several Sanskrit names, including Lanka, for that country, and one of these is Sinhala or Singhala." A word easily Anglicized into "Senegalese."

How, then, did the soup make its way here? Via England? No English cookbook I consulted speaks of Senegalese Soup and that includes the exhaustively researched *Cooking of the British Isles* (1969) by Adrian

Bailey, one of the volumes in Time-Life's Foods of the World series. Nor do I find any reference to or recipe for Senegalese Soup in any French source or culinary dictionary. Did some American chef dream it up and name it Senegalese?

In *American Taste* (1982), James Villas praises "the famous Senegalese at the '21' Club in New York," but gives no clue as to origin. And in her headnote for Crème Senegalese, Mimi Sheraton (*The Whole World Loves Chicken Soup*, 1995) writes: "Old cookbooks from various parts of the United States credit New York with this version, at both the '21' Club and the erstwhile Delmonico's." Yet Lately Thomas makes no mention of it in *Delmonico's: A Century of Splendor* (1967). Nor is it listed on the extensive Delmonico's menu reproduced at the front of the book. The recipe does appear, however, in *The "21" Cookbook* (1995) by Michael Lomonaco with Donna Forsman, together with this headnote: "This rich, cold curried soup is more familiar in Europe (especially England) than in the U.S. It has been served at '21' for years, and we may be one of the few restaurants in this country where you can still find it. At '21,' the classic garnish for this soup is diced poached chicken." But the cookbook version substitutes ½ teaspoon chutney (per portion).

Once again, I am left wanting—and wondering.

BOULA-BOULA

SYLVIA LOVEGREN (*Fashionable Food,* 1995) writes that "Boula has a more documented history than does Mongole Soup." She adds that it was known in this country "as early as the 1830s," but provides no proof.

No early-nineteenth-century cookbook I checked mentions boula (boula-boula, boola, or boola-boola). Green turtle soup, yes, but no combination of green turtle and green pea. In her decade-by-decade review of "fashionable foods," Lovegren slots boula into the 1930s and offers a recipe for it from *Much Depends on Dinner* (1939) by Mary Grosvenor Ellsworth, who obtained the recipe from an "M. Derouet, the maître d'hôtel of the Chemists' Club." In what city, Lovegren does not say.

Apparently it was a specialty at the Plaza Hotel's Persian Room in the '30s, a signature dish of Chef de Cuisine Joseph Boggia. Diana Ashley's *Where to Dine in '39* includes Boggia's recipe:

½ cream green pea soup, ½ green turtle soup; add 1 tbls., per cup, of diced turtle meat; add dessertspoon, per cup, of dry sherry; pour in cups and add spoonful whipped cream; place under broiler until whipped cream is browned.

Craig Claiborne remembers his mother making boula-boula when he was a child, which would push the date back into the 1920s. In *The New York Times Food Encyclopedia* (1985), Claiborne reminisces: "In my childhood, boula-boula was a soup to be served on fancy occasions. It was made with a blend of two canned soups, a cream of green pea and a green turtle." He adds that the crowning touch was a dollop of stiffly whipped cream, ladled on just before serving and "run briefly under the broiler until the cream was lightly browned."

Just where did Boula-Boula originate? No one seems to know. An unnamed source Claiborne quotes in *The New York Times Food Encyclopedia* says: "It is an American soup . . . that originally came from the Seychelles"—presumably because of the availability of green turtles in this Indian Ocean island group. (These are now an endangered species.)

Norman Odya Krohn (*Menu Mystique: The Diner's Guide to Fine Food & Drink,* 1983) dismisses the Seychelles connection. "Although this soup is about as American as apple pie," he writes, "it has nothing to do with the college song that has been popular at Yale University since 1901. Nor," he continues, "has it any connection with the Seychelles Islands, contrary to whatever our English friends contend." No English source I consulted mentions boula and unfortunately, Krohn sheds no light on how he came to this conclusion. Perhaps it was because the Seychelles were once a British crown colony.

Sylvia Lovegren writes that René Verdon, White House chef during the Kennedy years, served boula at the White House (according to *The First Ladies Cook Book,* 1969, it was JFK's favorite soup). Lovegren writes, too, that Verdon credits the Kennedys with "jokingly" renaming "the soup boula-boula, after the Harvard song." Not likely. A Harvard man, Kennedy would have known that "Boula-Boula" belonged to Yale. Lovegren also believes the soup was called Boula-Boula before the Age of Camelot. I agree. I knew it in the 1950s before JFK and Jackie were known to one and all.

James Beard's Boula-Boula

Makes 6 Servings

✳

"I DON'T know if this name is derived from the famous Yale song," James Beard writes in his massive *American Cookery* (1972), from which this recipe is adapted, "but I do know that in the last fifty years the soup has become a top-drawer soup for company." Beard's boula, unlike many, does not consist merely of equal parts canned green pea soup and canned green turtle soup. He begins with frozen peas and enriches the mix with butter-sautéed onion.

NOTE: My good friend and colleague Jeanne Voltz tells me that with green turtles now an endangered species, cooks are substituting canned clams and bottled clam juice for green turtle soup. For this recipe you will need two (10-ounce) cans diced clams, drained, 2 (8-ounce) bottles clam juice, and 1 cup water.

SOUP

¼ cup (½ stick) butter
3 tablespoons minced yellow onion
2 (10-ounce) packages frozen green peas
½ cup chicken broth or water
½ teaspoon salt (or to taste)
¼ teaspoon hot red pepper sauce
3 cups canned green turtle soup (see Note above)
1 cup heavy cream
¼ cup medium-dry sherry

TOPPING
1 cup heavy cream, stiffly whipped

1. Melt butter in large heavy saucepan over moderate heat. Add onion and sauté until glassy—2 to 3 minutes.

2. Add peas, broth, salt, and red pepper sauce, cover, and cook until peas are tender—about 5 minutes.

3. Meanwhile, strain turtle soup; dice turtle meat and set aside; add liquid to peas and cook 5 minutes longer.

4. Puree pea mixture in electric blender at high speed, in food processor fitted with metal chopping blade, or by forcing through food mill.

5. Preheat broiler. Return pea mixture to pan, add cream, sherry, and diced turtle meat, and bring just to serving temperature. Taste for salt and adjust as needed.

6. Divide soup among 6 flameproof bowls or small crocks and "frost" each with whipped cream.

7. Set bowls on heavy-duty baking sheet and broil 4 to 5 inches from heat just until cream is tipped with brown—2 to 3 minutes. Serve at once.

TIMELINE

1910

Kitchen cabinets appear; pantries begin to disappear.

....

Hawaii pineapple growers begin canning pineapple and shipping it to the U.S.

1910–20

The era of the "combination stove" (gas plus wood or coal).

1911

Procter & Gamble develops hydrogenated vegetable shortening and calls it Crisco.

....

Canned chili goes on sale.

....

The New York Electric Exhibition introduces "electrified" chafing dishes, skillets, grills, percolators, toasters, waffle irons.

Chunky Chicken Noodle Soup with Vegetables

Makes 8 Servings

✳

THIS EASY recipe is adapted from *Lipton Creative Cookery Made Easy with Lipton Soup Mix,* published in 1987 by Thomas J. Lipton, Inc. The particular soup mix it calls for is Lipton Soup Secrets Noodle Soup Mix with Real Chicken Broth.

> 2 envelopes noodle soup mix
>   with real chicken broth
> 6 cups water
> 2 cups torn escarole
> 1 large rib celery, trimmed and
>   thinly sliced
> 1 small carrot, peeled and
>   thinly sliced
> ¼ cup frozen green peas
>   (optional)
> 1 small clove garlic, peeled and
>   minced
> ½ teaspoon dried leaf thyme,
>   crumbled
> 2 whole cloves
> 1 whole bay leaf
> 2 cups diced cooked chicken
> 1 tablespoon minced fresh parsley

1. Place soup mix, water, escarole, celery, carrot, peas, if desired, garlic, thyme, cloves, and bay leaf in large heavy saucepan; stir well.

2. Bring to boiling over moderate heat, reduce heat so mixture bubbles gently, and simmer, uncovered, until vegetables are tender—about 15 minutes.

3. Mix in chicken and parsley and bring just to serving temperature. Remove and discard bay leaf and cloves.

4. Ladle into heated soup bowls and serve.

Buttermilk Gazpacho

Makes 4 Servings

✳

I CAN'T say who originated this soup or when, exactly. I do know that I first tasted it in the early '60s and have loved it ever since. The good news is that this low-calorie, low-fat soup brims with health-

giving vegetables, and if only hard-cooked egg whites are used, the cholesterol levels plummet. This version is my own.

> 2 hard-cooked eggs, peeled and
>   halved
> 1½ cups canned tomato or
>   tomato-vegetable juice
> 1½ cups buttermilk
> ⅔ cup finely diced Spanish or
>   Bermuda onion
> ½ cup diced celery
> ⅓ cup diced green bell pepper
> ⅓ cup diced red bell pepper
> 1 tablespoon snipped fresh dill
> ¼ teaspoon salt (or to taste)
> ⅛ teaspoon black pepper (or to
>   taste)
> 1 lime, thinly sliced (optional)

1. Sieve egg yolks into large mixing bowl. Add tomato juice, buttermilk, onion, celery, green and red pepper, dill, salt, and black pepper; stir well to mix.

2. Cover and refrigerate several hours or overnight. Mince egg whites, wrap in plastic wrap, and refrigerate.

3. To serve, spoon a little minced egg white into each of four soup bowls, pour in gazpacho and, if desired, float a lime slice on each portion.

Garlic Soup

Makes 4 to 6 Servings

✳

ALTHOUGH MANY countries consider garlic soup a staple, it didn't win many fans here until the shift toward vegetarianism in the '60s and '70s. And only a decade or so later did it break into the mainstream by appearing on the menus of America's innovative young chefs. Few would deny that Deborah Madison belongs at the top of this list. After working with Alice Waters at Chez Panisse, she became founding chef at Greens, the celebrated vegetarian restaurant overlooking San Francisco Bay. This recipe is adapted from Madison's *The Savory Way* (1990). In the headnote, she writes that this particular garlic soup "lends itself to adornments and additions, such as croutons, a spoonful of cooked rice, tiny stellar *pastini,* or small pieces of boiled potatoes." She goes on to say that it can be "poured over grilled bread, covered with grated Parmesan or Gruyère cheese," and suggests that a few herby, ricotta-filled ravioli can be floated in each portion.

1 large bulb garlic, separated
   into cloves
2 quarts water
1 tablespoon fruity olive oil
2 whole cloves
8 large branches fresh flat-leaf
   parsley
10 large fresh sage leaves or
   ½ teaspoon dried leaf sage,
   crumbled
6 medium sprigs fresh thyme or
   ¼ teaspoon dried leaf thyme,
   crumbled
1 teaspoon salt (or to taste)
Pinch saffron, crumbled
4 tablespoons freshly grated
   Parmesan cheese
4 tablespoons minced fresh
   chervil or flat-leaf parsley

1. With flat side of heavy chef's knife, smash each garlic clove; remove and discard peel.

2. Drop garlic into large heavy saucepan, add water and all remaining ingredients except Parmesan and minced chervil. Bring to boiling, adjust heat so water bubbles gently, set lid on askew, and simmer 30 minutes.

3. Strain soup, discarding solids, return to pan and bring just to serving temperature. Taste for salt and adjust as needed.

4. Ladle into bowls and top each portion with Parmesan and minced chervil.

TIMELINE

1912

....

Soft, hamburger-size yeast buns are manufactured.

....

The Oreo cookie debuts.

....

Jell-O's newest recipe booklet features creations by six of America's most famous cooks: columnist and cookbook author Marion Harland (Lemon Jell-O Whip with Prunes), Sarah Tyson Rorer of *The Ladies' Home Journal* (Queen Mab Pudding, Frozen), *Boston Cook Book* author Mary J. Lincoln (Strawberry Mousse), *Boston Cooking School Magazine* editor Janet McKenzie Hill (Raspberry Jell-O Supreme), Butterick Publishing's Emma Paddock Telford (Lemon Jell-O Split), and household economist Christine Terhune Herrick (Chocolate Blanc Mange with Nuts). There are even Jell-O recipes from actress Ethel Barrymore and singer Madame Ernestine Schumann-Heink. *But note the absence of Fannie Farmer.*

Roasted Eggplant Soup

Makes 4 Servings

✳

ROASTED VEGETABLE soups came into fashion in the '80s, and there's none better than this one made with pureed roasted eggplant. It's adapted from Linda Ziedrich's *Cold Soups* (1995) and requires baked elephant garlic, which is milder and sweeter than regular garlic. Ziedrich prepares it thus: "Remove loose outer skin from 1 bulb elephant garlic, set garlic in small baking dish, and top with 3 tablespoons fruity olive oil. Sprinkle, if desired, with salt and pepper and tuck in a fresh thyme sprig. Cover and bake in preheated 275°F oven 30 minutes; uncover and bake 1 to 1½ hours more, basting now and then, until garlic is soft. This, by the way, makes a wonderful spread for bread."

NOTE: If you like food less "hot," use 1 to 2 chilies.

> *1 large eggplant (about 2 pounds)*
> *2 cloves baked elephant garlic, peeled (see headnote above)*
> *1 tablespoon oil from baked garlic*
> *2 cups chicken broth*
> *1 cup heavy cream*
> *3 serrano chilies, seeded and chopped*
> *½ to 1 teaspoon salt (or to taste)*
> *1 red bell pepper, roasted, peeled, seeded, and chopped (optional)*

1. Preheat oven to 400° F. With large kitchen fork, pierce eggplant in several places, then place in ungreased shallow baking pan.

2. Bake eggplant, uncovered, until very soft—about 1 hour.

3. Halve eggplant lengthwise and scoop flesh into electric blender cup or food processor fitted with metal chopping blade. Add garlic, oil, broth, cream, chilies, and ½ teaspoon salt and puree until smooth. Taste for salt and adjust as needed.

4. Serve soup at room temperature or chill well and serve cold. Top each portion, if desired, with chopped roasted red pepper.

Cold Cucumber Soup

Makes 6 Servings

✳

SMOOTH AS silk and cool as a—well—cucumber, this recipe is adapted from one in William Rice's splendid *Feasts of Wine and Food* (1987).

NOTE: Zucchini or yellow summer squash may be substituted for cucumbers. The soup may also be served hot, but I prefer it cold.

3 pounds medium cucumbers,
  peeled and chunked
2 quarts chicken broth (about)
1 small yellow onion, peeled
  and quartered
1 large bunch fresh dill,
  stemmed and washed
3 tablespoons farina (Cream of
  Wheat)
2 tablespoons white wine
  vinegar
1 cup sour cream
½ teaspoon salt (or to taste)
⅛ teaspoon white pepper (or to
  taste)

GARNISHES
6 thin unpeeled cucumber slices
2 tablespoons snipped fresh dill

1. Cook cucumbers in chicken broth with onion, dill, farina, and vinegar in partially covered large heavy saucepan over moderate heat until cucumbers are mushy—about 30 minutes.

2. Cool 15 minutes, then puree in electric blender at high speed or in food processor equipped with metal chopping blade. Strain puree through coarse sieve into large bowl.

3. Smooth in sour cream, tablespoon by tablespoon, then mix in salt and pepper. Soup should be consistency of vichyssoise; if too thick, thin with a little additional chicken broth.

4. Cover and chill several hours or overnight. Taste for salt and pepper and adjust as needed.

5. Ladle into bowls and garnish with cucumber slices and snipped dill.

Clam and Tomato Consommé

Makes 6 Servings

✳

QUICK SOUPS containing a can of this or bottle of that persisted well into the '60s thanks to continued support by the women's magazines. As late as November 1965, *McCall's* ran a feature called "First Course by the Fireplace." And every one of its soup recipes began with a can of something. This clam-tomato combo surfaced, I think, in the '50s when bottled clam juice became widely available. I remember experimenting with it when I was a recipe tester at *The Ladies' Home Journal* in the late '50s/early '60s. This one, never published, is my favorite. It's good hot or cold; in fact, I prefer it well chilled, drifted with yogurt, and sprigged with dill.

2 (8-ounce) bottles clam juice
2 (10¾-ounce) cans consommé
  madrilène
1 cup tomato juice
1 tablespoon fresh lemon juice
1 tablespoon finely grated
  yellow onion
2 teaspoons sugar
½ teaspoon Worcestershire sauce
¼ teaspoon hot red pepper
  sauce
⅛ teaspoon black pepper
6 small sprigs fresh dill or
  parsley

1. Bring all ingredients except dill to boiling in medium-size, heavy enameled or stainless steel saucepan over moderate heat—5 to 7 minutes. Reduce heat to lowest point and simmer, uncovered, 10 minutes.

2. Ladle into soup cups, sprig with dill and serve. Or chill well and serve cold.

Tomato and Orange Consommé

Makes 4 Servings

✳

ONE OF the more interesting quick twentieth-century soups is this orange juice–tomato juice combo. There are many variations on this theme. This one is adapted from *Gourmet's Menu Cookbook* (1963).

2 cups canned tomato juice
2 cups fresh orange juice,
  strained
1 tablespoon fresh lemon juice
  (or to taste)
½ teaspoon celery salt (or to
  taste)
¼ teaspoon hot red pepper
  sauce
1 tablespoon snipped fresh
  chives

1. Bring tomato juice and orange juice to simmering in small heavy saucepan over moderate heat.

2. Remove from heat, add lemon juice, celery salt, and red pepper sauce. Taste and adjust lemon juice and celery salt as needed.

3. Ladle into soup cups, sprinkle with chives, and serve hot. Or chill well and serve cold.

Campbell's Soup Combinations

IN 1949, the Campbell Soup Company published a recipe booklet called *Easy Ways to Good Meals* and devoted several pages to "Soup Combinations." To introduce them, the copywriter pulled out all the stops:

Let's combine one soup with another! For soups that are new and different, try combining some of your favorites. Taste the unusual deliciousness of cream of asparagus coupled with the rich savoriness of chicken soup—or the luscious new flavor of tomato when paired with green pea soup. Try all thirteen of the following recipes, and then invent new combinations of your own. There's practically no end to the delicious discoveries you'll be making.

Here, then, the 1949 Campbell's combos:

HIGHLAND VEGETABLE BROTH

Makes 6 servings

1 can Campbell's Scotch Broth
1 can Campbell's Vegetable Soup
2 cans water (using soup can as measure)

COMBINE the soups; add water. Heat to simmer 3 minutes.

❋

CHILLED TOMATO-CHICKEN SOUP

Makes 4–5 servings

1 can Campbell's Cream of Chicken Soup
1 can Campbell's Tomato Soup
1½ cans milk

MIX soups, stirring until smooth. Add milk; chill.

CHICKEN SOUP TREAT

Makes 4 servings

1 can Campbell's Cream of Mushroom Soup
1 can Campbell's Chicken Noodle Soup
1 can water

EMPTY cream of mushroom soup into a saucepan; stir well. Add chicken noodle soup, stirring constantly. Add water; heat to boiling and serve.

HUNGRY MAN'S CHOICE

Makes 6 servings

1 can Campbell's Ox Tail Soup
1 can Campbell's Vegetable-Beef Soup
2 cans water

COMBINE the soups; add the water. Heat to simmer 3 minutes.

❋

CREAM OF ASPARAGUS AND CHICKEN SOUP

Makes 6 servings

1 can Campbell's Cream of Asparagus Soup
1 can Campbell's Chicken with Rice Soup
2 cans milk

STIR asparagus soup until smooth. Combine soups; add milk. Heat, but do not boil.

SOUPS

PUREE MONGOLE

Makes 4 servings

1 can Campbell's Tomato
   Soup
1 can Campbell's Green Pea
   Soup
1 can milk

COMBINE soups; add milk.
Heat, but do not boil.

✳

BUFFET SUPPER SOUP

Makes 8 servings

1 can Campbell's Cream of
   Mushroom Soup
1 can Campbell's Cream of
   Asparagus Soup
1 can Campbell's Chicken with
   Rice Soup
2 cans milk
1 can water

COMBINE soups; add milk and
water. Heat, but do not boil.

✳

DELICIOUS MEAL SOUP

Makes 6 servings

1 can Campbell's Beef Soup
1 can Campbell's Beef Noodle
   Soup
2 cans water

COMBINE soups; add water;
simmer 3 minutes.

CREOLE CLAM BISQUE

Makes 4 servings

1 can Campbell's Clam
   Chowder
1 can Campbell's Chicken
   Gumbo Soup
1 can light cream

MIX the soups; add cream.
Heat, but do not boil.

✳

CREOLE TOMATO SOUP

Makes 6 servings

1 can Campbell's Tomato
   Soup
1 can Campbell's Chicken
   Gumbo Soup
2 cans water

COMBINE soups; add water.
Heat to simmer 3 minutes.

CREAM OF MUSHROOM AND ASPARAGUS SOUP

Makes 6 servings

1 can Campbell's Cream of
   Mushroom Soup
1 can Campbell's Cream of
   Asparagus Soup
2 cans milk

COMBINE soups; add milk.
Heat, but do not boil.

✳

MUSHROOM SAINT GERMAIN

Makes 6 servings

1 can Campbell's Cream of
   Mushroom Soup
1 can Campbell's Green Pea
   Soup
2 cans milk

COMBINE soups; add milk.
Heat but do not boil.

✳

VEGETABLE SOUP— PEASANT STYLE

Makes 6 servings

1 can Campbell's Vegetable
   Soup
1 can Campbell's Bean with
   Bacon Soup
2 cans water

COMBINE the soups; blend in
the water. Heat to simmer 3
minutes.

Meatball Soup

Makes 8 Servings

✳

THIS IS sometimes called *Italian* meatball soup, erroneously I think, because few classic Italian soups contain *polpettine* (meatballs). And if they do, they are more likely to be made with veal than beef. I suspect, but cannot prove, that this soup came out of America's big-city Italian restaurants early this century, where to accommodate the U.S. appetite for beef, cooks added meatballs to soups just as they did to pasta sauces. This recipe is my own.

MEATBALLS

½ pound ground beef chuck
¼ cup finely minced yellow onion
¼ cup fine dry bread crumbs
¼ cup freshly grated Parmesan cheese
1 small clove garlic, peeled and crushed
½ teaspoon salt
⅛ teaspoon black pepper
3 to 4 tablespoons cold water or beef broth (just enough to bind meatballs)

SOUP

1 meaty beef shank, about 4 inches long
3 quarts water
1 tablespoon salt (or to taste)
¼ teaspoon black pepper (or to taste)
½ small rutabaga, peeled and finely diced

1 large baking potato, peeled and finely diced
4 medium carrots, peeled and thinly sliced
2 large ribs celery, trimmed and thinly sliced
2 medium yellow onions, peeled and coarsely chopped
1 small red or green bell pepper, cored, seeded, and coarsely chopped
¼ small cabbage, cored and coarsely chopped
3 large vine-ripe tomatoes, cored and coarsely chopped or 1½ cups canned crushed tomatoes

1. **MEATBALLS:** Using hands, mix all ingredients thoroughly, shape into ½-inch balls, and set aside.

2. **SOUP:** Simmer beef shank in water with salt and pepper 30 minutes in uncovered large heavy kettle over moderate heat, skimming off froth as it collects.

3. Add rutabaga, potato, and meatballs, cover, and simmer slowly about 1 hour, stirring now and then.

4. Add carrots, celery, onions, and red pepper to kettle, cover, and simmer 15 minutes.

5. Add cabbage and tomatoes, cover, and simmer about 30 minutes until all vegetables are tender and flavors well blended. Taste for salt and pepper and adjust as needed. Remove beef shank, cut off all meat, and mix into soup; discard bone.

6. Ladle into heated large soup plates and serve at once. Pass freshly grated Parmesan cheese, if you like, and put out chunks of crusty Italian bread.

Cioppino

Makes 8 Servings

✳

THE ONLY thing definite about cioppino is that no one knows for sure when it originated. In researching the recipe, I found a wide range of dates—from Gold Rush Days to the 1930s. Most food historians and cookbook authors don't even try to fix the recipe in time, although all point to San Francisco as the place of origin. It's true, certainly, that cioppino wasn't well known beyond the Bay area (or at least outside California) until after World War II.

John Thorne, a masterful writer and meticulous researcher, describes in the September/October 1996 issue of his newsletter, *Simple Cooking,* how he came upon a vintage (1921) cookbook that discusses cioppino in detail. That book, *Fish Cookery* by Evelene Spencer of the U.S. Bureau of Fisheries and John N. Cobb, director of the College of Fisheries at the University of Washington, offers a recipe for cioppino that had appeared three years earlier in an article by H.B. Nidever in *California Fish and Game.* Thorne believes that it may be one of the first, if not *the* first, ever published. He also points to this passage in Nidever's article, which suggests that cioppino originated in the fishing grounds off the coast of California, not in San Francisco:

When fishermen are out on trips for days at a time, the only supplies that are taken are bread, wine, a little coffee, and the ingredients that are used to make up a cioppino, depending on their luck to catch the needed fish.

Those ingredients would have included olive oil, canned tomatoes, onions, and garlic, of which Spencer and Cobb write: "Garlic should certainly be tried by the housewife in this dish, even if she has never used it before." They do, alas, suggest substituting corn, cottonseed, or "any preferred brand of salad oil" for olive oil with "equal results."

Yet according to Coleman Andrews, a food writer/historian I respect, there is a classic Genoese fisherman's soup called *il ciuppin*. Its name, as he explains in *Flavors of the Riviera* (1996), is "simply a corruption of the Genoese word *sûppin*, meaning 'little soup.'" Take the linguistic corruption one step further, and you get cioppino.

And here's Helen Evans Brown, another writer I admire, on the subject. In her *West Coast Cook Book* (1952), she writes: "This is one of California's most famous dishes and one that we can claim is ours, all ours. It is a versatile dish, as it was invented by fishermen who made it with whatever the ocean was inclined to yield." Mrs. Brown adds that California fishermen of Italian and Portuguese descent both make cioppino, the latter adding potatoes

as a thickener. Brown dismisses one oft-told tale: "That San Francisco's fishermen did *not* introduce cioppino to California, but that an Italian named Bazzuro, who ran a restaurant on a boat anchored off Fisherman's Wharf, is responsible. What's more," Brown writes, "it was supposed to have been an old recipe, well known in Italy. This back in the 1850s. I refuse to believe it!"

The recipe below is adapted from one in *American Cooking: The Great West* (1971), a volume in Time-Life Books Foods of the World series.

NOTE: This recipe calls for fish stock. If you do not want to make it yourself, you will find frozen fish stocks in many specialty groceries. In a pinch, you can also substitute a half-and-half mixture of bottled clam juice and water.

¼ cup fruity olive oil
1 large yellow onion, peeled and coarsely chopped
2 cloves garlic, peeled and minced
1 quart fish stock
3 medium vine-ripe tomatoes, peeled, cored, and pureed or 1 cup canned tomato puree
1 cup dry white wine

2 tablespoons minced fresh flat-leaf parsley
2 (1½-pound) cooked, cleaned, and quartered Dungeness crabs or 3 pounds live blue crabs
3 dozen unshucked mussels, scrubbed and bearded
2 dozen unshucked littleneck or cherrystone clams, scrubbed
½ teaspoon salt (or to taste)
2 pounds fresh cod steaks, cut into 8 pieces of equal size

1. Heat olive oil in large heavy kettle over moderate heat 1 minute. Add onion and garlic and stir-fry until glassy—3 to 5 minutes.

2. Add stock, tomato puree, wine, and parsley and bring to a boil, stirring occasionally. Adjust heat so mixture bubbles gently, set lid on askew, and simmer 15 minutes.

3. Arrange Dungeness, or failing that, live whole blue crabs, in ungreased 6- to 8-quart enameled, flameproof casserole. Lay mussels and clams on top, then pour in tomato-fish stock mixture. Bring to a boil over high heat, adjust heat so liquid barely trembles, cover, and cook 10 minutes.

4. Meanwhile, salt cod on both sides, dividing total amount evenly.

5. Add cod to casserole, cover, and simmer gently 8 to 10 minutes longer, until mussels and clams open —discard any that do not. Taste for salt and adjust as needed.

6. Ladle into soup bowls, making sure each person gets plenty of liquid.

Tuna-Vegetable Chowder

Makes 2 to 4 Servings

✳

CHOWDERS ARE hardly a twentieth-century invention, but tuna chowder *is* because it wasn't until 1903 that canned tuna became available. This recipe is adapted from one that appeared in a booklet called *Starkist Sensational Tuna* (1993).

> ½ cup diced carrot (about 1 small)
> 1 cup quartered small mushrooms
> 1 cup small broccoli florets
> 2 tablespoons butter or margarine
> ¼ cup finely minced yellow onion
> 4 tablespoons all-purpose flour
> 2⅔ cups milk (low-fat or regular) or buttermilk
> 1 cup chicken broth
> 1 (6⅛-ounce) can tuna, drained and flaked
> ½ teaspoon dried dillweed
> ½ teaspoon dried leaf marjoram, crumbled
> ½ teaspoon dried leaf basil, crumbled
> ½ teaspoon salt
> ¼ teaspoon black pepper
> 2 tablespoons dry sherry (optional)

1. Steam carrot, mushrooms, and broccoli together over simmering water until almost tender—8 to 10 minutes. Set aside.

2. Melt butter in large heavy saucepan over moderate heat. Add onion and stir-fry until glassy—about 3 minutes.

3. Blend in flour, add milk and broth, and cook, stirring constantly, until mixture thickens and no raw starch taste remains—about 5 minutes.

4. Add reserved steamed vegetables, tuna, dillweed, marjoram, basil, salt, and pepper and cook and stir just until heated through—3 to 5 minutes.

5. Stir in sherry, if desired, ladle into soup bowls, and serve.

Sweet Red Pepper Bisque

Makes 6 Servings

✳

AS BEST I can tell, this soup emerged during the go-go days of "New American Cooking" in the late '70s and early '80s. Innovative chefs on both coasts began making sweet pepper soups—red, yellow, orange—sometimes swirling two or more colors in a single bowl. But sweet red pepper soup seemed everyone's favorite. Mine, certainly. After tasting it in the early '80s in more than one restaurant, I rushed home to "crack" the recipe. This is my own version, a recipe I created for a story I was writing for *Food & Wine* magazine and one that's been well received at dinner parties. Sometimes I serve the soup hot, sometimes cold. It's good both ways.

SOUP

> 2 large sprigs fresh rosemary
> 2 medium sprigs fresh marjoram
> 3 tablespoons fruity olive oil
> 6 large red bell peppers, cored, seeded, and cut into ½-inch strips
> 6 medium leeks (white part only), washed and thinly sliced
> 2 large cloves garlic, peeled and minced
> ¼ teaspoon black pepper (or to taste)
> 2½ cups beef stock or broth
> ¾ cup crème fraîche *or* sour cream
> Salt, if needed, to taste

GARNISHES

> 6 tablespoons crème fraîche *or* sour cream
> 6 tiny sprigs fresh rosemary

1. SOUP: Tie rosemary and marjoram sprigs in cheesecloth and wring lightly to release volatile oils. Set aside.

2. Heat olive oil in large heavy saucepan over high heat 1 minute. Add red peppers and stir-fry until lightly softened—about 2 minutes.

Add leeks and garlic and stir-fry 2 minutes more.

3. Add cheesecloth bag of herbs and black pepper. Reduce heat to very low, cover tight, and cook until vegetables release considerable juice and peppers are soft—about 1 hour.

4. Discard cheesecloth bag, then puree saucepan mixture in batches in electric blender at high speed or in food processor fitted with metal chopping blade.

5. Strain puree into saucepan, add stock, and cook, uncovered, just until hot—2 to 3 minutes. Smooth in *crème fraîche,* season to taste with salt, and adjust black pepper as needed.

6. Ladle into heated soup plates and garnish each serving with 1 tablespoon of *crème fraîche* and 1 tiny rosemary sprig. Or, if you prefer, chill well, then serve topped by *crème fraîche* and rosemary sprigs.

Alice Waters's Carrot and Red Pepper Soup

Makes 8 Servings

✱

WHEN SHE opened Chez Panisse in Berkeley in 1971, Alice Waters had no idea that her small kitchen would be a training ground for many of the innovative young chefs who've shaken up American cooking—Joyce Goldstein, Deborah Madison, Mark Miller, and Jeremiah Tower, to name four of the more visible. From the outset, Waters used only the finest, freshest produce available and treated it with reverence, as this signature soup clearly demonstrates. She calls this "our first double soup," then goes on to explain that "the carrot soup acts as a backdrop for the more pungent red pepper flavor." The recipe here is adapted from Baba S. Khalsa's *Great Vegetables from the Great Chefs* (1990).

CARROT SOUP
¼ cup (½ stick) butter
4½ cups water
6 large carrots (about 1¼ pounds), peeled and cut into ½-inch dice
1 small yellow onion, peeled and cut into ¼-inch dice
1 teaspoon salt (or to taste)
⅛ teaspoon black pepper (or to taste)
1½ teaspoons fresh lemon juice

RED PEPPER SOUP
2 tablespoons butter
3 medium red bell peppers, cored, seeded, and diced
¾ cup water
¼ teaspoon salt (or to taste)
⅛ teaspoon black pepper (or to taste)
Few drops red wine vinegar (optional)
8 small sprigs fresh chervil (optional)

1. CARROT SOUP: Melt butter in large heavy saucepan over moderate heat, add 1 cup water, carrots, and onion. Bring to simmering, adjust heat so mixture barely bubbles, cover, and cook until carrots are very soft and almost all water has evaporated—about 30 minutes. Add remaining 3½ cups water and bring to boiling. Cool 5 minutes.

2. Puree mixture in small batches in electric blender at high speed or in food processor fitted with metal chopping blade until smooth—about 3 minutes per batch. Mix in salt, pepper, and lemon juice, taste, and adjust salt and pepper as needed. Keep soup warm.

3. RED PEPPER SOUP: Melt butter in medium heavy saucepan over moderate heat, add red peppers and water. Bring to simmering, adjust heat so mixture bubbles slowly, cover, and cook until peppers are very soft—about 20 minutes. Cool slightly.

4. Puree peppers with cooking liquid until smooth in electric blender at high speed or in food processor fitted with metal chopping blade—about 1 minute. Strain red pepper puree, return to pan, and season to taste with salt and black pepper. Taste and, if soup lacks depth, mix in vinegar. Also thin, if necessary, with a little water until soup is same consistency as carrot soup.

5. TO SERVE: Pour ⅔ cup carrot soup into each of 8 heated soup plates, then spoon 2 tablespoons red pepper soup into center of each and swirl lightly with a thin-blade knife or spatula to marbleize. Garnish with chervil sprigs.

Soups

that Entered the American Mainstream
During the Twentieth Century, with Their Source

....

(* Recipe Included)

FRANCE
*Billi-Bi, Bouillabaisse
*French Onion Soup Gratinée
Soupe au Pistou

✳

ITALY
*Minestrone, *Pasta e Fagioli

✳

GREECE
Avgolemono Soup

✳

RUSSIA/MIDDLE EUROPE
*Borscht, Matzoh Ball Soup
Hungarian Sour Cherry Soup

✳

SPAIN & PORTUGAL
Garbanzo Bean Soup, *Gazpacho, *White Gazpacho
*Caldo Verde (Portuguese Green Soup)

✳

MEXICO/CARIBBEAN/
LATIN AMERICA
Black Bean Soup, *Tortilla Soup
Sopa de Albondigas

✳

ASIA
Egg-Drop Soup
Hot and Sour Soup
Wonton Soup
*Thai Shrimp, Mushroom, and Lemon Grass Soup

Minestrone

Makes 6 to 8 Servings

✳

A HUSKY Italian vegetable soup so mainstream you can buy it by the can. No brand, however, can match the minestrone you make yourself. The beauty of this recipe (my own, by the way) is that once the basics are in the pot, you can go about your business. The minestrone can simmer the better part of the day. In fact, it's better if it does. Just make sure the burner heat is as low as it can go (use a flame-tamer, if necessary)—the soup should never boil. In northern Italy, near Genoa in particular, cooks often stir a bit of pesto (page 214) into their minestrone just before serving.

NOTE: If you chop and slice the vegetables by food processor, even the prep is a breeze. This soup keeps well in the refrigerator for about a week and also freezes well.

> ¼ pound salt pork, coarsely chopped
> 2 large yellow onions, peeled and coarsely chopped
> 2 large cloves garlic, peeled and minced
> 2 large ribs celery, trimmed and coarsely chopped
> 3 large leeks, trimmed, washed well, and thinly sliced
> 3 large carrots, peeled and coarsely chopped
> 1 large all-purpose potato, peeled and coarsely chopped

4 large vine-ripe tomatoes, cored and coarsely chopped or 3 cups canned crushed tomatoes
1 quart rich beef broth (about)
1 whole bay leaf
1 teaspoon dried leaf basil, crumbled
½ teaspoon dried leaf thyme, crumbled
½ teaspoon dried leaf marjoram, crumbled
¼ pound tender young wax or green beans, tipped and cut into 1-inch lengths
2 tender young zucchini, trimmed and thinly sliced
¼ small cabbage, trimmed, cored, and thinly sliced
1½ teaspoons salt (or to taste)
½ teaspoon black pepper (or to taste)
2 cups, rinsed and drained, cooked or canned cannellini beans

1. Sauté salt pork in large heavy kettle over moderate heat until crisp and brown—12 to 15 minutes. With slotted spoon transfer crisp brown bits to paper towels to drain.

2. Sauté onions in drippings until limp—about 5 minutes. Add garlic, celery, and leeks and stir-fry until limp—3 to 5 minutes. Add carrots and potato, turn heat to lowest point, and sauté, stirring occasionally, until tender and golden but not brown—about 20 minutes.

3. Add tomatoes, broth, bay leaf, basil, thyme, and marjoram. Bring to a gentle simmer, cover, and cook *very* slowly 3 to 4 hours, stirring occasionally and adding additional broth if kettle threatens to cook dry.

4. Add wax beans, zucchini, cabbage, salt, and pepper, cover, and simmer slowly 1 to 1½ hours, until very tender.

5. Add cannellini beans and reserved browned salt pork, cover, and simmer until flavors mellow—20 to 30 minutes longer. Taste for salt and pepper and adjust as needed.

6. Discard bay leaf. Ladle into heated large soup plates and serve with crusty chunks of Italian bread.

Pasta e Fagioli

Makes 6 Servings

✳

LIKE SO many Italian recipes now in the American vernacular, *pasta e fagioli,* a classic dried-bean-and-pasta soup, moved from big-city Italian neighborhoods outward into the rest of America. This particular recipe is adapted from one that appears in *From the Farmer's Market,* a wonderful book that my good friend and colleague Sandra Gluck coauthored with Richard Sax.

SOUP

2 tablespoons fruity olive oil
2 large yellow onions, peeled and thickly sliced
2 small carrots, trimmed, peeled, and thickly sliced
½ medium red bell pepper, cored, seeded, and cut into 1 × ¼-inch strips
4 cloves garlic, peeled and minced
½ cup chopped fresh basil or 1 teaspoon dried leaf basil, crumbled
⅛ teaspoon dried leaf oregano, crumbled
½ pound boneless smoked ham, cut into ¼-inch dice
1 cup canned crushed tomatoes
6 cups chicken or vegetable broth
4 cups dried cooked or canned beans (Great Northern, cranberry, or red kidney), rinsed and drained well
2½ cups small pasta shells or elbow macaroni
1½ teaspoons salt (or to taste)
¼ teaspoon black pepper (or to taste)
¾ cup thinly sliced mushrooms

TOPPING

⅓ cup thinly sliced green scallion tops (3 to 4 large)
2 tablespoons fruity olive oil
Freshly grated Parmesan cheese

1. SOUP: Heat olive oil in medium heavy kettle over moderately high heat 1 minute. Add onions, carrots, and red pepper and stir-fry until limp—6 to 8 minutes. Add garlic, 3 tablespoons fresh basil (or 1 teaspoon dried), oregano, and ham and cook and stir 2 minutes.

2. Add tomatoes and cook, uncovered, stirring often, until consistency of pasta sauce—5 to 6 minutes.

3. Add broth and beans and bring to boiling. Mash about one-fourth of beans against side of kettle, reduce heat, cover, and simmer slowly 20 minutes.

4. Add pasta and boil gently, uncovered, until not quite *al dente*—5 to 7 minutes.

5. Remove from heat and skim off as much fat as possible; season to taste with salt and pepper. Scatter mushrooms on top of soup, cover, and let stand 5 minutes.

6. Return soup to heat and bring just to boiling. Taste for salt and pepper and adjust as needed. Stir in remaining fresh basil.

7. Ladle into large soup bowls, and top each portion with scallion tops and olive oil, dividing amounts evenly. Pass freshly grated Parmesan.

Billi-Bi

Makes 4 to 6 Servings

✳

A TWENTIETH-CENTURY French classic that leapt the Atlantic early on, Billi-Bi was, by most accounts, created by Chef Louis Barthe in 1925. In *The Dictionary of American Food and Drink,* Revised Edition (1994), John Mariani says there's some discrepancy as to whether Barthe created this cold mussels soup at Maxim's in Paris, the restaurant with which it's most closely associated, or at Ciro's in Deauville. There is less question, however, that Billi-Bi was named in honor of American William Brand, a Maxim's regular. The recipe here is adapted from one of my favorite books, *American Taste* (1982) by James Villas.

NOTE: Many high-end groceries now carry frozen fish stock and it's a good substitute for homemade. Be forewarned: Only "essence of mussels," i.e., the juices, are used in this recipe. As for the steamed mussels themselves, serve warm or cold in a fine vinaigrette, add to a good marinara sauce and serve over pasta, or freeze and add later to a favorite fish soup or stew.

6 dozen unshucked mussels, scrubbed and bearded
1 quart fish stock
1 cup dry white wine
2 carrots, peeled and sliced
3 medium yellow onions, peeled and chopped
¾ pound mushrooms, wiped clean and chopped
3 medium ribs celery, trimmed and chopped
½ cup minced fresh flat-leaf parsley
½ teaspoon salt (or to taste)
¼ teaspoon white pepper (or to taste)
1½ cups light cream, scalded

1. Bring mussels, fish stock, wine, carrots, onions, mushrooms, celery, parsley, salt, and pepper slowly to boiling in large heavy kettle over moderately low heat. Adjust heat so mixture bubbles gently, cover, and simmer just until mussels open—about 5 minutes. Discard any mussels that do not open and reserve the balance for another use.

2. Cool kettle mixture to room temperature. Strain mussels broth into a medium saucepan and discard solids.

3. Boil mussels broth, uncovered, over high heat until reduced by half —10 to 15 minutes.

4. Off heat, stir in cream and cool mixture to room temperature. Transfer soup to bowl, cover tight, and refrigerate several hours or overnight.

5. Taste for salt and pepper and adjust as needed, then ladle into well-chilled soup bowls and serve.

TIMELINE

1912

Life Savers appear.

The Oyster Bar opens in New York's Grand Central Terminal.

Morton introduces free-flowing, granulated table salt.

Whitman Candy Company boxes a mixture of chocolates, calls it a "Sampler," and prints a chart inside the lid to identify each piece.

1913

Fruit cocktail is created by a California canner.

Campbell's cans cream of celery soup.

1914

Vitamin A is isolated.

1914–18

World War I.

French Onion Soup Gratinée

Makes 6 Servings

✳

ALTHOUGH THIS soup was known early this century, and perhaps somewhat earlier, it was hardly a "household name" until after World War II when GIs came home from France with a taste for it. I first dipped into French Onion Soup when I was an undergraduate at Cornell in the 1950s. Today's sophisticated cooks may consider it a cliché. Still, nothing beats it for warming up a wintry day.

¼ cup (½ stick) butter
4 large yellow onions (about 2 pounds), peeled and thinly sliced
6 cups rich brown stock or broth, preferably homemade
½ teaspoon salt (or to taste)
¼ teaspoon black pepper (or to taste)
12 (½-inch-thick) slices French bread (about 1 medium loaf)
¾ cup coarsely shredded Gruyère cheese
¼ cup freshly grated Parmesan cheese

1. Preheat oven to 300° F. Melt butter in large heavy saucepan over moderately low heat, add onions, and cook, uncovered, stirring occasionally, until golden brown, 15 to 20 minutes.

2. Add stock, salt, and pepper and simmer, uncovered, stirring occasionally, about 15 minutes.

3. Meanwhile, spread bread slices on ungreased baking sheet and toast until crisp and golden, about 15 minutes. Remove toast from oven and preheat broiler.

4. Taste soup and adjust salt and pepper as needed. Arrange 2 slices of toast in each of six 8- to 10-ounce flameproof soup bowls, ladle in soup, and sprinkle with Gruyère, then with Parmesan, dividing all amounts evenly.

5. Place bowls on heavy-duty baking sheet, set 4 inches from broiler unit, and broil just until cheese melts and is tipped with brown, about 2 minutes. Serve at once.

Gazpacho

Makes 6 to 8 Servings

✳

PERHAPS MARY RANDOLPH and Sheila Hibben (see box, opposite) were right to call this cold soup a salad. James Peterson (*Splendid Soups,* 1994) concurs: "I always think of gazpacho as a wonderful vegetable salad with all the ingredients so finely chopped that you can drink it." This recipe here is one I developed for the food processor. The soup itself can be prepared by processor, and some of the garnishes, too (the sliced scallions, minced parsley, and green pepper). But the rest you must do by hand—the croutons, the diced cucumber and tomato—because the machine will cut them too fine.

SOUP

- 1 medium Spanish onion, peeled and chunked
- 1 medium clove garlic, peeled
- 1 medium green bell pepper, cored, seeded, and cut in 1-inch pieces
- 1 medium cucumber, peeled, seeded, and chunked
- 4 fully ripe tomatoes, peeled, cored, and chunked
- ¼ cup tarragon vinegar
- 2 slices firm-textured white bread, broken into small pieces
- 1 tablespoon honey
- ½ teaspoon salt (or to taste)
- ¼ teaspoon black pepper
- ⅛ teaspoon ground hot red pepper (cayenne)
- ⅔ cup fruity olive oil

GARNISHES

- 1 cup minced parsley
- 1 cup diced green bell pepper
- ½ cup thinly sliced scallions
- 1 cup diced, cored, seeded tomato
- 1 cup dried, peeled, seeded cucumber
- 3 cups croutons lightly browned in olive oil (about 6 slices firm-textured white bread)

1. SOUP: Puree onion and garlic in food processor fitted with metal chopping blade; empty into large ceramic bowl. Puree green pepper and cucumber same way and add to bowl. Puree tomatoes, two at a time, and add to bowl.

GASPACHA—SPANISH

....

*P*UT SOME SOFT BISCUIT *or toasted bread in the bottom of a sallad bowl, put in a layer of sliced tomatas with the skin taken off, and one of sliced cucumbers, sprinkled with pepper, salt, and chopped onion; do this until the bowl is full, stew some tomatas quite soft, strain the juice, mix in some mustard and oil, and pour over it; make it two hours before it is eaten.*—MARY RANDOLPH, *The Virginia House-wife*, 1824

It seems impossible that this recipe would crop up in so early an American cookbook, yet here it is sandwiched between HOW TO MAKE AN OMELETTE and EGGS AND TOMATAS. Karen Hess, who provided Historical Notes and Commentaries for the facsimile edition of *The Virginia House-wife* (1984), suggests that the *gaspacha*, one of what she calls "a group of Spanish recipes of exceptional interest . . . must have been personally collected because such home recipes were not deemed worthy of entry in Spanish cookbooks. . . . I suggest that they may well have come from Harriet Randolph Hackley, Mary Randolph's sister, who seems to have spent some time in Cadiz."

Mary Randolph's *gaspacha* aside, this cold Spanish soup did not become widely known here until this century. In *The National Cookbook* (1932), Sheila Hibben gives a Pensacola recipe for "Guspachy." She, too, calls it a salad.

2. Add vinegar, bread, honey, salt, black and cayenne peppers to processor and churn to paste. With motor running, drizzle olive oil down feed tube in fine stream and after all oil is incorporated, churn 10 seconds more. Mix into bowl of pureed vegetables. Cover and chill several hours or overnight.

3. GARNISHES: Place garnishes in separate small bowls and set on table.

4. TO SERVE: Stir gazpacho well, taste for salt, and adjust as needed. Transfer to large tureen, set on table, and surround with bowls of garnishes. Ladle gazpacho into soup plates and let everyone help himself to garnishes.

WOMAN'S FAVORITE

Cook Book

THREE BOOKS IN ONE VOLUME

White Gazpacho

Makes 4 Servings

❋

THIS ALMOND-AND-GRAPE-BASED gazpacho from Málaga has only recently become popular in this country. This recipe is adapted from one in *365 Great Soups & Stews* (1996), written by my good friend Georgia Chan Downard with Jean Galton.

1 cup blanched almonds
2 cloves garlic, peeled and
    halved
3 slices day-old bread, crusts
    removed
¼ cup water
1 quart cold chicken broth
¼ cup fruity olive oil
3 tablespoons white wine
    vinegar
½ teaspoon salt (or to taste)
1 cup seedless green grapes,
    halved
½ cup lightly toasted croutons

1. Preheat oven to 350° F. Spread almonds in pie tin and bake, uncovered, stirring now and then, until lightly toasted—about 15 minutes. Cool.

2. Pulse almonds and garlic until uniformly fine in electric blender or food processor fitted with metal chopping blade.

3. Soak bread in water in small bowl and squeeze dry. Add bread to blender or processor and pulse to incorporate. Add chicken broth, olive oil, vinegar, and salt, and churn until smooth.

4. Press soup through medium sieve into bowl, extracting as much liquid as possible; discard solids.

5. Cover tight and chill several hours or overnight. Taste for salt and adjust as needed.

6. Stir in grapes, spoon into well-chilled soup bowls, and scatter croutons on top.

Caldo Verde (Portuguese Green Soup)

Makes 6 to 8 Servings

❋

FIRST POPULAR in such Portuguese–American enclaves as New Bedford and Gloucester, Massachusetts, this green soup is now fairly well known across the country. It can be made with kale or turnip greens, but to be authentic, you must use collards *(couve gallego)*. To slice them razor-thin, stack four or five leaves, roll into a tight "cigar," then slice with a chef's knife. This recipe is adapted from my book, *The Food of Portugal* (1986).

NOTE: *Chouriço* is a dry Portuguese sausage made with plenty of garlic that's plentiful here wherever the Portuguese have settled—New England, New Jersey, California, Hawaii. In flavor and texture it resembles the more widely available Spanish chorizo, which can be substituted for it. So can Italian pepperoni, even Polish kielbasa.

¼ cup fruity olive oil
2 medium yellow onions, peeled
    and coarsely chopped
3 large cloves garlic, peeled and
    minced
4 large baking potatoes, peeled
    and thinly sliced
2 quarts cold water
¼ pound chouriço, chorizo,
    pepperoni, or other dry,
    garlicky sausage, in one piece
1½ teaspoons salt (or to taste)
⅛ teaspoon black pepper (or to
    taste)
1 pound young collards,
    trimmed of stems and very
    thinly sliced

1. Heat olive oil 1 minute in large heavy saucepan over moderate heat. Add onions and garlic and stir-fry until limp and golden—3 to 4 minutes. Add potatoes and cook, stirring often, until golden—2 to 3 minutes.

2. Add water and *chouriço,* cover, and cook until potatoes are mushy—about 30 minutes. Set off heat, remove *chouriço,* and cool. With potato masher, mash potatoes in pan but leave some lumps. Slice *chouriço* thin and return to soup. Add salt and pepper to taste, cover, and simmer 5 minutes.

3. Toss in collards and simmer, uncovered, just until soup turns emerald green—about 5 minutes.

4. Ladle into heated soup plates and serve with a rough country bread.

Tortilla Soup

Makes 4 to 6 Servings

✻

NO STRANGER to the border states (Texas, New Mexico, and Arizona), this frugal but sustaining soup began to be featured in women's magazines about twenty-five years ago and is now known and appreciated in all fifty states. The following recipe is adapted from *Better Homes & Gardens Mexican Cook Book* (1977).

1 cup canned crushed tomatoes
1 medium yellow onion, peeled and chunked
1 large clove garlic, peeled
2 tablespoons snipped fresh coriander (cilantro) or flat-leaf parsley
½ teaspoon sugar
1 quart chicken broth
6 (6-inch) tortillas
Vegetable oil for shallow frying
1 cup coarsely shredded Monterey Jack, longhorn, or Cheddar cheese

1. Churn tomatoes, onion, garlic, coriander, and sugar until nearly smooth in electric blender at high speed or food processor fitted with metal chopping blade.

2. Transfer to large heavy saucepan, add broth, and bring to boiling. Adjust heat so liquid bubbles easily, cover, and simmer 20 minutes.

3. Meanwhile, cut tortillas into ½-inch strips. Pour oil into medium heavy skillet to depth of ½ inch, set over moderate heat and, when tortilla strip will sizzle, add all strips and fry until crisp and lightly browned—about 1 minute. Drain on paper towels.

4. Divide tortilla strips and cheese among 4 to 6 heated soup plates, ladle in soup, and serve at once.

....

Thai Shrimp, Mushroom, and Lemon Grass Soup

Makes 4 Servings

✻

I FIRST tasted this celestial soup in the late '70s in a Thai restaurant on Eighth Avenue in New York City. It seemed then the most skillful mingling of flavors—and still does. Fortunately, Thai restaurants have proliferated across the U.S., so it's no longer necessary to travel far to enjoy it. This recipe is adapted from *365 Great Soups & Stews* (1996) by Georgia Chan Downard and Jean Galton.

NOTE: Lemon grass, Thai fish sauce, and canned straw mushrooms are available at Asian or specialty groceries.

2 stalks lemon grass or 2 (2× 1-inch) strips lemon zest
2 cups chicken broth
2 cups water
2 (2× 1-inch) strips lime zest
1 tablespoon Thai fish sauce (nam pla) or soy sauce
1 tablespoon fresh lime juice
1 teaspoon brown sugar
¼ teaspoon ground hot red pepper (cayenne)
½ pound shelled and deveined medium shrimp
½ cup canned straw mushrooms or 1 (4-ounce) can sliced mushrooms
2 scallions, trimmed and thinly sliced

1. Discard tough lemon grass tops and outer leaves. Cut lemon grass into 2-inch lengths and smash with flat side of chef's knife; set aside.

2. Bring chicken broth and water to boiling in large heavy saucepan over moderate heat. Add lemon grass, lime zest, fish sauce, lime juice, sugar, cayenne, shrimp, and mushrooms. Cook just until shrimp turn pink—2 to 3 minutes.

3. Stir in scallions, ladle into heated soup bowls, and serve.

Borscht

Makes 6 Servings

❋

BETWEEN THE closing decades of the nineteenth century and 1914, waves of Eastern Europeans entered this country, among them thousands of Russian Jews who brought their cherished Old Country recipes to New York and the other big metropolitan enclaves where they settled. A particular favorite was—and is—Borscht. Yet it would be decades before the rest of America would taste it. I, for example, who grew up in a very Waspy part of the South, had never heard of Borscht until I went north to school toward the end of the '50s. My favorite lunch while I was at the Columbia Graduate School of Journalism was a bowl of Borscht (hot in winter, cold in summer) at the late, lamented Russian Tea Room on West 57th Street ("slightly to the left of Carnegie Hall," the radio commercials used to say). It came with a crisp, cheese-filled borek—more than enough to keep me going until dinner at the dorm. This recipe is the result of my effort to crack that ambrosial RTR recipe.

2 tablespoons vegetable oil
1 large yellow onion, peeled and coarsely chopped
1¾ cups finely sliced cabbage
2 tablespoons minced fresh flat-leaf parsley
2⅔ cups rich beef broth, preferably homemade
2 (16-ounce) cans sliced beets, with their juice, coarsely chopped or finely julienned
2 tablespoons red wine vinegar
1½ tablespoons tomato paste
1 teaspoon sugar
½ teaspoon salt (or to taste)
¼ teaspoon black pepper (or to taste)
6 tablespoons sour cream
2 tablespoons snipped fresh dill

1. Heat oil in large heavy saucepan over moderately high heat. Add onion, cabbage, and parsley and sauté, stirring occasionally, until cabbage is glossy and crisp-tender, 8 to 10 minutes.

2. Add broth, half the beets, the vinegar, tomato paste, sugar, salt, and pepper, reduce heat to low, and simmer, uncovered, 15 minutes.

3. Meanwhile, puree remaining beets and beet liquid in an electric blender at high speed or food processor fitted with metal chopping blade. Add to pan and bring just to serving temperature.

4. Ladle into heated soup bowls, top each portion with sour cream and a sprinkling of dill, and serve. Or chill well and serve cold, topped with sour cream and dill.

TIMELINE

1915

....

Fannie Farmer dies.

....

On May 27, Corning introduces Pyrex baking dishes at Jordan Marsh in Boston and two days later at Gimbel's in New York.

....

Corning runs its first national Pyrex ad in the October *Good Housekeeping* with a testimonial from cookbook author Sarah Tyson Rorer: "Mrs. Rorer uses Pyrex exclusively."

....

Frigidaire markets a "self-contained" electric refrigerator.

....

A & P (founded as the Great Atlantic and Pacific Tea Company in the late nineteenth century) now has 1,726 grocery stores.

1916

....

Campbell's publishes *Helps for the Hostess* to show women how to use canned soups as recipe ingredients.

MEATS,
FISH, FOWL

THE WONDERFUL
LITTLE GIANT MEAT CUTTER.

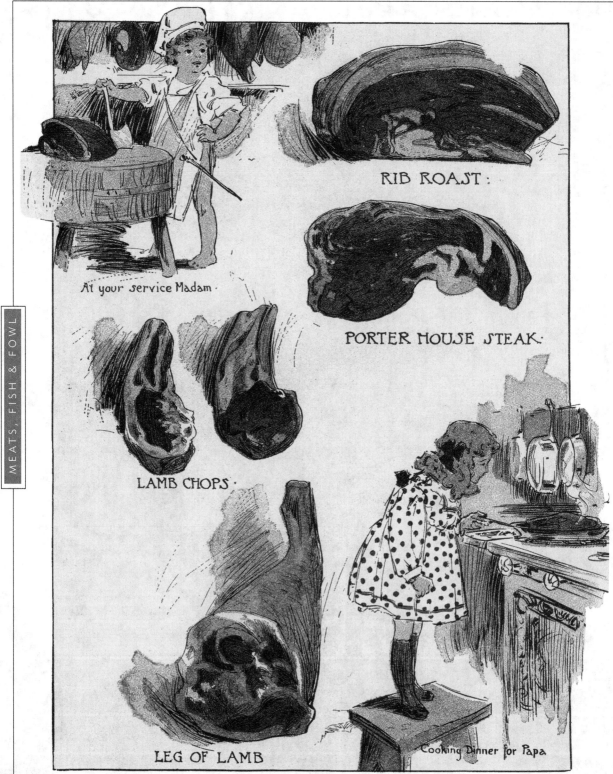

At your service Madam.

RIB ROAST:

PORTER HOUSE STEAK:

LAMB CHOPS.

LEG OF LAMB

Cooking Dinner for Papa

FLIP THROUGH any late-nineteenth- or early-twentieth-century cookbook and you'll notice few recipes for meat, fish, or fowl. The chapters devoted to them deal largely with basic methods of cooking—boiling, braising, roasting, frying, and so forth. Also with butchering, food conservation, and preservation—important subjects before reliable home refrigeration.

The original *Boston Cooking-School Cook Book* (1896) devotes exactly 100 of its 536 pages to fish and shellfish, beef, lamb and mutton, veal, sweetbreads (these merit a chapter), pork and ham, poultry, and game. Things improved slightly for the 1906 edition. These sections got an extra thirteen pages, mainly to make room for French classics such as Steak Mirabeau. *Mrs. Rorer's New Cook Book* (1902) skimps on meat, fish, and fowl, also, allotting only 140 out of 701 pages to all three.

Both Sarah Tyson Rorer and Fannie Farmer seem obsessed with the nutritional value of meat, fish, and fowl. Farmer includes full-page "composition" tables for each, showing percentages of refuse, protein (which she quaintly calls "proteid"), fat, mineral matter, and water. Occasionally she slips in a carbohydrate count. But there is no talk of vitamins.

Rorer introduces her fish chapter with the breakdown of water, fat, salts, and nitrogenous matter in flounder and salmon. "Fish," she writes, "belong to the nitrogenous group of foods [which] builds and repairs muscular flesh and tissues. Is digested principally in the stomach, proper."

To their credit, both Fannie Farmer and Sarah T. Rorer had a healthy regard for foods few mainstream Americans will touch today: tripe, heart, sweetbreads, kidneys, brains, turtle, frog's legs, pig's trotters, and calf's head.

Recipe variety seems to begin after 1910. Women's magazines, now flourishing, had advertisers to please.

And food companies' products to push. In 1915, *Larkin Housewives' Cook Book* offers a recipe for Michigan Hash, a layered casserole of hamburger, tomatoes, Larkin Rice, Larkin Macaroni, Larkin Salt, Larkin Black Pepper, and Larkin Celery Salt. The very next year, Campbell's published *Helps for the Hostess,* which shows, for the first time, how to use its soups as ingredients in recipes, among them Chicken Jelly Loaf made with "1 pound chopped chicken, 3 hard-boiled eggs, 2 rounding tablespoonfuls granulated gelatin, and 1 can Campbell's Consommé or Bouillon."

After World War I, meat, fish, and fowl recipes veered toward the international. Or to be more accurate, their titles did because few of these dishes had any connection with the countries for which they were named. To wit, these from *Good Housekeeping's Book of Menus, Recipes and Household Discoveries* (1922): Arabian Stew (pork chop, tomato, and rice casserole), Filipino Roast (beef and pork loaf baked in tomato sauce), Mexican Lamb Stew (with tomatoes, canned green peas, and corn), Spanish Lamb (diced cooked lamb reheated in a chafing dish with onions, green pepper, tomatoes, and rice).

By the 1930s, recipe developers—most of them home economists hired by magazines or food companies— were going gangbusters. Check this Stewed Chicken à l'Espagnol from *Good Housekeeping's Meals Tested, Tasted and Approved* (1930): In addition to chicken it calls for "1 10 oz. bottle green olives, 1 No. 2 can tomatoes, 1 No. 2 can peas, and 1 No. 2 can mushrooms."

And so it went right through the '50s and into the '60s when the counterculture found its way back to the soil. Then along came Julia Child and her French Chef television series. Suddenly slow-cooking meats, fish, and fowl were in, quickie casseroles out. We tried Julia's *Boeuf à la Bourguignonne,* her *Coq au Vin,* her *Homard Thermidor.*

We were cooking from scratch and we loved it.

MEATS,
FISH, FOWL

Mom's Swiss Steak Dinner

Makes 4 Servings

＊

INTRODUCED IN 1947, Reynolds Wrap Aluminum Foil encouraged cooks "to line your pans and save your hands." One of its earliest recipes was Swiss steak. "The secret to perfect results," a headnote promises, "is to line and cover the baking pan with heavy-duty aluminum foil. The results are tender and delicious, without involved preparation. Baked with added potatoes and frozen vegetables, Mom's Swiss Steak is an 'all-in-one' meal for today's busy lifestyles." The recipe here is a variation of the Reynolds original.

2 (1-pound) beef chuck steaks

1 medium yellow onion, peeled and sliced

8 small unpeeled new potatoes, quartered (about ¾ pound)

1 (10¾-ounce) can cream of mushroom soup, undiluted

1 (14½-ounce) can stewed tomatoes, with their juice

1 tablespoon Worcestershire sauce

½ teaspoon dried leaf thyme, crumbled

¾ teaspoon salt

¼ teaspoon garlic powder

¼ teaspoon black pepper

1 (9-ounce) package frozen whole green beans, separated

1. Preheat oven to 425° F. Line 13 × 9 × 2-inch baking pan with heavy-duty aluminum foil, leaving 1½-inch overhang all around.

2. Cut steaks into 4 equal portions and place in pan. Top with half the onion slices, the potatoes, then remaining onion slices; set aside.

3. Combine soup, tomatoes, Worcestershire sauce, thyme, salt, garlic powder, and pepper in medium bowl, whisking until well blended.

4. Pour over steak and vegetables. Cover pan with large sheet of heavy-duty foil and roll edges tightly with overhang to seal.

5. Bake 1½ hours. Uncover pan, add green beans, distributing evenly, reseal pan with foil, and bake 15 to 20 minutes longer, until beans and steak are tender. Stir well before serving.

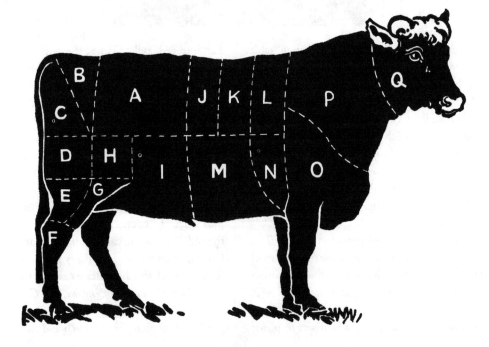

Swiss Steak

THE FIRST RECIPE I've been able to find for Swiss Steak appears in *Larkin Housewives' Cook Book* (1915). Nothing more than browned, inch-thick beef round baked in water with bottled onion extract, it barely resembles the tomato-rich versions we know and love today. Two years later Ida Bailey Allen *(Mrs. Allen's Cook Book)* offers a Swiss Steak nearer our own *except* that it cooks stovetop. The tomatoey baked variety seems to have surfaced in the 1930s. In *Meals, Tested, Tasted, and Approved*, a 1930 *Good House-keeping* cookbook, there is an early Swiss steak called Tomato Steak (see below).

In 1934, John MacPherson, radio's famous "Mystery Chef," offers a true Swiss Steak and calls it that, too, in *The Mystery Chef's Own Cook Book*.

Swiss Steak remains popular to this day, partly due to the fact that it can be cooked in aluminum foil. Some cooks simply bundle all ingredients in heavy-duty foil, wrap tight, set on a baking sheet, and shove into a slow oven.

TOMATO STEAK

Serves 6

3 tablespoonfuls fat	1 large onion	2 cupfuls canned tomatoes
2½ lbs. round steak 2" thick	3 carrots	2 teaspoonfuls salt
	2 white turnips	⅛ teaspoonful pepper

HEAT fat in a frying pan, add meat, and sear it brown on all sides. Then arrange in a casserole and cover with onion, carrots, and turnips which have been peeled and chopped very fine, tomatoes, salt, and pepper. Cover tightly and bake in a slow oven of 275°F for 3 hours. The gravy may be thickened if desired.

THE MYSTERY CHEF'S SWISS STEAK

2 lbs. round or flank steak	1 medium sized onion, chopped fine	1 teaspoon salt
1 small can tomatoes		½ cup sifted flour
3 tablespoons drippings or shortening	1 cup water	
	¼ teaspoon pepper	

SPRINKLE a little water over steak. Sift flour into large bowl or onto large plate, then put steak into flour and press as much flour into the steak as you can.

PUT drippings or shortening into a large frying pan and when sizzling hot put the floured steak in. Brown the steak thoroughly on both sides. The steak can either be cooked on top of the stove or in the oven; whichever way you cook it the pot or baking pan should have a lid. Grease the pot or baking pan with a little dripping and transfer the browned steak to it. Now put the cup of water into the frying pan the steak was browned in, and let the water boil while you run a fork over the pan to loosen up any of the steak juices and flour that may be sticking to the pan. Then pour the boiling water from the frying pan over the steak, add 1 medium onion, finely chopped, and add a small can of tomatoes; add salt and pepper. Bring to a boil, then turn the flame down and cover the pan or pot with a lid, and allow to simmer for 2 hours. If cooked in the oven, cover the baking pan and bake in a slow oven for 2 hours.

SERVE with mashed potatoes.

$25,000 Grecian Skillet Rib Eyes

Makes 2 Servings

✽

AT THE National Beef Cook-Off in Little Rock, Arkansas, in September 1995, this recipe prepared by Pennsylvanian Fran Yuhas took the $25,000 grand prize.

SEASONING MIX
1½ teaspoons dried leaf basil, crumbled
1½ teaspoons dried leaf oregano, crumbled
1½ teaspoons garlic powder
½ teaspoon salt
⅛ teaspoon black pepper

STEAKS
2 well-trimmed (1-inch-thick) beef rib-eye steaks
1 tablespoon olive oil
1 tablespoon fresh lemon juice
2 tablespoons crumbled feta cheese
1 tablespoon chopped, pitted Kalamata or ripe olives

1. SEASONING MIX: Combine all ingredients.

2. STEAKS: Press seasoning mix on both sides of each steak.

3. Heat oil in large, heavy nonstick skillet over moderately high heat 1 minute. Add steaks and cook, turning once, 10 to 14 minutes according to taste.

4. Transfer steaks to heated platter, sprinkle with lemon juice, then scatter with feta cheese and chopped olives. Serve at once.

Carpetbag Steak

THOUGH POPULAR in Australia, this unusual steak stuffed with oysters is apparently of American origin. It takes its name from the cloth satchel travelers used around the time of the Civil War. Just before the turn of the century, when broiled steaks were coming into vogue, a popular way to serve them was under a coverlet of oysters. This recipe simply takes that late-nineteenth-century recipe one step further. Who's responsible? Perhaps Chasen's restaurant, which opened in Hollywood in 1936 (and closed in 1995). Carpetbagger Steak, as Chasen's called it, was a house specialty. Or was Louis Diat the creator? He includes this recipe for it in *Cooking à la Ritz* (1941):

LOUIS DIAT'S CARPET-BAG STEAK

HAVE butcher cut steak from the sirloin 1½ to 2 inches thick, and then cut through the center to make a pocket. Stuff this pocket with raw oysters, seasoned with salt and pepper. Then sew the edges of pocket together. Broil about fifteen minutes on each side. Serve with any desired potatoes.

Steak Diane

Makes 4 Servings

✽

I ALWAYS associated this recipe with New York City's Colony Restaurant because that was where I first tried it. Yet I find no mention of it in *The Colony* (1945), Iles Brody's portrait of that restaurant. It is featured, however, in Michael Lomonaco's *The "21" Cookbook* (1995) together with this description: "At '21' Steak Diane is traditionally prepared tableside by the captains or Maître d' Walter Weiss. The beef, sizzling in a large copper pan with brandy flaming and sauce bubbling, makes a wonderful show reminiscent of the days when Humphrey Bogart and friends would bound in at midnight following the newest opening on Broadway." Here, then, my adaptation of the "21" Traditional Steak Diane, which Chef Lomonaco says should be prepared one at a time and kept warm in a 350°F oven.

2 tablespoons unsalted butter
4 (6-ounce) shell steaks,
    butterflied and pounded
    ¼ inch thick with meat
    tenderizer
1 teaspoon salt (or to taste)
½ teaspoon black pepper
    (or to taste)
3 tablespoons minced shallots
¼ cup good brandy
¼ cup dry white wine
1 teaspoon prepared hot English
    mustard
¾ cup beef broth
¼ cup heavy cream
3 tablespoons snipped fresh
    chives

1. Preheat oven to 350°F.

2. Heat large heavy skillet over moderate heat 1 minute, add ½ tablespoon butter. Meanwhile, sprinkle steaks on both sides with salt and pepper.

3. When butter foams, sear first steak 1 to 2 minutes on each side; transfer to hot ovenproof platter. Brown remaining steaks in butter the same way, transferring each to platter.

4. Add shallots to skillet and stir-fry until glassy—2 minutes. Remove skillet from heat and carefully add brandy. Return to low heat and reduce—do not flame—to glaze. Add wine, raise heat to moderate, and boil down to glaze.

5. Set platter of steaks, uncovered, in oven to warm. Blend mustard into skillet and cook 1 minute. Mix in beef broth, boil 1 minute, then add cream and bring just to boiling.

6. Transfer steaks to four heated serving plates. Stir chives into sauce, taste for salt and pepper, adjust as needed, then pour over steaks and serve at once.

The Famous "21" Burger

Makes 4 Servings

❋

IN 1975, New York's famous "21" Club came up with what is by most accounts the world's best burger. Certainly it's the most expensive (1996 price: $21.40 for lunch, $24 at night). A story "21" likes to tell involves Mrs. David West, owner of a Georgia eatery where newsmen hung out during Jimmy Carter's run for office. When Mrs. West came to New York, the first thing she wanted

to eat was the pricey "21" burger (then $12), which she'd been hearing about. Was it any better than her 75-center? Mrs. West liked the "21" burger but, no, she didn't think it any better. She attributed the inflated price to "21"'s high-rent district (her cafe occupied a mobile home). More steak than burger, the "21" comes to table "nude"—no bun or bread (for the history of the hamburger as sandwich, see Breads & Sandwiches, page 348). The recipe here is adapted from *The "21" Cookbook* by Michael Lomonaco (1995).

NOTE: Because of the danger of ground meat's being contaminated with E. coli, U.S. Department of Agriculture food experts recommend cooking all meat well done. Of course, the burgers will not be as succulent.

BURGER
    ¼ cup finely diced celery
    ¼ cup chicken broth
    2 pounds ground top sirloin
    ¼ teaspoon freshly grated
        nutmeg
    Dash Worcestershire sauce
    ¼ cup soft bread crumbs
    1 teaspoon salt
    ¼ teaspoon black pepper
    3 tablespoons butter

OPTIONAL BROWN SAUCE
    3 tablespoons butter
    3 tablespoons flour
    1 cup beef broth
    Salt and black pepper to taste

1. Preheat oven to 350°F.

2. Poach celery in chicken broth in small heavy saucepan over lowest heat 20 minutes; drain, and cool.

3. Using hands, mix celery with sirloin, nutmeg, Worcestershire, bread crumbs, salt, and pepper in large mixing bowl, taking care not to compact mixture. Shape into 4 large patties, again being careful not to compact.

4. Melt butter in very large heavy skillet with heat-proof handle over moderate heat. When butter turns amber, add burgers and brown 6 minutes on each side. Set skillet, uncovered, in oven and cook burgers 6 to 8 minutes more for medium rare, a few minutes longer for medium or well done.

5. *Meanwhile, prepare Sauce, if desired:* Melt butter in small heavy saucepan over moderate heat and blend in flour. Add broth and cook, stirring constantly, until thickened, smooth, and no raw flour taste remains—about 3 to 5 minutes. Season to taste with salt and pepper.

6. To serve, arrange burgers on heated plates and, if desired, drizzle sauce over each.

VINTAGE RECIPES

Meat Loaves

WAS MEAT loaf too homely a recipe to make American cookbooks published in the nineteenth century or earlier? I wonder. In his book, *White House Chef* (1957), François Rysavy, who served the Eisenhowers, includes a recipe for what he calls "Martha Washington's Meat Loaf," yet there is no such recipe in *Martha Washington's Booke of Cookery,* newly available (1995) with introduction and commentary by food historian Karen Hess.

In fact, I find no meat loaves in American cookbooks before the 1880s; these were primarily veal loaves (a more economical meat early on than beef) and altogether different from the meat loaves so familiar today. This one appears in *The Boston Cook Book* (1883) by Mrs. Mary J. Lincoln:

Parboil two pounds of lean veal. Chop fine with one fourth of a pound of salt pork or bacon; add flour, butter crackers, pounded, two eggs, well beaten, two teaspoonfuls of salt, one saltspoonful of pepper, and half a saltspoonful of nutmeg or mace. Moisten with the meat liquor, mould into an oval loaf, and put into a shallow tin pan. Add a little of the water in which the meat was boiled. Bake till quite brown, basting often. Serve hot or cold, cut in slices. Raw veal may be used in the same way, baking it two hours or more.

Three years later, Sarah Tyson Rorer offers a slightly more elaborate veal loaf in *Mrs. Rorer's Philadelphia Cook Book* along with something called "Cannelon," which is clearly a precursor of meat loaf as we know it today.

Here is the Cannelon, just as it appears in her 1886 cookbook.

```
┌─────────────────── CANNELON ───────────────────┐
```

CANNELON

1 pound of uncooked beef,
    chopped fine
Yolk of one egg
1 tablespoonful of
    chopped parsley
1 tablespoonful of butter

2 tablespoonfuls of bread
    crumbs
1 teaspoonful of lemon
    juice
1 teaspoonful of salt
3 dashes of black pepper

MIX all the ingredients together, then form into a roll about six inches long and four inches in diameter; wrap in greased paper, put in a baking-pan, and bake in a quick oven thirty minutes, basting twice with melted butter. When done, remove the paper, place the roll in the center of a hot dish, and serve with mushroom or brown sauce poured over it.

The original *Boston Cooking-School Cook Book* (1896) by Fannie Farmer includes two recipes for veal loaf, one a cold pressed veal, the second a mixture of raw veal and fat salt pork forced through a *meat chopper* (the first time I've seen this piece of equipment mentioned), rolled common crackers, melted butter, egg, salt, pepper, and sage. This, too, is served cold.

Cannelons appear in cookbooks right into the 1920s, although by this time meat loaves were outnumbering them. Were meat loaves slow to come because of the lack of meat grinders? Or was it because of unreliable refrigeration (ground raw meat is extremely perishable)? Possibly a bit of both, but I can't say for sure.

In *Mrs. Rorer's New Cook Book* (1902) there's a simple Beef Loaf made with raw beef, and in *The Settlement Cook Book* (1903) a Beef Loaf that combines one pound chopped round steak with one teaspoon chopped onion, one-half cup each of bread crumbs and cold water, plus salt and pepper to season. That same year the *Good Housekeeping Everyday Cook Book* offered this *Meat Loaf,* which more closely resembles the meat loaves of today:

Two pounds of chopped beef, one pound of chopped pork, two eggs, four teaspoons of milk, five crackers, rolled fine, salt and pepper. Mix in loaf with bits of butter on top. Bake one hour.

Though simple loaves of chopped meat may have been made during America's infancy and adolescence, only in the twentieth century did meat loaves truly arrive. What appear on these pages are some of the most beloved. And, yes, many of them did come out of big food company test kitchens. Like it or not.

Old-Fashioned Meat Loaf

Makes 8 Servings

✳

THIS RECIPE and the Italian Stuffed Meat Loaf (page 96) come from *The Quaker Oats Treasury of Best Recipes,* a collection of the most popular recipes created over the years in the test kitchens of The Quaker Oats Company. Both are used courtesy of The Quaker Oats Company.

> *1½ pounds lean ground beef*
> *¾ cup rolled oats (quick-*
>   *cooking or old-fashioned)*
> *½ cup chopped yellow onion*
> *½ cup tomato sauce or ketchup*
> *1 egg, slightly beaten*
> *½ teaspoon salt*
> *¼ teaspoon black pepper*

1. Preheat oven to 350° F. Lightly coat 8 × 4 × 2¾-inch loaf pan with nonstick cooking spray and set aside.

2. Using hands, mix all ingredients well in large bowl and pack into prepared pan.

3. Bake, uncovered, 55 to 60 minutes, then cool in pan on wire rack 5 to 10 minutes before slicing.

Italian Stuffed Meat Loaf

Makes 6 Servings

✳

ANOTHER "MOST requested" from *The Quaker Oats Treasury of Best Recipes,* reprinted here courtesy of The Quaker Oats Company.

MEAT LOAF

1 pound lean ground beef
1 cup rolled oats (quick-cooking or old-fashioned)
1 (15½-ounce jar) spaghetti sauce
½ cup chopped yellow onion
⅓ cup grated Parmesan cheese
1 egg, slightly beaten
1 tablespoon Worcestershire sauce
½ teaspoon black pepper

FILLING

⅓ cup sliced pitted ripe olives
⅓ cup shredded mozzarella cheese
⅓ cup sliced butter-sautéed mushrooms

TOPPING

½ cup shredded mozzarella cheese
¼ cup sliced pitted ripe olives

1. Preheat oven to 350° F. Grease 8 × 8 × 2-inch baking pan; set aside.

2. MEAT LOAF: Using hands, mix beef, oats, ½ cup spaghetti sauce, onion, Parmesan, egg, Worcestershire, and pepper well in large bowl. Place remaining spaghetti sauce in saucepan; set aside.

ABOUT CHOPPED MEAT

W HEN CHOPPED MEAT *is offered for sale at a low price, it almost certainly contains a high percentage of fat, and sometimes a great deal of water, for it is just as easy to "pump" beef as chicken or oysters. It is more economical to pay a little more and get honest meat. If the butcher will not let you see his meat chopped, it is wise to grind the meat at home.*
—*Mrs. Allen's Cook Book* (1917) by Ida Bailey Allen

3. Divide meat mixture in half and shape into two 7-inch patties. Place one patty in prepared pan and layer FILLING ingredients on top, leaving ½-inch margin all around. Top with second patty and press edges to seal; smooth into rounded loaf.

4. Bake, uncovered, 50 minutes. Toward end of baking, set reserved spaghetti sauce over low heat and heat, just until mixture steams, stirring occasionally.

5. Remove meat loaf from oven and top at once with hot spaghetti sauce, mozzarella, and olives.

6. Cut into wedges and serve.

Beef and Sausage Loaf

Makes 8 to 10 Servings

✳

A SUPREMELY flavorful, juicy meat loaf that I developed myself.

1½ pounds ground lean beef chuck
1 pound sweet Italian sausages, casings removed
½ pound ground lean pork shoulder
2 cups moderately coarse Italian bread crumbs
2 large yellow onions, peeled and minced
1 small red bell pepper, cored, seeded, and minced
2 small ribs celery, trimmed and minced

2 cloves garlic, peeled and minced

1 cup canned crushed tomatoes

¼ cup dry red or white wine

2 eggs

1 teaspoon dried leaf basil, crumbled

½ teaspoon dried leaf oregano, crumbled

¼ teaspoon dried leaf thyme, crumbled

1 tablespoon anchovy paste

1 teaspoon finely grated lemon zest

½ teaspoon salt

¼ teaspoon black pepper

1. Preheat oven to 350° F. Coat 9 × 5 × 3-inch loaf pan with non-stick cooking spray and set aside.

2. Using hands, mix all ingredients thoroughly in large bowl. Pack into prepared pan.

3. Bake, uncovered, until loaf pulls from sides of pan and is richly browned—about 1½ hours.

4. Cool loaf in pan on wire rack 15 minutes; drain off drippings.

5. Slice and serve warm.

Best-Ever Meat Loaf

Makes 8 Servings

✳

THIS 1950S meat loaf developed in the Campbell's Soup test kitchens couldn't be easier. Included in *Campbell's Best-Ever Recipes, 125th Anniversary Edition* (1994), it uses two popular Campbell's soups, one canned, one dry.

1 (10½-ounce) can condensed tomato or cream of mushroom soup, undiluted

2 pounds ground beef

1 pouch dry onion soup and recipe mix

½ cup dry bread crumbs

1 egg, well beaten

¼ cup water

1. Preheat oven to 350° F. Lightly coat 2-quart oblong baking dish with nonstick cooking spray and set aside.

2. Using hands, mix ½ cup tomato soup, ground beef, onion soup mix, bread crumbs, and egg in large bowl until well blended. Shape into 8 × 4-inch loaf and place in prepared baking dish.

3. Bake, uncovered, until meat thermometer inserted in center of loaf registers 160° F and meat is no longer pink—about 1¼ hours. Remove from oven and spoon off fat, reserving 1 to 2 tablespoons drippings.

4. Mix remaining tomato soup with water and reserved drippings in small heavy saucepan, set over moderate heat and cook, stirring occasionally, just until mixture steams.

5. Slice meat loaf and top with tomato sauce.

1916

A Hong Kong cook living in America invents the fortune cookie.

Nathan Handwerker, a Polish shoemaker, opens a hot dog stand at Coney Island; it's soon known as "Nathan's."

Piggly Wiggly opens a self-service grocery in Memphis.

1916–17

Sarah Tyson Rorer, well in her sixties, crisscrosses the U.S. and Canada demonstrating how to use Pyrex baking dishes.

1917

Vichyssoise is created by Chef Louis Diat at New York's Ritz-Carlton Hotel.

Marshmallow Fluff is invented and bottled by Durkee-Mower in Lynn, Massachusetts.

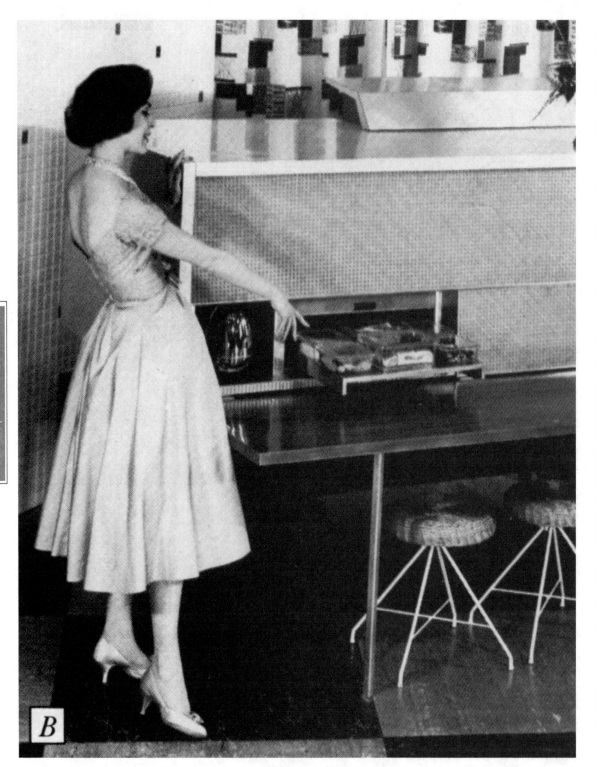

B

Slimmed-Down Meat Loaf

Makes 8 Servings

✳

A FAN of meat loaf and plagued by weight problems, I decided to trim the fat and calories from some of my favorites. They appeared in a 1993 issue of *Family Circle* and of them all, this is a particular favorite. The counts per serving: 330 calories, 14 grams fat, and 2 milligrams cholesterol.

MEAT LOAF

¾ pound lean ground beef round
¾ pound lean ground turkey
2 cups fine soft bread crumbs
1 large yellow onion, peeled and minced
1 clove garlic, peeled and minced
1 cup canned stewed tomatoes, with their juice
1 tablespoon dried leaf marjoram, crumbled
1 tablespoon paprika
¼ teaspoon black pepper
⅓ cup no-cholesterol fat-free thawed frozen egg product

GRAVY

1 small yellow onion, peeled and minced
1 tablespoon vegetable oil
2 tablespoons flour
¾ cup condensed beef broth
½ cup water

1. MEAT LOAF: Preheat oven to 375° F. Coat 6-cup ring mold with nonstick cooking spray and set aside.

2. Using hands, mix all ingredients thoroughly in large bowl. Pack into prepared mold.

3. Bake, uncovered, until loaf pulls from sides of mold—about 1 hour.

4. Unmold on heated platter, cover loosely, and keep warm.

5. GRAVY: Stir-fry onion in oil in small heavy pan over moderate heat until limp—2 to 3 minutes. Blend in flour, add broth and water, and cook, stirring constantly, until thickened, smooth, and no raw flour taste lingers—3 to 5 minutes.

6. Spoon gravy over meat loaf and serve.

....

Frosted Meat Loaf

Makes 8 Servings

✳

IN THE '50s and '60s, cooks seemed to work overtime concocting new meat loaves. One of the most successful was a beef loaf frosted with mashed potatoes. Every woman's magazine printed its own version. This one is liberally adapted from a recipe in the "Hamburger Cook Book" (*House & Garden*, January 1965).

MEAT LOAF

2 pounds lean ground beef chuck
2 eggs
2 cups milk
2 teaspoons salt
1 teaspoon Worcestershire sauce
½ teaspoon dried leaf thyme, crumbled
½ teaspoon parsley flakes
¼ teaspoon black pepper
1 medium yellow onion, peeled and minced

FROSTING

3 cups seasoned mashed potatoes
2 tablespoons butter, melted
Paprika

1. MEAT LOAF: Preheat oven to 350° F. Coat 9 × 5 × 3-inch loaf pan with nonstick cooking spray and set aside.

2. Using hands, mix all ingredients thoroughly in large bowl. Pack into pan.

3. Bake, uncovered, until loaf pulls from sides of pan—about 1½ hours.

4. Cool loaf in pan on wire rack 15 minutes; drain off drippings. Raise oven temperature to 450° F.

5. FROSTING: Turn loaf onto ovenproof platter. Frost top and sides with mashed potatoes, brush with melted butter, and blush with paprika.

6. Return to oven and bake, uncovered, until tipped with brown—about 10 minutes. Serve at once.

Lamb, Apple, and Two-Grain Loaf

Makes 8 to 10 Servings

✳

NOT EVERYONE makes meat loaves with lamb, but my mother often did. This recipe evolved from one of hers. I make it often, even for parties. It's equally good warm or cold.

1 cup bulgur wheat
1 cup apple juice
2 pounds lean ground lamb shoulder
1 pound lean ground pork shoulder
2 medium yellow onions, peeled and chopped
1 medium tart green apple, peeled, cored, and chopped
2 medium carrots, peeled and finely chopped
½ cup rolled oats (quick-cooking or old-fashioned)
1 cup tomato sauce
¼ cup minced chutney
¼ cup minced fresh parsley
3 tablespoons minced fresh mint
3 eggs
½ teaspoon dried leaf marjoram, crumbled
¼ teaspoon dried leaf rosemary, crumbled
1½ teaspoons salt
¼ teaspoon black pepper

1. Preheat oven to 350° F. Coat 9 × 5 × 3-inch loaf pan with non-stick cooking spray and set aside.

2. Soak bulgur in apple juice in large mixing bowl 1 hour. Add all remaining ingredients and using hands, mix thoroughly. Pack into prepared pan.

3. Bake, uncovered, until loaf pulls from sides of pan and is richly browned—about 1¾ hours.

4. Cool loaf in pan on wire rack 30 minutes; drain off drippings.

5. Slice and serve warm, or chill well and serve cold.

PRESIDENTIAL PREFERENCES

I N THE course of researching this book, I came across *The First Ladies Cook Book* (1969), which features our presidents' favorite recipes—from George Washington (Beefsteak and Kidney Pie) to Richard Nixon (Beef Wellington). My focus here: All the twentieth-century presidents' favorite main dishes (meat, fish, fowl, etc.). They provide an interesting timeline of changing tastes.

WILLIAM MCKINLEY
(1897–1901)
Bacon and Eggs

THEODORE ROOSEVELT
(1901–09)
Roast Suckling Pig

WILLIAM HOWARD TAFT (1909–13)
Lobster à la Newburg

WOODROW WILSON
(1913–21)
Roast Turkey with
Corn Bread Stuffing

WARREN G. HARDING
(1921–23)
Roast Filet Mignon with Sherried Mushrooms

CALVIN COOLIDGE
(1923–29)
Baked Beans

HERBERT HOOVER
(1929–33)
Corned Beef Hash with
Tomato Sauce

FRANKLIN DELANO ROOSEVELT
(1933–45)
Boiled Salmon with Egg Sauce

HARRY S. TRUMAN
(1945–53)
Meat Loaf with Tomato Sauce
(also Tuna-Noodle Casserole)

DWIGHT D. EISENHOWER
(1953–61)
Quail Hash

JOHN F. KENNEDY
(1961–63)
Beef Stroganoff

LYNDON BAINES JOHNSON
(1963–69)
Pedernales River Chili

RICHARD M. NIXON
(1969–74)
Beef Wellington

GERALD FORD (1974–77)
Spareribs with Sauerkraut
(also Spaghetti and Meatballs)

JIMMY CARTER (1977–81)
Brunswick Stew with Buttermilk Biscuits
(also Pork Chops with
Corn Bread Stuffing)

RONALD REAGAN
(1981–89)
Broiled Swordfish with Lemon Butter
(also Homemade Mushroom,
Onion, Sweet Red
and Green Pepper Pizza)

GEORGE BUSH (1989–93)
Broiled Steak and Baked Potato

BILL CLINTON (1993–)
Chicken Enchiladas
(also Hamburgers)

CHILI

IT'S TRUE that chili predates the twentieth century, but it is also true that it was neither "Americanized" nor widely known until the 1920s, my reason for including it here.

Few subjects are more incendiary than chili and few dishes are of less certain origin. By some accounts, we have Texas cowboys to thank for chili. Or at least a primitive dried-beef-and-chili "pemmican" from which our favorite dish descends. On roundups, they would carry this chili pemmican in their saddlebags—it was light, imperishable, and when boiled in water, became a rib-sticking stew.

Another theory holds that in the 1820s the San Antonio poor stretched their meat by lacing it with chili peppers. And perhaps with dried beans as well. The first chili powder was mixed up in 1835 by "Anglos" living in San Antonio; it may have been America's first spice blend. There's no denying that America's first "chili parlors" were pushcarts that appeared in San Antonio plazas sometime around 1880. They were decorative affairs presided over by equally decorative "chili queens," some of whom attracted customers with serenading musicians.

For purists, chili will forever be "the bowl of red" —no tomatoes, no beans. Just beef and suet— coarsely chopped—chilies, garlic, oregano, cumin, and enough water to keep the pot from boiling dry.

For most Americans, however, chili is a dried red bean stew chock-a-block with onions, peppers sweet and hot, and as much chili powder as you can stand. In the old days, there was chili and chili *con carne* (with meat)—nearly everyone's preference today.

Thumbing through early twentieth-century cookbooks, I find no mention of chili before the 1906 edition of Fannie Farmer's *Boston Cooking-School Cook Book*. "Chili Con Carni," she calls it. And any resemblance to today's chili ends there:

Clean, singe, and cut in pieces for serving, two young chickens. Season with salt and pepper, and sauté in butter. Remove seeds and veins from eight red peppers, cover with boiling water, and cook until soft; mash, and rub through a sieve. Add one teaspoon salt, one onion finely chopped, two cloves of garlic finely chopped, the chicken, and boiling water to cover. Cook until chicken is tender. Remove to serving dish, and thicken sauce with three tablespoons each butter and flour cooked together; there should be one and one-half cups sauce. Canned pimentos may be used in place of red peppers.

This is chili? The Chili Con Carni (again Fannie's spelling) in the *Larkin Housewives' Cook Book* (1915) is equally off-track, even though canned chili had been available since 1911. Here's the Larkin version:

Put one pound each of veal and beef, also one large onion through a Larkin Food-Chopper. Cover with water and simmer one and one-half hours. When almost cooked, add one cup boiled Larkin Short-Cut Macaroni, one can Larkin Tomatoes, and one can of Larkin Peas. Season with salt and red pepper. Will serve nine.

According to Cheryl Alters Jamison and Bill Jamison (*Texas Home Cooking*, 1993), "You can follow the progression of chili across the country, and see it move from hot to mild, in the ingredients that were added over time." They add that beans went into the pot in the 1920s, tomatoes a decade or two later.

A dandy way to stretch precious meat—or to get protein into the diet without it—chili, now plumped with beans and tomatoes, came to the rescue during the Great Depression. And again during World War II when there was plenty of chili but little *carne*.

Chili aficionados are legion and number in their ranks everyone from actress Elizabeth Taylor to President Lyndon Johnson to outlaw Jesse James who, it's said, spared one small-town bank just because his favorite chili parlor was nearby.

Chasen's Famous Chili

Makes about 1 Gallon

✽

ELIZABETH TAYLOR was so fond of Chasen's chili she would have the Hollywood restaurant ship it to wherever she was when hunger struck: to Rome, where she was filming *Cleopatra;* to Mexico, where Richard Burton was making *Night of the Iguana.* It was a favorite, too, of actor Jack Lemmon, as I learned when I interviewed him in the 1960s for *The Ladies' Home Journal.* Almost from the day it opened in 1936, Chasen's was Hollywood's power-lunch-and-dinner place. Then, sadly, phased out by trendier restaurants such as Drai's and Spago, it closed in 1995. Chasen's graciously gave me their chili recipe to accompany my Jack Lemmon article. This is my adaptation.

NOTE: Skip the MSG, if you like.

½ pound dried pinto beans, picked over and washed
5 cups canned crushed tomatoes
3 medium green bell peppers, cored, seeded, and coarsely chopped
1½ tablespoons vegetable oil
4 medium yellow onions, peeled and coarsely chopped
2 cloves garlic, peeled and minced
½ cup finely chopped fresh parsley
½ cup (1 stick) butter
2½ pounds ground lean beef chuck
1 pound ground lean pork shoulder
⅓ cup chili powder
2 tablespoons salt
1½ teaspoons black pepper
1½ teaspoons ground cumin
1½ teaspoons monosodium glutamate (MSG) (optional)

1. Soak beans overnight in large heavy kettle in cold water to cover by 2 inches.

2. Next day, cover and simmer beans in soaking water until tender —about 1 hour. Add tomatoes and simmer 5 minutes longer.

3. Stir-fry green peppers in oil in very large heavy skillet over moderate heat until limp—about 5 minutes. Add onions and stir-fry until glassy—5 to 8 minutes. Stir in garlic and parsley and set aside.

4. In second very large heavy skillet, melt butter over moderately high heat. Add beef and pork and sauté, stirring often, 15 minutes. Add meat to onion mixture, blend in chili powder, and cook, stirring occasionally, 10 minutes.

5. Add meat mixture to beans, along with salt, black pepper, cumin, and, if desired, MSG. Bring to boiling, adjust heat so chili bubbles gently, cover, and simmer 1 hour. Remove cover and cook, stirring now and then, 30 minutes longer.

6. Skim as much fat from chili as possible, ladle into heated soup bowls, and serve.

1918

America begins canning mushrooms.

....

Arnaud's opens in New Orleans.

1919

The first "built-in" refrigerator goes on sale.

....

Beta-carotene is crystallized from carrots at the University of Wisconsin and its vitamin A activity noted.

....

KitchenAid introduces a standing electric mixer (its design remains little changed today).

1920s

Prohibition begins.

....

Iodized salt is developed to reduce incidence of goiter in America's heartland, where diets lack iodine (from saltwater fish).

Pedernales River Chili

Makes 6 Servings

✻

UNTIL HE had a heart attack, President Lyndon B. Johnson doted on the greasy chili-parlor chilis of Texas. Once his doctor put him on a low-fat, low-cholesterol diet, however, the chili prepared on his beloved LBJ Ranch had to be modified. The recipe here, the slimmed-down version, is adapted from the one in Cheryl Alters Jamison and Bill Jamison's *Texas Home Cooking* (1993), which was, in turn, provided by Lady Bird Johnson.

4 pounds coarsely ground lean beef chuck or venison shoulder
1 large yellow onion, peeled and coarsely chopped
2 cloves garlic, peeled and minced
1 teaspoon dried leaf oregano, crumbled (preferably Mexican oregano)
2 tablespoons chili powder (or to taste)
1 teaspoon ground cumin
1½ teaspoons salt (or to taste)
2 to 6 dashes hot red pepper sauce
2 cups water
1½ cups canned crushed tomatoes

1. Stir-fry beef, onion, and garlic in large heavy kettle over moderate heat until lightly browned—about 10 minutes.

2. Add all remaining ingredients, bring to boiling, adjust heat so mixture bubbles gently, then simmer, uncovered, stirring now and then, until flavors marry. Skim off excess fat, taste for chili powder and salt, and adjust as needed.

3. Ladle into heated soup bowls and serve. Good with soda crackers.

Porcupine Meat Balls

Makes 6 Servings

✻

THE SORT of easy, novelty recipe that appealed to cooks in the '30s, yet it appears to have been developed during World War I as a way to stretch meat. In *Conservation Recipes* (1918) compiled by the Mobilized Women's Organizations of Berkeley and published by the Berkeley Unit, Council of Defence Women's Committee, there is something called "Rice Meat Balls," a clear forerunner of the recipe here, which is adapted from *My Better Homes & Gardens Cook Book* (1939). The 1918 version plumps up a pound of round steak with 1 cup crumbs and ¾ cup rice. The *Better Homes* recipe specifies beef neck, shank, or plate ground to order—not readily available today. I've substituted ground chuck.

1½ pounds ground beef chuck
½ cup uncooked converted rice
1 teaspoon salt
¼ teaspoon black pepper
1 tablespoon minced yellow onion
1 (10½-ounce) can condensed tomato soup
1 soup can water

1. Using hands, mix beef, rice, salt, pepper, and onion well and shape into 1-inch balls.

2. Mix tomato soup and water in medium heavy kettle and bring to simmering over moderate heat.

3. Add meatballs, adjust heat so mixture bubbles very gently, cover, and simmer 1 hour. Serve accompanied by a crisp green salad.

Hamburger Stroganoff

Makes 4 to 6 Servings

✻

THIS EASY knockoff of the Russian classic (see Beef Stroganoff, page 125) was a favorite among hostesses in the late '50s and early '60s. This particular recipe was given to me by actress Natalie Wood whom I profiled for *The Ladies' Home Journal* back in 1961. It was a party dish she liked to serve, which says something about the way Hollywood entertained in those days. Note the ersatz salts, a kitchen staple then.

3 tablespoons butter

2 pounds ground beef round

1 teaspoon seasoned salt

1 teaspoon garlic salt

½ teaspoon salt (or to taste)

¼ teaspoon black pepper (or to taste)

1 medium yellow onion, peeled and chopped

½ medium green bell pepper, cored, seeded, and chopped

10 medium mushrooms, wiped clean and thinly sliced

2 ribs celery, trimmed and chopped

1½ cups canned crushed tomatoes

1 cup sour cream

½ pound wild rice, cooked by package directions

1. Melt butter in large heavy skillet over moderate heat, add ground round, seasoned salt, garlic salt, salt, and pepper and stir-fry, breaking up large clumps of meat, until nicely browned—about 10 minutes.

2. Add onion, green pepper, mushrooms, and celery and cook, stirring occasionally, until onion is limp and golden—3 to 5 minutes.

3. Mix in tomatoes, adjust heat so mixture bubbles gently, cover, and simmer 20 minutes.

4. Smooth in sour cream and bring just to serving temperature—do not boil or cream may curdle. Taste for salt and pepper and adjust as needed.

5. Serve over wild rice.

RECOMMENDED BY DUNCAN HINES

DUNCAN HINES, a traveling salesman from Kentucky, didn't set out to become a food and lodging guru; he simply enjoyed good food. Early on, he began keeping track of the restaurants where he ate, jotting down descriptive notes on palatability, prices, and service. In 1935, he listed his favorites on the back of his Christmas cards—and soon was deluged with requests for copies of the list from total strangers as well as from friends.

The next year he published a modest booklet, *Adventures in Good Eating*, precursor to the famous guide that sold a quarter of a million copies and went through forty-six editions. Why were so many people so eager to take Hines's advice? The time was right. By the late '30s, the automobile had put millions of Americans—with no previous travel experience and little faith in their own judgment—on the road. Most restaurants, hotels, and the new "motels" were locally owned and might be terrific or terrible. Who knew?

Duncan Hines knew. It was said that he traveled fifty thousand miles a year, sometimes ate six meals a day, and never accepted a free dinner or room that might compromise his integrity. "Recommended by Duncan Hines" soon became the ultimate seal of approval. Establishments sought it. Travelers looked for it.

AMERICAN CHOP SUEY

O F COURSE "real" chop suey is American, too, a nineteenth-century creation, it's said, of the Chinese who cooked for men laying track for the Pacific Railroad.

This altogether different, twentieth-century chop suey enjoyed a certain faddishness in the teens and '20s. This recipe is reprinted from the *Larkin Housewives' Cook Book* (1915):

Cook one-half package of Larkin Short-Cut Macaroni in boiling salted water for twenty minutes. While this is cooking put two onions and one-half pound of round steak through a Larkin Food-Chopper. Brown in a hot pan with a piece of butter or beef drippings. Drain water from macaroni, add one can of Larkin Tomatoes, season with Larkin Salt and Pepper, then add steak and onions and cook slowly for thirty minutes. Serve piping hot.

Larkin, as this recipe makes clear, not only processed and packaged a wide array of food but also sold a variety of kitchen gadgets. Founded in 1875, Larkin "Pure Food Specialists" had offices in Buffalo, Chicago, Peoria, and Philadelphia.

Baked Herb-Stuffed Pork Chops

Makes 4 Servings

✳

STRANGELY, EARLY-twentieth-century cookbooks short-shrift pork. The 1906 edition of *The Boston Cooking-School Cook Book* offers a lonely two recipes. Even *Good Housekeeping's Book of Menus, Recipes and Household Discoveries* (1922) gives only one—for crown roast of pork at that. Stuffed pork chops seem to be a '30s innovation. *My Better Homes & Gardens Cook Book* (1939) prints a basic recipe for stuffing six double pork chops with "½ recipe Bread Dressing" and baking for 45 minutes in a moderately slow oven. After World War II, however, when meat became more widely available and cooks more creative, pork chops were being stuffed with everything from spinach to minced oysters. They don't get much better, however, than this recipe, with its herby apricot-mushroom stuffing, adapted from *Family Circle Recipes America Loves Best* (1982).

NOTE: Make sure the skillet in which you bake the chops has a heat-proof handle.

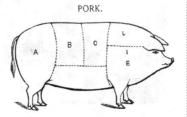

PORK.

½ pound medium mushrooms, wiped clean and thinly sliced
⅓ cup chopped yellow onion
⅓ cup chopped celery
½ cup (1 stick) butter or margarine
1 cup dry bread crumbs
¼ teaspoon ground sage
½ cup minced fresh parsley
¼ cup minced dried apricots
4 double center-loin pork chops with pockets cut between the two rib bones
½ teaspoon salt
¼ teaspoon black pepper
1 cup dry white wine

1. Preheat oven to 350° F.

2. Stir-fry mushrooms, onion, and celery in half the butter in large heavy ovenproof skillet 3 minutes; mix in bread crumbs, sage, parsley, and apricots; set aside.

3. Sprinkle pork chops inside and out with salt and pepper, then stuff mushroom mixture loosely into pockets and fasten with toothpicks.

4. Wipe skillet clean, set over moderately high heat, add remaining butter and, when it sizzles, add chops and brown 3 to 5 minutes on each side.

5. Pour wine around chops, cover skillet, transfer to oven, and bake until chops are tender—about 1 hour. Serve at once.

Baked Pork Chops with Roasted Peanut Stuffing

Makes 6 Servings

✳

THIS RECIPE dates to the '70s when stuffings became a popular potato substitute. Today stuffing mixes can be stirred on top of the stove. In this recipe—my own—the stuffing is made from scratch and goes on top of the chops, not inside them.

> 1 tablespoon butter
> 1 small yellow onion, peeled and minced
> 1 cup fine soft bread crumbs
> ½ cup finely minced roasted peanuts
> ½ teaspoon salt
> ¼ teaspoon ground hot red pepper (cayenne)
> ½ cup evaporated milk
> 6 (1-inch-thick) center-loin pork chops

1. Preheat oven to 350° F.

2. Melt butter in medium heavy skillet over moderate heat, add onion and stir-fry until glassy—2 to 3 minutes. Mix in crumbs, peanuts, salt, cayenne, and evaporated milk. Spread on top of pork chops, dividing total amount evenly.

3. Place chops, stuffing-side-up, in shallow roasting pan and bake, uncovered, 45 minutes to 1 hour, or until stuffing is lightly browned and pork chops are well done. Serve at once.

"HAM WHAT AM"

SPAM, THAT plump pink loaf of gelatin-glazed spiced ham, will forever be associated with World War II. Yet it had its origin much earlier when a Hormel executive, faced with a windfall of several thousand pounds of pork shoulder, decided to chop it with some ham, spice it, and can it in a gelatin preservative. Aware that its new product was a potential gold mine, Hormel asked the public to suggest catchy names for it, and paid $100 for Spam—a contraction of "spiced" and "ham." In one of America's first singing commercials, Hormel launched its "new miracle meat in a can" in 1937 to the tune of "My Bonnie Lies Over the Ocean."

During World War II, as Nikita Khrushchev later recalled, it was primarily Spam that saved Russian troops from starvation. Margaret Thatcher remembers eating this "wartime delicacy," accompanied by lettuce and peaches, during the Christmas holidays of 1943.

GIs joked about Spam and complained about having to eat it three times a day, but after the war they continued to buy it. Today, Americans scarf down more than 122 million cans of Spam a year. Where is the most Spam sold? Hawaii, Alaska, Arkansas, Texas, and Alabama in this country; the United Kingdom and South Korea worldwide.

Today, Spam recipe contests are held at sixty-eight state and regional fairs. And a Spam-carving contest is popular in Seattle, where recent winners have included "Spamhenge" and "Spammy Wynette."

Skinnier Ham Loaf

Makes 6 Servings

✻

HERE'S ANOTHER favorite meat loaf from which I've subtracted considerable fat and calories. Like my Slimmed-Down Meat Loaf (page 99), it ran in *Family Circle*. The counts per serving: 257 calories, 13 grams fat, and 20 milligrams cholesterol.

3 tablespoons fine dry bread crumbs
½ pound ground lean smoked ham
1 pound ground lean turkey
20 no-fat soda crackers, finely crushed
3 medium carrots, peeled and finely chopped
1 medium yellow onion, peeled and finely chopped
1 medium red bell pepper, cored, seeded, and finely chopped
¼ cup evaporated skim milk
¼ cup no-cholesterol fat-free thawed frozen egg product
½ teaspoon dry mustard
½ teaspoon ground allspice
¼ teaspoon ground ginger

1. Preheat oven to 350° F. Lightly coat 8 × 4 × 2¾-inch loaf pan with nonstick cooking spray, add fine dry bread crumbs and tilt from side to side to coat evenly; tap out excess crumbs and set pan aside.

2. Using hands, mix all remaining ingredients well in large bowl and pack into prepared pan.

3. Bake, uncovered, 55 to 60 minutes until browned and springy to touch, then cool in pan on wire rack 10 minutes before slicing.

Good Basic Ham Loaf with Sour Cream-Mustard Sauce

Makes 8 to 10 Servings

✻

STRANGELY, HAM loaves do not begin appearing in cookbooks until the first quarter or third of this century. At least I've found none earlier. This one—my own—is plenty spicy. It's good cold, perfect for a party buffet.

GLAZE

½ to 1 cup tart red jelly
OR
½ cup firmly packed brown sugar

HAM LOAF

1½ pounds ground smoked ham
1 pound lean ground pork shoulder
2 cups fine soft bread crumbs
2 medium yellow onions, peeled and minced
¼ cup minced fresh parsley
1 cup buttermilk, milk, or sour milk
2 eggs
2 tablespoons Dijon mustard
2 tablespoons ketchup
2 tablespoons India relish
¼ cup drained small capers (optional)
¼ teaspoon ground ginger
¼ teaspoon ground cloves
¼ teaspoon ground allspice
⅛ teaspoon freshly grated nutmeg
¾ teaspoon salt
¼ teaspoon black pepper

SOUR CREAM-MUSTARD SAUCE

2 cups sour cream
3 tablespoons Dijon mustard
¼ cup drained small capers
1 tablespoon prepared horseradish
2 tablespoons snipped fresh dill

1. Preheat oven to 350° F. Coat 9 × 5 × 3-inch loaf pan with non-stick cooking spray and set aside.

2. GLAZE: Spoon jelly or brown sugar into pan, spreading evenly over bottom.

3. HAM LOAF: Using hands, mix all ingredients thoroughly in large bowl. Pack into prepared pan.

4. Bake, uncovered, until loaf pulls from sides of pan and is richly browned—about 2 hours.

5. Set pan on wire rack, loosen loaf around edges, then cool in pan to room temperature; drain off drippings.

6. SAUCE: Mix all ingredients and refrigerate until ready to serve.

7. Slice ham loaf and arrange on platter. Spoon some sauce on top and pass the rest.

Cranberry-Glazed Ham

Makes 16 to 20 Servings

✳

AN EASY recipe from Ocean Spray, which surfaced in a '50s pamphlet called *Cranberry Dishes for Holidays and Special Occasions.* "What could be prettier than a tulip-red cranberry glaze for Easter ham?" reads the photo caption. "Not only does it taste good, but the cranberry sauce has a tenderizing effect on the ham." Perhaps. The ham shown has a hefty outer layer of fat, which the ten-derizingly acidic cranberry glaze would be unlikely to penetrate. No matter. Few of today's hams need tenderizing.

> 1 (8- to 10-pound) smoked ham, trimmed of rind and excess fat
> 2 dozen whole cloves (about)
> 1 (1-pound) can jellied cranberry sauce
> ½ cup firmly packed light brown sugar

1. Bake ham according to package directions.

2. Thirty minutes before ham is done, remove from oven and pour all drippings from pan. Score ham crisscross fashion in diamond pattern with sharp knife and stud each "diamond" with a clove.

3. Crush cranberry sauce with fork, add brown sugar, and blend until smooth. Spread over ham.

4. Return ham to oven and bake ½ hour longer, basting occasionally with pan drippings.

5. Just before serving, spoon cranberry sauce from bottom of pan over ham until it glistens.

TIMELINE

1920

Italian immigrants in California begin growing and popularizing broccoli (known since Thomas Jefferson's day, it had been enjoyed mainly by a privileged few).

Breakstone packages cream cheese for mass distribution.

Curtiss Candy Company creates a chocolate-covered, caramel-peanut bar, calls it Kandy Kake, then renames it Baby Ruth.

1921

Wonder Bread hits the market (in Indianapolis, Indiana).

An Iowa confectioner coats a vanilla ice cream bar with chocolate, calls it I-Scream, then renames it Eskimo Pie.

Baked Spicy Pineapple Balinese Chicken

Makes 4 Servings

❋

MARY LOUISE Lever of Rome, Georgia, says she got the inspiration for this recipe on a trip to the South Pacific. It won the $25,000 top prize at the 41st National Chicken Cooking Contest in Atlanta in 1995.

CHICKEN

4 boned and skinned chicken breast halves (about 1¼ pounds)
3 tablespoons Dijon mustard
½ cup gingersnap crumbs

SPICY PINEAPPLE SAUCE

1 tablespoon vegetable oil
1 medium red onion, peeled and chopped
1 clove garlic, peeled and minced
¼ cup rice wine vinegar
1 cup canned unsweetened crushed pineapple
¼ teaspoon ground allspice
¼ teaspoon crushed red pepper flakes
2½ teaspoons Dijon mustard
2 tablespoons finely chopped fresh basil
¼ cup diced red bell pepper

1. CHICKEN: Coat 11 × 7 × 2-inch baking dish with nonstick cooking spray and set aside.

2. Place chicken breasts between sheets of plastic wrap and pound to uniform thickness. Spread on both sides with mustard, then dredge in gingersnap crumbs. Refrigerate in baking dish 20 minutes.

3. Preheat oven to 350° F. Bake chicken, uncovered, 20 minutes, until no longer pink in center.

4. Meanwhile, prepare SAUCE: Heat oil in large heavy skillet over moderate heat 1 minute. Add onion and garlic and stir-fry 2 minutes. Mix in vinegar, pineapple, allspice, red pepper flakes, and mustard; cook and stir 3 to 4 minutes until bubbly and slightly thickened. Puree mixture in electric blender at high speed or food processor fitted with metal chopping blade. Return to skillet and stir in basil and bell pepper and bring to serving temperature.

5. To serve, puddle sauce on four heated plates, dividing amount evenly, and top with chicken.

....

King Ranch Chicken

Makes 6 Servings

❋

KAREN HARAM, food editor of the San Antonio *Express-News,* tells me that though Texans claim this recipe, no one knows where it originated. Or how it came to be named for the King Ranch, whose claims to fame are its immense acreage, its oil, and its Santa Gertrudis cattle, a breed developed there to replace the sinewy Texas longhorns. Certainly the King Ranch was never known for chicken. "Maybe," Haram speculates, "it's because this recipe is so rich." The one here is adapted from *Texas Home Cooking* (1993) by Cheryl Alters Jamison and Bill Jamison.

SAUCE

2 tablespoons butter
2 cloves garlic, peeled and minced
¼ teaspoon ground hot red pepper (preferably ancho)
⅛ teaspoon ground cumin
2 tablespoons flour
¾ cup chicken broth
½ cup milk
2 tablespoons sour cream
½ teaspoon salt (or to taste)
¼ teaspoon black pepper (or to taste)

FILLING

1 tablespoon butter
1 small yellow onion, peeled and chopped
½ medium green bell pepper, cored, seeded, and chopped
¼ cup chopped roasted green chilies
6 ounces mushrooms, wiped clean and finely chopped
½ cup canned crushed tomatoes
2 tablespoons minced pimiento

TORTILLAS

Vegetable oil for frying
8 corn tortillas

CHICKEN AND OTHER LAYERS

3 cups diced cooked chicken
1½ cups coarsely shredded mild Cheddar cheese
¼ cup sliced pimiento-stuffed olives
¼ cup thinly sliced scallions

1. Preheat oven to 350° F. Coat 11 × 7 × 2-inch baking dish with nonstick cooking spray and set aside.

2. SAUCE: Melt butter in medium heavy skillet over moderate heat. Add garlic, red pepper, and cumin and stir-fry 1 minute. Blend in flour, add broth and milk, and cook, stirring constantly, until thickened and smooth—about 3 minutes. Smooth in sour cream, salt, and black pepper to taste; set aside.

3. FILLING: Melt butter in large heavy skillet over moderate heat. Add onion, green pepper, green chilies, mushrooms, tomatoes, and pimiento, and cook, stirring often, until vegetables soften and flavors meld—10 to 15 minutes.

4. TORTILLAS: Pour oil to depth of ½ inch in small heavy skillet, set over moderate heat, and heat until ripples appear on skillet bottom. Holding tortillas by tongs, dip one by one into oil just long enough to soften—5 to 10 seconds. Drain on paper towels.

5. TO LAYER: Arrange half of tortillas in bottom of prepared baking dish, then build up layers this way, distributing each evenly: ½ chicken and ⅓ sauce; ½ each filling, cheese, olives, and scallions, and ½ remaining sauce; remaining tortillas, chicken, filling, cheese, olives, scallions, and finally, remaining sauce.

6. Bake, uncovered, until bubbly—about 30 to 35 minutes. Serve at once.

CHICKEN DIVAN

THIS 1930S recipe remains popular, though mostly in the heartland where it's a staple of fund-raiser cookbooks. These versions have veered far from the original Chicken Divan by turning it into a canned-soup casserole. The one thing I discovered while researching this recipe was that precious little had been written about it. Then a friend steered me toward a book I hadn't known, *New York Holiday* (1950), by travel writer Eleanor Early. In her coverage of New York restaurants, she not only discusses the mid-Manhattan restaurant that created Chicken Divan but also describes the original recipe in some detail:

DIVAN PARISIEN at 17 East 45th Street was once voted the seventh most popular restaurant in America. Most people go to the Divan because of a specialty called Chicken Divan. Which is a wonderful dish that you can make at home, and I'll tell you how. You start with a good big fowl, which you have boiled until it is delectably tender. Then you make a rich sauce. I use two cups of the chicken stock and a cup of cream; but I understand that the chef at the Divan uses two cups of ordinary white sauce, to which he adds half a cup of whipped cream and half a cup of Hollandaise sauce. My way is easier. Add to the sauce a few tablespoons of sherry, a pinch of nutmeg and a teaspoon of Worcestershire sauce. Cook a package of frozen broccoli, drain and arrange in a casserole or deep serving platter. Sprinkle the broccoli with grated Parmesan cheese, and over it spread slices (or chunky pieces) of the breast and leg meat. Pour the sauce over all, and sprinkle generously with more Parmesan. Use about a cup of Parmesan altogether. Place the dish about five inches below a hot broiler flame and cook until brown and bubbly. This makes four generous servings.

The restaurant Divan Parisien, alas, is now out of business. Has been for more than forty years. But Chicken Divan, the American classic it created, may live forever.

Caribbean Chicken Drums

Makes 4 Servings

✳

WITH THIS quick, colorful recipe, Rosemarie Berger of Jamestown, North Carolina, won $25,000 in the 40th National Chicken Cooking Contest held in 1993 in Richmond, Virginia.

> *8 broiler-fryer chicken drumsticks*
> *2 tablespoons vegetable oil*
> *1 (14½-ounce) can whole, peeled tomatoes, drained and cut into chunks*
> *1 (4-ounce) can diced green chilies, drained*
> *1 tablespoon brown sugar*
> *¼ teaspoon ground allspice*
> *¼ cup mango chutney, chopped*
> *1 tablespoon fresh lemon juice*
> *¼ cup dark seedless raisins*
> *1 large banana, peeled and sliced*
> *1 ripe mango, peeled and sliced*

1. Brown drumsticks well in oil in large heavy skillet over moderate heat—about 10 minutes.

2. Add tomatoes, chilies, brown sugar, and allspice. Bring to boil, cover, reduce heat to low, and cook 20 minutes.

3. Add chutney, lemon juice, and raisins. Cover and cook about 15 minutes or until fork can be inserted in chicken with ease. Remove chicken to heated serving platter.

4. Skim fat from skillet mixture. Add banana and bring just to serving temperature.

5. Spoon fruit and a little of the sauce over chicken. Garnish with mango slices. Pass remaining sauce separately.

Chicken Imperial

Makes 4 to 6 Servings

✳

CREATED IN the late 1950s in the New York test kitchens of *The Ladies' Home Journal,* this may be the best chicken recipe ever. It's also one of the earliest "oven-fried" chickens and the inspiration, quite possibly, for today's popular "shake and bake" method.

NOTE: Begin this recipe the day before you serve it. For 2 cups soft, fine bread crumbs, you'll need one

KENTUCKY FRIED CHICKEN

IN 1956, Colonel Harland Sanders, already past retirement age, took his fried chicken on the road. He had been frying chicken for a quarter of a century in Corbin, Kentucky, had been made a Kentucky Colonel for his contribution to the state's cuisine, and had a good head for business.

What he didn't have was money. Various misfortunes, such as having a new Interstate highway bypass his restaurant, had forced him to pack up his fifty-pound container of eleven secret herbs and spices and his indispensable pressure cooker, and peddle franchises from restaurant door to restaurant door.

The unorthodox method worked: Sanders swapped his recipe and gave restaurant owners a crash cooking course in exchange for a four-cent royalty on every chicken sold; by 1964 he had more than six hundred franchises grossing $37 million a year. By the time he died (having sold his interest in the company for $2 million), Kentucky Fried Chicken was grossing more than $2 *billion* a year.

firm-textured, unsliced loaf, trimmed of crusts. Grate on the coarse side of a four-sided grater or tear into chunks and buzz to crumbs in a food processor.

> 2 cups soft, fine bread crumbs
> ¾ cup grated Parmesan or
>   Romano cheese
> ¼ cup minced fresh parsley
> 1 clove garlic, peeled and
>   crushed
> 2 teaspoons salt
> ¼ teaspoon black pepper
> 2 (2½- to 3-pound) broiler-
>   fryers, cut up
> 1 cup (2 sticks) butter, melted

1. Spread crumbs on large tray and dry overnight at room temperature.

2. Next day, mix crumbs with cheese, parsley, garlic, salt, and pepper.

3. Preheat oven to 350°F.

4. Dip each chicken piece into melted butter, then crumb mixture, coating well on all sides.

5. Arrange crumbed chicken in single layer in an open, shallow roasting pan. Drizzle remaining butter over all.

6. Bake, uncovered, 1 hour until fork-tender, basting frequently with pan drippings.

7. Serve hot, at room temperature, or chill well and serve straight from the refrigerator.

ROCK CORNISH HENS

IT'S BEEN said that these bantam-weight chickens, a cross between the Cornish, a meaty British breed, and the White Rock, were introduced in 1965. Not so! We were cooking them in the late 1950s when I was beginning my food career as a recipe tester at *The Ladies' Home Journal*. Indeed, *The Ladies' Home Journal Cook Book* (1960) includes three recipes for Rock Cornish Game Hens.

In *Cooks, Gluttons, and Gourmets* (1962), Betty Wason writes that Wild-Rice-Stuffed Rock Cornish Hens with Madeira Sauce were among the things cooked by the winning team of American chefs at the Tenth International Culinary Olympics in Frankfurt, Germany. The year: 1960.

Jim Fobel, author of *The Whole Chicken Cookbook* (1992), says that Cornish hens have been around since the 1940s, when cross-breeding techniques were perfected. He adds, moreover, that no birds can be labeled "Cornish Hens" or "Rock Cornish Game Hens" unless they contain bloodlines from both the Cornish and White Rock breeds.

In the masses of literature sent me by Perdue Farms in Salisbury, Maryland, there's this statement: "In the beginning (about 1887), the rock Cornish game hen was developed by cross-breeding America's hardy Plymouth rock chicken and England's flavorful Cornish. Chefs hailed the new arrival, but it wasn't sold to consumers until the 1970s." That date of course is wrong. Frozen Rock Cornish Game Hens were widely available in the late 1950s. Perdue began marketing the fresh in 1975.

What makes Cornish hens so appealing is that they're practically all breast and because of their infancy, supremely tender. These babies come to market five or six weeks old and weigh in at about 1½ pounds.

Rock Cornish Hens with Wild Rice Stuffing

Makes 6 Servings

✻

THIS RECIPE, adapted from *The Ladies' Home Journal Cook Book* (1960) on which I worked, allows one whole bird per person. Today, half a bird is a more reasonable portion. I've also reduced the amount of butter in the stuffing.

STUFFING

¼ cup (½ stick) butter
1 small yellow onion, peeled and chopped
½ pound mushrooms, wiped clean and coarsely chopped
1½ cups diced cooked ham
1 cup wild rice, cooked by package directions
½ teaspoon salt
½ teaspoon dried leaf marjoram, crumbled
½ teaspoon dried leaf thyme, crumbled

BIRDS

6 (1- to 1½-pound) Rock Cornish Hens
1 teaspoon salt
12 slices bacon
2 tablespoons butter

1. STUFFING: Melt butter in large heavy skillet over moderate heat; add onion, mushrooms, and ham and sauté, stirring often, 5 minutes. Mix in rice, salt, marjoram, and thyme; set aside.

2. BIRDS: Preheat oven to 350°F. Sprinkle cavities of birds with salt. Spoon stuffing lightly into body and neck cavities of birds; fold neck skin against backs and secure with toothpicks. Drape 2 slices bacon over each bird.

3. Arrange breast-side-up and not touching in large shallow roasting pan, drop in butter and roast, uncovered, basting often, until no signs of pink show in center of breasts—1 to 1¼ hours. Serve at once.

Rock Cornish Hens with Olive Stuffing

Makes 4 Servings

✻

THIS RECIPE is my own. It's a good choice for a small dinner party.

STUFFING

2 tablespoons fruity olive oil
1 medium yellow onion, peeled and chopped
1 clove garlic, peeled and minced
1 small rib celery, diced
1 teaspoon rubbed sage
¼ teaspoon dried leaf marjoram, crumbled
¼ teaspoon dried leaf thyme, crumbled
2 cups soft bread crumbs
2 hard-cooked eggs, peeled and chopped
¼ cup minced fresh parsley
2 tablespoons minced, pitted green olives
½ teaspoon salt
¼ teaspoon black pepper
2 tablespoons butter, melted
2 tablespoons dry white wine

BIRDS

4 (1-pound) Rock Cornish Hens
¼ cup (½ stick) butter, melted
1 tablespoon fruity olive oil
2 tablespoons dry white wine

1. STUFFING: Heat olive oil in small heavy skillet over moderate heat 1 minute, add onion, garlic, and celery and stir-fry until limp—3 minutes. Mix in sage, marjoram, and thyme and mellow 1 minute. Dump skillet mixture into large bowl, add all remaining stuffing ingredients, and toss well; set aside.

2. BIRDS: Preheat oven to 375°F. Spoon stuffing lightly into body and neck cavities of birds; fold neck skin against backs and secure with toothpicks. Wrap any remaining stuffing in foil.

3. Arrange birds breast-side-up and not touching in large shallow roasting pan. Add foil bundle of extra stuffing. Mix melted butter, olive oil, and wine and brush on birds.

4. Roast birds, uncovered, brushing often with butter mixture, until no pink shows in center of breasts—1 to 1¼ hours. Serve at once.

IRMA ROMBAUER
AND THE JOY OF COOKING

FTER HER husband committed suicide in 1930, a St. Louis widow decided to gather up favorite family recipes, add others that were popular at the time, and publish them in a little book. Her daughter, not yet married and still living at home, supported the idea. The project, she believed, would keep her mother's mind off her troubles and maybe make a little money, too.

Although Irma Rombauer's *The Joy of Cooking* would be the first American cookbook to offer a serious challenge to Fannie Farmer's *Boston Cooking-School Cook Book,* and although it was destined to become one of the beloved cookbooks of all time, the way Irma and her daughter Marion went about getting it into print was disarmingly casual.

"We simply called in a printer," Marion Rombauer Becker recalled years later. "He arrived laden with washable cover fabrics, type and paper samples. In a few hours all decisions were made." Since that first privately printed 1931 edition of 3,000 copies, eight subsequent editions (about half of them genuine revisions) were published by Bobbs-Merrill. Until Irma fell ill (she had the first of a series of strokes in 1955 and died in 1962), she devoted much of her time and energy to updating subsequent editions of *Joy.*

According to Anne Mendelson (*Stand Facing the Stove: The Story of the Women Who Gave America The Joy of Cooking,* 1996), from the time Irma's daughter Marion married architect John Becker and moved to Cincinnati in 1932 until 1948, Marion was only "tangentially involved" with *The Joy of Cooking.* She was a full-fledged collaborator, however, on the 1951 edition, and was responsible for the first truly encyclopedic *Joy* (1963).

Marion's own health faltered in the '70s (as did her husband's), yet "working under a death sentence," as Anne Mendelson calls it, she managed to revise and update the final Rombauer/Becker edition. It appeared in 1975, just a year before Marion died of cancer.

A '90s *Joy* is now on the way from Scribner, its chapters being parceled out to a stable of food writers to modernize and reshape. Fortunately, Irma Rombauer's grandson Ethan Becker still has the last word.

The Joy of Cooking spans two-thirds of a century of culinary change: thrifty use of leftovers during the Depression . . . sugarless, meatless recipes for World War II . . . interest in nutrition health during the '50s and '60s . . . and, in the '70s, emphasis on international cuisine and the use of ingredients available through modern technology and transport.

But despite all the changes, the cookbook reflects Irma Rombauer's beliefs that "all *Joy of Cooking* readers are amateurs in the kitchen" and that "inexperienced cooks cannot fail to make successful soufflés, pies, cakes, soups, gravies, and so forth if they follow the clear instructions."

Pompano en Papillote

Makes 6 Servings

✳

THE YEAR: 1901. The place: New Orleans. The occasion: The visit of French hot-air balloonist Alberto Santos-Dumont. To honor the event, Jules Alciatore, proprietor of Antoine's, created a special recipe—a fillet of pompano baked in parchment with creamed shrimp and crab. When it came from the oven, it was puffed—just like Santos-Dumont's ascension balloon. Before long, Antoine's new recipe was the talk of the town and other chefs scrambled to "crack" it. It's said that while shooting *The Pirate's Lady* in New Orleans in 1937, film director Cecil B. DeMille was so taken with *pompano en papillote* he worked it into his movie. This despite the fact that the New Orleans of his period piece film predated Antoine's, which opened in 1840. So much for history. The recipe here is adapted from the original *pompano en papillote* in *Antoine's Restaurant Since 1840 Cookbook* (1980) by Roy F.

Guste, Jr., the restaurant's fifth-generation proprietor.

NOTE: For the *papillotes,* you will need six hearts cut out of baking parchment (or foil), each about 10 inches long and 14 inches across at the widest point.

SAUCE

3 tablespoons butter
3 tablespoons flour
½ teaspoon salt
⅛ teaspoon white pepper
2 cups fish stock or 1 cup each bottled clam juice and water

POMPANO

3 tablespoons butter
1 cup finely chopped scallions
1 cup raw peeled and deveined shrimp
1½ cups dry white wine
2 cups Sauce (above)
1 cup lump crabmeat, picked over for bits of shell
2¼ teaspoons salt
⅛ teaspoon white pepper
⅛ teaspoon ground hot red pepper (cayenne)
6 (6-ounce) skinned pompano fillets
1 medium yellow onion, peeled and thinly sliced
5 peppercorns
2 whole bay leaves
Juice of 1 lemon

1. SAUCE: Melt butter in small heavy saucepan over moderate heat, blend in flour, salt, and pepper, add fish stock, and cook, stirring constantly, until thickened and smooth—3 to 5 minutes. Set off heat but keep warm.

2. POMPANO: Melt butter in large heavy skillet over moderate heat, add scallions and sauté, stirring often, until limp—2 to 3 minutes. Add shrimp and 1 cup wine; bring to boiling. Blend in sauce, then add crab, ¼ teaspoon salt, white and cayenne peppers. Adjust heat so mixture bubbles lazily, and simmer, uncovered, stirring occasionally, 10 minutes.

3. Preheat oven to 400°F. Coat large baking sheet with nonstick cooking spray and set aside.

4. Poach pompano fillets 1 to 2 minutes in very large nonreactive skillet with onion, 2 teaspoons salt, peppercorns, remaining ½ cup wine, bay leaves, lemon juice, and enough water to cover. The minute fish begins to flake, drain and keep warm.

5. FOR *PAPILLOTES:* Fold each parchment heart (see Note above) in half lengthwise, then open flat. Spoon about ¼ cup shrimp mixture slightly to right of center fold of each parchment heart, placing as near middle of half-heart as possible. Lay pompano fillets on top, fold paper over to enclose, then seal by tightly rolling edges over several times.

6. Slide *papillotes* onto baking sheet and bake until paper puffs and begins to brown—about 15 minutes.

7. Transfer *papillotes* to six heated dinner plates and serve with ceremony. To open, slit tops of *papillotes* with a sharp knife.

LOBSTER FRA DIAVOLO

A RECIPE OF elusive origin. I'd always thought Lobster Fra Diavolo Italian, probably *southern* Italian, but I do not pretend to be an expert on the cooking of that extraordinary country.

Then, just as I was putting this book to bed, along comes a *New York Times* article (May 29, 1996) suggesting that this rich dish—chunks of lobster, still in the shell, bedded on pasta and smothered with a spicy tomato sauce—was created early this century by Italian immigrants in or around New York City. Like spaghetti and meatballs.

I know the author of that article—Florence Fabricant. And I know her to be painstaking about her facts. She doesn't proclaim that Lobster Fra Diavolo is American. Instead, she queries the experts, such respected writers on and teachers of Italian cooking as Marcella Hazan, Giuliano Bugialli, and Anna Teresa Callen. And such highly regarded New York restaurateurs as Tony May, owner of the elegant San Domenico on Central Park South.

Hazan remembers eating Lobster Fra Diavolo in 1940 at Grotta Azzurra, a restaurant opened in New York's Little Italy in 1908 that's still going strong.

"I remember the dish clearly," Fabricant quotes Hazan as saying, "because it was so heavy and typical of Italian cooking in America. We don't eat like that in Italy." Anna Teresa Callen concurs. "It's not an Italian dish," she tells Fabricant. "It's really another Italian-American invention. I have never seen it in Italy and suspect that it came from Long Island."

Bugialli, like Hazan and Callen, scoffs at the notion that Lobster Fra Diavolo is an Italian classic.

"We don't even have American lobsters in Italy,"

he explains to Fabricant. "And a heavy tomato sauce with hot peppers, seafood, and pasta all in one dish is not Italian cooking. I think it came from a restaurant that was near the old Met, around Thirty-eighth Street and Broadway."

Would that have been the old Mama Leone's? It opened behind the Met in 1906.

Restaurateur Tony May, a Neapolitan, says he'd never heard of Lobster Fra Diavolo until he arrived in New York in 1963. He thinks Vesuvio, a midtown Manhattan restaurant, might have invented it.

But Frank Scognamillo, the owner of Patsy's, another midtown Italian restaurant, begs to differ. His father, Pasquale, emigrated from Naples to New York in the early 1920s and opened Patsy's in 1944. Lobster Fra Diavolo was a house specialty. Frank Sinatra loved it, although he did ask for the garlic to be toned down.

Scognamillo says his father told him Lobster Fra Diavolo was a Neapolitan dish, and that like many other spicy, tomatoey recipes of southern Italy, it was handed down for generations.

Connie Davino, owner of Grotta Azzurra where Marcella Hazan first tried Lobster Fra Diavolo nearly sixty years ago, said that his father also told him the recipe was Neapolitan.

"We have different lobsters in Naples," he tells Fabricant. "But they had a dish like that. We've been serving it as long as I can remember."

With all due respect to Scognamillo and Davino —also to food writer/historian John Mariani, whose mother told him she learned to prepare Lobster Fra Diavolo from her mother-in-law who was born in Abruzzi, an area known for its peppery sauces—I tend to think Hazan, Bugialli, Callen "and company" nearer the mark.

Salmon-Pimiento Loaf

Makes 8 to 10 Servings

❋

ALTHOUGH CANNED salmon was available before the turn of the century, it apparently wasn't being made into loaves. Only in the 1903 *Good Housekeeping Everyday Cook Book* do I come upon a salmon loaf: *Take one can of salmon, drain off the juice and chop fine. Add yolks of four eggs beaten very light, one-half cup of grated bread crumbs, four tablespoons of melted butter, one-half teaspoon of pepper (scant), one-half teaspoon of salt, and a little finely chopped parsley. Beat whites of egg stiff and add last. Put in buttered pan and bake half an hour.*

The following recipe is my mother's, jazzed up with fresh herbs.

2 (14.5-ounce) cans salmon, drained and flaked
2½ cups soft bread crumbs
3 eggs, lightly beaten
½ cup evaporated milk
½ cup finely chopped yellow onion
¼ cup finely chopped pimientos
¼ cup minced fresh parsley
3 tablespoons snipped fresh dill or 1 teaspoon dillweed
3 tablespoons snipped fresh chives or frozen chives
¼ cup fresh lemon juice
½ teaspoon finely grated lemon zest
½ teaspoon salt
¼ teaspoon black pepper
⅛ teaspoon hot red pepper sauce

1. Preheat oven to 350° F. Coat 9 × 5 × 3-inch loaf pan with non-stick cooking spray and set aside.

2. Using hands, mix all ingredients thoroughly in large bowl. Pack into pan.

3. Bake, uncovered, until loaf pulls from sides of pan and is lightly browned and firm—45 to 50 minutes.

4. Cool loaf in pan on wire rack 15 minutes; drain off drippings.

5. Slice and serve warm. Or chill well and serve cold.

Microwaved Ginger Sea Bass

Makes 4 Servings

❋

NEARLY SIXTY years ago, scientists discovered that if they bombarded a beaker of water with microwaves, it would boil. Still, it took many more decades before microwave ovens came to the modern home kitchen. And only in the 1980s did we learn that these speed demons could do more than pop corn or thaw frozen food. The microwave cooks fish to perfection as this recipe readily proves. It's adapted from *Micro Ways* (1990), which I coauthored with Elaine Hanna.

NOTE: If sea bass is unavailable, use bluefish or striped bass. With more and more home cooks absorbed with Asian cooking, dark soy sauces, chili oil and roasted sesame oil, once the province of Asian groceries, are carried by many upscale supermarkets.

4 (½-inch-thick) sea bass fillets (1½ pounds)
1 tablespoon minced fresh ginger
1 clove garlic, peeled and minced
1 tablespoon dry sherry
2 tablespoons dark roasted sesame oil
2 tablespoons Japanese soy sauce
¼ teaspoon chili oil
2 teaspoons cornstarch
2 tablespoons clam juice mixed with 2 tablespoons water
¼ cup minced scallions (include green tops)

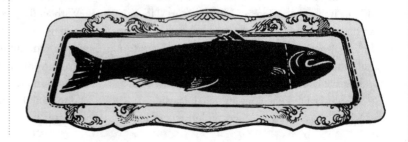

1. Fold tapering fillet ends in toward center, then arrange fillets ½ inch apart around edge of shallow 3-quart baking dish, thickest parts outward.

2. Mix ginger, garlic, and sherry and spread over fillets; mix sesame oil, soy sauce, and chili oil and sprinkle over fillets. Cover with plastic wrap and refrigerate 1 hour, turning in marinade after 30 minutes.

3. Roll one corner of plastic wrap back, then microwave fish on HIGH (100 percent power) 4 to 5 minutes, rotating 180° at halftime, just until it begins to flake. Transfer fillets to heated platter, cover with foil, and let stand.

4. Mix cornstarch and clam juice mixture, blend into baking dish liquid and microwave, uncovered, on HIGH (100 percent power) about 2 minutes, stirring at halftime, just until thickened.

5. Pour evenly over fish, scatter scallions on top, and serve.

Paul Prudhomme's Blackened Redfish

Makes 6 Servings

✳

CAJUN CHEF Paul Prudhomme set the culinary world on fire in 1979. Almost literally. That was the year he opened his own restaurant in New Orleans, K-Paul's Louisiana Kitchen, and began serving blackened redfish, which was bounced in and out of a white-hot cast-iron skillet. Prudhomme recommends heating the skillet over very high heat at least 10 minutes—"beyond the smoking stage," he says in *Chef Paul Prudhomme's Louisiana Kitchen* (1984), until "you see white ash in the skillet bottom (the skillet cannot be too hot for this dish)." Soon chefs coast to coast were blackening everything.

The recipe here, adapted from *Chef Paul Prudhomme's Louisiana Kitchen*, requires courage and care.

SEASONING MIX

1 tablespoon sweet paprika
2½ teaspoons salt
1 teaspoon onion powder
1 teaspoon garlic powder
1 teaspoon ground hot red pepper (cayenne)
¾ teaspoon white pepper
¾ teaspoon black pepper
½ teaspoon dried leaf thyme, crumbled
½ teaspoon dried leaf oregano, crumbled

FISH

¾ pound (3 sticks) unsalted butter, melted
6 (8- to 10-ounce) redfish, pompano, or tilefish fillets, cut about ½-inch thick

1. SEASONING MIX: Mix all ingredients in small bowl; set aside.

2. FISH: Pour 2 tablespoons melted butter into each of 6 individual ramekins and keep warm. Pour remaining melted butter into pie tin. Dip each fish fillet into melted butter in tin, then sprinkle both sides with seasoning mix, patting on firmly.

3. One at a time, char fish fillets in dry, ungreased, white-hot cast-iron skillet (see headnote), allowing about 2 minutes per side. As soon as each fillet goes into skillet, drizzle 1 teaspoon melted butter (from pie pan) over it, taking care it doesn't catch fire. Turn fish and spoon on a second teaspoon melted butter.

4. Serve blackened redfish with ramekins of melted butter.

SHRIMP WIGGLE

I INCLUDE THIS only as a curiosity. Around the turn of the century, college girls kept chafing dishes in their dormitory rooms and cooked on the sly. A favorite production was Shrimp Wiggle: canned peas and shrimp heated in a basic white sauce, then served on toast. If the girls were living dangerously, they might sneak in a little "cooking sherry." The dish remained a ladies' lunch staple well into this century with crisp patty shells replacing toast points.

Shrimp de Jonghe

Makes 4 Servings

❋

AT THE turn of the century, a Dutch family, the De Jonghes, owned a Chicago hotel, and this recipe was the house specialty. Although the hotel is long gone, the recipe lives on—an American classic. The version here is adapted from one supplied by Carol Haddix of the *Chicago Tribune* to a delightful little cookbook called *Food Editors' Hometown Favorites* (1984), published by the Newspaper Food Editors and Writers Association, Inc.

3 quarts water
1 small yellow onion, peeled and thinly sliced
2 celery tops
6 peppercorns
1 whole bay leaf
1¼ teaspoons salt
2 pounds medium raw shrimp in the shell
½ cup (1 stick) butter, melted
2 tablespoons dry sherry
1½ cups fine white bread crumbs
2 tablespoons minced fresh parsley
1 clove garlic, peeled and crushed
½ teaspoon paprika
⅛ teaspoon ground hot red pepper (cayenne)

1. Preheat oven to 350° F. Butter 6-cup shallow casserole and set aside.

2. Bring water, onion, celery tops, peppercorns, bay leaf, and 1 teaspoon salt to boiling in large heavy kettle over moderate heat. Add shrimp, cover, and return just to boiling. Drain shrimp at once, cool slightly, shell, and devein.

3. Place shrimp in large bowl, add ¼ cup melted butter and sherry; toss well; set aside.

4. In separate bowl, toss bread crumbs with remaining ¼ cup butter, parsley, remaining ¼ teaspoon salt, garlic, paprika, and cayenne.

5. Arrange half the shrimp in casserole and top with half the crumb mixture. Add remaining shrimp, then remaining crumb mixture.

6. Bake, uncovered, until browned and bubbly—35 to 40 minutes.

- - - - - - - - - - - - - - - - - - -

Crabmeat Norfolk

Makes 4 Servings

❋

ACCORDING TO Craig Claiborne (*Craig Claiborne's Southern Cooking,* 1987), "Crab Norfolk is a specialty of Norfolk, Virginia, where it was first created by W.O. Snowden of the once popular, now defunct Snowden and Mason Restaurant, which opened in that city in 1924." Claiborne goes on to say that the recipe was originally cooked in "specially designed, small oval aluminum pans." In some Norfolk restaurants,

it still is. Claiborne's version calls for cooking the crab on top of the stove. I've always had it baked and as a child who spent part of every summer on Chesapeake Bay, I ate an awful lot of Crabmeat Norfolk. This baked version is my mother's.

NOTE: An alternate method is to toss all ingredients lightly except for the butter. It should be ice cold, cut into small chips, then strewn lavishly over the crab mixture before it's baked.

1 pound lump crabmeat, bits of shell and cartilage removed
2 tablespoons vinegar (white or cider)
⅓ cup butter, melted
¼ teaspoon salt
¼ teaspoon hot red pepper sauce
⅛ teaspoon black pepper

1. Preheat oven to 375° F.

2. Place crab in large bowl, add remaining ingredients, and toss gently, taking care not to break up crab lumps.

3. Spoon mixture into ungreased, shallow 1-quart casserole or *au gratin* pan and bake, uncovered, just until bubbly—15 to 20 minutes.

4. Serve at once with fluffy boiled rice.

MEAT, FISH & POULTRY RECIPES
that Entered the American Mainstream
During the Twentieth Century with Their Source

....

(*Recipe Included)

FRANCE/BELGIUM
Beef Bourguignon
*Carbonnades à la Flamande
(Beef Carbonnade)
Choucroute Garni
*Steak au Poivre
Steak Béarnaise
Steak Mirabeau
Veal Cordon Bleu
*Pork à la Boulangère
*Cassoulet
Chicken Cordon Bleu
Chicken Marengo
Chicken with 40 Cloves of Garlic
Coq au Vin
*Duckling à l'Orange
*Coquilles St. Jacques
Lobster l'Américaine
Lobster Thermidor
❋

IRELAND
Beef Wellington
❋

GERMANY/AUSTRIA/
SWITZERLAND
Beef Fondue
*Émincé de Veau
*Königsberger Klopse
Rouladen
Sauerbraten
*Wiener Schnitzel

SCANDINAVIA
*Beef à la Lindstrom
Swedish Meatballs
❋

RUSSIA/
MIDDLE EUROPE
*Beef Stroganoff
Veal Orloff
Chicken Kiev
Chicken Pojarski
*Chicken Paprikash
Coulibiac of Salmon
❋

ITALY
*Calf's Liver Venetian Style
*Osso Buco
Piccata
Veal Parmigiana
Veal alla Marsala
*Vitello Tonnato
*Saltimbocca alla Romana
Scaloppine alla Milanese
*Chicken Cacciatore
Fish Florentine
*Scampi
❋

GREECE/TURKEY/
MIDDLE EAST
Gyros
Kofta Kebabs
Shish Kebabs
Circassian Chicken
❋

SPAIN & PORTUGAL
Paella

NORTH AFRICA
Couscous
❋

MEXICO/CARIBBEAN/
LATIN AMERICA
*Picadillo
Arroz con Pollo
*Chicken Mole
Red Snapper Veracruz
❋

ASIA/PACIFIC
Orange Flavor Beef
*Szechuan Shredded Beef
Moo Shu Pork
Sukiyaki
Tandoori
Teriyaki
Thai Beef (chicken or shrimp)
with Fresh Basil Sauce
Thai Red or Green Curry (with
beef, chicken, or shrimp)
Biryani (lamb, chicken, shrimp,
or vegetarian)
Vindaloo (lamb, chicken, or fish)
*Hawaiian Sweet-Sour Spareribs
Chicken Tikka Masala
Lemon Chicken
Moo Goo Gai Pan
Shredded Hunan Chicken
Peking Duck
Sushi
Tempura

STEAK AU POIVRE

AMERICA DIDN'T fall in love with steak until the waning years of the last century. For good reason. Before railroads, beef, marched to market, was shoe-leather tough. Once cattle could be shipped "on the hoof" to slaughterhouses, once steers were penned and fattened, steak was the meat every American longed to sink his teeth into.

In the beginning, steaks were baked, broiled, or grilled and seasoned with nothing more than salt, pepper, and perhaps a pat of butter (except in the Midwest and Plains States, where they were pounded, floured, and "chicken-fried").

Steak remained the red meat of choice until the '60s and '70s ascent of vegetarianism. And despite the recent multimedia blitzes extolling the nutritional virtues of beef, it has yet to regain its former preeminence.

Still, the classic French *Steak au Poivre* (pepper steak), a restaurant showpiece demanding pyrotechnical skills, remains popular in some quarters. The recipe appears to be relatively new: Escoffier doesn't include *Steak au Poivre* in *Ma Cuisine* (1934) but his contemporary, Henri-Paul Pellaprat, does give a recipe for it in *Modern Culinary Art* (1935).

However, in *The New York Times Food Encyclopedia* (1985), Craig Claiborne suggests that the recipe may not only date back to the early nineteenth century but also that its cre-

BEEF.

ator may have been Leopold I of Bavaria whose second wife was the beautiful Louise Marie of Orléans, daughter of King Louis Philippe of France. These two royals, the story goes, loved to cook. Quoting *Bull Cook and Authentic Historical Recipes and Practices* (1960) by George Leonard Herter and Berthe E. Herter (an amusing book of questionable reliability), Claiborne includes this passage on how to make Steak Leopold, which may or may not be the original *Steak au Poivre:*

Now take your beefsteak . . . [and] salt both sides to taste. Now take your peppermill and grind a thin coating of pepper berries over one side of the steak . . . and press the pieces of the pepper berries into the meat as much as possible. Turn the steak over and do the same for the other side. Now broil the steak . . . remove when done as you desire it and quickly take a heaping spoonful of butter and spread it over the entire steak.

Food historians of solid reputation dismiss the Prince Leopold theory as apocryphal. Or pure fantasy. Whatever its origin, though, *Steak au Poivre* became the culinary tour de force of many stylish big-city American restaurants early this century. Although it is still sometimes simply topped with butter à la Prince Leopold or merely drizzled with pan juices, many maîtres d'hôtel prefer to pull out all the stops and end their tableside preparation in a blaze of glory.

Steak au Poivre

Makes 2 Servings

✳

STEAK AU POIVRE is a last-minute dish that requires careful choreography. To keep things moving smoothly, measure out all ingredients before you begin and line up all necessary utensils. During the freewheeling '80s when green and red peppercorns nearly eclipsed the "basic black," chefs began preparing the recipe with these hot new peppercorns. Or sometimes a particolored mix of them. At Maxim's in Paris, *Steak au Poivre* is made with crushed white peppercorns (only there it's called *Steak Albert*). I frankly like a fifty-fifty mix of the green and black. I also like to use unsalted butter, as indeed do all professional chefs.

NOTE: *Demi-glace,* or meat glaze, is now sold by the jar in specialty food shops.

STEAK
- ½ teaspoon moderately coarsely crushed green peppercorns
- ½ teaspoon moderately coarsely crushed black peppercorns
- 2 (1½-inch-thick) center-cut slices beef tenderloin, trimmed of excess fat
- 2 tablespoons butter

SAUCE
- 3 tablespoons cognac
- 1 tablespoon butter
- ½ teaspoon Dijon mustard
- 2 tablespoons demi-glace (meat glaze)

1. STEAK: Pound green and black peppercorns into both sides of each tenderloin steak and let stand at room temperature 30 minutes.

2. Melt butter in medium heavy skillet over moderately high heat and when foam subsides, add steaks and brown 3 to 4 minutes per side for rare, 4 to 5 for medium-rare, and 5 to 6 for medium. Transfer steaks to small heated platter and keep warm.

3. SAUCE: Remove skillet from heat, add cognac, and stir to loosen browned bits. Blaze with a match and when flames die, add butter, mustard, and *demi-glace.* Return to moderate heat and cook and stir just until smooth.

4. Pour sauce over steaks and serve at once.

Carbonnades à la Flamande (Beef Carbonnade)

Makes 4 to 6 Servings

✳

BEFORE WORLD War II—make that before the late '50s—only well-traveled Americans had ever heard of this Belgian beef-and-beer stew, let alone tasted it. What a difference a few decades make. The recipe here is adapted from *The New York Times Cook Book* (1961), edited by Craig Claiborne. Serve with tiny new potatoes boiled in their skins. And frosty glasses of beer.

- 1 cup unsifted flour
- 1 teaspoon salt (or to taste)
- ½ teaspoon black pepper (or to taste)
- 2 pounds boned beef chuck, trimmed of excess fat and cut into 1-inch cubes
- 2 tablespoons butter
- 2 tablespoons vegetable oil
- 6 medium yellow onions, peeled and thinly sliced
- 1 clove garlic, peeled and minced
- 1½ cups flat beer
- 1 whole bay leaf
- 1 tablespoon minced fresh parsley
- ¼ teaspoon dried leaf thyme, crumbled

1. Place flour, salt, and pepper in paper bag, shake to mix, then dredge beef, a few pieces at a time, by shaking in seasoned flour.

2. Heat butter and oil in large heavy kettle over moderately low heat and stir-fry onions and garlic until limp and golden but not brown—8 to 10 minutes. Transfer to large bowl and reserve.

3. Brown beef well in drippings in batches. Return onion mixture to kettle, add beer, bay leaf, parsley, and thyme and bring to a boil. Adjust heat so mixture bubbles gently, cover, and simmer slowly until beef is fork-tender—about 1½ hours. Remove and discard bay leaf.

4. Taste for salt and pepper, adjust as needed, and serve.

Szechuan Shredded Beef

Makes 4 Servings

✳

WHEN PRESIDENT Nixon reopened relations with China in the 1970s, Americans discovered that there was more to Chinese cooking than the bland Cantonese dishes served by nearly every Chinese-American restaurant. By the late '70s, Szechuan was hot in more ways than one. I couldn't get enough of this peppery stuff, which is to Chinese cooking as Tex-Mex is to American. Neither stints on chilies. This recipe was—and is—a particular favorite of mine.

MARINADE
> *1 clove garlic, peeled and*
> * minced*
> *2 tablespoons finely minced*
> * fresh ginger*
> *3 tablespoons dry sherry*
> *3 tablespoons dark soy sauce*
> *1 tablespoon dark roasted*
> * sesame oil*
> *¼ teaspoon pulverized star*
> * anise or ground anise*
> *¼ teaspoon ground cloves*
> *¼ teaspoon ground cinnamon*
> *¼ teaspoon crushed dried red*
> * chili peppers*

BEEF
> *1 pound beef tenderloin,*
> * trimmed of fat and cut into*
> * 2 × ¼ × ¼-inch strips*
> *3 tablespoons peanut oil (about)*
> *2 medium carrots, peeled and*
> * cut into 2 × ⅛ × ⅛-inch*
> * strips*

> *2 medium ribs celery, trimmed*
> * and cut into 2 × ⅛ × ⅛-*
> * inch strips*
> *6 medium scallions, trimmed*
> * and cut into 2 × ¼ × ¼-inch*
> * strips (include some green*
> * tops)*

1. MARINADE: Mix all ingredients in large shallow bowl.

2. BEEF: Add beef to marinade, toss well, cover, and let stand at room temperature 1 hour.

3. Heat 2 tablespoons oil in large heavy skillet over high heat until ripples appear on skillet bottom—1 to 1½ minutes. Add carrots, celery, and scallions, and stir-fry until limp—about 3 minutes.

4. Spoon remaining 1 tablespoon oil into skillet, add beef and marinade, and stir-fry just until beef is no longer red—2 to 3 minutes.

5. Serve at once with fluffy boiled rice.

Beef Stroganoff

Makes 4 Servings

✳

THIS IS the Stroganoff I've been serving since the 1960s.

> *1½ pounds beef tenderloin,*
> * trimmed of fat and cut into*
> * 2 × ½ × ½-inch strips*
> *½ teaspoon salt (or to taste)*
> *½ teaspoon black pepper*
> * (or to taste)*
> *1 large yellow onion, peeled*
> * and thinly sliced*

> *¼ cup (½ stick) butter*
> *2 tablespoons flour*
> *1 cup beef broth*
> *2 teaspoons Dijon mustard*
> *⅓ cup sour cream (at room*
> * temperature)*

1. Spread tenderloin on wax-paper-lined counter, sprinkle with salt and pepper, and toss well to mix. Cover with onion slices and toss well again. Cover loosely with wax paper and let marinate 1 hour.

2. Melt 2 tablespoons butter in large heavy skillet over moderately low heat and blend in flour. Add broth and cook, stirring constantly, until thickened and smooth—about 3 minutes; blend in mustard and set off heat.

3. In second large heavy skillet, melt remaining 2 tablespoons butter over moderately high heat. Add tenderloin and onion and brown well—8 to 10 minutes.

4. Add browned tenderloin—*but not onion*—to first skillet, set over low heat, and simmer, stirring now and then, 10 minutes.

5. Off heat, smooth in sour cream. Taste for salt and pepper, adjust as needed, and serve with noodles.

BEEF STROGANOFF

ALTHOUGH CONSIDERED a '50s dish, Beef Stroganoff began appearing in American cookbooks at least two decades earlier. The first recipe for it I find is in John MacPherson's *Mystery Chef's Own Cook Book* (1934). Two Stroganoffs appear in Diana Ashley's *Where to Dine in '39,* a 1939 guide to New York City restaurants, one from the defunct Russian Kretchma on East 14th Street, the second from The Russian Tea Room, "slightly to the left of Carnegie Hall" on West 57th Street, now also gone but expected to reopen under new ownership. Both recipes seem to me Americanized: both contain Worcestershire sauce, both are made with sweet cream rather than sour, and both contain mushrooms, which a Russian friend told me is not authentic. Indeed, they do not appear in Alexandra Kropotkin's recipe in *The Best of Russian Cooking* (1964). A Russian princess and writer on Russian food, Kropotkin had this to say about the recipe's origin:

Beef Stroganoff—to translate it into English—was named for a noted Russian gourmet, Count Paul Stroganoff, who flourished in the Gay Nineties of the last century. He was a dignitary at the court of Tsar Alexander III and a member of the Imperial Academy of Arts in St. Petersburg. The record doesn't tell us whether it was he himself who invented the delectable treat which has immortalized him, or whether his chef conjured it up. At any rate, the name Stroganoff has become familiar throughout the world to lovers of fine food.

Quite so. Beef Stroganoff—with mushrooms and sour cream—shows up in *The Joy of Cooking* (1943 edition). Unfortunately, America was then immersed in World War II, red meat was strictly rationed, and few cooks could afford the luxury of Beef Stroganoff. Once the war was over, however, and beef again became plentiful, Beef Stroganoff became the signature dish of "gourmet" cooks across the country. Following *The Joy of Cooking*'s lead, many added mushrooms to their Stroganoff, first the canned, and then when they became widely available, the fresh. Even in that early *Joy,* Irma Rombauer calls for fresh mushrooms. Of course, she lived in St. Louis, a city large enough and European enough for fresh mushrooms to be commonplace. In the North Carolina Piedmont where I grew up, fresh mushrooms were "a special order" well into the '60s.

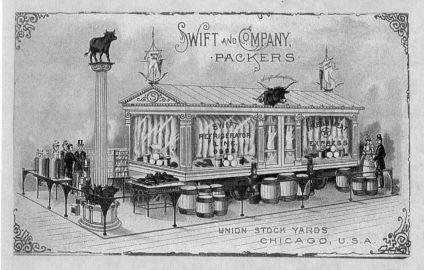

BEEF WELLINGTON

UNTIL I began researching Beef Wellington, I assumed the recipe hailed from New Zealand or Australia. Apparently not. Jane Garmey includes it in *Great British Cooking: A Well Kept Secret* (1981), but admits that the recipe's origin is a mystery. "I have never been able to find a reference to Beef Wellington in any British cookery book, old or new," she writes in her recipe headnote. "However, since . . . cooking meat in a pastry case was fairly common at the end of the eighteenth century and since this is a rather special way to prepare a beef fillet, it would seem unfair to omit Beef Wellington for its dubious heritage." Strangely, Adrian Bailey makes no mention of Beef Wellington in *The Cooking of the British Isles* (1969), a time when this fussy recipe was in vogue in this country (it was said to be President Nixon's favorite).

Craig Claiborne does shed light on Beef Wellington's "dubious heritage" in *The New York Times Food Encyclopedia* (1985). He says that Theodora Fitz-Gibbon, a well-known writer on Irish food, attributes the recipe to Ireland and its name to Arthur Wellesley, the Duke of Wellington. According to Fitz-Gibbon, "Steig [steak] Wellington," as the recipe was known in Ireland, was much admired by "The Iron Duke," who was born in Ireland in 1769.

Beef Wellington, a complicated, costly recipe that involves spreading a beef tenderloin with duxelles and/or *pâté de foie gras,* then baking it in a puff pastry wrapper, became the showpiece of ambitious '60s hostesses.

The September 1968 issue of *House & Garden* made Beef Wellington the centerpiece of a feature, "Beef at Its Finest," and in flowery prose Philip S. Brown introduces it thus: "Once served only in the grandest of restaurants, it is now a favorite *pièce de résistance* at party tables, since the widespread interest in haute cuisine has amply demonstrated that elaborate dishes like this one are not necessarily difficult to prepare." Maybe not, yet Brown needs one full page in the magazine and seven thumbnail diagrams to tell how to construct it.

NOTE: The *House & Garden* recipe calls for both duxelles and *pâté de foie gras.*

Three months later, in the December *American Home,* Food Editor Virginia T. Habeeb writes, "For the holidays this year, why not serve beef—but instead of the traditional Roast Ribs of Beef —make it Filet of Beef Wellington! This is a delicate tenderloin of beef, browned to perfection, coated with a savory mushroom filling, and wrapped in a tender, flaky pastry. Not only is it spectacular, it's elegantly delicious served with a rich Madeira sauce!" Habeeb's version requires a page and a half of text and nine step-by-step photographs. Hers, too, is an over-the-top Beef Wellington with duxelles and *pâté* and a crust decorated with puff paste poinsettias.

Before long, however, there were shortcut versions with canned liver paste substituting for *foie gras,* canned mushrooms for duxelles, and refrigerator crescent rolls or frozen patty shells for puff pastry. There was even Hamburger à la Wellington (*House Beautiful,* January 1970).

By the '80s, however, it was over. Beef Wellington had lost its cachet.

Picadillo

Makes 6 Servings

✳

I DON'T believe that this spicy Mexican minced meat was well known beyond the border states until the '60s or '70s. I know I first met up with it in the '60s. In *The Border Cookbook* (1995), Cheryl Alters Jamison and Bill Jamison write that *picadillo* "inspired the dreadful ground-beef mixture that goes into most North American fast-food tacos." They add that "many cooks serve *picadillo* by itself as an entrée instead of in a taco" . . . dressed up "with additions such as tomatoes, raisins, almonds, green olives, and *canela* [cinnamon] or even cloves for some extra spice." Texans, they say, add a "copious amount of chili and cumin" to their *picadillo*. And Mexicans zip things up with fresh serrano chilies. This recipe is adapted from the Jamisons' superior *picadillo* in *The Border Cookbook*.

3 tablespoons vegetable oil
1 large yellow onion, peeled and minced
6 cloves garlic, peeled and minced
2 pounds ground beef chuck
1 tablespoon flour
1 teaspoon dried leaf oregano, crumbled
½ teaspoon ground hot red pepper (cayenne)
1 medium baking potato, parboiled, peeled, and finely diced
½ cup beef broth
½ teaspoon salt (or to taste)

1. Heat oil in large heavy skillet over moderate heat 1 minute. Add onion and garlic and stir-fry until golden —2 to 3 minutes. Add beef and stir-fry, breaking up clumps, until all red color vanishes. Blend in flour, oregano, and cayenne.

2. Mix in potato, broth, and salt, adjust heat so mixture barely bubbles, and simmer, uncovered, stirring often, until potatoes are tender and *picadillo* is thick but still moist —about 5 minutes. Taste for salt and adjust as needed.

3. Serve in tacos or, following suggestions in the headnote, serve as a main course.

······································

Beef à la Lindstrom

Makes 4 to 6 Servings

✳

THESE BEEF, beet, and potato patties seem to have "arrived" in the 1930s—the first recipe I find for them appears in Inga Norberg's *Good Food from Sweden* (1939). Then Irma Rombauer offers two versions in the 1943 edition of *The Joy of Cooking* (a meatball one and a meat patty one). According to Dale Brown (*The Cooking of Scandinavia*, 1968), "*Biff à la Lindström* may look rather like a hamburger on the outside, but it is something else again inside—a piquant and juicy blend of beef, finely diced beets, chopped onions, and capers." He adds that Swedes developed the recipe as a way to ten-

derize beef. Brown's Swedish recipe contains no potatoes, but Inga Norberg's does. And so do most American versions (like *Beef à la Lindstrom II* in the 1943 *Joy of Cooking*), providing a neat way to stretch beef *and* use up leftover potatoes and beets. This recipe is my own.

1 pound ground beef chuck
¾ cup finely chopped, well-drained, cooked beets
1 cup finely minced boiled potatoes
2 tablespoons finely minced yellow onion
1 tablespoon finely minced capers
2 egg yolks, lightly beaten
2 tablespoons light cream
¼ teaspoon salt
⅛ teaspoon black pepper
3 tablespoons butter

1. Mix beef, beets, potatoes, onion, capers, egg yolks, cream, salt, and pepper well; cover, and chill 3 to 4 hours until firm enough to shape.

2. Preheat oven to 250° F. Shape beef mixture into patties 2 to 2½ inches across.

3. Heat butter in large heavy skillet over moderately high heat until it melts, foams up, and subsides. Brown patties in two batches—3 to 5 minutes per side. When first batch is done, transfer to paper-towel-lined shallow baking pan and set, uncovered, in oven to keep warm.

4. Serve as soon as all patties are nicely browned.

Emincé de Veau

Makes 4 Servings

✳

THIS SWISS dish isn't difficult. But there are a few points to bear in mind: First, have all ingredients and implements at the ready. Once you begin, there's no time to hunt for this or that. Also, make sure the butter in the skillet sizzles before you add the veal. Finally, do not brown the veal, merely cook until milky— no more than a minute or two. And the best accompaniment for it? A starch to catch the creamy sauce— a fried, shredded potato cake (*rösti*), boiled noodles, or rice. You'll find a recipe for *rösti* on page 256.

¼ cup (½ stick) butter
1 pound veal scaloppine, cut into 2½ × ⅜ × ⅜-inch strips
2 medium shallots, peeled and minced
⅛ teaspoon dried leaf thyme, crumbled
⅛ teaspoon freshly grated nutmeg
½ pound medium mushrooms, wiped clean and thinly sliced
⅓ cup dry white wine
1½ cups heavy cream (at room temperature)
½ teaspoon salt (or to taste)
⅛ teaspoon black pepper (or to taste)

1. Heat 1½ tablespoons butter in large heavy skillet over high heat until sizzling—1 to 1½ minutes.

Add half the veal and stir-fry until milky—1 to 2 minutes. Using slotted spoon, lift to large bowl and reserve. Stir-fry remaining veal in 1½ tablespoons butter the same way; add to bowl.

2. Melt remaining 1 tablespoon butter in skillet, reduce heat to moderately low, add shallots, and stir-fry until limp—about 2 minutes. Mix in thyme and nutmeg and mellow 1 to 2 minutes.

3. Add mushrooms and stir-fry 1 minute; turn heat to low, cover, and cook until mushrooms give up their juices—about 10 minutes. Add wine and boil, uncovered, over high heat until juices reduce to a thick glaze—3 to 5 minutes.

4. Add cream and boil, uncovered, until reduced by half—3 to 5 minutes.

5. Return veal to skillet along with accumulated juices, reduce heat to low, and bring just to serving temperature. Mix in salt and pepper, taste, adjust as needed, and serve.

Osso Buco

Makes 6 Servings

✳

I DO not believe that this classic Italian way to deal with tough veal shanks was well known in this country until after World War II. At least not beyond large metropolitan areas or pockets where Italians had settled. This recipe was given to me by a Napa wine-grower's wife, a first-generation American of Italian extraction.

6 (2-inch-thick) veal shanks
¾ cup unsifted flour
5 tablespoons fruity olive oil
1½ teaspoons salt (or to taste)
¼ teaspoon black pepper (or to taste)
2 medium yellow onions, peeled and chopped
2 cloves garlic, peeled and minced
2 tablespoons minced fresh basil
2 tablespoons minced fresh parsley
2 teaspoons minced fresh marjoram or ½ teaspoon dried leaf marjoram, crumbled
1 teaspoon minced fresh rosemary or ¼ teaspoon dried leaf rosemary, crumbled
1 large vine-ripe tomato, peeled, cored, and coarsely chopped (reserve juice but remove seeds)
1¼ cups dry white wine
1 (2-inch) strip lemon zest

1. Dredge veal shanks well in flour, shaking off excess.

2. Brown shanks in two batches in olive oil in large heavy kettle over moderate heat—8 to 10 minutes per batch. As shanks brown, drain on paper towels, and season well with salt and pepper.

3. Sauté onions, garlic, basil, parsley, marjoram, and rosemary in drippings over very low heat, stirring occasionally, until limp—15 to 20 minutes. Do not allow mixture to brown. Add tomato and its juice, cover, and simmer 10 minutes.

4. Stand browned veal shanks in kettle, spooning tomato mixture on top. Add wine and lemon zest, adjust heat so mixture bubbles very gently, cover, and simmer slowly until veal nearly falls from bones—3½ to 4 hours. Taste for salt and pepper and adjust as needed.

5. To serve, stand veal shanks on large platter and spoon kettle mixture on top.

NOTE: If you have them, put out marrow spoons so guests can extract it from inside the bones with ease. If you don't, steak knives work almost as well.

TIMELINE

1921

The Quaker Oats Company introduces quick-cooking oatmeal, one of America's first convenience foods.

Vitamin C is isolated and identified.

Betty Crocker is "born."

A drive-in restaurant opens in Dallas.

America's first hamburger chain—White Castle—begins in Wichita, Kansas.

1922

The magazine destined to become one of America's publishing phenomena is launched in Des Moines, Iowa. Its name—for the first two years anyway—is *Fruit, Garden, and Home.*

An electric milk shake blender is patented in Racine, Wisconsin, home of Horlick's malted milk.

Wiener Schnitzel

Makes 4 Servings

✳

FROM THE early nineteenth century on, these breaded veal scallops were known in the German-American communities of New York, Milwaukee, Minneapolis, Cincinnati, and St. Louis. Yet *Wiener Schnitzel* didn't become a "household name" for more than a hundred years. I grew up on the *Wiener Schnitzel* my mother had learned to make during the years she and my father lived in Vienna as "young marrieds" and was pleased to see that when I came to New York in the late 1950s, there were plenty of German restaurants and plenty of *Wiener Schnitzel.* My favorite was Luchow's on 14th Street. All dark paneling, giant beer steins, and oompah bands, it was the quintessential German restaurant and had been ever since it opened in 1882. Up in the East Eighties in heavily German Yorkville, there were a half dozen more top German restaurants. But unhappily, nearly all have vanished —even Luchow's.

NOTE: The hallmark of perfect *Wiener Schnitzel* is a crisp crumb jacket that does not cling to the meat—you should be able to slide a knife between the two. The trick is to bread and cook the scallops right away—the slightest delay will make the crumb coating stick.

1 pound veal scaloppine,
    pounded very thin
½ teaspoon salt
⅛ teaspoon black pepper
⅓ cup unsifted flour
3 eggs, lightly beaten
1½ cups fine dry bread crumbs
¼ cup (½ stick) butter
2 tablespoons peanut or other
    vegetable oil
4 lemon wedges

1. Preheat oven to its keep-warm setting (200° to 250°F). Halve any scaloppine that are large, sprinkle both sides of each piece with salt and pepper, and let stand at room temperature 10 to 15 minutes.

2. On counter near stove, line up three pie plates: In first plate place flour, in second, beaten eggs, and in third, bread crumbs.

3. Heat butter and oil in very large heavy skillet over moderately high heat until bread cube will sizzle— about 2 minutes.

4. Dredge half of scaloppine in flour, shaking off excess, dip into egg, then coat well with bread crumbs, again shaking off excess.

5. Brown in hot butter mixture— about 3 minutes per side. Remove to shallow pan lined with paper towels and set, uncovered, in oven to keep warm.

6. Quickly bread and brown remaining scaloppine the same way.

7. Serve hot with lemon wedges.

Vitello Tonnato (Cold Sliced Veal with Tuna Mayonnaise)

Makes 6 Servings

✳

MY FIRST taste of *vitello tonnato* on a summer visit to New York in the early '50s was for me a sort of epiphany. Several years later on a trip abroad, I ordered it everywhere in Northern Italy and vowed to learn to make it as soon as I got home. This is my own recipe, made with boned and rolled veal shoulder or rump because round costs the earth. If your butcher rolls the cut tight enough and if you use a sharp knife to slice it, the slices should hold together. If you can afford veal round, the traditional cut for *vitello tonnato,* by all means use it.

NOTE: You can substitute turkey breast for veal (many restaurants do), but the meat will be blander, drier. Freeze leftover kettle puree and use as a base for soups or stews. Or make a double batch of Tuna Sauce and use to dress hot pasta or cold chicken, turkey, or tuna salad.

VEAL

3½ pounds boned, tightly
    rolled veal shoulder, rump, or
    round
3 tablespoons fruity olive oil
3 medium yellow onions, peeled
    and chopped
1 clove garlic, peeled and
    minced

3 medium ribs celery, sliced
2 large carrots, peeled and
   sliced
4 large sprigs fresh parsley
1 large bay leaf, crumbled
2 medium sprigs fresh
   marjoram or ½ teaspoon
   dried leaf marjoram,
   crumbled
1 medium sprig fresh thyme or
   ¼ teaspoon dried leaf thyme,
   crumbled
1 small sprig fresh rosemary or
   ¼ teaspoon dried leaf
   rosemary, crumbled
1 (2-inch) strip lemon zest
1 cup dry white wine
1 (7-ounce) can white tuna,
   drained and flaked
2 teaspoons anchovy paste
¼ teaspoon black pepper

TUNA SAUCE
   1½ cups mayonnaise
   2 cups pureed kettle mixture
      (above)
   ¼ cup fresh lemon juice
   2 teaspoons anchovy paste

GARNISHES
   2 tablespoons drained small
      capers
   2 tablespoons finely minced
      fresh parsley

1. VEAL: Lightly brown veal on all sides in olive oil in large heavy kettle over moderately high heat; transfer veal to large plate and reserve.

2. Reduce heat to moderate, add onions, garlic, celery, and carrots, and stir-fry until limp and golden (do not brown)—about 10 minutes.

Add parsley, bay leaf, marjoram, thyme, rosemary, and lemon zest and mellow 2 to 3 minutes over moderate heat.

3. Add wine, tuna, anchovy paste, and pepper, adjust heat so mixture barely simmers, then return veal to kettle. Spoon some of vegetables on top of veal, cover, and simmer until fork will pierce veal with only slight resistance—2 to 2½ hours.

4. Remove veal to large heat-proof bowl and set aside. Puree kettle mixture in three to four batches in electric blender at high speed or in food processor fitted with metal chopping blade. Pour puree over veal, cover, and refrigerate at least 24 hours.

5. Next day, remove veal from bowl and scrape any puree clinging to it back into bowl. Rinse veal lightly in cool water and pat dry. Remove all strings and set veal aside.

6. TUNA SAUCE: Mix mayonnaise with 2 cups pureed kettle mixture, lemon juice, and anchovy paste, whisking or processing until smooth.

7. TO ASSEMBLE: Carefully carve veal into thin slices. Arrange, slightly overlapping, on platter, spooning a little Tuna Sauce over each slice. Cover, and marinate 2 to 3 hours in refrigerator. Also cover and refrigerate remaining Tuna Sauce.

8. Just before serving, ladle a little more Tuna Sauce artfully over veal. Garnish with scatterings of capers and parsley. Pass remaining sauce, if any, in small sauce boat.

Saltimbocca alla Romana (Veal Scaloppine with Prosciutto and Sage)

Makes 4 Servings

✳

AFTER WORLD WAR II, millions of Americans living beyond the reach of such big cities as New York, Chicago, and Los Angeles who'd never eaten veal discovered scaloppine and few recipes demonstrated its versatility better than this one. Originally the province of chefs, *saltimbocca alla Romana* is easy enough for home cooks, even the inexperienced.

NOTE: Because the scaloppine for this recipe will be folded and wrapped in prosciutto, you'll need four to five very thin, large pieces—roughly 7×4 inches each after pounding.

> 1 pound veal scaloppine, pounded thin
> Light sprinkling salt
> Light sprinkling black pepper
> ¼ pound thinly sliced prosciutto
> 2 tablespoons finely minced fresh sage or 1 teaspoon rubbed sage
> ¼ cup (½ stick) butter
> ⅔ cup dry white wine
> 2 (10-ounce) packages frozen chopped spinach, cooked by package directions, drained, and seasoned to taste with salt, pepper, and butter

1. Lightly sprinkle scaloppine on both sides with salt and pepper. Cover each veal scallop with prosciutto, overlapping and piecing as needed. Fold in half so prosciutto is on outside, making almost square "envelopes," then just before sealing, sprinkle a little sage inside each. Fasten with toothpicks.

2. Heat butter in large heavy skillet over high heat until sizzling—about 1 minute. Reduce heat to moderately high, add veal packets, and sauté quickly until lightly browned—2 to 3 minutes per side. Transfer to heated platter, remove toothpicks, cover loosely, and keep warm.

3. Pour wine into skillet and boil, stirring constantly, until browned bits dissolve and sauce thickens slightly—about 2 minutes.

4. To serve, spoon spinach onto small heated platter, center *saltimbocca* on top, one packet overlapping the next, then drizzle skillet sauce evenly over veal.

....

Calf's Liver Venetian Style

Makes 6 Servings

✳

FOR MOST of us, liver and bacon went together like ham and eggs until after World War II when we discovered this slightly sweet-sour recipe loaded with onions. Not every onion will do, however. Choose a variety that's naturally sweet—Spanish, Bermuda, Vidalia, or Walla-Walla.

> ⅔ cup white wine vinegar
> ¼ cup fruity olive oil
> 2 medium Spanish or Vidalia onions, peeled and thinly sliced
> 1 teaspoon salt (or to taste)
> 2 pounds calf's liver, cut into 3×½×½-inch strips
> ⅛ teaspoon black pepper (or to taste)
> ¼ cup minced fresh parsley

1. Boil vinegar slowly in small, heavy nonreactive pan over low heat until reduced to about 2 tablespoons —8 to 10 minutes.

2. Meanwhile, heat olive oil in large heavy skillet over moderate heat 1 minute. Add onions and stir-fry until limp and golden but not brown—about 5 minutes. Sprinkle onions with salt, reduce heat to low, cover, and steam 1 minute. Uncover, and stir-fry onions 3 to 5 minutes longer until almost all accumulated liquid has evaporated.

3. Raise heat to high, add liver, and stir-fry just until no longer red—3 to 5 minutes.

4. Off heat, mix in reduced vinegar, pepper, and parsley. Taste for salt and pepper, adjust as needed, and serve.

Königsberger Klopse (German Meatballs with Anchovies and Capers)

Makes 4 to 6 Servings

❋

THOUGH THESE meatballs were popular in tightly knit German communities before the turn of the century, the rest of America did not discover them until the 1900s.

NOTE: Using club soda as the liquid ingredient makes the meatballs light and fluffy.

MEATBALLS

1 pound ground veal shoulder
½ pound ground pork shoulder
2 cups fine soft bread crumbs
2 tablespoons minced fresh parsley
1 tablespoon minced drained capers
1 tablespoon finely grated lemon zest
1 egg, lightly beaten
2 teaspoons anchovy paste
¼ teaspoon salt
⅛ teaspoon white pepper
¾ cup club soda

POACHING LIQUID

2 cups beef broth
1 quart water

SAUCE

Poaching Liquid (above)
3 tablespoons butter

2 medium shallots or scallions, peeled and minced
3 tablespoons flour
¼ cup drained small capers
½ cup sour cream, at room temperature

1. MEATBALLS: With hands, mix all ingredients together well; cover, and chill until firm enough to shape —2 to 3 hours. Roll into 1- to 1½-inch balls, arrange in single layer on large tray lightly coated with non-stick cooking spray, cover, and chill 2 hours.

2. TO POACH: Bring broth and water to simmering in large heavy saucepan over moderate heat. Add half the meatballs and when liquid returns to simmer, adjust heat so it barely trembles. Poach meatballs, uncovered, 20 minutes; using slotted spoon, transfer to large heatproof bowl, cover loosely, and keep warm. Poach remaining meatballs the same way, add to bowl, cover, and keep warm.

3. SAUCE: Boil poaching liquid, uncovered, until reduced to 2 cups —about 20 minutes. Meanwhile, melt butter in small heavy saucepan over low heat; add shallots and stir-fry until golden—2 to 3 minutes. Blend in flour and mellow 2 to 3 minutes. Whisk 1 cup reduced poaching liquid into flour paste, stir back into large pan with poaching liquid, and cook, stirring constantly, until thickened and smooth—3 to 5 minutes. Stir in capers.

4. Return meatballs to pan, set lid on askew, and bring slowly to serving temperature. Gently smooth in sour cream and serve.

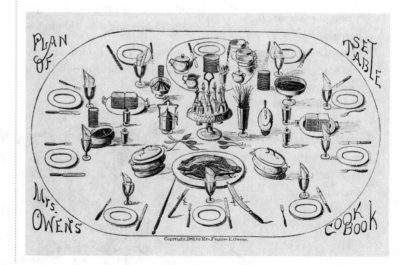

PLAN OF SET TABLE

Mrs. OWEN'S COOK BOOK

Copyright, 1883, by Mrs. Frances E. Owens.

Pork à la Boulangère

Makes 8 to 10 Servings

✳

I ALWAYS thought Julia Child taught us to roast pork the French baker's wife's way—on a bed of sliced potatoes and chopped onions. Yet I find no recipe for *Rôti de Porc à la Boulangère* in either volume of *Mastering the Art of French Cooking.* There is, however, a similar one, *Rôti de Porc Grand'Mère,* in which the pork roasts *en casserole* with *whole* small potatoes and onions. No matter. Americans appear to have discovered this easy way of roasting pork about the time Julia burst upon us—in other words, the '60s. This recipe is adapted from *The Doubleday Cookbook* (1975), which I coauthored with Elaine Hanna.

1 (5-pound) center-loin pork
   roast
3 cloves garlic, peeled and
   minced
3½ pounds medium all-
   purpose potatoes
2 large yellow onions, peeled
   and coarsely chopped
⅓ cup minced fresh parsley
¼ cup (½ stick) butter,
   melted
1 teaspoon minced fresh
   marjoram or ½ teaspoon
   dried leaf marjoram,
   crumbled
2 teaspoons salt
½ teaspoon black pepper

1. Preheat oven to 350° F.

2. Arrange pork fat-side-up in very large, shallow roasting pan and rub well with garlic. Roast, uncovered, 1 hour.

3. Meanwhile, peel potatoes and slice very thin, letting slices fall into large bowl of ice water. To prevent darkening, keep potatoes submerged.

4. When pork has roasted 1 hour, remove from pan and pour off drippings. Raise oven temperature to 400° F.

5. Drain potatoes well and place in roasting pan. Add onions, parsley, butter, marjoram, salt, and pepper and toss well to mix.

6. Place pork fat-side-up on bed of potatoes and roast, uncovered, 1 to 1½ hours longer until meat thermometer, inserted into lean, not touching bone, registers 155° to 160° F. Stir potato mixture occasionally as pork roasts, and if it seems dry, sprinkle with a little water or chicken broth. Let roast stand 15 minutes at room temperature before serving.

7. To serve, center pork on large heated platter and surround with potato mixture.

Hawaiian Sweet-Sour Spareribs

Makes 4 Servings

✳

ONCE CANNED pineapple juice became available in the early 1900s, women's magazines raced to offer new and exotic "Hawaiian" recipes. This is one of the better ones. Small wonder it's one of the most dog-eared cards in my mother's index file. Serve with boiled rice and a salad of tropical fruits—any combination you fancy.

NOTE: Also good as an appetizer.

SPARERIBS
4 pounds spareribs
1 quart boiling water

GLAZE
1 cup Japanese soy sauce
1 cup pineapple juice
¼ cup brandy
½ cup firmly packed light
   brown sugar
3 cloves garlic, peeled and
   finely minced
2 tablespoons finely minced
   fresh ginger

HOW TO SELECT THEM.

1. **SPARERIBS:** Preheat oven to 350° F. Spread ribs in very large roasting pan, add water, cover snugly with foil, and bake 1 hour.

2. **GLAZE:** Mix all ingredients in very large bowl; set aside.

3. Cool ribs until easy to handle; drain off all pan drippings. Cut ribs into serving pieces, 2 to 3 ribs wide.

4. Place ribs in glaze and turn well to coat. Cover, and marinate 24 hours in refrigerator, turning ribs in glaze several times.

5. Preheat oven to 350° F. Arrange ribs in large shallow roasting pan, pour glaze over all, and bake, uncovered, until meat almost falls from bones—1 to 1¼ hours. As ribs bake, turn in glaze every ½ hour. If glaze threatens to boil away, add a little hot water.

6. As soon as ribs are tender and richly glazed, mound onto heated platter and serve.

Mabel Hoffman

Slow-Cooker Cassoulet

Makes 6 Servings

✳

MY REASON for including this particular recipe is to show just how far knowledge of this French country classic had spread by 1975. That was the year Mabel Hoffman's *Crockery Cookery* appeared, the book that taught mass America how to throw a meal in an electric pot and let it cook slowly, unattended. This recipe is adapted from that award-winning, five-million-copy best-seller.

1 (3- to 3½-pound) broiler-
   fryer, cut up
1 leek, trimmed, washed, and
   thinly sliced
1 clove garlic, peeled and
   minced
3 tablespoons minced fresh
   parsley
½ teaspoon salt
¼ teaspoon black pepper
2 (15-ounce) cans white kidney
   beans, drained
½ pound smoked sausage links,
   sliced ½-inch thick
¼ cup dry white wine

1. Place chicken in slow cooker and sprinkle evenly with leek, garlic, parsley, salt, and pepper. Spoon beans and sausage on top, distributing evenly.

2. Pour in wine, cover, and cook on LOW until chicken is tender and meatiest pieces show no signs of pink in center—5 to 6 hours.

3. Serve at once, accompanying with boiled rice or small new potatoes cooked in their skins.

Duckling à l'Orange

Makes 4 Servings

❋

ALTHOUGH FANCY big-city restaurants were serving this French classic before the turn of the century, it did not become the province of the home cook until well after World War II. This unorthodox version was developed by my good friend Ben Etheridge as a way to reduce the fat and "give the sauce more pizzazz."

NOTE: Upmarket groceries sell bottled *demi-glace* (brown meat glaze).

DUCKLING

*1 (5-pound) oven-ready
    duckling
Julienned zest of 1 navel orange
1 quart cold water (about)
¼ teaspoon salt*

SAUCE

*Duckling giblets
3 tablespoons vegetable oil
2 medium yellow onions, peeled
    and thinly sliced
2 medium carrots, peeled and
    thinly sliced
3½ cups beef broth (about)
4 large sprigs fresh parsley
1 whole bay leaf
Pinch dried leaf thyme,
    crumbled
Julienned zest of 2 navel
    oranges
1 quart boiling water
3 tablespoons sugar
¼ cup red wine vinegar*

*2½ tablespoons cornstarch
    mixed with 3 tablespoons dry
    Madeira
2 teaspoons demi-glace (brown
    meat glaze)
⅔ cup dry Madeira
3 tablespoons Grand Marnier
2 teaspoons fresh lemon juice
½ teaspoon salt (or to taste)
2 tablespoons butter*

1. DUCKLING: Remove as much fat from duckling as possible, cut off tail and oil glands at base of tail. Rinse bird inside and out under cold running water. Place orange zest in body cavity, place bird on footed rack in kettle big enough to accommodate it without cramping. Add water, making sure it does not touch bird. Bring to simmering over moderate heat, cover, and steam 1½ hours. Check pot occasionally and add more water, if needed.

2. SAUCE: Coarsely dice giblets and pat dry on paper towels. Divide oil between two medium heavy skillets and set each over moderate heat. Add giblets to one, onions and carrots to other; brown simultaneously, stirring often, 6 to 8 minutes.

3. Transfer giblets and vegetables to medium heavy saucepan. Add broth, parsley, bay leaf, and thyme. If broth does not cover giblets and vegetables, add water until it does. Bring to simmering over moderately low heat, set pan lid on askew, and simmer 1½ hours. Strain broth, discarding solids; also skim fat from broth. Measure giblet stock; it should total 2 cups. If there is too much, boil, uncovered, over moderate heat until reduced to 2 cups; if too little, round out measure with beef broth.

4. When duckling is tender, lift gently from kettle taking care not to break skin; cool on rack to room temperature.

5. Meanwhile, finish SAUCE: Blanch julienned orange zest in boiling water 15 minutes; drain and reserve. Mix sugar and vinegar in medium, nonreactive heavy saucepan, and reduce over moderate heat until only an amber glaze remains on pan bottom. Off heat, stir in a little of the 2 cups giblet stock, stirring until hardened bits of glaze dissolve. Add remaining stock, whisk in cornstarch mixture and reserved orange zest, and cook, stirring constantly, over moderate heat until thickened and clear—3 minutes. Blend in *demi-glace* and set off heat.

6. Boil Madeira in small heavy saucepan over moderately high heat until reduced to 2 to 3 tablespoons; mix into sauce.

7. TO FINISH DUCKLING: Preheat broiler. Remove and discard orange zest in body cavity. With poultry shears, halve breast lengthwise. Turn bird over, cut along both sides of backbone, and remove. Twist off first two wing joints. Carefully remove breast bone and all other bones, including wing bone attached to shoulder; leave drumsticks intact. Trim away ragged pieces of skin, then halve each duckling half horizontally.

8. Place duckling on counter skin-side-up and flatten gently with palms, then arrange skin-side-up on broiler pan. Sprinkle evenly with ¼ teaspoon salt and broil 4 inches from heat 5 to 8 minutes; if any areas brown too fast, cover with bits of foil.

9. Meanwhile, add Grand Marnier, lemon juice, and salt to sauce, set over low heat, and swirl in butter; keep sauce warm but do not boil.

10. To serve, arrange duck on heated platter, top with some of sauce, and pass the rest.

1922

The Colony Restaurant opens in New York City and becomes a celebrity hangout.

Vitamin D is identified and named.

Vitamin E is discovered.

1923

Sanka decaffeinated coffee comes to America.

Henry Ford manufactures charcoal briquets to recycle mountains of sawdust—fallout from the Model T's wooden roof supports.

The last Delmonico's closes.

Inventor J.L. Rosefield develops a new process that keeps peanut butter from separating. Swift's quickly adopts it for its Peter Pan brand.

To publicize the healthfulness and versatility of his cereals (and not coincidentally to pump up sales), W.K. Kellogg hires home economist Mary Barber to set up a company test kitchen to develop new recipes that use plenty of "product." Kellogg's is one of the first major American food companies to do so.

Chicken Paprikash

Makes 4 Servings

✳

ALTHOUGH CHICKEN Paprika appears in the 1906 edition of *The Boston Cooking-School Cook Book*, Americans who didn't cook the Fannie Farmer way weren't likely to know this dish until it showed up in *The Joy of Cooking* more than three decades later. Today nearly every cookbook offers it. This one, adapted from *The Good Housekeeping Cookbook* (1973), is authentic.

> 1 (2½- to 3-pound) broiler-fryer, cut up
> 1¼ teaspoons salt
> 2 teaspoons Hungarian sweet rose paprika
> 3 tablespoons vegetable oil
> ½ cup water
> 1 medium yellow onion, peeled and coarsely chopped
> ¾ cup sour cream (at room temperature)
> 1 tablespoon minced fresh parsley

1. Rub chicken with 1 teaspoon each salt and paprika and let stand at room temperature 30 minutes.

2. Heat oil in large heavy skillet over moderately high heat 1 to 1½ minutes until ripples appear on skillet bottom. Add chicken and brown well on all sides—about 10 minutes. Pour all drippings from skillet.

3. Add water and onion to skillet, bring to boiling, adjust heat so water bubbles gently, cover, and simmer until chicken is fork-tender—about 35 minutes.

4. Transfer chicken to heated platter, cover loosely, and keep warm.

5. Smooth sour cream, remaining 1 teaspoon paprika, and ¼ teaspoon salt into skillet and bring just to serving temperature. Do not boil or mixture may curdle.

6. Pour sauce over chicken, sprinkle with parsley, and serve.

Chicken Cacciatore

Makes 4 Servings

✳

SOME FOOD writers have declared this recipe to be of Italian-American ancestry. Yet that dean of Italian cookbook writers, Marcella Hazan, offers a recipe for *Pollo alla Cacciatora* in *The Classic Italian Cook Book* (1962). I have little doubt, however, that most Americans first tasted this Italian "hunter's" chicken in an Italian-American restaurant. Perhaps in the 1930s, maybe even earlier. The first recipe I've been able to find for Chicken Cacciatore appears in *The Mystery Chef's Own Cook Book* (1934) by John MacPherson. The recipe here is adapted from *Family Circle Recipes America Loves Best* (1982).

> ⅓ cup plus 1 tablespoon flour
> 2½ teaspoons salt
> 1 teaspoon black pepper
> 1 (3-pound) broiler-fryer, cut up
> 3 tablespoons olive oil
> 1 large yellow onion, peeled and thinly sliced
> 3 cloves garlic, peeled and minced
> ½ pound medium mushrooms, wiped clean and thinly sliced
> 6 medium vine-ripe tomatoes, cored and cut into wedges
> ¼ cup dry red wine
> 1 tablespoon Italian seasoning
> 1 (6-ounce) can tomato paste
> 2 tablespoons cold water
> 1 large green bell pepper, cored, seeded, and cut lengthwise into strips ¼-inch wide

1. Place ⅓ cup flour, 1 teaspoon salt, and ½ teaspoon black pepper in paper bag and shake to mix. Add chicken, a few pieces at a time, and shake well in seasoned flour to dredge.

2. Heat olive oil in medium Dutch oven 1 minute over moderate heat. Brown chicken in oil in two or three batches, allowing 8 to 10 minutes for each; lift browned chicken to paper towels to drain.

3. Pour drippings from Dutch oven, measure out 1 tablespoon, and return to pot. Add onion, garlic, and mushrooms, and sauté 1 minute. Add tomatoes, wine, remaining 1½ teaspoons salt and ½ teaspoon black pepper, and Italian seasoning. Adjust heat and simmer, gently, stirring now and then, 15 minutes.

4. Blend in tomato paste, return chicken to Dutch oven, cover, and simmer over low heat until fork-tender—about 1 hour.

5. Transfer chicken to heated platter, cover loosely, and keep warm. Blend remaining 1 tablespoon flour with cold water, add to Dutch oven, and mix into tomato mixture. Add green pepper and cook, stirring constantly, 3 to 5 minutes just until sauce thickens slightly and no raw flour taste lingers.

6. Spoon tomato mixture over chicken and serve.

Chicken Mole

Makes 6 Servings

＊

A MEXICAN classic that spread across the U.S. during the twentieth century. Jane Butel (from whose *Tex-Mex Cookbook* [1980] this recipe is adapted) says *pollo mole* is "Mexico's most unusual dish." She adds that turkey can be substituted for chicken.

> *1 (4-pound) roasting chicken, cut up*
> *2 to 3 celery tops*
> *1 large carrot, peeled and quartered*
> *1 small yellow onion, peeled and quartered*
> *2½ teaspoons salt*
> *1 slice dry white bread*
> *2 tablespoons seedless raisins*
> *½ ounce unsweetened chocolate*
> *2 tablespoons finely minced yellow onion*
> *3 tablespoons blanched almonds*
> *1 medium green bell pepper, cored, seeded, and finely chopped*
> *1 large vine-ripe tomato, cored and quartered*

> *1 clove garlic, peeled and minced*
> *3 tablespoons flour*
> *1 tablespoon hot chili powder*
> *¼ teaspoon ground cinnamon*
> *¼ teaspoon ground cloves*
> *2½ cups chicken stock (from cooking chicken)*

1. Place chicken in large heavy kettle, add cold water to cover, also celery tops, carrot, quartered onion, and 2 teaspoons salt. Bring to boiling, adjust heat so mixture bubbles gently, cover, and cook until chicken is nearly tender—about 40 minutes. Cool chicken in stock. Reserve chicken; strain stock, and reserve 2½ cups for sauce; discard solids. Save leftover stock for soup or stew.

2. Tear bread into chunks and pulse with raisins, chocolate, minced onion, almonds, green pepper, tomato, and garlic in electric blender at high speed or in food processor fitted with metal chopping blade until uniformly fine.

3. Transfer to medium heavy kettle, blend in flour, chili powder, cinnamon, and cloves, then add stock and remaining ½ teaspoon salt. Cook and stir over moderate heat until thickened and smooth—3 to 5 minutes.

4. Add chicken to sauce, adjust heat so mixture simmers slowly, cover, and cook, basting frequently, until flavors meld and chicken is tender —about 30 minutes.

5. Serve at once with rice as a main course.

Scampi

Makes 6 Servings

＊

WE SEEM not to have discovered this simple Italian way of cooking shrimp until after World War II. Certainly *scampi* weren't familiar beyond big metropolitan areas. Today they can be had in some fast-food restaurants. This recipe—my own—adds fresh rosemary and wine. If fresh rosemary isn't available, skip it; the dried is a poor substitute.

> *3 pounds jumbo shrimp in the shell*
> *6 tablespoons fruity olive oil*
> *3 large cloves garlic, peeled and quartered*
> *4 whole bay leaves*
> *6 small sprigs fresh rosemary*
> *¼ cup dry white wine*
> *⅛ teaspoon black pepper*

1. Place shrimp in large shallow bowl, add 3 tablespoons olive oil, garlic, bay leaves, and rosemary. Toss well, cover, and marinate in refrigerator 4 hours.

2. Heat remaining 3 tablespoons oil in very large heavy skillet over moderately high heat 1 minute, dump in shrimp mixture, and stir-fry 6 to 8 minutes until bright pink. Transfer to heated platter, remove bay leaves and rosemary, and keep shrimp warm.

3. Add wine and pepper to skillet and cook and stir 1 minute over high heat. Pour over shrimp and serve.

JAMES BEARD, DEAN OF AMERICAN COOKERY

H E'D PLANNED to be an opera singer. Or an actor. But he failed at both because he was larger than life—six feet, three inches tall and, at top weight, more than three hundred pounds.

James Beard, America's first full-fledged food celebrity, found his calling by accident. Reared in Portland, Oregon, Beard was the only child of a worldly British mother and a father descended from Iowa pioneers who'd followed the Oregon Trail west. From his earliest years, Beard loved good food; his mother had run a boardinghouse and was known for the tables she set. Mary Beard taught her son much, not least of which was the importance of seasonal, home-grown produce. Of freshly caught local fish and shellfish, of local cheese, butter, eggs, and cream. He grew up well fed.

Expelled after six months at Reed College in Portland, Beard spent the next half-dozen years hacking about—London, Paris, New York, Hollywood, San Francisco. He got minor acting jobs along the way, his booming baritone was heard on radio, but after years on the road, Beard returned to Portland and plunged into community theater.

When his arty Portland friends began defecting to New York, Beard followed, settling there more or less permanently in 1937 and supporting himself by doing what he did best—cooking. Down the years Beard had prepared rehearsal snacks for the productions with which he was involved, he'd cooked dinners for actor friends and planned a few theater parties, and he'd even given cooking lessons. In 1939, he and Bill and Irma Rhode opened Hors d'Oeuvre,

Inc. Within months, they catered a reception for the New York chapter of The International Wine and Food Society that wowed its distinguished members and opened a new world to Beard.

Beard's first cookbook, *Hors d'Oeuvre and Canapés* (M. Barrows, 1940) demonstrated how imaginative cocktail food could be. Even with America on the edge of war, Beard's little book sold well. It is still in print.

A savvy self-promoter, Beard wrote cookbooks and articles till the end of his days (often with the aid of "ghosts"). For a time he reviewed restaurants for *Gourmet* magazine, he opened a cooking school, he endorsed products, and he became America's first television chef.

By the '70s Beard had become an icon, a father figure and mentor to squads of up-and-coming American cooks. Though he roamed the globe, Beard was first, last, and always an American cook, a booster of the best this country had to offer. His biggest and by many accounts his best work is *James Beard's American Cookery* (Little, Brown, 1972).

Beard died in 1985 at the age of 81, a superstar in the culinary theater.

Today his Greenwich Village town house is headquarters for The James Beard Foundation, a nonprofit organization whose purpose is to recognize excellence not only among food journalists and cookbook authors but also among this country's rising young chefs. The kitchen where Beard taught has become a stage where chefs from East Coast and West, from New England, the South, and heartland come to strut their stuff. And the lunches and dinners they prepare are nearly always sold out.

James Beard would be pleased.

Coquilles St. Jacques

Makes 6 to 8 Servings

✳

FEW AMERICANS knew this wonderful French gratin of scallops until Julia Child taught us how easy it was to make it in the 1960s. This recipe is adapted from *The Doubleday Cookbook* (1975), which I coauthored with Elaine Hanna.

SCALLOPS

1½ cups dry white wine
4 medium shallots, peeled and finely chopped
1 whole bay leaf
1 large sprig fresh parsley
½ teaspoon salt
4 peppercorns
1½ pounds bay scallops, washed
½ pound mushrooms, wiped clean and minced
1½ cups water (about)

SAUCE

Scallops cooking liquid
¼ cup (½ stick) butter
5 tablespoons flour
¾ cup heavy cream
2 egg yolks, lightly beaten
1 tablespoon fresh lemon juice
¼ teaspoon salt
⅛ teaspoon white pepper

TOPPING

1¼ cups soft white bread crumbs
⅓ cup finely grated Gruyère cheese
¼ cup (½ stick) butter, melted

1. SCALLOPS: Simmer wine, shallots, bay leaf, parsley, salt, and peppercorns, uncovered, in large nonreactive saucepan 5 minutes. Add scallops, mushrooms, and enough water to cover, cover, and simmer just until scallops turn milky —3 to 4 minutes. Drain, reserving cooking liquid, bay leaf, and parsley. Set mushrooms aside; slice scallops crosswise about ⅛ inch thick and set aside also.

2. SAUCE: Return scallops cooking liquid, bay leaf, and parsley to pan and boil, uncovered, over moderate heat until reduced to ¾ cup—5 to 8 minutes; set aside.

3. Melt butter in small heavy saucepan over low heat and blend in flour. Strain reduced cooking liquid into pan, add cream, and cook, stirring constantly, until thickened and smooth—3 to 5 minutes.

4. Blend a little hot sauce into egg yolks, stir back into pan, and cook and stir 1 minute. Off heat, mix in lemon juice, salt, pepper, reserved mushrooms and scallops.

5. TO ASSEMBLE: Preheat broiler. Butter 6 to 8 large scallop shells or individual *au gratin* dishes well. Divide scallop mixture among shells. Mix TOPPING ingredients and sprinkle evenly over each shell.

6. Set shells on large baking sheet and broil 5 inches from heat 3 to 4 minutes until bubbly and tipped with brown. Serve at once.

TIMELINE

1924

The Popsicle—frozen fruit ice on a stick—is patented.

Fruit, Garden, and Home, the magazine launched two years earlier in Des Moines, Iowa, changes its name to *Better Homes & Gardens* and soon becomes one of America's most popular magazines. Many of the recipes we now consider American classics were first published in "BH & G."

Caesar Salad is created by Caesar Cardini at his restaurant in Tijuana, Mexico, and it immediately becomes a "Southern California classic."

Wheaties go on sale.

CASSEROLES

FAVORITE RECIPES *of*
Home Economics Teachers

Casseroles
INCLUDING BREADS

O F COURSE American cooks were *scalloping* food—creaming and baking it—early on. And I suppose that's a sort of casserole. Then, too, late nineteenth-century cookbooks include a few recipes for baking meat or poultry *en casserole*. Scarcely what *casserole* means to us today, however.

The index to the original *Boston Cooking-School Cook Book* (1896) shows one casserole entry: Casserole of Rice and Meat. But a look at the recipe shows that by today's definition, it is nothing of the sort:

Line a mould, slightly greased, with steamed rice. Fill the centre with two cups cold, finely chopped, cooked mutton, highly seasoned with salt, pepper, cayenne, celery salt, onion juice, and lemon juice; then add one-fourth cup cracker crumbs, one egg slightly beaten, and enough hot stock or water to moisten. Cover meat with rice, cover rice with buttered paper to keep out moisture while steaming, and steam forty-five minutes. Serve on a platter surrounded with Tomato Sauce. Veal may be used in place of mutton.

Elsewhere in that same *Boston Cooking-School Cook Book*, Fannie Farmer includes a layered oyster and macaroni combo, a more casserolelike affair, as are her Luncheon Chicken (leftovers reheated in the oven with carrots), Beefsteak Pie (leftover beef, gravy, and potatoes baked underneath a biscuit crust), and Cottage Pie (Shepherd's Pie variation).

Still, casseroles did not play a major role until this century.

Here's what Marion Harland has to say about them in 1903 *(Marion Harland's Complete Cook Book)*. As far as I can tell, Harland is the first American cookbook author to devote a chapter to casseroles (albeit a slim one). She begins it thus:

The French name "casserole" has a certain amount of terror for the American housewife. The foreign word startles her and awakens visions of cooking as done by a Parisian chef, or by one who has made the culinary art his profession. She, a plain, everyday housekeeper, would not dare aspire to the use of a casserole.

And yet the casserole itself is no more appalling than a saucepan. It is simply a covered dish, made of fireproof pottery, which will stand the heat of the oven or the top of the range. And the dainty cooked in this dish is "casserole" of chicken, rice, etc., as the case may be. Like many another object of dread this, when once known, is converted into a friend.

Here is one of Harland's more interesting recipes:

CASSEROLE OF CHICKEN

Clean and joint a tender spring chicken. Put into a frying-pan three tablespoonfuls of butter and fry in this a small onion and a carrot, both cut into tiny dice. When these vegetables are lightly browned, turn into the casserole, add to them two cupfuls of clear soup stock, in which three bay leaves and a little thyme have been boiled and then removed. In this consommé lay the jointed chicken, put the closely-fitting cover on the casserole and set it in a steady oven. It should cook for an hour. At the end of this time stir into the chicken a dessertspoonful of tomato catsup. Recover and cook for half an hour longer. Then add two dozen small French mushrooms which have been previously stewed for ten minutes, lastly, a glass of sherry. Season the whole to taste with pepper and salt and leave uncovered in the oven long enough for the chicken to brown.

In 1912, Marion H. Neil, Principal, Philadelphia Practical School of Cooking, and *Ladies' Home Journal* recipe editor, published a book of "casserole dishes," and two years later Olive M. Hulse's *200 Recipes for Cooking in Casseroles* appeared, "driven," suggests Russ Parsons in a 1994 *Los Angeles Times* article on casseroles, by "the proliferation of American pottery factories" producing low-cost earthenware. What also fueled casserole mad-

CASSEROLES

ness, I believe, were World War I, when cooks were urged to use every scrap of food (what better catch-all than a casserole?), and second, the publication in 1916 of Campbell's *Helps for the Hostess,* which shows for the first time how canned soups can be used as recipe ingredients, doubling, in particular, for long-winded sauces. Here, a trend-setting page from that little booklet:

ONE OF THE MOST *important and economical uses of* CAMPBELL'S SOUPS *is for sauces. Instead of taking time to make and season an elaborate sauce, you need only use one of the many kinds of* CAMPBELL'S SOUPS. *Many times unattractive "left-overs" are thrown away when, by using a can of* CAMPBELL'S SOUPS, *they could be made into an attractive, appetizing dish. You can combat the high cost of living by using* CAMPBELL'S SOUPS *as sauces, thus making a second meal at low expense and the quality of the sauces obtained in this way leaves nothing to be desired.*

BEEF, PORK, AND MUTTON *left-overs combine best with Tomato, Mock Turtle, Ox Tail, Beef or Vegetable Soup.* NOODLES AND MACARONI *combine best with Tomato-Okra, Bouillon or Consommé.* RICE *combines best with Mulligatawny (curry flavor).* VEAL, EGGS, CHEESE, CHICKEN, AND FISH *left-overs combine best with Tomato, Chicken, Chicken-Gumbo, Asparagus, Celery, or Pea Soups.*

THE GENERAL RULE FOR MAKING CAMPBELL'S SAUCES IS:

1 cup CAMPBELL'S SOUPS.
1 tablespoonful flour.
1 tablespoonful butter.

Melt butter, add flour, blend, and pour on soup. Then add chopped 'left-over' and serve in one of various ways: Use on toast, with rice, with pastry shell or vol-au-vent, or bake and scallop in oven for few minutes, or pour over macaroni or noodles.

Another important, but time-taking task in cooking is the making of "stock." Think of the boiling, straining, and labor it means! And yet you seldom need more than one or two cups at any time. Here is where CAMPBELL'S *will save you time and labor. In any recipe where it says "stock," use a can of* CAMPBELL'S BOUILLON, CONSOMMÉ,

JULIENNE *or if you want small dainty vegetables,* PRINTANIER. *No work, no cooking, no straining: just as many cups of "stock" as you wish instantly at hand. The housewife who does it the "CAMPBELL way" will save both labor and money.*

In 1917, *Mrs. Allen's Cook Book* by Ida Bailey Allen rolled off the presses and although it contains no casserole chapter, it doesn't lack for them—fish casseroles, meat casseroles, poultry casseroles, vegetable casseroles. There's even a fruit casserole. I counted twenty-five in all.

Allen discusses casseroles twice, first in a chapter called "Short-Cut Preparation of Meals," then again in a section devoted to the basic methods of cooking. Here she calls it "En Casserole," and writes:

Cooking en casserole is a combination of stewing and braising. In this case the meat is usually browned, then put into the casserole with vegetables, rice, crumbs, or macaroni, water or stock, covered, and slowly cooked in the oven until tender. It should not boil.

Earlier on she includes this more expansive paragraph on "Casserole Cooking," which speaks only of *oven* casseroles:

Most American housewives understand too little about the possibilities of cooking in the oven. The mind turns instantly to the casserole and the tougher cuts of meat, but these by no means exhaust the resources of the oven. There is no better way to make a chicken or other tender meat "go far" than en casserole; there is no more delicious way to cook fish, game, both dried and fresh vegetables, puddings, many cereals, dried and fresh fruits, than in the oven.

Casseroles got their biggest boost, perhaps, in the '30s. First, the Depression taught people to skimp and recycle. Second, and even more important, perhaps, was the arrival in 1934 of Campbell's Cream of Mushroom Soup, the perfect casserole "binder." It was no longer necessary to make cream sauce.

By 1939, *My Better Homes & Gardens Cook Book* had given casseroles equal time in its "Eggs and Casseroles" chapter, if not a chapter of their own. Two years later, Marian and Nino Tracy's *Casserole Cookery* hit the stores and climbed the best-seller charts. The first paragraph of its introduction explains why.

Being lazy and liking to cook and to entertain, we struggled futilely for a long time over how to combine these features pleasantly. Finally the thing came to us—that thing being a casserole. Stews and other wrongly demeaned dishes take on a dash of simplicity and sophistication when prepared in a casserole. Essentially a one-dish meal, it requires little watching, a side serving of some green salad, bread, and your preference in drink. We can come home late, put a casserole in the oven, and relax—a unique indulgence. Our motto is: Pamper self and stomach, but let the food take care of itself.

The 1943 *The Joy of Cooking,* in its section on "Quick Casserole Dishes," offers some dozen-and-a-half recipes. But with barely half that, the 1948 edition of *The Boston Cooking-School Cook Book* lags far behind.

The casserole craze continued well into the '50s and '60s, due to Poppy Cannon's *Can-Opener Cook Book* (1951), James Beard's *The Casserole Cookbook* (1955), and in 1960, Peg Bracken's *The I Hate to Cook Book.* Bracken's book was such a blockbuster it was reissued in 1986 as *The Compleat I Hate to Cook Book.*

Casseroles remain the busy cook's trump card right across the country. And thanks to the thousands of community cookbooks freighted with casserole recipes, old and new, they are not likely to drop from sight anytime soon. Even purist, back-to-scratch cooks are turning once again to casseroles, more, I think, for comfort than as a way to shortcut kitchen time.

Clearly, there is not space here to include every popular twentieth-century casserole. I've exercised my writer's privilege and selected a representative group.

Johnny Marzetti (Johnny Mazetti)

Makes 10 to 12 Servings

✳

A '50s/early '60s party favorite. The version here is adapted from Peg Bracken's *The I Hate to Cook Book* (1960). And who, pray tell, is "Johnny Marzetti?" According to John Mariani (*The Dictionary of American Food and Drink,* Revised Edition, 1994), he is the brother of the owner of the Marzetti Restaurant in Columbus, Ohio, where the recipe was created in the 1920s.

NOTE: Bracken's recipe calls for 1 can mushrooms—"the more the better."

3 tablespoons olive or vegetable oil
1 large yellow onion, peeled and chopped
¾ pound medium mushrooms, wiped clean and thinly sliced
2 pounds ground lean beef
3½ cups canned tomato sauce
1½ pounds sharp Cheddar cheese, coarsely shredded
1 pound elbow macaroni, cooked and drained by package directions

1. Preheat oven to 350° F. Lightly grease 14 × 11½ × 2¼-inch baking dish and set aside.

2. Heat olive oil in very large heavy skillet over moderate heat 1 minute. Add onion and stir-fry until limp—about 3 minutes. Add mushrooms and stir-fry until juices are released and evaporate—about 5 minutes. Add beef and cook and stir, breaking up clumps, until no longer red—about 5 minutes. Off heat, mix in tomato sauce and all but 1 cup cheese.

3. Transfer to baking dish, add macaroni, and toss gently but thoroughly to mix. Scatter remaining 1 cup cheese on top.

4. Bake, uncovered, until browned and bubbling—35 to 40 minutes—and serve.

The Origin of Tamale Pie

CASSEROLES

IN *THE Dictionary of American Food and Drink* (revised edition, 1994), John Mariani writes that the term "tamale pie" first appeared in print in 1911. It may be so, but my own search has turned up nothing that predates World War I. Then, as during World War II, women were urged to save meat. *Conservation Recipes* (1918), a booklet compiled by the Mobilized Women's Organizations of Berkeley and published by the Berkeley Unit, Council of Defence Women's Committee, offers five recipes for Tamale Pie,

each from a different woman. All are completely meatless and all contain corn, cornmeal, and tomatoes in some form (puree, sauce, canned tomatoes, etc.). Some enrich the mix with ripe olives or cheese, and some don't.

Tamale Pie also appears in *Everyday Foods in Wartime* (1918) by Mary Swartz Rose, assistant professor, Department of Nutrition, Teachers College, Columbia University, New York, New York. Hers, however, contains ground beef and is much nearer to the recipes we know today:

TAMALE PIE

Corn meal, 2 cups	Onion, 1	Cayenne pepper, ½ teaspoon or
Salt, 2½ teaspoons	Fat, 1 tablespoon	Chopped sweet pepper, 1 small
Boiling water, 6 cups	Hamburgh steak, 1 pound	Salt, 1 teaspoon
	Tomatoes, 2 cups	

Make a mush by stirring the corn meal and one and one-half teaspoons salt into boiling water. Cook in a double boiler or over water for 45 minutes. Brown the onion in the fat, add the Hamburgh steak, and stir until the red color disappears. Add the tomatoes, pepper, and salt. Grease a baking-dish, put in a layer of corn meal mush, add the seasoned meat, and cover with mush. Bake 30 minutes. Serves six.

The Tamale Loaf in *Good Housekeeping's Book of Menus, Recipes and Household Discoveries* (1922) also adds ground beef, only here it's cooked, *then* ground. The method, however, is wholly different: Meat, tomatoes, onion, and chili powder are boiled into sauce, the cornmeal goes in, forming a sort of gruel into which chopped ripe olives are stirred. The mix is spooned into molds, chilled, then reheated in a steamer and served with tomato sauce.

The July 1941 issue of *Sunset* published a tamale pie in its popular "Kitchen Cabinet" column and called it a version of "a long-time Western favorite." A Chicken Tamale Pie (with canned corn) makes the 1943 edition of *Joy of Cooking* and another chicken variation, the 1948 *Boston Cooking-School Cook Book*.

Tamale pie surged in popularity after World War II, when, according to Gerry Schremp (*Kitchen Culture: Fifty Years of Food Fads*, 1991), it became the darling of potluck suppers.

Tamale Pie

Makes 6 Servings

✳

THE RECIPE here, adapted from Jean Hewitt's *The New York Times Heritage Cook Book* (1972), closely parallels the recipe I remember my mother making—with a bottom crust of cornmeal mush. Modern variations skip the bottom crust and cover the filling with corn bread. I like this more authentic version.

CORNMEAL CRUST
4 cups water
¾ teaspoon salt
1½ cups cornmeal
2 tablespoons butter or lard
(not vegetable shortening)

FILLING
2 tablespoons bacon drippings or vegetable oil
1 medium yellow onion, peeled and chopped
1 small green bell pepper, cored, seeded, and chopped
1 clove garlic, peeled and minced
1¼ pounds lean ground beef chuck
1 tablespoon chili powder
½ teaspoon ground cumin
1 cup canned crushed tomatoes
½ cup beef broth
¾ teaspoon salt (or to taste)

1. CRUST: Preheat oven to 350°F. Grease 2½-quart casserole; set aside.

2. Bring water and salt to boiling in medium heavy saucepan over high heat. Whisking vigorously, add cornmeal gradually and continue beating until thick and smooth; beat in butter. Spoon three-fourths of mixture into casserole and with spoon, press over bottom and up sides. Set aside. Keep remaining cornmeal mixture covered until ready to use.

3. FILLING: Heat drippings in large heavy skillet over moderate heat 1 minute, add onion, green pepper, and garlic, and stir-fry until limp, about 5 minutes. Add beef, chili powder, and cumin and cook, breaking up clumps, until meat is no longer pink—about 5 minutes. Add tomatoes, broth, and salt and cook and stir 5 minutes. Taste for salt and adjust as needed.

4. Spoon meat mixture into cornmeal "crust" and cover with remaining cornmeal mush.

5. Bake, uncovered, until browned and bubbly—30 to 35 minutes.

New Quick Taco Bake

Makes 8 to 10 Servings

✳

YOU MIGHT call this a "'90s Tamale Pie." It comes from Bisquick and uses not only biscuit mix but also taco seasoning mix, canned tomato sauce, and canned whole-kernel corn. Not for the purist, however busy working moms will appreciate the speed with which it all goes together. Serve, if you like, with sour cream, chopped ripe tomato, and crisp shredded lettuce.

FILLING
1 pound lean ground beef chuck
½ cup chopped yellow onion
1 (1¼-ounce) envelope taco seasoning mix
1 (15-ounce) can tomato sauce
1 (15½-ounce) can whole-kernel corn, drained
2 cups shredded sharp Cheddar cheese

TOPPING
2 cups biscuit mix
1 cup milk
2 eggs, lightly beaten

1. Preheat oven to 350°F.

2. FILLING: Brown beef and onion in large heavy skillet over moderate heat, breaking up clumps, until no trace of pink shows, about 5 minutes. Spoon into ungreased 13 × 9 × 2-inch baking pan and mix in seasoning mix, tomato sauce, and corn. Sprinkle with cheese and set aside.

3. TOPPING: Mix all ingredients in large mixing bowl and pour over beef mixture.

4. Bake, uncovered, 35 minutes until bubbly and lightly browned.

"Casserole Cookery"
Round Steak with Mushroom
Soup and Peas

THE RECIPE here is reprinted just as it appeared in Marian and Nino Tracy's best-selling *Casserole Cookery* (1941).

INGREDIENTS   **TIME:** *1¼ hours*

1½ lbs. round steak cut in 1½-inch squares—
*   top round is best, costs the most*
1 No. 2 can tiny new potatoes drained
1 package frozen peas
1 can condensed
*   mushroom soup*
pinch of mint
pinch of marjoram
salt and pepper

Season the meat with salt and pepper. Sauté in olive oil. Remove to low buttered casserole. Add potatoes, peas, mushroom soup, and seasoning. Mix well and bake in 350°F oven for 40 minutes. Serves 4.

Mustcohola

Makes 6 to 8 Servings

THIS RECIPE became very popular in the Midwest in the 1930s, possibly because it was a good way to stretch meat—one pound feeds as many as eight. As for the title, I think it's a corruption of *mostaccioli* (little mustaches)—better known here as penne—although a Mustacholi in *The Mystery Chef's Own Cook Book* (1934), attributed to Spain, ladles the meat mixture over noodles or macaroni instead of baking everything *en casserole*. The recipe here calls for small shells or elbow macaroni and does put everything into one dish.

  2 tablespoons bacon drippings
  2 large yellow onions, peeled
  *   and chopped*
  2 medium green bell peppers,
  *   cored, seeded, and chopped*
  ¼ pound mushrooms, wiped
  *   clean and thinly sliced*
  ¾ pound lean ground beef
  ¼ pound lean ground pork
  1 tablespoon chili powder
  ¾ teaspoon salt
  ¼ teaspoon black pepper
  2 cups canned crushed tomatoes
  ½ pound small pasta shells or
  *   elbow macaroni, cooked and*
  *   drained by package directions*

1. Heat drippings in large heavy kettle over moderate heat 1 minute; add onions and green peppers and stir-fry until limp—3 to 5 minutes. Push to one side, add mushrooms and stir-fry 5 minutes.

2. Add beef and pork and stir-fry, breaking up clumps, until no longer pink—about 5 minutes. Blend in chili powder, salt, and black pepper.

3. Add tomatoes and simmer, uncovered, until slightly thickened —about ¾ hour.

4. Toward end of cooking, preheat oven to 350° F. Also coat 2½-quart casserole with nonstick cooking spray and set aside.

5. Mix macaroni into kettle mixture, then transfer to casserole and bake, uncovered, stirring occasionally, until no longer soupy and flavors marry—40 to 45 minutes.

Stroganoff Casserole

Makes 6 to 8 Servings

✳

A '70s/'80s party pleaser that I dug out of my personal recipe file.

> *1½ pounds lean ground beef chuck*
> *1 large yellow onion, peeled and coarsely chopped*
> *1 clove garlic, peeled and minced*
> *½ teaspoon dried leaf marjoram, crumbled*
> *¼ teaspoon dried leaf thyme, crumbled*
> *1 (8-ounce) can tomato sauce*
> *1 cup cream-style cottage cheese*
> *½ (8-ounce) package cream cheese, diced*
> *½ pound medium egg noodles, cooked and drained by package directions*
> *½ teaspoon salt (or to taste)*
> *¼ teaspoon black pepper (or to taste)*
> *½ cup coarsely shredded sharp Cheddar cheese*

1. Preheat oven to 350° F. Coat 2½- to 3-quart casserole with nonstick cooking spray and set aside.

2. Stir-fry beef, onion, and garlic in very large heavy nonstick skillet over moderate heat, breaking up clumps, until meat is uniformly brown— about 5 minutes. Stir in marjoram and thyme and cook, stirring often, 3 to 4 minutes.

3. Mix in tomato sauce, cottage cheese, cream cheese, noodles, salt, and pepper. Taste for salt and pepper and adjust as needed.

4. Turn into casserole, scatter Cheddar evenly on top and bake, uncovered, until browned and bubbly— 25 to 30 minutes.

Chickpea, Tomato, and Pepperoni Casserole

Makes 6 Servings

✳

THIS IS one of my special favorites. The recipe was given to me in the '60s by my New York piano teacher, Stanley Lock, who was almost as well known for his cooking as he was for his keyboard dexterity. Stanley made this a party staple and his guests invariably came back for seconds—and requested the recipe. It's quick to make, filling, and frugal.

  *2 pepperoni sausages, thinly
    sliced*
  *1 large yellow onion, peeled
    and coarsely chopped*
  *1 small green bell pepper, cored,
    seeded, and coarsely chopped*
  *1 clove garlic, peeled and
    minced*
  *½ teaspoon dried leaf oregano,
    crumbled*
  *½ teaspoon dried leaf basil,
    crumbled*
  ¼ teaspoon salt (or to taste)
  *2 tablespoons minced fresh
    parsley*
  2 (8-ounce) cans tomato sauce
  ½ cup dry white wine
  1 tablespoon brown sugar
  *2 (1 pound, 4-ounce) cans
    chickpeas, drained well*
  *½ cup coarsely shredded sharp
    Cheddar cheese*

Hunt...
for the best

1. Preheat oven to 375° F. Lightly grease 2-quart casserole; set aside.

2. Brown pepperoni 2 to 3 minutes in large heavy skillet over moderate heat; transfer to paper towels to drain. Pour off all drippings, then measure out and return 3 tablespoons to skillet.

3. Add onion, green pepper, and garlic to skillet and stir-fry until limp —3 to 5 minutes. Add oregano, basil, salt, parsley, tomato sauce, wine, and brown sugar and cook and stir 5 minutes. Taste for salt and adjust as needed.

4. Dump chickpeas into casserole, add cheese and pepperoni, and toss well to mix. Stir in skillet mixture.

5. Bake, uncovered, stirring twice, until lightly browned—about 1 hour.

Pork Chop and Rice Casserole

Makes 4 Servings

✳

THERE'S AN early version of this recipe in *Good Housekeeping's Book of Menus, Recipes and Household Discoveries* (1922). Called "Arabian Stew," it is nonetheless the layered casserole of browned chops and rice plus slices of onion and green pepper that became so popular in the late '30s. The *Good Housekeeping* recipe gets "three to four hours in an oven registering 350° F.," but this one, adapted from *My Better Homes & Gardens Cook Book* (1939), trims baking time by parboiling the rice.

NOTE: Drain rice well after it's parboiled. Also, if casserole seems dry at halftime, add a little water.

> 4 loin or rib pork chops,
>   cut 1-inch thick
> ½ teaspoon salt
> ¼ teaspoon black pepper
> ½ cup unsifted flour
> 2 tablespoons vegetable oil
> 4 green bell pepper rings
> 4 slices yellow onion
> ⅔ cup long-grain rice, par-
>   boiled 10 minutes in lightly
>   salted water and drained
> 1½ cups canned crushed
>   tomatoes

1. Preheat oven to 350° F. Grease shallow 2-quart casserole; set aside.

2. Sprinkle chops with salt and pepper, then dredge in flour, shaking off excess.

3. Heat oil 1 minute in large heavy skillet over moderately high heat. Add chops and brown 3 to 5 minutes on each side.

4. Transfer chops to casserole. Top each with green pepper ring, then onion slice, then mound of parboiled rice, dividing full amount equally. Pour tomatoes into casserole around chops so as not to disturb the rice.

5. Cover snugly with foil and bake until chops show no signs of pink in center, about 1 hour, and serve.

One-Dish Chicken and Rice Bake

Makes 4 Servings

✻

CAMPBELL'S, WHENCE this '90s recipe comes, calls it a "one-dish wonder." It goes together in five minutes, bakes in forty-five. Best of all, it's mixed *and* baked in the same casserole.

> 1 (10¾-ounce) can cream of
>   mushroom soup
> 1 cup water
> ¾ cup uncooked long-grain rice
>   (not quick-cooking)
> ½ teaspoon paprika
> ½ teaspoon black pepper
> 4 boned and skinned chicken
>   breast halves

1. Preheat oven to 375° F.

2. Mix soup, water, rice, and ¼ teaspoon each paprika and pepper in ungreased shallow 2-quart casserole.

3. Lay chicken on top and sprinkle with remaining paprika and pepper.

4. Cover, and bake until bubbly and chicken shows no signs of pink in center—about 45 minutes.

TIMELINE

1925

Howard Johnson opens an eatery in Wollaston, Massachusetts.

Tomato juice is canned and becomes an instant hit.

The number of A & P stores reaches 14,000.

The first "green giant" appears, a marketing icon for Minnesota Valley Canning of Minneapolis. According to *Memoirs of a Giant: Green Giant Company's First 75 Years (1903–1978),* he was white, dwarfish, a figure out of Grimms fairy tales who "wore a scowl and a scruffy bearskin rather than a suit of leaves and a smile." A makeover ten years later made him *jolly* and *green.*

1926

Thiamin (vitamin B1) is shown to cure beri-beri.

The original Brown Derby Restaurant opens in Los Angeles.

1927

A Nebraska chemist concocts Kool-Aid.

Chicken and Artichoke Bake

Makes 6 Servings

✳

MY MISSISSIPPI friend Jean Todd Freeman introduced me to this wonderful casserole. Fiction editor of *The Ladies' Home Journal* in the early '60s, Jean lived just around the corner from me in Greenwich Village. As I remember, this was her favorite "company" dish. Alas, I've lost the recipe she wrote out for me, so the one here is adapted from *Celebrations on the Bayou* (1989), a nostalgic collection of Deep South recipes published by the Junior League of Monroe, Louisiana. Serve this casserole with fluffy boiled rice.

3 whole chicken breasts, split
1½ teaspoons salt
¼ teaspoon black pepper
1 teaspoon paprika
¼ cup vegetable oil
¼ cup (½ stick) butter or
* margarine*
¾ pound medium mushrooms,
* wiped clean and thinly sliced*
3 tablespoons flour
1½ cups chicken broth
¼ cup dry sherry
2 (13¾-ounce) cans artichoke
* hearts, rinsed and drained*
* well*

1. Preheat oven to 375° F. Lightly butter shallow 3-quart casserole and set aside.

2. Remove excess fat from chicken breasts and discard. Mix salt, pepper, and paprika and rub over both sides of chicken breasts.

3. Heat oil and butter in large heavy skillet over moderately high heat until butter melts—about 1½ minutes. Brown chicken breasts in two batches on both sides, allowing about 3 to 4 minutes per side. Drain well on paper towels.

4. Pour off all drippings, then measure out and return 3 tablespoons to skillet. Add mushrooms and stir-fry until juices are released and these evaporate—about 5 minutes. Blend in flour, then add broth and sherry, and cook, stirring constantly, until thickened and smooth—3 to 5 minutes. Continue simmering, uncovered, 5 minutes longer, stirring occasionally.

5. Arrange chicken in casserole, not overlapping, pour mushroom mixture over all, cover, and bake 45 minutes.

6. Halve artichoke hearts and tuck in and around chicken, cover, and bake until chicken shows no signs of pink in center—about 10 minutes longer.

Savory Peanut 'n' Turkey Casserole

Makes 8 Servings

✳

THE WINNER in the 1979 Cook-A-Peanut Contest sponsored by Grower's Peanut Food Promotions, which was held at the North Carolina-Virginia Peanut Trade Show. The blue-ribbon cook? Mrs. Hunter Daughtrey of Suffolk, Virginia. In addition to putting peanuts to good use, her recipe deliciously recycles "the big bird."

10 slices day-old white bread
2 tablespoons butter or
* margarine (at room*
* temperature)*
½ cup chopped yellow onion
½ cup diced celery
½ cup chopped green bell pepper
½ teaspoon curry powder
½ teaspoon salt
¼ teaspoon black pepper
1 cup frozen peas and carrots
* (no need to thaw)*
¾ cup mayonnaise
3 cups diced cooked turkey
3 eggs, lightly beaten
2 cups milk
1 (10¾-ounce) can condensed
* cream of celery soup*
¾ cup chopped roasted peanuts
½ cup shredded sharp Cheddar
* cheese or freshly grated*
* Parmesan cheese*

1. Lightly butter shallow 3-quart baking dish and set aside.

2. Trim crusts from 2 slices bread; butter each slice, using 2 teaspoons

butter, then cut in ½-inch cubes and set aside. Cut 8 unbuttered slices into 1-inch squares and set aside also.

3. Stir-fry onion, celery, and green pepper in remaining 4 teaspoons butter in small heavy skillet over moderate heat until glassy—about 5 minutes. Blend in curry powder, salt, and black pepper.

4. Transfer to large bowl, add peas and carrots, mayonnaise, and turkey and toss well to mix; set aside.

5. Place half the unbuttered bread squares in baking dish, add turkey mixture, then remaining unbuttered bread squares.

6. Mix eggs and milk and pour evenly over all. Cover and refrigerate at least 1 hour.

7. Preheat oven to 325° F. Spread celery soup smoothly over surface of casserole and top with reserved buttered bread cubes. Scatter peanuts evenly over all.

8. Bake, uncovered, until filling is set—about 40 minutes. Top with cheese and bake just until cheese melts—about 5 minutes longer.

Microwaved Flounder Florentine Casserole

Makes 4 Servings

✳

NOT EVERY casserole microwaves well, but this one does. It's adapted from *Micro Ways* (1990), a basic microwave cookbook I coauthored with Elaine Hanna.

SAUCE

    ¼ cup (½ stick) butter
    2 tablespoons minced yellow
        onion
    4 tablespoons flour
    2½ cups milk (about)
    ½ teaspoon salt (or to taste)
    ⅛ teaspoon white pepper
    Pinch leaf thyme, crumbled
    ¼ bay leaf (do not crumble)
    Pinch freshly grated nutmeg
    ⅓ cup grated Gruyère cheese
    ¼ cup freshly grated Parmesan
        cheese

FLOUNDER

    1½ pounds flounder fillets
    1½ cups chopped, hot buttered
        spinach
    1½ cups Sauce (above)
    ¼ teaspoon paprika (about)

1. SAUCE: Place butter and onion in 6-cup measure, cover with wax paper, and microwave on HIGH (100 percent power) until glassy—about 1½ minutes. Blend in flour and microwave, uncovered, on HIGH until foamy—30 seconds.

2. Slowly blend in milk, then mix in salt, pepper, thyme, bay leaf, and nutmeg, and microwave, uncovered, again on HIGH, whisking after 2 minutes, until sauce boils and thickens—4½ to 5½ minutes. Whisk again.

3. Strain sauce, return to measure, add Gruyère and Parmesan, cover with wax paper, and microwave on MEDIUM (50 percent power) until cheese melts—about 1 minute. If sauce seems thick, thin with a little milk. Taste for salt and adjust as needed; set aside.

4. FLOUNDER: Arrange fish fillets ½ inch apart in large shallow baking dish, thickest portions outward; fold tapering ends in toward center. Cover with paper towels and microwave on HIGH, turning dish 180° at halftime, just until fish is opaque—5 to 7 minutes. Cover with foil and let stand 2 minutes.

5. TO ASSEMBLE FLORENTINE: Spread spinach in ungreased 2½-quart shallow oval casserole. Arrange flounder on top in single layer, thicker portions toward edge. Smooth sauce over fish and blush with paprika.

6. Cover with wax paper and microwave on MEDIUM (50 percent power), turning dish 180° at halftime, until bubbling—4 to 5 minutes. Pass remaining sauce.

SWANSON TV DINNERS

IN 1954, the Swanson Company decided to put its very first frozen meals in boxes designed to look like television screens, and to call them "TV Dinners," hoping to draw a parallel between the magic of television and the magic of heat-and-serve food. The company didn't mean people had to eat the TV dinners while watching TV —but that's what people did, and furthermore what people continued to do with the many frozen entrées that followed Swanson in supermarket freezers: all were called TV dinners, and all were consumed in front of the TV set.

Carl Swanson, founder of the company, arrived in Nebraska at the turn of the century a poor young Swedish immigrant, rose from grocery clerk to wholesale grocer to turkey processor, and left a thriving business to his two sons, who moved from poultry to frozen chicken and turkey potpies. Their first frozen dinner (turkey and dressing) cost 98 cents and is still a favorite choice today, along with Salisbury steak and fried chicken. But the divided aluminum trays, once avidly collected and much prized by thrifty or poor people, are no longer part of the Swanson package—they were retired in 1984 as unsuitable for the microwave.

Salmon-Rice Casserole

Makes 6 Servings

❋

THIS RECIPE and the Shrimp Creole that follows come from *Pyrex Prize Recipes,* published in 1953 by Corning Glass Works. Both represent the types of jiffy casseroles that were so popular in the '50s. The headnote for this one says, "The gourmet touch is supplied by the olives."

> ½ cup milk
> ½ pound processed pimiento cheese
> ½ teaspoon salt
> ¼ teaspoon black pepper
> 3 cups cooked rice
> 1 (7¾-ounce) can salmon, drained and flaked
> ¼ cup chopped or sliced pimiento-stuffed olives

1. Preheat oven to 350° F. Butter 1½-quart glass ovenware casserole well and set aside.

2. Mix milk, cheese, salt, and pepper in top of double boiler set over boiling water; heat and stir until smooth.

3. Arrange half the rice in casserole and top with half the salmon, olives, and cheese sauce. Repeat layers, ending with cheese sauce. If desired, arrange final layer of olives around edge of casserole as a garnish.

4. Bake, uncovered, 30 minutes until lightly browned.

Shrimp Creole

Makes 6 Servings

❋

IS THE 1950s when this Corning recipe was published, fresh shrimp was available mainly to those living within the sound of the surf. Deepest America had to settle for canned. Today fresh—or at least flash-frozen shrimp—is a supermarket staple and I urge you to use one of these.

> 4 (4½-ounce) cans shrimp or 1 pound cooked, shelled, and deveined jumbo shrimp
> ¼ cup (½ stick) butter or margarine
> ¾ teaspoon salt
> ⅛ teaspoon black pepper
> 2½ cups canned tomatoes, with their juice
> ½ cup minced yellow onion
> 1 cup diced celery
> 1 cup diced mushrooms
> 4 tablespoons flour

> ¾ cup water
> ½ cup shredded sharp Cheddar cheese

1. Preheat oven to 350° F. Grease a 2-quart glass ovenware casserole and set aside.

2. Simmer shrimp in butter with salt and pepper in large heavy skillet 2 minutes over moderate heat. Remove from heat.

3. Add tomatoes, onion, celery, and mushrooms.

4. Mix flour and water to form a smooth paste and add to tomato-shrimp mixture. Return to heat and cook gently, stirring often, until sauce thickens and no starchy taste remains—about 10 minutes.

5. Pour all into casserole and sprinkle with cheese.

6. Cover, and bake 15 to 20 minutes until bubbly and cheese is melted. Serve with boiled rice.

WORLD WAR I
ADVICE ON BEING
ECONOMICAL AND PATRIOTIC
AT THE SAME TIME

THE FIRST step in food economy (aside from saving of waste) is to emphasize the use of cereal foods. *[Note: The author gives high marks to oatmeal, graham flour, rye flour, and cornmeal.]*

A second measure which generally makes for good economy is to emphasize the use of dried fruits and vegetables. *[Note: Highly rated are dried beans, peas, apples, figs, prunes, and raisins.]*

A pound of eggs (8 or 9) gives about the same nutrient return as a pound of medium-fat beef, but to be as cheap as beef at thirty cents a pound, eggs must not cost over forty-five cents a dozen. Eggs must be counted among the expensive foods, to be used very sparingly indeed in an economical diet. Nevertheless the use of eggs as a means of saving meat is a rational food conservation movement, to be encouraged where means permit.

Fats are not as cheap as milk and cereals if they cost over ten cents a pound. The best way to economize is by saving the fats without much flavor, and cutting the total fat in the diet to a very small amount, not over two ounces per person a day. This is also good food conservation since fats are almost invaluable in rationing an army, and those with decidedly agreeable flavor are needed to make a limited diet palatable.

The saving of sugar, while a necessary conservation measure, is contrary to general food economy since sugar is a comparatively cheap fuel food and has the great additional value of popularity.

Sugar substitutes are not all as cheap as sugar by any means, but molasses on account of its large amount of mineral salts, especially of calcium, has a score value of 2,315 as against 725 for granulated sugar, and may be regarded with favor by those economically and patriotically inclined.

—*Everyday Foods in Wartime* (1917) by Mary Swartz Rose, assistant professor, Department of Nutrition, Teachers College, Columbia University, New York, New York.

Classic Tuna-Noodle Casserole

Makes 4 Servings

✳

FEW CASSEROLES are more beloved than this one created some fifty years ago by the Campbell Soup Company. There's no need to make white sauce to bind ingredients. Just open a can of condensed cream of celery or cream of mushroom soup. Reprinted in 1994 in *Campbell's Best-Ever Recipes, 125th Anniversary Edition,* the recipe carries this headnote: "Before World War I, tuna was seldom served and was available only in fresh fish markets. With the war's scarcity of meat, sardine canners began to put tuna in cans, and tuna casseroles became important in the American diet." *Author's Note: Tuna was first canned in 1903. Russ Parsons of* The Los Angeles Times *thinks a precursor of this Campbell classic was the béchamel-bound "Escalloped Tuna Fish" in Ida Bailey Allen's* Modern Cookbook *(1932).*

1 (10¾-ounce) can condensed
cream of celery or mushroom
soup
½ cup milk
2 cups hot cooked medium egg
noodles, drained
1 cup cooked green peas, drained
2 tablespoons chopped, canned
pimiento (optional)
2 (6-ounce) cans tuna, drained
and flaked
¼ cup shredded Cheddar cheese
(optional)
2 tablespoons dry bread crumbs
1 tablespoon butter or
margarine, melted

1. Preheat oven to 400° F. Lightly
butter 1½-quart casserole.

2. Mix soup and milk in casserole.
Stir in noodles, peas, pimiento, if
using, and tuna.

3. Bake, uncovered, 20 minutes; stir.

4. Mix cheese, if using, crumbs, and
butter in small bowl. Scatter evenly
over tuna mixture, bake 5 minutes
more, until lightly browned.

Cheese-Swirled
Tuna Casserole

Makes 6 Servings

✳

WITH ITS topping of pinwheel
biscuits, this tuna casserole took first
prize in its category (seafood) in an
annual recipe contest sponsored by
the Marion, Indiana, newspaper—
The Chronicle-Tribune. The winning cook? Carolyn R. Butt of

Huntington. I featured her casserole
in "The Recipes that Took the Ribbons," an article I wrote for the June
3, 1980, issue of *Family Circle*.

TUNA MIXTURE
¼ cup minced yellow onion
⅓ cup minced green bell pepper
3 tablespoons butter or
margarine
6 tablespoons flour
1 teaspoon salt
1 (10¾-ounce) can condensed
cream of chicken soup
1½ cups milk
1 (6-ounce) can tuna, drained
and flaked
1 tablespoon fresh lemon juice

CHEESE SWIRL BISCUITS
2 cups sifted flour
3 teaspoons baking powder
½ teaspoon salt
¼ cup vegetable shortening
⅔ cup milk
½ cup shredded sharp Cheddar
or American cheese
¼ cup minced, canned
pimientos, drained

1. Preheat oven to 425° F. Lightly
butter 1½- to 2-quart casserole and
set aside.

2. TUNA MIXTURE: Stir-fry
onion and green pepper in butter in
large heavy skillet over moderate
heat until lightly browned—5 to 8
minutes. Blend in flour and salt,
then soup. Add milk and heat, stirring constantly, until thickened and
smooth—3 to 5 minutes. Mix in
tuna and lemon juice; set off heat,
but keep warm.

3. CHEESE SWIRL BISCUITS:
Sift flour, baking powder, and salt
together into large mixing bowl.
Add shortening and cut in with pastry blender until texture of coarse
meal. Add milk and fork briskly to
make soft dough.

4. Roll on floured pastry cloth with
floured stockinette-covered rolling
pan pin to 12 × 8 × ¼-inch rectangle. Scatter cheese and pimientos
evenly on top, then roll jelly-roll style,
starting from short end, to form
chunky roll 8 inches long. With
floured sharp knife, slice 1-inch thick.

5. Spoon tuna mixture into casserole. Space biscuits evenly on top,
arranging so spiral designs show.

6. Bake, uncovered, until biscuits
puff and brown lightly—about 20
minutes.

OF POTS AND
PRESIDENTS

·····························

I N 1938, a young
chemist named Roy J.
Plunkett was working in the
research laboratories of Du
Pont, hoping to find a useful
refrigerant. Instead, he discovered a substance that nothing
else would stick to. Marketed
as Teflon, it eventually coated
75 percent of the pots and pans
sold in the United States—and
was said to protect at least one
American President.

CASSEROLES

Spinach and Egg Casserole

Makes 4 to 6 Servings

✱

THERE ARE several versions of this recipe. Instead of slicing the hard-cooked eggs, some cooks like to devil them and bury them in the middle of the casserole. If that's your choice, you'll need three hard-cooked eggs. As for the deviling, use your favorite recipe.

¼ cup (½ stick) butter or margarine
4 tablespoons flour
¼ teaspoon ground hot red pepper (cayenne)
1½ teaspoons salt
1½ cups milk
1 cup soft white bread crumbs
2 (10-ounce) packages frozen chopped spinach, cooked and drained by package directions
2 hard-cooked eggs, peeled and thinly sliced or 3 hard-cooked eggs, deviled
1 cup finely shredded sharp Cheddar cheese
1 strip lean bacon, diced

1. Preheat oven to 350° F. Butter 6-cup casserole and set aside.

2. Melt butter in small heavy saucepan over moderate heat, blend in flour, cayenne, and salt. Add milk and heat, stirring constantly, until thickened and smooth—about 3 minutes.

3. Layer ingredients into casserole this way: half each of bread crumbs, spinach, and eggs *(Note: If using deviled eggs, add at this point, arranging right-side-up);* next, one-third of sauce and half of cheese; then, remaining spinach and egg, another third of sauce and remaining cheese; finally, remaining sauce and crumbs. Dot bacon over top.

4. Bake, uncovered, until bubbly and browned—40 to 45 minutes.

Corn and Sausage Bake

Makes 6 Servings

✱

THIS SOUTHERN specialty is plenty hearty. Not for dieters!

NOTE: Some of today's sausage is so lean it won't yield the 4 tablespoons drippings needed for this recipe. If that should happen, drizzle the bread crumbs with 2 tablespoons melted butter or margarine.

1 pound bulk sausage meat
1 large yellow onion, peeled and chopped
1 small green bell pepper, cored, seeded, and chopped
2 (15-ounce) cans cream-style corn
4 eggs, lightly beaten
¼ teaspoon salt
¼ teaspoon black pepper
⅛ teaspoon dried leaf thyme, crumbled
⅛ teaspoon freshly grated nutmeg
2 cups soft white bread crumbs

1. Preheat oven to 400° F. Butter 9×9×2-inch baking dish; set aside.

2. Brown sausage in large heavy skillet over moderately high heat, breaking up clumps; continue cooking

TABLE SET FOR DINNER.

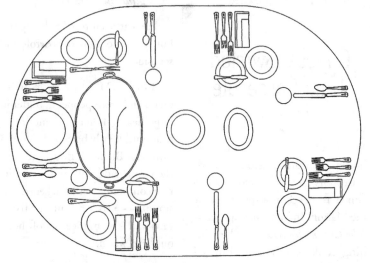

160

until uniformly brown—10 to 15 minutes. With slotted spoon, transfer sausage to medium bowl and set aside. Drain off all drippings, then spoon 2 tablespoons back into skillet. Also, reserve 2 more tablespoons drippings.

3. Add onion and green pepper to skillet and sauté until lightly browned—8 to 10 minutes. Transfer to second bowl, then mix in corn, eggs, salt, black pepper, thyme, and nutmeg.

4. Spoon half of mixture into baking dish, layer sausage on top, cover with remaining corn mixture, then bread crumbs, then drizzle with remaining 2 tablespoons sausage drippings.

5. Bake, uncovered, until bubbly and tipped with brown—about 30 minutes.

Yellow Squash Casserole

Makes 4 to 6 Servings

❋

AN ALL-TIME favorite down South where I grew up. This recipe is my mother's.

NOTE: I sometimes substitute zucchini for yellow squash, olive oil for butter, and Italian bread crumbs for cracker crumbs. And I usually cook a clove of garlic along with the squash and onion.

6 medium yellow squash, trimmed and cut into ½-inch dice
1 large yellow onion, peeled and coarsely chopped
⅓ cup water
1 teaspoon salt
¼ teaspoon black pepper
3 tablespoons butter (at room temperature)
2 eggs, well beaten
¾ cup soda-cracker or rich round cracker crumbs
1 teaspoon light brown sugar
⅛ teaspoon freshly grated nutmeg

TOPPING
½ cup fine soda-cracker crumbs
4 teaspoons melted butter or margarine

1. Preheat oven to 350°F. Butter 6-cup casserole well and set aside.

2. Cook squash and onion in water in covered very large heavy saucepan over moderately low heat 25 minutes until soft. Drain well, mash, and mix in salt, pepper, and butter. Beat in eggs, then stir in cracker crumbs, sugar, and nutmeg. Spoon into casserole.

3. TOPPING: Toss crumbs with melted butter and scatter evenly over casserole.

4. Bake, uncovered, until nicely browned—40 to 45 minutes.

TIMELINE

1927

Harry Lender emigrates from Poland to Connecticut and begins making Old World Jewish bagels.

Stainless-steel cutlery appears.

The automatic toaster arrives.

Milk is homogenized.

Fruit canners agree upon a single "recipe" for canned fruit cocktail.

1928

Riboflavin (vitamin B2) is identified.

Loaves of bread are factory-sliced.

1929

Chiffon pies become the rage.

Classic Green Bean Bake

Makes 6 Servings

✳

CAMPBELL'S SOUP home economists created this recipe in 1955, and it's been popular ever since. For many reasons, explains the headnote accompanying the recipe in *Campbell's Best-Ever Recipes, 125th Anniversary Edition* (1994): "It's delicious and easy to make, easy to remember and leaves room for creativity." I include the original recipe here plus two quick variations from Campbell.

> 1 (10¾-ounce) can condensed cream of mushroom soup
> ½ cup milk
> 1 teaspoon soy sauce
> Pinch black pepper
> 2 (9-ounce) packages frozen green beans, cooked and drained, or 2 (1-pound) cans green beans, drained
> 1 (2.8-ounce) can French fried onions

1. Preheat oven to 350° F. Lightly butter 1½-quart casserole.

2. Mix soup, milk, soy sauce, and pepper in casserole. Stir in beans and half the onions.

3. Bake, uncovered, 25 minutes until bubbling; stir well.

4. Top with remaining onions, bake 5 minutes more, and serve.

——— VARIATIONS ———

CORN AND BEAN AMANDINE: Prepare as above, substituting 1 (10¾-ounce) can condensed golden corn soup for mushroom. After baking 25 minutes, mix in ¼ cup toasted slivered almonds; proceed as directed. Makes 6 servings.

BROCCOLI BAKE: Prepare as directed, substituting 1 (10¾-ounce) can condensed cream of broccoli soup for mushroom and 1 (20-ounce) package frozen broccoli cuts or 4 cups cooked and drained broccoli florets for beans. Makes 6 servings.

Asparagus Casserole

Makes 6 Servings

✳

ONCE CAMPBELL'S taught Americans how to cook with canned soups in the early part of this century (especially how to substitute them for cream sauces in casseroles), every cook began collecting casserole recipes and concocting a few of her own. One of the beloved vegetable dishes to emerge from the canned-soup-casserole craze is this one.

CASSEROLE

> 3 (15-ounce) cans asparagus, drained or 3 (10-ounce) packages frozen asparagus spears, cooked by package directions and drained
> 2 hard-cooked eggs, peeled and chopped
> ¾ cup coarsely shredded sharp Cheddar cheese
> ½ cup blanched slivered or sliced almonds
> 1 (10¾-ounce) can condensed cream of mushroom or celery soup
> ½ cup milk

TOPPING

> ¼ cup coarsely shredded sharp Cheddar cheese
> ¼ cup blanched slivered or sliced almonds

1. CASSEROLE: Preheat oven to 350° F. Lightly butter shallow 2-quart casserole.

2. Build up alternate layers in casserole of asparagus, eggs, cheese, and almonds. Mix soup and milk and pour evenly over all.

3. TOPPING: Scatter cheese, then almonds over top of casserole.

4. Bake, uncovered, until bubbly and tipped with brown—about 30 minutes.

NOTE: Some cooks like to top this casserole with crushed potato chips instead of cheese and almonds.

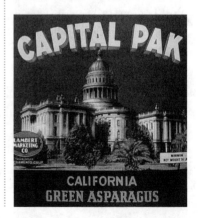

Festive Broccoli Bake

Makes 8 Servings

✳

A 1995 "put-together" from the McCormick/Schilling test kitchens that goes together zip-quick.

1 (16-ounce) bag frozen broccoli
    florets, thawed and drained
2 (14½-ounce) cans stewed
    tomatoes, with their juice
2 tablespoons cornstarch
1 teaspoon sugar
¼ teaspoon black pepper
1 teaspoon Italian seasoning
1½ cups shredded mozzarella
    cheese
¼ cup (½ stick) butter or
    margarine, melted
2 tablespoons freshly grated
    Parmesan cheese
2 cups unseasoned dry bread
    cubes, crushed to coarse
    crumbs

1. Preheat oven to 350° F.

2. Arrange broccoli in single layer in ungreased 3-quart baking dish, halving any large florets.

3. Mix tomatoes, cornstarch, sugar, pepper, and ¾ teaspoon Italian seasoning and pour over broccoli. Scatter mozzarella evenly on top.

4. Mix melted butter with remaining ¼ teaspoon Italian seasoning and Parmesan and toss with dry bread crumbs. Sprinkle evenly over broccoli mixture.

5. Bake, uncovered, until bubbly and browned—about 30 minutes.

VINTAGE RECIPE

THIS RECIPE is reprinted just as it appeared in Marian and Nino Tracy's *Casserole Cookery* (1941).

"CASSEROLE COOKERY"
FRANKFURTERS WITH SAUERKRAUT

INGREDIENTS   **TIME: 35 min.**
1 lb. frankfurters
1 quart sauerkraut, drained
1 tablespoon celery seed

Put a layer of sauerkraut at the bottom of a deep casserole, sprinkle with celery seed, then a layer of frankfurters and repeat until all the ingredients are used. Cover tightly and bake in a medium oven (350°) for 30 minutes. Serves 4.

Better living with your new
G-E FOOD FREEZER

ICE CREAM
FROZEN PEAS
Orange Juice

GENERAL ⓖ ELECTRIC

CASSEROLE RECIPES

*that Entered the American
Mainstream During
the Twentieth Century
with Their Source*

....

*(*Recipe Included)*

FRANCE
*Cassoulet (see Meats, Fish,
& Fowl)

❊

GREECE
*Moussaka
*Pastitsio

❊

ITALY
*Lasagne

❊

SPAIN
*Arroz con Pollo
Paella

Anne Mead's Best-Ever Lasagne

Makes 6 to 8 Servings

✱

THOUGH LASAGNE recipes began showing up in specialty cookbooks in the '30s (there's one in Diana Ashley's *Where To Dine in '39: New York Restaurant Guide and Cook Book*), lasagne didn't catch on until the '60s. According to Gerry Schremp (*Kitchen Culture: Fifty Years of Food Fads*, 1991), "During the 1960s, Americans discovered that there was more to Italian food than spaghetti and meatballs." An early favorite, she adds, was lasagne. For several reasons: It was cheap, it was versatile, and it put a husky main course in one dish. I believe that one of the first, if not *the* first, all-purpose cookbooks to include it was *The Ladies' Home Journal Cook Book* (1960), on which I worked. In fact, we included two lasagne recipes, a "like Mama used to make" one and a quick (jazzed-up frozen lasagne). The recipe here is from my good friend Anne Mead, who makes the best lasagne I have ever eaten.

She began making lasagne in the early '60s, starting with a back-of-the-box recipe, then adding her own touches. The result is a light (almost soufflé-light) lasagne. It's the recipe Anne's family requests the most. So whenever "the troops" gather for Thanksgiving or Christmas, she's bound to have a couple of batches of lasagne sauce in the freezer. The rest goes together fast.

TOMATO-MEAT SAUCE
1 pound ground beef chuck
1 medium yellow onion, peeled and chopped
1 (28-ounce) can crushed tomatoes
1 (6-ounce) can tomato paste
4 teaspoons salt
1 whole bay leaf
1/8 teaspoon ground hot red pepper (cayenne)
1/4 teaspoon dried leaf basil, crumbled
1/4 teaspoon dried leaf oregano, crumbled
2 cups water

LASAGNE
10 lasagne noodles (about 1/2 pound)
1 tablespoon salt
1 pound ricotta cheese
1/2 pound mozzarella cheese, thinly sliced
Tomato–Meat Sauce (above)
1/2 cup freshly grated Parmesan cheese

1. TOMATO-MEAT SAUCE: Brown beef in large, heavy nonstick skillet over moderately high heat, breaking up large clumps, until no traces of red remain, about 5 minutes. Transfer to very large, deep heavy saucepan, add all remaining ingredients, and simmer, uncovered, over low heat, stirring occasionally, until flavors meld—about 1 1/2 hours. Discard bay leaf. Set sauce aside.

2. LASAGNE: Preheat oven to 325° F.

3. Cook noodles in large kettle of boiling water with 1 tablespoon salt until very tender, stirring frequently; rinse under cold running water and drain well.

4. To Assemble: Arrange 5 wet noodles lengthwise in ungreased 11¾ × 7½ × 1¾-inch baking dish, then top with half each of ricotta, mozzarella, and sauce. Repeat layers. Sprinkle with Parmesan.

5. Bake, uncovered, until bubbly and tipped with brown—about 45 minutes.

6. Cool lasagne 15 minutes, then cut into squares and serve.

Arroz con Pollo

Makes 6 Servings

✳

IN THE early '70s, I wrote an article on casseroles for *Family Circle* and among its recipes was this Spanish classic, in which the chicken bakes neatly in a casserole with saffron rice, tomatoes and green peas. I shortcut the classic by using frozen green peas, canned tomatoes and chicken broth.

> 1 (3-pound) broiler-fryer,
>   cut up
> 3 tablespoons fruity olive oil
> 1 teaspoon salt
> ¼ teaspoon black pepper
> ½ teaspoon paprika
> 1 large yellow onion, peeled
>   and chopped
> 1 clove garlic, peeled and
>   minced
> ¼ teaspoon crushed saffron
>   threads
> ½ teaspoon dried leaf oregano,
>   crumbled
> 1 cup chicken broth
> 2 cups canned crushed tomatoes
> 1 whole bay leaf
> 1¼ cups raw converted rice
> 1 (10-ounce) package frozen
>   green peas, thawed
> ¼ cup slivered canned
>   pimientos

1. Preheat broiler.

2. Rub chicken with 1 tablespoon olive oil, then sprinkle with ¼ teaspoon salt, ⅛ teaspoon pepper, and all the paprika. Broil, skin-side-up, in foil-lined shallow baking pan 5 inches from heat until nicely browned—8 to 10 minutes; set aside. Reduce oven temperature to 375° F.

3. Heat remaining 2 tablespoons olive oil in large heavy skillet over moderately high heat 1 minute. Add onion and garlic and stir-fry until limp—about 5 minutes. Mix in saffron and oregano and cook and stir 1 to 2 minutes. Add broth, tomatoes, bay leaf, remaining ¾ teaspoon salt and ⅛ teaspoon pepper, and cook and stir 2 minutes. Add rice and bring to boiling.

4. Transfer to ungreased 3-quart casserole and arrange browned chicken on top, pushing slightly down into liquid.

5. Cover, and bake 45 minutes. Fork up rice, add peas and pimientos, distributing in and around chicken.

6. Cover, and bake until chicken shows no signs of pink in center—about 15 minutes. Discard bay leaf and serve.

TIMELINE

1929

....

"21" Club opens in New York City as a speakeasy.

....

7UP goes on sale.

....

Gerber's introduces canned baby food.

1930s

....

Pressure cookers, developed for military use, become the rage among homemakers.

....

Beta-carotene is identified as precursor of vitamin A.

....

The Great Depression. Popular "frugal" foods: macaroni and cheese, creamed chipped beef on toast, salmon loaf, meat loaf, spaghetti with meatballs, roast beef hash, casseroles.

....

A Youngstown, Ohio, ice cream shop owner puts a chocolate-covered ice cream bar on a stick and calls it a Good Humor bar.

Moussaka

Makes 10 Servings

✳

ALTHOUGH NO stranger to Americans of Greek heritage, moussaka, like lasagne, did not gain fans beyond ethnic neighborhoods until the '60s. I first tasted it in Greece in 1963. I came home a fan. The recipe here, liberally adapted from *The New Good Housekeeping Cookbook* (1986), shows how "mainstream" moussaka has become.

NOTE: For best results, do not peel the eggplants.

FILLING

- ¼ cup fruity olive oil (about)
- 2 (2-pound) eggplants, trimmed and sliced ¼-inch thick
- 1½ pounds lean ground lamb shoulder
- 1 large yellow onion, peeled and chopped
- 2 cloves garlic, peeled and minced
- ¼ teaspoon dried leaf oregano, crumbled
- ¼ teaspoon dried leaf thyme, crumbled
- ⅛ teaspoon ground cinnamon
- 1 cup crumbled feta cheese (about ¼ pound)
- ½ cup tomato sauce
- ½ cup fine dry bread crumbs
- ¼ cup dry red wine
- ¼ cup minced fresh flat-leaf parsley
- 1 egg, lightly beaten
- 1½ teaspoons salt
- ¼ teaspoon black pepper

SAUCE

- ⅓ cup butter or margarine
- ½ cup unsifted flour
- ½ teaspoon salt
- ¼ teaspoon white pepper
- ⅛ teaspoon ground cinnamon
- 1¾ cups chicken broth
- 1 cup milk
- 2 tablespoons freshly grated Parmesan cheese

1. Preheat oven to 350° F. Lightly coat 13 × 9 × 2-inch baking pan with nonstick cooking spray and set aside.

2. FILLING: Heat olive oil in very large heavy skillet over moderately high heat until ripples show on skillet bottom—1 to 1½ minutes. Brown eggplant slices in oil in batches, adding additional oil, if needed. Drain well on paper towels.

3. Reduce heat under skillet to moderate, add lamb, onion, and garlic and stir-fry, breaking up clumps, until lamb is uniformly brown—about 5 minutes. Mix in oregano, thyme, and cinnamon and mellow over moderate heat 1 minute.

4. Remove from heat and mix in feta, tomato sauce, bread crumbs, wine, parsley, egg, salt, and black pepper. Set aside.

5. SAUCE: Melt butter in medium heavy saucepan over moderate heat, blend in flour, salt, white pepper, and cinnamon, then add broth and milk and cook, stirring constantly, until thickened and smooth—3 to 5 minutes. Remove from heat and stir in Parmesan.

6. TO ASSEMBLE MOUSSAKA: Arrange half of eggplant over bottom of pan, spread lamb mixture evenly on top, cover with remaining eggplant, then smooth sauce evenly over all.

7. Bake, uncovered, until bubbling and tipped with brown—about 30 minutes. Cool 15 minutes, then cut into squares and serve.

Vegetarian (Meatless) Moussaka

Makes 8 Servings

✳

HERE'S A recipe I developed in 1973 for an article I was writing for *Family Circle* called "Melting-Pot Money-Savers." I'd eaten meatless moussakas in Greece and think this one every bit as good as the richer versions containing a pound or more of ground lamb.

NOTE: For best results, do not peel the eggplants.

EGGPLANT

- 2 (2-pound) eggplants, trimmed and sliced ½-inch thick
- 2 teaspoons salt
- ¼ cup fruity olive oil

TOMATO SAUCE

- 2 tablespoons fruity olive oil
- 3 medium yellow onions, peeled and chopped
- 2 cloves garlic, peeled and minced

2 cups canned crushed tomatoes

¼ teaspoon dried leaf rosemary, crumbled

2 tablespoons minced fresh mint

2 tablespoons minced fresh flat-leaf parsley

2 teaspoons sugar

½ teaspoon salt (or to taste)

¼ teaspoon black pepper (or to taste)

1 (8-ounce) can tomato sauce

CHEESE FILLING

2 cups cream-style cottage cheese

1 egg, lightly beaten

2 tablespoons freshly grated Parmesan cheese

⅛ teaspoon dried leaf rosemary, crumbled

⅛ teaspoon freshly grated nutmeg

¼ teaspoon salt

⅛ teaspoon white pepper

FOR LAYERING

⅔ cup freshly grated Parmesan cheese

1. EGGPLANT: Sprinkle eggplant slices well on both sides with salt and place between several thicknesses paper towels, top with a large baking sheet, and weight by placing large unopened cans of food on top. Let stand 1 hour.

2. TOMATO SAUCE: Heat olive oil in large heavy skillet over moderate heat 1 minute. Add onions and stir-fry until glassy—about 5 minutes. Add garlic and stir-fry 2 minutes. Mix in tomatoes and all remaining sauce ingredients except tomato sauce. Reduce heat to low, cover, and simmer, stirring occasionally, until flavors meld—45 minutes to 1 hour. Mix in tomato sauce and simmer, uncovered, 15 minutes, stirring often. Set aside.

3. CHEESE FILLING: Mix all ingredients and set aside.

4. Preheat broiler. Brush eggplant slices on both sides with olive oil and broil about 4 inches from heat until browned—about 2 minutes per side. Reduce oven heat to 375°F.

5. TO ASSEMBLE MOUSSAKA: Spoon half of tomato sauce over bottom of ungreased 13 × 9 × 2-inch baking pan and sprinkle generously with some of the ⅔ cup "layering" Parmesan. Lay half the eggplant slices on top in single layer, cover with cheese filling, smoothing to corners, and again sprinkle generously with Parmesan. Add remaining eggplant slices, sprinkle with Parmesan, top with remaining tomato sauce and Parmesan.

6. Bake, uncovered, until bubbly and tipped with brown—about 45 minutes. Let stand 15 minutes, then cut into squares and serve.

FIFTEEN CENTS A COPY

AMERICAN COOKERY

FORMERLY

THE BOSTON
COOKING-SCHOOL MAGAZINE

OF·CULINARY·SCIENCE AND DOMESTIC·ECONOMICS

FEBRUARY, 1917
Vol. XXI   No. 7

$1.50 A YEAR

15 CENTS A COPY

PUBLISHED
BY
THE BOSTON COOKING
SCHOOL MAGAZINE Cº
221 COLUMBUS AVᴱ
BOSTON MASS.

Pastitsio

Makes 6 Servings

✳

THIS LAYERED Greek lamb and macaroni casserole became fashionable in the '70s. Today it is as popular as moussaka. The recipe is my own, the result of a long vacation in Greece.

MEAT LAYER

2 tablespoons fruity olive oil
1 large yellow onion, peeled and chopped
1 clove garlic, peeled and minced
1 pound lean ground lamb shoulder
2 tablespoons tomato paste
1 tablespoon minced fresh mint
¼ teaspoon ground cinnamon
¼ teaspoon dried leaf rosemary, crumbled
¼ teaspoon dried leaf thyme, crumbled
½ teaspoon salt
¼ teaspoon black pepper

MACARONI LAYER

¼ cup (½ stick) butter or margarine
7 tablespoons flour
1 teaspoon salt
⅛ teaspoon white pepper
⅛ teaspoon freshly grated nutmeg
2 cups milk
½ pound elbow macaroni, cooked and drained by package directions
1 egg, lightly beaten
½ cup freshly grated Parmesan cheese

1. Preheat oven to 350° F. Butter 9 × 9 × 2-inch baking; set aside.

2. MEAT LAYER: Heat oil in large heavy skillet over moderate heat 1 minute; add onion and stir-fry until limp and lightly browned—about 5 minutes. Add garlic and stir-fry 1 minute. Add lamb, breaking up large clumps, and stir-fry until no longer pink—3 to 5 minutes. Blend in remaining ingredients, turn heat to low, and cook, uncovered, stirring occasionally, while preparing Macaroni Layer.

3. MACARONI LAYER: Melt butter in large heavy saucepan over moderate heat. Blend in flour, salt, white pepper, and nutmeg and cook and stir 1 minute. Add milk and cook, stirring constantly, until thickened and smooth—3 to 5 minutes.

4. Stir ¾ cup sauce into macaroni in medium bowl. Blend a little remaining sauce into egg, stir back into pan, and reserve.

5. Layer half the macaroni mixture into baking dish and sprinkle with 2 tablespoons Parmesan. Add all meat mixture, pressing firmly onto macaroni, sprinkle with 2 more tablespoons Parmesan and top with remaining macaroni mixture. Finally, sprinkle with another 2 tablespoons Parmesan, spread reserved sauce on top, and scatter remaining Parmesan evenly over all.

6. Bake, uncovered, until brown—about 45 minutes. Cool 15 minutes before serving.

TIMELINE

1930

The electric range arrives.

Bird's Eye introduces its line of "frosted foods."

Thanks to the "congealed" salads fad, Jell-O introduces a new flavor—lime—that's ideal for appetizers, main dishes, desserts, *and* salads.

Ruth Wakefield invents the chocolate chip cookie at the Toll House, her historic inn near Whitman, Massachusetts.

Twinkies are created by a Hostess plant manager.

Better Homes & Gardens publishes its first cookbook.

1931

Vitamin C is crystallized out of lemon juice.

Free-standing sinks give way to built-ins.

General Electric introduces the "monitor top" electric refrigerator.

EGGS, CHEESE, PASTA, GRAINS

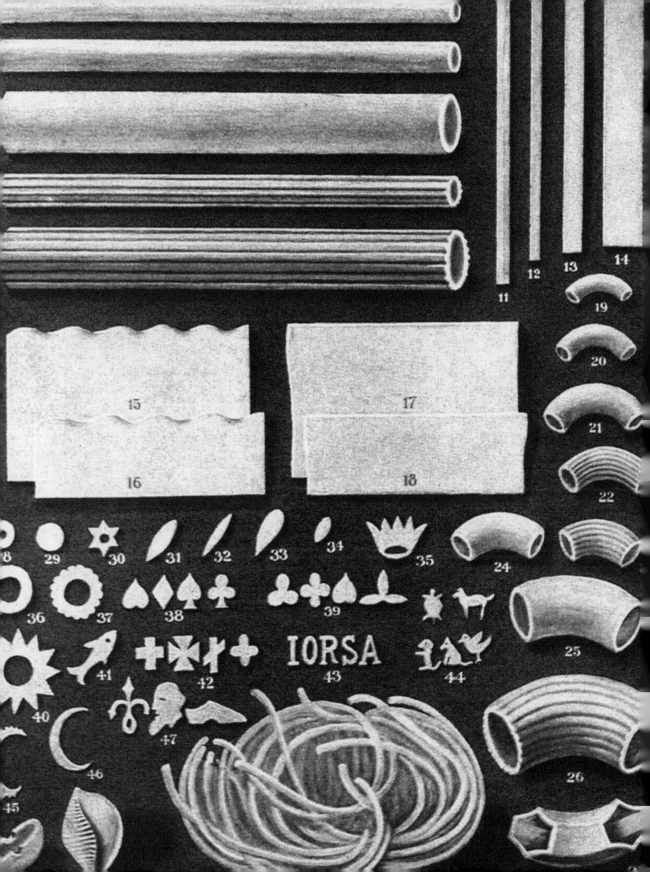

Good Housekeeping

AUGUST 1924

35 CENTS IN CANADA

25 CENTS

The SECRET of LASTING YOUTH by MARY GARDEN

George Weston — Gene Stratton — Porter — Sabatini
Louise Dutton — Edith Barnard Delano — Mrs. Keyes

T HUMBING THROUGH early American cookbooks produces some surprises. Soufflés abound. Omelets abound. Stuffed eggs and curried eggs abound. And polenta goes all the way back to Thomas Jefferson.

There are rarebits, Golden Bucks (rarebits on toast crowned with poached eggs) and Blushing Bunnies (chafing dish macaronis and cheese with tomatoes). There are cheese puddings, cheese ramekins, cheese "fondus" (mock soufflés). Rice recipes proliferate, especially in southern cookbooks. Scarcely surprising—rice made men rich in the South Carolina Lowcountry. Still, I don't think it incorrect to say that rice came into its own in this century, in particular the last half of it, when arborio and basmati rices landed in the corner supermarket together with brown rice and such aromatic varieties as "popcorn" and "jasmine." Wild rice (the "rice" that isn't "rice") came of age this century, too. From the '60s and '70s onward, we learned to cook rice the Indian way, the Turkish way, the Chinese way. More important, we discovered the beauties of *risotto*.

We made friends with couscous, thanks to Paula Wolfert's ground-breaking *Couscous and Other Good Food from Morocco* (1973). But more than anything, we fell head over heels for pasta. Not that pasta didn't exist here before 1900—Thomas Jefferson imported it from Italy and served it often. But few cooks knew what to do with it. Our early cooking teachers—Mary Lincoln, Fannie Farmer, Sarah Tyson Rorer, and so on—were nearly all Anglo-Saxon.

Mrs. Rorer's Philadelphia Cook Book (1886) devotes a brief chapter to macaroni. But no Italian would recognize her "Macaroni à l'Italienne"—a stovetop macaroni and cheese. By today's standards, her eight other macaroni recipes—for the most part creamed—are lackluster, too. Still, Mrs. Rorer earns points for recogniz-

ing the importance of pasta and informing her readers.

Fannie Farmer (*The Boston Cooking-School Cook Book,* 1896) lumps macaroni in with cereals and offers recipes no more imaginative than Mrs. Rorer's. She does, however, single out spaghetti:

Spaghetti may be cooked in any way in which macaroni is cooked, but is usually served with tomato sauce.

It is cooked in long strips rather than broken in pieces; to accomplish this, hold quantity to be cooked in the hand, dip ends in boiling salted water; as spaghetti softens it will bend, and may be coiled under water.

According to Richard J. Hooker (*Food and Drink in America,* 1981), few immigrants had a greater impact on our eating habits than the Italians, who began arriving by the boatload late in the nineteenth century and settling in Boston, New York, Philadelphia, and other big cities.

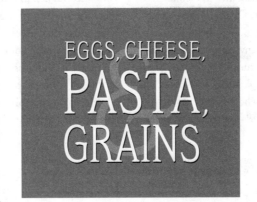

EGGS, CHEESE, PASTA, GRAINS

Hooker says New Yorkers discovered spaghetti in the 1890s because it had begun to be manufactured on Staten Island and served in Italian restaurants in Manhattan. "Italian" pasta recipes appear with increasing regularity in cookbooks in the opening decades of this century. But only in the '20s and '30s do they approach authenticity.

Sheila Hibben's *National Cookbook* (1932) includes among its luncheon dishes "Spaghetti (as cooked on Catharine Street, Philadelphia)" and "Noodles with Ham (New York's Italian Quarter)."

John MacPherson, radio's famous "Mystery Chef" of the 1930s, offers in his *Mystery Chef's Own Cook Book* (1934) a Ravioli, which he calls "The National Dish of Italy," plus an Italian Spaghetti Sauce, a red clam sauce, and an anchovy sauce. Pungent stuff.

However, the 1930s writer who plunges more deeply into pasta than any other is *House Beautiful* Food Editor Mary Grosvenor Ellsworth. In *Much Depends on Dinner* (1939), she gives pasta its own chapter and begins thus:

Under this heading the Italian groups all the shapes, sizes, and varieties of edibles he molds of hard wheat flour and water. Spaghetti, macaroni, vermicelli, ravioli, gnocchi, shaped in elbows, shells, whorls, rosettes, cushions, and ribbons, all very much alike except in form, all practically tasteless, all hearty, nourishing inexpensive food.

Ellsworth then goes on to say that we of English background: . . . cooked them [pastas] too much, we desecrated them with further additions of flour, we smothered them in baking dishes and store cheese. Unless there was some tincture of Latin blood in the family or an unusual interest in Continental cooking, most American households met spaghetti et al, only in this debased form.

Ellsworth says that our love of real Italian pasta began during Prohibition because many speakeasies were run by Italians. It may be so. At any rate, of all the cookbooks I've explored, hers offers the most authentic collection of pastas and pasta sauces to date. Twelve pages' worth.

World War II, even more than Prohibition, sharpened our appetite for pasta. Many were meatless, filling, and cheap. Moreover, GIs returning from Italy after World War II had tasted the real thing. In Naples. In Rome. In Sicily. And they knew how good it could be.

From the '50s and '60s onward—with Angelo Pelle-grini, Ada Boni, Marcella Hazan, Giuliano Bugialli, Anna Teresa Callen, and others to cheer us on—we began to explore the world of pasta in earnest.

But the "pasta avalanche," as James Beard called it, began about 1980. Suddenly pasta was no longer the province of smoky dives with red-checked tablecloths and drippy candles thrust into the necks of Chianti bottles. It moved uptown to stylish restaurants. By 1981, Americans were second only to Italians in quantities of pasta consumed.

Pasta cookbooks began spewing off the presses and pasta machines, both manual and electric, became the gadgets du jour. Pasta shops opened coast to coast and take-out stores added pasta salads, soups, and sauces to their inventories.

The more passionate of us sailed off to Italy to study the fine art of pasta making with Marcella Hazan or Giuliano Bugialli and to discover, as Hazan once said, that "the warmth of the hand makes for elasticity and body more than any kind of machine."

Our pilgrimage continues.

Clearly, it is impossible to include all—or even half—of the egg, cheese, pasta, or grain recipes that joined our culinary repertoire this century. The best I can do is offer this representative sampling.

Eggs Sardou

Makes 4 Servings

✳

THIS FIRST of New Orleans's poached-egg extravaganzas was, according to Rima and Richard Collin (The New Orleans Cookbook, 1975), created at Antoine's to honor French playwright Victorien Sardou, who came visiting in 1908. Eggs Sardou is now a signature dish at Brennan's, the restaurant founded in 1946 that's synonymous with luxurious breakfasts. The Brennan's recipe here is adapted from The Best of Food & Wine: 1988 Collection.

8 medium artichokes, stemmed, stripped of tough outer leaves, then all but 1½ inches of base cut away
2 quarts water mixed with juice of 1 lemon (acidulated water)
1 cup (2 sticks) plus 3 tablespoons butter
1 tablespoon flour
¾ cup milk
⅛ teaspoon freshly grated nutmeg
1 teaspoon salt
¼ teaspoon hot red pepper sauce
¼ cup minced scallions
2 (10-ounce) packages frozen chopped spinach, thawed and squeezed dry
⅜ teaspoon white pepper
3 egg yolks
2 tablespoons fresh lemon juice
8 poached eggs

1. Boil artichoke bottoms in acidulated water in large heavy nonreactive pan until tender—about 25 minutes. Cool in cooking liquid until easy to handle, then with spoon, scrape out prickly chokes. Set artichoke bottoms aside.

2. Melt 1 tablespoon butter in small heavy saucepan over moderate heat. Blend in flour and cook and stir 1 minute. Add milk and cook, stirring constantly, until thickened and smooth—3 to 5 minutes. Reduce heat to low and continue cooking, stirring often, 15 minutes until no raw starch taste lingers. Mix in nutmeg, ¼ teaspoon salt, and hot red pepper sauce. Set off heat and reserve.

3. Melt 2 tablespoons butter in large, heavy nonreactive skillet, add scallions, and stir-fry over moderate heat until limp—2 to 3 minutes. Add spinach and cook and stir 2 minutes. Blend in reserved sauce, ½ teaspoon salt, and ¼ teaspoon white pepper. Cover, set off heat, and keep warm.

4. Melt remaining 1 cup butter in small heavy saucepan over moderate heat and keep warm.

5. Whisk egg yolks and lemon juice in double boiler top, set over simmering water, and whisk until fluffy—about 5 minutes. Add melted butter in fine stream, whisking until hollandaise thickens. Mix in remaining ¼ teaspoon salt and ⅛ teaspoon white pepper.

6. TO ASSEMBLE: Nest ½ cup warm spinach on each of 4 heated plates. Arrange 2 artichoke hearts on top and cup a poached egg in each. Ladle hollandaise over eggs and serve.

Baked Eggs on Ham and Cheddar with Bell Pepper Sauce

Makes 2 Servings

✳

THIS QUICK recipe appeared in *Gourmet's* popular "In Short Order" column and is adapted from *Gourmet's In Short Order* (1993).

> *2 slices rye bread, toasted*
> *2 thin slices Cheddar cheese,*
>   *cut to fit bread*
> *⅔ cup chopped cooked ham*
> *2 eggs*
> *½ teaspoon salt*
> *¼ teaspoon black pepper*
> *⅓ cup chicken broth*
> *⅓ cup heavy cream*
> *1 small red bell pepper, cored,*
>   *seeded, and chopped*

1. Preheat oven to 350° F.

2. Place toast in ungreased 9-inch pie tin, top with cheese, then ham, shaping into little nests. Break an egg into each nest and sprinkle with ¼ teaspoon salt and ⅛ teaspoon black pepper, dividing amounts evenly.

3. Bake, uncovered, just until yolks set—about 15 minutes.

4. Meanwhile, mix broth and cream in small heavy saucepan, add red pepper, and boil, uncovered, until reduced by half; season with remaining salt and black pepper.

5. Transfer toast to heated serving plates, wreathe with sauce, and serve.

TIMELINE

1931

St. Louis housewife Irma Rombauer pays to have 500 recipes from family, friends, and acquaintances published in book form. *The Joy of Cooking,* she calls it.

General Mills develops Bisquick.

The Countess Fal de St. Phalle Gives You This Latest Idea for a Bisquick Waffle Luncheon

1932

Family Circle, "the first supermarket magazine," debuts in groceries, but it is at first entertainment-oriented.

Corn chips appear.

1933

Prohibition ends.

J.L. Rosefield, the man who learned to keep peanut butter from separating, produces his own brand. He calls it "Skippy Peanut Butter" and packs it in rectangular red-white-and-blue tins.

Eggs Florentine

ALTHOUGH LATE nineteenth-century/early twentieth-century cookbooks team spinach with hard-cooked eggs, I don't find Eggs Florentine—poached in spinach nests or served on a bed of buttered spinach—appearing before the 1920s. My hunch is that this was a hotel or restaurant recipe that appealed to the cookbook authors who held forth in the early years of this century.

Chef Louis Diat, who came to New York's Ritz-Carlton in 1910 and stayed for forty years, includes this shortcut recipe in *Cooking à la Ritz* (1941):

POACHED EGGS FLORENTINE

Place poached eggs on a bed of cooked and buttered spinach. Coat with Mornay Sauce, sprinkle with grated Parmesan cheese and brown under a broiler.

A somewhat fancier Sardi's version (*Curtain Up at Sardi's* by Vincent Sardi, Jr., and Helen Bryson, 1957) puts the spinach "in the bottom of shirred-egg dishes," tops with poached eggs, blankets with Sardi Sauce (a velouté-hollandaise blend fluffed with whipped cream and spiked with sherry), then scatters with grated Parmesan and browns under the broiler.

As for home versions of Eggs Florentine, the first I find is this one, which showed up in the 1923 edition of *The Boston Cooking-School Cook Book:*

FLORENTINE EGGS IN CASSEROLES

Finely chop cooked spinach and season with butter and salt. Put one tablespoon spinach in each buttered individual casserole, sprinkle with one tablespoon grated Parmesan cheese, and slip into each an egg. Cover each egg with one tablespoon Béchamel Sauce and one-half tablespoon grated Parmesan. Bake until eggs are set and eat immediately.

We can't improve on that recipe today.

Tuna-Stuffed Eggs on Rice with Curry Sauce

Makes 6 Servings

✳

AN UNUSUAL recipe adapted from a 1953 Corning cookbook called *Pyrex Prize Recipes.* The headnote says it all: "Here is an easy-to-prepare, inexpensive Friday dish—hard-cooked eggs stuffed with a delicious tuna mixture, baked in a bed of rice, and covered with a rich curry sauce. An epicurean delight!"

3 cups cooked rice
2 tablespoons butter or
    margarine
6 hard-cooked eggs, peeled
1/3 cup finely flaked tuna
    (1/2 of a 6 1/2-ounce can)
1/3 cup mayonnaise
1/2 teaspoon salt

CURRY SAUCE
1/4 cup (1/2 stick) butter or
    margarine
4 tablespoons flour
3/4 teaspoon salt
1/2 teaspoon curry powder
2 cups milk

1. Preheat oven to 325° F. Grease a 1 1/2-quart (8 1/4-inch-round) glass ovenware cake dish well.

2. Spoon rice into cake dish and dot with butter.

3. Halve eggs lengthwise, scoop out yolks, mash, then mix in tuna, mayonnaise, and salt. Fill whites with tuna mixture and arrange on top of rice.

4. CURRY SAUCE: Melt butter over low heat, remove from heat, and blend in flour, salt, and curry powder. Add milk and cook, stirring constantly, over moderate heat until thickened and no raw starch taste remains—about 10 minutes. Pour over stuffed eggs.

5. Bake, uncovered, until bubbly— 15 to 20 minutes.

1. Whisk soup until smooth in medium bowl.

2. Beat eggs in, two by two, then mix in pepper.

3. Melt butter in heavy 10-inch skillet over low heat, add egg mixture, and scramble softly. Serve at once.

Campbelled Eggs

Makes 4 Servings

❋

BACK IN the '50s, this recipe began showing up in cartons of eggs, courtesy of the Campbell Soup Company. According to company spokesmen, the recipe is one of the "all-time favorites" ever developed by Campbell's. It appears in *Campbell's Best-Ever Recipes, 125th Anniversary Edition* (1994), and according to the accompanying headnote, "is a great way to add flavor to everyday scrambled eggs." I've adapted the recipe here—for style, not content.

> 1 (10¾-ounce) can condensed
>   Cheddar cheese or cream of
>   chicken soup
> 8 eggs
> Pinch black pepper
> 2 tablespoons butter or
>   margarine

Wisconsin's Favorite Macaroni and Cheese

Makes 4 to 6 Servings

❋

THIS RECIPE from the Wisconsin Milk Marketing Board contains broccoli and is thus more nutritionally correct than the macaroni-and-cheeses of old. It needs nothing more for accompaniment than a salad of crisp greens and fruit for dessert.

> ½ cup chopped yellow onion
> 3 tablespoons butter
> 2 teaspoons prepared mustard
> 1 (16-ounce) container
>   Wisconsin Cold Pack
>   Cheddar Cheese
> ½ cup milk or skim milk
> ⅛ teaspoon black pepper
> ½ pound (about 2¼ cups)
>   elbow macaroni, cooked and
>   drained

> 1 bunch broccoli, cut into
>   florets, boiled 3 minutes, and
>   drained
> ⅓ cup crushed soda crackers

1. Preheat oven to 375° F. Butter 2½- to 3-quart casserole well and set aside.

2. Sauté onion in 2 tablespoons butter in large heavy saucepan over moderate heat 3 minutes. Blend in mustard. Add cheese, milk, and pepper and cook and stir until cheese melts and mixture is smooth. Stir in macaroni.

3. Spoon half of macaroni mixture into casserole, arrange broccoli on top, and cover with remaining macaroni mixture.

4. Melt remaining 1 tablespoon butter, mix with cracker crumbs, and use as casserole topping.

5. Bake, uncovered, 25 to 30 minutes until bubbling and brown. Let stand 10 minutes before serving.

Macaroni and Cheese:
A Long Journey into Mainstream America

THE SURPRISE of this humble recipe is that it dates at least as far back as Thomas Jefferson. (So why include macaroni and cheese in a book devoted to twentieth-century classics? Because the recipe as we now know it took several centuries to evolve and become a staple cross-country.) At Monticello, Jefferson served both a sweet macaroni pudding and a savory one baked with grated cheese and an equal amount of butter.

According to food historian Karen Hess, who with husband John, a journalist, wrote *The Taste of America* (1977, Viking/Grossman), Mary Randolph "likely gave many Americans their first macaroni-and-cheese recipe." Mrs. Hess speaks of the recipe in *The Virginia*

House-Wife (originally published in 1824 and now available in a facsimile edition with historical notes by Mrs. Hess). Mary Randolph directs the reader to "Boil as much macaroni as will fill your dish, in milk and water till quite tender, drain it on a sieve, sprinkle a little salt over it, put a layer in your dish, then cheese and butter as in the polenta [a recipe given directly above], and bake in the same manner."

No fan of macaroni and cheese, Mrs. Hess believes that it "started out as a misconception of an Italian dish."

In Sarah Rutledge's *The Carolina Housewife* (1847), I find this recipe, clearly a precursor of macaroni and cheese as we know it today:

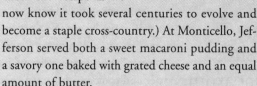

TO DRESS MACARONI À LA SAUCE BLANCHE

Take a quarter of a pound of macaroni, boil it in water, in which there must be a little salt. When the macaroni is done, the water must be drained from it, and the saucepan kept covered; roll two table-spoonfuls of butter in a little flour; take a pint of milk, and half a pint of cream; add the butter and flour to the milk, and set it on the fire, until it becomes thick. This sauce ought to be stirred the whole time it is boiling, and always in the same direction. Grate a quarter of a pound of parmesan cheese; butter the pan in which the macaroni is to be baked, and put in first, a layer of macaroni, then one of grated cheese, then some sauce, and so on until the dish is filled; the last layer must be of cheese, and sauce with which the macaroni is to be covered. Ten minutes will bake it in a quick oven. —Italian Receipt.

By the end of the nineteenth century, Italians had established themselves in many major America cities, among them Philadelphia. To introduce her non-Italian readers to macaroni, which she considered more exotic than the egg noodles of the Pennsylvania Dutch, cooking school teacher Sarah T. Rorer

wrote in *Mrs. Rorer's Philadelphia Cook Book* (1886): *Macaroni, as an article of food, is rather more valuable than bread, as it contains a large proportion of gluten. It is the bread of the Italian laborer. In this country, it is a sort of luxury among the upper classes; but there is no good reason, considering its price, why it should not enter more extensively into the food of our working classes.*

Still, macaroni didn't go mainstream right away. According to James Trager (*The Food Chronology,* 1995), "large-scale pasta production" began in the U.S. only in 1914 when World War I made it impossible to import supplies from Italy. Food historians point to the 1930s, specifically the Depression, as the great popularizer of macaroni (by now available in convenient "elbows") and cheese: Here was a dish that was easy, rib-sticking, and cheap. Recipes in Kraft cheese ads and fliers no doubt helped although macaroni and cheese recipes had been appearing in cookbooks from the late nineteenth century on.

The original *Boston Cooking-School Cook Book* by Fannie Merritt Farmer (1896) offers this recipe for Baked Macaroni with Cheese:

> Put a layer of boiled macaroni in buttered baking dish, sprinkle with grated cheese, repeat, pour over White Sauce, cover with buttered crumbs, and bake until crumbs are brown.

Four years later, in her chatty cookbook *I Go A-Marketing*, Henrietta ("Henriette") Sowle, includes a somewhat different version:

> The macaroni with cheese you know all about, I dare say. Is this your way of doing it? Break the macaroni into two-inch lengths and drop into boiling salted water. When it is quite tender, pour cold water over it, drain and stir about in plenty of melted butter—till each piece is well-covered, then put into a baking-dish, strew grated Parmesan cheese over it and let brown in a hot oven. Just a little bit of cayenne added to the cheese improves the flavor wonderfully, to my thinking.

The first edition of *The Settlement Cook Book* compiled in 1903 by Mrs. Simon Kander and Mrs. Henry Schoenfeld of Milwaukee leads off its chapter of "Entrées, Scalloped Dishes and Chafing Dishes" with Baked Noodles with Cheese. The recipe closely resembles Fannie Farmer's *Baked Macaroni with Cheese*—with one major difference. It calls for broad noodles instead of macaroni. This collection of recipes, unlike those in *The Boston Cooking-School Cook Book,* was aimed at recent immigrants from Germany and Middle Europe, who knew egg noodles but not Italian macaroni.

Who simplified the classic recipe for macaroni and cheese by adding the cheese to the sauce? Right through the 1950s, *Fannie Farmer* continues layering the macaroni and cheese as did the original volume; however cheese sauce variations began creeping in in the 1940s and 1950s. And in the Twelfth Edition revised by Marion Cunningham (1979), the only recipe given calls for cheese sauce.

Down the years *Joy of Cooking* has offered somewhat richer renditions—eggs to bind the macaroni instead of white sauce. There's even a version in which sour cream substitutes for sauce. But I find no macaroni and cheese made with cheese sauce.

James Beard's American Cookery (1972) offers two recipes for macaroni and cheese, neither one made with cheese sauce.

The first resembles the original Fannie Farmer recipe (macaroni, shredded cheese, and white sauce layered into a casserole, the lot topped with buttered crumbs).

The second recipe is nearer Mary Randolph's—nothing more than layers of butter-dotted macaroni and grated Cheddar. Mary Randolph doesn't call for a topping of buttered crumbs. James Beard makes it optional.

The earliest recipe I've found made with an honest-to-goodness cheese sauce (apparently a twentieth-century innovation) is this one from the *Larkin Housewives' Cook Book* (1915), published by the Larkin Co., Pure Food Specialists. They call it English Style Macaroni.

ENGLISH STYLE MACARONI

Cook one cup Larkin Short-Cut Macaroni in boiling salted water until tender [on the previous page, Larkin recommends boiling macaroni rapidly for twenty-five or thirty-five minutes!]. Rinse with cold water. Make a sauce by melting three tablespoons butter in a double-boiler. Add three tablespoons flour. When bubbling add one and one-half cups sweet milk. Stir constantly until thickened, add two-third cup grated cheese or four ounces cheese thinly sliced. Stir until melted. Add one-half teaspoon salt and a little pepper. Mix together sauce and Macaroni, reheat in kettle or put into baking dish and bake about twenty minutes until brown.

Larkin attributes this recipe to a Mrs. I.F. Knee of Omaha, Nebraska.

Fifteen years later, in 1930, the Good House-keeping Institute's *Meals Tested, Tasted and Approved:*

Favorite Recipes and Menus from Our Kitchens to Yours appeared with this fancier recipe. It, too, calls for cheese sauce but pumps up the flavor with layers of shredded cheese.

MACARONI AND CHEESE

1 1/2 cupfuls macaroni broken in pieces
3 tablespoonfuls butter or margarine

3 tablespoonfuls flour
1/2 teaspoonful salt
1/8 teaspoonful pepper
Dash paprika

1 1/2 cupfuls milk
1 1/2 cupfuls grated cheese
1/2 cupful buttered crumbs

Cook the macaroni as directed and drain. Melt fat in top of double-boiler, add flour and seasonings and blend thoroughly. Pour in milk and stir until thick and smooth. Cook for 5 minutes longer, then add 1 cup grated cheese and stir until all is melted. Put 1/2 of macaroni in greased baking dish, cover with 1/2 the sauce and 1/4 cup of grated cheese. Repeat, using remaining ingredients. Sprinkle buttered crumbs on top and bake in a moderate oven of 375° F. for 20 minutes or until well browned. Serves 6.

Few people, alas, bother to make macaroni and cheese from scratch these days. It's available canned, frozen, and of course as "instant dinners."

Kraft was the first to introduce an instant macaroni and cheese dinner. The year was 1937 and soon Kraft, during commercial breaks in the Kraft Music Hall radio program, was promising American cooks that a Kraft Dinner was "A meal for four in nine minutes for an everyday price of 19 cents."

In 1937 alone, eight million Kraft Dinners were sold, but their popularity soared tenfold during World War II because they were not only good meat substitutes but also required just one ration coupon. "Don't hurry, puff and wheeze," Kraft Dinner commercials now urged. "There's a main dish that's a breeze."

All women had to do was open the familiar blue box, cook and drain the noodles, then mix in the packet of dried cheese and watch it magically turn into sauce. Even today Kraft sells hundreds of millions of Kraft Dinners every year (or "Blue Boxes"), making them top supermarket sellers.

"Kraft Dinner is one of our all-time favorite comfort foods," Jane and Michael Stern admit in *Square Meals* (1984). When they heard that it might be phased out in favor of the Deluxe Kraft Dinner, the Sterns say, "The thought of life without macaroni and cheese à la Kraft was so intolerable that . . . we raided every supermarket in town, buying case lots to hoard in our basement."

The Sterns needn't have worried. The original Kraft Dinner lives.

Wait till you taste this macaroni-and-cheese! And I'll have it ready in a "jif"!

Lightened Up Macaroni and Cheese

Makes 6 Servings

❋

THIS RECIPE, adapted from one developed by L. Alyson Moreland, *Cooking Light* magazine's recipe editor, was printed in the March 1995 issue. It has been trimmed of much of its fat—calories and cholesterol, too. Per serving, it weighs in at 11.2 grams total fat (5.2 grams saturated), 63 milligrams cholesterol, and 356 calories. Yet it's as delicious as the old-fashioned "artery-clogging" macaroni and cheese we all grew up on.

   2 cups elbow macaroni, cooked and drained by package directions
   2 cups shredded reduced-fat sharp Cheddar cheese (about 8 ounces)
   1 cup 1 percent low-fat cottage cheese
   ¾ cup nonfat sour cream
   ½ cup skim milk
   2 tablespoons grated yellow onion
   4½ teaspoons reduced-calorie stick margarine, melted
   ½ teaspoon salt
   ¼ teaspoon black pepper
   1 egg, lightly beaten
   ¼ cup dry bread crumbs
   ¼ teaspoon paprika

1. Preheat oven to 350° F. Coat 2-quart casserole with nonstick cooking spray and set aside.

2. Mix macaroni, Cheddar and cottage cheeses, sour cream, milk, onion, 1½ teaspoons melted margarine, salt, pepper, and egg well and spoon into casserole.

3. Toss remaining 3 teaspoons melted margarine with bread crumbs and paprika and sprinkle over macaroni.

4. Cover, and bake 30 minutes; uncover, and bake 5 minutes more until set.

Campbell's Macaroni and Cheese

Makes 6 Servings

❋

A JIFFY macaroni and cheese that substitutes a couple of cans of condensed Cheddar cheese soup for a from-scratch cheese sauce. The recipe here is adapted from *Campbell's Best-Ever Recipes, 125th Anniversary Edition* (1994), the company whose motto is "Never Underestimate the Power of Soup."

   2 (10¾-ounce) cans condensed Cheddar cheese soup
   1 soup can milk
   2 teaspoons prepared mustard
   ¼ teaspoon black pepper
   4 cups hot cooked corkscrew pasta (about 3 cups uncooked)
   2 tablespoons dry bread crumbs mixed with 1 tablespoon melted butter or margarine

1. Preheat oven to 400° F. Lightly coat 2-quart casserole with nonstick cooking spray.

2. Mix cheese soup, milk, mustard, and pepper in casserole. Add pasta and toss gently but thoroughly. Top with bread crumb mixture.

3. Bake, uncovered, until bubbling—about 25 minutes. Serve as a main dish accompanied by a crisp green salad.

STOUFFER'S CLASSY MACARONI AND CHEESE

AFTER WORLD War II—with women demanding convenience foods and returned soldiers accustomed to GI rations—frozen foods rapidly gained acceptance in American homes. But the early "frosted" foods were packaged separately and simply. Combining meat and sauces or entrée and vegetables in one box was still almost a decade away. One of the earliest participants in the frozen entrée sweepstakes, along with Swanson, was Stouffer's.

Mahala Stouffer and her husband, Abraham, had started out in 1922 with a small Cleveland restaurant that became famous for its corned beef hash, baked beans, lasagne, and apple pie, all cooked by Mahala. Gradually she and Abraham opened branches in Detroit, Pittsburgh, Philadelphia, and New York, each time maintaining their standard of high-quality food at fair prices.

One of the restaurants, located near a subway stop, was so busy its manager decided to freeze the most demanded meals and sell them for home consumption. This led to the building of a frozen food factory and the introduction of twenty-five Red Box specialties, including macaroni and cheese and spinach soufflé. Despite stiff competition from the company's Lean Cuisine and Lunch Express lines, those two old Red Box favorites are still among Stouffer's best sellers.

Cheese Strata

Makes 6 Servings

✳

THIS RECIPE—buttered slices of bread layered into a casserole with grated Cheddar and topped with beaten eggs and milk—begins appearing under various aliases shortly after the turn of the century. Sarah Rorer (*Mrs. Rorer's New Cook Book,* 1902) calls it "Cheese Pudding." And *Good Housekeeping Everyday Cook Book* (1903) titles it "Escalloped Cheese." A few books even call it "Cheese Fondue." Being meatless, filling, and frugal, Cheese Strata was popular during World War I and the Depression. In fact, my mother served it often during World War II. This is her recipe.

> 6 slices firm-textured white
> bread
> ¼ cup (½ stick) butter or
> margarine (at room
> temperature)
> 3 cups coarsely shredded sharp
> Cheddar cheese
> 3 eggs
> 2½ cups milk
> 1 teaspoon prepared mustard
> 1 teaspoon salt
> ¼ teaspoon ground hot red
> pepper (cayenne)

1. Preheat oven to 325° F.

2. Spread each slice of bread with butter on one side, then quarter the slices. Layer bread and cheese alternately in ungreased 2- to 2½-quart casserole, beginning with bread and ending with cheese.

3. Whisk together eggs, milk, mustard, salt, and cayenne and pour evenly over bread mixture.

4. Bake, uncovered, until set like custard—40 to 45 minutes.

Spaghetti Sauce with Meatballs

Makes 1 Gallon

＊

IN THE beginning (around the turn of the century) Italian-American restaurants did not serve meatballs with their spaghetti. These were added to satisfy America's hunger for red meat. Of course there are dozens of variations on the theme. But the best, to my mind, is this make-ahead spaghetti sauce with meatballs cooked up by Sharon Bates, a recipe I featured in a 1992 *Family Circle* article. The judges at the Skowhegan State Fair in Maine agreed. They awarded Bates their top prize. She makes huge batches of spaghetti sauce with meatballs and keeps them in her freezer. Come dinnertime, all she has to do is heat the sauce and cook the spaghetti.

MEATBALLS
1¼ pounds lean ground beef
1 egg
¼ cup Italian-seasoned dry bread crumbs
½ teaspoon salt
⅛ teaspoon black pepper

SAUCE
¾ pound hot Italian sausage, thickly sliced
5 (14½-ounce) cans stewed tomatoes, with their juice
1 (15-ounce) can tomato puree
1 (6-ounce) can tomato paste
½ pound mushrooms, wiped clean and chopped
2 large ribs celery, chopped
¼ cup chopped green bell pepper
1 clove garlic, peeled and minced
1½ teaspoons Italian herb seasoning
1 teaspoon salt
½ teaspoon black pepper

1. MEATBALLS: Preheat oven to 375° F. Coat 15½ × 10½ × 1-inch jelly-roll pan with nonstick cooking spray; set aside.

2. Using hands, mix all meatball ingredients thoroughly. Shape into 1-inch balls, arrange on pan, and bake until uniformly brown—12 to 15 minutes.

3. SAUCE: Brown sausages in large heavy kettle over moderately high heat until most of drippings cook out—8 to 10 minutes; pour off drippings. Reduce heat to moderate, add meatballs and all sauce ingredients, and bring to boiling. Adjust heat so mixture bubbles gently, cover, and simmer very slowly 3 hours, stirring as needed to prevent sticking and using flame tamer, if necessary.

4. Cool mixture, ladle into freezer containers, date, label, and store in 0° F freezer.

TIMELINE

1934

Vitamin K is discovered.

Nabisco comes up with a round, buttery cracker so rich the only name that will do is Ritz.

Campbell's adds chicken-noodle and cream of mushroom to its line of canned soups.

Refrigerators are streamlined with the exterior compressor ("monitor top") buried inside the cabinet.

Girl Scout Troop 129 in Philadelphia bakes and sells cookies to raise funds for summer camp.

The Rainbow Room opens atop 30 Rockefeller Center in New York City.

MSG (monosodium glutamate) is manufactured in the U.S.

Fusilli with Sweet Red Pepper Sauce

Makes 4 to 6 Servings

✳

NOT EVERY red pasta sauce owes its color solely to tomatoes. Roasted red bell peppers redden and mellow this mix, which is my own invention.

NOTE: For how-tos on roasting peppers, see page 246.

SAUCE

3 tablespoons fruity olive oil
4 medium scallions, trimmed and thinly sliced (white part only)
2 cloves garlic, peeled and halved
¼ teaspoon dried leaf marjoram, crumbled
¼ teaspoon dried leaf rosemary, crumbled
3 large red bell peppers, roasted, peeled, stemmed, and seeded (see headnote), then patted dry
1 (8-ounce) can tomato sauce (not tomato paste)
½ teaspoon salt (or to taste)
¼ teaspoon black pepper (or to taste)

PASTA

1 pound fusilli (corkscrew pasta), cooked al dente *by package directions and drained well*
Freshly grated Parmesan cheese

1. SAUCE: Heat olive oil in small heavy skillet over moderate heat 1 minute. Add scallions and garlic and

stir-fry until limp—2 to 3 minutes. Turn heat to lowest point, add marjoram and rosemary, cover, and "sweat" 15 minutes; if mixture threatens to scorch, add 1 to 2 tablespoons water.

2. Scrape skillet mixture into electric blender cup or food processor fitted with metal chopping blade, add all remaining sauce ingredients, and puree until smooth. Transfer to medium saucepan, set over moderate heat and cook, stirring often, just until mixture steams—3 to 5 minutes. Taste for salt and pepper and adjust as needed.

3. PASTA: Mound hot pasta in large shallow bowl, ladle sauce on top, and toss well to mix. Serve with plenty of freshly grated Parmesan.

Liver-Mushroom Spaghetti Sauce

Makes 6 to 8 Servings

✳

THIS CARUSO-esque pasta sauce (see *Spaghetti alla Caruso* box, page 188) is adapted from the *Ladies' Home Journal Cook Book* (1960).

2 slices bacon
½ pound mushrooms, wiped clean and thinly sliced
1 medium yellow onion, peeled and chopped
1 clove garlic, peeled and minced
1 cup water (about)
½ (6-ounce) can tomato paste
1 cup canned crushed tomatoes

½ teaspoon dried leaf oregano,
   crumbled
¼ teaspoon dried leaf basil,
   crumbled
¼ teaspoon dried leaf thyme,
   crumbled
¾ teaspoon sugar
¾ teaspoon salt
¼ teaspoon black pepper
½ pound chicken livers,
   trimmed of membranes and
   diced
Freshly grated Parmesan cheese

1. Brown bacon in large heavy skillet over moderate heat 3 to 4 minutes; lift bacon with slotted spoon to paper towels to drain.

2. Stir-fry mushrooms, onion, and garlic in drippings over moderate heat until lightly browned—about 5 to 8 minutes.

3. Add water, tomato paste, tomatoes, oregano, basil, thyme, sugar, salt, and pepper. Bring to boiling, adjust heat so mixture bubbles gently, cover, and simmer very slowly until flavors meld—about 2 hours. Stir from time to time and if sauce thickens too fast, add a little extra water.

4. Crumble in bacon, add chicken livers, cover, and cook slowly 15 to 20 minutes more.

5. Ladle over hot spaghetti and accompany with freshly grated Parmesan.

WHEATIES:
BREAKFAST OF CHAMPIONS

CHILDREN WHO followed the radio adventures of Jack Armstrong, All-American Boy, in the 1930s are today's grandparents, and chances are they're still eating Wheaties.

Discovered by accident when an early dabbler in health food dropped a spoonful of gruel on a hot stove and liked the crispy result, Wheaties went on the market in 1924 but failed to excite consumers until General Mills hit on the novel idea of boosting sales with singing commercials, box-top premiums, and radio shows aimed at kids. So many boys and girls rushed to collect box tops for the Jack Armstrong "Hik-a-Meter" that from New York to California Wheaties virtually disappeared from grocery shelves.

The cereal's long and lucrative association with sports figures began in the '30s with endorsements from Johnny Weismuller, Babe Ruth, Jack Dempsey, and the exotic Maria Rasputin, wild animal trainer of Barnum & Bailey fame. More recent faces to grace the Wheaties box include gymnast Mary Lou Retton, tennis great Chris Evert, and basketball star Michael Jordan.

And then there was the young sportscaster from Des Moines who in 1937 won a Wheaties contest and received, as a prize, a trip to Los Angeles and a screen test. After years in the movies, he went into politics and became our fortieth president. His name? Ronald Reagan.

Spaghetti alla Caruso

HERE'S ANOTHER twentieth-century American classic about which there's little agreement. Whose idea was it to sauce pasta with chicken livers? There are three theories:

(1) That the recipe originated at Caruso, a small New York City Italian restaurant chain famous for its chicken and pasta. Chef Antonia Riconda's recipe is a basic mushroom-tomato sauce into which sautéed diced chicken livers are stirred just before serving. The recipe appears in Diana Ashley's *Where To Dine in '39*.

(2) That it was concocted by Enrico Caruso himself—despite the fact that he was said to loathe chicken livers. Carol Truax, a New York food writer

who edited the *Ladies' Home Journal Cook Book* (1960) and whom I got to know while working on that project, always claimed that one evening when her father, Judge Truax, was entertaining at his East Sixties town house, the great Neapolitan tenor marched into the kitchen, donned an apron, and whipped up a pasta sauce containing chicken livers.

(3) That the dish was named in honor of Enrico Caruso. Louis DeGouy, for years the chef at New York's Knickerbocker Hotel, claims the recipe as his own. Here it is, just as it appears in his *Gold Cook Book* (1947). Note that DeGouy's recipe contains no chicken livers.

SPAGHETTI ALLA CARUSO
(ORIGINAL RECIPE AS PREPARED BY THIS WRITER)

TOMATO paste is precious, invaluable. Buy some good Italian tomato paste if you would honor a party of chosen guests. With an authentic dish of spaghetti, but buy also 3 pounds of good lean beef, a veal knuckle, a slice of ham, some fat bacon and leeks, celery, carrots, parsley, chervil . . . and, of course, plenty of garlic. Thrifty Italians grow sweet basil in their gardens, on their kitchen windowsills; and you should get some of the fresh herb if you possibly can; otherwise, use a pinch of dried basil.

FRY 4 slices of diced bacon and ¼ pound lean ham in an iron skillet, then chop them and put them into a large stew pot. Dredge the beef lightly with powdered sugar, and sear it fiercely in the hot bacon fat, turning it over and over till it is nearly black and all crusty and glistening. Put it in the stew pot with the chopped ham and bacon, the well washed, split veal knuckle, 1 whole bunch of well cleaned and washed leeks, three stalks of celery, scraped and chopped, 2 carrots, scraped and chopped, 1 tablespoon each of parsley and chervil, also finely chopped, 2 large bay leaves, tied with 2 sprigs of thyme, 2 cloves of garlic, sliced thinly; but, if you have conscientious scruples, you may substitute 6 shallots. Season with a tablespoon of salt, 1 of black pepper, 4 whole cloves, and either the fresh or dried sweet basil, then pour in boiling water to cover; bring to a boil, and simmer 3 or 4 hours, or until the fiber of the meat is broken down and all its essence is in the sauce. Strain through a colander, pressing through all the soft pulp and leaving behind only the lumps and shreds. Add 1 cup of the tomato paste and ½ cup of Marsala, sherry, or Madeira wine.

NOW, take 1 medium truffle from a tin, wash and brush it, slice it thinly, and cut the slices into julienne strips. Peel ½ pound of fresh mushrooms, chop the stems and slice the caps thinly in transverse sections. Add of these to the sauce and simmer very gently, while the spaghetti is boiling.

USING a large kettle of salted boiling water, put in 2 packages of whole length spaghetti, without breaking. Twelve to 18 minutes is the time depending on the hardness of the paste. Italians—AND CARUSO WAS ONE *[Caps mine.—J.A.]*—when I prepared this dish of dishes in the kitchen of the ninth floor, at the old Knickerbocker Hotel, prefer it not too tender, not too soft; just *al dente*, that is, a little crackling, a little chewy; but some Americans like it as soft as boiled rice. While it boils, grate your cheese, rubbing the granite-like block of Parmesan furiously on a fine grater, till you have a mountain of light and feathery flakes. The dry and tasteless grated Parmesan that comes in bottles or cartons is an insult to spaghetti and to cheese. Incidentally, if Parmesan is a bit too much for you, in bouquet and tang, you may grate a little Swiss, Gruyère or old Cheddar along with it.

WHEN done, drain the spaghetti, then pile it on a huge platter, and pour the golden bronze sauce over it with luxurious abandon; be sure to make a small mountain of the cheese in the middle, and have an extra dish of cheese on the table. How does one eat it? Well, an Italian can turn the trick with elegance, by catching up the strands on a fork and twirling them into a neat bolus in the bowl of soup spoon. Try it.

Louis Diat's Spaghetti à la Caruso (*Cooking à la Ritz*, 1941) does contain diced chicken livers, also "4 or 6 diced artichoke bottoms." Otherwise, it's a robust, beef-gravy-based fresh mushroom-tomato sauce with plenty of onions (but no garlic).

There's a similar recipe in *The Longchamps Cookbook* (1954) by Max Winkler. The Spaghetti Longchamps sauce is a medley of fresh mushrooms, tomatoes, garlic, shallots, and butter-sautéed chicken livers, these last added just before serving. There's no stinting here on butter. This recipe for four contains nearly half a pound but, strangely, no olive oil.

Because Carol Truax maintained that Caruso created Spaghetti alla Caruso in her father's kitchen, I flipped through the *Ladies' Home Journal Cook Book*, which she edited.

There is no Spaghetti alla Caruso, but on page 492, I find something quite like it—Liver-Mushroom Spaghetti Sauce (see page 184).

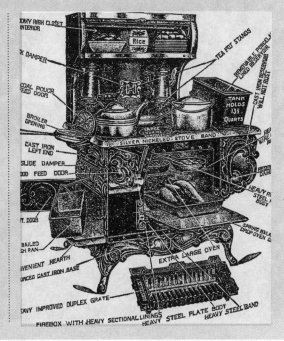

Turkey (or Chicken) Tetrazzini

Makes 8 Servings

❋

THERE'S PLENTY of speculation about this recipe but scanty documentation. What is known is that it was created early this century for the Italian coloratura soprano Luisa Tetrazzini, who made her American debut in 1908 at the Metropolitan Opera House in New York. Tetrazzini toured the U.S. from 1910 to 1913 and was a member of the Chicago Opera Company during the 1913–14 season. According to James Beard (*James Beard's American Cookery,* 1972), she of the "astounding girth and thrilling voice" loved San Francisco and that's where he believes the recipe was created. Beard's recipe is made with chicken although Louis DeGouy (*The Gold Cook Book,* 1947) says the original contained turkey. Barbara Haber, Curator of Books, The Schlesinger Library at Radcliffe College, traced Turkey Tetrazzini to a 1912 printing of *The Boston Cooking-School Cook Book.* Yet according to Barbara Kuck, director of the Culinary Archives and Museum at Johnson & Wales University, Providence, R.I., no Tetrazzini (turkey or otherwise) appears in *The Sunday American Cook Book,* an uncatalogued pamphlet of the singer's favorite recipes published in 1911 by *The American,* a Hearst newspaper in New York City. Ironically, the cover shows Madame Tetrazzini dipping into a steaming pot of pasta.

> 5 tablespoons butter
> 3 tablespoons flour
> 2 cups chicken broth
> 1 cup cream
> 2 tablespoons dry sherry or Madeira
> ¾ cup freshly grated Parmesan cheese
> ¼ teaspoon black pepper
> ¾ pound medium mushrooms, wiped clean and thinly sliced
> 3 medium scallions, trimmed and thinly sliced
> 1 pound spaghetti, cooked al dente *by package directions and drained well*
> ½ cup diced canned pimientos
> 4 cups diced cooked turkey or chicken

1. Preheat oven to 375° F. Lightly coat 13 × 9 × 2-inch baking dish with nonstick cooking spray and set aside.

2. Melt 3 tablespoons butter in medium heavy saucepan over moderate heat. Blend in flour, add broth, then cook, stirring constantly, until thickened and smooth—about 3 minutes. Mix in cream, sherry, ¼ cup Parmesan, and pepper. Cook and stir 2 minutes, then set off heat.

3. Melt remaining 2 tablespoons butter in large heavy skillet over

Luisa Tetrazzini

moderate heat. Add mushrooms and scallions and stir-fry until limp—about 3 minutes.

4. Toss spaghetti in large bowl with sauce, mushroom mixture, pimientos, and turkey. Transfer to prepared baking dish and scatter remaining 1/2 cup Parmesan evenly over all.

5. Bake, uncovered, until bubbling and brown—20 to 25 minutes.

Souper Chicken Tetrazzini

Makes 4 Servings

✳

CREDIT FOR popularizing chicken and turkey Tetrazzini must go to this shortcut version, which substitutes a can of cream of mushroom soup for sauce. The recipe here is adapted from *Campbell's Best-Ever Recipes, 125th Anniversary Edition* (1994).

1 (10¾-ounce) can condensed cream of mushroom soup
½ cup milk or evaporated skim milk
1 small yellow onion, peeled and chopped
¼ cup freshly grated Parmesan cheese
¼ cup sour cream
1½ cups diced cooked chicken or turkey
1 small zucchini, halved lengthwise and thinly sliced
1½ cups cooked spaghetti (3 ounces uncooked)

A Handy Index for Your Convenience

OTHER HELPFUL SUGGESTIONS IN THIS BOOK

1. Preheat oven to 375° F. Lightly coat 1½-quart casserole with non-stick cooking spray and set aside.

2. Mix mushroom soup, milk, onion, Parmesan, and sour cream in large bowl. Mix in chicken and zucchini. Add spaghetti and toss gently.

3. Turn into casserole and bake, uncovered, until bubbly and tipped with brown—about 30 minutes.

4. Serve at once, accompanied with additional grated Parmesan.

Spinach Fettuccine with Fresh Tomatoes and Basil

Makes 4 Servings

✳

IN THE 1980s, pasta became available in rainbow colors: red (tomato), hot pink (beet), yellow (pumpkin, carrot, or saffron), brown (buck-

wheat), black (squid ink). Most of these have faded from view, but the green (spinach) pasta is more popular than ever. This is my favorite summer meal. I sometimes substitute fresh arugula for basil, doubling the amount and cutting the leaves into thin strips instead of chopping. Try it.

1 pound green fettuccine, cooked al dente *by package directions and drained well*
4 large vine-ripe tomatoes, cored, seeded, and diced but not peeled
½ cup coarsely chopped fresh basil
1 clove garlic, peeled and minced
2 tablespoons fruity olive oil
½ teaspoon salt (or to taste)
¼ teaspoon black pepper (or to taste)
Freshly grated Parmesan cheese

1. Place still-warm fettuccine in large shallow bowl.

2. Mix tomatoes, basil, garlic, olive oil, salt, and pepper in medium bowl; taste for salt and pepper and adjust as needed. Pour over fettuccine and toss gently to mix.

3. Serve at once, accompanied by a bowl of Parmesan so everyone can help himself.

Michael McLaughlin's Stuffed Shells Baked in Jalapeño Tomato Sauce

Makes 4 Servings

✳

OUR LOVE of stuffing things— tomatoes, green or red bell peppers, onions, squash—predates Fannie Farmer. Yet only recently did we discover giant pasta shells just begging to be stuffed. In a move that also illustrates the '80s trend toward cross-cultural cooking, chef/food writer Michael McLaughlin puts the heat of the Southwest in a fairly classic Italian pasta sauce. The recipe here is adapted from *The Best of Food & Wine, 1988 Collection.*

SAUCE

3 tablespoons fruity olive oil
1 large yellow onion, peeled and chopped
4 cloves garlic, peeled and minced
1 fresh jalapeño pepper, cored, seeded, and minced
1 (28-ounce) can Italian tomatoes, crushed, with their juice

FILLING

1 pound mild goat cheese (at room temperature)
½ pound ricotta cheese (at room temperature)
1 (10-ounce) package frozen chopped spinach, thawed, drained, and squeezed dry
½ cup heavy cream
1 egg
2 cups tightly packed fresh basil leaves, minced
¼ cup freshly grated Parmesan cheese
¼ teaspoon black pepper

SHELLS

½ pound large pasta shells, cooked al dente *by package directions and drained well*

TOPPING

2 tablespoons fresh bread crumbs mixed with 2 tablespoons freshly grated Parmesan cheese

1. SAUCE: Heat olive oil in medium heavy saucepan over moderate heat 1 minute. Add onion, garlic, and jalapeño, reduce heat to low, cover, and cook until soft—about 15 minutes.

2. Add tomatoes and their juice, bring to boiling, adjust heat so sauce bubbles gently, set lid on askew, and

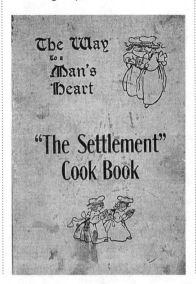

simmer, stirring occasionally, until flavors meld—about 30 minutes. Remove lid and continue simmering until slightly thickened—about 30 minutes more.

3. FILLING: Mix all ingredients and set aside.

4. Slide top oven rack into upper third of oven; preheat oven to 400° F.

5. SHELLS: Spoon 1 heaping tablespoon filling into each pasta shell. Spread 1 cup sauce over bottom of ungreased 11¾ × 7½ × 1¾-inch baking dish, then arrange shells, filling-side-up, in rows in sauce. Cover with remaining sauce and scatter TOPPING evenly over all.

6. Bake on top oven rack until browned—about 40 minutes.

7. Cool 10 minutes and serve.

Savory Orzo-Stuffed Zucchini Boats

Makes 6 Servings

✳

IN THE '80s, we not only discovered that pasta came in rainbow colors but also in shapes we'd never heard of. Orzo, for example, are seed-shaped pasta no bigger than grains of rice. And like rice, they're perfect for stuffing vegetables. This recipe, a hit from the makers of Hellmann's and Best Foods mayonnaise, is adapted from *Over 100 Ways to Bring out the Best* (1990), published by the Best Foods division of CPC International, Inc. It can be made with "real" (old-fashioned) mayonnaise, "light," or "low-fat" mayonnaise dressing. These zucchini boats are not baked but served cold.

> 3 large zucchini
> 1/3 cup mayonnaise
> 1/4 cup milk
> 1 tablespoon Dijon mustard
> 1 tablespoon fresh lemon juice
> 1/4 teaspoon salt
> 1/4 teaspoon black pepper
> 1/2 pound cooked ham, cut into small matchstick strips
> 1/4 pound Jarlsberg cheese, cut into small matchstick strips
> 2 cups well-washed, coarsely chopped raw spinach leaves
> 2/3 cup orzo, cooked al dente by package directions and drained well
> 1/4 cup minced scallions

1. Halve zucchini lengthwise, scoop out pulp, leaving shells 1/4-inch thick; discard pulp.

2. Parboil zucchini shells in boiling water just until crisp-tender—2 to 3 minutes. Drain upside-down on paper towels.

3. Blend mayonnaise with milk, mustard, lemon juice, salt, and pepper in large bowl. Add ham, cheese, spinach, orzo, and scallions and toss well to mix.

4. Mound into zucchini shells and serve.

PASTA PRIMAVERA

F EW PEOPLE, I think, would disagree that this is America's grandest contribution to the pasta repertoire. And as often happens with truly great recipes, it came about quite by chance. In the late '70s. Here's what Ella Elvin, former food editor of New York's *Daily News,* had to say about it in the February 1, 1978 paper:

Pasta Primavera is a specialty at Le Cirque at 58 E. 65th St. Sirio Maccioni, co-owner, says it came onto his menu rather obliquely. He and friends had once had a few fun days of cooking wild boar and lobster in Canada, when his wife served pasta with briefly cooked fresh vegetables. "It's something we do a lot in Italy," says Sirio, "but on this occasion it tasted spectacularly good to everyone, and we then tried it as an item for friends here at the restaurant. When Paul Bocuse came, we suggested it as an appetizer and he said: 'I want it as the main course.' It's a matter of using fresh vegetables that are in season. Heat olive oil with a touch of garlic and sauté the mushrooms first with the pignoli nuts, add broccoli that has been chopped and dipped briefly in boiling water. Heat but don't cook.

"When it comes to a boil, remove from heat. Sauté the chopped tomatoes separately with a bit of garlic, heat, don't cook." The cooked pasta is tossed with creamy mascarpone cheese and grated Parmesan.

"We don't use cream," says Sirio. "If you can't get mascarpone, use ricotta."

The pasta is topped with spoonfuls of both vegetable sautés and pepper is ground over the top. It is a juicy, delectable saucing of fine spaghetti, not the least bit heavy. Sirio agreed that you don't completely drain the spaghetti.

Pasta Primavera was a breakthrough recipe, the dish that taught us there are better ways to dress spaghetti than with a gloppy red sauce.

Le Cirque's Spaghetti Primavera

Makes 4 Servings

✻

LE CIRQUE'S Pasta Primavera varies according to the season, even the chef's whim. Former *New York Times* Food Editor Craig Claiborne and his associate, Pierre Franey, include the recipe in *Craig Claiborne's Favorites from The New York Times, Volume Four* (1978) from which this recipe is adapted. In the headnote, Claiborne writes: "The dish as served in the restaurant is the collaboration of Jean Vergnes, the French owner-chef, and Sirio Maccioni, his elegant Italian co-owner and the majordomo of the dining room." The two drove out to Claiborne's kitchen in East Hampton to demonstrate the making of their famous dish.

NOTE: Although Maccioni tells the *Daily News (see Box, page 191)* that he uses no cream in his Primavera, he calls for it in the *Times* version.

1 medium bunch broccoli, trimmed and divided into small florets
1½ cups matchstick strips unpeeled zucchini (about 2 small)
4 (5-inch) asparagus spears, cut in thirds
1½ cups 1-inch lengths green beans
½ cup fresh or frozen green peas
¾ cup fresh or frozen snow pea pods (optional)
1 tablespoon peanut or vegetable oil
2 cups thinly sliced mushrooms
1 teaspoon minced red or green chili pepper
¼ cup minced fresh parsley
6 tablespoons olive oil
1 teaspoon minced garlic
3 cups 1-inch cubes vine-ripe tomatoes
¼ cup minced fresh basil
¼ cup (½ stick) butter
2 tablespoons chicken broth
½ cup heavy cream (about)
⅔ cup freshly grated Parmesan cheese
1 pound spaghetti or spaghettini cooked al dente *and drained*
Salt to taste
Black pepper to taste
⅓ cup pignoli (pine nuts)

1. Cook broccoli, zucchini, asparagus, and green beans one by one in same large heavy kettle of boiling salted water, allowing 5 minutes for each. Also blanch green peas and, if desired, pea pods 30 seconds in same kettle. Drain vegetables and quick-chill in ice water; drain well again and place in large mixing bowl; toss lightly and set aside.

2. Heat peanut oil 1 minute in large heavy skillet over moderate heat. Add mushrooms and stir-fry 2 minutes, shaking skillet; add to bowl of vegetables along with chili pepper and parsley.

3. Heat 3 tablespoons olive oil in large heavy saucepan over moderate heat 1 minute. Add half the garlic and all the tomatoes and cook, stirring gently, until hot—3 to 4 minutes. Mix in basil and set off heat.

4. Heat remaining 3 tablespoons olive oil in large heavy skillet over moderate heat 1 minute, add remaining garlic and reserved vegetable mixture and cook, stirring carefully, just until hot—2 to 3 minutes.

5. Melt butter in large heavy kettle over moderately low heat. Add chicken broth, cream, and Parmesan. Cook, stirring gently, until smooth.

6. Add spaghetti and toss quickly to coat. Add half the vegetable mixture and drain liquid from tomatoes into kettle; toss gently. Add remaining vegetable mixture and if sauce seems thick, add a little extra cream—but not enough to make things soupy. Season to taste with salt and black pepper, add *pignoli*, and toss just enough to mix.

7. Divide among four large heated plates, top each portion with basil-tomato mixture, and serve.

PUFFED RICE/PUFFED WHEAT:
OUT OF THE CANNON'S MOUTH

T THE St. Louis World's Fair in 1904, gawkers crowded around the Quaker Oats Company booth to see a battery of Spanish-American War cannons loaded with rice, then fired. With each thunderous explosion, hundreds of snow-white rice puffs sailed through the air like a storm of popcorn. As promotion for a new kind of cereal, it was expensive but enormously impressive.

Quaker's method of "exploding" rice kernels (which did not in fact require cannons) had been hit upon accidentally by Alexander Pierce Anderson, a botanist researching starches. Seeing the possible commercial value of "puffed" cereal, Quaker set Anderson up in a secret lab to continue his experiments and hired an engineer to perfect a gun that could puff grains in quantity.

By 1909 the company began selling puffed rice and wheat as cereal "shot from guns." When Anderson's patent expired in 1929, other companies started selling puffed cereal, and Quaker had to think up new advertising gimmicks. Celebrity endorsements (from Shirley Temple, Babe Ruth, and Bing Crosby) kept sales high during the '30s and '40s.

Then in the '50s one adman caused a near disaster with a scheme to give away 21 million "deeds" to one-inch-square parcels of land in the Yukon—the setting for a company-sponsored TV series. On discovering the deeds tucked in their cereal boxes, thousands of excited customers wanted to know (by phone) the exact location of their land and its precise value. A few attempted to collect enough one-inch squares to make an acre!

He Invented the Foods
Shot from Guns

You owe these puffed foods, and all your delight in them, to Prof. A. P. Anderson.

He was seeking a way to break up starch granules so the digestive juices could get to them.

He was aiming to blast the starch granules to pieces by an explosion of steam.

When he did this, he found that he had created the most enticing cereal foods in existence.

Note the curious process

The whole wheat or rice kernels are put into sealed guns. Then these guns are revolved, for forty minutes, in a heat of 550 degrees.

This terrific heat turns the moisture in the grain to steam, and the pressure becomes tremendous.

Then the guns are fired. Instantly the steam explodes every granule into myriads of particles.

The kernel of grain is expanded eight times. It becomes four times as porous as bread.

Yet the wheat or rice berry remains shaped as before. We have simply the magnified grain.

Puffed Wheat, 10c—Puffed Rice, 15c

There was never a cereal food half so delicious. Never one more digestible.

Think of unbroken wheat or rice berries puffed to eight times their size.

They are so porous that they melt in the mouth. Yet they are crisp.

Let the Children Know

Get one package of the Quaker Puffed Rice, and one of the Quaker Puffed Wheat.

Get both, because they differ vastly. Let the children decide what they want.

Don't wait till tomorrow — order them now. For you are missing a food that's better than any you know.

Exact Size of Grains After Being Puffed

Made only by The Quaker Oats Company

MINUTE RICE

O NE DAY in 1941 a stranger approached a General Foods executive with a pot, a hotplate, and a packet of rice, claiming he could cook the rice in ten minutes. Greatly impressed with the on-the-spot demonstration, and perhaps also with the stranger's credentials (he was Ataullah K. Oazi Durrani, a cousin of the King of Afghanistan), the executive rushed him to a lab to perfect his method of precooking and quick-drying rice in large quantities.

While experiments were under way, America went to war and the U.S. government commandeered General Foods' test facilities in

hopes of creating an "instant" rice for C-rations. This arrangement, which provided General Foods with the U.S. Armed Forces as a captive test market, was mutually beneficial.

In 1949, Minute Rice appeared in grocery stores, its arrival trumpeted by ads, the crowning of an International Rice Queen, and newspaper features with how-to recipes contrasting the "easy, quick, and sure-

to-be wonderful" Minute Rice with the unpredictable long-cooking variety. So successful was this campaign that for a quarter of a century only die-hards insisted on cooking rice the old-fashioned way.

And now for the health-conscious, there is even Minute Brown Rice.

Spanish Rice

Makes 6 to 8 Servings

❋

S PANISH OMELETS appear in plenty of cookbooks before the twentieth century, but not, as far as I can see, Spanish rice. I first find it in *Mrs. Rorer's New Cook Book* (1902) in a section devoted to Jewish dishes. But this recipe calls for stewing a chicken "in pot with just enough water to keep it from burning," then seasoning "highly with onion, red pepper, and salt." About halfway through Mrs. Rorer adds "a can of tomatoes," then an hour later, "a cup of rice," and just before serving, "a bunch of parsley, chopped fine." A recipe much nearer our idea of Spanish Rice shows up a year later in *Marion Harland's Complete Cook Book* (1903). "Very nice," Harland comments, then tells her readers how to assemble this casserole of cooked rice, salt pork, green pepper, and tomato sauce. She adds a topper of fine crumbs, then shoves it into the oven. By the '30s Spanish Rice was a fairly common side dish. But the nearly meatless years of World War II gave it its biggest boost and elevated it to main-dish status. This is my mother's 1940s recipe with a few of my innovations.

4 strips bacon, snipped
  crosswise into julienne strips
1 small yellow onion, peeled
  and chopped
1/2 cup minced green bell pepper
1/2 teaspoon dried leaf basil,
  crumbled

3 cups cooked long-grain rice
2 cups canned crushed tomatoes
1 tablespoon light brown sugar
1 teaspoon salt
¼ teaspoon black pepper

1. Preheat oven to 350° F. Lightly coat 2-quart casserole with nonstick cooking spray and set aside.

2. Fry bacon in large heavy skillet over moderately high heat until fat cooks out and only crisp brown bits remain; with slotted spoon, transfer to paper towels to drain.

3. Stir-fry onion and green pepper in bacon drippings over moderate heat until limp and golden—3 to 5 minutes. Mix in basil and mellow over low heat 1 to 2 minutes.

4. Mix in rice, tomatoes, brown sugar, salt, pepper, and bacon, then spoon into casserole.

5. Bake, uncovered, until bubbly—about 30 minutes.

Tex-Mex Rice

Makes 6 Servings

✳

AN EASY recipe that has been popular with Texans of Mexican descent since the first decades of this century. It does not stint on garlic or cumin. Serve with roast pork or chicken as a potato substitute.

2 tablespoons vegetable oil
1 small yellow onion, peeled and chopped

½ cup minced green bell pepper
1 clove garlic, peeled and minced
1 cup long-grain rice
1 (8-ounce) can tomato sauce
1¾ cups water
¼ teaspoon crushed cumin seeds
½ teaspoon salt
¼ teaspoon black pepper

1. Heat oil in large heavy saucepan over moderate heat 1 minute. Add onion, green pepper, garlic, and rice and stir-fry until onion and pepper are limp—about 5 minutes.

2. Mix in tomato sauce, water, cumin seeds, salt, and black pepper and bring to boiling.

3. Adjust heat so mixture bubbles lazily, cover, and simmer until rice is tender and all liquid absorbed—25 to 30 minutes. Dish up and serve.

Green Rice Casserole

Makes 8 Servings

✳

THERE'S A Green Rice Pudding—actually a sort of soufflé—in *My Better Homes & Gardens Cook Book* (1939), the green supplied by a cup of minced parsley. Broccoli and peas do the job in this somehat similar recipe adapted from the July 1995 issue of *Southern Living*. With two kinds of cheese, it's hearty enough to be a main dish.

1¼ cups coarsely shredded Monterey Jack cheese
1 cup ricotta cheese
1 cup mayonnaise (can use low-fat)
1 clove garlic, peeled and crushed
¼ teaspoon black pepper
3 cups cooked long-grain rice
1 (10-ounce) package frozen chopped broccoli, thawed and drained well
1 cup frozen green peas, thawed
¼ cup thinly sliced scallions

1. Preheat oven to 375° F. Lightly coat 2-quart casserole with nonstick cooking spray and set aside.

2. Mix 1 cup Monterey Jack with ricotta, mayonnaise, garlic, and pepper in large bowl. Add rice, broccoli, peas, and scallions and mix well.

3. Turn into casserole and bake, uncovered, 20 minutes.

4. Scatter remaining ¼ cup Monterey Jack on top and continue baking until cheese melts—about 5 minutes.

5. Dish up and serve.

Brown Rice, Mushrooms, and Scallions

Makes 6 Servings

✳

TO MY great surprise, brown rice shows up in *Good Housekeeping's Book of Menus, Recipes and Household Discoveries* (1922), baked *en casserole* with milk, eggs, and gobs of grated cheese. It surfaces again—paired less winningly this time with sardines and curry powder—in *Good Housekeeping's Meals, Tested, Tasted, and Approved* (1930). Still, brown rice didn't go big time until the '60s and '70s counterculture made vegetarianism fashionable. Once the province of health food stores, brown rice can now be found on every supermarket shelf. The newest arrival: quick-cooking brown rice. The recipe here and the one that follows are adapted from ones developed by USA Rice Federation in Houston, Texas. Serve as an accompaniment to meat, fish, or fowl.

1 cup brown rice
2½ cups beef broth
1 tablespoon butter or
*   margarine*
2 tablespoons fruity olive oil
½ pound mushrooms, wiped
*   clean and thinly sliced*
4 medium scallions, trimmed
*   and thinly sliced (include*
*   tops)*
¼ teaspoon salt (or to taste)
¼ teaspoon black pepper (or to
*   taste)*

1. Bring rice, broth, and butter to boiling in large heavy saucepan over high heat. Adjust heat so broth bubbles gently, cover, and simmer until rice is tender and broth absorbed—45 to 50 minutes. Fluff with fork and keep warm.

2. Heat olive oil in large heavy skillet over moderate heat 1 minute. Add mushrooms and scallions and stir-fry until golden—about 5 minutes.

3. Add rice, salt, and pepper and toss gently but thoroughly. Taste for salt and pepper, adjust as needed.

Vegetable-Brown Rice Pancakes

Makes 6 Servings

✳

YOU MIGHT call these pancakes created by USA Rice Federation "vegetarian burgers." Top with yogurt or sour cream.

1 cup brown rice
2½ cups water
1 tablespoon butter or
*   margarine*
1½ teaspoons salt
2 medium carrots, peeled and
*   finely grated*
1 small yellow onion, peeled
*   and finely chopped*
1 clove garlic, peeled and
*   minced*
¼ teaspoon black pepper
2 eggs, lightly beaten
½ cup unsifted whole-wheat or
*   all-purpose flour*
¼ cup minced fresh parsley
¼ cup vegetable oil

1. Bring rice, water, butter, and salt to boiling in large heavy saucepan over high heat. Adjust heat so water bubbles gently, cover, and simmer until rice is tender and water absorbed—45 to 50 minutes. Fluff with fork.

2. Dump rice into large bowl, add carrots, onion, garlic, pepper, eggs, flour, and parsley and mix well. Shape into 12 thin patties of equal size, pressing firmly to compact.

196

3. Heat oil in large heavy skillet over moderately high heat until ripples appear on skillet bottom—1 to 1½ minutes.

4. Brown patties in oil in two batches, allowing about 2 minutes per side. Drain on paper towels and serve hot.

Wild Rice and Carrot Bake

Makes 6 Servings

❋

I DEVELOPED this recipe in the 1960s and still serve it often. It's delicious with roast game, game birds, pork, turkey, or chicken and can even become the main course of a light lunch or supper.

NOTE: A Chippewa Indian, a member of a family of wild rice gatherers, taught me this way of cooking it and it has never failed me.

1½ cups wild rice, well washed
2½ cups cold water
2 teaspoons salt
4 slices bacon, snipped crosswise into julienne strips
1 large yellow onion, peeled and coarsely chopped
¼ pound medium mushrooms, wiped clean and thinly sliced
2 medium carrots, peeled and finely grated
½ cup light cream
1 egg, lightly beaten

1. Bring wild rice, water, and salt to boiling in large heavy saucepan over moderately high heat, then boil, uncovered, vigorously, 10 minutes. Set off heat, cover, and let stand until rice absorbs water—about 20 minutes.

2. Preheat oven to 325° F. Lightly butter 6-cup casserole and set aside.

3. Brown bacon in large heavy skillet over moderate heat until crisp—3 to 5 minutes. Lift bacon to paper towels to drain.

4. Stir-fry onion, mushrooms, and carrots in bacon drippings until limp and golden—about 5 minutes. Add reserved bacon and wild rice and toss gently but thoroughly to mix.

5. Mix cream and egg in small bowl; fold into wild rice mixture.

6. Turn into casserole, cover, and bake 30 minutes. Remove cover, fork up mixture, then bake, uncovered, 30 minutes, forking again at halftime. Dish up and serve.

TIMELINE

1935

First issue of *Yankee* magazine appears.

"The Jolly Green Giant," Chicago adman Leo Burnett's reincarnation of the dour 1925 original, begins appearing on canned food labels.

Margaret Rudkin of Fairfield, Connecticut, develops a sturdy, additive-free, whole-grain bread for her asthmatic son—the first Pepperidge Farm loaf.

1936

Clementine Paddleford, one of America's most beloved food writers, begins a column for *The New York Herald Tribune*.

Corning rolls out Pyrex Flameware skillets and saucepans (with detachable wire handles) that can be set directly on gas burners.

Duncan Hines's *Adventures in Good Eating* is published. Later editions become the unofficial guides to America's best restaurants, and millions of copies are sold. Before long, the very name "Duncan Hines" is synonymous with "quality."

Marie Simmons's Wild Rice with Grapes, Raisins, and Toasted Almonds

Makes 4 to 6 Servings

✳

MARIE SIMMONS, a New York food writer for whom I have both affection and respect, wrote a wonderful book called *Rice, The Amazing Grain* (1991). This easy skillet recipe is adapted from that book. It is, according to Simmons, "a great side dish with roasted chicken, broiled duck breasts, or roast beef. It is easy to make but sophisticated enough for a special dinner." Quite so.

NOTE: The Simmons method of cooking wild rice differs from mine but is equally good.

1 cup wild rice, rinsed in
*   warm water and drained*
3 cups chicken broth
¼ cup sliced unblanched
*   almonds*
2 tablespoons butter
2 tablespoons fruity olive oil

Wild Rice

ALTHOUGH THIS aquatic grass was well known early on in some quarters—to the Native Americans who harvested it, to those living in Wisconsin and Minnesota where it grew, to the wealthy who could afford it—wild rice was hardly a "marquee name" to the rest of America until after World War II.

My search through late-nineteenth- and early-twentieth-century cookbooks turned up no mention of wild rice before the 1930s. Strangely, I discovered the first recipe for it in the *Watkins Cook Book* (1938), a ring-binder of recipes published by the J.R. Watkins Company, whose door-to-door salesmen fanned out across the country selling everything from extracts and flavorings to aftershave lotions and antiseptics. The much-spattered volume in my possession belonged to my Aunt Florence, who lived on a farm in central Illinois from the '20s through the '50s. A meat-and-potatoes kind of cook, I doubt that Aunt Florence ever washed and cooked wild rice as Watkins directed. The pristine nature of the page tends to corroborate that.

WILD RICE

2 cups wild rice   1 teaspoon salt
2 cups cold water

Wash rice in several waters, mix equal amount of rice and water, soak all day. Cook 1 hour in double boiler, cover. Rice should be dry, serve hot.

Perhaps the "soak all day" turned Aunt Florence off. *My Better Homes & Gardens Cook Book* (1939) calls only for washing wild rice, then boiling in salted water without stirring "20 minutes or until very tender." Once the wild rice is drained, *Better Homes* suggests fluffing it "over very low heat 10 to 15 minutes." A perfectly good way to cook wild rice.

This book also offers a recipe for wild rice baked with chopped green bell pepper, celery, and onions—plus plenty of butter. The recipe sounds good.

In *The Philadelphia Cook Book* (1940), Anna Wetherill Reed mixes butter-sautéed mushrooms and green bell pepper or chicken livers into boiled wild rice just before serving. But her method of cooking wild rice is alone enough to discourage most cooks.

> Wash rice in cold water. Cover with boiling water and let stand 20 minutes. Drain. Repeat 4 times using fresh boiling water each time and adding salt last time. Drain, season, and serve.

Reed then redeems herself with this simpler method:

> Wash rice in cold water and drain. Put on to boil in cold water using about 5 cups water to ¾ cup rice, adding 1 teaspoon salt. Let boil for exactly 25 minutes watching it carefully. The exact time is the whole secret of the cooking. Do not stir or disturb the rice in any way while boiling. Take from fire and drain thoroughly in a wire strainer. Set in a warm place on back of range to dry out.

Reed next offers a recipe for Wild Rice Croquettes that requires the rice to be soaked overnight, then boiled 25 minutes. The croquettes are bound with egg yolks and cream sauce, breaded, fried "in very hot deep fat," then served "with currant jelly on each croquette."

By the 1940s, wild rice was familiar enough to appear in *The Good Housekeeping Cook Book* (1942), which introduces readers to it with this brief paragraph:

Wild rice is the seed of a shallow water grass. The grains are long, spindly and grayish in color and require a special method of cooking. It is more expensive than white or brown rice, and is especially good with game.

This cookbook gives two recipes for wild rice: boiling in water and baking in canned condensed consommé in the company of butter-browned mushrooms.

Wild rice makes the 1943 edition of *The Joy of Cooking* (Wild Rice Ring [with garlic and onions], Browned Wild Rice with Mushrooms, and Wild Rice Dressing for Game [with giblets, chopped onion, celery, and green bell pepper]).

From the '50s onward, wild rice appears in ever more imaginative ways. And today, wild rice is a supermarket staple. It still grows wild in the Great Lakes region, but since the 1960s (thanks, in part, to Uncle Ben's–driven research), wild rice has been cultivated in Minnesota and California, which brings the price down within reason.

Then, too, there are rice/wild rice blends that don't cost the earth.

½ cup chopped red onion
1½ cups small seedless red grapes, stemmed and rinsed
½ cup dried currants
¼ teaspoon salt (or to taste)
¼ teaspoon black pepper (or to taste)

1. Bring wild rice and broth to boiling in large heavy saucepan over moderately high heat. Adjust heat so broth bubbles gently, cover, and simmer until rice is tender—about 45 minutes. Set off heat and let stand until rice absorbs all broth—15 to 20 minutes.

2. Heat large heavy skillet over moderate heat about 1 minute—no fat needed. Add almonds and toast, shaking skillet constantly, until pale tan—2 to 3 minutes; transfer to small bowl and reserve.

3. Melt butter in skillet with olive oil, add onion and stir-fry until limp—about 3 minutes. Add grapes and currants and cook, stirring gently, until coated with butter. Add wild rice, salt, and pepper, tossing gently, and bring just to serving temperature.

4. Taste for salt and pepper and adjust as needed. Scatter with toasted almonds and serve.

Baked Grits and Cheese

Makes 6 to 8 Servings

✳

FEW NON-SOUTHERNERS can understand the Southern passion for grits. This recipe will help to explain why they love grits so much.

1 quart milk
½ cup (1 stick) butter or margarine
1 teaspoon salt
⅛ teaspoon black pepper
1 cup hominy grits (not instant)
⅓ cup melted butter or margarine
¼ cup freshly grated Parmesan cheese
1 cup shredded sharp Cheddar cheese
½ teaspoon paprika

1. Generously coat 9 × 9 × 2-inch baking dish with nonstick cooking spray and set aside.

2. Bring milk, ½ cup butter, salt, and pepper to boiling in large heavy saucepan over moderate heat.

3. Reduce heat to moderately low, then gradually whisk in grits. Continue whisking until thick. Remove from heat and beat at highest electric mixer speed 3 to 4 minutes.

4. Pour grits into baking dish and chill until hard—3 to 4 hours. With knife dipped in warm water, cut grits into strips ½-inch wide, then quarter each strip so you have four domino-shaped pieces.

5. Wash baking dish and recoat with nonstick cooking spray. Preheat oven to 350° F.

6. Stand grits "dominoes" on end but slightly tilted in snug rows in baking dish. Drizzle with melted butter, then sprinkle with Parmesan and Cheddar. Blush with paprika.

7. Bake, uncovered, until bubbly and tipped with brown—about 45 minutes. Serve as a potato substitute.

Garlicky Cheese Grits

Makes 6 Servings

✳

ANOTHER IMMENSELY popular way to prepare grits down South that came into vogue about the time garlic cheese, a soft Cheddar-type packaged in chunky links, went on sale—shortly after World War II, if memory serves. This recipe uses modern quick-cooking grits instead of the old-fashioned kind. Although some people serve these grits as a side dish, I like to make a meal of them—but only once in a great while because they're loaded with saturated fat, calories, and cholesterol.

3 cups water
2 cups milk
1 teaspoon salt
1¼ cups quick-cooking grits
1 clove garlic, peeled and finely minced
½ cup (1 stick) butter
1 (6-ounce) roll garlic cheese, diced
¾ pound mild Cheddar cheese, coarsely shredded
2 teaspoons Worcestershire sauce
½ teaspoon ground hot red pepper (cayenne)

1. Bring water, milk, and salt to boiling in large heavy saucepan over moderate heat.

2. Add grits slowly, beating all the while, then add garlic and cook, stirring, until thick and creamy—3 to 5 minutes.

3. Turn heat to lowest point, add butter, garlic cheese, Cheddar, Worcestershire sauce, and cayenne and stir just until cheeses have melted.

4. Dish up and serve accompanied by a salad of tartly dressed greens.

Vegetable-Bulgur Pilaf

Makes 4 Servings

✳

THUMB THROUGH nineteenth-century American cookbooks and you will find pilafs, even "Turkish Pilafs." All are made with rice, an important crop in the Carolina Lowcountry until the Civil War. Pilafs made with other grains—this bulgur one, for example, and the barley one that follows (see page 202), are twentieth-century innovations. At least in this country. Serve with roast beef, lamb, or pork.

2 tablespoons fruity olive oil
1 medium yellow onion, peeled and chopped
1 large carrot, peeled and finely chopped
¼ teaspoon dried leaf thyme, crumbled
⅛ teaspoon ground coriander
1 cup bulgur
1¾ cups beef or chicken broth
½ teaspoon salt (or to taste)
¼ teaspoon black pepper (or to taste)

1. Heat olive oil in large skillet over moderate heat 1 minute. Add onion and carrot and stir-fry until lightly browned—8 to 10 minutes. Add thyme and coriander and mellow 1 to 2 minutes.

2. Add bulgur and stir-fry just until grains are golden and begin to look translucent—2 to 3 minutes.

3. Add broth, salt, and pepper, bring to boiling, adjust heat so broth bubbles gently, and simmer, uncovered, until all liquid is absorbed—about 20 minutes. Bulgur should be tender but have a certain amount of crunch, too.

4. Taste for salt and pepper, adjust as needed, then serve in place of potatoes.

KRAFT CHEESE

THE AVERAGE American used to eat less than a pound of cheese a year. Today it's more than twenty times that. And there's considerable evidence to suggest that this dramatic increase is due to the efforts of the country's leading cheesemakers, the Kraft brothers. James Kraft started his career with eleven inauspicious years as a grocery clerk in Ontario, Canada. Yet this experience was valuable. When he moved to Chicago and began delivering cheese by horse and buggy, he recalled the giant wheels of smelly, dried-out cheese in the over-heated general stores of his youth, and began wrapping his own cheese in protective tinfoil.

In 1915, he invented a unique method of grinding, blending, and pasteurizing cheese to retard spoilage and make it easier to cut. The resulting "process" cheese is the cheese Americans fell in love with at first taste. In a single year after the new process cheese was introduced, company sales jumped from $5,000 to $150,000. James Kraft called on his four brothers for help just as the U.S. government ordered six million tons of cheese to feed the troops during World War I.

After the war, Kraft wrapped five-pound rectangles of cheese in foil, packaged them in reusable wooden boxes—and could hardly meet the demand. It was no accident that these five-pound cheeses, sliced, precisely fit sandwich-size sliced bread. The next step—presliced cheese—was inevitable. Many Americans would agree it's the greatest thing since sliced bread.

Baked Bulgur with Toasted Walnuts

Makes 6 to 8 Servings

❋

LIKE BROWN rice, bulgur or cracked wheat is one of the whole grains we learned to appreciate in the '60s and '70s. I use this recipe as a baked-separately Thanksgiving stuffing.

1 cup walnuts
½ ounce dried mushrooms
1¾ cups boiling water
1 cup bulgur
1 cup boiling chicken broth
2 tablespoons fruity olive oil
2 cloves garlic, peeled and minced
1 medium yellow onion, peeled and coarsely chopped
2 large ribs celery, trimmed and coarsely chopped
4 medium carrots, peeled and coarsely chopped
1½ teaspoons minced fresh marjoram or ½ teaspoon dried leaf marjoram, crumbled
1½ teaspoons minced fresh lemon thyme or ¼ teaspoon dried leaf thyme, crumbled
½ teaspoon minced fresh rosemary or ¼ teaspoon dried leaf rosemary, crumbled
½ teaspoon finely grated orange zest
½ teaspoon finely grated lemon zest
½ (11-ounce) box mixed dried fruits, coarsely chopped
½ teaspoon salt (or to taste)
¼ teaspoon black pepper (or to taste)

1. Preheat oven to 350° F. Lightly coat 2-quart casserole with nonstick cooking spray and set aside.

2. Spread walnuts in pie tin and set, uncovered, in oven until crisp and lightly browned—10 to 12 minutes. Coarsely chop and reserve. Raise oven temperature to 375° F.

3. Soak dried mushrooms in 1 cup boiling water in small heat-proof bowl 20 minutes. Meanwhile, soak bulgur in large heat-proof bowl in boiling broth and remaining ¾ cup boiling water until all liquid is absorbed—about 30 minutes.

4. Strain mushroom soaking water through coffee-filter-lined small sieve; set aside. Rinse mushrooms, pat dry, chop, and reserve.

5. Heat olive oil in large heavy skillet over moderate heat 1 minute. Add garlic, onion, and celery and stir-fry until limp and golden—3 to 5 minutes. Add carrots, marjoram, thyme, rosemary, orange and lemon zests, and ¼ cup mushroom soaking liquid. Turn heat down low, cover, and "sweat" 15 minutes.

6. Add skillet mixture to bulgur along with toasted walnuts, dried fruits, chopped mushrooms, remaining mushroom soaking liquid, salt, and pepper. Toss well, taste, and adjust salt and pepper as needed.

7. Turn into casserole, cover snugly with foil, and bake 35 to 40 minutes. Fluff with fork and serve.

Pilaf of Barley and Mushrooms

Makes 6 Servings

❋

THIS UNUSUAL pilaf comes from Joanne Lamb Hayes, food editor of *Country Living,* and Bonnie Tandy Leblang, syndicated newspaper columnist. The recipe here is adapted from their book *Grains* (1995). Serve as a substitute for potatoes.

2 tablespoons fruity olive oil
1 large yellow onion, peeled and coarsely chopped
1 pound medium mushrooms, wiped clean and thinly sliced
1 cup medium-pearl barley, rinsed and drained
2¾ cups chicken or vegetable broth
½ teaspoon salt (or to taste)
¼ teaspoon black pepper (or to taste)

1. Heat oil in large heavy saucepan over moderately high heat 1 minute. Add onion and mushrooms and stir-fry until mushrooms release their juices and these evaporate—about 5 minutes.

2. Add barley and stir-fry until lightly browned—about 1 minute. Add broth, salt, and pepper, bring to boiling, then adjust heat so mixture bubbles gently. Cover, and cook until barley is tender and all liquid absorbed—35 to 45 minutes.

3. Set off heat and let stand 5 minutes. Fluff with fork, taste for salt and pepper, adjust as needed, and serve.

EGG, CHEESE, PASTA & GRAIN RECIPES

that Entered the American Mainstream

During the Twentieth Century with Their Source

(*Recipe Included)

FRANCE
*Pipérade
*Quiche Lorraine

SWITZERLAND
*Cheese Fondue
Raclette

GERMANY
*Spaetzle

RUSSIA/MIDDLE EUROPE
*Kasha Varnishkes (Kasha with Bow Tie Pasta)
Poppy Seed Noodles

ITALY
*Frittata
*Gnocchi
*Lasagne (see Casseroles)
*Fettuccine Alfredo

Spaghetti alla Bolognese
*Spaghetti alla Carbonara
*Pasta al Pesto
Polenta
*Spaghetti alla Puttanesca
Ravioli
Tortellini
*Risotto
Cannelloni
Manicotti
*Linguine with White Clam Sauce
Spaghetti with Red Clam Sauce

NORTH AFRICA/ GREECE/ TURKEY/MIDDLE EAST
*Bulgur
*Tabbouleh (see Salads & Salad Dressings)
Couscous

MEXICO/CARIBBEAN/ LATIN AMERICA
*Huevos Rancheros
Chilies Rellenos

ASIA/PACIFIC
Eggs Foo Yung
Fried Rice
Lo Mein
*Szechuan Sesame Noodles
Steamed Dumplings (pork or vegetable)
Wontons (pot stickers)
Pad Thai
Fried Tofu
Tofu with Ginger Sauce

Huevos Rancheros

Makes 6 Servings

✳

IN SHEILA Hibben's *National Cookbook* (1932) I came across this rudimentary "Eggs Rancheros" attributed to Arizona: "Fry the number of eggs needed; put them on a hot platter, and on the side of each put a spoonful of Red Chili Sauce." Hardly the classic, yet it's the earliest recipe I've found for this peppery breakfast dish. The 1943 and 1946 editions of *The Joy of Cooking* do not include Huevos Rancheros (although later ones do) and the recipe makes no edition of *The Boston Cooking-School Cook Book*. The one here is adapted from *Better Homes & Gardens Mexican Cook Book* (1977).

3 tablespoons vegetable oil
6 (6-inch) corn tortillas
1 small yellow onion, peeled and chopped
1 clove garlic, peeled and minced
3 cups canned crushed tomatoes
1 (4-ounce) can diced green chilies, well drained
¼ teaspoon salt
6 eggs
1 tablespoon water
1 cup coarsely shredded Monterey Jack cheese (about 4 ounces)

1. Preheat broiler.

2. Heat 2 tablespoons oil in small heavy skillet over moderately high heat 1 minute. Using tongs, dip tortillas in oil one by one and hold there until limp—about 10 seconds. Line ungreased 10 × 6 × 2-inch flameproof baking dish with tortillas and keep warm.

3. Add onion and garlic to skillet and stir-fry over moderate heat until limp—about 3 minutes. Mix in tomatoes, chilies, and salt and simmer, uncovered, 10 minutes. Spoon tomato sauce over tortillas.

4. Add remaining 1 tablespoon oil to large heavy skillet and set over moderate heat. Break eggs into oil, spacing well. When egg whites set, add water, cover, and cook until yolks almost set—2 to 3 minutes more.

5. Ease eggs on top of tomato sauce, spacing evenly, sprinkle with cheese, and broil 3 to 4 inches from heat until cheese melts—1 to 2 minutes.

Pipérade

Makes 6 Servings

✳

THIS SHOWY, open-face Basque omelet became stylish brunch fare in the '60s. The version here is adapted from *American Home All-Purpose Cook Book* (1966), a collection of recipes that had appeared in *American Home*. Sadly, that magazine no longer exists.

> 5 tablespoons butter
> 1 medium yellow onion, peeled and thinly sliced
> 1 small green bell pepper, cored, seeded, and cut into matchstick strips
> 1 cup julienned cooked ham
> 1 medium vine-ripe tomato, cored and diced
> 8 eggs
> ½ teaspoon salt
> ⅛ teaspoon black pepper

1. Melt 3 tablespoons butter in medium heavy skillet over moderate heat, add onion and green pepper, and stir-fry just until limp—2 to 3 minutes. Transfer to medium bowl and reserve. Brown ham in butter remaining in skillet and add to onion mixture along with tomato.

2. Melt remaining 2 tablespoons butter in well-seasoned 10-inch omelet pan over moderate heat. Quickly whisk eggs with salt and black pepper, pour into pan, and fork briskly, just until eggs begin to set.

3. Spoon tomato mixture on top and fork lightly into eggs, leaving onion, green pepper, ham, and tomatoes clearly visible.

4. Continue cooking pipérade just until set—1 to 2 minutes longer. Cut into wedges and serve.

Spinach-Parmesan Frittata

Makes 4 Servings

✳

ALTHOUGH MANY of us enjoyed these pancakelike omelets in *trattorias* while we traveled about Italy in the '60s and '70s, I don't think it occurred to us to cook them at home until the '80s when there was an explosion of interest in all things Italian. And yet as early as 1952 a recipe for Frittata alla Marechiaro appeared in the food pages of *The New York Times*. The *frittata* here is adapted from a cookbook I love, Patricia Wells's *Trattoria* (1993).

> 6 eggs, at room temperature
> 4 cups loosely packed tender young spinach leaves, washed, patted dry on paper towels and finely chopped
> ¼ teaspoon freshly grated nutmeg
> ¾ teaspoon salt
> ¼ teaspoon black pepper
> 1 cup freshly grated Parmesan cheese
> 1 tablespoon fruity olive oil

1. Preheat broiler.

2. Fork eggs lightly in large bowl. Add spinach, nutmeg, salt, pepper, and half the Parmesan, again forking lightly to mix.

3. Heat olive oil 1 to 1½ minutes in well-seasoned 9-inch cast-iron skillet with flameproof handle over moderate heat, tilting from side to side to coat skillet bottom evenly.

4. Add mixture, reduce heat to low, and cook, gently forking on top but leaving bottom undisturbed so it will brown. After 3 to 5 minutes, when *frittata* top is softly set, loosen around edges. Sprinkle with remaining ½ cup Parmesan.

5. Transfer to broiler, setting 5 inches from heat, and broil just until cheese melts, browns lightly, and eggs are set—about 2 minutes.

6. Cool *frittata* in skillet on wire rack 2 minutes. Invert on large plate, cool to room temperature, then cut into wedges and serve.

Leek Frittata

Makes 4 Servings

✳

A GOOD way to track late-twentieth-century trends, I've always thought, was to flip in chronological order through the works of those two cutting-edgers, Julee Rosso and Sheila Lukins, whose *Silver Palate* cookbooks caught the Yuppie fancy in the '80s. A case in point: The original *Silver Palate Cookbook* (1979) ignores *frittata. The Silver Palate Good Times Cookbook* (1984) contains one *frittata,* and their third, *The New Basics Cookbook* (1989), offers four. A little further digging, however, turns up Frittata Italiana in *The New York Times Cook Book* (1961), edited by Craig Claiborne. According to food historian/author Anne Mendelson, reviewing *The New York Times Cook Book* (revised edition, 1990) for *The Journal of Gastronomy,* this recipe originally appeared in the *Times* in 1952 as Frittata alla Marechiaro. That was five years before Claiborne's arrival at the paper. *Times* home economist Ruth P. Casa-Emellos had adapted the recipe for the paper, giving as her source the chef of the Italian Line's steamship *Saturnia.* Still, I think it fair to say that these flat Italian omelets made little culinary impact on this side of the Atlantic until the '80s. They are the perfect vehicle for recycling leftovers—snippets of meat, fish, fowl, vegetables. However, the more-American-than-Italian *frittata* here, adapted from *The Silver Palate Good Times Cookbook,* begins with a dozen fresh leeks and proceeds to goat cheese or *crème fraîche.* There's nothing secondhand here.

¼ cup (½ stick) butter
2 tablespoons fruity olive oil
12 medium leeks, trimmed, washed well, and sliced ¼-inch thick
Juice of ½ small lemon
1 teaspoon sugar
7 eggs
½ cup chèvre or crème fraîche
½ teaspoon salt
⅛ teaspoon black pepper
½ (8-ounce) package cream cheese

1. Heat 3 tablespoons butter and the olive oil in large heavy skillet over moderate heat until butter melts—1 to 2 minutes. Add leeks and stir-fry until limp—3 to 5 minutes. Mix in lemon juice and sugar, reduce heat to lowest point, cover, and cook until very soft—about 30 minutes.

2. Preheat broiler. Butter 10- to 12-inch cast-iron skillet with flameproof handle with remaining 1 tablespoon butter; set aside.

3. Whisk eggs with chèvre, salt, and pepper in large bowl. Mix in leeks and pour into skillet. Set over moderately low heat and cook, stirring occasionally, just until bottom is set—3 to 5 minutes.

4. Dot surface of *frittata* with cream cheese, transfer to broiler, setting about 5 inches from heat, and broil just until cheese melts and top is set—about 2 minutes.

5. Cool 10 to 15 minutes, cut into wedges, and serve warm or at room temperature.

Quiche Lorraine

Makes a 9-inch Pie, 8 to 10 Servings

✳

ALTHOUGH A rudimentary quiche appeared in Irma Rombauer's self-published *Joy of Cooking* (1931), Hot Quiche Lorraine Tartlets in *June Platt's Plain and Fancy Cookbook* (1941), and a full-size Quiche Lorraine in the 1951 *Joy of Cooking,* quiche madness didn't descend upon us until the late '70s and go-go '80s, when chefs outdid themselves dreaming up off-the-wall combos— yam and ham quiche, to name one. The Alsatian classic, however, is still the best. This recipe, my own, has served me well for years.

PASTRY
1¼ cups sifted all-purpose flour
½ teaspoon salt
⅓ cup well-chilled lard or vegetable shortening
4 to 5 tablespoons ice water

FILLING
½ pound lean smoky bacon, snipped crosswise at ½-inch intervals
½ pound Gruyère cheese, coarsely shredded
4 eggs, lightly beaten
½ teaspoon salt
⅛ teaspoon white pepper
⅛ teaspoon ground hot red pepper (cayenne)

*⅛ teaspoon freshly grated
   nutmeg
1 cup half-and-half
¾ cup heavy cream
1 tablespoon butter, melted*

1. **PASTRY:** Preheat oven to 425° F. Mix flour and salt in medium bowl, add lard and, using pastry blender, cut in until texture of uncooked oatmeal. Briskly fork in ice water just until mixture holds together.

2. Shape pastry into ball on lightly floured pastry cloth, then with floured, stockinette-covered rolling pin, roll into 12-inch circle. Fit into 9-inch pie pan or tart tin and trim so pastry overhangs pan 1 inch all around. Roll overhang under onto rim and crimp into high fluted edge.

3. Prick bottom and sides of pastry lightly, lay large square of wax paper in pie shell, and fill with pie weights or dried beans. Bake, uncovered, 10 to 12 minutes until pale tan. Lift out paper and pie weights, then cool pie shell in pan on wire rack to room temperature.

4. **FILLING:** Brown bacon in medium heavy skillet over moderate heat until crisp—3 to 5 minutes. Pour off drippings and drain bacon well on paper towels.

5. Scatter bacon and cheese over bottom of pie shell. Whisk together eggs, salt, white pepper, cayenne, nutmeg, half-and-half, heavy cream, and melted butter in medium bowl.

6. Set pie shell on heavy-duty baking sheet, then strain egg mixture directly into pie shell.

7. Bake, uncovered, at 425° F for 15 minutes, reduce oven temperature to 350° F, and bake until knife inserted midway between rim and center comes out clean—10 to 15 minutes more.

8. Cool quiche in pan on wire rack 15 to 20 minutes.

9. Cut into wedges and serve.

Cheese Fondue

Makes 4 Servings

✻

THUMB THROUGH almost any basic, late-nineteenth-century cookbook and you will find something called "fondu" or "fondue." But this is not the Swiss classic that became so popular in the '50s and '60s. Those early fondues were mock cheese soufflés plumped with bread crumbs. The traditional Swiss fondue here is adapted from *The Doubleday Cookbook* (1975), which I coauthored with Elaine Hanna.

NOTE: To keep the fondue from lumping or "stringing," use only well-aged, imported Swiss Gruyère and Emmentaler. Inferior cheeses won't melt smoothly. If at any time the mixture becomes too thick, blend in a little warm wine.

*10½ ounces well-aged Gruyère,
   cut into ¼-inch dice*

*5¼ ounces well-aged
   Emmentaler, cut into ¼-inch
   dice
3 tablespoons flour
½ teaspoon paprika
¼ teaspoon freshly grated
   nutmeg
⅛ teaspoon ground hot red
   pepper (cayenne)
1 clove garlic, peeled and
   halved
1¾ cups dry white wine
1 tablespoon fresh lemon juice
2 tablespoons kirsch
¼ teaspoon baking soda
6 cups 1½-inch cubes day-old
   French bread*

1. Toss Gruyère and Emmentaler with flour, paprika, nutmeg, and cayenne in large bowl; set aside.

2. Rub an earthenware fondue pot *(caquelon)* well with garlic; discard garlic. Add wine and heat, uncovered, over low heat just until bubbles begin to appear on bottom of *caquelon.*

3. By handfuls, add cheese mixture, stirring all the while in figure eights. Add lemon juice. Mixture will clump, but no matter; after 15 minutes of vigilant stirring, the fondue will again be creamy. Smooth in kirsch and soda.

4. Set *caquelon* over its alcohol burner and adjust flame so fondue stays just below the bubble.

5. Serve with bread cubes and fondue forks so everyone can spear the cubes and twirl them in the bubbling fondue.

Marcella Hazan's Potato Gnocchi

Makes 6 Servings

❋

THE RECIPE that follows is adapted from Marcella Hazan's benchmark *Classic Italian Cook Book* (1973). In the headnote, she writes that potato gnocchi can be sauced a number of ways. To her, "three particularly happy combinations" are tomato sauce, pesto, or a creamy Gorgonzola, the sauce included here.

NOTE: While shaping gnocchi keep hands, surface, and fork well floured.

GNOCCHI
 1½ pounds medium all-
   purpose potatoes
 1 cup unsifted all-purpose flour
   (about)
 ⅔ cup freshly grated Parmesan
   cheese

GORGONZOLA SAUCE
 ¼ pound Gorgonzola cheese
 ⅓ cup milk
 3 tablespoons butter
 Salt to taste

1. GNOCCHI: Boil unpeeled potatoes in medium saucepan until tender—30 to 35 minutes. Test only toward end of cooking lest water seep into fork punctures and make potatoes soggy. Drain potatoes, return to pan, and shake over moderate heat a few seconds to drive off excess moisture.

2. Peel potatoes when cool enough to handle, force through ricer or food mill set over large bowl. Knead

Gnocchi

MUCH TO my surprise, Fannie Farmer includes this recipe in the original *Boston Cooking-School Cook Book* (1896) and in subsequent editions right through the 1920s (by which time the title had been changed to *Gnocchi à la Romana*).

GNOCCHI À LA ROMANA

¼ cup butter	*2 cups scalded milk*
¼ cup flour	*Yolks 2 eggs*
¼ cup corn-starch	*¾ cup grated cheese*
½ teaspoon salt	

MELT butter, and when bubbling, add flour, corn-starch, salt, and milk, gradually. Cook three minutes, stirring constantly. Add yolks of eggs slightly beaten, and one-half cup cheese. Pour into a buttered shallow pan, and cool. Turn on a board, cut in squares, diamonds, or strips. Place on a platter, sprinkle with remaining cheese, and brown in oven.

By Italian standards, this hardly qualifies as gnocchi. Nearer the mark is Gnocchi II in *Much Depends on Dinner* (1939) by Mary Grosvenor Ellsworth, food editor of *House Beautiful*. Her Gnocchi I is amusing, so I include it here as well as the more authentic second recipe. Both appear just as she wrote them.

GNOCCHI I

SCALD in a saucepan three cups of milk and a cup of cream with half an ounce of butter. This should boil about five minutes. Meantime sift a pound of flour with half a teaspoon of salt, a generous pinch of cayenne, and an ounce of grated Parmesan (yes, this time the cheese goes in). Pour the milk on the flour slowly, stirring hard with a wooden spoon. Keep on stirring a couple of minutes after the last of the milk has gone in, till the whole thing is smooth, then break in an egg and stir again till smooth. This batter now goes into boiling salted water in small gobbets which may be collected on the end of a knife or spoon and pushed off into the water with your favorite finger. Get them all in as quickly as you can so they will be done together. This takes about six minutes. Lift out, drain, rinse, and serve on a hot dish with any trimmings you elect.

GNOCCHI II

THIS time scald a pint of milk and when it just boils, shake into it a quarter of a pound of semolina. Season with salt, pepper, and a trace of nutmeg; cook slowly for twenty minutes. Then take it off the fire, stir in an egg yolk, then spread it out thin on a buttered sheet. Let it [cool], then cut in small squares and arrange in a baking dish, sprinkling each layer with grated Parmesan and distributing dabs of butter throughout. Brown it quickly on top in a hot oven.

Still, it would be a good many more years before most of us enjoyed real Italian gnocchi on this side of the Atlantic. Certainly, few of us would have dreamed of making it until Marcella Hazan's *Classic Italian Cook Book* (1973) set us straight on this and other Italian classics.

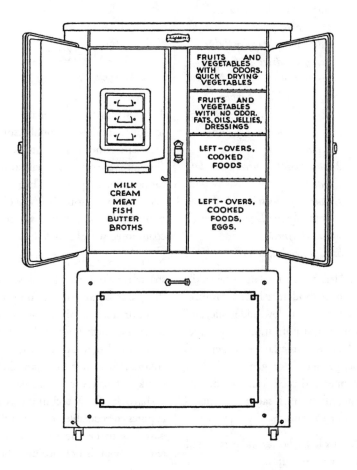

in ⅔ cup flour, then add remaining ⅓ cup flour gradually, kneading until smooth and soft but still a bit sticky. If dough is too soft to shape, knead in a little more flour.

3. Working on well-floured surface with well floured hands, roll dough into ropes about ¾-inch thick; slice at ¾-inch intervals.

4. Flour hands well again, then holding well-floured fork horizontally—parallel to well-floured work surface—with concave side of bowl facing you, press chunks of dough one by one with index finger against bowl of fork, leaving fork imprints on one side and fingerprint on other. As you press dough into little cresents, flip toward fork handle, then let drop onto well floured counter. Repeat until all gnocchi are shaped.

5. SAUCE: Mash Gorgonzola into milk and butter in small heavy enameled-iron saucepan and set over low heat. Cook and stir until creamy—about 1 minute. Add salt to taste, set aside, and keep warm.

6. TO COOK GNOCCHI: Drop about 20 gnocchi into large saucepan of boiling salted water and as soon as they float—after 1 to 2 minutes—cook 8 to 10 seconds more.

7. With skimmer, scoop gnocchi to large heated platter and top with a little Gorgonzola sauce.

8. Cook remaining gnocchi in batches the same way, adding to platter along with a little sauce. Top with any remaining sauce, mix in Parmesan, and serve hot.

Spaghetti alla Puttanesca

Makes 4 to 6 Servings

❋

ONLY IN the '80s did knowledge of this gutsy pasta sauce move beyond America's big metropolitan areas. Today nearly every supermarket stocks jars of it. Roughly translated, *alla puttanesca* means "in the style of the whore" and there are two theories as to the origin of the name. The first is that it takes no longer to prepare than it does to turn a trick. The second holds that prostitutes lured customers with its heady aroma. The recipe here is adapted from *365 Ways to Cook Pasta* (1988), written by my friend Marie Simmons.

NOTE: Because of the saltiness of the olives, capers, and anchovies, this recipe is not likely to need salt. But taste before serving.

> *3 tablespoons fruity olive oil*
> *2 cloves garlic, peeled and minced*

1 (1-pound, 12-ounce) can crushed tomatoes
¼ cup chopped, pitted, salt-cured black olives
2 teaspoons rinsed, drained small capers
1 teaspoon red pepper flakes
½ teaspoon dried leaf oregano, crumbled
⅛ teaspoon black pepper
1 (2-ounce) tin anchovy fillets, drained, patted dry and diced
2 tablespoons minced fresh flat-leaf parsley
1 pound spaghetti, cooked al dente *by package directions and drained*
Salt, if needed, to taste

1. Heat olive oil in large heavy skillet over moderate heat 1 minute. Reduce heat to low, add garlic, and stir-fry just until limp—1 minute. Mix in tomatoes, olives, capers, red pepper flakes, oregano, and black pepper and cook, uncovered, stirring often, until sauce thickens—about 15 minutes.

2. Mix in anchovies and parsley and simmer 2 minutes.

3. Pile hot spaghetti into large shallow bowl, add sauce, and toss well to mix. Taste for salt and add, if needed. Toss again and serve.

Spaetzle

Makes 4 Servings

❋

THESE LITTLE German pasta squiggles are now so popular some high-end supermarkets stock the "instant" variety—a poor substitute for homemade spaetzle. The recipe here is adapted from *The New German Cookbook* (1993), which I coauthored with Hedy Würz.

NOTE: Specialty food shops sell spaetzle makers, which look something like potato ricers. You prop them on a kettle of boiling salted water and slowly push the batter in. You can also force it through a colander but deft German chefs whisk it off of a wooden paddle with a sharp knife, a technique that requires considerable practice. If the batter is to be the right consistency—about that of medium white sauce—you must use a good all-purpose flour and sift it before you measure it. If the flour in your area contains much hard wheat, you may need to use only ⅞ cup.

> 1 cup plus 2 tablespoons sifted
>   all-purpose flour
> ¼ teaspoon freshly grated
>   nutmeg
> ½ teaspoon salt
> 1 egg
> 6 tablespoons milk
> ¼ cup (½ stick) butter, melted

1. Mix flour, nutmeg, and salt in small mixing bowl; make well in center. Whisk egg and milk together in second small bowl. Add to well in dry ingredients and beat hard until smooth and elastic.

2. Push batter through spaetzle maker into large kettle of vigorously boiling salted water and cook, uncovered, just until spaetzle firm up and no longer taste of raw flour—8 to 10 minutes. Drain and quick-chill at once in ice water.

3. Drain spaetzle well, then warm with butter in large heavy skillet 4 to 5 minutes. Serve in place of potatoes.

Kasha

Makes 4 Servings

✳

ALTHOUGH KASHA (buckwheat groats) was brought to this country by early settlers (by the Dutch, Bert Greene writes in *The Grains Cookbook,* 1988), it was used at first as fodder. Only early in this century, when waves of Jewish settlers arrived here from Russia and other Eastern European countries, did kasha take its place at the dinner table—and then mostly in ethnic enclaves. Kasha's breakout occurred, by most accounts, during the surge of vegetarianism in the '60s and '70s. For those unaccustomed to its slightly medicinal flavor, kasha is an acquired taste. This basic way of preparing it is adapted from Mimi Sheraton's deliciously nostalgic *From My Mother's Kitchen,* Revised Edition (1991). As a variation, Sheraton suggests stirring butter-browned onions or mushrooms into the kasha instead of plain butter.

> 1 cup coarse or medium-grain
>   kasha
> 1 egg, lightly beaten
> 2 cups boiling water
> 1 tablespoon butter
> ¾ teaspoon salt (or to taste)

1. Fork kasha briskly with egg in large shallow bowl until grains absorb egg. Transfer to large heavy skillet and cook over moderately high heat, stirring often, until kasha grains dry and separate.

2. Add water, shaking skillet to distribute evenly. Adjust heat so water bubbles gently, cover, and simmer 10 to 15 minutes. Add butter and salt, cover, and cook until kasha puffs and all liquid is absorbed—10 to 15 minutes.

3. Taste for salt, adjust as needed, and serve.

TIMELINE

1936

American Airlines begins serving meals on its DC3s.

The Waring Blendor arrives.

Bobbs-Merrill prints a trade edition of *The Joy of Cooking.*

Commercially baked Girl Scout cookies, a shortbread type shaped like the Scout badge, go on sale at 25 cents a box.

1937

Kraft rolls out its "instant" macaroni and cheese dinner.

Margaret Rudkin's home-baked breads are so successful she founds Pepperidge Farm, Inc.

Woman's Day, the first food-oriented supermarket magazine, is published by A & P for distribution in its stores.

Hormel introduces Spam.

The gas home refrigerator arrives.

The modern electric "dashboard" range is introduced.

JULIA CHILD

WHO WOULD have dreamed that this Pasadena native, this Smith graduate (class of '34), this six-foot-two redhead who seemed built more for shooting baskets than for making bouillabaisse, would change the way America ate?

Certainly not Julia McWilliams Child. She admits that she didn't cook until she was in her thirties and then only as an act of survival. Stationed in China by the OSS (now CIA) during World War II, she took up cooking to avoid eating in the army mess.

"The army cooks were terrible," Julia told Baba S. Khalsa in an interview for *Great Vegetables from the Great Chefs* (1990). "Dried potatoes, canned tomatoes, and water buffalo. Awful!"

But there was one bright note. China was where Julia fell in love with future husband, colleague, and life partner, Paul Child. She dabbled at cooking after the two returned to the U.S., trying recipes from *The Joy of Cooking* and *Gourmet*. But only in 1948, when the U.S. Information Agency dispatched Paul to Paris, did Julia, then thirty-six, get serious about cooking. She who had never baked a cake.

Her first move: To enroll in the Cordon Bleu. Here she met Simone Beck and Louisette Bertholle, the two good French cooks who eventually coauthored *Mastering the Art of French Cooking*, Volume I (1961) with Julia.

Julia's television career began in 1962, a direct result of that book. Sent on tour to promote it, she appeared on "I've Been Reading" on WGBH, Boston's public television channel. Impressed by her directness, her ability to make complicated things sound simple, her rapport with the camera, the producers asked her to prepare three pilots for a series tentatively titled "The French Chef." It began airing in 1963, and the rest, as they say, is history.

Nearly all of today's emerging cookbook authors, food writers, chefs, and television chefs were weaned on "The French Chef." The timing for its television debut was perfect. With jets hurdling the Atlantic in seven hours, Americans began traveling as never before. They toured Paris, the French provinces, and elsewhere, experiencing, as did Julia, a gastronomic epiphany.

As a result, *coq au vin* began phasing out Southern fried chicken, *boeuf à la Bourguignonne* beef stew,

tarte tatin Mom's apple pie. Julia was there every week on TV to demystify French cooking. She was ebullient, a born teacher who made it all seem easy. Sure, there was the occasional goof. But Julia laughed at her foibles as heartily as we did. We loved her for that.

In the mid-'70s, Julia shifted gears and began to explore the glories not only of regional American cooking but also of other national cuisines. So her subsequent PBS series—among them *Julia Child & Company, Julia Child & More Company*—taught us to make everything from Gazpacho Salad and Gravlaks to Peking Wings, Potato Gnocchi, and Chocolate-Chip Spice Pound Cake.

Today, thanks to regular appearances on ABC-TV's *Good Morning America* not to mention new shows and reruns of her various PBS series, Julia Child is inspiring a whole new generation of American cooks.

Has anyone this century done more to shape and reshape the way we eat, the way we cook? Not likely.

Kasha Varnishkes (Kasha with Bow Tie Pasta)

Makes 6 to 8 Servings

✳

THIS EASTERN/Middle European classic only recently became well known in this country beyond the Jewish community. The recipe here is adapted from *Grains* (1995) written by my good friends Joanne Lamb Hayes, food editor of *Country Living Magazine,* and Bonnie Tandy Leblang, whose syndicated column, "Supermarket Sampler," appears in more than 100 newspapers. The traditional accompaniment for Kasha Varnishkes? Hayes and Leblang say braised beef.

1 cup medium-grain kasha
1 egg, lightly beaten
1 tablespoon vegetable oil
1 large yellow onion, peeled and coarsely chopped
2 cups chicken or vegetable broth
½ teaspoon salt (or to taste)
¼ teaspoon black pepper (or to taste)
2 cups bow tie pasta, cooked al dente *by package directions and drained*
2 tablespoons butter

1. Fork kasha with egg in small bowl until grains are uniformly coated.

2. Heat medium heavy saucepan over high heat 1 minute, turn heat to low, and add kasha. Cook and stir, breaking up clumps, until golden brown—5 to 10 minutes. Scoop kasha into bowl and reserve.

3. Add oil to pan and heat 1 minute over high heat. Add onion, reduce heat to moderate, and stir-fry until richly browned—10 to 15 minutes. Scrape into second bowl and reserve.

4. Return kasha to pan, add broth, salt, and pepper and bring to boiling over high heat. Adjust heat so mixture bubbles gently and cook, uncovered, stirring often, until all broth is absorbed—10 to 15 minutes.

5. Place hot bow tie pasta in large bowl, add butter, browned onions, and kasha and toss well. Taste for salt and pepper, adjust as needed, and serve.

Fettuccine Alfredo

Makes 4 Servings

✳

THE STORY goes that while honeymooning in Rome in 1927, Douglas Fairbanks and Mary Pickford dined almost daily on this rich pasta at Alfredo's restaurant, and in gratitude, presented restaurateur Alfredo Di Lelio with a golden pasta fork and spoon at the end of their stay. Journalists picked up the story and spread news of Fettuccine Alfredo across the Atlantic. Before long, American chefs were improvising. According to Marie Simmons, a good friend, fellow cookbook author, and food writer who is of Italian heritage, an authentic Fettuccine Alfredo is not tricked out with cream or mushrooms or green peas or garlic. It's a mix of sweet creamery butter, Parmigiano-Reggiano, homemade fettuccine, and black pepper. Nothing more, nothing less. The recipe here is adapted from Marie's *365 Ways To Cook Pasta* (1988).

NOTE: Use only imported Parmigiano-Reggiano; domestic "Parmesans" just don't "cut it."

1 pound fresh fettuccine
½ cup (1 stick) unsalted butter (at room temperature)
½ cup freshly grated Parmesan cheese
Black pepper

1. Cook fettuccine until *al dente* according to package directions in large kettle of boiling salted water—about 2 minutes.

2. Meanwhile, dice butter into heated large bowl.

3. Quickly drain pasta, turn into bowl, add Parmesan, and toss well. Add several grinds of the peppermill and serve at once.

Pasta Carbonara

Makes 6 Servings

❋

LET ME say at the outset that this is not the all-stops-out Roman original freighted with cheese, bacon, and eggs. It is a slimmed-down version developed by Vanessa Taylor Johnson, test kitchen director at *Cooking Light* magazine, in response to a reader plea. The magazine regularly reworks high-fat, high-cholesterol, high-calorie classics, a valuable reader service. This recipe, adapted from the Pasta Carbonara in the April 1996 *Cooking Light,* miraculously slashes fat to 6 grams per serving (2 grams saturated), cholesterol to 23 milligrams, and calories to 284. P.S. It's delicious.

> 6 ounces turkey bacon, diced
> 2 cloves garlic, peeled and
>   minced
> ¾ pound thin spaghetti, cooked
>   al dente *by package
>   directions and drained well*
> ¼ cup freshly grated Parmesan
>   cheese
> 2 tablespoons minced fresh
>   parsley
> ¼ teaspoon black pepper
> 1 cup 2-percent low-fat milk
> 6 tablespoons thawed frozen
>   nonfat egg product

1. Brown bacon in large, heavy nonstick skillet over moderately high heat 3 to 4 minutes until crisp. Add garlic and stir-fry until soft—about 1 minute.

2. Reduce heat to low, add spaghetti, Parmesan, parsley, and pepper.

3. Whisk milk and egg product together in small bowl. Pour into skillet and cook, stirring constantly, just until sauce thickens—about 3 minutes.

4. Dish up and serve.

Microwave Linguine with White Clam Sauce

Makes 6 Servings

❋

THE LINGUINE isn't microwaved (it cooks the old-fashioned way) but the clam sauce *is.* By the time you've cooked and drained the pasta, it's ready to ladle on top. This recipe is adapted from *Micro Ways* (1990), a basic microwave cookbook I coauthored with Elaine Hanna that's now available in paperback.

SAUCE

> 2 cloves garlic, peeled and
>   minced
> ¼ cup fruity olive oil
> 2 tablespoons flour
> 2 cups bottled clam juice
> 1½ cups minced raw fresh
>   clams
> 1 tablespoon minced fresh
>   parsley (about)
> ⅛ teaspoon black pepper
> 1 tablespoon butter, diced

PASTA

> 1½ pounds linguine, cooked al
>   dente *by package directions
>   and drained*

1. SAUCE: Microwave garlic in oil in uncovered 2-quart measure on HIGH (100 percent power) until golden—about 2 minutes.

2. Blend in flour and microwave, uncovered, also on HIGH, until foamy—about 30 seconds.

3. Smooth in clam juice and microwave, uncovered, again on HIGH, whisking at halftime, until lightly thickened and smooth—4½ to 5½ minutes.

4. Add clams, parsley, and pepper, cover with wax paper, and microwave on MEDIUM (50 percent power), stirring at halftime, until flavors meld—about 4 minutes. Stir in butter.

5. Pour over hot pasta, toss well, and serve, accompanied, if desired, by additional minced parsley.

Pasta al Pesto

Makes 4 Servings

❋

IN THE late '70s/early '80s, when fresh basil could be had at most farmer's markets, pesto became the pasta sauce of choice. I am so fond of pesto that whenever fresh basil is in season (May through August), I make huge batches of it and freeze in half-pint containers so that I can enjoy it all winter long. The food processor has revolutionized the making of pesto and put it within the realm of every cook who can lay her hands on a hefty supply of basil. For each pound of pasta, you'll need about ¾ cup pesto, so the recipe here, one I developed especially for the food processor, makes twice the amount of sauce needed to dress the one pound of pasta called for. No matter, refrigerate or freeze the balance. Today pesto is so commonplace supermarkets sell bottles of it, also refrigerated containers of the "freshly made." Neither can compare, however, with the pesto you make yourself.

NOTE: To toast pignoli, spread in a pie tin and set in a 325°F oven for 5 to 10 minutes.

> 2 cups firmly packed fresh basil leaves, well washed and patted very dry on paper towels
> 2 tablespoons lightly toasted pignoli (pine nuts—see headnote)
> 2 cloves garlic, peeled
> ½ cup fruity olive oil
> ½ teaspoon salt
> ⅛ teaspoon black pepper
> 1 pound thin spaghetti, cooked al dente by package directions and drained well
> 2 tablespoons butter or olive oil
> Freshly grated Parmesan cheese

1. Place basil, pignoli, garlic, olive oil, salt, and pepper in food processor fitted with metal chopping blade and churn 30 seconds nonstop.

2. Scrape down work bowl sides with rubber spatula and buzz 30 seconds longer. If not smooth, churn 30 to 60 seconds more.

3. Return drained hot pasta to kettle in which it cooked, add butter, and toss well to coat. Add half the pesto sauce and toss well again.

4. Serve at once with freshly grated Parmesan.

Szechuan Sesame Noodles

Makes 6 Servings

✳

WHEN I was living on New York's Upper East Side in the 1970s, a new Chinese restaurant opened a few blocks away on Second Avenue. Called Szechuan East, it served peppery food wholly unlike the bland Chinese dishes I'd known as a child (during my youth, there was a popular restaurant in Raleigh, North Carolina, called The Canton; my parents took me there often). Szechuan cooking was something else again—as peppery as Tex-Mex. A Szechuan East specialty I ordered every time I went were these noodles dressed with sesame-peanut sauce. I spent weeks trying to crack the recipe and came up with this.

NOTE: Asian sesame paste and chili oil can be found in Chinese groceries and specialty food shops, even today in high-end supermarkets.

SAUCE

> ¾ cup hot chicken broth
> ⅔ cup cream-style peanut butter
> ⅓ cup Asian sesame paste or tahini
> ¼ cup dry sherry
> ¼ cup rice wine vinegar
> ¼ cup Japanese soy sauce
> 2 tablespoons chili oil
> 1½ tablespoons dark roasted Asian sesame oil
> 1 (1½-inch) cube peeled fresh ginger, halved
> 2 cloves garlic, peeled and halved

PASTA

> 2 tablespoons peanut oil
> 4 medium scallions, trimmed and cut into matchstick strips (include tops)
> ½ cup finely slivered prosciutto or baked Virginia ham
> ½ small cucumber, peeled, seeded, and cut into matchstick strips
> 1 pound thin spaghetti, cooked al dente by package directions and drained
> ⅓ cup minced fresh coriander (cilantro) or parsley

1. SAUCE: Puree all ingredients in electric blender at high speed or in food processor fitted with metal chopping blade; set aside.

2. PASTA: Heat peanut oil in small heavy skillet over moderately high heat 1 minute. Add scallions and stir-fry just until limp—1 to 2 minutes. Off heat, add ham and cucumber and toss lightly.

3. Place skillet mixture in heated large shallow bowl, add hot drained spaghetti, then sauce. Toss well. Add fresh coriander and toss again, more gently this time, and serve.

Risotto

Makes 4 Servings

✳

ALTHOUGH FANNIE Farmer includes a "Rissoto Creole" (spelling hers) in the revised *Boston Cooking-School Cook Book* (1906) and Ida C. Bailey Allen offers what she calls "Risotto alla Milanese" in *Mrs. Allen's Cook Book* (1917), risotto can hardly be said to have made the grade until well after World War II. I credit Marcella Hazan (*The Classic Italian Cook Book,* 1973) with putting it on the culinary map of America. Certainly it was she who taught us how to prepare risotto properly. Still, only when arborio (short-grain rice) became widely available (the '80s) did many American cooks attempt risotto in earnest. Today whole books are devoted to the art of making risotto. And hip chefs are dreaming up *risotti* of decidedly American flavor (see recipes that follow my basic one here).

NOTE: Cooking risotto takes time and patience. Do not rush the process by raising the heat—the rice will gum up. When you have added about half the liquid, you will note that the rice grains have doubled in size and become gelatinous on the outside. From this point on, stir slowly so you don't bruise, break, or mash the rice.

> 1 large shallot, peeled and
>   minced
> 2 tablespoons butter
> 1 tablespoon fruity olive oil
> 1 cup arborio (short-grain) rice
> 1¾ cups simmering chicken
>   broth
> 1¼ cups simmering water
> Salt to taste
> Black pepper to taste

1. Stir-fry shallot in butter and olive oil in medium heavy saucepan over moderate heat until limp—2 to 3 minutes.

2. Add rice and stir until every grain is golden and translucent—about 2 minutes. Reduce heat to moderately low.

3. Mix chicken broth and water and adjust heat so mixture simmers slowly. Add ⅓ cup hot broth mixture to rice and cook, stirring constantly, until all liquid is absorbed—3 to 4 minutes. Continue adding broth mixture, ⅓ cup at a time, stirring all the while and waiting until all liquid is absorbed before adding more.

4. When nearly all broth mixture has been incorporated, taste a grain of rice. When done, rice will be creamy, tender-firm all the way through with no crumbly center or taste of raw starch.

5. Season to taste with salt and pepper and serve in place of potatoes.

——— **VARIATION** ———

CHEESE RISOTTO: Prepare as directed, but with final addition of broth mixture, add 5 tablespoons freshly grated Parmesan cheese and 1 tablespoon butter. Stir just until butter and cheese melt, then serve. Makes 4 servings.

Barbara Kafka's Fabulous Microwave Risotto

Makes 6 Servings

✳

EVER THE intrepid culinary pioneer, Barbara Kafka began tinkering with *risotti* in the 1980s. I can hear her saying, "To hell with it! There must be an easier way." She found it, of course, in that instrument that cooks at near supersonic speed, the microwave. Kafka's microwave risotto is revolutionary and as she, herself, says, "It doesn't get much better than this." Quite so. The recipe here is adapted from Kafka's *Microwave Gourmet* (1987), a breakthrough book that showed us that the microwave is more than a warming oven. Much, much more.

> *2 tablespoons butter*
> *2 tablespoons fruity olive oil*
> *½ cup minced yellow onion*
> *1 cup arborio rice*
> *3 cups chicken broth*
> *2 teaspoons kosher salt*
> *¼ teaspoon black pepper*
> *¼ cup freshly grated Parmesan cheese (optional)*

1. Microwave butter and olive oil, uncovered, in 10-inch deep-dish pie plate on HIGH (100 percent power) 2 minutes.

2. Add onion, stir well, cover, and microwave, again on HIGH, 4 minutes.

3. Add rice, stir until grains glisten, and microwave, uncovered, once again on HIGH, 4 minutes.

4. Stir in broth, and microwave, uncovered, on HIGH, 18 minutes, stirring well at halftime.

5. Let risotto stand on counter 5 minutes, stirring often, until all liquid is absorbed.

6. Mix in salt, pepper, and if desired, grated Parmesan. Serve as an accompaniment to meat.

TIMELINE

1936

Trader Vic's opens in Oakland, California.

Cyclamate is approved as an artificial sweetener (a known carcinogen, it is now banned).

Niacin (nicotinic acid), the pellagra preventive, is recognized as a vitamin.

1938

The Food, Drug and Cosmetic Act zeros in on toxic food additives.

Pots and pans go glamorous with copper-bottomed Revere Ware.

Corning makes Pyrex Flameware percolators and saucepans with improved handles (secured with metal bands).

1939

Vitamin tablets become a national obsession; only laxatives outsell them.

Scott Howell's Caramelized Onion Risotto with Corn and Bacon

Makes 4 Servings

✳

SCOTT HOWELL is the brilliant young chef-proprietor at Nana's in Durham, North Carolina. Although he learned to make a classic risotto at San Domenico in Imola, Italy, he now injects lusty Tar Heel flavors. I profiled Howell for the September 1995 issue of *Food & Wine,* and among his recipes featured by the magazine was this stellar down-home risotto.

NOTE: The sweet corn Howell prefers is Silver Queen, and the sweet onions he uses are Vidalias.

3 medium ears sweet corn, desilked but not shucked
7 tablespoons butter
3 large sweet onions, peeled and thinly sliced
¼ pound slab bacon, cut into 2 × ¼ × ¼-inch strips
8 cups low-sodium chicken broth (about)
1 medium yellow onion, peeled and finely chopped
1 small carrot, peeled and finely chopped
1 small rib celery, trimmed and finely chopped
2 cups arborio rice
1 cup dry white wine
¼ cup freshly grated Parmesan cheese

Salt to taste
Black pepper to taste

1. Light grill or preheat oven to 350° F. Grill or oven-roast corn, turning now and then, until tender—about 15 minutes. Cool slightly, shuck, and cut kernels from cobs into bowl; reserve cobs.

2. Melt 3 tablespoons butter in large heavy saucepan over high heat. Add sliced onions and stir-fry until richly caramelized—about 25 minutes; add to corn.

3. Stir-fry bacon in same pan over high heat until crisp and brown— about 3 minutes. Drain on paper towels. Pour off all drippings, and return 2 tablespoons to pan.

4. Bring chicken broth and corn cobs to boiling in second large heavy saucepan; adjust heat so broth bubbles gently and keep hot.

5. Add chopped onion, carrot, and celery to pan with bacon drippings and stir-fry until limp—about 3 minutes. Add rice and turn to coat evenly with fat. Add wine and cook, stirring constantly, until nearly all absorbed, about 2 minutes. Mix in reserved corn, caramelized onions, and bacon.

6. Add 1 cup hot chicken broth and cook and stir over moderate heat until absorbed. Add remaining broth, ½ cup at a time, stirring each time until all liquid is absorbed. Continue cooking just until rice is tender and creamy—the risotto-making process will take about 25 minutes in all.

7. Stir in remaining 4 tablespoons butter, also Parmesan, salt, and pepper to taste. If risotto seems thick or sticky, add a little additional broth. Serve at once.

Michael Romano's Pumpkin Risotto

Makes 6 Servings

✳

MICHAEL ROMANO is the gifted chef at Danny Meyer's Union Square Cafe in New York's trendy Flatiron District. Romano makes a specialty of risotto. This one, adapted from *The Union Square Cafe Cookbook* (1994), is one of his best.

PUMPKIN BROTH
   1 tablespoon butter
   1 medium yellow onion, peeled
      and thinly sliced

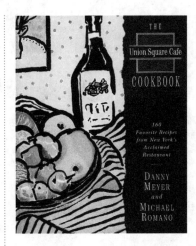

   2 medium carrots, peeled and
      thinly sliced
   1 medium rib celery (with
      tops), thinly sliced
   1 medium leek, washed and
      thinly sliced
   2 cups canned solid-pack
      pumpkin (not *pie mix*)
   8 cups low-sodium chicken
      broth
   1 whole bay leaf
   6 black peppercorns
   4 whole allspice
   ¼ teaspoon freshly grated
      nutmeg
   ¼ cinnamon stick
   2 tablespoons pure maple
      syrup

RISOTTO
   ¼ cup fruity olive oil
   1¾ cups arborio rice
   1½ cups ½-inch dice fresh
      pumpkin or winter squash
   ½ cup dry white wine
   6 to 7 cups Pumpkin Broth
      (above)
   1 tablespoon minced fresh
      sage

   2 cups arugula, washed and
      chopped
   ⅓ cup diced fresh mozzarella
   1 teaspoon kosher salt
   ¼ teaspoon black pepper
   ¼ cup freshly grated Parmesan
      cheese
   3 tablespoons butter

1. PUMPKIN BROTH: Melt butter in large heavy saucepan over moderate heat, add onion, carrots, celery, and leek and stir-fry until tender, about 10 minutes. Mix in canned pumpkin and cook and stir 3 minutes. Add all remaining ingredients, cover, and simmer 45 minutes. Put broth through fine strainer without forcing vegetables through; discard solids. Return broth to pan and keep hot.

2. RISOTTO: Heat olive oil 1 minute over moderate heat in second large heavy saucepan. Add rice and diced pumpkin and stir with wooden spoon until rice is well coated with oil.

3. Add wine and cook and stir until wine is absorbed. Add ½ cup hot pumpkin broth and cook and stir until absorbed. Add enough remaining pumpkin broth, ½ cup at a time, and stirring after each addition until absorbed, until risotto is *al dente* but creamy. This will take 20 to 25 minutes.

4. Stir in sage, arugula, mozzarella, salt, pepper, and 2 tablespoons Parmesan; smooth in butter.

5. Spoon into heated bowls and top with remaining 2 tablespoons Parmesan.

VEGETABLES

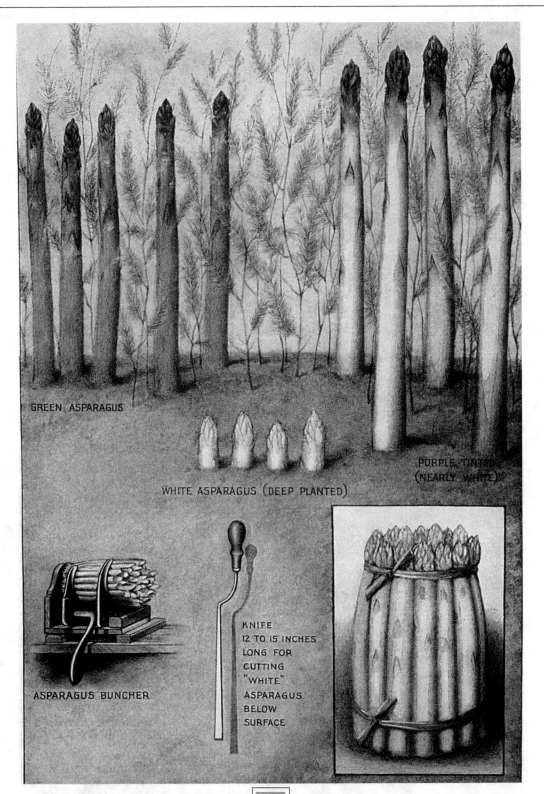

GREEN ASPARAGUS

WHITE ASPARAGUS (DEEP PLANTED)

PURPLE TINTED
(NEARLY WHITE)

ASPARAGUS BUNCHER

KNIFE
12 TO 15 INCHES
LONG FOR
CUTTING
"WHITE"
ASPARAGUS
BELOW
SURFACE

T HE TWENTIETH century, particularly the last half of it, added immeasurably to our repertoire of vegetables. But at the same time old favorites fell from grace, virtually disappearing from grocery shelves and from cookbooks—parsnips, salsify, cymlings, parched corn, poke, and beet greens to name six— although hip young chefs are beginning to rediscover the first two at least.

In the late-nineteenth and early-twentieth centuries, the preferred ways to cook vegetables were to boil, to bake, and to fry—more or less in that order. Seasonings were, for the most part, uninspired. Before World War I, most cookbooks offered few options: Butter, salt, and pepper, or white sauce. A particular favorite —Ambushed Asparagus—called for serving creamed asparagus in biscuits.

Now and then a cauliflower recipe might call for a cheese sauce. Beets might be pickled and served cold (as were Jerusalem artichokes); cucumbers and radishes were often boiled in broth and served hot. Lettuce, Belgian endive, and dandelion greens were wilted with hot dressings.

Vegetable casseroles barely made a statement before the twentieth century. In Maria Parloa's *Appledore Cook Book* (1872), a recipe for Baked Tomatoes tells the cook to layer whole peeled tomatoes into a dish with salt, pepper, and cracker crumbs, to dot with butter, and bake.

To my surprise, baked stuffed potatoes (what we call "Twice-Baked Potatoes") were a mainstay well before the turn of the century. I found this recipe for them in *Buckeye Cookery and Practical Housekeeping* (1880):

POTATOES IN JACKETS
Bake as many potatoes as are needed; when done, take off a little piece from one end to permit them to stand, from the other end cut a large piece, remove carefully the inside,

and rub through a fine sieve, or mash thoroughly; put on the fire with half an ounce of butter and one ounce of grated cheese to every four fair-sized potatoes; and add boiling milk and pepper and salt as for mashed potatoes; fill the potato shells, and sprinkle over mixed bread-crumbs and grated cheese; and put in hot oven and brown. Many prefer to omit cheese and bread-crumbs, filling the shells heaping full and then browning.

Three years later, *Mrs. Lincoln's Boston Cook Book* (1883) gives two different versions of twice-baked potatoes: "Potatoes in the Half-Shell," in which beaten egg whites are added to puff the potato filling, and "Stuffed Potatoes," with meat and mashed potatoes mounded into scooped-out potatoes.

Other baked stuffed vegetables were in vogue before the twentieth century, too—cabbage, tomatoes, and turnips, plus the occasional stuffed artichoke, onion, and winter squash—rather than the eggplant, mushrooms, and summer squash we favor today. Fannie Farmer, apparently, introduced us to stuffed peppers via *The Boston Cooking-School Cook Book* (1896). I find there two recipes for stuffed bell peppers, the first filled with a rice, meat, and tomato farce; the second, peppers filled with a mixture of bread crumbs, onion, and cream.

Canned vegetables were also known to the nineteenth-century cook. Indeed, Sarah Tyson Rorer includes "To Cook Canned Peas" in *Mrs. Rorer's Philadelphia Cook Book* (1886). But frozen vegetables are thoroughly twentieth century (see *Clarence Birdseye: Father of the Frozen Food Industry,* page 239), as are dehydrated vegetables and instant mashed potatoes.

Although early-twentieth-century cookbooks salute the nutritional value of vegetables, most instruct the cook to boil them to death. Even "international nutritional authority" Ida C. Bailey Allen, one of the first cookbook authors to write an entire volume on vegetables (*Vital Vegetables,* 1927), counsels the cook thus:

Partial view of Burpee's Fordhook Farms

BOILED GREEN PEAS
Cook peas in boiling water to barely cover containing 1 teaspoon salt to the quart. If peas are old, add a teaspoon sugar also. Simmer until tender—from twenty to thirty-five minutes. Add to liquid a little pepper and a tablespoon of butter for each pound of peas, and serve.

Right through the '40s and '50s we continued to overcook vegetables. And at about the same time, we began adding pinches of baking soda to the water in which we cooked green beans and asparagus, even broccoli and spinach. "To keep them bright green," the women's magazines told us. What they didn't say, and probably didn't know, was that the soda made the vegetables soapy and destroyed the vitamin C.

A typical recipe of the times is this one from *The June Platt Cook Book* (1958). Mrs. Platt, one of the powerful voices in the food field during the '30s, '40s, and '50s, for many years wrote a monthly recipe column for *House & Garden*.

Yet, she too, for all her sophistication, advocated "the pinch of soda" for green vegetables:

STRING BEANS ALMONDINE
Serves 6–8
3 pounds fresh string beans
1/2 pound butter
pinch of soda
1/2 cup shelled almonds
1 tablespoon chopped parsley

. . . Wash 3 pounds string beans in cold water. With a sharp knife, remove strings and cut fine lengthwise. This

is known as "Frenching the beans." Cook them in plenty of boiling salted water to which you have added a large pinch of soda to keep them green. Be sure to skim them. Do not overcook; 10–12 minutes should be sufficient . . .

By today's standard, Mrs. Platt was overcooking her beans. And another dozen years would pass before we would begin to see the light.

By most accounts, the one who led us out of the darkness was Alice Waters, a young Montessori teacher and passionate hobby cook. Advanced $10,000 from her parents back in New Jersey, Waters opened *Chez Panisse* restaurant in the summer of '71 in Berkeley, California. Her straightforward food *sans* fancy sauces showcased the finest, freshest produce available, and she cooked it only enough to coax out the natural flavors.

Waters turned our theories of vegetable cookery upside-down and launched the movement known as "California Cuisine," which in turn spawned what is now commonly called "New American Cooking."

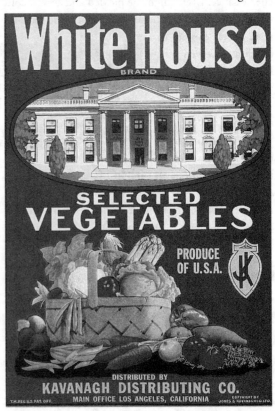

Microwaved Asparagus, Sweet Red Pepper, and Water Chestnuts

Makes 4 to 6 Servings

❋

ONE FACT surfaced from the microwave madness of the 1980s: This speed demon cooks vegetables to perfection and none better than asparagus. Not only does it emerge crisply succulent but also with most of its vitamins and minerals intact because there's no cooking water for them to leach out into and because the cooking itself is so swift. This recipe is adapted from *Micro Ways* (1990), a basic microwave cookbook I coauthored with Elaine Hanna.

> 1½ pounds asparagus, trimmed
>   of tough stem ends
> 1 medium red bell pepper,
>   cored, seeded, and cut into
>   2 × ⅛-inch strips
> 2 tablespoons roasted Asian
>   sesame oil
> ¼ cup thinly sliced water
>   chestnuts
> ¼ teaspoon salt
> ⅛ teaspoon black pepper

1. Snap off asparagus tips and set aside; slice stems on bias ½-inch thick. Arrange tips in center of microwave-safe 11- to 12-inch round platter.

2. Cover with red pepper strips and wreathe asparagus stems around edge. Sprinkle all evenly with oil.

3. Cover with vented plastic wrap and microwave on HIGH (100 percent power) 4 minutes.

4. Toss vegetables well, cover, and microwave 1 to 2 minutes longer just until crisp-tender.

5. Mix in water chestnuts, salt, and pepper, cover, and let stand 2 minutes before serving.

Roasted Asparagus

Makes 4 to 6 Servings

❋

THE '90S launched a new fad: roasted vegetables, especially *delicate* ones like asparagus. Here's my way of doing it.

> 2 tablespoons fruity olive oil
> 1½ pounds asparagus, trimmed
>   of tough stem ends
> 2 tablespoons freshly grated
>   Parmesan cheese
> ¼ teaspoon salt
> Black pepper

1. Preheat the oven to 375°F.

2. Pour oil into 13 × 9 × 2-inch baking pan, lay asparagus in pan one layer deep, then shake pan lightly to coat asparagus evenly with oil.

3. Roast, uncovered, shaking pan once or twice, 10 to 12 minutes until asparagus is lightly browned and crisp-tender.

4. Sprinkle with Parmesan and salt, add several grinds of pepper, and serve.

1939

Nestlé develops the chocolate "morsel."

Actor-singer James Beard opens a catering business in New York City.

1939–41

The New York World's Fair is held in Flushing Meadow with pavilions from fifty-eight foreign countries; the restaurant in the French pavilion reopens in New York City as Le Pavillon.

1940

Continuous countertop kitchens become state of the art.

James Beard's first cookbook—*Hors d'Oeuvre and Canapés*—is published.

Pre-cut, pre-packaged meats in cellophane wrappers go on sale in A & Ps.

Aunt Sammy

BEGINNING IN 1926 and continuing through the Great Depression until 1944, the U.S. Department of Agriculture broadcast a sort of "home ec of the air," fifteen minutes each weekday, coast to coast. The "anchor" was Aunt Sammy, a mythical Uncle Sam female counterpart with a friendly voice, who taught women how to cook dinner, make a dress, fix a drippy faucet and, most important, stretch a dollar. Aunt Sammy's recipes were such a hit they were bound into a book, which sold more than a million copies *during* the Depression. Mostly this was comfort food that taxed neither the budget nor the cook. Here's a sample, just as it appeared in *Aunt Sammy's Radio Recipes* in the 1930s:

SCALLOPED ASPARAGUS AND SPAGHETTI

1½ cups spaghetti broken into small pieces.

1 pint canned or cooked asparagus and liquid.

2 tablespoons flour.

2 tablespoons melted butter.

1 cup rich milk.

3 or 4 drops tabasco sauce.

½ teaspoon salt.

1 cup buttered bread crumbs.

Cook the spaghetti in salted boiling water for 20 minutes, and drain. Drain the liquid from the asparagus and cut the stalks in short pieces. Prepare a sauce of the flour, fat, milk, and asparagus water, and add the tabasco sauce and salt. In a greased baking dish put a layer of the cooked spaghetti, then one of asparagus, cover with the sauce, and continue until all the ingredients are used. Cover the top with the buttered bread crumbs. Bake in a moderate oven for about 20 minutes or until the crumbs are golden brown.

Baby Limas with Bacon and Sour Cream

Makes 6 Servings

❋

FROZEN VEGETABLES, which became widely available only after World War II, revolutionized the way Americans cooked. Today, with greenmarkets proliferating, few serious cooks will admit to using frozen fruits and vegetables. But in the '50s and '60s, this recipe was extremely popular among trendy hostesses. Sour cream gave it a "gourmet" touch.

6 slices bacon, cut crosswise into julienne strips

2 tablespoons butter or margarine

2 tablespoons minced yellow onion

2 (10-ounce) packages frozen baby lima beans

⅔ cup water

1 teaspoon salt

¼ teaspoon black pepper

½ teaspoon paprika

1 tablespoon minced fresh parsley

1 cup sour cream, at room temperature

1. Brown bacon in large heavy skillet over moderate heat 3 to 5 minutes until all fat cooks out; drain crisp brown bits on paper towels and reserve.

2. Melt butter in large heavy saucepan over moderate heat, add

onion and sauté, stirring often, about 2 minutes until limp.

3. Add beans, water, salt, pepper, and paprika, reduce heat to low, cover, and cook, stirring occasionally, 20 to 25 minutes, until beans are tender; drain well.

4. Remove from heat, stir in parsley, sour cream, and reserved bacon bits, and serve.

Harvard Beets

Makes 6 Servings

❋

I ALWAYS assumed this recipe predated the twentieth century. Yet I find no Harvard Beets in the dozen or so nineteenth-century cookbooks I consulted. *The Original Boston Cooking-School Cook Book* (1896) doesn't include them, but the 1906 edition does:

Wash twelve small beets, cook in boiling water until soft, remove skins, and cut beets in thin slices, small cubes, or fancy shapes, using French vegetable cutter. Mix one-half cup sugar and one-half tablespoon corn-starch. Add one-half cup vinegar and let boil five minutes. Pour over beets and let stand on back of range one-half hour. Just before serving add two tablespoons butter.

The recipe's name, it's said, comes from the crimson color of the beets —a perfect match for the official color of Harvard College (the vinegar in the sauce is what turns the beets a dazzling red). In *The Dictionary of American Food and Drink* (revised edition, 1994), John Mariani offers another theory set forth in a reader letter to *The New York Times*. It seems that Harvard Beets were created in the seventeenth century in England at a pub called Harwood's. According to Mariani, Harwood's "customers included a Russian emigré who, in 1846, opened up a restaurant in Boston under the same name." He served Harwood Beets here, only he pronounced the name more like "Harvard." So if the story is true, England's Harwood Beets became America's Harvard Beets. Whatever their origin, this much is certain: Harvard Beets became popular coast-to-coast only in the twentieth century.

> *2 pounds medium beets, tops*
> *removed*
> *⅓ cup sugar*
> *2 tablespoons cornstarch*
> *1 teaspoon salt*
> *¼ teaspoon black pepper*
> *1 cup cider vinegar*
> *¼ cup water*
> *3 tablespoons butter or*
> *margarine*

1. Boil beets in skins in covered, large heavy saucepan of lightly salted boiling water 40 to 45 minutes until tender. Drain, quick-chill in ice water, then peel and trim off stem and root ends. Slice beets thin and reserve.

2. Mix sugar, cornstarch, salt, and pepper in pan and slowly blend in vinegar. Add water and butter and cook over moderate heat, stirring constantly, 3 to 5 minutes until mixture thickens and clears.

3. Return beets to pan and turn gently in sauce. Reduce heat to lowest point, cover, and simmer beets 10 minutes. Serve at once.

Broccoli Italian Style

Makes 4 Servings

❋

ITALIANATE RECIPES for broccoli began appearing in mass magazines in the 1960s and never stopped. This recipe, my own, has served me well for years.

> *1 pound bunch broccoli*
> *3 tablespoons fruity olive oil*
> *1 clove garlic, peeled and*
> *slivered*
> *¼ teaspoon salt*
> *¼ teaspoon black pepper*
> *2 tablespoons balsamic vinegar*
> *2 anchovy fillets, mashed*

1. Trim tough leaves and stems from broccoli and cut into small florets; wash and drain well.

2. Heat oil in large deep skillet 2 minutes over moderate heat. Add broccoli, garlic, salt, and pepper and sauté 6 to 8 minutes, stirring constantly, until broccoli is crisp-tender.

3. Blend vinegar and anchovies, add to broccoli, toss well, and serve.

BROCCOLI

ISCUSSING VEGETABLES that gained popularity in the 1920s, Richard J. Hooker (*A History: Food and Drink in America,* 1981) writes: "Italian immigrants did not introduce but popularized broccoli, which by 1920 was being grown commercially." Waverley Root and Richard de Rochemont go into more detail in *Eating in America* (1976): "We are accustomed to think of broccoli as a twentieth-century revelation; but John Randolph, in *A Treatise on Gardening by a Citizen of Virginia,* written just before the Revolution, speaks of it as if it were well known in his time . . . ."

Still, broccoli recipes did not show up in American cookbooks with any regularity until the late 1920s, and there was precious little variety until after World War II. The original *The Boston Cooking-School Cook Book* (1896) by Fannie Merritt Farmer never mentions broccoli. Nor do the 1906, 1918, or 1923 editions.

Ida C. Bailey Allen, Chautauqua circuit lecturer and author of *Good Housekeeping's* "Three Meals a Day" column, who claimed the culinary limelight after Fannie Farmer's death in 1915, is, as far as I can determine, the first cookbook author to discuss broccoli at some length. In *Vital Vegetables* (1927), Mrs. Allen instructs:

Wash, soak in cold salted water thirty minutes to remove any insects [today broccoli is washed three times before it goes to market]*, cut in coarse dice or trim in even lengths, and tie in cheesecloth. If to be steamed, first sprinkle with salt. If to be boiled, add one teaspoon salt to a quart of boiling water. Cook twenty to thirty minutes and season with one tablespoon butter to three cups of prepared vegetable and salt and pepper to taste.*

"When plain cooked," she continues, "serve with the main dish at luncheon or dinner. When served with an elaborate sauce use as an entrée." Her "elaborate sauces" are a "savoury egg or cream sauce, drawn butter, hollandaise or mousseline sauce or green pepper sauce."

Elsewhere in the book, Mrs. Allen gives a recipe for a cream of broccoli soup (ladled onto squares of buttered toast and topped "as desired" with grated cheese) and another for broccoli salad ("arrange cooked broccoli cut in inch lengths in nests of lettuce or cress and use with French dressing").

Continuing to track broccoli, I find in *Good Housekeeping's Meals, Tested, Tasted and Approved* (1930) a recipe for Broccoli on Toast (smothered with white sauce and chopped hard-cooked eggs). And two lackluster recipes in Sheila Hibben's fairly sophisticated *National Cookbook* (1932): Boiled Broccoli and Broccoli with Cheese.

It remained for Italian immigrants in California and elsewhere to teach us how versatile broccoli is. And most of us didn't catch on until a couple of decades after World War II.

Broccoli-Cheese Potato Topper

Makes 4 Servings

✳

BY THE time the Campbell Soup Company published *Campbell's Best-Ever Recipes* in 1994, broccoli had become such a mainstay that nearly a fourth of the book's recipes contain it, among them a Chicken-Broccoli Divan. The original Divan, created in the 1930s at the Divan Parisien Restaurant in New York City, is generally credited with making broccoli a household word (see box, page 111). This recipe and the one that follows are two of the broccoli recipes from Campbell's *Best-Ever* book, a brief but telling timeline of culinary Americana.

> 1 (10¾-ounce can) condensed
>   Cheddar cheese soup
> 2 tablespoons sour cream or
>   plain yogurt
> ½ teaspoon Dijon mustard
> 1 cup cooked broccoli florets
> 4 hot baked potatoes, halved
>   lengthwise

1. Mix soup, sour cream, and mustard in small heavy saucepan; add broccoli. Set over moderate heat and bring just to serving temperature, stirring occasionally.

2. Pinch each potato half to fluff meat inside, arrange two halves on each of four dinner plates, ladle broccoli mixture on top, and serve.

Vegetables with Broccoli-Lemon Sauce

Makes 8 Servings

✳

NOTE THAT the base for the sauce is Campbell's Condensed Cream of Broccoli Soup. It was introduced in 1990 and, despite former President George Bush's highly public broccoli-bashing, became, according to Campbell's, its "most successful new product launch and the first new product to break the top-ten list of popular soups in fifty-five years."

> 3 pounds small new potatoes,
>   quartered
> 2 cups fresh broccoli florets
> 1 large red bell pepper, cored,
>   seeded, and cut into rings
> 1 (10¾-ounce) can condensed
>   cream of broccoli soup
> ½ cup mayonnaise
> ¼ cup finely chopped scallions
> 1 tablespoon fresh lemon juice
> ¼ teaspoon dried leaf thyme,
>   crumbled

1. Cook potatoes in 1-inch boiling water in large heavy saucepan over high heat 10 minutes.

2. Add broccoli and red pepper and cook 5 minutes; drain all well.

3. Mix soup, mayonnaise, scallions, lemon juice, and thyme in small saucepan. Bring to serving temperature over moderate heat, stirring occasionally.

4. Arrange vegetables on deep platter, pour sauce over all, and serve.

THE TUPPERWARE PARTY

ONE OF the most remarkable marketing successes of the '50s was achieved by the aptly named Brownie Wise, who persuaded housewives to demonstrate and sell to their friends vast quantities of plastic containers that had been languishing on store shelves. The polyethylene storage containers designed by Earl S. Tupper and introduced in 1946 really were flexible, unbreakable, airtight, and superior to earlier plastics. Still, skeptical homemakers needed convincing, and that's when Wise, hired specially to solve the problem, came up with the Tupperware Party.

The idea was perfect for the '50s—that decade of togetherness, *kaffee klatsches,* and backyard barbecues. In split-level ranch houses all over America women gathered for light refreshments and a chance to examine the Tupperware merchandise and "burp" the lids. Party-givers earned commissions, party-goers got discounts if they sold any Tupperware to their friends, and everybody was happy.

Especially Mr. Tupper.

Sautéed Broccoli Rabe

Makes 4 Servings

✳

LIKE BROCCOLI, this member of the cabbage family with deeply serrated, dark green leaves and tiny bud clusters, made its way from Italian-American communities into the mainstream. But its journey was much slower—only in the late '80s did broccoli rabe begin showing up with any regularity in supermarkets. Its flavor is biting and its nutritional value impressive. Broccoli rabe is a powerhouse of iron, calcium, potassium, and vitamins A, C, and K. This quick-and-easy recipe is adapted from *The Woman's Day Cookbook* (1995).

1¼ pounds broccoli rabe
2 tablespoons fruity olive oil
1 clove garlic, peeled and
  minced
½ teaspoon salt

1. Trim ½ inch from broccoli rabe stem ends. Stack leaves and cut crosswise into 1-inch strips.

2. Heat oil 1 minute in large, deep nonstick skillet over moderate heat. Add garlic and stir-fry 1 minute.

3. Add salt and half the broccoli rabe. Cook and stir briefly until broccoli rabe cooks down, then add remaining broccoli rabe. Cover, and cook 6 to 7 minutes until leaves are wilted and stems tender; turn broccoli rabe occasionally as it cooks and add 3 tablespoons water if it threatens to scorch.

4. Cook, uncovered, 2 minutes until juices evaporate, and serve.

Michael McLaughlin's Broccoli-Leek Puree

Makes 12 Servings

✳

AN INNOVATIVE young American chef, Michael McLaughlin collaborated on the best-selling *Silver Palate Cookbook* (with Silver Palate shop owners Sheila Lukins and Julee Rosso), then went on to write several first-rate cookbooks of his own. This stellar broccoli puree, a far cry from the boring broccoli we were force-fed in the '30s, '40s, and '50s, is adapted from a recipe in *The New American Kitchen* (1990), Michael's book of "casual menus for good friends, easy times, and great food."

The recipe feeds an army but Michael points out that "this bright green puree loses nothing by being prepared a day in advance." In fact, it keeps well for several days in the fridge and can be heated up, a portion or two at a time.

3 medium bunches broccoli
  (about 4½ pounds total)
5 teaspoons salt (or to taste)
¾ cup (1½ sticks) butter
6 large leeks, white part only,
  trimmed, cleaned, and
  chopped
1 teaspoon freshly grated
  nutmeg
1 teaspoon black pepper

1. Trim broccoli of coarse leaves and stalks; peel tender stalks and divide tops into florets.

2. Add 3 teaspoons salt to large kettle of boiling water, drop in broccoli stalks, and cook, uncovered, 5 minutes. Add florets and cook, uncovered, 5 to 7 minutes longer, until very tender. Drain, quick-chill in ice bath, then drain well again.

3. Melt butter in large heavy skillet over moderate heat; add leeks, reduce heat to low, cover, and cook, stirring now and then, until very tender—about 20 minutes.

4. Puree broccoli in batches until satiny in electric blender at high speed or in food processor fitted with metal chopping blade, then puree leeks with their butter.

5. Mix broccoli and leek purees; stir in nutmeg, pepper, and remaining 2 teaspoons salt.

Microwaved Brussels Sprouts with Garlic and Cream

Makes 4 Servings

✳

A POPULAR vegetable around the turn of the century, Brussels sprouts had fallen from favor by World War II. Then frozen sprouts became available, then the microwave, which cooks fresh Brussels sprouts quickly and kindly. Today nearly every quality supermarket carries little tubs of fresh Brussels sprouts in season, and they're a staple at most farmer's markets. This recipe is adapted from *Micro Ways* (1990), a microwave handbook Elaine Hanna and I wrote together.

1 pound Brussels sprouts, trimmed and sliced crosswise ¹⁄₁₆-inch thick (discard hard cores)
½ clove garlic, peeled and minced
2 tablespoons chicken broth
¼ cup heavy cream
½ teaspoon salt (or to taste)
¼ teaspoon freshly grated nutmeg
⅛ teaspoon black pepper (or to taste)

1. Mix sprouts, garlic, and broth in 2-quart microwave-safe casserole.

2. Cover with lid and microwave on HIGH (100 percent power) 6 to 8 minutes, stirring at halftime.

3. Mix in cream, salt, nutmeg, and pepper, cover, and microwave on MEDIUM (50 percent power) 2 minutes to blend flavors.

4. Toss mixture well, taste for salt and pepper, adjust as needed, and serve.

....

Carrots and Green Pepper in Sour Cream Sauce

Makes 2 to 4 Servings

✳

IN COOKBOOKS published in the waning years of the nineteenth century and right through the first decades of this century, parsnip recipes outnumbered carrot recipes four to one. Maria Parloa dismisses carrots with a single sentence in *The Appledore Cook Book* (1872): "Prepare, boil, and serve the same as parsnips." Eleven years later Mary Lincoln had this to say about them in *Mrs. Lincoln's Boston Cook Book:* "Carrots are not a favorite vegetable for the table." Her successor at the Boston Cooking School, Fannie Merritt Farmer, doesn't do much better by them in *The Original Boston Cooking-School Cook Book* (1896): "... carrots are chiefly used for flavoring soups, and for gar-

nishing, on account of their bright color." She did, however, introduce that tiresome combo, carrots and peas. Here's a better one—carrots with sweet green pepper. The original recipe was given to me in the 1950s by Mildred Sieber, a home economist with the Duke Power Company, who traveled all over North Carolina demonstrating unusual recipes. I've fine-tuned it over the years and call this version my own.

6 medium carrots, peeled and coarsely grated
½ medium green bell pepper, cored, seeded, and finely chopped
2 tablespoons butter or margarine
½ cup water
¼ teaspoon salt
⅛ teaspoon black pepper
⅛ teaspoon freshly grated nutmeg
½ cup sour cream

1. Simmer carrots, green pepper, butter, water, salt, pepper, and nutmeg in covered medium heavy saucepan over moderately low heat until carrots are tender—about 10 minutes.

2. Uncover, and cook 5 to 10 minutes until almost all water evaporates.

3. Smooth in sour cream and serve.

Orange-Glazed Carrots

Makes 4 Servings

✳

BY THE 1930s, cooks had begun to treat carrots like sweet potatoes, that is, to candy or glaze them. I fished this battered, splattered recipe out of my mother's recipe file and note that the date on it is 1938. Usually meticulous about crediting her recipe sources, Mother failed to do so for these carrots.

NOTE: In those days we liked carrots good and soft, so you may want to trim the cooking times.

> 8 large carrots, peeled and halved crosswise
> 2 cups water
> 3 tablespoons butter or margarine
> Juice of ½ lemon or 1 lime
> 2 tablespoons light brown sugar
> 1 tablespoon orange or ginger marmalade
> ¼ teaspoon salt
> ⅛ teaspoon black pepper

1. Boil carrots in water in covered, large heavy saucepan over moderate heat 30 to 35 minutes until tender; drain well.

2. Return to heat and shake pan gently to drive excess moisture from carrots.

3. Add butter, lemon juice, brown sugar, marmalade, salt, and pepper, and simmer, uncovered, over lowest heat 30 minutes, shaking pan often, until carrots are richly glazed.

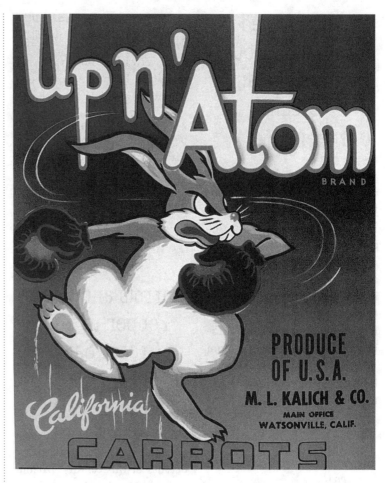

Shredded Carrots with Lemon

Makes 4 to 6 Servings

✳

A BETA-CAROTENE-RICH 1990s recipe that I spun off the classic *carottes râpées* of the south of France. Note that the cooking fat is olive oil.

> 1½ pounds medium carrots, peeled and coarsely shredded
> 1 large red onion, peeled and chopped

> 1 medium clove garlic, peeled and minced
> ¼ cup fruity olive oil
> ½ teaspoon dried leaf marjoram, crumbled
> ¼ teaspoon dried leaf thyme, crumbled
> ¼ cup fresh lemon juice
> ¼ teaspoon salt (or to taste)
> ⅛ teaspoon black pepper (or to taste)

1. Stir-fry carrots, onion, and garlic in olive oil in large heavy skillet over moderately high heat until crisp-tender—about 5 minutes.

VEGETABLES

2. Add marjoram and thyme and stir-fry 1 to 2 minutes longer.

3. Add lemon juice, salt, and pepper and toss lightly. Serve hot, at room temperature, or cold.

Microwaved Corn-on-the-Cob

Makes 2 Servings

✻

WHAT A wonder the microwave is when it comes to cooking corn-on-the-cob. The ears needn't be shucked or desilked and there're no kettles of boiling water to cope with. Here's my favorite way to microwave corn. Rule Number One: Choose super-fresh ears of uniform size. Next, consider your own preferences and the wattage of your microwave oven. Some people like corn-on-the-cob practically raw. I don't, so I microwave it until no raw starchy taste lingers. If you belong to the "raw" school, reduce the microwave time suggested by 2 or 3 minutes. My microwave oven is a 650-watter and the times given here are for those in the 550–650 range. If yours is more powerful, reduce overall cooking time a couple of

minutes. If of lower wattage, increase microwave time accordingly. You'll soon discover the time that suits your oven and taste precisely.

NOTE: To trim fat and calories, I often skip the butter and squeeze a little fresh lime juice over the ears of corn. Not bad.

> *4 large ears sweet corn in the husk*
> *Butter or margarine*
> *Salt to taste*
> *Black pepper to taste*

1. Line counter with several thicknesses newspaper and set out a sharp, heavy chef's knife.

2. Arrange unhusked corn on microwave oven floor, spacing 1½ inches apart and alternating direction of ears: tip facing forward, tip facing backward, and so on.

3. Microwave on HIGH (100 percent power) 8 to 10 minutes.

4. Using dish towel, lift hot ears to newspaper-covered counter. Slice off stalk ends and tips, then unfurl husks (most silks will come away with husks).

5. Butter ears of corn, sprinkle with salt and pepper, and serve.

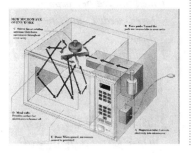

M OST PEOPLE had never heard the word "microwave" in 1945 when Dr. Percy L. Spencer, a scientist working for the electronics firm Raytheon, made the newspapers by successfully popping corn with microwaves. A few years later, Raytheon introduced its Radarange—but for commercial use only. It stood five feet tall, weighed nearly half a ton, and cost several thousand dollars.

During the early '50s, Raytheon brought out better and cheaper microwave ovens; in 1955 Tappan introduced a $1,295 model designed for home use, with Hotpoint and General Electric not far behind. And at last, in 1967, Amana Refrigeration, Inc. (then a Raytheon subsidiary) came out with a 115-volt countertop microwave priced at just $495. American cooks could no longer resist the temptation to try out the new technology—and in the beginning they tried to make these speed demons do everything, only to be disappointed. Foods neither brown nor crisp in a microwave oven. But how perfectly it cooks fish, grains, and vegetables!

Buttercrust Corn Pie with Fresh Tomato Salsa

Makes 6 Servings

✳

A 1990s twist on a World War I classic—Tamale Pie (page 149)—that takes the tomatoes out of the pie and puts them in a salsa, America's turn-of-the-twenty-first-century passion. The recipe here, a *Southern Living* reader letter from Linda Magers of Clemmons, North Carolina, is adapted from the version in the July 1995 issue.

NOTE: The salsa recipe makes about two cups and is a good all-round topper for tacos or other Tex-Mex favorites.

FRESH TOMATO SALSA
2 cups cored, peeled, and chopped vine-ripe tomatoes (about 2 medium)
1 medium jalapeño pepper, cored, seeded, and minced or 1 (4.5-ounce) can chopped green chilies, well drained
½ cup thinly sliced scallions
Juice of ½ lemon or 1 lime
½ teaspoon dried leaf oregano, crumbled
½ teaspoon salt
⅛ teaspoon black pepper
2 tablespoons minced fresh coriander (cilantro) or parsley

CORN PIE
1¼ cups fine soda-cracker crumbs

¼ cup freshly grated Parmesan cheese
½ cup (1 stick) butter or margarine, melted
1¼ cups milk
2 cups fresh or frozen whole-kernel corn
1 teaspoon onion salt
¼ teaspoon white pepper
2 tablespoons flour
¼ cup chopped, pitted ripe olives
½ cup thinly sliced scallions
2 eggs, lightly beaten
½ teaspoon paprika

1. FRESH TOMATO SALSA: Toss together all ingredients except coriander in medium nonreactive bowl, cover, and refrigerate until flavors blend—3 to 4 hours. Mix in fresh coriander and mellow at room temperature about ½ hour.

2. Meanwhile, prepare CORN PIE: Preheat oven to 400° F.

3. Toss cracker crumbs with Parmesan and melted butter well; measure out and reserve 2 tablespoons. Pat remaining mixture over bottom and up sides of ungreased 9-inch pie plate; set aside.

4. Bring 1 cup milk, the corn, onion salt, and white pepper to boiling in medium heavy saucepan over moderate heat. Adjust heat so mixture bubbles gently, then simmer, uncovered, 3 minutes.

5. Blend remaining ¼ cup milk with flour, add slowly to corn mixture, and stir vigorously, then cook and stir until thickened—about 1 minute.

6. Remove from heat and mix in olives and scallions. Blend about ½ cup hot mixture into eggs, stir back into pan, and mix well.

7. Spoon into crumb crust, sprinkle with reserved crumb mixture, and add a blush of paprika.

8. Bake, uncovered, until set like custard—about 20 minutes.

9. Cut into wedges and accompany with Fresh Tomato Salsa.

Mexicali Corn

Makes 4 to 6 Servings

✳

ALSO CALLED "Spanish Corn," "Calico Corn," and "Confetti Corn" because of its bright dots of red, green, and yellow, this recipe has been a favorite for more than half a century. The original called for canned whole-kernel corn, but I make it with frozen whole-kernel corn and think it's better. You can also substitute sweet corn, freshly cut from the cob (you'll need about eight good-size ears).

1 medium green bell pepper, cored, seeded, and finely diced
1 medium red bell pepper, cored, seeded, and finely diced
1 medium yellow onion, peeled and finely chopped
¼ cup (½ stick) butter or margarine
2 (10-ounce) packages frozen whole-kernel corn, thawed

¼ teaspoon salt (or to taste)
¼ teaspoon black pepper (or to taste)

1. Stir-fry green and red peppers and onion in butter in large heavy skillet 5 to 8 minutes over moderate heat.

2. Add corn, salt, and black pepper, cover, turn heat to low, and simmer just until corn is done, about 5 minutes; stir occasionally and if corn threatens to stick, add a few tablespoons hot water.

3. Taste for salt and black pepper, adjust as needed, and serve.

Slow-Cooker Eggplant and Artichokes with Parmesan

Makes 4 to 6 Servings

✳

MABLE HOFFMAN, from whose best-selling *Crockery Cookery* (1975) this recipe is adapted, won millions of fans for her ability to make carefree cooking of long-winded recipe classics. There's no denying that the recipe here goes together zip-quick and cooks completely unattended.

1 medium eggplant (about 1 pound)
¾ teaspoon salt
1 (14-ounce) jar marinara sauce
1 (9-ounce) package frozen artichoke hearts, thawed and quartered
2 tablespoons well-drained capers
2 teaspoons snipped fresh rosemary or ½ teaspoon dried leaf rosemary, crumbled
¼ teaspoon black pepper
⅓ cup freshly grated Parmesan cheese

1. Slice unpeeled eggplant crosswise ¾-inch thick, halve slices, and sprinkle with salt.

2. Layer eggplant alternately into slow cooker with marinara sauce, artichoke hearts, and capers, sprinkling as you go with rosemary and pepper.

3. Cover and cook on HIGH until eggplant is tender—4 to 5 hours.

4. Sprinkle with Parmesan and serve.

TIMELINE

1941

M&M's Plain Chocolate Candies ("The milk chocolate melts in your mouth—not in your hand.") debut in six colors: red, green, yellow, orange, brown, and violet. Eight years later, tan replaces violet.

THE MAGAZINE OF GOOD LIVING

Gourmet magazine debuts. Publisher Earl MacAusland names as editor Pearl Metzelthin, author of *The World Wide Cook Book* (1939).

General Electric introduces the garbage Disposall.

The Federal Enrichment Act passes; millers, bakers, and cereal manufacturers must bring nutritive content of their products to that of whole wheat by restoring iron, thiamin, riboflavin, and niacin lost in milling or processing.

1941–45

World War II.

Corn dogs are sold at the State Fair of Texas.

Roasted Garlic

WHEN DID we fall in love with roasted garlic? Late '70s? Early '80s? "I think *late* '80s," says Sara Moulton, chef of the Executive Dining Room at *Gourmet* magazine, star of the Food Network's popular *Cooking Live,* and frequent guest on ABC-TV's *Good Morning America.* "It was when trendy Italian restaurants began bringing fresh-baked bread to the table and pouring out a little olive oil as a dip. In some restaurants they'd also bring you a little dish of roasted garlic to spread on the bread."

Sara likes to smooth roasted garlic on toast and squeeze it directly from the bulb into sauces—"it's a great thickener and flavorer." Sara adds that it's good, too, in soups, gravies, and many vegetable dishes.

SARA MOULTON'S METHOD FOR ROASTING GARLIC

1. Cut about 1 inch off the top of a head or bulb of garlic, just enough to expose the flesh of each clove.

2. Drizzle the cut side of the garlic with olive oil, wrap head in foil, and roast about 1 hour at 350°F or until the garlic feels soft.

3. Squeeze the hot garlic flesh out of the head and use in any of the ways suggested above.

Baked Fennel

Makes 4 Servings

✳

ELIZABETH ("SUSIE") Schneider, a food journalist for whom I have enormous respect both as a writer and as a researcher, says in her benchmark book *Uncommon Fruits & Vegetables: A Commonsense Guide* (1986): "Perhaps it is because I was raised near Little Italy in Greenwich Village that I have always taken for granted this crisp, fragrant vegetable/herb, which I have just recently come to realize is relatively hard to find in much of the country." I, on the other hand, who grew up in Raleigh, North Carolina, perhaps ten years before Susie, had never heard of fennel until I came to New York to work in the late 1950s. Today, with nearly every town of even moderate size boasting a green-market, fennel (or *finocchio,* as Italians know it,) is not as scarce as it was ten years ago when Susie's book was published. She includes ten fennel recipes in the book, among them this supremely easy one, which I've adapted here.

> *2 medium fennel bulbs (about*
>   *1½ pounds minus tops)*
> *2 tablespoons fruity olive oil*
> *½ teaspoon coarse kosher salt*
> *½ cup dry white wine*
> *¼ cup water*
> *½ cup freshly and finely grated*
>   *Parmesan cheese*

1. Preheat oven to 350°F.

2. Quarter fennel bulbs and remove tough bases and hard lower cores. Slice quarters thin and arrange in baking/serving dish just large enough to hold them.

3. Drizzle oil evenly over fennel and sprinkle with salt. Pour in wine and water. Place oiled sheet of wax paper over fennel, tucking in around edges. Crimp large sheet of foil over baking dish to seal.

4. Bake fennel 35 to 45 minutes until tender. Remove foil and wax paper and stir gently. Return to oven and bake, uncovered, 30 minutes longer until almost all liquid has evaporated.

5. Sprinkle cheese over fennel and serve hot, warm, or at room temperature.

Sautéed Fennel and Red Peppers

Makes 6 Servings

❊

A LOVELY recipe from *Chicago Tribune* food columnist William Rice, which he included in *Feasts of Wine and Food* (1987). The book and the recipe, adapted slightly here, are favorites of mine. Serve with baked fish or roast chicken.

6 medium red bell peppers, roasted as directed on page 246

4 medium fennel bulbs, trimmed (about 3 pounds minus tops) and cut into julienne strips
5 tablespoons butter
½ teaspoon anise liqueur
Black pepper to taste

1. Peel red peppers, quarter lengthwise, discard pith and seeds; set aside.

2. Sauté fennel in 3 tablespoons butter in large heavy skillet over moderate heat 3 to 5 minutes until crisp-tender; add liqueur and a sprinkling of black pepper and toss well; set aside.

3. Melt remaining butter in second large heavy skillet over moderate heat. Add red peppers and heat, turning in butter, just until serving temperature. Sprinkle with black pepper and toss gently.

4. To serve, mound red peppers in center of platter and wreathe with fennel.

Leeks au Gratin

Makes 4 to 6 Servings

❊

A LUMINARY in the food field during the '50s, '60s, and '70s, Nika Hazelton not only edited the valuable *Woman's Day Encyclopedia of Cooking* but also wrote several excellent cookbooks of her own including *The Unabridged Vegetable Cookbook* whence this recipe is adapted.

12 medium to large leeks
1¼ cups beef or chicken broth (about)
1 cup dry white wine
4 tablespoons butter or margarine
4 tablespoons flour
1 cup coarsely shredded Swiss cheese or 1 cup freshly grated Parmesan cheese
Salt to taste
Black pepper to taste

1. Preheat oven to 425°F. Butter 6-cup *au gratin* pan and set aside.

2. Trim leeks of root ends and all but 2 inches tops, then halve lengthwise. Wash well in several changes of water; drain.

3. Bring broth and wine to boiling in large heavy skillet over high heat. Reduce heat to low, add leeks, cover, and simmer 5 to 7 minutes until barely tender; drain, reserving cooking liquid. Arrange leeks in *au gratin* pan.

4. Melt butter in small heavy saucepan over moderate heat, then blend in flour. Measure reserved cooking liquid and if there are not 2 cups, add broth to round out measure. Add to flour mixture and cook, stirring constantly, 3 to 5 minutes until thickened and smooth. Mix in ¾ cup cheese and stir until cheese melts; season to taste with salt and pepper.

5. Pour cheese sauce over leeks, top with remaining ¼ cup cheese, and bake, uncovered, until nicely browned—about 20 to 25 minutes.

Leeks Vinaigrette

Makes 4 Servings

✳

"THE LEEK is a very hardy, and of easy culture, succeeding best in a light but well-enriched soil," instructs *Burpee's Farm Annual* of 1888. "The whole plant is edible, employed in soups, boiled with meat, etc., reputed more delicate in flavor than the Onion." Quite so. And yet cookbooks virtually ignore the leek until the 1960s, certainly the leek as vegetable. *Mrs. Rorer's New Cook Book* (1902) by Sarah Tyson Rorer—the first cookbook I was able to find in which leeks were given any space in the vegetable chapter—had only this to say: "The bulb of the leek is greatly elongated, and the leaves broadly linear. They are used principally as flavoring for soups but are sometimes boiled and served with cream sauce. The old and popular dish, cock-a-leekie, a chicken soup, is thickened with leeks." The 1943 edition of *Joy of Cooking* includes leeks—but just barely. *The New York Times Cook Book* (1961), edited by Craig Claiborne, offers a lone recipe—for Braised Leeks. And his *The New York Times Menu Cook Book* (1966) also gives a single recipe, this time for Leeks with Red Wine. Julia Child, I feel sure, was the first to teach us how lovely leeks can be. In *Mastering the Art of French Cooking* (1961) she gives us Braised Leeks, Leeks Browned with Cheese, Leeks à la Grecque, Leek and Potato Soup, Leek Gratin with Ham, and Flamiche (a leek quiche). Cold cooked vegetables topped with a simple oil and vinegar dressing had been the province of big-city American chefs from the mid-nineteenth century on, but Leeks Vinaigrette did not enter the average home cook's repertoire for a hundred years. The version here is adapted from Linda and Fred Griffith's *Onions, Onions, Onions* (1994).

8 slender leeks, trimmed to include tender green part
1 teaspoon kosher salt (or to taste)
1 tablespoon fresh lemon juice
2 tablespoons Champagne vinegar or white wine vinegar
1 teaspoon Dijon mustard
⅓ cup fruity olive oil
2 tablespoons minced fresh flat-leaf parsley
1 tablespoon minced shallots
1 tablespoon minced fresh tarragon or 1 teaspoon dried leaf tarragon, crumbled
1 teaspoon minced lemon verbena or lemon balm leaves or ½ teaspoon finely grated lemon zest
Salt and black pepper to taste

1. Halve leeks lengthwise; rinse carefully to remove grit.

2. Fill large saucepan with water, add 1 teaspoon kosher salt, and bring to boiling over high heat. Add leeks, reduce heat to low, and cook just until tender—8 to 10 minutes. Drain carefully and refresh leeks in ice water.

3. Mix lemon juice, vinegar, and mustard in small bowl. Slowly whisk in olive oil, then stir in parsley, shallots, tarragon, and lemon verbena. Season to taste with salt and pepper.

4. Arrange leeks in single layer in shallow nonreactive dish. Pour vinaigrette evenly over all, turn leeks gently to coat, then cover, and refrigerate at least 1 hour.

5. Let leeks stand at room temperature for about 1 hour before serving.

CLARENCE BIRDSEYE:
FATHER OF
THE FROZEN FOOD INDUSTRY

IN 1914 while on a winter expedition to Labrador with the U.S. Fish and Wildlife Service, a young Brooklyn scientist named Clarence Birdseye discovered that the fish he pulled from icy waters froze rock-hard before he could take them off the hook. To his further surprise, these fish could be kept for weeks, and when cooked, tasted remarkably fresh.

From that day onward, Birdseye began to experiment with different ways of freezing food. He'd seen Eskimos bury their catch in ice only to retrieve it weeks later, cook it, and enjoy it. One winter while out trapping, he followed their lead, dressing some caribou steaks and burying them in ice. Some days later, he chipped away the ice, broiled the steaks, and pronounced them first-rate.

After World War I, Birdseye went to work in the fishery business in Gloucester, Massachusetts. But his real interests lay elsewhere—in his off-hours experiments with frozen food. By now he'd determined that the more quickly foods were frozen and the lower the temperature inside his mechanical freezer (in this case well below 0° F), the higher their quality. This held true for frozen meats, fish, fowl, fruits, vegetables—even such baked goods as breads, cakes, and pies.

Convinced that his quick-frozen foods were supe- rior to canned foods and every bit as good as the fresh, Birdseye's next step was to go into production. To raise capital, he cooked a series of frozen-food dinners for prospective investors. And when a skep- tical Wall Streeter refused to travel to Gloucester to dine *chez* Birdseye, Birdseye dispatched a frozen din- ner to the millionaire's Westchester home together with instructions for preparing it.

"Mr. Wall Street" was so impressed he ponied up enough to help launch Bird- seye's frozen foods. In 1929, Birdseye merged his firm with the Postum Company, creating the food-company giant General Foods.

General Foods rolled out its new Birds Eye Frosted Foods in 1930 and enticed groceries into stocking them with the offer of free freezer cabinets. But with the coun- try sunk in the Depression, it would seem that General Foods could not have picked a worse time to introduce an important new food line.

Apparently not. Even though its frozen foods cost more than the fresh or canned, even though they required "t.l.c." from plant to store to rental freezer locker (for this was all that was available before home freezers) to kitchen, even though they involved new cooking techniques, Birds Eye Frosted Foods caught on.

And by the mid-1940s they had become absolutely indispensable.

Compote of Leek and Wild Mushrooms

Makes 2 to 4 Servings

✳

FEW WOULD deny that Dean Fearing, executive chef at The Mansion on Turtle Creek, a landmark Dallas hotel, is one of America's most innovative young cooks. This simple dish, adapted from *The Mansion on Turtle Creek Cookbook* (1987), shows what he can do given five ingredients. Fearing serves this compote as an accompaniment to medallions of venison with blackberry-sage sauce, but it is equally delicious with roast beef, lamb, or pork.

NOTE: Fearing says the compote can be prepared several hours ahead and kept warm or gently reheated.

1 large leek, white part only
1 cup julienned assorted wild
*   mushrooms (morels,*
*   pleurotes, shiitake, or cèpes)*
½ cup heavy cream
Salt to taste
Juice of ½ lemon (or to taste)

1. Cut leek into 2-inch lengths and cut each into fine julienne strips.

2. Bring leek, mushrooms, and cream to boiling in medium heavy saucepan over moderate heat; reduce heat to low and cook until cream thickens, about 5 minutes.

3. Off heat, season to taste with salt and lemon juice and serve.

Paprika Mushrooms

Makes 6 Servings

✳

CRAIG CLAIBORNE, who joined *The New York Times* in 1957, did more to expand our knowledge of food and introduce us to new recipes than anyone until Julia Child came along a few years later. When I first tried these mushrooms many, many years ago, I remember thinking "how easy, how exotic!" They hardly seem so today, yet I still prepare them often. The recipe here is adapted from *The New York Times Cook Book* (1961), which Claiborne edited. Although the *Times* recipe doesn't call for it, I sometimes add a tablespoon snipped fresh dill.

3 tablespoons butter
1 medium yellow onion, peeled
*   and coarsely chopped*
¾ pound medium mushrooms,
*   wiped clean and sliced*
½ teaspoon salt
⅛ teaspoon black pepper
1 teaspoon Hungarian sweet
*   rose paprika*
1½ tablespoons flour
⅔ cup sour cream (at room
*   temperature)*
1 tablespoon snipped fresh dill
*   (optional)*

1. Melt butter in large heavy skillet over moderate heat, add onion and sauté 2 to 3 minutes until golden.

2. Add mushrooms and sauté, stirring often, 3 to 4 minutes.

3. Mix in salt, pepper, paprika, and flour and cook, stirring now and then, 5 minutes.

4. Remove from heat, mix in sour cream and, if desired, dill.

5. Serve at once as an accompaniment to meat or spoon over toast or into patty shells and serve as a light luncheon entrée.

Baked Stuffed Mushrooms

Makes 6 Servings

✳

EVEN BEFORE the turn of the century, Fannie Farmer and her peers were urging women to stuff sweet peppers, onions, tomatoes, even beets and turnips. But stuffed mushrooms came later, mostly because mushrooms were hard to come by.

The first stuffed mushrooms I ever tasted were created by Louella G. Shouer, food editor of *The Ladies' Home Journal* when I went to work there in 1957. Few magazine food editors were more creative than Louella, who had worked with the legendary Ann Batchelder at the *Journal,* then succeeded her as food editor. Louella's shining years were the 1940s and 1950s, and right up to the end, she was busily creating new recipes. This is one of her best.

1 pound medium mushrooms
1 cup chopped pecans
*3 tablespoons minced fresh
   parsley*
¼ cup (1 stick) butter, softened
*1 clove garlic, peeled and
   crushed*
*¼ teaspoon dried leaf thyme,
   crumbled*
½ teaspoon salt
Pinch black pepper
½ cup heavy cream (about)

1. Preheat oven to 350° F.

2. Wipe mushrooms with damp cloth; remove stems. Arrange caps in shallow baking dish, hollow sides up. Chop stems and mix with pecans, parsley, butter, garlic, thyme, salt, and pepper. Mound into mushroom caps, pressing down firmly. Carefully pour cream over mushrooms.

3. Cover, and bake 30 to 45 minutes until mushrooms are tender, basting once or twice with cream in dish. Add a little more cream, if necessary, to keep dish from boiling dry. Serve hot as a meat platter garnish.

French-Fried Onion Rings

Makes 2 to 4 Servings

MUCH TO my surprise, Sarah Tyson Rorer offers a recipe for deep-fried onion rings in *Mrs. Rorer's New Cook Book* (1902), but these are not dredged. The French-fried onion rings added to the 1906 edition of *The Boston Cooking-School Cook Book* are, however: "Peel onions," Fannie Farmer writes, "cut in one-fourth-inch slices, and separate into rings. Dip in milk, drain, and dip in flour. Fry in deep fat, drain on brown paper, and sprinkle with salt." Still, the crispy sweet, golden brown onions didn't catch our fancy until forty-some years later when fast-food stands made them a staple. This recipe is my own. Self-rising flour

MRS RORER'S
NEW
COOK BOOK

A MANUAL
OF
HOUSEKEEPING

By
SARAH TYSON RORER

Author of Mrs. Rorer's Philadelphia Cook Book,
Canning and Preserving, Bread and Bread Making,
and other valuable works on cookery

PHILADELPHIA
ARNOLD AND COMPANY
420 SANSOM STREET

makes the onions twice as light and paprika adds a blush.

Vegetable oil for deep frying
*1 large Spanish onion (about 1
   pound), peeled and sliced ¼-
   inch thick*
¾ cup unsifted self-rising flour
½ teaspoon paprika
¾ cup buttermilk

1. Begin heating oil in deep-fat fryer over moderate heat; insert deep-fat thermometer. Preheat oven to 250° F. Separate onion slices into rings.

2. Mix flour and paprika in pie pan. Place buttermilk in second pie pan.

3. When fat approaches 375° F, quickly dip a few onion rings into buttermilk, then into flour mixture, shaking off excess.

4. Deep-fry at 375° F about 1 minute until golden; using tongs, turn onion rings and brown flip sides 30 to 60 seconds.

5. Drain onion rings on paper-towel-lined baking sheet and keep warm by setting, uncovered, in 250° F oven.

6. Scoop any charred bits from oil in deep-fat fryer and continue dredging and browning onion rings as before. Serve hot.

Onion Supreme

Makes 6 Servings

✳

THIS RECIPE, a '50s favorite of test kitchen home economists at Corning Glass Works in Corning, New York, is best when baked in a Pyrex pie plate because heat-proof glass crisps the biscuit crust better than a metal tin. The original recipe headnote (in *Prize Pyrex Recipes*) says that "Onion Supreme is a delicious accompaniment to a Pot Roast."

BISCUIT CRUST
2 cups sifted all-purpose flour
3 teaspoons baking powder
½ teaspoon salt
⅓ cup cold vegetable shortening
⅔ cup milk (about)

FILLING
7 cups thinly sliced yellow onions (about 1½ pounds)
¼ cup (½ stick) butter or margarine
½ cup milk
½ cup buttermilk
1 egg, well beaten
1 teaspoon salt

1. Preheat oven to 425°F.

2. BISCUIT CRUST: Sift flour, baking powder, and salt together into large bowl. Using pastry blender, cut in shortening until mixture resembles coarse meal. Fork in enough milk to make a soft dough that's easy to roll.

3. Pat or roll dough on floured surface into 13-inch circle about ¼-inch thick and fit into an ungreased 9½-inch glass ovenware pie plate. Trim overhang and crimp into high fluted edge.

4. FILLING: Brown onions in butter in large heavy skillet over moderate heat about 5 minutes. Remove from heat and mix in milk, buttermilk, egg, and salt.

5. Spoon filling into crust and bake until golden brown—about 20 minutes.

Sugar Snap Peas with Scallions

Makes 4 Servings

✳

SUGAR SNAP Peas, a snow pea/green pea hybrid eaten pods and all (like the French *mange-tout*), were virtually unknown in this country until the 1980s. It was then that home gardeners began growing them and crying out for recipes. Today Sugar Snaps are practically a spring and summer staple at greenmarkets. This recipe, adapted from one published in *Cook's Simple and Seasonal Cuisine* (1988), couldn't be easier.

½ pound Sugar Snap Peas, strings removed
2 tablespoons peanut oil
1 tablespoon soy sauce
½ teaspoon roasted Asian sesame oil
2 medium scallions, trimmed and finely chopped

1. Parboil Sugar Snaps 5 minutes in large kettle of lightly salted boiling water. Drain and quick-chill in ice water; drain well again.

2. Heat peanut oil 1 minute in large heavy skillet over moderately high heat. Dump in Sugar Snaps and stir-fry 3 minutes.

3. Stir in soy sauce, sesame oil, and scallions, remove from heat, and serve.

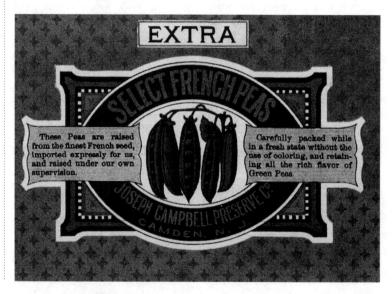

Slow-Cooker Beef-and-Corn-Stuffed Green Peppers

Makes 5 Servings

✳

STUFFED PEPPERS are not a twentieth-century invention, but *slow-cooker* stuffed peppers definitely are. This recipe is adapted from Mabel Hoffman's best-selling *Crockery Cookery*, which first appeared in 1975. In 1995 an updated edition was published with several new recipes plus all the old favorites, among them these stuffed peppers.

> 5 large green bell peppers
> ½ pound lean ground beef chuck
> 1 small yellow onion, peeled and finely chopped
> 1 tablespoon minced pimiento
> ½ teaspoon salt
> 1 (11- or 12-ounce) can whole-kernel corn, well drained
> 1 tablespoon Worcestershire sauce
> 1 teaspoon prepared mustard
> 1 (10¾-ounce) can condensed tomato soup, undiluted

1. Slice tops off peppers; core and seed, remove all pithy parts, then level bottoms as needed to make peppers stand straight. Drain peppers upside-down on several thicknesses paper towel.

2. Mix beef with onion, pimiento, salt, and corn in medium bowl, breaking up beef clumps so mixture is uniformly crumbly. Spoon mixture into peppers, dividing evenly. Stand peppers in slow cooker, spacing evenly.

3. Whisk Worcestershire sauce, mustard, and soup together in small bowl. Pour over peppers.

4. Cover, and cook on LOW until peppers are fork-tender—7 to 8 hours. Serve at once, ladling plenty of tomato sauce over each portion.

TIMELINE

1942–45

Food rationing: first sugar and coffee, then meat, butter, margarine, cheese, and canned goods.

1943

National Wartime Nutrition Program establishes *Basic 7 Food Groups* as good nutrition guideline for Americans.

....

A deep-dish pizza—bubbling layers of cheese, sausage, and tomatoes baked in a thick, high-sided crust—is created by Ric Riccardo and Ike Sewell and served at Pizzeria Uno, their nothing-fancy eatery on Chicago's North Side. Before long, it is famous as "The Chicago Deep Dish Pizza."

Mid-'40s

....

Instant coffee arrives.

1946

....

Enter Tupperware.

....

Minute Maid launches frozen orange juice concentrate.

243

Baked Potatoes with Sour Cream and Chives

Makes 4 Servings

✳

WHEN I first went to California in the late 1950s, I couldn't get enough of these baked potatoes. I'd never had them with sour cream and chives, only with gobs of butter. I thought these infinitely superior. They're a shade less caloric, too. Today, of course, you can trim fat and calories significantly by using one of the new low- or no-fat sour creams. Or yogurt. The effect is much the same. Did this recipe originate in California? I suspect so but I can't prove it.

NOTE: Try substituting fresh dill for chives. It's equally delicious.

4 large baking potatoes, scrubbed
1 teaspoon salt
½ teaspoon black pepper
1 cup sour cream or plain yogurt
¼ cup snipped fresh chives

1. Preheat oven to 425° F. Pierce potatoes deeply with sharp fork to allow steam to escape as they bake (this makes them fluffy).

2. Place potatoes, not touching, directly on middle oven rack and bake 1 hour until tender.

3. Score tops of potatoes with Xs, then pinch potatoes gently to force flesh up. Sprinkle with salt and pepper, then top with sour cream and chives, dividing all amounts evenly. Serve at once.

Union Square Cafe Mashed Sweet Potatoes with Balsamic Vinegar

Makes 4 Servings

✳

CONSISTENTLY AT the top of every best-restaurant-in-New York survey, Danny Meyer's Union Square Cafe is known for its imaginative treatment of vegetables. This recipe, adapted from one that appeared in the award-winning *Union Square Cafe Cookbook* (1994), shows just how far we've come from those days of marshmallow-frosted sweet potato casseroles. Meyer and chef Michael Romano say these "gently spiced and sweetly tart" sweet potatoes can be served with "roast pork, duck, even lamb chops." I think they're equally delicious with roast chicken or turkey.

4 to 5 large sweet potatoes (4 pounds), scrubbed
2 tablespoons butter
⅛ teaspoon ground cinnamon
⅛ teaspoon freshly grated nutmeg
1 cup milk
1 teaspoon salt (or to taste)
Black pepper to taste
1 to 2 teaspoons balsamic vinegar

1. Preheat oven to 400° F.

2. Bake sweet potatoes until easily pierced by a paring knife—about 50 minutes. Cool until easy to handle, peel, and put through a food mill or potato ricer; set aside.

3. Melt butter in medium heavy saucepan over moderate heat and let it brown. Mix in cinnamon and nutmeg. Off heat, stir in milk.

4. Return to heat, add sweet potatoes, and beat with wooden spoon until creamy. Season with salt, pepper, and balsamic vinegar to taste and serve.

IDAHO® POTATOES

Marshmallow-Topped Sweet Potato Casserole

LATE-NINETEENTH- and early-twentieth-century cookbooks dish up plenty of recipes for candied sweet potatoes and attribute most of them to the South, or if achingly sweet, to Georgia. But these are boiled sweet potatoes, peeled, sliced, then drizzled with melted butter and molasses or sugar syrup (a recipe in *Good Housekeeping's Book of Menus, Recipes and Household Discoveries* [1922] calls for "1 to 1½ cupfuls sirup from canned peaches"). Often the sweet potatoes are layered into a baking dish with dots of butter and sprinklings of brown sugar (the Georgia-style adds a pralinelike topping of chopped pecans).

The sweet potato casserole is something else again and appears to date to the 1920s. The potatoes are mashed and mixed with sugar (and sometimes canned crushed pineapple or mashed bananas and vanilla). The crowning touch: marshmallows. This recipe from Ida C. Bailey Allen's *Vital Vegetables* (1928) is the earliest sweet potato casserole I could find that calls for marshmallows:

BROWNED SWEET POTATO WITH MARSHMALLOWS

3 cups mashed sweet potato	¾ teaspoon salt	1 egg, well beaten
2 tablespoons butter	1 tablespoon sugar	12 marshmallows

Butter a baking dish. Beat together potato, butter, salt, sugar, and egg, pile in a dish, making the top rather rough; cover with the marshmallows and "dots" of butter and cook in a moderate oven—350 degrees F—till browned.

The following recipe, printed exactly as it appears in *River Road Recipes* (1959) by The Junior League of Baton Rouge, Inc., is more typical of the sweet potato casseroles popular in the '50s and '60s. They (or one of many variations on the theme) are still popular down South. Often crushed pineapple substitutes for milk and sometimes the potatoes are spiked with sherry.

RIVER ROAD BAKED SWEET POTATOES WITH MARSHMALLOWS

8 medium-size sweet potatoes	3 tablespoons sugar	1 tablespoon orange juice
1 cup milk	½ stick butter	Marshmallows
1 teaspoon vanilla	¼ teaspoon cinnamon	
	Few dashes of nutmeg	

BAKE sweet potatoes in 350°F oven until done. Peel hot potatoes and put through ricer until mashed. Scald milk and add vanilla, sugar and butter. To potatoes add cinnamon, nutmeg and orange juice. Stir. Add milk mixture to potatoes. [Note: A line has been dropped from recipe at this point, but layer half the potato mixture into a buttered casserole, add] a layer of marshmallows, remaining potatoes and bake at 350°F until very hot. Add a top layer of marshmallows and brown. Serves 8 to 10.

Spaghetti Squash

A CCORDING TO James Traeger (*The Food Chronology*, 1995), the person who introduced us to spaghetti squash was Frieda Caplan, founder of Frieda's Finest (now simply Frieda's), a Los Angeles-based produce company specializing in exotic fruits and vegetables. The year: 1962. It was then that Frieda's purple-tagged-and-bagged exotics began appearing in America's high-end supermarkets. Nothing quite caught the national fancy, however, like spaghetti squash, which could be boiled or microwaved, forked into strands, then sauced like spaghetti. Needless to add, this "pasta" is low-cal. To acquaint cooks with her unusual produce, Frieda accompanied each item with an informative label. Here, for example, are the instructions printed on a Frieda's spaghetti squash label:

SPAGHETTI SQUASH

TO PREPARE: Cut squash in half lengthwise and clean out seeds.

BOILED: Place squash cut side down in a pot with 2" water, cover and boil 20 minutes.

IN MICROWAVE: Place squash cut side up in a dish with ¼ cup water. Cover with clear wrap and cook 7–8 minutes. Run fork over inside of cooked squash to get spaghetti-like strands.

NOTE: The microwave instructions don't tell what power to use; it should be HIGH (100 percent).—J.A.

Roasted Sweet Peppers

✳

SOMETIME IN the '50s, we learned that nothing mellowed sweet peppers or developed their sweetness like a stint in the oven or broiler. Once roasted, the slightly smoky peppers could be slivered into salads, pastas, and stuffings or pureed into soups and sauces. All sweet peppers can be roasted—the red, the yellow, the orange, and green—although these last will lose color. (Chilies can be roasted, too, but are trickier to handle.) Every cook has a pet method for roasting peppers, but the one I prefer comes from *From the Farmer's Market* (1986), a cookbook written by two close friends, Richard Sax and Sandra Gluck.

BASIC METHOD

1. Preheat broiler.

2. Lay whole peppers on their sides on foil-lined baking sheet.

3. Place in broiler, 4 to 6 inches from heat.

4. Broil, turning with tongs, until lightly charred on all sides—8 to 10 minutes in all.

5. Remove peppers from broiler and cover with foil (or place peppers in paper bag and close top). Let stand at least 20 minutes to loosen skins.

6. Peel peppers, discarding skins. Remove stems and seeds, but reserve juices.

7. Use as recipes direct. Or arrange peppers on platter with their juices and a whole peeled garlic clove. Sprinkle lightly with salt and pepper, then drizzle lightly with balsamic or red wine vinegar and olive

Watch Your Grocers Shelves for these Labels

oil; let stand at room temperature for at least 1 hour; discard garlic clove and serve. In season, some chopped fresh basil is a nice touch.

Sweet Red Peppers Stuffed with Spaghetti Squash, Mushrooms, and Basil

Makes 4 Servings

✳

THIS RECIPE, adapted from one in a leaflet, *Frieda's Exotic & Healthy Foods* (1992), shows how versatile spaghetti squash is. It also calls for three other Frieda's items: shiitake mushrooms, fresh basil, and thyme.

NOTE: For directions on how to cook spaghetti squash, see the box at left.

- *¼ cup chicken broth*
- *1 cup chopped zucchini, yellow crookneck, pattypan, or other summer squash*
- *½ cup chopped shiitake or brown mushrooms*
- *¼ cup thinly sliced scallions*
- *1 tablespoon chopped fresh basil or 1 teaspoon dried leaf basil, crumbled*
- *1 tablespoon chopped fresh thyme or 1 teaspoon dried leaf thyme, crumbled*
- *1 clove garlic, peeled and minced*
- *½ teaspoon salt*
- *¼ teaspoon black pepper*
- *1½ cups cooked spaghetti squash strands (about ½ medium squash)*
- *4 medium red bell peppers*
- *¼ cup coarsely shredded Swiss or Cheddar cheese*

1. Preheat oven to 375° F. Coat 8 × 8 × 2-inch baking dish with nonstick cooking spray; set aside.

2. Bring broth to boiling in medium heavy skillet over moderate heat. Add zucchini, shiitake, scallions, basil, thyme, garlic, salt, and black pepper and simmer, uncovered, stirring occasionally, until all vegetables are tender—4 to 5 minutes. Mix in spaghetti squash and keep warm.

3. Slice tops off red peppers and reserve; scoop out and discard pith and seeds. Also, if needed, level bottoms of peppers so they stand straight in baking dish without wobbling.

4. Spoon skillet mixture into peppers, dividing total amount evenly, and top each with cheese, again dividing amount evenly. Replace tops on peppers.

5. Cover with foil, bake peppers 30 to 35 minutes until fork-tender, and serve.

1946

French's introduces instant mashed potatoes.

Brennan's opens in New Orleans.

America's first serious cooking school opens in New Haven, Connecticut. It later becomes the CIA (Culinary Institute of America) and relocates to Hyde Park, New York.

1946–47

James Beard hosts *I Love to Eat* on WNBC-TV, America's first television cooking show.

1947

Reynolds Metals rolls out aluminum foil.

Raytheon manufactures the Radarange "electronic oven," the forerunner of the modern microwave.

1947–48

General Mills and Pillsbury launch cake mixes.

Spinach with Sour Cream and Nutmeg

Makes 4 Servings

❋

WITH THE availability of commercial sour cream, cooks began smoothing it into everything. I cannot say who came up with this delicious side dish. When. Or where. I do know that I first tasted it in the mid-'50s. I know, too, that it remains a favorite among busy cooks across the U.S.

> 2 tablespoons butter or
>   margarine
> ¼ cup minced yellow onion
> 2 (10-ounce) packages frozen
>   chopped spinach, thawed
>   and drained well
> ¼ teaspoon freshly grated
>   nutmeg
> 1 teaspoon salt
> ¼ teaspoon black pepper
> ½ cup sour cream (at room
>   temperature)

1. Brown butter lightly in large heavy saucepan over moderate heat. Add onion and sauté, stirring often, 2 to 3 minutes until limp.

2. Add spinach, nutmeg, salt, and pepper, stir well, then cover and cook over low heat 8 to 10 minutes until steaming hot, stirring now and then.

3. Smooth in sour cream and bring just to serving temperature. Do not boil or sour cream may curdle.

Microwaved Summer Squash with Garlic and Fresh Dill

Makes 2 Servings

❋

WHENEVER I want a vegetable in a hurry, I rustle up this easy dish. Sometimes I make it with zucchini, sometimes with straightneck yellow squash. Both work equally well. This method produces golden brown rounds of squash and doesn't require constant turning.

NOTE: Because of the lemony-ness of the fresh dill, I rarely add salt.

> 1 large clove garlic, peeled and
>   slivered lengthwise
> 2 medium zucchini or yellow
>   squash, trimmed, scrubbed
>   and sliced ⅛-inch thick
> 1½ tablespoons fruity olive oil
> 1 tablespoon snipped fresh dill
> ⅛ teaspoon black pepper
> Salt, if needed, to taste
> Freshly grated Parmesan cheese
>   (optional topping)

1. Place garlic, zucchini, oil, dill, and pepper in 5-cup, microwave-safe *au gratin* dish and toss well until garlic slivers and zucchini rounds are evenly coated with oil, pepper, and dill. Spread in even, thin layer across bottom of dish.

2. Microwave, uncovered, on HIGH (100 percent power) 10 to 12 minutes until golden brown. Sprinkle, if desired, with Parmesan.

Olive-Sautéed Shredded Zucchini with Onion

Makes 6 Servings

❋

LIKE BROCCOLI, these slim green summer squash were popularized by Italian immigrants, primarily those settling in California. Food writer/historian John Mariani says the time was the 1920s. Yet as late as 1968, Alex D. Hawkes wrote in *A World of Vegetable Cookery*: "This is an extremely desirable vegetable, yet, except in the kitchens of persons of Mediterranean antecedents, it is somewhat neglected in the United States." Within ten years, that would change with home gardeners bringing in "gushers" of zucchini and cooks trying desperately to cope. This recipe and the two that follow are my favorites.

> 3 tablespoons fruity olive oil
> 1 large Spanish onion, peeled
>   and coarsely chopped
> 3 pounds tender young
>   zucchini, trimmed and
>   coarsely shredded
> ½ teaspoon dried leaf
>   marjoram, crumbled
> ¼ teaspoon dried leaf rosemary,
>   crumbled
> 1 teaspoon salt (or to taste)
> ¼ teaspoon black pepper

1. Heat olive oil in large heavy skillet over moderate heat 2 minutes.

2. Add onion and brown 3 to 5 minutes. Add zucchini, marjoram, rosemary, salt, and pepper and sauté, stirring often, 5 minutes. Cover, and simmer 5 minutes.

3. Uncover, simmer 5 to 10 minutes more until juices evaporate.

Stuffed Zucchini

Makes 6 Servings

✱

ADELE VOLPI, a wonderful California cook of Italian heritage, gave me this recipe back in the 1970s.

6 medium zucchini, trimmed of stem ends
1 quart lightly salted water
½ pound sweet Italian sausages
1 medium yellow onion, peeled and finely minced
⅓ cup chopped fresh basil
¼ cup chopped fresh flat-leaf parsley
¼ teaspoon dried leaf marjoram, crumbled
½ cup freshly grated Parmesan cheese
¼ cup moderately fine dry bread crumbs
1 egg
½ teaspoon salt
¼ teaspoon black pepper

1. Preheat oven to 350° F. Halve zucchini lengthwise; arrange in single layer in large shallow roasting pan. Set over moderate heat, add lightly salted water, cover with baking sheet, and parboil 10 to 12 minutes until barely tender. Gently lift zucchini to paper towels to drain.

2. With teaspoon, scoop out seedy portions, leaving zucchini shells ¼-inch thick. Chop scooped-out portions fine and reserve.

3. Slit sausage casing, scoop meat into large heavy skillet, and sauté 5 to 8 minutes over moderately low heat, breaking up clumps, until no traces of pink remain.

4. Add onion, basil, parsley, and marjoram, reduce heat to lowest point, and cook 5 to 8 minutes; continue breaking up sausage until fine and crumbly.

5. Off heat, mix in reserved chopped zucchini, Parmesan, bread crumbs, egg, salt, and pepper.

6. Fill zucchini shells with mixture, dividing evenly and mounding slightly.

7. Arrange filled zucchini—touching so they support one another—on ungreased baking sheet and bake, uncovered, 30 minutes until lightly browned. Serve hot.

Zucchini and Potato Pancakes

Makes about 1 Dozen

✱

THIS RECIPE, adapted from *From the Farmer's Market* by Richard Sax and Sandra Gluck (1986), shows how gifted cooks put zucchini to good use. "Don't count on saving these crispy pancakes for a meal if you've got people wandering through the kitchen as you fry them," they caution in their recipe headnote.

1½ cups coarsely grated zucchini (about 2 medium)
1¼ cups grated Idaho potato (about 1 large)
1 small yellow onion, peeled and grated
2 tablespoons cornmeal
2 tablespoons flour
¾ teaspoon salt
1 egg, lightly beaten
2 tablespoons vegetable oil (about)
Sour cream

1. Preheat oven to its keep-warm setting. Place zucchini in colander and press firmly to extract as much liquid as possible.

2. Transfer to mixing bowl and mix with potato and onion. Stir in cornmeal, flour, and salt; then add egg and stir until well combined.

3. Heat vegetable oil in large heavy skillet over moderate heat 1 to 2 minutes until ripples appear in pan.

4. Working in batches and using about 2 tablespoons zucchini mixture per pancake, brown pancakes 3 to 4 minutes on a side, flattening each lightly with a pancake turner.

5. As pancakes brown, transfer to plate lined with paper towels and set, uncovered, in keep-warm oven while you fry the balance. Also add additional oil to skillet as needed.

6. Serve pancakes hissing-hot with sour cream.

Sautéed Cherry Tomatoes with Basil

Makes 6 Servings

✳

WHEN CHERRY tomatoes first began appearing in groceries after World War II, they were the novelty every hostess had to serve. Often they were put out as an appetizer to be dunked in seasoned salt. Often they were sliced or quartered into green salads. And more often they were clustered on dinner plates to add a blast of color. Then someone —I wish I knew who—thought to warm cherry tomatoes gently in butter or oil, which mellowed and intensified their flavor all at the same time. This recipe, a little fancier than most, is adapted from *The Family*

Circle Cookbook: New Tastes for New Times (1992). Serve them as an accompaniment to beef, lamb, pork, or poultry.

> 1 tablespoon fruity olive oil
> 1 small red onion, peeled and thinly sliced
> 1 clove garlic, peeled and minced
> 2 pints red and/or yellow cherry tomatoes, stemmed
> ½ cup packed fresh basil leaves, thinly sliced
> ¼ teaspoon salt
> ⅛ teaspoon black pepper
> 2 teaspoons balsamic vinegar

1. Heat oil in large heavy skillet 1 minute over moderate heat. Add onion and garlic and stir-fry until tender—3 to 4 minutes.

2. Add cherry tomatoes, basil, salt, and pepper and cook, stirring, just until tomato skins start to wrinkle —about 2 minutes.

3. Drizzle in vinegar, turning tomatoes gently, heat about 1 minute longer, and serve.

Vegetarian Black Bean Chili

Makes 6 Servings

✳

A 1960S recipe that won "Best of the 1991 New York State Fair" for Pat Steer of Syracuse. It's a recipe she began making in college, a spicy black bean chili or *feijoada* (Brazilian bean stew) ladled over rice. The recipe was featured in "Blue-Ribbon Winners," a story I wrote for the August 21, 1992, issue of *Family Circle.* I must confess I never thought I'd like a vegetarian chili, but this one hooked me. It's low in fat (4 grams per serving), calories (334), and cholesterol (zero) but doesn't lack protein (12 grams per serving).

> 1 tablespoon fruity olive oil
> 1 large yellow onion, peeled and coarsely chopped
> 3 cloves garlic, peeled and minced
> 2 teaspoons ground cumin
> 1 teaspoon dried leaf oregano, crumbled
> 1 cup chopped green bell pepper
> 1 cup chopped red bell pepper
> 1 medium jalapeño pepper, cored, seeded, and minced
> ½ cup coarsely chopped celery
> 3 cups cooked or canned black beans, drained

2 cups canned crushed tomatoes

1 small orange, peeled, seeded, and coarsely chopped

1 teaspoon frozen orange juice concentrate, thawed

1 teaspoon fresh lemon juice

1 teaspoon hot red pepper sauce

1 teaspoon molasses

4 cups cooked brown or white rice

OPTIONAL TOPPING

1 tablespoon chopped green bell pepper

1 tablespoon chopped red bell pepper

1½ teaspoons chopped jalapeño pepper

1 tablespoon chopped fresh coriander (cilantro)

1. Heat oil in medium heavy kettle over moderate heat 1 minute. Add onion, garlic, cumin, and oregano and stir-fry until glassy—about 3 minutes. Add green and red peppers, jalapeño, and celery and stir-fry 3 minutes more.

2. Add 2½ cups beans, the tomatoes, orange, orange juice concentrate, lemon juice, red pepper sauce, and molasses. Bring to boiling, adjust heat so mixture bubbles gently, cover, and simmer 5 minutes.

3. Mash remaining ½ cup beans, stir into kettle, cover, and simmer 15 minutes.

4. Mound bean mixture in large, deep platter and wreathe with rice.

5. OPTIONAL TOPPING: Toss all ingredients together lightly and sprinkle over chili and rice.

B & M BAKED BEANS

....

L ONG BEFORE the Pilgrims landed, Native Americans dried beans so they'd keep. Then they would soak them, season them with deer fat, and bake them in clay pots sunk in the ground. It wasn't long before the Massachusetts colonists took up the habit.

At the turn of the twentieth century, a few farsighted Yankee grocers were baking huge vats of beans and selling portions over-the-counter. But it was Burnham and Morrill (B & M) of Portland, Maine, that began canning New England-style baked beans for America at large. The year: 1927.

Today, as in colonial days, B & M bakes beans the old-fashioned way. Pea beans (mostly from Michigan) arrive at the factory by railroad car, a thousand tons per hopper, are stored in giant silos, then transported in batches to mechanical shakers that sort out the pebbles and debris. After two washings, the beans are dumped into huge pots along with molasses, mustard, salt, and salt pork, and baked in brick ovens at 500° F to 600° F. Only then are they put into cans, about a million of them every week.

Many people are surprised to learn that pea beans aren't native to New England. We don't know for sure where the Native Americans got theirs, but we do know that during the Gold Rush, New England clipper ships carrying supplies to California returned with pea beans as ballast. Thrifty New Englanders, instead of dumping the ballast, baked it.

HOW TO USE YOUR CUISINART™ FOOD PROCESSOR

WHEN THE Cuisinart Food Processor was unveiled at the Chicago housewares show in January 1973, it was hardly a hit. Indeed, myopic store buyers saw it as a souped-up blender with an exorbitant price tag. In other words, a white elephant.

Some white elephant. In just six years it spawned a score of imitations and turned America into a food-processor society. No one knows (or rather, will say) how many zillions of food processors have been sold across the U.S. since Cuisinart's inauspicious debut, but what is known is that, in 1977, a half-million of them were bought for Mother's Day in the New York City area alone.

All because Carl G. Sontheimer, a retired electronics engineer and hobby chef from Connecticut, haunted the French housewares show in Paris in 1971 looking for a project to occupy his spare time. That project turned out to be a powerful, compact French machine called *Le Magix-Mix*, which could grind, chop, mince, slice, puree, pulverize, mix, and blend with stunning speed. Sontheimer and his wife, Shirley, were fascinated. They tracked down the machine's inventor, Pierre Verdun, who had also developed its precursor, *Le Robot-Coupe*, a heavy-duty restaurant version, which

chefs had dubbed "the buffalo chopper."

Sontheimer obtained U.S. distribution rights for *Le Magix-Mix*, then shipped a dozen of them back to Connecticut. In his garage, he took them apart, reassembled them, took them apart again, analyzing their strengths and shortcomings. He kitchen-tested them, his wife kitchen-tested them, and he tinkered some more. He refined the French design, improved its slicing and shredding discs, incorporated safety features, and rechristened it the Cuisinart.

Undaunted by the Cuisinart's tepid reception at the Chicago housewares show, Sontheimer went on the road, demonstrating his machine's prowess to America's top food editors and cookbook authors.

Smart man. His food processor won their unanimous blessings and was praised to the skies—in print. Suddenly, the food processor was the new must-have kitchen gadget. And the rest of us rushed out to buy them.

Today, the food processor is indispensable to professional chefs and home cooks alike. Indeed, it's one of the few trendy appliances that hasn't been relegated to a top pantry shelf. Most cooks keep the machine on the kitchen counter. In fact, I have three food processors at the ready, a mini-chopper, a medium-size one, and a heavy-duty professional model sturdy enough to knead a couple of pounds of bread dough.

Cuisinart
EXPANDED FEED TUBE KIT
COVER, PUSHERS, 2mm AND 4mm EXPANDED BLADE SLICING DISCS

CFP-4,5,5A,9,9A ACCESSORY
MODEL FP-755

VEGETABLE RECIPES

*that Entered the American Mainstream
During the Twentieth Century with Their Source*

....

(*Recipe Included)

FRANCE
Brussels Sprouts Braised with Chestnuts
Carrots Vichy, Celery Amandine
Leeks (Celery) à la Grecque
*Garlic-Mashed Potatoes
Pommes Soufflées, Potatoes Anna
*Ratatouille
Vegetable Quiches (Broccoli, Corn, Spinach, Tomato, etc.)

❋

SCANDINAVIA
*Jansson's Temptation

❋

GERMANY
*Red Cabbage Cooked in Red Wine

❋

SWITZERLAND
*Rösti

❋

ITALY
Stuffed Artichokes, Eggplant Parmigiana
*Fried Zucchini Sticks

❋

**EASTERN MEDITERRANEAN (GREECE, TURKEY,
MIDDLE EAST)**
*Spanakopita

❋

CARIBBEAN/MEXICO/LATIN AMERICA
Black Beans and Rice, Refried Beans

❋

CHINA
Szechuan Dry-Sautéed Green Beans
*Snow Peas with Fresh Shiitakes

❋

INDIA
*Curried Cabbage

VEGETABLES

Curried Cabbage

Makes 4 Servings

A '70s favorite brought back from India by those trekking to the subcontinent on voyages of self-discovery. I was one of them, and it was my guide who gave me this recipe.

> 2 teaspoons mustard seeds
> 2 tablespoons ghee (clarified
>   butter)
> 1 tablespoon peanut oil
> 1 medium yellow onion, peeled
>   and chopped
> 2 tablespoons finely minced
>   green bell pepper (or if you
>   can find it, 1 tablespoon
>   minced Indian pepper leaf)
> 2 teaspoons finely minced fresh
>   ginger
> 2 teaspoons curry powder
> Pinch ground cinnamon
> Pinch freshly grated nutmeg
> 1 (2-pound) green cabbage,
>   quartered, cored, and thinly
>   sliced
> ½ teaspoon salt (or to taste)
> ¼ teaspoon black pepper (or to
>   taste)

1. Stir-fry mustard seeds in ghee and oil in very large heavy skillet over moderately high heat until they sputter and dance—about 2 minutes.

2. Reduce heat to moderate, add onion, green pepper, and ginger, and stir-fry until limp—3 to 5 minutes.

3. Smooth in curry powder, cinnamon, and nutmeg and mellow over moderate heat 1 minute.

4. Add cabbage and stir-fry until nicely glazed—about 5 minutes. Reduce heat to low and cook cabbage, uncovered, stirring often, 5 to 10 minutes, until as crisp or tender as you like.

5. Season to taste with salt and black pepper and serve.

Red Cabbage Cooked in Red Wine

Makes 6 Servings

✳

SPLENDID WITH roast pork, turkey, chicken, or venison, this recipe is adapted from one given me by my Bavarian friend Hedy Würz.

3 tablespoons butter or margarine
1 tablespoon sugar
1 large yellow onion, peeled and finely chopped
2 large tart green apples, peeled, cored, and coarsely chopped
1 (2-pound) red cabbage, quartered, cored, and thinly sliced
¼ cup red wine vinegar
1 cup beef broth
½ teaspoon salt
2 whole bay leaves
2 tablespoons flour
1 cup dry red wine
2 tablespoons red currant jelly

1. Melt butter in very large heavy skillet over moderate heat, sprinkle in sugar and cook and stir just until dissolved—2 to 3 minutes.

2. Add onion and apples and stir-fry until golden—about 5 minutes.

3. Add cabbage and stir-fry until nicely glazed—about 5 minutes.

4. Add vinegar and ½ cup broth and bring to simmering. Adjust heat so mixture bubbles gently, add salt and bay leaves, cover, and simmer until cabbage is crisp-tender—20 to 25 minutes.

5. Sprinkle flour over cabbage and toss well. Add wine and remaining ½ cup broth and cook, stirring gently, 3 to 5 minutes until thickened and no raw starch taste remains.

6. Remove bay leaves, smooth in jelly, and toss lightly to mix. Heat 5 minutes longer and serve.

Garlic-Mashed Potatoes

Makes 6 Servings

✳

PURÉE DE *Pommes de Terre à l'Ail* (Potato Puree with Garlic) is what Julia Child calls these in *Mastering the Art of French Cooking* (1961), the book that changed the way most of us cook and eat. But her recipe is fairly complex: She blanches the garlic, peels it, and cooks it slowly in butter; next she blends in flour, then boiling milk, salt, and pepper. The potatoes are cooked separately, pureed, and seasoned. Next, the hot garlic sauce is vigorously beaten in, then heavy cream and minced parsley. *Chicago Tribune* food columnist Bill Rice has whipped up an easier but equally ambrosial version, from which this recipe is adapted. He featured his Garlic-Mashed Potatoes in *Feasts of Wine and Food* (1987), pairing them with broiled duck breast. I like them with roast beef.

6 medium all-purpose potatoes, peeled
4 medium cloves garlic, peeled and thinly sliced
2 cups steaming-hot heavy cream
½ cup (1 stick) butter
½ teaspoon fresh lemon juice
Pinch ground hot red pepper (cayenne)
Salt to taste
White pepper to taste

1. Boil potatoes and garlic in large heavy saucepan of lightly salted water over moderate heat until potatoes are soft—35 to 40 minutes; drain well.

2. Rice potatoes and garlic directly into large heated bowl.

3. Beat in cream, then butter, bit by bit. Season with lemon juice, cayenne, salt, and white pepper.

4. Serve at once.

Snow Peas with Fresh Shiitakes

Makes 6 Servings

✳

FEW AMERICANS know more about the Asian ingredients now flooding our greenmarkets than Bruce Cost, who has devoted much of his adult life to researching these exotics and writing about them. This recipe is adapted from one that appeared in his indispensable book, *Bruce Cost's Asian Ingredients* (1988). Shaoxing wine, he explains, is "China's most famous rice wine, from Shaoxing in Zhejiang Province," where it has been made for "over 2,000 years."

> 2 tablespoons chicken broth
> 1 tablespoon Shaoxing wine or medium-dry sherry
> 1 teaspoon salt
> 1 teaspoon sugar
> 5 tablespoons peanut oil
> ¼ pound fresh shiitake mushrooms, thinly sliced
> 1 pound snow peas, strings removed

1. Mix broth, wine, salt, and sugar in small ramekin; set aside.

2. Heat oil in wok or large heavy skillet over high heat until ripples show on pan bottom. Add mushrooms and stir-fry until they wilt and release their juices—2 to 3 minutes.

3. Add snow peas and stir-fry 1½ to 2 minutes. Add reserved broth mixture and stir until all liquid evaporates and peas are crisp-tender. Serve at once.

Rösti (Swiss Shredded Potato Pancake)

Makes 4 to 6 Servings

✳

NOT EVERY potato makes good *rösti*. If this skillet-size pancake is to hold together, you must use a waxy variety. The best are California Long Whites or red-skin potatoes because they form a fairly sturdy crisp-crusted pancake. Even so, turning *rösti* is tricky. To minimize breakage, loosen pancake carefully, slide onto a dinner plate, then invert in the skillet.

NOTE: If you shred the potatoes in a food processor, as I do, use the medium shredding disc.

> ¼ cup (½ stick) butter or margarine
> 12 medium California Long White potatoes, peeled and moderately coarsely shredded
> ½ teaspoon salt (or to taste)
> ¼ teaspoon black pepper (or to taste)

1. Heat 3 tablespoons butter in well-seasoned, heavy 10-inch iron skillet over moderately high heat until frothy; tilt skillet in circular motion to coat skillet sides with butter.

2. Dump in shredded potatoes and press hard, flattening into single large pancake. Brown 5 minutes, continuing to press and flatten pancake.

3. Lower heat to moderate, cover, and cook 5 minutes. Uncover, and cook 5 to 8 minutes, again compacting pancake, until surface looks quite dry.

4. Loosen pancake, slide onto dinner plate. Scrape up any stubborn bits of potato in skillet and pat onto pancake.

5. Heat remaining 1 tablespoon butter in skillet till foamy and ease pancake back into skillet, raw-side-down. Raise heat to moderately high and brown about 5 minutes—*rösti* should be crusty brown on both sides.

6. Season to taste with salt and pepper, cut into wedges, and serve.

Jansson's Temptation

Makes 6 Servings

✳

MORE THAN one writer has declared that this classic is American, not Swedish. That it's named for Erik Janson, a self-styled prophet who led a band of Swedes to Bishop Hill, Illinois, last century. Though

Clark C. Dildine, the Clothier, Dundee, N.Y.

RICE'S SEEDS.

I SAY – THE MURPHYS are a noted family – among them
NEW EARLY SUNRISE
Has proved itself the earliest of all, producing potatoes fit for
the table in fifty two days from time of planting.
(12) largest potatoes in a crop grown from one (1) pound in
sixty-seven (67) days weighed twenty-five (25) pounds.

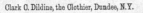

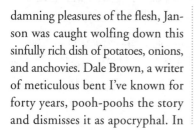

PARKER & WOOD.

ica, and its briny taste seems to give people a feeling of being in instant communication with the sea." Jansson's Temptation is traditionally made with minced anchovy fillets, but I prefer anchovy paste because it blends smoothly with the cream and spreads the anchovy flavor more evenly throughout the potatoes and onions.

NOTE: The anchovy paste provides all the salt this recipe needs.

4 medium yellow onions, peeled and thinly sliced
3 tablespoons butter
6 large baking potatoes, peeled and cut into 2 × ¼ × ¼-inch matchsticks
¼ teaspoon black pepper
3 tablespoons anchovy paste
2 cups light cream

1. Preheat oven to 400° F. Butter 2½-quart shallow casserole well and set aside.

2. Sauté onions in butter in large heavy skillet over moderate heat 8 to 10 minutes until very limp and golden but not brown.

3. Beginning and ending with potatoes, arrange three layers of potatoes and two of onions in casserole, dividing amounts evenly and sprinkling with pepper as you go.

4. Whisk together anchovy paste and cream and pour evenly into casserole.

5. Bake, uncovered, 1½ to 2 hours until richly browned and potatoes are tender. Serve at once.

damning pleasures of the flesh, Janson was caught wolfing down this sinfully rich dish of potatoes, onions, and anchovies. Dale Brown, a writer of meticulous bent I've known for forty years, pooh-poohs the story and dismisses it as apocryphal. In

The Cooking of Scandinavia (1968) he writes, "Jansson and Janson are not even spelled the same way—but it [the story] does serve to show what the dish can do to a Swede. Its popularity in Sweden is roughly comparable to that of pizza in Amer-

Spanakopita

Makes 8 to 10 Servings

✳

THIS SPINACH/feta cheese pie wrapped in wispy phyllo pastry moved from Greek-American communities into the mainstream in the late '70s or early '80s. With frozen phyllo leaves now stocked by many supermarkets, to say nothing of frozen chopped spinach, *spanakopita* is no longer the labor-intensive recipe it once was. The recipe here is my own.

FILLING

¼ cup fruity olive oil
1 cup coarsely chopped scallions, including some green tops (about 8 scallions)
3 (10-ounce) packages frozen, chopped spinach, thawed and drained very well
½ cup loosely packed minced fresh flat-leaf parsley
½ cup loosely packed snipped fresh dill
1 teaspoon salt
¼ teaspoon black pepper
8 ounces feta cheese, finely crumbled
3 eggs, lightly beaten

CRUST

½ (1-pound) package frozen phyllo pastry, thawed by package directions
½ cup (1 stick) butter or margarine, melted

1. Preheat oven to 375° F. Butter 13×9×2-inch baking pan well and set aside.

2. FILLING: Heat olive oil in large heavy skillet over moderate heat 1 minute. Add scallions and stir-fry until limp and golden—about 2 minutes.

3. Add spinach, reduce heat to low, cover, and cook 10 minutes. Uncover, mix in parsley, dill, salt, and pepper and cook 10 minutes longer, stirring often, until very dry. Cool, uncovered, 30 minutes.

4. Mix in feta cheese and eggs and set aside.

5. CRUST: Following package directions for working with phyllo pastry, line pan with 6 leaves phyllo, brushing each well with melted butter before adding the next, and trimming so there's only a 1-inch overhang all around.

6. Spread spinach filling smoothly over phyllo, then top with 6 more phyllo leaves, brushing each with melted butter and trimming as before.

7. If phyllo overhang is still pliable, roll on top of *spanakopita,* forming a rolled edge; if it is too brittle to roll, trim all round until level with rim of pan (phyllo will ruffle as it bakes).

8. Bake, uncovered, 45 to 50 minutes or until phyllo is golden brown.

9. Cool *spanakopita* 10 to 15 minutes, cut into large squares, and serve.

Electric BRAND

GARDEN SPINACH

Distributed by

OLNEY & FLOYD,

WESTERNVILLE, ONEIDA CO., N.Y.

Ratatouille

Makes 8 to 10 Servings

✳

MUCH TO my surprise, there's a recipe for Ratatouille Niçoise (and a reasonably authentic one at that) in the 1946 edition of *The Boston Cooking-School Cook Book.* Still, it wasn't until the '60s that this bright Provençal stew of green peppers, zucchini, tomatoes, and eggplant became the "status" recipe among aspiring cooks. Most, alas, over-cooked it to mush instead of pre-serving the identity of each vegetable. The ratatouille here is my adaptation of the one served at New York's La Côte Basque restaurant. Chef/owner Jean-Jacques Rachou's classic ratatouille appeared in *Great Vegetables from the Great Chefs* (1990).

1 cup fruity olive oil
2 medium yellow onions, peeled and chopped
2 medium green bell peppers, cored, seeded, and cut into small dice
6 small zucchini, trimmed and cut into small dice
3 medium eggplants, trimmed and cut into small dice
6 medium vine-ripe tomatoes, peeled, seeded, and diced
2 cloves garlic, peeled and minced
1 teaspoon salt (or to taste)
¼ teaspoon black pepper (or to taste)
1 tablespoon chopped fresh thyme or 1 teaspoon dried leaf thyme, crumbled
2 whole bay leaves

1. Heat ½ cup olive oil in large heavy skillet over moderate heat 1 minute. Add onions and green peppers and stir-fry until golden—about 3 minutes.

2. Heat remaining ½ cup olive oil in second large heavy skillet over moderate heat 1 minute. Add zucchini and eggplant, cover, and cook until tender—10 to 15 minutes.

3. Add to first skillet along with tomatoes, garlic, salt, pepper, thyme, and bay leaves. Cover, and cook over moderate heat 45 minutes to 1 hour.

4. Remove bay leaves, taste for salt and pepper, and adjust as needed. Serve warm or at room temperature.

Fried Zucchini Sticks

Makes 6 Servings

✳

IN THE 1960s and 1970s, Amer-ica's better Italian restaurants made crisply fried zucchini sticks as pop-ular as French fries. They still are.

NOTE: For best results, use un-waxed zucchini and choose those no more than eight inches long. Also, dredge zucchini sticks lightly in flour *before* dipping in batter. When fry-ing, keep the temperature of the fat as near to 400° F as possible. If it drops below 375° F, the zucchini sticks will be greasy.

8 medium zucchini (about 2¼ pounds)
1½ cups unsifted all-purpose flour (plus flour for dredging)
1¼ teaspoons salt
½ teaspoon white pepper
1¼ cups cold water
Vegetable oil for deep frying

1. Preheat oven to its keep-warm setting. Trim zucchini, scrub, and pat dry. Halve crosswise, then cut into sticks the size of French fries. Spread on several thicknesses paper towels and set aside.

2. Whisk flour, salt, and pepper together in medium shallow bowl. Add water and whisk until smooth.

3. Heat oil in deep-fat fryer to 400° F.

4. Dredge 10 to 12 zucchini sticks lightly in flour; into batter to coat evenly, then with two-pronged, long-handled fork, ease, one by one, into hot fat. Fry 3 to 4 minutes until golden brown; with skimmer, trans-fer to large baking sheet covered with several thicknesses paper tow-els. Set, uncovered, in oven to keep warm.

5. Continue browning zucchini sticks in batches as before and drain-ing on paper towels. Never pile browned zucchini sticks one layer on another, and never cover them; they will go soggy.

SALADS
SALAD DRESSINGS

*R*egardless of price the World affords no finer Salad Oil than Mazola

This simple French Dressing recipe will prove this Statement ᔓ ᔓ Try it

¹/₂ cup Mazola
3 tablespoons vinegar

¹/₂ teaspoon salt
¹/₈ teaspoon white pepper

Beat thoroughly and use with any vegetable, meat or fish salad. If a sweeter dressing is desired add 1 teaspoon Karo Red Label.

1928

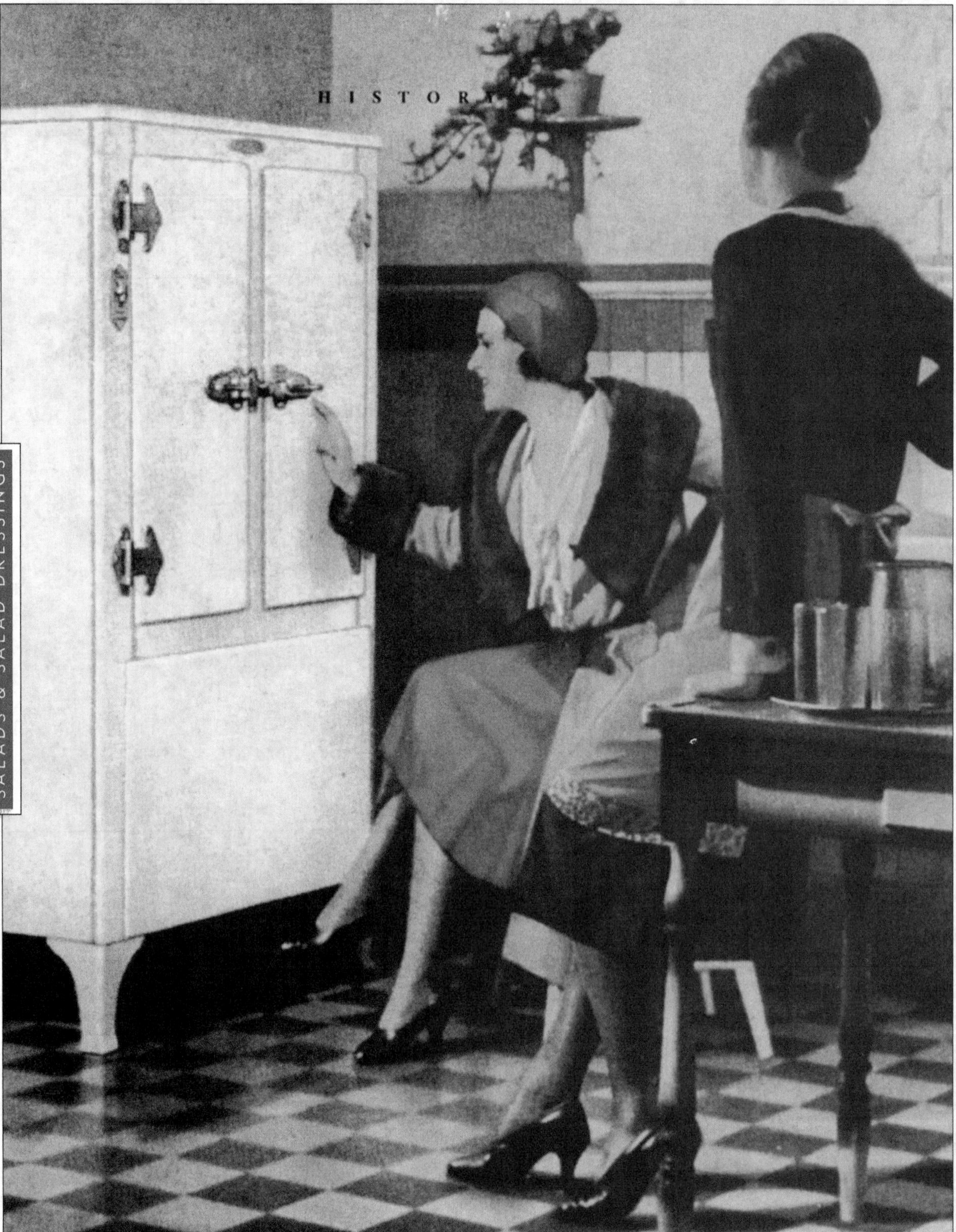

YOU MIGHT call this "The Century of the Salad." To be sure, salads existed before the twentieth century; in fact, Waldorf Salad, that dice of apples and celery bound with mayonnaise, was invented in 1893 by Oscar Tschirky, the haughty maître d'hôtel of New York City's old Waldorf-Astoria Hotel. But before the twentieth century, most salads were looked upon as repositories for leftovers. Thus, meat, chicken, and fish salads were common (though not tuna, which arrived only after tuna was put into cans in 1903). Fruit salads were popular, as were tartly dressed mélanges of cold vegetables. There was tomato aspic, too, molded first with calf's foot jelly (made from scratch), then with sheet gelatin, then, just at the turn of the century, with Mr. Knox's new granulated gelatin.

Jell-O dramatically changed the salad course, nudging it ever nearer dessert. And frozen fruit salads (the July 1912 *Ladies' Home Journal* devotes an entire article to them) pushed it over the edge. These sweet salads still have their fans in the South and heartland.

Green salads, for the most part, meant a wedge of iceberg doused with Russian or Thousand Island dressing. Yet as early as 1939, Irma Rombauer, in her now forgotten *Streamlined Cooking,* writes: "The constant stress by scientists and physicians on the importance of uncooked vegetables and fruits in our everyday diet brings the salad into prominence." She goes on to suggest rubbing a salad bowl with garlic and filling it with crisp cold lettuce. "Use iceberg," she recommends, "romaine, endive, watercress (this is supposed to be like eating your way across a lawn), etc. Young spinach is sometimes substituted for lettuce."

Still, green salads didn't come into their own after World War II. For many reasons. Americans began traveling abroad as never before, getting acquainted with mesclun and mâche in France, arugula and radicchio in Italy, fresh snow peas and bean sprouts in China.

As demands for the unusual grew, boutique farmers began supplying chefs, then greenmarkets, even better supermarkets, with broad palettes of greens: Bibb, Boston, and butterhead lettuce, Belgian endive, oak-leaf and ruby lettuce, mizuna, mesclun, arugula, sorrel, peppergrass, watercress, purslane, and dandelions.

Herb gardens proliferated, putting fresh basil, borage, burnet, chervil, chives, coriander, dill, fennel, lovage, marjoram, mint, nasturtium, oregano, and tarragon just blocks—sometimes just steps—away.

We discovered flavored oils—fruity virgin olive oils, of course, but also avocado oil, grapeseed, hazelnut, sesame, and walnut. Red and white wine vinegars became cupboard staples, as did tarragon and the mellow brown Italian *aceto balsamico.* We experimented with Asian rice wine vinegars and Spanish sherry vinegars, not to mention half a dozen different berry vinegars.

From the early '60s onward, there seemed to be a new salad exotic every month in the produce section of our supermarkets. This was thanks primarily to Frieda Caplan, the "Kiwi Queen" (see page 278), who introduced us not only to that fuzzy little green-fleshed fruit but also to elephant garlic, jicama, tomatillos, tamarillos, and, oh, so many other strange fruits and vegetables.

Salads remain a work in progress, with chefs constructing them of ever odder, ever more artful (or architectural) couplings.

That said, the twentieth century has already given us these all-star classics: Caesar Salad, Chef's Salad, Cobb Salad, Celery Victor, Green Goddess Salad, Palace Court Salad, Raw Spinach Salad with Hot Bacon Dressing, Three-Bean Salad, Overnight Layered Salad, Crab Louis, Tuna Salad, and yes, Perfection Salad, that shimmery gelatin that kicked off The Era of the Molded Salad back in 1905.

SALADS
SALAD DRESSINGS

CAESAR SALAD

CONSIDERED A "California" classic, Caesar Salad actually originated at Caesar's Place, a restaurant in Tijuana, Mexico. It dates to Prohibition days when movie stars headed South of the Border on weekends to party. The weekend that gave us Caesar Salad was the Fourth of July, 1924.

In a 1995 article on Caesar Salad, *New York Newsday* food writer Cara De Silva quotes Julia Child, who recalled visiting Caesar's Place as a girl. "I remember this great big fellow with his salad bowl making the salad at the table, which was the way it always used to be made. And you were supposed to eat it with your hands." That would have been shortly after Caesar Salad was created. Here's how it happened. Jonathan Norton Leonard, in *American Cooking: The Great West* (one in Time-Life's valuable "Foods of the World" series), writes:

. . . one evening Caesar Cardini's restaurant almost ran out of food. The local stores were either cleaned out or closed, and Caesar desperately took inventory of his storeroom. All he found was crates of romaine lettuce (in those days a little-known delicacy), a huge slab of Romano cheese, some bread, some bottles of olive oil, and half a crate of eggs.

His hastily improvised salad—crisp romaine torn into bite-size pieces, olive-oil browned croutons, and grated Romano tossed up with a lemony dressing in a wooden bowl rubbed with garlic. But the secret ingredient was a one-minute coddled egg, which made the dressing stick.

In a 1995 article on the rewards of culinary improv, which included the story of Caesar Salad, *New York Daily News* food columnist Arthur Schwartz wrote that Cardini's attitude was "Give the show people a little show and they'll never realize it's only salad." So Cardini "sent his dining room captains out to the tables with salad bowls and those rummaged ingredients, to make a show of the salad preparation."

According to Jonathan Norton Leonard, the show people were so delighted they didn't ask for anything else, "and the fame of Caesar's Salad spread across the continent."

Inevitably, others began fiddling with Caesar's recipe, adding minced anchovies, substituting blue cheese or Parmesan for Romano, using raw egg instead of coddled.

In footnotes to his story on Caesar Salad, Arthur Schwartz wrote:

[1] *The original Caesar was made with only small, whole leaves of romaine and was meant to be eaten with the fingers.*

[2] *There were no anchovies mashed into the original dressing—and definitely none topping the salad—but those who sought to reproduce the salad tasted the anchovies that are in Worcestershire sauce and mistakenly added them to the dressing.*

There's some dispute, however, as to whether Cardini added Worcestershire sauce to his original dressing. In *American Taste,* James Villas, a particularly painstaking researcher, includes it in his "Classic Caesar Salad." On the other hand, *James Beard's American Cookery* does not (however, the version of his Caesar Salad printed in the *Salads* volume of Time-Life's "The Good Cook" series calls for "12 to 15 oil-packed flat anchovy fillets, rinsed, patted dry and finely cut").

Alas, we may never know whether Worcestershire sauce went into the original dressing. Cardini failed to write down the recipe. That's understandable, forgivable even. His first priority that Fourth of July weekend in 1924 was to please the movie folk who'd driven down to Tijuana to dine.

The recipe that follows is generally acknowledged to be the classic.

Caesar Salad

Makes 6 Servings

✳

TRUE CAESAR Salad calls for raw or barely cooked egg—risky business these days with salmonella infecting much of our egg supply (only thorough cooking will kill the bacteria). There is a solution: Use one of the frozen egg products recommended for people with high blood cholesterol. They are available in every supermarket and they are perfectly safe.

NOTE: The best bread to use for the croutons is French, Italian, or firm-textured white bread. The croutons can be made a day or two ahead and stored in an airtight container at room temperature. The romaine can also be prepared a day ahead of time; in fact, it will be crisper if it is. Separate into leaves, wash in several changes of cool water, spin-dry in a salad spinner, then layer into plastic bags with paper towels, and store in the refrigerator.

2½ cups ½-inch white bread cubes
⅓ cup plus 1 tablespoon fruity olive oil
1 large clove garlic, peeled and halved lengthwise
1 large head romaine, washed, spun dry, and crisped in the refrigerator
½ teaspoon salt
¼ teaspoon black pepper
1 soft-boiled (1-minute) egg or ¼ cup frozen egg product, thawed
3 tablespoons fresh lemon juice
½ teaspoon Worcestershire sauce (optional)
¼ cup freshly grated Romano cheese

1. Preheat oven to 450°F. Toss bread cubes with 1 tablespoon olive oil in large bowl, then spread on baking sheet. Bake, uncovered, 8 to 10 minutes, turning occasionally, until uniformly golden brown. Drain on paper towels and reserve.

2. Rub large wooden salad bowl well with garlic; discard garlic. Break romaine into bowl in bite-size pieces, drizzle with remaining ⅓ cup oil, and sprinkle with salt and pepper.

3. Break egg into bowl or drizzle egg product evenly over greens. Pour lemon juice over greens combined, if desired, with Worcestershire sauce. Sprinkle in cheese.

4. Toss until every leaf glistens, top with croutons, then serve.

NOTE: An alternative—easier—way to dress the salad is simply to whisk together until creamy the lemon juice, soft-boiled egg or egg substitute, Worcestershire, salt, and pepper. Add remaining ⅓ cup olive oil in fine stream, whisking vigorously until creamy. Finally, mix in cheese. Pour dressing over romaine in large bowl and toss until well coated. Top with croutons and serve.

PALACE COURT SALAD

WE HAVE San Francisco's historic Palace Hotel to thank for this twentieth-century American classic as well as for Green Goddess, which follows. Here's what Doris Muscatine, speaking of the last time she lunched at the Palace, has to say about it in *A Cook's Tour of San Francisco* (1963):

The cold buffet includes . . . assorted salads including the original Palace Court Salad: a mound of either tuna, prawns, shrimp, chicken, or crab pyramided atop an artichoke base and a slice of tomato, skirted with lettuce ruffles and chopped egg, accompanied by a boat of Thousand Island dressing.

And here's Helen Evans Brown on the same subject in her *West Coast Cook Book* (1952):

Palace Court Salad: Shredded lettuce, thick slices of ripe tomato, heart of artichoke filled with crab salad. Serve with Thousand Island dressing, and garnish with chopped hard-cooked egg yolk.

And James Beard in *American Cookery* (1972); note that he changes the recipe name to "Crab Legs Palace Court:"

The first one I remember consisted of a slice of tomato arranged on lettuce leaves, on which was placed a large artichoke bottom. This was topped with a mound of Russian salad and crab legs were set in a design around and over the salad. It was served with a masking of Russian dressing. Helen Brown, who got the recipe directly from Lucien, chef at the Old Palace Court, states that although the dish was originally made with crabmeat it was subsequently made with shrimp or lobster and sometimes with a mixture of all three. Nowadays the Palace Court serves the crab salad on an artichoke bottom decorated with Russian dressing and garnished with hard-boiled eggs and pimiento strips.

None of these three writers dates the salad's creation, nor could a call to the hotel—now lavishly renovated and reopened April 3, 1991, as the Sheraton Palace. What is known for sure is that Palace Court Salad belongs to this century and that it most likely predates 1942, when the Palace Court was rechristened the Garden Court.

In its article "Hotels with Histories," *Sunset* magazine (April 1991) says: "A remarkable amount of painstaking work was undertaken to restore the Garden Court [often called just Palace Court] to its original grandeur.

"The 70,000 pieces of leaded glass that make up the vast domed ceiling, yellowed by decades of tobacco smoke, were all removed, then cleaned or replaced." And ten 700-pound crystal chandeliers were also cleaned and restored, these for the very first time.

Sunset goes on to say that the Garden Court, which in days past had often been closed for private affairs, will now allow regular diners to bask "in its wonderful natural light" at breakfast, lunch, afternoon tea, and dinner.

Palace Hotel
San Francisco, Ca.

Green Goddess Salad

Makes 6 Servings

✳

IN THE mid-1920s, actor George Arliss starred in a William Archer play called *The Green Goddess*. During the San Francisco run, he stayed at the Palace Hotel and dined often at its Palm Court Restaurant. To honor Arliss, chef Philip Roemer created a new mixed green salad with a creamy herb dressing. "Green Goddess," he called it. Like most dressings, this one will taste better if made one day and served the next. The recipe here makes about 3 cups, more than you'll need for a single salad. No matter. Stored tightly covered in the refrigerator, Green Goddess dressing keeps well for about a week.

DRESSING

- 1 cup loosely packed fresh parsley sprigs
- ¼ cup coarsely snipped fresh chives
- ¼ cup loosely packed fresh tarragon leaves
- 1 large scallion (including about half the tops), chunked
- 1 small clove garlic, peeled
- 5 anchovy fillets or 2 tablespoons anchovy paste
- ¼ cup tarragon vinegar
- 1½ cups mayonnaise
- ½ cup sour cream
- 1 to 2 tablespoons buttermilk (as needed to thin dressing)

SALAD

- 1 clove garlic, peeled and halved
- 1 medium head romaine
- 1 medium head Boston lettuce
- ½ medium bunch chicory

1. DRESSING: Place all ingredients in work bowl of food processor fitted with metal chopping blade, then pulse 8 to 10 times until smooth and creamy, scraping work bowl sides down 2 or 3 times. If mixture seems too thick (it should be slightly thicker than medium white sauce), pulse in 1 to 2 tablespoons buttermilk. Pour into 1-quart jar, cover tight, and set in refrigerator. Shake well before using.

2. SALAD: Rub large wooden salad bowl well with garlic; discard garlic. Break greens into bowl in bite-size pieces and drizzle in about 1½ cups dressing. Toss lightly, then if each leaf doesn't glisten nicely with dressing, drizzle in a little more dressing, and toss again. Taste, and if the greens don't seem properly dressed, add a bit more dressing and toss again. The flavor of the dressing should not overpower that of the greens, but the salad shouldn't seem anemic, either.

TIMELINE

1948

Chiffon cakes become a national obsession.

McDonald's installs drive-through service in its San Bernardino, California, hamburger stand and eliminates carhops.

1949

Diners Club issues a credit card to boost business.

KitchenAid introduces a home electric dishwasher.

The National Chicken Cooking Contest—America's first big cook-off—is staged on the Delmarva Peninsula on the Chesapeake's Eastern Shore.

A Chicago baker names his new company for his nine-year-old daughter: Sara Lee.

Framingham, Massachusetts, medical researchers begin a long-range heart study that will link high blood cholesterol to heart disease.

Brown Derby Cobb Salad

Makes 4 to 6 Servings

*

ACCORDING TO Christie McFerren of the Walt Disney World publicity department, the recipe for Cobb Salad first saw print in *The Brown Derby Cookbook.* She adds that the dressing became so popular among Hollywood stars that Bob Cobb bottled it for home use. The adapted dressing recipe here makes 3½ cups, far more than you'll need for this amount of salad. No matter. Store it tightly covered in the refrigerator and use to dress any green salad.

NOTE: The water is optional—it ups the yield and trims per-serving counts for fat and calories. A trick not lost on image-conscious Hollywood. In fact, stars have been known to quadruple the amount of water.

BROWN DERBY FRENCH DRESSING

¼ cup water (optional)

¾ cup red wine vinegar

1 teaspoon sugar

Juice of ½ small lemon

¾ teaspoon salt (or to taste)

1 teaspoon black pepper (or to taste)

1 tablespoon Worcestershire sauce

1 teaspoon dry English mustard

1 clove garlic, peeled and minced

1 cup olive oil

1 cup vegetable oil

COBB SALAD

4 cups finely cut iceberg lettuce (about ½ head)

2 cups finely cut watercress (about ½ bunch)

5 cups finely cut chicory (about 1 small bunch)

4 cups finely cut romaine (about ½ head)

2 medium vine-ripe tomatoes, peeled and cored

2 cooked chicken breasts (about 1 pound) (preferably roasted), boned

6 strips bacon, crisply cooked

1 medium avocado, halved, pitted, and peeled

3 hard-cooked eggs, peeled and finely chopped

2 tablespoons snipped fresh chives

½ cup finely grated (or crumbled) Roquefort cheese

1. DRESSING: Shake water (if using), vinegar, sugar, lemon juice, salt, pepper, Worcestershire, mustard, and garlic in 1-quart shaker jar. Add olive and vegetable oils and shake well. Taste for salt and pepper and adjust as needed. Cover tight and store in refrigerator. Shake well before using.

2. SALAD: Arrange iceberg lettuce, watercress, chicory, and romaine in artful clumps in large shallow salad bowl or deep platter. Halve tomatoes, seed, cut into fine dice, and arrange in strip across middle of greens. Dice chicken and arrange on top of greens. Crumble or chop bacon fine and sprinkle over salad. Finely dice avocado and wreathe around edge of salad. Decorate with hard-cooked eggs, chives, and Roquefort. Just before serving, add 1 cup dressing, bring to the table, and toss well in front of guests.

COBB SALAD

ABOUT THE time mass America became motorized, architects had a field day designing restaurants in the shape of hot dogs, chickens, pigs, even hoopskirted plantation cooks. But none caught America's fancy like The Brown Derby, which opened in 1926 directly across Wilshire Boulevard from the Ambassador Hotel.

Why a Derby? There are several legends. According to Betty Goodwin (*Hollywood du Jour,* 1993), "the Derby was chosen as a classy symbol for the newly moneyed and sophisticated folk of Hollywood." Or it might have been because restaurant cofounder Wilson Mizner liked "the hat worn by Al Smith, governor of New York, on a visit to Los Angeles." Soon the Derby was packing in the

celebrities—John Barrymore, Charlie Chaplin, W.C. Fields—who liked the fact that they could hang out there until four in the morning.

A second Brown Derby opened three years later at the corner of Hollywood and Vine. And though of more conventional design, it was even more popular thanks to its proximity to major movie studios and to such star-power "regulars" as the two Joans (Bennett and Crawford), Jean Harlow, Katharine Hepburn, and William Powell. Robert Cobb bought the Derbies in 1934, and before long there were two more—one in Beverly Hills and another in Los Feliz.

Like so many classic recipes, Bob Cobb's salad was tossed together out of odds and ends. Arthur Schwartz, *New York Daily News* columnist, says the year was 1937 and that it happened one midnight when Cobb needed to rustle up something for his good buddy Sid Grauman (of Grauman's Chinese Theater). Cobb opened the huge restaurant refrigerator and "pulled out this and that: a head of lettuce, an avocado, some romaine, watercress, tomatoes, some cold breast of chicken, a hard-boiled egg, chives, cheese, and some old-fashioned French dressing. He started chopping. Added some crisp bacon—swiped from a busy chef." Grauman liked Cobb's spur-of-the-moment salad so much he ordered it the next day for lunch and pretty soon studio boss Jack Warner was sending his chauffeur over for takeout. "Since 1937," Schwartz adds, "more than four million Cobb Salads have been sold at Brown Derby restaurants."

Mesclun Salad with Toasted Goat Cheese

Makes 4 Servings

✳

BY THE late 1980s, mesclun (a South-of-France salad mix of baby greens, herbs, and edible flowers that's pronounced roughly *MES-klune*) was on the menu of every with-it chef and hostess. So was goat cheese, which some enterprising cook thought to toast and serve with mesclun.

This recipe is adapted from one that appeared in a *Country Living* "Food of the '80s" article written by the magazine's food editor, Joanne Lamb Hayes.

NOTE: Most specialty greengrocers, even high-end supermarkets, sell mesclun. You can also buy seed packets of it and grow your own.

DRESSING

2 tablespoons balsamic vinegar
1½ teaspoons minced shallots
1 teaspoon honey
1 clove garlic, peeled and
    minced
½ teaspoon Dijon mustard
¼ teaspoon salt
⅛ teaspoon cracked black
    pepper
6 tablespoons fruity olive oil

The Evolution of Chef's Salad

WHAT CHEF dreamed up this salad? Food writer/historian John Mariani attributes Chef's Salad to California in general but to no one in particular. Evan Jones, on the other hand, says in his head-note to Chef's Salad recipe in *American Food: The Gastronomic Story* (1975): "The origin of this salad is not, apparently, a matter of record, but it may have been made first in the kitchen of the Ritz-Carlton where a recipe used by Louis Diat called for smoked ox tongue as one of the meats and watercress as the only green leaf." Louis Diat includes this recipe in *Cooking à la Ritz* (1941):

CHEF'S SALAD

Place separately in a salad bowl equal amounts of chopped lettuce (placed on the bottom of the bowl), boiled chicken, smoked ox tongue and smoked ham, all cut in julienne style. Add ½ hard-cooked egg for each portion. Place some watercress in the center and serve with French Dressing.

A year earlier, Edith Barber, food editor of *The New York Sun*, offered this Chef's Salad in *Edith Barber's Cook Book* (1940). Her recipe differs significantly from Chef Louis's and like him, she doesn't say where she obtained the recipe. Here it is, word for word:

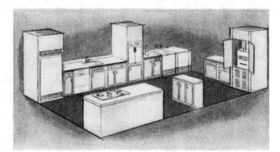

Mixed Green Salad (Chef's Salad)

Salad greens, sliced cucumbers, radishes, and scallions or minced chives, shredded raw carrots, shredded cabbage, chopped green peppers, flowerets of raw cauliflower, diced celery, quartered or sliced tomatoes, sliced hard-cooked egg, in any combination or proportions may be used with French Dressing for a green vegetable salad. Thin shreds of chicken, turkey, ham, or tongue are often added. Cucumbers may be pared or not, and should be sliced or diced and soaked in salt water for half an hour before using. Longer soaking is not desirable, as it causes wilting. Tomatoes should be skinned after they are dipped in boiling water and chilled before slicing or quartering. Tomatoes may be marinated in the dressing for an hour or more, but other vegetables and greens should be added just before the salad is to be served. The bowl may be rubbed with garlic before the salad is mixed. After greens and vegetables have been tossed with French dressing, the salad should be tasted, and more salt added, if necessary.

The original Chef's Salad was, if memory serves, "diet fare," which lends credence to Mariani's theory that it comes from California. Could it have originated in a Hollywood restaurant (or perhaps a studio commissary ordered to serve stars low-cal lunches)? The vegetable version of Edith Barber's salad, even with a few slivers of chicken breast, would surely be slimming if not inundated with dressing.

Over time chef's salads became fancier, weightier. In *American Gourmet* (1991), Jane and Michael Stern write: "At its worst, chef's salad is nothing more than cold cuts on top of lettuce, smothered in Thousand Island dressing. At its best, as it has been for many summers in the Four Seasons Bar Room, it is a distinguished warm-weather meal, needing only a chewy crusted loaf of bread on the side and a bowl of fresh berries to follow."

According to the Sterns, the secret of the Four Seasons dressing is the addition of tuna, an idea borrowed from the Italian *Vitello Tonnato* (slices of cold roast veal napped with tuna mayonnaise). The Four Seasons version of Chef's Salad doesn't stint on vegetables: carrots, zucchini, celery, red and green bell pepper, and daikon radish, all neatly julienned. There's plenty of protein, too: boiled ham, mortadella, Genoa salami, Parmesan cheese. And to complete the picture: romaine; small bunches of arugula, mâche, dandelion, and watercress; quartered pimientos, and clusters of Niçoise olives.

Scarcely diet fare.

Salad

1 pound mesclun, washed and
spun dry in a salad-spinner
8 (¼-inch) slices French bread
2 tablespoons butter
1 tablespoon fruity olive oil
2 cloves garlic, peeled and sliced
8 (¼-inch) slices goat cheese
about 2 inches in diameter

1. **Dressing:** Whisk together vinegar, shallots, honey, garlic, mustard, salt, and pepper. Gradually beat in oil and continue whisking until creamy; set aside.

2. **Salad:** Preheat oven to 400° F. Place mesclun in salad bowl; set aside.

3. Arrange bread slices on baking sheet. Heat butter with olive oil and garlic in small saucepan over moderate heat until butter melts and garlic turns golden; discard garlic.

4. Brush half of butter mixture over bread slices and bake until lightly toasted—about 5 minutes. Turn, brush with remaining butter mixture, and toast 2 to 3 minutes longer. Remove from oven and set aside.

5. Preheat broiler. Place goat cheese slices on greased baking sheet and broil 3 inches from heat until soft and touched with brown. With metal spatula, carefully transfer warm cheese slices to toast slices.

6. Quickly whisk dressing, drizzle over mesclun, and toss well.

7. Divide salad among four plates, then garnish with cheese-topped slices of toast.

Overnight Layered Chicken Salad

Makes 10 to 12 Servings

✳

SUNSET, FOUNDED IN 1929, was always in the avant-garde when it came to food because so many "all-American" classics first saw the light of day in that California magazine. A case in point: Overnight Layered Chicken Salad, which *Sunset* includes in its book of *All-Time Favorite Recipes* (1993). "The idea of an overnight layered salad was still new when we published this recipe in the mid-'70s," reads the head-note. "Favored by *Sunset* editors for its simplicity and creamy curry-flavored dressing, the salad has become a make-ahead classic."

SALAD

6 cups shredded iceberg lettuce
¼ pound fresh bean sprouts, washed and drained well
1 (8-ounce) can water chestnuts, drained and sliced
½ cup thinly sliced scallions
1 medium cucumber, thinly sliced
4 cups (2- to 3-inch-long) cooked chicken strips
2 (6-ounce) packages frozen snow peas, thawed and drained

DRESSING

2 cups mayonnaise
2 teaspoons curry powder
1 tablespoon sugar
½ teaspoon ground ginger

GARNISHES

½ cup Spanish peanuts
12 to 18 cherry tomatoes, halved

1. SALAD: Spread lettuce evenly in wide glass serving bowl, then layer on top in this order: bean sprouts, water chestnuts, scallions, cucumber, chicken, and snow peas.

2. DRESSING: Combine all ingredients and spread over snow peas.

3. Cover salad and chill overnight.

4. Garnish with peanuts and cherry tomatoes.

5. To serve, lift out portions with spoon and fork, scooping to bottom of bowl to include all layers.

Classic Layered Salad

Makes 8 Servings

✳

FOOD WRITER/chef Michael McLaughlin says in *More Back of the Box Gourmet* (1994) that he first encountered layered salads in a restaurant salad bar in his Colorado home town in the '80s. "What is *that?*" he asked the man ahead of him in line. "Looks like a train wreck," the man snorted, then helped himself to a hefty portion. McLaughlin tried the mess himself and had to admit that "it tasted wonderful." In his amusing little book of "hit recipes from American food packages" McLaughlin offers a Seven-Layer Salad from Kraft—shredded lettuce, chopped tomatoes, sliced raw mushrooms, thawed frozen green peas, and red onion rings layered into a 2-quart bowl with cubes of Kraft Cheddar, the lot frosted with Kraft's Miracle Whip. Could Kraft have originated the recipe? It does make a dandy show-case for two of its best-sellers. The recipe here comes from *The Best of Family Circle Cookbook* (1985). It's more typical of the layered salads popular during the 1980s than the *Sunset* recipe that precedes.

4 cups shredded romaine
4 medium carrots, peeled and cut into matchstick strips
1 cup small macaroni shells, cooked and drained by package directions
1 (10-ounce) package frozen green peas, thawed
1 small red onion, peeled, halved lengthwise, sliced crosswise, and separated into crescents
2 cups cubed cooked ham
½ cup shredded Swiss cheese
1½ cups mayonnaise
2 tablespoons snipped fresh dill or 1½ teaspoons dillweed

1. Layer ingredients evenly in 3-quart clear glass bowl as follows: romaine, carrots, macaroni, peas, onion, ham, and cheese.

2. Mix mayonnaise and dill and spread over top layer.

3. Cover with plastic food wrap and chill several hours or overnight.

4. Just before serving, toss well to incorporate mayonnaise mixture.

ALICE WATERS

SHE'S BEEN called the "Mother of California Cooking," even the "Mother of the New American Cuisine." But Alice Waters dismisses the notion.

From the moment in 1971 she opened Chez Panisse restaurant in Berkeley, California, her mission was to lay her hands on the freshest produce available, then treat it with respect.

Like so many of our culinary gurus, Alice Waters did not set out to be a cook. Indeed, this New Jersey native, a picky childhood eater, was training to be a Montessori teacher. Then, at the age of nineteen, she flew off to France for her "year abroad," and that year forever changed her life.

In French village markets where produce was laid out as carefully as gems in a jewelry store, Alice discovered the glories of top-quality produce rushed from field to kitchen: tomatoes, red to the core, that tasted of sunshine; potatoes and carrots blessed with earthy richness; garlic both sweet and pungent; bouquets of freshly plucked basil, rosemary, tarragon, and thyme.

She also discovered green-gold olive oils that tasted of olives, silken goat cheeses, and not least, the works of Elizabeth David, the British author who wrote so eloquently about regional French cooking.

Alice Waters came home in love with French food, with *fresh* food, and, "cooking her way through Elizabeth David," produced such splendid dinners her friends urged her to open a restaurant.

Chez Panisse began as a simple place where Berkeley students could "hang" over Alice's awesome salads—offbeat combinations of lettuces, vegetables, and herbs that always seemed to work. As Alice gained confidence and indulged her creative urges, as boutique organic gardeners broke ground in California, the menu at Chez Panisse expanded. So, too, did the hours. To help make ends meet, Alice began serving dinner but kept it *prix fixe* like lunch.

Pretty soon word got around that something extraordinary was happening in Berkeley. And it wasn't long before America's culinary hotshots came to dinner.

James Beard called Chez Panisse "an extraordinary dining experience" thanks to Alice Waters's "brilliant gastronomic mind, her flair for cooking and her almost revolutionary concept of menu planning."

That revolutionary concept might pair lobster with cabbage leaves and roasted peppers . . . or baked goat cheese with garden lettuces . . . or poached salmon with fresh basil and olive butters . . . or fresh cherries and ripe Italian fontina cheese.

The combinations were so dazzling, so original, they inspired nearly every chef who worked at Chez Panisse. Four of them, now stars in their own right, are Jeremiah Tower, Mark Miller, Joyce Goldstein, and Deborah Madison.

Alice Waters continues to inspire—in cookbooks as well as in the kitchen, meaning those who never make it to Berkeley can still dine *chez* Waters.

Raw Spinach Salad
with Hot Bacon Dressing

IN *FIFTY-TWO Sunday Dinners* by E.O. Hiller (1915), there's something called Spinach Salad—a misnomer, for this is nothing more than chopped cooked spinach and bacon packed into little molds, chilled, then turned out on slices of baked ham and served cold with mayonnaise or tartar sauce. Fannie Farmer offers the same recipe (but minus the bacon) in the original *Boston Cooking-School Cook Book* (1896). She, too, calls it Spinach Salad. *Raw* spinach salad with hot bacon dressing came later.

In *Food Editors' Hometown Favorites Cookbook* (1984) by members of the Newspaper Food Editors and Writers Association, Peggy Daum of *The Milwaukee Journal* writes: "In many restaurants in the Milwaukee area, spinach salad with hot bacon dressing is a specialty. The idea originated with the city's German population, but the recipe has spread far beyond German homes and restaurants." To me the German connection is plausible; that country's classic potato salad is warmed with a hot bacon dressing. Germans also wilted lettuce with hot dressings. Many late-nineteenth-century American cookbooks contain recipes for Wilted Lettuce, sometimes called Dutched Lettuce (for the Pennsylvania Dutch, many of whom were German).

Then, leafing one day through *Mrs. Rorer's New Cook Book* (1902) by Sarah Tyson Rorer of Philadelphia, I came upon this recipe.

DANDELION SALAD, GERMAN FASHION

2 ounces bacon
2 tablespoonfuls of vinegar

1 saltspoonful of paprika
1 quart of fresh dandelion leaves
1 saltspoonful of salt

1 tablespoonful of chopped
onion or chives

Cut the bacon into strips; put it in a frying pan with two tablespoonfuls of water. Let the water evaporate and the bacon fry carefully until crisp, but not dry. Lift, and stand it aside while you shake the dandelions perfectly dry, and cool the bacon fat. Arrange the dandelions in your salad bowl and put over the slices of bacon. Add to the bacon fat the vinegar, salt, pepper *[not given in the ingredient list above]* and onion or chives; mix and pour over the dandelions and serve at once.

The leap from dandelions to spinach, from cold bacon dressing to hot is hardly a quantum one. Yet my perusal of cookbooks of the '20s, '30s, and '40s shows that it took several decades. Peggy Daum doesn't tell when spinach salad became popular in Milwaukee restaurants, but my introduction to it took place in the late 1950s. In California.

The *Ladies' Home Journal Cook Book* (1960), on which I worked, includes a fairly classic raw spinach salad, called here Wilted Spinach, except that one chopped hard-cooked egg is added to the hot bacon dressing. The 1965 *Better Homes and Gardens Cook Book* offers something similar, a Chafing-Dish Spinach Salad. First a hot bacon dressing is made at table in the chafing dish, then spinach is piled in and wilted along with sliced scallions.

Today, chafing dishes are passé. Besides, pouring a boiling dressing over tender young spinach leaves does a good job of wilting them.

Raw Spinach Salad with Hot Bacon Dressing

Makes 4 to 6 Servings

✳

HERE IS my own recipe for Spinach Salad with Hot Bacon Dressing—a little spicier than the Milwaukee classic (its dressing contains three ingredients only: bacon plus equal parts sugar and white vinegar).

1 pound tender young spinach, trimmed of coarse stems
6 slices bacon, snipped crosswise into julienne strips
4 scallions, trimmed, washed, and thinly sliced
1 clove garlic, peeled and crushed
1 tablespoon ketchup
½ cup cider or red wine vinegar
½ teaspoon salt
¼ teaspoon black pepper

1. Wash spinach well in several changes of cold water, spin dry, then bundle in paper towels and refrigerate. When ready to proceed, mound spinach in large heat-proof salad bowl.

2. Brown bacon in large heavy skillet over moderate heat 3 to 5 minutes, until all fat cooks out; drain crisp brown bits on paper towels and reserve.

3. Add scallions and garlic to bacon drippings and sauté over low heat about 2 minutes until limp. Mix in ketchup, vinegar, salt, and pepper. Bring all to boiling, pour over spinach, sprinkle in bacon bits, and toss well to mix. Serve at once.

TIMELINE

1949

Pillsbury holds a Grand National Recipe and Baking Contest in New York City, the forerunner of its biennial Bake-Off Cooking and Baking Contest.

James Beard becomes the restaurant critic for *Gourmet*.

1950s

The "Casserole Decade."

World War II veterans' appetite for sukiyaki, shish kebabs, pizzas, and beef Bourguignon heightens interest in foreign food.

Chickens begin to be sold as "parts," but account for only 5 percent of the market.

The "Kraft Television Theater" begins airing on network TV and its commercials are how-to cooking demonstrations.

Girl Scout cookies become available in flavors other than "basic shortbread."

Three-Bean Salad

Makes 10 to 12 Servings

✳

THOUGH MY first encounter with Three-Bean Salad occurred in New York in the late '50s, I felt that the recipe must surely predate that. Apparently not. Flipping through early-twentieth-century cookbooks, I find green bean salads, even kidney bean salads, but no "three-bean." Forties editions of "Fannie" and "Joy" and *Better Homes and Gardens* cookbooks offer no recipes for it, nor does James Beard's best-selling *Fireside Cook Book* (1949). Sylvia Lovegren (*Fashionable Food,* 1995) attributes it to Stokely-Van Camp, specifically a 1955 recipe booklet of theirs called "Let's Eat Outdoors." Sounds plausible—Stokely-Van Camp's line of canned goods included beans. The first recipe I could find for Three-Bean Salad appeared in June 1956, in *Sunset's* "Kitchen Cabinet," a column devoted to reader recipes. Submitted by a J.W.D. of Winthrop, Washington, it began with this headnote: "You may like to add a little sliced celery for additional crunchiness." This 1995 version from *Sunset Kitchen Cabinet,* a collection of more than 500 favorite recipes printed since the column's inception in 1929, is stripped of some of the fat and sugar "in keeping with modern tastes in salad dressings." *Sunset* also advises the cook, "For best flavor, prepare salad a day in advance to give vegetables time to absorb flavor."

SALAD
> 1 (15-ounce) can cut green beans
> 1 (15-ounce) can cut yellow wax beans or garbanzo beans
> 1 (15-ounce) can red kidney beans
> 1 small green bell pepper, cored, seeded, and finely chopped
> 1 small yellow onion, peeled and finely chopped

DRESSING
> ¼ cup sugar
> ¼ cup vegetable oil
> ⅓ cup white vinegar
> ½ teaspoon salt
> ¼ teaspoon black pepper

1. SALAD: Dump green beans, wax beans, and kidney beans into large colander and rinse well under cold running water. Drain well, then place in large bowl (not metal). Add green pepper and onion and mix gently.

2. DRESSING: Whisk together all ingredients, pour over salad, and mix gently.

French Dressing

● 5 ingredients (see above)
MIX the salt, sugar and paprika together. Add vinegar and oil— beat thoroughly.

3. Cover salad and marinate in refrigerator at least 24 hours. Mix gently once again.

4. To serve, lift salad with slotted spoon to individual plates.

Hot Bean Sprout Salad

Makes 6 to 8 Servings

✳

JOAN FONTAINE prepared this wonderful salad for me in 1959 when I was interviewing the actress for a *Ladies' Home Journal* article. The salad was new to me then, but I have served—and been served—it many times since. Nowadays, with fresh bean sprouts so widely available, it is almost commonplace. The recipe here has been adapted from the Fontaine original, which appeared in *The Ladies' Home Journal.*

SALAD
> 2 quarts fresh bean sprouts, well washed
> 8 slices bacon, snipped crosswise into julienne strips
> 10 to 12 large scallions, trimmed, washed, and thinly sliced
> 3 tablespoons minced green bell pepper
> 2 tablespoons minced pimiento

DRESSING
> ⅓ cup bacon drippings (reserved from bacon above)
> ⅓ cup red wine vinegar
> 1 clove garlic, peeled and crushed

¾ teaspoon salt
½ teaspoon Worcestershire sauce
⅛ teaspoon dry mustard
⅛ teaspoon black pepper

1. **SALAD:** Mound bean sprouts in large colander, set under hot water tap and run water over them—hard —2 to 3 minutes to wilt.

2. Meanwhile, brown bacon in large heavy skillet over moderate heat 3 to 5 minutes until all fat cooks out; drain crisp brown bits on paper towels and reserve. Also reserve ⅓ cup drippings for Dressing.

3. Drain sprouts well, transfer to large heat-proof bowl; add scallions, green pepper, and pimiento but do not toss. Set aside.

4. **DRESSING:** Bring drippings, vinegar, garlic, salt, Worcestershire sauce, mustard, and black pepper to boiling in small skillet over moderate heat, stirring constantly.

5. Pour boiling dressing over salad and toss well. Let marinate at room temperature 45 minutes to 1 hour. Add reserved bacon bits, toss well again, and serve.

Celery Victor

Makes 4 Servings

✳

HERE'S A less labor-intensive version I've worked out for today's cook. In her *West Coast Cook Book*, Helen Evans Brown notes that at the St. Francis, Celery Victor was often topped with alternating slices of

hard-cooked egg and tomato. And sometimes with cold cracked crab legs, or with crisscrosses of anchovy fillets or pimiento. But she doesn't say whether this was during Victor Hirtzler's reign or afterward. Suit yourself.

SALAD
　　8 small celery hearts
　　6 cups chicken broth
　　2 large sprigs fresh parsley
　　1 carrot, peeled and chunked
　　1 whole bay leaf
　　4 peppercorns

DRESSING
　　¼ cup fruity olive oil
　　2 tablespoons tarragon white
　　　　wine vinegar
　　2 tablespoons water
　　¼ teaspoon salt
　　⅛ teaspoon black pepper

GARNISH
　　4 teaspoons minced fresh
　　　　chervil or tarragon

1. **SALAD:** Poach celery hearts in broth with parsley, carrot, bay leaf, and peppercorns in covered shallow pan over low heat just until tender —25 to 30 minutes.

2. Cool celery hearts in broth, drain well (reserve broth for soup), then with hands gently press out as much remaining broth as possible. Trim hearts of excess leaves and arrange two hearts on each of four salad plates.

3. **DRESSING:** Whisk together all ingredients and drizzle evenly over celery hearts.

4. Sprinkle hearts with minced chervil and serve.

VICTOR IS Victor Hirtzler, chef de cuisine at San Francisco's elegant Hotel St. Francis during the early part of this century. Here's Celery Victor just as it appears in Hirtzler's *Hotel St. Francis Cook Book* (1919).

CELERY VICTOR

Wash six stalks of large celery. Make a stock with one soup hen or chicken bones, and five pounds of veal bones, in the usual manner, with carrots, onions, bay leaves, parsley, salt, and whole pepper. Place celery in vessel and strain broth over same, and boil until soft. Allow to cool in the broth. When cold, press the broth out of the celery gently with the hands and place on plate. Season with salt, fresh-ground black pepper, chervil, and one-quarter white wine tarragon vinegar to three-quarters of olive oil.

FRIEDA CAPLAN: "QUEEN OF KIWIFRUIT"

KIWIS ARE merely one of the exotic fruits and vegetables this Los Angeles produce wizard has brought into our lives. And it all began with mushrooms—California brown mushrooms in 1957.

Then working as a bookkeeper in a Los Angeles produce company owned by her husband's relatives, Frieda Caplan was left in charge while they went off on a two-week holiday just before Thanksgiving. Could she, a major store-chain buyer wanted to know, fulfill orders for fresh mushrooms if he were to advertise them as a Thanksgiving special? Without batting an eye, Frieda said she could, unaware that (1) mushroom supplies plummeted at that time of year and (2) demand for them soared.

Undaunted, Frieda kept her promise, even going so far as to help harvest, pack, and deliver the mushrooms herself in her station wagon, sometimes with her new baby Karen on board (Karen Caplan is now president and CEO of Frieda's, Inc., as the company is known today).

On April 2, 1962, Frieda launched her own business, Produce Specialties, Inc., at Los Angeles's 7th Street Market, dealing almost exclusively with fresh mushrooms, then available mostly by the can. Frieda's open mind and go-with-the-flow attitude turned a fluke into a marketing coup: When the sign painter arrived to letter her firm's first sign, the only color he had (other than basic black) was an orchidy shade of purple.

That purple, now gracing every package of Frieda's produce, every label, every brochure, every "Hot Sheet" (newsletter) instantly identifies Frieda's brand-name produce and other food specialties (won ton wrappers, egg roll wrappers, tofu, crêpes, etc.).

The specialty that made Frieda a household name was the Chinese gooseberry, an ovoid fruit with fuzzy brown skin, jade-green flesh, pale custardy heart, and perfumey flavor. When a Safeway buyer asked Frieda back in 1962 if she'd ever heard of a Chinese gooseberry, she had to admit that she hadn't. Scarcely six months later, a broker offered her a load of them and she snapped them up only to discover that there were few takers.

A marketer of enviable skill, Frieda decided that what this wallflower fruit needed was a good PR job. So she rechristened the Chinese gooseberry the "kiwifruit," naming it after the bird (and emblem) of New Zealand, the country from whence this strange fruit came.

Frieda next persuaded a local pastry chef to create a special kiwifruit pastry and sweet-talked produce buyers into setting up kiwifruit displays in their stores. Then, to teach wary customers about kiwifruit, she produced display posters and recipe fliers. Soon, California farmers began growing kiwifruit and in 1971, Frieda introduced the first domestic crop. Before long, "New American" chefs were hip to kiwis, churning them into sorbets, slicing them into tarts, dicing them into fruit salads and salsas. So the cool green fruit became hot. Frieda calls it her "eighteen-year overnight success story."

Among Frieda's other successful fruit and vegetable launches: Cactus pears, cherimoyas, elephant garlic, dried red tomatoes, enoki and shiitake mushrooms, jicama, Sugar Snap Peas, tamarillos, and tomatillos. Look for them in your supermarket.

Salad of Kiwi, Orange, Grapefruit, and Watercress

Makes 4 Servings

✻

ELIZABETH SCHNEIDER, a New York food journalist of rare devotion, has written one of the twentieth century's most valuable cookbooks/references: *Uncommon Fruits & Vegetables, A Commonsense Guide.* In it, she profiles the exotic produce that joined our larder during the last half of this century. Among these, to be sure, is the Chinese gooseberry, or, as it's better known, the kiwi. This recipe is adapted from Schneider's book. She introduces it with this headnote: "Colorful, and pleasantly bittersweet, this salad works particularly well with roasted pork or smoked meats. For a deliciously garish change, substitute thin ribbons of radicchio rosso for watercress."

DRESSING

2 tablespoons fresh lemon juice
1 tablespoon rice vinegar
¼ teaspoon salt
⅛ teaspoon ground hot red pepper (cayenne)
2 teaspoons flowery honey
3 tablespoons corn oil
Juices from cut orange, grapefruit, and kiwi (below)

SALAD

1 medium bunch watercress, trimmed, rinsed, and dried
1 large navel orange, peeled, halved lengthwise, and each half thinly sliced
1 large pink or red grapefruit, peeled, halved lengthwise, and each half thinly sliced
3 large kiwis, peeled and cut into thin rounds

1. DRESSING: Place all ingredients in small shaker jar, screw cap on tight, and shake well to mix. Set aside until ready to use.

2. SALAD: Wreathe watercress around edge of large serving plate. Spiral orange and grapefruit slices around plate just inside watercress, alternating the fruits. Arrange kiwi rounds in center. Cover and chill until ready to serve.

3. Just before serving, shake dressing well, then pour evenly over salad.

Avocado and Grapefruit Salad

Makes 6 to 8 Servings

✻

AVOCADOS, INDIGENOUS to Central and South America, were first planted in Florida in 1833 and fifteen years later in California just east of Los Angeles (today most of our crop comes from California). Only in the 1950s, however, did "alligator pears," as avocados used to be called, become trendy salad ingredients. Two classic combos are given here: grapefruit and avocado and orange and avocado. The recipes were adapted from ones developed by the California Avocado Advisory Board (now the California Avocado Commission) for its booklet, *The Avocado Bravo.*

SALAD

3 ripe medium California avocados, pitted, peeled, and sliced
3 medium grapefruits, peeled, sectioned, and seeded
1 head Bibb lettuce, separated into leaves, washed and patted dry
3 to 5 sprigs watercress

DRESSING

⅓ cup vegetable oil
¼ cup tarragon vinegar
¼ cup fresh grapefruit juice
1 tablespoon fresh lemon juice
1 teaspoon sugar
½ teaspoon salt
½ cup crumbled Roquefort cheese (optional)

1. SALAD: Fan avocado slices and grapefruit sections out on bed of lettuce in large bowl, alternating the fruits.

2. DRESSING: Whisk together oil, vinegar, grapefruit juice, lemon juice, sugar, and salt until creamy; mix in Roquefort, if desired.

3. Spoon dressing evenly over salad, garnish with watercress, and serve.

--- **VARIATION** ---

AVOCADO AND ORANGE SALAD: Prepare as directed, substituting 3 cups orange or mandarin orange segments for grapefruit; in dressing, use orange juice in place of grapefruit juice. Makes 6 to 8 servings.

I ALWAYS assumed this was a Southern salad because it appeared so regularly in my grammar school cafeteria in Raleigh, North Carolina. Also, because when I went north to school in the 1950s, no one had ever heard of it. Although there may be earlier recipes for macaroni salad, the first one I've been able to track down in print is this one, which appeared in *Mrs. Allen's Cook Book* (1917) by Ida Bailey Allen:

MACARONI SALAD

1¼ cupfuls macaroni, broken into pieces

1¼ cupfuls diced celery

23 stuffed olives, sliced

Mayonnaise or boiled dressing

Lettuce or cress

Boil the macaroni until tender, and cool it. Combine with the remaining ingredients, chill and serve on a bed of the salad green. Garnish with whole olives.

The macaroni salad of my childhood was slightly different. Usually it contained a spoon or two of yellow mustard, occasionally some celery seeds, and sometimes leftover ham, and/or peas and carrots. And if a cook was feeling intrepid, she might grate in a little onion. The dressing was always mayonnaise—and plenty of it.

DRESSING

¼ cup fresh orange juice

¼ cup olive oil or vegetable oil

1 teaspoon Dijon mustard

1 tablespoon chopped fresh coriander (cilantro)

¼ teaspoon chili powder

¼ teaspoon salt

SALAD

2 medium navel oranges, peeled, thinly sliced, and each slice quartered

2 cups torn lettuce leaves

4 thin slices red onion

1 cup peeled, julienned jicama

1. DRESSING: Place all ingredients in small shaker jar, screw lid down tight, and shake well to mix.

2. SALAD: Place oranges, lettuce, red onion, and jicama in large salad bowl. Drizzle dressing evenly over all and toss gently but thoroughly to mix. Serve at once.

Jicama, Orange, and Onion Salad

Makes 4 Servings

✱

JICAMA (pronounced HEE-kama) came into its own in the mid-'80s thanks to Frieda Caplan (see "Queen of Kiwifruit" box, page 278) and innovative young Southwestern chefs like Dean Fearing of Dallas's Mansion on Turtle Creek. On the subject of this fleshy Mexican tuber, Frieda Caplan writes: "Jicama, one of our all-time favorites, is a crunchy, sweet snack that is so low in calories you can eat it all day without guilt!

Its crisp texture resembles a raw potato; peel off the brown skin, slice, chop, or cut into sticks." The recipe here is adapted from one in *Frieda's Exotic & Healthy Foods* leaflet (1992).

Jim Villas's Ham and Macaroni Salad

Makes 6 Servings

✱

MY GOOD friend and fellow Tar Heel, Jim Villas, included this macaroni salad in *My Mother's Southern Kitchen,* the book he wrote with his mother, Martha Pearl Villas. It's a little fancier than the macaroni salads of my Raleigh childhood because it contains hard-cooked eggs and Swiss cheese as well as ham, and it's moistened with a Mustard Buttermilk dressing. I've adapted Jim's recipe—but only the language. To introduce the recipe, Jim wrote this headnote: "This type of simple, old-fashioned salad evolved in the South long before Americans ever heard the word 'pasta.' Today, it might be looked down upon by more 'sophisticated' cooks, but to Southern ladies like my mother, it is still the perfect salad to serve at club meetings and on a large luncheon buffet. Personally, I love it." So do I, Jim.

DRESSING

- ½ cup buttermilk
- ½ cup mayonnaise
- 1 tablespoon prepared yellow mustard
- ¼ teaspoon Worcestershire sauce
- Black pepper to taste

SALAD

- 3 cups cooked elbow macaroni, well drained
- 1 pound lean cooked ham, cut into ½-inch cubes
- ½ pound Swiss cheese, cut into ½-inch cubes
- 2 hard-cooked eggs, peeled and chopped
- 2 ribs celery, chopped
- ½ cup chopped sweet pickles
- Cherry tomatoes (for garnish)

1. DRESSING: Whisk all ingredients together in small bowl; cover, and refrigerate until ready to use.

2. SALAD: Toss macaroni in large bowl with ham, cheese, eggs, celery, and pickles; add dressing and toss again. Garnish with cherry tomatoes and serve.

IT'S SMOOTHER— CREAMIER— DIFFERENT

LARGEST SELLING Prepared Mustard in the U.S.A. today

French's PURE PREPARED MUSTARD CREAM SALAD BRAND

Crab Louis

Makes 6 Servings

✳

THERE'S CONSIDERABLE dispute about who created this recipe, when, and where. To quote Helen Evans Brown (*West Coast Cook Book,* 1952): "Just which Louis invented this West Coast specialty I am not prepared to say, but only because I don't know. I do know, however, that it was served at Solari's, in San Francisco, in 1914, for Clarence Edwords gives their recipe for it in his epicure's guide, *Bohemian San Francisco.*" *The Sunset Cookbook* (1965) says Solari's was serving Crab Louis as early as 1911. John Mariani (*Dictionary of American Food and Drink,* Revised Edition, 1994) suggests Crab Louis might have been created by the chef at Seattle's Olympic Club (as does *The American Heritage Cookbook,* 1964), or perhaps by the chef at the St. Francis Hotel in San Francisco. Indeed, Victor Hirtzler includes this recipe for it in his *Hotel St. Francis Cook Book* (1919):

Arrange lettuce leaves around the inside of a salad bowl, with a few sliced leaves on the bottom. Put crabmeat on top of the sliced leaves, and a few sliced hard-boiled eggs and sliced chives on top of the crabmeat. In another bowl mix one-half cup French dressing with one-half cup Chili sauce, two spoonfuls of mayonnaise, salt, pepper, and one teaspoonful of Worcestershire sauce. Pour over the salad, and serve very cold.

The recipe that follows is adapted from one that appeared in *American Cooking: The Great West* (1971) by Jonathan Norton Leonard, one of the volumes in Time-Life Books splendid "Foods of the World" series. It calls for mounding the crab mixture in avocado halves, a practice that's been popular at least since the 1950s.

LOUIS DRESSING

1½ cups mayonnaise
¼ cup chili sauce
3 tablespoons finely minced scallions (include some green tops)
3 tablespoons finely minced green bell pepper
1 tablespoon fresh lemon juice
1½ teaspoons Worcestershire sauce
¼ teaspoon hot red pepper sauce

SALAD

1½ pounds lump crabmeat (preferably Dungeness), bits of shell and cartilage removed

2 heads Bibb or Boston lettuce, separated into leaves, washed, and spun dry in a salad spinner
3 large firm-ripe avocados, halved, pitted, and peeled
2 medium vine-ripe tomatoes, cored and cut into 6 wedges
3 hard-cooked eggs, peeled and quartered lengthwise

1. LOUIS DRESSING: Whisk together all ingredients in large bowl.

2. SALAD: Add crab to dressing and turn until evenly coated.

3. Bed lettuce leaves on each of six salad plates. Mound crab mixture into avocado halves and center on leaves. Garnish with tomatoes and hard-cooked eggs, dividing total amounts evenly, and serve.

Tuna Salad

Makes 6 to 8 Servings

✳

THE REASON tuna salad belongs to the twentieth century (for American women had been making fish and shellfish salads forever) is that fresh tuna was unavailable and canned tuna went on sale only in 1903. This recipe is one I developed in the 1970s for the food processor.

NOTE: If you have no processor, hand-chop the herbs, onions, and celery, flake the tuna, then combine all ingredients.

1 cup loosely packed, washed, and dried fresh parsley sprigs

⅓ cup loosely packed, washed, and dried fresh dill sprigs

4 (6- or 7-ounce) cans chunk white tuna, well drained

3 medium yellow onions, peeled and cut into slim wedges

2 medium celery ribs, washed, trimmed of tops, and cut into 2-inch chunks

1 cup mayonnaise

¼ cup small capers, drained

3 to 4 tablespoons milk, light cream, or water

¼ teaspoon black pepper

Salt to taste

1. Pulse parsley and dill in food processor equipped with metal chopping blade 3 to 5 times until coarsely chopped; empty into large mixing bowl.

2. Flake tuna in two batches in food processor by pulsing 3 to 4 times; transfer to bowl.

3. Coarsely chop onions and celery in food processor with 8 to 10 pulses; add to bowl.

4. Add mayonnaise, capers, 3 tablespoons milk, and pepper to processor work bowl and pulse quickly to mix.

5. Pour over salad and toss well to mix; if mixture seems stiff, add remaining 1 tablespoon milk. Taste for salt and season as needed.

6. Cover, and chill several hours before serving.

THESE QUIVERY crowns, rings, and towers strewn with diced fruits, meats, and/or vegetables caught America's fancy early in the twentieth century and remained popular well into the '60s. Indeed, throughout the South and heartland, they're still a party staple.

In her meticulously researched book, *Perfection Salad,* Laura Shapiro writes that turn-of-the-century American women were obsessed with tidying up their salads, with containing the disparate and sometimes messy ingredients in lettuce cups or hollowed-out vegetables or tiaras constructed of hard-cooked eggs. But the "tidiest and most thorough way to package salad," Shapiro continued, "was to mold it in gelatin."

The molded-salad movement might be said to have begun in 1893 when Philadelphia Cooking School teacher Sarah Tyson Rorer suggested to the Knox Gelatine Company that it granulate its sheets and shreds of gelatin, eliminating the need for a preliminary half-hour soak in cold water.

Knox paid attention and barely a year later introduced "Sparkling Granulated Gelatine" together with a free recipe booklet, *Dainty Desserts for Dainty People,* to teach women how to use this new convenience food. It begins:

Knox's Sparkling Calves Foot Gelatine (the purest made) is recognized to-day as the Standard by all users of pure food. It has no odor or taste to disguise, so requires less flavoring than any other; is clear and sparkling, needs no clarifying.

You have no doubt noticed, while pouring the hot water on some gelatines, a sickening odor which will arise from it (this never will happen in pure gelatines), and shows that the stock is not pure, so is unfit for food.

Gelatine should dissolve quickly; two to five minutes' soaking in cold water is long enough. Where it takes longer, it is more of a gluey nature, and should be used in cabinetwork only. You never have to cook pure gelatine to dissolve it. Soak it in cold water, five minutes at most, then pour on your boiling water, when it should all dissolve instantly. Knox Gelatines are made by the same process used in making calf's foot jelly. You can have same results without the labor of preparing the feet, etc.

MOLDED SALADS

Dainty Desserts for Dainty People then proceeds to list some three dozen "Teachers of Cookery" who have "used and approved Knox Gelatine," among them Mrs. Sarah Tyson Rorer, Principal, Philadelphia Cooking School; Mrs. Mary J. Lincoln, author, "Boston Cook Book" (the precursor of the best-selling "Fannie Farmer"), and Miss Fannie M. Farmer, Principal, Boston School of Cookery.

In the beginning, writes Shapiro, the new granulated gelatin "was used much as the old shredded gelatins had been—to make puddings, mousses, charlottes, and jellies as well as the occasional main dish, or tomato aspic—but the possibilities for salad making soon became evident."

Before long women were begging their favorite magazines for gelatin recipes. An 1896 letter to Mary Lincoln, columnist for *American Kitchen Magazine,* requested "directions for a jelly where pieces of oranges, bananas, white grapes, are used and are seen in the jelly." Mrs. Lincoln obliged by telling her how to layer fruits into an orange gelatin dessert.

In 1905, Charles Knox ran a recipe contest that launched the Age of the Molded Salad. Mrs. John Cooke of New Castle, Pennsylvania, submitted her recipe for Perfection Salad, a tart gelatin mold strewn with bits of cabbage, celery, and sweet red pepper, which the judges —Fannie Farmer among them—awarded third prize. The first- and second-place winners have been forgotten, but not Mrs. Cooke's Perfection Salad (see box, page 286). Knox printed the recipe in its next recipe booklet and continued to offer it in subsequent pamphlets printed throughout the twentieth century, updating it now and then to suit the times.

Perfection Salad inspired cooks as few recipes have. And the rise of Jello-O at approximately the same time, the proliferation of its fruity flavors, and the industry of its advertising staff in "papering" the country with Jello-O recipes fueled the molded-salad boom. Soon every woman had her particular favorites, shimmering, lollipop-colored affairs reserved for special company.

My mother's battered edition of *The Joy of Cooking*

(1946) includes a huge section on what Irma Rombauer calls "Aspic Salads." She introduces it with this bit of advice: "Any clever person can take a few desolate-looking icebox left-overs and glorify them into a tempting aspic salad." Irma then offers eighteen pages of molded salads (69 recipes!) that range from Clam Juice Ring to Golden Glow Salad to Molded Horseradish Salad.

Only in the late '60s did molded salads fall from favor and then mostly in sophisticated metropolitan areas where chefs were beginning to experiment with composed salads and an exotic new palette of greens. Some say the hippie counterculture was to blame because it rejected anything tainted by corporate America, not the least of which was processed food. These "flower children" also taught the rest of America the nutritional benefits of "eating clean, eating green."

Starting at the beginning—with Perfection Salad—I offer recipes for some of America's most beloved twentieth-century molded salads, the ones that continually crop up in community cookbooks.

In the box on page 286, just as the Knox Gelatine Company printed it in a leaflet announcing the winners of its 1905 recipe contest (and reprinted it in *Family Album* on the occasion of the company's Diamond Jubilee), is the original Perfection Salad.

Perfection Salad

Makes 6 Servings

✳

HERE'S KNOX'S somewhat more modern version of Perfection Salad.

2 envelopes unflavored gelatin
1 cup cold water
1½ cups boiling water
½ cup sugar
½ cup cider vinegar
2 tablespoons fresh lemon juice
1 teaspoon salt
1½ cups finely shredded
   cabbage
1½ cups chopped celery
¼ cup diced green bell pepper
¼ cup chopped pimientos
Salad greens (optional)

1. Sprinkle gelatin over cold water in large heat-proof bowl; let stand 1 minute. Add boiling water and stir until gelatin dissolves completely, about 5 minutes.

2. Stir in sugar, vinegar, lemon juice, and salt.

3. Chill, stirring occasionally, until mixture is consistency of unbeaten egg white, 45 to 50 minutes.

4. Fold in cabbage, celery, green pepper, and pimientos.

5. Turn into 6-cup mold or bowl and chill 3 hours or until firm.

6. To serve, unmold on serving platter and garnish, if desired, with salad greens.

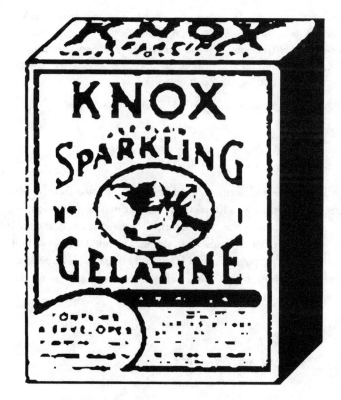

The 1905 Salad That Became a Classic

KNOX'S GELATINE: THE ONLY odorless—the absolutely pure —the one guaranteed Gelatine. It may not be in highest favor with poorly informed or indifferent housewives, but it certainly is pronounced the best by all the rest.

THIRD PRIZE WINNER
A $100 Sewing Machine

PERFECTION SALAD

½ package Knox's Gelatine
½ cup cold water
½ cup vinegar
Juice of 1 lemon
1 pt. boiling water
½ cup sugar
1 teaspoon salt

2 cups celery, cut in small pieces
1 cup finely shredded cabbage
¼ can sweet red peppers, finely cut

Soak Gelatine in cold water two minutes, add vinegar, lemon juice, boiling water, sugar and salt. Strain, and when beginning to set add remaining ingredients. Turn into a mold and chill. Serve on lettuce leaves with mayonnaise dressing, or cut in dice and serve in cases made of red and green peppers.

A delicious accompaniment to cold sliced chicken or veal.

MR. CHARLES B. KNOX,
Dear Sir,

Enclosed please find receipt for salad. It is one of the finest salads I have ever had, was made with Knox's Gelatine and can be served in so many different ways. I am going to have this salad served at our next church supper, if I can, where we always feed from two hundred to two hundred and fifty people. This salad is especially fine with fried oysters. I never use anything except Knox's Gelatine because it "jells" so quickly. Trusting this will meet with your approval, I remain,

Yours,
Mrs. John E. Cooke
174 Boyles Ave., New Castle, Pa.

Avocado and Tomato Salad Mold

Makes 8 to 10 Servings

✳

TOMATO ASPIC is nothing new, but layering it in a decorative mold with avocado aspic is a '50s innovation. This recipe is adapted from one that appeared in *The Sunset Cookbook* (1960), a collection of "best recipes" from that trend-setting California magazine.

AVOCADO ASPIC

1 envelope unflavored gelatin
¼ cup cold water
1 cup boiling water
1 teaspoon sugar
2 tablespoons fresh lemon or lime juice
1 cup mashed avocado (1 large)
½ cup sour cream
½ cup mayonnaise
1 teaspoon salt
¼ teaspoon hot red pepper sauce

TOMATO ASPIC

1 envelope unflavored gelatin
¼ cup cold water
1 cup boiling water
2 tablespoons sugar
1 tablespoon fresh lemon juice
1¼ cups canned tomato/ vegetable juice
¼ teaspoon salt
⅛ teaspoon hot red pepper sauce

GARNISH

*8 to 10 Bibb lettuce leaves,
washed and patted dry*

1. AVOCADO ASPIC: Soften gelatin in cold water in large heat-proof bowl, pour in boiling water, and stir until dissolved. Mix in sugar and 1 tablespoon lemon juice; set in refrigerator until consistency of unbeaten egg white—about 30 minutes. Immediately after mashing avocado, mix in remaining 1 tablespoon lemon juice.

2. When gelatin mixture is consistency of unbeaten egg white, add mashed avocado, sour cream, mayonnaise, salt, and red pepper sauce and blend until smooth.

3. Pour into decorative 2-quart mold and chill until almost set, 1½ to 2 hours. Surface should still be tacky.

4. Meanwhile, prepare TOMATO ASPIC: Soften gelatin in cold water in large heat-proof bowl, pour in boiling water, and stir until dissolved. Mix in sugar, lemon juice, tomato/vegetable juice, salt, and red pepper sauce. Pour over congealed avocado aspic in mold.

5. Return mold to refrigerator and chill several hours, or until set.

6. To serve, arrange lettuce on serving plate, carefully loosen aspic, and unmold on greens.

Jellied Gazpacho

Makes 8 Servings

✳

A '60s recipe from *Knox On-Camera Recipes,* which demonstrates America's growing interest in foreign food and low-calorie food (this salad weighs in at just 20 calories per serving). Because gazpacho was hardly a household word in 1960, *Knox* introduces the recipe with this headnote: "Along with castles, olives and sherry, Spain has its beloved cold soup, gazpacho, doubly delicious jellied."

*1 envelope unflavored gelatin
1½ cups cold water
1 bouillon cube
⅓ cup red wine vinegar
½ teaspoon salt
1 teaspoon sweet paprika
½ teaspoon dried leaf basil,
    crumbled
¼ teaspoon ground cloves
⅛ teaspoon hot red pepper
    sauce
1 clove garlic, peeled and
    minced
2 tablespoons finely chopped
    onion
¼ cup finely chopped celery
½ cup finely chopped green bell
    pepper
1½ cups finely chopped vine-
    ripe tomatoes
Sour cream (optional topping)*

1. Soften gelatin in ½ cup cold water in medium nonreactive saucepan; set over low heat and stir until dissolved.

2. Off heat, add bouillon cube and stir until dissolved. Add remaining 1 cup water, vinegar, salt, paprika, basil, cloves, and hot red pepper sauce; chill until consistency of unbeaten egg white—about 30 minutes.

3. Fold in garlic, onion, celery, green pepper, and tomatoes; cover, and chill 1 hour or until softly set.

4. Spoon into soup bowls and drift, if desired, with sour cream.

JELL-O

ELL-O, THAT wiggly-jiggly delight of childhood, first appeared in 1897, but it took the turn of a century to change the luck of what would soon be this country's best-selling prepared dessert. In fact, Orator Woodward, founder of the Genesee Pure Food Company, which produced Jell-O, was so discouraged in 1899 that he tried to sell out for $35. Less than three years later Jell-O sales zoomed to $250,000, and by 1906 they had reached $1 million. Clever advertising hastened this reversal of fortune. Early ads portrayed attractive housewives serving "America's most famous dessert." Booklets illustrated by popular artists Maxfield Parrish and Norman Rockwell offered the favorite Jell-O recipes of actress Ethel Barrymore and opera diva Madame Ernestine Schumann-Heink.

Rose O'Neill, creator of the Kewpie doll, drew an even cuter Kewpie—the Jell-O Girl—for Jell-O ads and boxes. In the 1930s, comedian Jack Benny's radio show featured a catchy commercial spelling "J-E-L-L-O" and listing its "Six delicious flavors: Strawberry, raspberry, cherry, orange, lemon, and lime!" Fifty years later, TV's Roseanne often serves Jell-O.

In the 1970s and 1980s when sales fell off, General Foods responded not only with a sugar-free Jell-O for the health-conscious but also with a new recipe no mother could resist—"Jigglers," which kids could cut out in animal shapes and eat with their hands.

To celebrate its centennial in 1997, Jell-O even dreamed up a new flavor—Sparkling White Grape, "the champagne of Jell-O."

Molded Cranberry Salad

Makes 8 to 10 Servings

❋

THIS THANKSGIVING classic comes from an undated Ocean Spray booklet, *Cranberry Dishes for Holidays and Special Occasions,* which surely belongs to the '50s (the photographs and art are dead giveaways). The salad is made with canned whole cranberry sauce instead of fresh cranberries (another giveaway, because the '50s culinary mindset was to use every prepared food possible). Strangely, Ocean Spray recommends this particular salad for Easter. "If you like turkey for your Easter dinner," reads the recipe headnote, "give your guests a choice of either cranberry sauce as an accompaniment or this delicious cranberry salad." And in case you prefer ham for your Easter feast, Ocean Spray offers Cranberry-Glazed Ham (page 109).

1 (3-ounce) package raspberry-flavored gelatin
1 cup hot water
½ cup cold water
1 small orange, peeled, segmented, and each segment halved
½ cup canned crushed pineapple, well drained
1 (1-pound) can whole cranberry sauce
¼ cup chopped nuts (pecans, blanched almonds, or walnuts)
8 to 10 lettuce leaves

1. Dissolve gelatin in hot water in large heat-proof bowl. Mix in cold water and chill until consistency of unbeaten egg white, about 30 minutes.

2. Fold orange, pineapple, cranberry sauce, and nuts into gelatin. Pour into decorative 1-quart mold or divide among 8 to 10 individual fluted molds and chill several hours or until firm, about 3 hours.

3. Unmold on lettuce leaves and serve.

Mother's Lime Gelatin Salad

Makes 12 to 15 Servings

✳

OF ALL the molded salads my mother made, this one and the Wales Salad that follows were the family favorites.

> 1 (3-ounce) package lime-flavored gelatin
> 1 (3-ounce) package lemon-flavored gelatin
> 2 cups boiling water
> 1 cup pineapple juice
> ⅓ cup fresh lemon juice
> ½ teaspoon salt
> ½ teaspoon prepared horseradish
> 1 cup evaporated milk, partially frozen
> 1 cup sieved cottage cheese
> ¼ cup mayonnaise
> 1½ cups canned crushed pineapple, well drained
> 1 cup coarsely chopped pecans
> Crisp lettuce leaves

1. Dissolve lime and lemon gelatins in boiling water in large heat-proof bowl. Mix in pineapple and lemon juices, salt, and horseradish. Chill until consistency of unbeaten egg white, about 40 minutes.

2. Whip evaporated milk until fluffy, then beat in gelatin mixture. Blend in cottage cheese and mayonnaise, then fold in pineapple and pecans.

3. Pour into a 3-quart ring mold or divide among 12 to 15 individual fluted molds and chill several hours, or until set, about 4 hours.

4. Unmold on lettuce leaves and serve.

What you can do with JELL-O

Wales Salad

Makes 10 Servings

✳

AN OFT-TOLD story in my family was that Daddy wouldn't marry Mother unless she served him salad every day. She did, and this was his favorite.

1 (3-ounce) package lemon-
   flavored gelatin
1 cup boiling water
1 cup shredded Cheddar cheese
½ cup coarsely chopped
   blanched almonds
½ cup chopped pimientos
½ cup thinly sliced pimiento-
   stuffed green olives
¼ teaspoon salt
2 tablespoons fresh lemon juice
1 cup heavy cream, softly
   whipped
Crisp lettuce leaves

1. Dissolve gelatin in boiling water in large heat-proof bowl and cool.

2. Mix in cheese, almonds, pimientos, olives, salt, and lemon juice. Chill until consistency of unbeaten egg white—about 30 minutes.

3. Fold in whipped cream. Divide among 10 individual fluted molds (or pour into a 6-cup ring mold) and chill several hours, or until set. Better yet, chill overnight.

4. Unmold on lettuce and serve.

Neapolitan Loaf

Makes 10 Servings

✳

THIS INTRICATELY layered gelatin loaf dates to a 1933 General Foods booklet entitled *What You Can Do with Jell-O*. It capitalizes on

the discovery that partially set gelatin can be whipped, also on the Great Depression fondness for affordable food in fancy dress. Even the salad's out-of-the-air name suggests elegance. Needless to add, there is nothing Neapolitan about it.

> 2 (3-ounce) packages orange-
> flavored gelatin
> 4 cups warm water
> ¾ cup halved, seeded green
> grapes
> 1 medium orange, peeled and
> segmented

1. Dissolve gelatin in warm water. Pour ¼-inch layer in 9 × 5 × 3-inch loaf pan; chill until tacky—10 to 15 minutes. Reserve 1 cup dissolved gelatin for whipping and chill until consistency of unbeaten egg white —25 to 30 minutes. Chill remaining gelatin separately until consistency of unbeaten egg white.

2. Arrange some of grapes in patterns, cut-sides-up, on tacky layer of gelatin in pan. Add enough of chilled remaining gelatin (about 1 cup) to anchor grapes; chill until tacky. Top with ½ cup chilled remaining gelatin to make first layer; chill until tacky.

3. Beat the 1 cup reserved, chilled gelatin in ice bath until as stiff and fluffy as whipped cream. Pour into pan and chill until tacky.

4. Fold orange and remaining grapes into remaining syrupy gelatin and pour over whipped layer; chill several hours, or until firm. To serve, slice about ¾-inch thick.

THIS MAY seem one of the hokier molded salads, but it has been adored down South ever since the recipe surfaced in the opening decades of this century.

COCA-COLA SALAD
Makes 6 Servings

1 envelope unflavored gelatin	1½ cups Coca-Cola
2 tablespoons sugar	1½ cups mixed diced fruits
¼ cup cold water	(fresh, frozen, or canned)
¼ cup fresh lemon juice	6 lettuce leaves

1. Combine gelatin and sugar in saucepan. Add water and lemon juice, set over low heat, and cook, stirring constantly, until gelatin and sugar dissolve.

2. Off heat, add Coca-Cola; chill until consistency of unbeaten egg white.

3. Fold in fruit, divide among 6 individual fluted molds, and chill several hours or until set.

4. Unmold on lettuce leaves and serve.

NOTE: There is also a Cherry Coke Salad, which came somewhat later. It begins with cherry Jell-O and contains dark pitted cherries, crushed pineapple, and chopped pecans as well as Coca-Cola.—J.A.

IN THE second decade of the twentieth century, canned fruits acquired a certain cachet, some food writers even proclaiming them superior to fresh. At the same time, America had begun to sweeten its savory dishes. Fannie Farmer, no less, suggested "brightening up a French dressing" with a tablespoon of ketchup and "enlivening" a fruit salad with marshmallows.

According to Sylvia Lovegren (*Fashionable Food,* 1995), frozen fruit salads date to the 1920s, when home-size electric refrigerators began replacing iceboxes. *Good Housekeeping's Book of Menus, Recipes and Household Discoveries* (1922) includes a recipe for Frozen Fruit Mayonnaise and calls for it to be sealed carefully and buried "in equal parts of ice and salt for four hours," which suggests that frozen fruit salads predate electric refrigerators. Laura Shapiro (*Perfection Salad,* 1986) traces them to the turn of the century—"fruits that had been frozen into a mold lined with mayonnaise and whipped cream" that were called "a Salad Mousse or a Frozen Fruit Salad." Shapiro is nearer the mark. In the July 1912 issue of *The Ladies' Home Journal,* there's an article on "Frozen Salads and Fruit Desserts."

There's no denying, however, that the electric refrigerator did much to launch the Age of the Frozen Fruit Salad. In 1929, the Frigidaire Corporation of Dayton, Ohio, published a little recipe booklet, *Frigidaire Frozen Delights,* which, the company said, was "especially prepared for apartments with Frigidaire." In it are Frozen Fruit Salad No. 1 and Frozen Fruit Salad No. 2.

FROZEN FRUIT SALAD No. 1

1 orange
1 banana
¾ cup white grapes or
   Royal Anne cherries
2 slices pineapple

1 cup fruit salad dressing
   No. 1 (see Page 23)
1 cup XX [heavy] cream
12 maraschino cherries

Free orange from all skin and rind. Cut pineapple fine and halve the cherries. Seed and peel grapes. Place fruit in Frigidaire to chill. Whip cream and combine salad dressing with cream. Combine fruits and add banana, sliced very thin. Add fruits to cream and salad dressing. Pour into tray and allow to freeze. When frozen, cut in cubes. Serve on lettuce leaf or serve directly on the salad plate covered with paper doily.

Sunshine Salad

Makes 6 Servings

✳

ALSO KNOWN as "Golden Glow Salad" or sometimes simply "Golden Salad," this one has been around for most of the twentieth century. The blender version here comes from *A Guide to Creative Gel Cookery* printed in 1972 by Knox Gelatine, Inc. It works equally well with the food processor, which was unveiled in 1973 at the Chicago Housewares Show.

1 envelope unflavored gelatin
¼ cup cold fresh orange juice
¾ cup boiling fresh orange juice
¼ cup sugar
⅛ teaspoon salt
1 lemon, peeled, halved, and
   seeded
1 cup peeled, chunked carrots

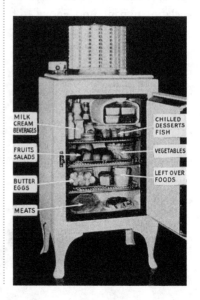

SALADS & SALAD DRESSINGS

1 (8½-ounce) can crushed
  pineapple or pineapple
  chunks in juice
Crisp salad greens (optional
  garnish)

1. Sprinkle gelatin over cold orange juice in electric blender cup or work bowl of food processor fitted with metal chopping blade. Let stand several minutes until gelatin is evenly moistened.

2. Add boiling orange juice and pulse or churn at low speed until gelatin dissolves.

3. Add sugar, salt, and lemon and churn at high speed until lemon liquefies.

4. Add carrots and pulse or churn at high speed until finely chopped.

5. Transfer all to bowl, add pineapple and juice, then chill, stirring occasionally, until consistency of unbeaten egg white—30 to 40 minutes.

6. Turn into decorative 3-cup mold and chill several hours, or until set.

7. Unmold and garnish, if desired, with crisp salad greens.

FROZEN FRUIT SALAD No. 2

One medium-sized can of fruit salad. Cut very fine, add two-thirds cup of either honey dressing or fruit dressing with two-thirds cup XX Cream.

Add fruit dressing to fruit mixture, then fold in whipped cream. Pour into Frigidaire tray and allow to freeze. Block out and serve either on lettuce leaf or on plate covered with doily. This needs no garnishing.

Many variations of this salad can be made by using different fruit combinations.

Frozen fruit salads remained popular right through the '70s. Down South where I grew up, they were nearly always served at bridge parties, with each hostess trying to outdo the others. Over time, cream cheese was added "to cut the richness" of a mix that already included mayonnaise, marshmallows, whipped cream, and, oh yes, maraschino cherries.

Fund-raiser cookbooks, Southern ones in particular, brim with recipes for frozen fruit salad, one richer than the next. This one is reprinted just as it appeared in *The Charlotte Cookbook,* published in 1971 by the Junior League of Charlotte, North Carolina.

FROZEN FRUIT SALAD

1 3-ounce package cream
  cheese
1 tablespoon cream
1/3 cup mayonnaise
1 tablespoon lemon juice
Dash of salt
1 cup canned pineapple,
  drained
1 cup orange sections,
  drained

1 cup Royal Ann cherries,
  drained, or green seedless
  grapes
1/2 cup maraschino cherries,
  drained
1 cup whipped cream
3 tablespoons sugar
1 cup miniature
  marshmallows

Blend softened cream cheese, cream and mayonnaise. Add lemon juice and salt. Add fruit, which has been cut in small pieces. (Any fruit may be substituted.) Whip cream, folding in sugar. Fold whipped cream, marshmallows, and fruit mixture together. Pour into refrigerator trays or square pan and freeze until firm. Serves 8.
—MRS. CHARLES WARNER

New Manhattan Salad

Makes 8 Servings

✳

ALTHOUGH GENERAL Foods calls this Jell-O gelatin salad "New Manhattan" in its 1933 booklet *What You Can Do with Jell-O,* it is actually a congealed Waldorf Salad and that's how it's generally known today. The first Waldorf Salad was created in New York City in 1893 by Oscar Tschirky, the formidable maître d'hôtel of the Waldorf-Astoria Hotel. The original recipe was nothing more than a mix of diced red-skinned apples, celery, and mayonnaise. The chopped nuts were added later (perhaps by Rector's, another Manhattan restaurant, for walnuts make the ingredient list of the Waldorf Salad in *The Rector Cook Book* [1928]). Snipped marshmallows and dates were added about the same time by Southern cooks whose families doted on all things sweet.

1 (3-ounce) package lemon-
    flavored gelatin
2 cups warm water
1 tablespoon cider vinegar
½ teaspoon salt
1 cup finely diced tart apples
½ cup coarsely chopped
    walnuts
1 cup finely diced celery
8 lettuce leaves

1. Dissolve gelatin in warm water; mix in vinegar and salt. Pour thin layer into decorative 5- to 6-cup mold. Chill until tacky—10 to 15 minutes. At same time, pour remaining gelatin into a large shallow pan and chill until consistency of unbeaten egg white—about 15 minutes.

2. Mix apples, walnuts, and celery and arrange on tacky layer in mold. Top with remaining gelatin and chill several hours or until firm.

3. To serve, unmold, cut into wedges, and serve on lettuce leaves.

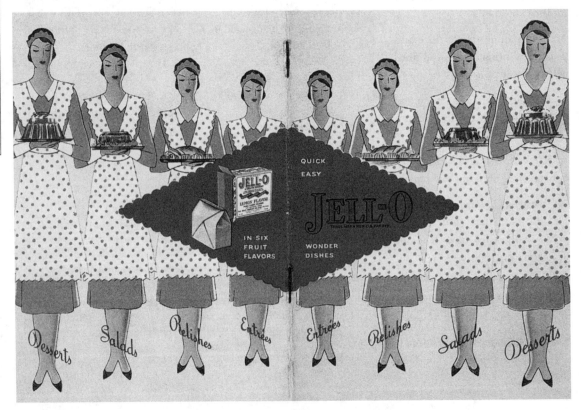

Ginger Ale Salad

Makes 6 Servings

❋

TO MY surprise, Fannie Farmer dreamed up this recipe in 1912 for a "February Luncheon Menu" for *The Woman's Home Companion*. In *Perfection Salad*, Laura Shapiro writes that Fannie "added a cup of ginger ale to the gelatin mixture and folded in some cut-up grapes, celery, apples, and pineapple." Although she called it a fruit salad, the idea of using soda pop in molded salads had been planted. By the 1940s, when *Joy of Cooking* replaced Fannie Farmer as the modern cook's Bible, Irma Rombauer introduced her Ginger Ale Salad by saying, "This is about the best molded fruit salad given." The recipe here is a World War II version of Ginger Ale Salad from Knox. Capitalizing on the built-in sweetness of ginger ale, it calls for a mere two tablespoons of sugar, which would scarcely have dented precious sugar allotments. "The youngsters will love this one," Knox promises, then suggests topping the salad with mayonnaise "to which a few spoonfuls of whipped cream have been added."

1 envelope unflavored gelatin
¼ cup cold water or fruit juice
¼ cup fresh orange juice or
*   other fruit juice*
2 tablespoons fresh lemon juice
2 tablespoons sugar
¼ teaspoon salt
1 cup ginger ale
1 cup diced fresh or canned
*   fruit (any combination)*
2 tablespoons chopped
*   crystallized ginger (optional)*
6 lettuce leaves

1. Soften gelatin in cold water in large heat-proof bowl, set bowl over boiling water and stir until gelatin dissolves. Mix in orange juice, lemon juice, sugar, and salt.

2. Cool to room temperature, add ginger ale, then chill until consistency of unbeaten egg white—about 30 minutes.

3. Fold in fruit and crystallized ginger, if desired, then divide among 6 individual molds and chill several hours, or until set—about 3 hours.

4. Unmold on lettuce and serve.

Molded Grapefruit Salad

Makes 8 Servings

❋

IN RALEIGH, North Carolina, where I grew up in "The Age of Jell-O," women were constantly swapping recipes, which is how my mother amassed a huge collection of molded salads. This one came, if memory serves, from our next-door neighbor Helen Collins. It's an unusual molded salad—the hollowed-out grapefruit halves serve as the molds. It is also unusually good—and like so many Southern salads, sweet enough to serve as dessert.

SALAD
2 large grapefruits, halved and
*   scooped out*
2 (3-ounce) packages lemon-
*   flavored gelatin*
¾ cup boiling water
1 cup canned crushed
*   pineapple, well drained*

DRESSING
1 tablespoon flour
2 tablespoons sugar
⅓ cup pineapple juice
¼ cup fresh lemon juice
1 egg yolk, well beaten
4 marshmallows, quartered
⅔ cup heavy cream, stiffly
*   whipped*

1. SALAD: Seed grapefruit sections, then coarsely chop. Measure out and reserve 3¼ cups chopped grapefruit and juice; save balance (if any) to use another time.

2. Dissolve gelatin in boiling water, cool to room temperature, then mix in chopped grapefruit and pineapple.

3. Fill grapefruit halves with gelatin mixture, leveling surface, and chill several hours, or until firm.

4. DRESSING: Mix flour, sugar, pineapple and lemon juices, and egg yolk in top of small double boiler. Cook and stir over simmering water until thickened. Add marshmallows and stir until melted. Cool dressing, then fold in whipped cream.

5. To serve, halve each grapefruit half and arrange one on each of eight salad plates. Top with generous ladlings of dressing.

LIKE SALADS, salad dressings metamorphosed this century. There were new additions: Green Goddess, Thousand Island, Russian, Roquefort, ranch.

But the bottling of dressings had greater impact. Hellmann's creamy "deli-style" mayonnaise went into the jar in 1915—a landmark (see the box on page 300). Kraft played a pivotal role early on, too, with a slim but select repertoire of bottled dressings including the ever popular Miracle Whip and coral-colored French dressing.

Busy cooks loved these "convenience" dressings. In fact many considered them superior to anything they themselves could make. So bottles of prepared dressings were upended over wedges of iceberg (the lettuce of choice

until after World War II), tossed with diced fruits or vegetables, folded into potato salads and slaws. How easy it was.

By the 1950s, there were also dried dressing mixes—Italian, herb, and so forth—that needed only to be shaken up in a bottle with oil and vinegar (Good Seasons even provided the bottles).

With the arrival of the blender and food processor, we learned to buzz raw eggs and olive oil into mayonnaise zip-quick. Then along came salmonella, a "bug" now raging through America's henhouses that renders raw or improperly cooked eggs risky to eat.

So, it's back to old-timey boiled dressing. Or bottled ones, which are pasteurized and perfectly safe.

Family French Dressing

Makes about 1¼ Cups

✳

THIS IS the dressing most of us grew up on. And until Julia Child taught us how to make vinaigrette in the 1960s, it was the one we ladled over wedges of iceberg or tossed with mixed greens. This particular recipe, from the Consumer Test Kitchens of H.J. Heinz in Pittsburgh, remains a favorite throughout the American heartland.

½ cup tomato ketchup
½ cup vegetable oil
¼ cup cider vinegar
1 tablespoon confectioners'
*   (10X) sugar*
1 clove garlic, peeled and split
¼ teaspoon salt
Pinch black pepper

1. Place all ingredients in 1-pint shaker jar and shake well to mix.

2. Refrigerate several hours to mellow flavors, discard garlic, then shake well before using.

Roquefort Dressing

Makes about 1¾ Cups

✳

I THINK of this as a '50s recipe, yet Ida Bailey Allen includes this recipe in *Mrs. Allen's Cook Book* (1917).

¼ cupful Roquefort cheese
¼ cupful olive oil
Dash paprika
2 tablespoonfuls vinegar
½ teaspoonful salt
⅛ teaspoonful pepper

Beat the cheese till creamy, gradually working in the oil, seasonings, and, lastly, the vinegar. Use at once.

Like Mrs. Allen's, early Roquefort dressings were basically vinaigrettes into which a little Roquefort was creamed or crumbled. Today they are more apt to be mayonnaise-based, like this rich '50s recipe, which I learned while at Cornell University (of course, in those days we made our own mayonnaise).

2½ ounces Roquefort or blue
*   cheese, crumbled*
2 tablespoons Dijon mustard
1¼ cups mayonnaise
¼ cup sour cream
1 tablespoon Worcestershire
*   sauce*
2 tablespoons red or white wine
*   vinegar or tarragon vinegar*

1. Mix all ingredients, cover, and refrigerate until just before serving.

2. Stir lightly and use to dress crisp mixed greens, allowing about 2 tablespoons dressing per person.

"21" Traditional Lorenzo Dressing

Makes about 1½ Cups

✳

AT NEW York's toney "21" Club, which opened during Prohibition, salads were traditionally made at table, usually by the captains or waiters. This American classic created by a waiter named Lorenzo was virtually the "house" dressing. Supremely versatile, Lorenzo dressing can be used to dress everything from tossed greens to shellfish salads (shrimp, crab, and lobster). It is even good on chicken salad. This recipe is adapted from *The "21" Cookbook* (1995), by Chef Michael Lomonaco with Donna Forsman.

> *1 teaspoon dry mustard*
> *blended with 2 tablespoons*
> *cold water*
> *½ teaspoon salt*
> *½ teaspoon black pepper*
> *¼ cup red wine vinegar*
> *⅔ cup fruity olive oil*
> *¼ cup bottled chili sauce or*
> *ketchup*
> *¼ cup finely chopped young*
> *watercress leaves*
> *¼ cup chopped crisply cooked*
> *bacon*

1. Pulse mustard paste, salt, pepper, and vinegar in electric blender or food processor fitted with metal chopping blade until well blended.

2. With motor running, add olive oil in thin stream, then churn until consistency of mayonnaise.

3. By hand, fold in chili sauce, watercress, and bacon.

Avocado Dressing

Makes about 3 Cups

✳

A RICH, creamy dressing for mixed green salads. Minus the onion, it's equally good on fruit salads, especially those made with citrus. This recipe is adapted from one in *The Avocado Bravo,* published in 1975 by the California Avocado Advisory Board (now the California Avocado Commission) to teach mass America that an avocado's uses don't begin and end with guacamole.

> *2 medium California avocados,*
> *pitted, peeled, and pureed*
> *1⅓ cups sour cream*
> *1 teaspoon salt*
> *2 tablespoons fresh lemon or*
> *lime juice*
> *1 teaspoon finely minced*
> *scallions or onion (optional)*
> *1 tablespoon minced fresh*
> *chervil or tarragon or ½*
> *teaspoon dried leaf chervil or*
> *tarragon, crumbled*
> *⅛ teaspoon hot red pepper*
> *sauce*

1. Mix all ingredients, cover, and refrigerate until ready to serve.

2. Whisk well and use to dress salads of mixed greens or fruits.

RANCH DRESSING

....

T WO PEOPLE claim to have invented this creamy buttermilk dressing. The first is David Bears, part owner of The Todds Food Company in Glendale, Arizona, who says he stirred up the magic mix in the 1980s.

His wasn't a salad dressing, however. It was a dip for fried zucchini sticks that he created especially for Bobby McGee's Restaurants.

Claimant number two? In *The Dictionary of American Food and Drink* (revised edition, 1994), John Mariani writes that the Chlorox Company of Oakland, California, bought trademark rights to the Hidden Valley Ranch Original Ranch salad dressing mix in 1972.

The sellers were the Henson family, owners of the Hidden Valley Ranch located near Santa Barbara. Chlorox insists that the Henson family developed the dry Ranch dressing mix shortly after World War II.

The garlicky, buttermilk dressings now featured in nearly every all-purpose cookbook today (not to mention scores of community fund-raisers) aren't called Ranch. But they are definitely Ranch-inspired.

FLAVORED VINEGARS

YOU MIGHT call the '80s The Decade of Flavored Vinegars, a trend initiated by cutting-edge chefs in New York and California. Others soon followed suit, and the H.J. Heinz Company of Pittsburgh, makers of quality vinegars, went to work developing a collection of flavored vinegar recipes for the home cook. The ones included here all come from Heinz's 1994 booklet, *Create a Classic: Making Flavored Vinegars.*

BASIL-GARLIC VINEGAR: Place ½ cup coarsely chopped fresh basil leaves and 2 cloves peeled and split garlic in sterilized 1-pint preserving jar. Heat 2 cups red wine vinegar or distilled white vinegar to simmering, pour into jar, seal, and let stand 3 to 4 weeks at room temperature. Strain vinegar, discarding solids. Pour into clean sterilized jar, tuck in well-washed fresh basil sprig or two, and seal tight. Use in dressings for rice or pasta salads, for antipasto, or flavored mayonnaises. Makes 1 pint.

RASPBERRY VINEGAR: Bruise 1 cup fresh raspberries lightly and place in sterilized 1-pint preserving jar. Heat 2 cups red wine vinegar or distilled white vinegar to simmering, pour into jar, seal, and let stand 2 to 3 weeks at room temperature. Strain vinegar, discarding solids. Pour into clean sterilized jar and seal tight. Use in dressings for mixed green or fruit salads or in marinades for chicken. Makes 1 pint.

LEMON-THYME (OR DILL) VINEGAR: Remove zest from 1 lemon in continuous spiral and place in sterilized 1-pint preserving jar along with 4 to 5 sprigs thyme, lemon thyme, or dill. Heat 2 cups distilled white vinegar to simmering, pour into jar, screw lid down tight, and let stand 3 to 4 weeks at room temperature. Strain vinegar, discarding solids. Pour into clean sterilized jar, tuck in well-washed fresh herb sprig and lemon zest spiral, and seal tight. Use in dressings for tossed green salads or vegetable marinades. Makes 1 pint.

TARRAGON-CHIVE VINEGAR: Lightly bruise 4 to 5 sprigs tarragon and place in sterilized 1-pint preserving jar along with ⅓ cup snipped fresh chives. Heat 2 cups apple cider vinegar or distilled white vinegar to simmering, pour into jar, screw lid down tight, and let stand 3 to 4 weeks at room temperature. Strain vinegar, discarding solids. Pour into clean sterilized jar, tuck in well-washed fresh tarragon sprig or two plus a few chives, and seal tight. Use in dressings for tossed green or pasta salads, also for Marinated Mushrooms (see page 17). Makes 1 pint.

Thousand Island Dressing

Makes about 1½ Cups

✳

ACCORDING TO Craig Claiborne (*Craig Claiborne's Southern Cooking*, 1987), this popular dressing may have been "created many years ago by the chef at the Drake Hotel in Chicago." Legend has it that when his wife saw the lumpy dressing, she said it "looked like the Thousand Islands, near Ontario, New York, which they had recently visited." No one at the Drake today is prepared to confirm or deny the story. Whatever its origin, Thousand Island dressing became popular early this century. I found a simplified recipe for it in *Mrs. Allen's Cook Book* (1917) by Ida Bailey Allen, which contains four ingredients only: mayonnaise, chili sauce, chopped pimiento, and chives. This recipe, adapted from one in *The Doubleday Cookbook* (1975), which I coauthored with Elaine Hanna, typifies what most of us consider the classic Thousand Island.

1 cup mayonnaise
¼ cup chili sauce
¼ cup minced pimiento-stuffed green olives
1 tablespoon minced green bell pepper
1 tablespoon minced onion, scallion, or chives
1 hard-cooked egg, peeled and finely chopped
¼ teaspoon hot red pepper sauce

1. Mix all ingredients, cover, and chill several hours.

2. Use to dress crisp wedges of lettuce or other green salads.

──── VARIATION ────

LOW-CALORIE THOUSAND ISLAND DRESSING: Prepare as directed, substituting yogurt for mayonnaise and 2 tablespoons minced fresh parsley for olives; use minced egg white only and reduce chili sauce to 1 tablespoon. Makes about 1 cup. About 10 calories per tablespoon.

Russian Dressing

Makes about 1½ Cups

✳

HERE'S ANOTHER dressing that came into vogue early this century (*Mrs. Allen's Cook Book* [1917] by Ida Bailey Allen was one of the first to include a recipe for it). What makes it Russian? Caviar. To quote *Cook's & Diner's Dictionary* (1968): "Originally, the recipe for this salad dressing called for a base of mayonnaise to which were added chili sauce, red and green peppers, and caviar."

Few cooks today can afford the extravagance of caviar, so Russian dressing has evolved into a "souped-up" Thousand Island dressing.

¾ cup mayonnaise
¼ cup chili sauce
¼ cup sour cream
3 tablespoons sweet pickle relish
2 tablespoons black or red caviar (optional)
2 teaspoons snipped fresh dill
1 teaspoon minced capers

1. Whisk together all ingredients, cover, and store in refrigrator until ready to use.

2. Whisk lightly and use to dress mixed green, cold vegetable, or shellfish salads.

Creamy Garlic-Buttermilk Dressing

Makes about 2 Cups

✳

THIS DRESSING will have better flavor if made ahead of time. Stored tightly covered in the refrigerator, it will keep well for four to five days.

1 cup buttermilk
½ cup sour cream
¼ cup mayonnaise
¼ cup cider vinegar

1 clove garlic, peeled and finely minced
2 tablespoons finely minced scallions
2 tablespoons minced fresh parsley
½ teaspoon black pepper
¼ teaspoon salt

1. Mix all ingredients by shaking in 1-quart jar with tight-fitting lid. Refrigerate until ready to serve.

2. Shake well and use to dress any salad of mixed greens. It's good, too, on any shrimp, crab, or lobster salad, also on boiled potatoes.

HELLMANN'S MAYONNAISE

BEFORE BLENDERS and food processors, making mayonnaise from scratch was tricky business, demanding that oil be beaten drop by drop into raw eggs until the mix thickened. Nevertheless, until commercial mayo was widely available, cooks did make it by hand, including the unidentified Spanish chef who first served it to Cardinal Richelieu in Mahon, Minorca, thus enabling the statesman to give the "sauce of Mahon" its name —*mahonnaise*. Three centuries later, German immigrant Richard Hellmann attained local fame for the salads he served in his Columbus Avenue deli in New York City. Correctly assuming his special mayonnaise was responsible for the salad's success, he spooned it into large glass jars tied with blue ribbons and displayed it on his countertop. Soon customers were clamoring for take-home orders, and by 1915 Hellmann had to get out of the deli business and devote himself full time to making and marketing mayonnaise. Today the Hellmann's Mayonnaise jar still boasts its blue ribbon, but the dressing within is no longer for salads and sandwiches only. Since 1937, it's been a main ingredient in a popular cake recipe invented by the wife of a company salesman and called, simply, "Chocolate Mayonnaise Cake" (see page 444).

Blender Mayonnaise

Makes 1⅓ Cups

✳

THE LADY who taught us to make perfect mayonnaise in 15 seconds was Ann Seranne, author of the definitive book on blender cookery. Here is what she has to say in *Ann Seranne's Good Food with a Blender* (1974):

Making mayonnaise is a typical example of how quickly your blender can homogenize a mixture of oil and egg. In other recipes for homemade mayonnaise, the oil must be beaten into the egg mixture with the utmost care, just drop by drop, or the oil, being of less density than the egg, will separate and float on top of the egg.

By using an electric blender, however, you can blend the ingredients together so thoroughly that they cannot separate or curdle IF YOU WILL FOLLOW THESE DIRECTIONS EXACTLY.

NOTE: When this book appeared more than twenty years ago, no one worried about an uncooked mayonnaise made with raw egg. Today there's the risk of salmonella poisoning, so make this recipe only if you know your eggs to be salmonella-free. Or look upon it as a bit of culinary history.

1 egg
2 tablespoons vinegar or fresh
    lemon juice
½ teaspoon dry mustard
¼ teaspoon salt
1 cup salad oil

1. Break egg into blender cup; add vinegar, mustard, salt, and ¼ cup oil. Cover, and blend on low speed.

2. Immediately remove inner cap on cover and pour in remaining oil in fast stream (*not* drop by drop). All oil must be in in 15 seconds.

3. A few drops oil may remain on surface of mayonnaise. Without turning blender off, switch to high and blend 3 seconds more.

SALADS

that Entered the American Mainstream
During the Twentieth Century with Their Source

....

(*Recipe Included)

FRANCE
*Celery Rémoulade
Salade Niçoise

❋

HAWAII/SOUTH PACIFIC
Pineapple Slaw

❋

ITALY
*Panzanella
Tomatoes, Mozzarella, & Basil
*Pasta Salads

❋

EASTERN MEDITERRANEAN
(GREECE, TURKEY, MIDDLE EAST)
*Tabbouleh
*Cacik

❋

SCANDINAVIA
Herring Salad
Beet Salad

❋

CARIBBEAN/MEXICO/LATIN AMERICA
*Taco Salad
*Guacamole
(see Appetizers & Snacks)

Celery Rémoulade

Makes 4 to 6 Servings

❋

CELERY ROOT is hard to the core, and the only way to attack it is with a razor-sharp chef's knife or cleaver. There's considerable waste because of the irregularity of the root and its thick, fibrous skin, but all the cutting is worthwhile. Celery Rémoulade can be served as an appetizer or cold vegetable as well as a salad.

NOTE: Rather than blanch the celery root strips, which may oversoften them, dress them well ahead of time and let the dressing "temper" the celery root as it seasons. Also, give the celery root a preliminary marinating in vinegar, lemon juice, and salt. Any leftover Rémoulade dressing can be used to dress cold cooked asparagus, broccoli, cauliflower, green beans, crab, lobster, or shrimp. *Unfortunately, the dressing calls for raw egg yolks—risky today with salmonella present in so many eggs. Know your egg source well if you intend to use raw yolks. Or play it safe and use hard-cooked yolks. The texture and taste won't be quite the same, but at least there's no danger of food poisoning.*

CELERY ROOT
　　1½ pounds celery root, trimmed, peeled, and cut into slim matchstick strips
　　1 tablespoon fresh lemon juice
　　1 tablespoon white wine vinegar
　　½ teaspoon salt

RÉMOULADE DRESSING

⅓ cup Dijon mustard
2 egg yolks (raw or hard-cooked)
¼ cup boiling water
2 tablespoons hot red wine vinegar
⅔ cup fruity olive oil
2 tablespoons minced fresh parsley
1 tablespoon minced fresh tarragon or 1 teaspoon dried leaf tarragon, crumbled
⅛ teaspoon black pepper

1. CELERY ROOT: Toss celery root with lemon juice, vinegar, and salt in large nonreactive bowl; cover, and marinate several hours in refrigerator.

2. RÉMOULADE DRESSING: Pulse mustard and egg yolks several times in food processor or electric blender until smooth. With motor running, drizzle in boiling water, then hot vinegar. With motor still running, add ¼ cup olive oil drop by drop; when mixture begins to emulsify, add remaining oil in fine stream. Continue beating 30 seconds at high speed until consistency of thin mayonnaise. Transfer to bowl, fold in parsley, tarragon, and pepper, cover, and refrigerate until ready to use.

3. TO ASSEMBLE SALAD: Toss celery root well, drain off all liquid, then add several heaping tablespoonfuls of Rémoulade and toss well. Add more dressing if needed to coat celery root generously. Cover, and marinate in refrigerator 6 to 8 hours or, better yet, overnight. Just before serving, toss well again, and add a bit more Rémoulade, if needed, to make salad good and moist.

Capellini with Sun-Dried Tomato "Pesto"

Makes 6 to 8 Servings

✳

THIS RECIPE, adapted from one that appeared in Viana La Place and Evan Kleiman's appealing book, *Cucina Fresca* (1985), shows how intrepid chefs had become about pasta salads in the mid-'80s. It

demonstrates, too, that these salads needn't be fussy.

1 cup olive oil from sun-dried tomatoes (if you don't have enough flavored oil, add olive oil to equal 1 cup)
1 cup sun-dried tomatoes, cut into thin strips
1½ teaspoons ground hot red pepper (cayenne)
1 pound capellini, cooked by package directions and drained well

1. Churn ¼ cup oil, ½ cup sun-dried tomatoes, and cayenne into rough paste in electric blender at high speed or in food processor equipped with metal chopping blade.

2. Empty into large salad bowl and mix in remaining oil.

3. Dump capellini into bowl and toss with tomato mixture. Scatter remaining sun-dried tomato strips over salad.

4. Cover, and let stand several hours, then serve cold or at room temperature.

Panzanella

(TUSCAN BREAD SALAD)
Makes 4 Servings

✳

THIS SIMPLE country salad surfaced on this side of the Atlantic in the 1980s with the proliferation of high-end Italian restaurants. There are dozens of variations on the theme; this straightforward version was created by my good friend Sandy Gluck, an endlessly (and enviably) creative chef/cookbook author. For best results, use fresh basil and freshly ground black pepper. Also, cut the tomatoes and cucumber into ½-inch dice.

DRESSING

⅓ cup fruity olive oil
¼ cup balsamic vinegar
2 anchovy fillets, mashed
½ teaspoon salt
¼ teaspoon black pepper

SALAD

1 large red bell pepper, halved and seeded
2 cups cored and diced firm-ripe plum tomatoes (6 to 8 small)
1 medium cucumber, peeled, halved lengthwise, seeded, and diced
1 small red onion, halved and thinly sliced
2 tablespoons chopped fresh basil or 2 teaspoons dried leaf basil, crumbled
1 tablespoon small capers, rinsed well and patted dry
4 ounces Italian bread, sliced ½-inch thick

1. DRESSING: Whisk oil with vinegar, anchovy fillets, salt, and black pepper in large nonreactive bowl until well combined. Set aside.

2. SALAD: Preheat broiler 10 minutes. Place red pepper cut side down on pan and broil 6 inches from heat until charred, about 10 minutes. Remove pepper from broiler and when cool enough to handle, peel and cut into strips ¼ inch wide.

3. Add pepper strips to bowl along with tomatoes, cucumber, onion, basil, capers, and bread. Toss well to combine.

4. Cover salad and refrigerate at least 2 hours or overnight. The salad should be moist. Spoon onto plates, lined, if you like, with arugola and/or radicchio and serve.

....

Cacik

(CUCUMBERS WITH YOGURT AND MINT)
Makes 6 to 8 Servings

✳

THIS TURKISH recipe, popular here since the Age of Yogurt (1960s), can be enjoyed as a salad or spooned into pita pockets and eaten like tacos.

3 large cucumbers, peeled and halved lengthwise
1 teaspoon salt
⅓ cup coarsely chopped fresh mint
1 cup plain yogurt (low-fat or regular)
¼ teaspoon black pepper
3 cups thinly sliced romaine

1. With teaspoon, scoop all seeds from cucumber halves; slice cucumbers crosswise ⅛-inch thick. Layer cucumber slices into shallow bowl, sprinkling with salt as you go. Let stand at room temperature 1 hour, then drain cucumbers as dry as possible.

2. Add mint, yogurt, and pepper to cucumbers and toss well. Cover and chill several hours.

3. To serve, divide romaine among 6 to 8 salad plates and ladle cucumber mixture on top.

Tabbouleh

(MIDDLE EASTERN SALAD OF BULGUR, TOMATO, AND MINT)
Makes 4 to 6 Servings

✳

THIS WHOLE-GRAIN salad entered our lives during the '60s vegetarian movement. It's nutritious, filling, and economical. Use only freshly squeezed lemon juice and freshly chopped mint—never bottled lemon juice or mint flakes. And for maxium flavor, use flat-leaf Italian parsley and the richest, fruitiest olive oil you can find.

1 cup bulgur
2½ cups boiling water
¼ cup minced fresh flat-leaf parsley
¼ cup minced fresh mint
1 small Bermuda or Spanish onion, peeled and chopped

1 large vine-ripe tomato, cored,
seeded, and coarsely chopped
3 to 4 tablespoons fresh lemon
juice
4 to 5 tablespoons fruity
olive oil
¾ teaspoon salt (or to taste)
¼ teaspoon black pepper (or to
taste)

1. Place bulgur in large heat-proof bowl, add boiling water, and let stand 20 minutes. Drain well, then bundle in clean dry towel, and squeeze out as much water as possible (important to keep salad from being mushy).

2. Return bulgur to bowl, add all remaining ingredients (3 tablespoons lemon juice and 4 of oil to start); toss lightly. Taste and adjust lemon juice, oil, salt, and pepper as needed. Toss lightly.

3. Cover, and refrigerate several hours. Toss again and serve—on crisp young romaine leaves, for a dressier presentation.

Taco Salad

Makes 4 Servings

✳

THIS SALAD arrived with the Tex-Mex fast-food franchises, which began to pepper the country in the '60s. According to John Mariani (*The Dictionary of American Food and Drink,* Revised Edition, 1994) the man who whetted our appetite for "hot and spicy" was Glen Bell, who opened the first "Taco Bell" in Downey, California. That was 1962.

Did Taco Bell originate the Taco Salad? I've been unable to prove that it did. Or didn't. The first recipe I could find for Taco Salad appeared in the May 1968 issue of *Sunset.* It was reprinted in *Sunset Kitchen Cabinet* (1995), a book of some 500 favorite reader recipes published in the "Kitchen Cabinet" column. The reader who submitted the Taco Salad back in 1968 was a Californian from Alhambra identified only as "A.R." This recipe is an adaptation.

1 pound lean ground beef
¼ cup finely chopped yellow
onion
2 teaspoons chili powder
½ teaspoon salt
1 (8-ounce) can tomato sauce
1 medium head iceberg lettuce,
shredded
⅓ cup shredded Cheddar cheese
2 medium tomatoes, peeled,
cored, and cut into wedges
1 medium avocado, pitted,
peeled, and sliced (optional)
1½ to 2 cups corn chips or
tortilla chips

1. Crumble beef into large nonstick skillet. Add onion and stir-fry over moderate heat until beef is no longer pink—6 to 8 minutes. Mix in chili powder, salt, and tomato sauce. Bring to a simmer and keep hot.

2. Divide lettuce among four dinner plates. Top with hot beef mixture and sprinkle with cheese. Divide tomato wedges, avocado slices, if using, and corn chips among the four plates, arranging as artfully as possible. Serve at once.

TIMELINE

1954

Butterball turkeys land on Thanksgiving tables.

M&M's introduces Peanut Chocolate Candies.

General Electric offers appliances in decorator colors: wood-tone brown, cadet blue, canary yellow, petal pink, and turquoise green.

Swanson introduces the frozen TV dinner.

1955

Bon Appétit begins as a free promotional booklet distributed through liquor stores.

Ray Kroc franchises McDonald's.

Tappan's home-size microwave oven goes on sale.

1956

The U.S. Department of Agriculture reduces the *Basic 7 Food Groups* to the *Basic 4,* consolidating some groups and deleting fat.

BREADS

SANDWICHES

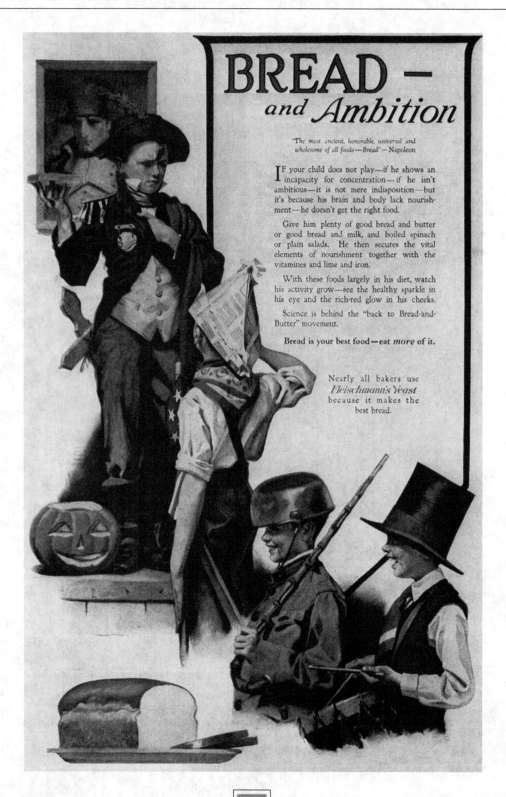

BREAD —
and Ambition

The most ancient, honorable, universal and wholesome of all foods — Bread" — Napoleon

IF your child does not play—if he shows an incapacity for concentration—if he isn't ambitious—it is not mere indisposition—but it's because his brain and body lack nourishment—he doesn't get the right food.

Give him plenty of good bread and butter or good bread and milk, and boiled spinach or plain salads. He then secures the vital elements of nourishment together with the vitamines and lime and iron.

With these foods largely in his diet, watch his activity grow—see the healthy sparkle in his eye and the rich-red glow in his cheeks.

Science is behind the "back to Bread-and-Butter" movement.

Bread is your best food—eat *more* of it.

Nearly all bakers use *Fleischmann's Yeast* because it makes the best bread.

W HEN IT COMES to bread, we've come full circle this century. Before 1900, baking loaves at home was the rule, not the exception—chewy yeast breads as well as biscuits, cornbreads, and muffins that could be mixed and baked in a jiffy.

A hot bread was expected at most meals—if not every meal—beginning with breakfast. And most home cooks happily obliged.

Then along came commercial breads, then commerically sliced breads, and the whiter and squishier the better. Many women still baked their own biscuits and muffins—especially in the South where they prided themselves on the "tenderness of their crumb."

But when it came to long-winded yeast breads, they were happy to settle for store-bought.

My own mother bucked the trend and continued to bake her own yeast bread long after cottony commercial loaves had overtaken supermarket shelves. These were the breads served in the school cafeteria and I'm ashamed to say I loved them so much they became the standard by which I judged all others.

One wintry day when I wanted a peanut butter sandwich to tide me over till dinner, Mother pulled a loaf from the oven and handed me a knife.

"Almost as good as store-bought," I said, meaning it as a compliment. Of course it was nothing of the sort.

During the '60s and '70s back-to-scratch movement, those weaned on cottony loaves plunged into yeast doughs and discovered the joys of kneading, shaping, and baking. These breads, for the most part, were chewy whole-grains loaves bursting with vitamins, minerals, and nut-sweet flavor.

Novelty yeast breads made the rounds in the burbs— Dilly Casserole Bread, Monkey Bread, and coffee cakes baked in Bundt pans.

But the breads that really arrived this century were quick loaves leavened with baking powder or soda instead of yeast (see box on pages 322–23). These could be mixed in minutes and shoved straight into the oven— no kneading, no first and second risings.

In the beginning, fruit-nut breads were the specialty— date-nut, banana-nut, cranberry-nut. Then we discovered carrot and zucchini bread and they were as rich as cake. Plain old-fashioned cornbreads no longer satisfied. So we folded in fresh corn kernels and turned up the heat with jalapeños.

Sandwiches went big time this century, too (see box on pages 340–41), mostly because of the automobile and soda fountain. As Americans took to the road, they needed something fast and affordable. And if it could be carried out and munched in the car, so much the better.

In time, drive-ins replaced soda fountains and diners because they were quicker and more convenient. Just drive up, give an order, then settle back and eat your burger in the privacy of your car.

Elsewhere in this chapter I discuss in detail the evolution of hot dogs, heroes, hamburgers, assorted sandwiches, muffins, fruit-nut breads, so I'll simply say that what follows is the most representative group of twentieth-century breads, sandwiches, and spreads that I could assemble.

Cornell Bread . . . Garlic Bread . . . Liberty Bread . . . Monkey Bread . . . Dilly Casserole Bread . . . Yogurt Batter Bread . . . Cranberry-Nut Bread . . . Zucchini Bread . . . Lemon Granola Bread . . . Jalapeño Corn Bread . . . Sticky Buns . . . Angel Biscuits . . . Spicy Pumpkin Muffins . . . Reubens . . . Club Sandwiches . . . Western Sandwiches . . . Sloppy Joes . . . Tuna Melts . . . Louisville Hot Browns . . . and Philadelphia Cheese-Steak Sandwiches.

They're all here, together with such foreign classics that came our way after 1900 as pizza, focaccia, and Portuguese sweet bread.

BREADS & SANDWICHES

Liberty Bread

Makes a 9 × 5 × 3-inch Loaf

✳

IN ITS March 1989 issue, *Country Living* devoted its food pages to "hard times" recipes and among them was this potato bread. In her headnote, Food Editor Joanne Lamb Hayes explains that during World War I, patriotic homemakers not only observed "wheatless" days but also stretched precious flour with other grains and starches—cornmeal, rice, cottonseed meal, buckwheat flour, peanut meal, barley, even potatoes.

> *1 large (¾-pound) baking potato, peeled and cut into eighths*
> *1 cup water*
> *1 envelope active dry yeast*
> *1 tablespoon butter, melted*
> *2 tablespoons sugar*
> *1 teaspoon salt*
> *3 to 3½ cups unsifted all-purpose flour*

1. Cook potato in water in covered 1-quart saucepan until soft; drain well, reserving liquid. Add enough water to cooking liquid to total 1 cup; cool to between 105° F and 115° F.

2. Place warm liquid in large bowl, sprinkle in yeast, and soften 5 minutes.

3. Mash potato and add to yeast mixture along with 2 teaspoons butter, the sugar, and salt; beat with electric mixer at moderate speed until smooth.

MAGIC YEAST RAISES

4. Stir in 3 cups flour and knead in bowl until soft dough forms.

5. Turn dough onto lightly floured cloth and knead 8 minutes until smooth and springy, adding remaining ½ cup flour only as needed to keep dough from sticking.

6. Shape dough into ball, place in buttered, warm, large bowl, then turn in bowl to butter all sides. Cover with cloth and let rise in warm, dry spot, away from drafts, about 30 minutes till doubled in bulk.

7. Preheat oven to 350° F. Grease 9 × 5 × 3-inch loaf pan well; set aside.

8. Punch dough down, shape into loaf, and fit into pan. Cover with cloth and let rise in warm, dry spot, away from drafts, until doubled in bulk, about 40 minutes.

9. Brush top of loaf with remaining 1 teaspoon melted butter and bake

55 to 65 minutes until golden brown and hollow-sounding when thumped.

10. Cool bread in pan on wire rack 5 minutes. Remove bread from pan and cool on rack to room temperature before cutting.

Honey Whole-Wheat Bread

Makes Two 9 × 5 × 3-inch Loaves

✳

IN THE '60s and '70s, the counterculture shunned store-bought bread, especially squishy white bread, in favor of husky home-baked whole-wheat loaves. Big food companies took note and wasted no time developing bread recipes using whole-grain and/or unbleached flours. The one here is used courtesy of the Betty Crocker Kitchens in Minneapolis.

> *3 cups unsifted stone-ground whole-wheat or graham flour*
> *⅓ cup honey*
> *¼ cup vegetable shortening*
> *3 teaspoons salt*
> *2 envelopes active dry yeast*
> *2¼ cups very warm water (120° to 130° F)*
> *3 to 4 cups sifted unbleached or all-purpose flour*
> *1 tablespoon butter or margarine, melted*

1. Place whole-wheat flour, honey, shortening, salt, and yeast in large electric mixer bowl. Add water and beat 1 minute at low speed, scraping bowl often. Raise mixer speed to medium and beat 1 minute, again scraping bowl often. Stir in enough unbleached flour, 1 cup at a time, to make a soft but manageable dough.

2. Turn dough onto lightly floured cloth and with floured hands, knead until smooth and elastic—about 10 minutes.

3. Shape dough into ball, place in buttered, warm, large bowl, then turn in bowl to butter all sides. Cover with cloth and let rise in warm, dry spot, away from drafts, until doubled in bulk—¾ to 1 hour.

4. Punch dough down, and divide in half, then with rolling pin, flatten each half into 18 × 9-inch rectangle. Fold each crosswise into thirds, overlapping two ends, then flatten into a 9-inch square and roll up tight, beginning with an open (unfolded) end, to form a loaf. As you roll, seal with thumbs after each turn, then press edges firmly to seal.

5. Tuck ends under loaves, place seam-side-down in greased 9 × 5 × 3-inch loaf pans, and brush tops lightly with melted butter. Cover with cloth and let rise until doubled in bulk—35 to 50 minutes.

6. Position rack in lower third of oven and preheat oven to 375°F.

7. Bake fully risen loaves until richly golden brown and hollow-sounding when tapped—40 to 45 minutes.

8. Turn loaves out of pans onto wire racks and cool to room temperature before slicing.

PEPPERIDGE FARM: A MOTHER'S DREAM

THE SQUISHY white bread so popular in the 1930s failed to impress Margaret Rudkin, a young Connecticut mother with three boys, one of them asthmatic. Advised by a doctor to limit her son's intake of additives often found in processed foods, Rudkin decided to make her own bread from scratch using stone-ground whole-wheat flour, whole milk, honey, butter, and molasses.

Although she later dismissed her first loaf as "from the Stone Age . . . hard as a rock and about one-inch high," she kept at it until she baked a loaf that pleased her, her son, his doctor—and so many of the doctor's patients and colleagues that Rudkin's country home-based bakery soon took over the garage, then the horse stables, and finally a state-of-the-art facility in Norwalk.

In the new quarters, Rudkin preserved the old name ("Pepperidge" for a species of gum tree at the farm) along with her commitment to wholesome ingredients. From the beginning she used the best, assuming correctly that customers would pay three times the going price (in the '30s) of a dime a loaf.

Later, when the company expanded into cookies and Rudkin decided to withdraw a certain Belgian chocolate type as too expensive to produce, public outcry was so insistent that she had to bring the cookie back—at a much higher price. After thirty years, Pepperidge Farm became part of Campbell's in 1961—and Rudkin remained active until her death six years later.

Cornell Bread

Makes Two 8½ × 4½ × 2¾-inch Loaves

✳

IN 1946, New York Governor Thomas E. Dewey asked Dr. Clive McCay, Cornell University professor of animal nutrition, to help plan a better diet for patients in the state mental hospitals. They were eating bread to the exclusion of almost everything else and as a result, many of them were suffering from malnutrition. McCay's solution: a protein-, vitamin- and mineral-packed bread. He made it a white bread because that's what the mental patients liked, but to the recipe he added soy flour, wheat germ, and nonfat dry milk, which supplied all the proteins humans need.

> 1 envelope active dry yeast
> 1½ cups very warm water
>   (110° to 115°F)
> ½ cup scalded milk
> 3 tablespoons sugar
> 3 tablespoons butter or
>   margarine
> 2 teaspoons salt
> 6 tablespoons soy flour
> 6 tablespoons nonfat dry milk
>   powder
> 2 tablespoons wheat germ
> 5 cups sifted unbleached all-
>   purpose flour (about)

1. Dissolve yeast in water in large warm bowl; set aside.

2. Mix milk, sugar, butter, and salt in small bowl, cool to lukewarm, and stir into yeast mixture.

3. Mix in soy flour, dry milk, wheat

germ, and 3 cups flour; beat hard. Beat in remaining flour, 1 cup at a time, to form soft but manageable dough.

4. On well-floured cloth, knead dough 8 to 10 minutes until smooth and springy, adding as little extra flour as possible.

5. Shape dough into ball, place in buttered, warm, large bowl, then turn in bowl to butter all sides. Cover with cloth and let rise in warm, dry spot, away from drafts until doubled in bulk, about 1 hour.

6. Punch dough down, let rest 5 minutes, then knead 2 minutes.

7. Shape into two loaves, place in greased 8½ × 4½ × 2¾-inch loaf pans, cover, and let rise 50 to 60 minutes till almost doubled in bulk. Toward end of rising, preheat oven to 400°F.

8. Bake loaves 30 to 35 minutes until nicely browned and hollow-sounding when tapped. Remove bread from pans and cool on wire rack before cutting.

VARIATION

PROCESSOR CORNELL BREAD: Omit Steps 1 through 4. Instead, pulse yeast and water in food processor fitted with metal chopping blade 2 to 3 times; let stand 5 minutes. Cool milk to lukewarm and add to processor along with sugar, butter, and salt; pulse 2 to 3 times to combine. Add soy flour, dry milk, wheat germ, and 3 cups flour, and pulse 2 to 3 times. Replace metal chopping blade with plastic dough blade. Pulse in remaining flour, 1 cup at a time, then churn 30 seconds. Let rest 1 minute, then churn 30 to 60 seconds longer until dough rolls into ball and rides up on central spindle. Proceed as directed in Steps 5 through 8. Makes two 8½ × 4½ × 2¾-inch loaves.

Monkey Bread

Makes a 10-inch Bundt or Tube Loaf

✳

THIS PULL-APART yeast bread, also known as "bubble loaf," began showing up in women's magazines and community cookbooks back in the '50s. There are two types, a savory and a sweet. The better known calls for rolling yeast dough thin, cutting into strips, dipping in melted butter, then layering in a Bundt or tube pan. This is the savory. The sweet is also known as bubble loaf because the dough is pinched off and rolled into balls. These are dipped in melted butter and then layered into the pan with a flavored sugar mixture or a caramel or brown sugar glaze (this is the version Judith and Evan Jones give in their wonderful *Book of Bread*, 1982). Sometimes dried currants and/or diced candied fruits are mixed into the dough before it's shaped. According to John Mariani (*The Dictionary of American Food and Drink*, Revised Edition, 1994), "Nancy Reagan made monkey bread a traditional dish of the White House Christmas celebration; she claims that the bread is so called 'because when you make it, you have to monkey around with it.'" It may be so. The Reagan recipe, which Mariani prints, contains no fruit. It calls for rolling balls of dough in gobs of melted butter (½ pound for a dough requiring only 3½ cups flour), but not for layering them with sugar or glaze. This version is mine.

NOTE: Begin this bread the day before you intend to serve it.

1 envelope active dry yeast
½ cup very warm milk (110°
*   to 115°F)*

1 egg, lightly beaten
½ cup vegetable oil
3 cups sifted all-purpose flour
¼ cup sugar
1 teaspoon salt
½ cup boiling water
¼ cup (½ stick) butter or
*   margarine, melted*

1. Dissolve yeast in warm milk in small bowl.

2. Place yeast mixture, egg, oil, flour, sugar, and salt in large bowl and beat until smooth.

3. Very slowly drizzle in boiling water, beating hard all the while. Cover bowl of dough with plastic wrap and refrigerate overnight.

4. Next day, coat 10-inch (12-cup) Bundt pan or 10-inch tube pan with nonstick cooking spray; set aside. Punch dough down, turn onto well-floured pastry cloth, and knead 1 minute. With floured, stockinette-covered rolling pin, roll dough into rectangle ¼-inch thick.

5. Cut into strips 3½ to 4 inches long and 1½ to 2 inches wide. Dip in melted butter, then arrange strips, overlapping, in pan.

6. Cover with cloth and let rise in warm, dry spot, away from drafts, 1½ hours until doubled in bulk. Toward end of rising, preheat oven to 350°F.

7. Bake 35 to 40 minutes until golden brown and loaf sounds hollow when tapped. Cool loaf in pan on wire rack 5 minutes, then turn out on rack and cool before serving.

TIMELINE

1956

Kentucky Fried Chicken becomes a fast-food franchise.

....

James Beard opens a cooking school in New York City.

1957

The sushi bar comes to America (in New York City).

....

Saccharin, previously available only as tablets, is pulverized, put up in individual portions in bright pink packets, and rechristened Sweet'n Low. Before long, it is the preferred coffee and tea sweetener among the calorie-conscious. The man who came up with the idea was Benjamin Eisenstadt, a tea-bag merchant whose business had fallen on hard times.

....

Craig Claiborne joins *The New York Times*.

Bubble Loaf

(MONKEY BREAD II)
Makes a 9-inch Tube Loaf

✳

A BUBBLE loaf can be sliced or it can be served whole with each person reaching in and pulling off the "bubbles."

BREAD
½ cup scalded milk
2 tablespoons butter or margarine, softened
¼ cup sugar
½ teaspoon salt
1 envelope active dry yeast
¼ cup very warm water (110° to 115°F)
1 egg, lightly beaten
3 cups sifted all-purpose flour (about)
⅓ cup butter or margarine, melted

GLAZE
¼ cup dark corn syrup
1 tablespoon butter or margarine, melted
1 teaspoon fresh lemon juice
½ teaspoon vanilla extract

1. BREAD: Mix milk, softened butter, sugar, and salt in large bowl; cool to lukewarm.

2. Dissolve yeast in warm water in small bowl; stir into cooled mixture along with egg.

3. Add 1½ cups flour and beat hard. Mix in remaining flour—dough should be soft but manageable. Turn onto lightly floured pastry cloth and knead until elastic.

4. Shape dough into ball, place in buttered, warm, large bowl, then turn in bowl to butter all sides. Cover with cloth and let rise in warm, dry spot, away from drafts, 1 hour till doubled in bulk.

5. Punch dough down and let rest 10 minutes. Coat 9-inch tube pan with nonstick cooking spray; set aside.

6. Pinch off bits of dough and roll into 1-inch balls. Dip in melted butter and arrange in pan, spacing ¼ inch apart. Cover and let rise 45 to 50 minutes till doubled in bulk. Toward end of rising, preheat oven to 350°F.

7. GLAZE: Mix all ingredients. When loaf is fully risen, drizzle glaze evenly over all.

8. Bake 40 to 45 minutes until golden brown and loaf sounds hollow when tapped. Cool loaf in pan on wire rack 5 minutes, then invert on rack and cool before serving.

——— VARIATION ———

ORANGE OR LEMON BUBBLE LOAF: Prepare dough and shape into balls as directed. Do not dip in melted butter; omit glaze. Instead, mix ⅓ cup sugar, 2 teaspoons finely grated orange or lemon zest, and ¼ teaspoon each ground cinnamon and nutmeg. Arrange half the balls in 9-inch tube pan and brush with 1 tablespoon melted butter. Sprinkle with half of zest mixture. Add remaining balls, brush with 1 tablespoon melted butter, and scatter remaining zest mixture on top. Let rise and bake as directed, reducing time by 5 minutes. Cool 5 minutes in pan on wire rack, invert on rack, and cool before serving. Makes a 9-inch tube loaf.

Dilly Casserole Bread

Makes an 8- or 9-inch Round Loaf

✳

FEW PILLSBURY Bake-Off Contest Grand Prize winners are more popular than this one, which has become an American classic. It was the creation of a good Nebraska cook named Leona P. Schnuelle, who entered it in the 1960 Bake-Off Contest. Since then, her casserole bread—or variations of it—has found its way into newspapers, women's magazines, and scores of community cookbooks. Both the original version and a quick food processor variation appear in the March 1995 Collector's Issue of *Classic Cookbooks* (a Pillsbury publication), which features all Bake-Off Grand Prize winners. According to the recipe headnote, "This dill and onion flavored bread is made with cottage cheese and is baked in a round casserole. It's easy and delicious!" Quite so.

2 to 2⅔ cups all-purpose or unbleached flour, lightly spooned into measure and leveled off
2 tablespoons sugar
2 to 3 teaspoons instant minced onion
2 teaspoons dill seeds
1 teaspoon salt
¼ teaspoon baking soda
1 envelope active dry yeast
¼ cup very warm water (110° to 115°F)
1 tablespoon margarine or butter
1 cup cream-style cottage cheese
1 egg
2 teaspoons margarine or butter, melted
¼ teaspoon coarse salt (optional)

1. Mix 1 cup flour well with sugar, onion, dill seeds, 1 teaspoon salt, soda, and yeast in large electric mixer bowl.

2. Heat water, 1 tablespoon margarine, and cottage cheese in small saucepan over moderately low heat until very warm (120° to 130°F).

3. Add warm liquid and egg to mixer bowl and beat at low speed until mixture is moistened. Raise mixer speed to medium and beat 3 minutes.

4. By hand, stir in remaining 1 to 1⅔ cups flour to form stiff batter.

5. Cover with cloth and let rise in warm, dry spot, away from drafts, 45 to 60 minutes till doubled in bulk. Toward end of rising, grease 1½- to 2-quart casserole well; set aside.

6. Stir batter down to release air bubbles. Turn into casserole, cover, and let rise until light and doubled in bulk, 30 to 45 minutes. Toward end of rising, preheat oven to 350°F.

7. Uncover casserole and bake bread 30 to 40 minutes until richly golden brown and hollow-sounding when tapped.

8. Immediately remove bread from casserole and set on wire rack. While loaf is still warm, brush with melted margarine and sprinkle, if you like, with coarse salt.

VARIATION

QUICK FOOD PROCESSOR DILLY CASSEROLE BREAD: Soften yeast in ¼ cup very warm water (110° to 115°F) in small bowl. Place 2 cups flour, the sugar, onion, dill seeds, 1 teaspoon salt, soda, and 1 tablespoon margarine in food processor fitted with metal chopping blade. Cover and churn 5 seconds. Add cottage cheese and egg and churn 10 seconds until well blended. With motor running, pour yeast mixture down feed tube and continue processing about 20 seconds until mixture is well blended, pulls from sides of work bowl, and forms a ball; add additional flour, if necessary. Transfer dough to greased large bowl, turn in bowl so greased side is up, cover loosely with greased plastic wrap and cloth towel. Let rise in warm, dry place, away from drafts, until doubled in bulk, 45 to 60 minutes. Proceed as original recipe (above) directs. Makes 1 round loaf, 8 or 9 inches across.

THE AMERICAN Institute of Baking in Manhattan, Kansas, receives so many queries about the origin of cinnamon or sticky buns that Dr. Ronald Wirtz, its director of Information Services, has researched them in depth. He begins, believe it or not, with the ancient Egyptians, Greeks, and Romans, then moves forward in time through Medieval Europe to present-day America.

Wirtz follows the spice trade, specifically that of cinnamon, which, writes Anne Wilson (*Food and Drink in Britain,* 1974) "was abundant and inexpensive in Britain by the thirteenth century," even being "sold in ground form, ready mixed with ground ginger and refined sugar as 'powder blanch' for use with a variety of foods."

Wirtz believes that our cinnamon roll or sticky bun owes "some of its origins to British cooking and baking, perhaps with a degree of influence from the Dutch and Germans." He points, in particular, to the Chelsea Bun, which Elizabeth David (*English Bread and Yeast Cookery,* 1980) describes as "Sugary, spicy, sticky, square and coiled like a Swiss roll . . . a pretty hefty proposition."

The originals, made at least as far back as the early eighteenth century, were apparently daintier, a favorite of Caroline of Ansbach, the German Queen of George II. Perhaps they reminded her of *Schnecken,* the snail-shaped sweet rolls of her homeland.

What I find particularly interesting in Wirtz's cinnamon-bun research is his mention of Mathew Malzbender's *Practical Manual for Confectioners, Pastry-cooks, Bakers and Candy Makers,* first published in Milwaukee in 1910 in both German and English. Wirtz says there's an easy explanation for this. At that time, one-third of America's professional bakers were German-speaking. The manual's directions for making cinnamon buns, according to Wirtz, call for a sweet dough to be "sheeted out and sprinkled with sugar, cinnamon and currants, rolled up and sliced just as in current practice." Also as in the preparation of *Schnecken,* Wirtz goes on to say that in the *Retail Bakers Reference Book* (1928), *Schnecken* and "rolled-up cinnamon buns" appear on the same page.

In *Taste of the States* (1992), Hilda Lee suggests that *Schnecken* became popular among bakers in Germantown, a Philadelphia suburb, as early as the 1680s. Judith and Evan Jones seem to agree. About the date, anyway. They introduce "Philadelphia Cinnamon Buns, Sticky Buns, or Pecan Rolls" in their *Book of Bread* by saying that the recipe probably "derives from a confection Mrs. William Penn and other Pennsylvania ladies called 'whig'."

That sent me scurrying to *Penn Family Recipes: Cooking Recipes of William Penn's Wife Gulielma* (facsimile, 1966). On page 61, I found:

TOO MAKE WHIGS
TAKE $\frac{1}{2}$ *a peck of flouer by mesure, then take a pound of butter and breke it into it with youre hands, the quantity of an oz: of nutmegs, mace and sinomen together in fine pouder, ¾ of a pound of Caraway*

BREADS & SANDWICHES

comfets, 1 pint and a ½ of yeist, the same of milke, it must bee blood warme, be suer you Do not over bake them—

In her accompanying notes, the book's editor Evelyn Abraham Benson explains that a Wig (also spelled Whig, Wigg, Wigge, and Wygge) is a "wedge-shaped cake, a kind of bun or small cake made of fine flour (1376–1888)." There's a 1688 definition, too: "Wigg is White Bread moulded long ways, and thick in the middle." (Elizabeth David says that whigs were "known in England at least as far back as the fifteenth century.")

Did Mrs. William Penn's whigs evolve over time into Philadelphia Sticky Buns? If so, the evolution was slow. And their introduction to the rest of America even slower.

No nineteenth- or early-twentieth-century cookbook I searched mentions them. Not *Mrs. Rorer's Philadelphia Cook Book* (1886), not *Mrs. Rorer's New Cook Book* (1902). Not *The Settlement Cook Book* (1903), not "Fannie Farmer" from the first edition (1896) right through the 1920s.

I did find in that first "Fannie" Swedish Rolls for which the yeast dough is rolled thin, spread with butter, sprinkled with cinnamon-sugar, "stoned raisins finely chopped" and chopped citron, then rolled up like jelly roll, sliced, and baked in a pan. There's no sticky glaze, however. Nor is there in a similar recipe—Sweet French Rolls—from that same book.

American Cooking: The Eastern Heartland (1971) in the "Time-Life Foods of the World" series acknowledges Philadelphia Cinnamon Buns only in passing:

There are other Philadelphia specialties that have managed to survive the transition to more contemporary eating patterns . . . there are the famous sticky or cinnamon buns on which many visitors love to breakfast.

Alas, there is no clue as to the recipe's date or origin. I do know this: The Time-Life recipe, which I've adapted (page 318) *is* twentieth century; its sticky glaze contains corn syrup, which was not introduced until 1902, in fact it specifies *light* corn syrup, which came some ten years later.

There's no word about Philadelphia Sticky Buns in *James Beard's American Cookery* (1972) or in Waverley Root and Richard de Rochemont's *Eating in America* (1976). But in *American Food: The Gastronomic Story,* Evan Jones writes:

Much of the American appetite for sweet rolls and cakes comes from these specific Germans [Pennsylvania Dutch] as well as from the Holland settlements that had so much early influence on New York, New Jersey, and Delaware. All of these early cooks made cinnamon-flavored breakfast- or coffee-cakes.

And yet Pennsylvania culinary historian William Woys Weaver has nothing to say about cinnamon buns—Philadelphia or otherwise—in *America Eats* (1989) or *Pennsylvania Dutch Country Cooking* (1993).

The earliest recipe for them I could find cropped up in 1922 in *Good Housekeeping's Book of Menus, Recipes and Household Discoveries.* Sheila Hibben includes Cinnamon Buns in *The National Cookbook* (1932) and attributes them to Philadelphia. And Anna Wetherill Reed opens her Breads, Waffles, Pancakes chapter in *The Philadelphia Cook Book* (1940) with Philadelphia Cinnamon Buns from the West Chester Inn—but has nothing further to say about them.

According to Dr. Wirtz of the American Institute of Baking, "recent history in the U.S. saw 'fad' popularity of large-size caramelized cinnamon rolls, combining the size and make-up of the Chelsea bun with the fillings and coatings of the rich *Schnecken* type roll."

He adds that "T.J. Cinnamons and Cinnamon Sam's, both based in Kansas City, spearheaded the fad."

Perhaps. But it's the bun's Philadelphia connection that stuck.

Philadelphia Cinnamon Buns

Makes 16

✳

I HAVE adapted this recipe from one that appears in the recipe binder of *American Cooking: The Eastern Heartland* (1971) from Time-Life's important "Foods of the World" series.

NOTE: If you prefer, substitute ½ cup coarsely chopped pecans for raisins.

> ¼ cup very warm water (110° to 115°F)
> 1 envelope active dry yeast
> ½ cup plus 1 teaspoon granulated sugar
> 4 to 4½ cups unsifted all-purpose flour (about)
> ½ teaspoon salt
> 2 egg yolks
> 1 cup very warm milk (110° to 115°F)
> 1½ cups firmly packed light brown sugar
> 6 tablespoons butter, melted
> ½ cup light corn syrup
> ½ cup seedless raisins
> 2 teaspoons ground cinnamon

1. Place water in small bowl, sprinkle in yeast and 1 teaspoon granulated sugar; let stand 2 to 3 minutes. Stir well, set in warm, draft-free spot 5 minutes until mixture froths and nearly doubles in volume.

2. Mix 4 cups flour, remaining ½ cup granulated sugar, and salt in large bowl; make well in center. Dump in yeast mixture, add egg

I USE
Alma Roller Mills
FLOUR,
ALMA, MICH.

yolks, and milk. With large spoon, slowly mix until dough is soft and smooth, and if necessary, adding ½ cup more flour until it can be gathered into a ball.

3. Knead on lightly floured surface 10 minutes until smooth and elastic, adding only enough flour to keep dough from sticking.

4. Shape dough into ball, place in well-buttered large bowl, turn in bowl so buttered side is up. Cover with clean cloth and let rise in warm spot, away from drafts, about 1 hour, until doubled in bulk.

5. Blend ¾ cup brown sugar, 2 tablespoons melted butter, and corn syrup into paste in small bowl. Divide between two 9-inch-round layer cake pans, spreading evenly to edges. In another small bowl, stir together remaining ¾ cup brown sugar, raisins, and cinnamon; set aside.

6. Punch dough down, knead quickly on lightly floured surface, then roll into 18 × 10-inch rectangle, ¼-inch thick. Brush with 2 tablespoons melted butter, then sprinkle evenly with sugar-raisin mixture.

7. Beginning at one long side of dough, roll up tight jelly-roll style, forming log 18 inches long and 2½ inches in diameter. With sharp knife, slice crosswise at 1¼-inch intervals.

8. Center one slice in each pan, then wreathe each with seven more slices, spacing evenly. Cover and let rise in warm spot, away from drafts, about 45 minutes until doubled in volume.

9. Preheat oven to 350°F. Brush tops of buns with remaining 2 tablespoons melted butter and bake on middle oven rack until golden brown, about 25 minutes.

10. Invert buns at once on racks set over wax-paper-covered surface. Serve warm—not hot.

Angel Biscuits

Makes 2½ Dozen

✳

YOU'LL HAVE to look long and hard to find a lighter, better biscuit than this one, a Southern favorite.

The dough can be covered, refrigerated, and kept for about a week. Simply reach in and remove whatever amount you'll need for the meal, then roll the dough, cut, and bake the biscuits as directed.

1 envelope active dry yeast
¼ cup very warm water (110°
  to 115°F)
5 cups sifted all-purpose flour
3 teaspoons baking powder
1 teaspoon baking soda
¼ cup sugar
2 teaspoons salt
1 cup vegetable shortening
2 cups buttermilk or sour milk

1. Preheat oven to 400°F.

2. Dissolve yeast in water in small bowl and set aside.

3. Sift flour with baking powder, soda, sugar, and salt into large bowl. Using a pastry blender, cut in shortening until mixture resembles coarse meal.

4. Add buttermilk and yeast mixture and toss briskly with a fork just until dough holds together.

5. Knead dough lightly on well-floured surface 1 minute. Roll to a thickness of ⅝ inch, then cut with well-floured 2½-inch biscuit cutter.

6. Bake on ungreased baking sheets for 15 minutes or until biscuits are puffed and pale tan. Serve at once.

ANGEL BISCUITS

I FIRST TASTED these heavenly biscuits on a trip home to North Carolina in the early '70s. I was interviewing farm women for the "America's Great Grass Roots Cooks" series I was writing for *Family Circle* magazine. Without exception, every woman I visited brought out this terrific "new" recipe.

Helen Moore, a freelance food writer living near Charlotte, says she got the recipe in the early '50s from a home economics professor at Winthrop College in South Carolina. "I remember her saying, 'I've got this wonderful new biscuit recipe. It's got yeast in it.'"

Who first dreamed up Angel Biscuits, or "Bride's Biscuits" as they're also called? York Kiker, formerly of the North Carolina Department of Agriculture, thinks it might have been a Southern miller. Like me, York first tasted them in the early '70s.

Kitty Crider of the *Austin American-Statesman* says in *Food Editors Hometown Favorite Cookbook* (1984) that "Alice Jarman, who served as director of Martha White Test Kitchens in Nashville for twenty-seven years, first encountered Angel Biscuits in the late '50s. They were called Alabama Biscuits then. She renamed them 'Riz' Biscuits and printed the recipe in a Martha White Flour leaflet. Somewhere along the way, either the bread or the baker was accorded the title 'angel,' because the flop-proof recipe goes by that name now." Or did *Southern Living* magazine coin the name "Angel"? They featured "Angel Biscuits" in their collection of all-time Christmas favorites.

A little digging turns up a recipe that dates at least as far back as 1941. It appears in *Southern Cooking* by Mrs. S.R. Dull, former editor of the Home Economics page of the Magazine Section of the *Atlanta Journal,* and though it's called "South Georgia Ice Box Rolls," it, like Angel Biscuits, contains three leavenings—yeast, baking powder, and soda. Indeed, the recipe closely resembles Angel Biscuits.

Food Processor Yogurt Batter Bread

Makes Two 9 × 5 × 3-inch Loaves

❋

TOO STICKY to knead, batter bread must be beaten forever to develop the gluten that forms its structure. In the old days, this had to be done by hand, but with the arrival of food processors in the 1970s, batter bread became a snap. Yogurt, needless to say, is a twentieth-century addition.

NOTE: Not every food processor will do. You must have a heavy-duty one with a sturdy motor that won't stall or die under the load of sticky dough. This bread freezes superbly. Wrap snugly in foil or several thicknesses plastic wrap, date, label, and quick-freeze by setting directly on floor of 0° F freezer. Use within three months.

> *2 packages active dry yeast*
> *⅓ cup very warm water (110° to 115°F)*
> *⅓ cup sugar*
> *2 (8-ounce) cartons plain yogurt*
> *¾ cup (1½ sticks) butter, melted*
> *6 cups sifted all-purpose flour*
> *1½ teaspoons baking powder*
> *1 teaspoon baking soda*
> *½ teaspoon salt*

1. Mix yeast, water, and sugar in small bowl; set aside.

2. Pulse yogurt and melted butter in food processor fitted with metal chopping blade until well blended. Pulse in yeast mixture.

3. Sift 3 cups flour with baking powder, soda, and salt. Add to processor, cup by cup, pulsing 4 to 5 times after each addition.

4. Add remaining 3 cups flour to processor, cup by cup, again pulsing 4 to 5 times to mix.

5. Beat hard, using 4 to 5 churnings of 10 seconds each until batter is elastic and beginning to blister.

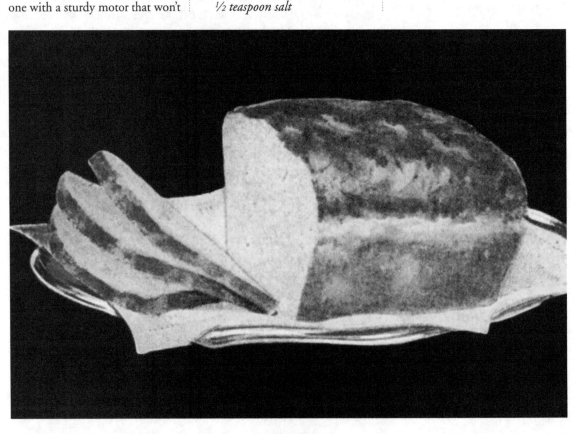

6. Turn batter into warm, buttered bowl and brush top with melted butter. Cover with cloth and let rise in warm, dry, draft-free spot 1 hour until doubled in bulk. Meanwhile, butter two 9 × 5 × 3-inch loaf pans well and set aside.

7. Stir batter down with wooden spoon, then beat hard 1 to 2 minutes to release large bubbles. Divide equally between two pans, smoothing surface. Cover with cloth and let rise about 30 minutes, until doubled in bulk. Toward end of rising, preheat oven to 350° F.

8. Bake loaves 40 to 45 minutes until nicely browned and hollow-sounding when thumped.

9. Cool loaves in pans on sides on wire racks 15 minutes. Loosen loaves, turn out, and cool right-side-up 1 hour before cutting.

Black Walnut-Raisin Bran Bread

Makes Two 9 × 5 × 3-inch Loaves

✳

MRS. CHARLES Seymour of Maryland's Eastern Shore gave me this recipe back in the 1970s when I was writing a series of articles on America's great grass roots cooks for *Family Circle* magazine. It is one of the best fruit-nut breads I know. If black walnuts are unavailable, substitute California walnuts or pecans, even toasted hazelnuts or toasted slivered almonds.

4 cups bran flakes
½ cup sugar
3 cups sifted all-purpose flour
½ teaspoon salt
1 cup coarsely chopped black walnuts
1 cup seedless raisins
2 eggs, well beaten
⅓ cup vegetable oil
2 cups milk
1 cup molasses mixed with 2 teaspoons baking soda

1. Preheat oven to 325° F. Grease and flour two 9 × 5 × 3-inch loaf pans well; set aside.

2. Stir bran flakes with sugar, flour, salt, walnuts, and raisins in large bowl until nuts and raisins are well dredged; make well in dry ingredients.

3. Beat eggs with oil and milk in small bowl just enough to blend.

4. Pour molasses-soda mixture into well in dry ingredients, then egg mixture and stir just enough to mix. Batter will be thin.

5. Divide batter between pans and bake about 1 hour until loaves have pulled from sides of pans and are springy to touch.

6. Cool loaves in pans on wire racks 10 minutes. Loosen around edges and turn out on racks. Cool thoroughly before slicing.

TIMELINE

1958

The Delaney Clause, added to the Pure Food and Drug Act, bans the addition of any carcinogen to food.

Pyroceram Corning Ware freezer- or fridge-to-oven casseroles change the way we cook.

1959

Reuben Mattus introduces a dense, super-rich ice cream and gives it a made-up Scandinavian name—Häagen-Dazs.

1960s

The Age of Granola and Tofu.

Macy's begins selling nonstick pans coated with Du Pont Teflon.

Fondue madness sets in.

New York restaurants become theater with such showy temples of gastronomy as the Forum of the Twelve Caesars, La Fonda del Sol, and the Four Seasons.

QUICK BREADS

CCORDING TO John Mariani (*The Dictionary of American Food and Drink,* Revised Edition, 1994), single-acting baking powders, commercial formulas of "sodium bicarbonate and an acid salt became popular in the 1850s" and double-acting baking powder was introduced in 1889.

What this meant was that cooks no longer had to rely on slow-growing yeasts to leaven their breads. Or the quicker but often unpredictable combination of vinegar, sour milk, molasses, or cream of tartar and saleratus (potassium or sodium bicarbonate).

Here is what *Mrs. Lincoln's Boston Cook Book* (1883) has to say on the subject of baking powders:

When your druggist or cook is not to be relied upon [to combine bicarbonate of soda and tartaric acid correctly for the purposes of leavening], *use a baking-powder which has been tested and proved pure. Pure baking-powders are soda and cream of tartar mixed by weight in the proper proportion, and combined with rice flour, cornstarch, or some harmless ingredient to insure their keeping. To allow for this starch the measure should be a little more than the combined amount of soda and cream of tartar* [meaning that mixed at home]; *three rounding teaspoonfuls of baking-powder being equal to one level teaspoon of soda and two full teaspoonfuls of cream of tartar. One even teaspoonful of baking-powder for each cup of flour is a convenient formula.*

Nearly twenty years later, Sarah Tyson Rorer includes several pages on baking powder breads in *Mrs. Rorer's New Cook Book* (1902). And she doesn't mince words about baking powder:

The true value of baking powder depends upon the amount of gas liberated in the dough. Tartaric compounds are expensive, and this induces many housewives to take the cheaper substitutes, usually "alum" powders, which are possibly injurious; the salts formed by the decomposition of bi-carbonate of soda and alum, are not readily absorbed. All good baking powders contain a small amount of dry starch, as fine flour or cornstarch, which prevents the active ingredients from becoming moist after the box is opened.

Alum phosphate baking powders were a concern right through the 1920s, the subject of a bitter controversy fueled, in part, by manufacturers of the more expensive tartrate baking powders. Claiming that soda alum (sodium aluminum sulfate) was hazardous to the health of all who used it, they fought to have it banned. But after years of legal wrangling, they lost. According to Andrew Lincoln Winton (*The Structure and Composition of Foods,* 1932), "their contention was not supported by the Referee Board of Consulting Scientists. As a consequence of the Board's report, the sale of alum baking powders is permitted in the United States by federal ruling."

It still is. Look on the label of a double-acting baking powder and you will see that it contains sodium aluminum sulfate, usually in combination with cornstarch, sodium bicarbonate (baking soda), and calcium phosphate. It is listed last, however, meaning that it's the ingredient used in the smallest proportion.

Back to 1902, Sarah Tyson Rorer, and *Mrs. Rorer's New Cook Book.* After giving two formulas for homemade baking powder (a tartaric acid powder and a cream of tartar one), she moves on to baking powder bread recipes. There are no surprises here. It's the usual repertoire: biscuits, scones (sweet milk, oatmeal), a variety of muffins plus several kinds of waffles and a batter bread. Certainly there is nothing resembling the fruit-nut breads or other quick loaves so popular today.

These appear to be a somewhat later twentieth-century phenomenon, probably because neither baking powders nor ovens were very reliable until the 1920s. In the original *Settlement Cook Book* (1903), I find a currant bread leavened with three teaspoons baking powder but it contains no shortening and only one tablespoon sugar. In fact, there are no directions for making or baking the bread.

A more promising Quick Nut Loaf leavened with 4 teaspoons baking powder appears in *Catering for Special Occasions with Menus & Recipes by Fannie Merritt Farmer* (1911). Strangely, baking powder loaves don't show up in *The Boston Cooking-School Cook Book* until the 1923 edition (eight years after Fannie Farmer's death) and one of those four is the 1911 Quick Nut Loaf, recycled.

In *Mrs. Allen's Cook Book* (1917), Ida Bailey Allen gives a recipe for a whole-wheat, quick nut loaf leavened with 3½ teaspoons baking powder. She also uses a combination of baking powder and soda to leaven a steamed prune bread, then offers a Quick Graham Bread raised the old-fashioned way with "1 teaspoonful soda and 2 teaspoonfuls cream of tartar."

The forerunner, surely, of today's ubiquitous fruit-nut breads is the Date and Nut Bread in *One Hundred Delights,* a recipe booklet published in 1922 by The Hills Brothers Company of New York, processors of Dromedary brand dates.

The introduction begins: "In compiling it [the booklet], we were assisted by the editor of a leading woman's magazine [unnamed], the domestic science department of a big university [unnamed], and the chef of a big New York hotel [also unnamed]. Recipes were assembled from housewives, social leaders, and domestic science teachers, and these favorites selected. We hope that *'One Hundred Delights'* will be of great assistance in your home." Here is that 1922 date-nut bread:

DATE AND NUT BREAD

3 cups flour	1 teaspoon cinnamon	1 egg
3 teaspoons baking powder	¾ cup broken walnuts	1½ cups milk
1 teaspoon salt	1 cup chopped Dromedary	
½ cup sugar	dates	

Stir flour, baking powder, salt, sugar and cinnamon together. Add nuts and dates and mix thoroughly. Add well beaten egg to milk. Add to flour mixture slowly, stirring constantly. Beat well and pour into greased bread pans. Cover and allow to stand 30 minutes. Bake in a moderate oven 1 hour. This makes 2 small loaves or 1 large loaf.

Note that the instructions call for the batter to stand in the pan for thirty minutes before the bread is baked, which says something about the efficacy of those early baking powders. In *Good Housekeeping's Book of Menus, Recipes and Household Discoveries* (1922), there is an orange-nut bread (made with candied orange rind) leavened with 4 teaspoons of baking powder; this one goes straight into the oven.

From the '30s on, fruit-nut breads grew in variety and popularity. *My Better Homes & Gardens Lifetime Cook Book* (1930) devotes a section to "Baking Powder Breads" and includes two nut breads, a date-nut loaf, a fruit gingerbread, and two coffee cakes.

Three years later, General Foods's *All About Home Baking* teaches—via step-by-step, black-and-white photographs—the correct way to make quick bread. "Here is the proper technic [spelling theirs] for making bread leavened by baking powder," the blurb announces.

In the beginning, fruit and fruit-nut loaves were not very sweet. But by the 1960s, when chocolate chips, crushed pineapple, carrots, and nearly everything else were being stirred into them, quick breads had become as rich as cake.

What follow are some of the signature quick breads of this century.

BISQUICK

LIKE SO many conveniences we wonder how we ever managed without, Bisquick was the result of a chance discovery. Late one night in 1930, a General Mills salesman named Carl Smith boarded a train for San Francisco and headed for the diner. He suspected a cold plate was the most he could hope for at that hour, yet to his surprise, dinner was speedily served, piping hot, and included fresh biscuits. Curious as to how anyone could produce fresh bread so fast, he spoke to the chef and discovered his secret: He premixed the dry ingredients and shortening and kept a batch in the icebox.

When Smith reported this curiosity to his bosses, they recognized the commercial potential of a biscuit mix but also saw technical problems: How could the shortening be kept fresh and the leavening potent over time? Once these problems were solved and Bisquick appeared on the market, it was a runaway hit. Within seven months, housewives had bought a half-million cases of the mix, and were discovering their own ways to use it as well as following recipes in the company booklet *101 Delicious Bisquick Creations.*

So eager were other companies to cash in on the Bisquick phenomenon that within a year of its appearance there were ninety-five similar mixes on the market. But so loyal were Bisquick fans that within another year, all but six competitors had vanished.

Given that today's cake, muffin, and pancake mixes descend from Bisquick, it's lucky that a hungry salesman met a clever chef that night sixty-seven years ago.

Apricot Bundt Coffee Cake

Makes a 10-inch Bundt Cake

❋

THIS RECIPE, featured in an article I wrote for *Family Circle,* comes from Minnesotan Marjorie Johnson, who has won more than a thousand ribbons for her baking. This coffee cake of hers took top honors at the Minnesota State Fair in 1991.

STREUSEL

    2 tablespoons firmly packed
        dark brown sugar, at room
        temperature
    2 tablespoons firmly packed
        light brown sugar
    1 tablespoon all-purpose flour
    1 tablespoon butter or
        margarine, at room
        temperature
    ½ teaspoon ground
        cinnamon
    ¼ teaspoon freshly grated
        nutmeg

COFFEE CAKE

    3 cups sifted all-purpose flour
    1½ teaspoons baking powder
    1 teaspoon baking soda
    ½ teaspoon salt
    1½ cups granulated sugar
    ¾ cup (1½ sticks) butter or
        margarine, at room
        temperature
    1 teaspoon vanilla extract
    ½ teaspoon almond extract
    4 eggs
    1¼ cups sour cream
    1 cup finely chopped dried
        apricots

GLAZE

1 cup confectioners' (10X) sugar
1 to 2 tablespoons milk
¼ to ½ teaspoon almond extract
Chopped dried apricots (optional)

1. Preheat oven to 350° F. Grease a 10-inch (12-cup) Bundt pan and set aside.

2. STREUSEL: Mix all ingredients in small bowl until crumbly; set aside.

3. COFFEE CAKE: Sift flour with baking powder, soda, and salt onto wax paper and set aside.

4. Cream sugar, butter, vanilla and almond extracts at low electric mixer speed 1 minute. Increase speed to medium-high and beat 4 minutes. Add eggs, one at a time, beating well after each addition.

5. By hand, add flour mixture alternately with sour cream, beginning and ending with flour mixture and stirring after each addition only enough to moisten dry ingredients. (Add dry ingredients in thirds, sour cream in two additions.) Stir in apricots.

6. Spoon half of batter into pan. Sprinkle Streusel over batter. Top with remaining batter, smoothing with spatula.

7. Bake 1 hour or until loaf is richly browned, begins to pull from sides of pan, and is springy to touch.

8. Cool in pan on wire rack 15 min-

utes. Loosen coffee cake around edge with thin metal spatula. Turn out on wire rack and cool.

9. GLAZE: Beat all ingredients until smooth in small bowl. Drizzle over cooled cake. Garnish with chopped apricots, if desired.

Quick Whole-Wheat Apricot Bread

Makes an 8½ × 4½ × 2¾-inch Loaf

✳

I'VE ALWAYS liked this fruit bread of my mother's because it isn't as sweet as most and because it's made of a fifty-fifty mix of unbleached and whole-wheat flour. An additional plus: The bread freezes wonderfully. Wrap snugly in foil or plastic freezer wrap; label, date, and store in a 0° F freezer. Use in three months.

1 cup sifted unbleached all-purpose flour
1 cup unsifted whole-wheat flour
2 teaspoons baking powder
½ teaspoon salt
½ cup firmly packed light brown sugar
1 cup coarsely chopped dried apricots
1 egg, lightly beaten
1 cup milk
⅓ cup vegetable oil

1. Preheat oven to 350° F. Grease 8½ × 4½ × 2¾-inch loaf pan well; set aside.

2. Mix unbleached flour, whole-wheat flour, baking powder, and salt in large bowl. Work in sugar, pressing out lumps; stir in apricots. Make well in center of dry ingredients.

3. Whisk together egg, milk, and oil in large measuring cup. Pour into well in dry ingredients and stir briskly just enough to mix—no longer or bread will be tough.

4. Spoon mixture into prepared pan, let stand on counter 10 minutes, then bake about 45 to 50 minutes until loaf begins to pull from sides of pan, is springy to touch, and a toothpick inserted in center comes out clean.

5. Cool loaf in pan on wire rack 10 minutes. Loosen around edge and turn out on rack. Cool thoroughly before slicing.

A Helping Hand for Homemakers

A 1915 Knox Gelatine booklet, *Dainty Desserts for Dainty People*, offers this recipe for stretching butter and introduces it with this note:

This mixture is intended for immediate use, and will do the work of two pounds of ordinary butter for table use and for baking cakes, muffins, etc., but is not used for frying purposes.

WORLD WAR I BUTTER-STRETCHER

1 pound good butter
2 pint bottles milk

1 heaping teaspoonful Knox Gelatine
2 teaspoonfuls salt.

Take the top cream of two pint bottles of milk, and add enough milk to make one pint.

Soak the gelatine in two tablespoonfuls of the milk ten minutes; place in a dish of hot water until gelatine is thoroughly dissolved.

Cut the butter in small pieces and place same in a dish over hot water until the butter begins to soften; then gradually whip the milk and cream and dissolved gelatine into the butter with a Dover egg beater. After the milk is thoroughly beaten into the butter, add the salt to taste.

If the milk forms, keep on beating until all is mixed in. Place on ice or in a cool place until hard. If a yellow color is desired, use butter coloring.

Spicy Banana-Nut Bread

Makes a 9 × 5 × 3-inch Loaf

❋

I HAVE a particular fondness for banana-nut bread, have had since I was a child. Of all the recipes I've tried, this one, adapted from McCormick's *Spices of the World Cookbook* (1964), is the one I like best.

1¾ cups sifted all-purpose flour
2 teaspoons baking powder
½ teaspoon salt
1 teaspoon ground cinnamon
⅛ teaspoon ground cardamom
⅛ teaspoon ground mace
⅓ cup vegetable shortening
⅔ cup sugar
2 eggs
1 teaspoon vanilla extract
1 cup pureed ripe bananas
½ cup coarsely chopped pecans

1. Preheat oven to 350° F. Grease 9 × 5 × 3-inch loaf pan well; set aside.

2. Sift flour, baking powder, salt, cinnamon, cardamom, and mace onto wax paper; set aside.

3. Cream shortening and sugar in large electric mixer bowl at medium speed until fluffy-light. Beat in eggs and vanilla.

4. By hand, add sifted dry ingredients alternately with bananas, beginning and ending with dry. Stir in pecans.

5. Spoon batter into pan, spreading to corners, and bake about 1 hour, until toothpick inserted in center of loaf comes out clean.

6. Cool loaf in pan on wire rack 10 minutes. Loosen around edge and turn out on rack. Cool thoroughly before slicing.

Pumpkin-Pecan Bread

Makes a 9 × 5 × 3-inch Loaf

❋

THE BEAUTY of this bread is that you can substitute pureed winter squash (either fresh or frozen) for pumpkin. You can also use walnuts (either black or California) in place of pecans. Lightly toasted hazelnuts are good, too.

1 cup granulated sugar
½ cup firmly packed light brown sugar

1 cup canned solid-pack pumpkin (not *pumpkin pie mix*) or 1 cup pureed cooked winter squash
½ cup vegetable oil
2 eggs
2 cups sifted all-purpose flour
1 teaspoon baking soda
½ teaspoon salt
½ teaspoon ground cinnamon
½ teaspoon freshly grated nutmeg
¼ teaspoon ground ginger
¼ cup water
1 cup seedless raisins
½ cup coarsely chopped pecans or walnuts

1. Preheat oven to 350° F. Grease and flour 9 × 5 × 3-inch loaf pan well; set aside.

2. Beat granulated sugar, brown sugar, pumpkin, oil, and eggs in large electric mixer bowl at medium speed 1½ to 2 minutes, until smooth.

3. Sift flour with soda, salt, cinnamon, nutmeg, and ginger onto wax paper. Mix into pumpkin mixture alternately with water, beginning and ending with dry ingredients. Fold in raisins and nuts.

4. Spoon batter into pan, smoothing to corners, and bake 60 to 65 minutes until bread pulls from sides of pan, is peaked, and springy to touch.

5. Cool bread in pan on wire rack 15 minutes. Loosen around edge, turn out on rack, and cool to room temperature before slicing.

Cranberry-Nut Bread

Makes a 9 × 5 × 3-inch Loaf

❋

THIS QUICK-AND-EASY bread from Ocean Spray has been popular from the mid-twentieth century on. With only ¼ cup (4 tablespoons) shortening, with orange juice the liquid ingredient instead of milk, it is also lower in fat than many fruit-nut breads. The original recipe called for a full teaspoon of salt, but I have halved that amount in my adaptation here.

NOTE: You can grate the orange zest in a food processor. Here's how: With a swivel-bladed vegetable peeler, remove zest of 1 medium orange in long thin strips. Add to food processor fitted with metal chopping blade, dump in sugar, and churn until uniformly fine—about 60 seconds. And here's another shortcut: Add sifted dry ingredients (flour, sugar, baking powder, soda, and salt) to zest mixture and pulse several times to combine. Transfer to large mixing bowl and proceed as recipe directs.

> 2 cups sifted all-purpose flour
> 1 cup sugar
> 1½ teaspoons baking powder
> ½ teaspoon baking soda
> ½ teaspoon salt
> ¼ cup vegetable shortening
> ¾ cup fresh orange juice
> 1 tablespoon finely grated
>   orange zest
> 1 egg, well beaten

> 1 cup fresh or frozen
>   cranberries, stemmed and
>   coarsely chopped
> ½ cup coarsely chopped pecans,
>   walnuts, or lightly toasted
>   slivered almonds

1. Preheat oven to 350° F. Coat 9 × 5 × 3-inch loaf pan with non-stick cooking spray; set aside.

2. Sift flour, sugar, baking powder, soda, and salt into large mixing bowl. Add shortening and use pastry blender to cut in until texture of cornmeal; make well in center.

3. Mix orange juice and zest with egg, dump into well in dry ingredients, and stir lightly—just enough to moisten. Fold in cranberries and pecans, again stirring lightly.

4. Spoon batter into pan, smoothing well to corners and making batter slightly higher around edge than in middle.

5. Bake 50 to 60 minutes until nicely browned and toothpick inserted in middle of loaf comes out clean.

6. Cool bread in pan on wire rack 10 minutes, loosen around edge, and turn out on rack. Cool to room temperature before slicing.

Carrot Loaf

Makes an 8½ × 4½ × 2¾-inch Loaf

❋

IN 1986 on the occasion of its seventy-fifth anniversary, the makers of Mazola Corn Oil gathered together the most successful recipes and printed them in a little booklet called *75 Years of Good Eating.* Among them, this spicy carrot bread.

> 1½ cups unsifted flour
> ½ cup firmly packed brown
>   sugar (light or dark)
> ½ cup granulated sugar
> 1½ teaspoons baking powder
> 1 teaspoon ground cinnamon
> ½ teaspoon salt
> 2 eggs, lightly beaten
> 1½ cups coarsely shredded
>   carrots (about 3 medium)
> ½ cup corn oil
> ½ teaspoon vanilla extract
> ½ cup coarsely chopped
>   walnuts or pecans

1. Preheat oven to 350° F. Grease and flour 8½ × 4½ × 2¾-inch loaf pan; set aside.

2. Mix flour, brown sugar, granulated sugar, baking powder, cinna-

mon, and salt in large bowl; make well in center.

3. Mix eggs, carrots, corn oil, and vanilla in small bowl. Dump into well in dry ingredients and stir just until well blended. Mix in walnuts.

4. Spoon into pan, spreading to corners, and bake about 1 hour until cake tester inserted in center comes out clean.

5. Cool bread in pan on wire rack 10 minutes. Loosen around edge, turn out on rack, and cool completely before slicing.

Zucchini Bread

Makes a 9 × 5 × 3-inch Loaf

✳

A DELICIOUSLY moist, full-flavored bread that became popular in the '60s and remains so today. It's a splendid way to cope with a summer gusher of zucchini because the bread freezes so well. This particular recipe comes from Mrs. Russell Harris of McLean County, Illinois, one of the natural-born cooks I interviewed in the early '70s for a series of articles I was writing for *Family Circle* magazine. This was my first encounter with zucchini bread but by no means my last. I have been offered zucchini bread recipes by cooks from all over the country but have yet to find a finer one.

NOTE: The best way to shred the zucchini is on the second coarsest side of a four-sided grater.

3 eggs
¾ cup vegetable oil
1½ cups sugar
2 cups peeled, moderately coarsely shredded zucchini (about 3 smallish zucchini)
1 teaspoon grated lemon zest
½ teaspoon vanilla extract
½ teaspoon orange extract
3 cups sifted all-purpose flour
¾ teaspoon salt
½ teaspoon ground cinnamon
¼ teaspoon ground ginger
2 teaspoons baking powder
1 teaspoon baking soda
½ cup chopped pecans

1. Preheat oven to 350° F. Grease and flour 9 × 5 × 3-inch loaf pan well; set aside.

2. Beat eggs at medium speed in large electric mixer bowl until foamy. Add oil slowly, beating all the while. Add sugar and beat at high speed until creamy and light. Stir in zucchini, lemon zest, vanilla and orange extracts.

3. Mix flour with salt, cinnamon, ginger, baking powder, and soda, then stir into batter, 1 cup at a time, beating only enough to combine. Fold in pecans.

4. Spoon into pan, spreading to corners, and bake 1 hour until bread pulls from sides of pan and browns.

5. Cool bread in pan on wire rack 15 minutes, loosen around edge, and turn out on rack. Cool to room temperature before cutting.

TIMELINE

1960s
....
Chuck Williams turns a small Sonoma, California, hardware store into a high-end cookware store and launches the Williams-Sonoma chain.

1960
....
Salton's electric Hotray becomes the "hot" appliance.

1961
....
Mastering the Art of French Cooking, by Julia Child, Simone Beck, and Louisette Berthold, is published.

....
"Fluffernutter" joins the lexicon of American food terms. Only the name, however, is new. Coined by an ad agency, it refers to that old New England lunchbox staple, the peanut butter and marshmallow fluff sandwich.

....
The New York Times Cook Book, edited by Craig Claiborne, rolls off the press.

Processor Parmesan Bread

Makes a 9×9×2-inch Loaf

✱

IN THE early '80s, when I was putting my new food processor through its paces, I developed this version of a favorite family quick bread. Use Parmigiano-Reggiano for this recipe, chunk, and whiz in food processor until uniformly fine. For 1 cup freshly grated Parmesan, you'll need about 5 ounces.

> 1½ cups sifted all-purpose flour
> 1 cup unsifted whole-wheat flour
> 3 teaspoons baking powder
> 1 teaspoon baking soda
> 2 tablespoons sugar
> 1½ teaspoons dried leaf marjoram, crumbled
> ½ teaspoon dried leaf rosemary, crumbled
> ½ teaspoon salt
> ½ teaspoon black pepper
> ¾ cup (1½ sticks) cold butter, cut into pats
> 1 cup freshly grated Parmesan cheese
> 1 cup buttermilk
> 2 eggs

1. Preheat oven to 400° F. Lightly grease 9×9×2-inch pan; set aside.

2. Pulse the two flours, baking powder, soda, sugar, marjoram, rosemary, salt, and pepper in food processor fitted with metal chopping blade several times to combine. Add butter and pulse until uni-formly crumbly and texture of coarse meal. Add Parmesan and pulse three to four times. Transfer to large bowl and make well in center.

3. Churn buttermilk and eggs in processor until foamy, pour into well in dry ingredients, and stir only enough to make a stiff dough.

4. Spoon into pan, spreading to corners, and bake 25 to 30 minutes, until springy to touch and toothpick inserted in center comes out clean.

5. Cool 10 minutes in pan on wire rack. Cut into squares and serve warm.

Peanut Butter Bread

Makes a 9×5×3-inch Loaf

✱

I'VE ALWAYS liked this recipe, which my mother adapted from one in *The Velvet Blend Book,* a Carnation leaflet published in 1946.

> 2 cups all-purpose flour
> ⅓ cup sugar
> 3 teaspoons baking powder
> 1 teaspoon salt
> ⅛ teaspoon ground hot red pepper (cayenne)
> ¾ cup firmly packed creamy peanut butter
> ¼ cup vegetable oil
> 1 egg
> ¾ cup evaporated milk blended with ½ cup water

1. Preheat oven to 350° F. Grease 9×5×3-inch loaf pan well; set aside.

2. Sift flour, sugar, baking powder, salt, and cayenne into large bowl. Cut in peanut butter with pastry blender until crumbly. Make well in center.

3. Whisk oil, egg, and milk mixture in small bowl; pour into well and mix thoroughly.

4. Turn batter into pan, smoothing to corners, and bake for about 50 to 60 minutes until nicely browned and springy to touch.

5. Cool loaf in pan on wire rack 10 minutes. Loosen bread around edges of pan, turn out on rack, and cool to room temperature before slicing.

Lemon-Granola Quick Bread

Makes a 9×5×3-inch Loaf

✱

SOME LEMON breads are nothing more than cake. Not this one made with whole-wheat flour and granola, adapted from Sunkist's *Cooking with Sunshine* (1986).

STREUSEL TOPPING
> 1 tablespoon all-purpose flour
> 1 tablespoon sugar
> 1½ teaspoons butter or margarine, softened
> 2 tablespoons granola
> Finely grated zest of ½ medium lemon

BREAD

1 cup sugar
1 cup sifted all-purpose flour
¾ cup unsifted whole-wheat flour
3 teaspoons baking powder
½ teaspoon salt
⅓ cup butter or margarine, melted
2 eggs, slightly beaten
½ cup water
Finely grated zest of 1 medium lemon
3 tablespoons fresh lemon juice
1 cup granola

1. STREUSEL: In small bowl, fork together flour, sugar, and butter; stir in granola and lemon zest; set aside.

2. BREAD: Preheat oven to 350° F. Grease and flour 9 × 5 × 3-inch loaf pan well; set aside.

3. Mix sugar, all-purpose and whole-wheat flours, baking powder, and salt in large bowl; make well in center.

4. Mix melted butter, eggs, water, lemon zest and juice in small bowl. Dump into well in dry ingredients and stir quickly just until dry ingredients are moistened. Mix in granola.

5. Turn batter into pan, spreading to corners. Sprinkle Streusel evenly on top. Bake 45 minutes, until toothpick inserted in center comes out clean.

6. Cool bread in pan on wire rack 10 minutes. Carefully loosen around edge, turn out on rack, and cool completely before cutting.

SCIENCE'S MOST THRILLING FOOD INVENTION!

Makes Anybody a Perfect Biscuit Maker!

1. NO MUSSING! — Add water or milk . . . Nothing else!

2. NO TROUBLE! — Put in oven . . . And . . .

3. NO FAILURES! — Have your husband say "Great!"

Ready For Oven in 90 Seconds!

Simply Add Water or Milk to Bisquick

To Have Biscuits Your Husband Will Say Are Better Than The Ones His Mother Used To Make!

Jalapeño Corn Bread

Makes a 9 × 9 × 2-inch Loaf

✳

THERE ARE jalapeño corn breads and jalapeño corn breads, but this one is as good as it gets. The recipe comes from *Quaker's Best Corn Meal Recipes* and is used courtesy of The Quaker Oats Company.

1¼ cups enriched cornmeal
¾ cup sifted all-purpose flour
4 teaspoons baking powder
1 tablespoon sugar (optional)
1 teaspoon salt
1 cup shredded Cheddar or Monterey Jack cheese
1 cup sour cream
1 cup cooked or canned whole-kernel corn, well drained
1 (4-ounce) can chopped green chilies, well drained
2 eggs, well beaten
2 tablespoons vegetable oil

1. Preheat oven to 400° F. Grease 9 × 9 × 2-inch pan well; set aside.

2. Mix cornmeal, flour, baking powder, sugar if desired, and salt in large bowl; make well in center.

3. Mix cheese, sour cream, corn, chilies, eggs, and vegetable oil in medium bowl. Dump into well in dry ingredients and mix only enough to blend.

4. Spoon batter into pan, spreading to corners, and bake 35 to 40 minutes until golden brown. Serve hot or at room temperature.

MUFFINS

WOMEN WERE making muffins well before the twentieth century, it's true. But these varied mainly according to the type of flour used —white, graham (whole-wheat), rye, corn. Sometimes a handful of chopped dates and/or raisins would be added, in which case the muffins became "Fruit Gems." Or perhaps a cup of cold leftover rice might be added to the batter. For the most part, however, muffins remained basic—plain—until well into the twentieth century.

For years we had a fairly set repertoire of muffins: bran, blueberry, corn, date, apple, oatmeal, and such. Then in the '70s and '80s, muffin madness set in. Muffins exploded to three or four times their normal size. They were made of pumpkin, zucchini, carrots, applesauce, even chocolate. They were strewn with chocolate chips, crowned with streusel or flavored sugars. They were glazed, they were frosted. And they were freighted with fat and calories. "Muffin" had become a euphemism for "cupcake."

In the pages that follow, I include only the more interesting—and successful—twentieth-century muffins.

The Best Bran Muffins

Makes about 1 Dozen

✳

KELLOGG'S, a cereal company begun as an offshoot of the Seventh Day Adventist Battle Creek Sanitarium run by vegetarian Dr. John Harvey Kellogg, believed early on in the value of whole grains. It was in 1894 that Kellogg and his brother W. K. invented flaked cereal. Quite by accident. To make the "San's" tasteless, tooth-bustingly-hard bread more palatable, they'd begun cooking wheatberries and forcing them through steel rollers into long sheets of dough. Called away one day before they could roll their last batch, the brothers fed the wheat grains into the rollers the next day and—presto—flakes. Once toasted, these were light, crisp and so good that "San" patients began ordering supplies to eat at home. Next came corn flakes, and W. K.'s defection to found the Battle Creek Toasted Corn Flake Company. The year was 1906. Ten years later, Kellogg introduced All-Bran cereal, which remains popular both as a breakfast cereal and as a recipe ingredient.

1¼ cups sifted all-purpose flour
½ cup sugar
3 teaspoons baking powder
¼ teaspoon salt
2 cups wheat bran cereal (not flakes)
1¼ cups milk
1 egg
¼ cup vegetable oil

1. Preheat oven to 400° F. Grease 12 (2 ½-inch) muffin-pan cups and set aside.

2. Sift flour, sugar, baking powder, and salt together onto wax paper and set aside.

3. Mix cereal and milk n large mixing bowl and let stand 5 minutes until cereal softens. Add egg and oil and beat well.

4. Add sifted dry ingredients and stir only enough to combine. Batter should be lumpy.

5. Divide batter evenly among muffin-pan cups and bake 20 minutes until lightly browned and springy to the touch. Serve warm.

Sweet Apple Muffins

Makes 1 Dozen

✳

TWO OF the most innovative, most dedicated food writers/chefs I know are Sandy Gluck and Richard Sax, who collaborated on a wonderful cookbook called *From the Farmer's Market* (1986). If you can find a copy, grab it! These heavenly muffins are from that book. Sandy and Richard like them "warm, with sweet butter and apple cider jelly."

MUFFINS

2¼ cups sifted all-purpose flour
¾ cup sugar
2 teaspoons baking powder
1 teaspoon baking soda
¾ teaspoon salt
1 egg
1 egg yolk
¾ cup buttermilk
⅜ cup vegetable oil
1½ cups moderately coarsely grated peeled apples (about 2 medium)

TOPPING

2 teaspoons sugar mixed with ¼ teaspoon ground cinnamon

1. Preheat oven to 400° F. Grease 12 (2½-inch) muffin-pan cups well; set pan aside.

2. Sift flour, sugar, baking powder, soda, and salt into large bowl; make well in center.

3. Whisk together egg, egg yolk, buttermilk, and oil in medium bowl until well blended. Stir in apples.

4. Dump apple mixture into well in dry ingredients and stir only enough to moisten.

5. Divide batter among muffin-pan cups and sprinkle with topping.

6. Bake muffins about 25 minutes until puffed and golden. Serve warm.

Low-Fat Blueberry Corn Muffins

Makes 1½ Dozen

✳

THE BLUEBERRY muffins familiar to most of us are cakelike and not particularly nutritious. These from the North American Blueberry Council in Folsom, California, made with cornmeal and whole-wheat flour, are low in fat (only 3.3 grams per muffin) and calories (a mere 138 per muffin).

>1½ cups sifted all-purpose flour
>½ cup unsifted whole-wheat flour
>½ cup cornmeal
>¾ cup sugar
>2½ teaspoons baking powder
>½ teaspoon baking soda
>½ teaspoon salt
>½ cup buttermilk
>½ cup fresh orange juice
>¼ cup (½ stick) butter or margarine, melted
>1 egg, well beaten
>1 tablespoon finely grated orange zest
>2 cups fresh blueberries

1. Preheat oven to 400° F. Grease 18 (2½-inch) muffin-pan cups well; set pans aside.

2. Mix all-purpose and whole-wheat flours, cornmeal, sugar, baking powder, soda, and salt in large bowl; make well in center.

3. Whisk together buttermilk, orange juice, melted butter, egg, and

orange zest in small bowl. Dump into well in dry ingredients and stir only enough to moisten. Fold in blueberries.

4. Divide batter among muffin-pan cups and bake 20 to 25 minutes until toothpick inserted in center of muffin comes out clean. Serve hot.

Grant Corner Inn Fresh Pear Muffins

Makes about 1½ Dozen

✳

AMERICAN B & Bs have done much to glorify muffins and none more so than the Grant Corner Inn of Santa Fe, New Mexico. Its breakfasts are so bountiful townspeople flock in for the morning feast. Among the popular muffins in innkeeper Louise Stewart's repertoire

are this one and the one that follows, both adapted from her *Grant Corner Inn Breakfast & Brunch Cookbook* (1986). For details on ordering, write the Grant Corner Inn, 122 Grant Avenue, Santa Fe, NM 87501.

>3 cups sifted all-purpose flour
>3 teaspoons baking powder
>⅛ teaspoon baking soda
>½ teaspoon salt
>½ cup (1 stick) butter
>1¼ cups sugar
>2 eggs
>¼ cup fresh lemon juice
>¾ cup bottled pear nectar
>1½ teaspoons vanilla extract
>2 ripe medium pears, peeled, cored, and coarsely chopped
>3 tablespoons sugar (for topping)

1. Preheat oven to 400° F. Line 18 (2½-inch) muffin-pan cups with crinkly paper cups; set pans aside.

2. Sift flour, baking powder, soda, and salt onto wax paper; set aside.

3. Cream butter and sugar in medium bowl until light; beat in eggs.

4. Mix lemon juice, pear nectar, and vanilla in large measuring cup. Add to creamed mixture alternately with dry ingredients, beginning and ending with dry. Fold in pears.

5. Divide batter among muffin-pan cups and sprinkle each muffin with sugar.

6. Bake about 20 minutes until lightly browned and springy to the touch. Serve hot.

Grant Corner Inn Carrot Muffins

Makes about 2 Dozen

✳

INNKEEPER LOUISE Stewart says that of all the hot breads she serves at her Grant Corner Inn in Santa Fe, these cake-rich muffins are the most popular. I've halved the original recipe and added a quick processor variation.

2 cups sifted all-purpose flour
¾ cup granulated sugar
2 teaspoons baking soda
2 teaspoons ground cinnamon
½ teaspoon ground mace
½ teaspoon salt
½ cup firmly packed light brown sugar
1½ cups finely grated carrots (about 3 medium)
½ cup golden seedless raisins
1 (8-ounce) can crushed pineapple, with juice
3 eggs, well beaten
½ cup vegetable oil
2 teaspoons vanilla extract

1. Preheat oven to 350° F. Grease 24 (2½-inch) muffin-pan cups well or line with crinkly paper cups; set pans aside.

2. Sift flour, granulated sugar, soda, cinnamon, mace, and salt into large bowl; work in brown sugar until uniformly fine. Add carrots and raisins, tossing well to dredge; make well in center.

3. Mix pineapple, eggs, vegetable oil, and vanilla in medium bowl. Dump into well in dry ingredients and stir only enough to blend.

4. Divide batter among muffin-pan cups and bake about 20 minutes until golden and springy to touch.

5. Cool muffins in pans at least 10 minutes before removing. Serve warm.

──────── VARIATION ────────

QUICK PROCESSOR CARROT MUFFINS: Pulse flour, granulated sugar, soda, cinnamon, mace, salt, and brown sugar in food processor fitted with metal chopping blade 10 to 15 times until uniformly fine; empty into large bowl. Add raisins and toss well to dredge; make well in center. Peel and chunk carrots, then process until fairly finely grated. Add pineapple, unbeaten eggs, oil, and vanilla and pulse several times to combine. Dump into well in dry ingredients, stir just enough to combine, then bake as directed above. Makes about 2 dozen.

- - - - - - - - - - - - - - - - -

Carrot-Oatmeal Muffins

Makes 1 Dozen

✳

THESE MUFFINS from the kitchens of Quaker Oats are less cake-like, more wholesome than the Grant Corner Inn Carrot Muffins, which precede. Especially if you omit the optional glaze.

MUFFINS
1⅓ cups sifted all-purpose flour
1 cup rolled oats (quick-cooking or old-fashioned)
¾ cup finely grated carrot (about 1 large)
½ cup seedless raisins
½ cup firmly packed brown sugar (light or dark)
3 teaspoons baking powder
½ teaspoon baking soda
1 teaspoon ground cinnamon
½ cup skim or low-fat milk
2 egg whites, lightly beaten
⅓ cup butter or margarine, melted
1 teaspoon vanilla extract

OPTIONAL GLAZE
½ cup confectioners' (10X) sugar mixed with 1 tablespoon skim or low-fat milk

1. Preheat oven to 375° F. Coat 12 (2½-inch) muffin-pan cups well with nonfat cooking spray; set pan aside.

2. Mix flour, oats, carrot, raisins, brown sugar, baking powder, soda, and cinnamon in large bowl; make well in center.

3. Whisk milk with egg whites, melted butter, and vanilla in second bowl. Dump into well in dry ingredients and mix only enough to moisten.

4. Divide batter among muffin-pan cups and bake about 25 minutes until golden and springy to touch.

5. If desired, drizzle muffins with glaze. Serve warm.

Spicy Pumpkin Muffins

Makes 1 Dozen

❋

GOLDEN OF hue, tender of crumb, aromatic of cinnamon and ginger. That's the way to describe these muffins from the Minneapolis test kitchens of Land O Lakes. The recipe was adapted from one in *Land O Lakes Treasury of Country Recipes,* a lavishly illustrated cookbook published in 1992.

2 cups sifted all-purpose flour
⅔ cup firmly packed brown
  sugar (light or dark)
⅓ cup granulated sugar
3 teaspoons baking powder
¼ teaspoon baking soda
1 teaspoon salt
1 teaspoon ground cinnamon
¼ teaspoon ground ginger
½ cup (1 stick) butter or
  margarine, melted
½ cup pureed cooked pumpkin
  or canned solid-pack
  pumpkin (not *pumpkin pie
  mix*)

⅓ cup buttermilk
2 eggs, lightly beaten

1. Preheat oven to 400°F. Grease 12 (2½-inch) muffin-pan cups well; set pan aside.

2. Mix flour, brown and granulated sugars, baking powder, soda, salt, cinnamon, and ginger in large bowl; make well in center.

3. Whisk melted butter in medium bowl with pumpkin, buttermilk, and eggs. Dump into well in dry ingredients and stir only enough to moisten.

4. Divide batter among muffin-pan cups and bake about 20 minutes, until golden and springy to touch.

5. Cool muffins in pan 5 minutes before removing. Serve warm.

Corn Kernel Muffins

Makes 12 to 14

❋

THESE UNUSUAL muffins were created by my friends Sandy Gluck and Richard Sax for their wonderful cookbook, *From the Farmer's Market.* This recipe is an adaptation.

1 cup unsifted all-purpose flour
3 teaspoons baking powder
1 teaspoon salt
½ teaspoon baking soda
½ teaspoon sugar
Pinch ground hot red pepper
  (cayenne)

1 cup cornmeal, preferably
   stone ground
2 eggs, lightly beaten
1¼ cups buttermilk
¼ cup (½ stick) butter or
   margarine, melted
1 cup fresh sweet corn kernels
   and milky pulp (about 2 ears)
⅓ cup grated sharp Cheddar
   cheese

1. Preheat oven to 425°F. Grease 14 (2½-inch) muffin-pan cups well; set pan aside.

2. Sift flour, baking powder, salt, soda, sugar, and cayenne into large bowl; stir in cornmeal and set aside.

3. Whisk eggs and buttermilk in second bowl until well blended; mix in melted butter and corn. Add to dry ingredients and stir only enough to moisten.

4. Divide batter among muffin-pan cups and sprinkle each muffin with cheese.

5. Bake muffins until golden brown and toothpick inserted in center of muffin comes out clean—about 25 minutes. Serve hot and don't stint on butter.

Bacon-and-Egg Muffins

Makes 1 Dozen

✳

FEW MUFFINS are more unusual —or delicious—than these adapted from White Lily's 100th anniversary cookbook, *Great Baking Begins with*
White Lily Flour (1982). They are a particular favorite "down South," as indeed is White Lily flour.

NOTE: To make with self-rising flour, omit baking powder and salt.

2 cups sifted all-purpose flour
2 tablespoons sugar
4 teaspoons baking powder
1 teaspoon dry mustard
½ teaspoon salt
¾ cup coarsely shredded sharp
   American or Cheddar cheese
1 egg, well beaten
¾ cup milk
¼ cup vegetable oil
2 hard-cooked eggs, peeled and
   coarsely chopped
4 slices bacon, crisply cooked,
   drained, and crumbled

1. Preheat oven to 400°F. Grease 12 (2½-inch) muffin-pan cups well; set pan aside.

2. Stir flour with sugar, baking powder, mustard, salt, and cheese in large bowl; make well in center.

3. Whisk egg, milk, and oil lightly in large measuring cup. Dump into well in dry ingredients and stir only enough to moisten.

4. Fill each muffin-pan cup one-third of the way with batter. Quickly mix hard-cooked egg and bacon and sprinkle into partially filled muffin-pan cups, dividing amount evenly. Top with remaining batter, again dividing evenly.

5. Bake about 20 minutes until golden and springy to touch. Serve warm.

TIMELINE

1961

Starkist launches its "Charlie the Tuna" commercials on network television, and the fish who wasn't good enough to become a Starkist tuna quickly becomes a beloved media icon. In addition, "Sorry, Charlie!" enters our vocabulary.

1962

Doubleday founds the Cook Book Guild.

The Kiwifruit arrives.

The French Chef Cookbook
Julia Child

1963

"The French Chef" with Julia Child comes to public television.

Weight Watchers is founded by Queens house-wife and former fattie Jean Nidetch together with Albert Lippert.

General Electric develops a self-cleaning oven.

Cheese Biscuits

Makes about 10

✳

BISCUITS HAVE been made in this country since Colonial days. But cheese biscuits, I believe, are a twentieth-century innovation. After hours of rummaging through late-nineteenth- and early-twentieth-century cookbooks looking for cheese biscuits, I finally turned up a recipe in the 1923 edition of "Fannie Farmer." It follows a recipe for —of all things—Sardine Biscuits, and contains ½ cup grated cheese. But given the proportion of shortening to flour—½ tablespoon each lard and butter to 1 cup bread flour —Fannie's biscuits could not have been very flaky. The recipe below is one I grew up on and if properly made, these biscuits will be light.

> 2 cups sifted all-purpose flour
> 4 teaspoons baking powder
> ¾ teaspoon salt
> ½ cup vegetable shortening
> 1 cup coarsely shredded sharp
>   Cheddar cheese
> ¾ cup milk

1. Preheat oven to 425° F. Sift flour, baking powder, and salt into large bowl.

2. Using pastry blender or two knives, cut in shortening until texture of peas. Add Cheddar and cut in until texture of coarse oatmeal.

3. Stir in milk, using fork, and mix lightly only until dough holds together.

4. Roll dough to thickness of 1 inch on lightly floured pastry cloth using lightly floured, stockinette-covered rolling pin.

5. With floured 2½- to 3-inch biscuit cutter, cut into rounds and place on ungreased baking sheet. Reroll and cut scraps.

6. Bake 10 to 12 minutes until puffy and golden brown. Serve hot.

Sticky Biscuits

Makes 9

✳

AS A child, I adored sticky buns. Rather than make yeast dough every time, my mother came up with this quick biscuit version.

GLAZE
> ¼ cup (½ stick) butter or
>   margarine
> ½ cup water or fresh orange
>   juice
> ½ cup firmly packed light
>   brown sugar
> 1 tablespoon finely grated
>   orange zest (optional)

BISCUITS
> 2 cups sifted all-purpose flour
> 3 teaspoons baking powder
> ½ teaspoon salt
> ¼ cup vegetable oil or butter or
>   margarine, melted
> ¾ cup milk

FILLING
> ¼ cup firmly packed light
>   brown sugar
> ½ teaspoon ground cinnamon
> ¼ teaspoon ground allspice

1. GLAZE: Grease 8 × 8 × 2-inch baking pan; set pan aside. Boil all glaze ingredients 2 minutes in small heavy saucepan. Spoon into pan and let stand while you prepare biscuits.

2. BISCUITS: Preheat oven to 450° F. Sift flour, baking powder, and salt into large bowl; make well in center. Combine oil and milk, dump into well in dry ingredients, and stir only enough to mix.

3. Roll dough into an 18 × 10-inch rectangle on lightly floured pastry cloth with lightly floured, stockinette-covered rolling pin.

4. FILLING: Mix brown sugar, cinnamon, and allspice; sprinkle evenly over biscuit dough.

5. Starting from a short side, roll up dough jelly-roll style so you have a log 18 inches long. Slice into 9 biscuits 2 inches thick.

6. Place biscuits cut-side-down in three rows in glaze in pan and bake 20 to 25 minutes until puffed and golden brown.

7. Invert pan at once on large platter so glaze runs down over biscuits. Serve hot.

Garlic Bread

Makes 6 Servings

✳

IN *AMERICAN Cooking* (1968), Dale Brown says that garlic bread is "a purely American invention." I remember its being served with ceremony at '50s dinner parties and always assumed it was a '50s innovation. Not so. In *Edith Barber's Cook Book* (1940), I find this recipe: *Slice French bread diagonally almost through loaf. Soften ½ cup butter, add 1 clove garlic, and let stand 15 minutes. Remove garlic, spread butter between slices, and bake in a moderately hot oven (400° F) about 5 minutes, until loaf is thoroughly heated. Serve hot with cheese platter or with salad course.*

Today we like a more garlicky bread. And we're more likely to serve it with the main course. Here's my recipe.

> 1 (10-ounce) long loaf French bread
> ½ cup (1 stick) butter or margarine, softened, or ½ cup fruity olive oil
> 1 large clove garlic, peeled and crushed

1. Preheat oven to 350° F. Slice bread on diagonal down to but not through bottom crust, making each slice about 1½ inches thick.

2. Mix butter and garlic and spread on both sides of each slice.

3. Wrap loaf in heavy-duty aluminum foil and heat 20 to 30 minutes until blisteringly hot. Unwrap and serve.

——— VARIATION ———
GARLIC-HERB BREAD: Prepare as directed, but add ¼ teaspoon each crushed dried rosemary (or basil) and marjoram to garlic butter. Makes 6 servings.

THE HERO

HIS IS not a single sandwich but a broad category of them masquerading under a half-dozen different names. All, however, are crusty, chewy French or Italian loaves split and mounded with everything from meatballs to cold cuts (usually salami and provolone) to fried oysters to veal parmigiana to roast beef, vegetables, and gravy. Where you live determines not only what you call them but also, to some extent, what goes into them.

When, where did the hero originate? Some point to the "Muffuletta" of New Orleans, a round Italian loaf piled with salami, cheese, and olive salad. According to John Mariani (*The American Dictionary of Food and Drink,* Revised Edition, 1994), this Sicilian-style sandwich was dreamed up by Salvatore Lupo at the Central Grocery in 1906. On the other hand, it may have evolved from that city's Po'Boy, a 1920s creation of Benny and Clovis Martin. A streetcar strike was on at the time and the story goes that the Martin Brothers Grocery treated the strikers to Po'Boys—French loaves stuffed with meat and/or cheese and/or oysters and/or tomatoes and gravy. Philadelphians argue that the hero—or "Hoagie," as they call it—began at Emil's Restaurant in South Philadelphia (an Italian enclave) in the 1930s.

The *New York Herald Tribune*'s popular food writer Clementine Paddleford is credited with bestowing the name "hero" shortly after she joined the paper in 1936. Confronted with one of these monster sandwiches, she snorted, "You'd have to be a hero to eat it!"

During World War II, "Grinders," as New Englanders called heros (because of all the tooth-grinding needed to get them down), came to be known as "Submarines" in and around the navy sub base at Groton, Connecticut. Grocer Benedetto Capaldo made a specialty of these

whopping Italian sandwiches and it was he who rechristened them "Submarines." Heros go by other names, too. Upstate New Yorkers call them "Bombers," Chicagoans "Italian Sandwiches" or "Italian Meat Sandwiches," Miami's "Little Havanans" know them as "Cuban Sandwiches," and cookbooks, especially those of the '50s, cast all of these names aside in favor of "A-Meal-in-a-Sandwich."

SANDWICHES & SANDWICH SPREADS

BEFORE THE turn of the twentieth century, cookbooks either neglected sandwiches or dismissed them with a few sentences.

In *The Appledore Cook Book* (1872), Maria Parloa lumps them together at the back of the book under "Miscellaneous Receipts." This is all she has to say on the subject of sandwiches:

Take the pieces of ham which are left on the bone after all the slices are cut off and chop rather fine. Cut bread into thin slices (the milk yeast is the best for this) and butter. Now spread with the ham, and lay another buttered slice over this. Trim the edges. This is a very nice dish for evening parties or picnics. Fold them in a damp towel until they are sent to the table. They may be made by putting slices of cold ham, tongue, beef, or chicken between slices of buttered bread.

Mrs. Lincoln's Boston Cook Book (1883) makes no mention of sandwiches. Nor does *Mrs. Rorer's Philadelphia Cook Book* (1886). And *Mrs. Rorer's New Cook Book* (1902) barely does any better:

Where salads are to be served for evening affairs, or wedding collations as the main course, pass them with appropriate sandwiches. Brown bread sandwiches are especially adapted to fish salads, cold fish with mayonnaise dressing, or lobster or crab salads. Serve nasturtium and caper sandwiches with mutton salad, nut sandwiches with chicken salad, chopped cress or parsley sandwiches with beef salad.

The first bonafide sandwich chapter I've found appears in *The Original Boston Cooking-School Cook Book* (1896) by Fannie Merritt Farmer. But Fannie's idea of a sandwich and ours are light-years apart. Among her recipes: Lettuce Sandwiches, Sardine

Sandwiches, Anchovy Sandwiches, Oyster Sandwiches, Nut and Cheese Sandwiches, Ginger Sandwiches (for which thinly sliced crystallized ginger is served between slices of bread), Fruit Sandwiches, and Brown Bread Sandwiches (layers of finely chopped peanuts or grated cheese and chopped English walnuts sandwiched together with slices of Boston Steamed Brown Bread). She also introduces several sandwiches still popular today: ham, ham salad, egg salad, chicken salad, lobster salad. I find her sandwich-making instructions quaint:

ROLLED BREAD

Cut fresh bread, while still warm, in as thin slices as possible, using a very sharp knife. Spread evenly with butter which has been creamed. Roll slices separately, and tie each with baby ribbon.

BREAD AND BUTTER FOLDS

Remove end slice from bread. Spread end of loaf sparingly and evenly with butter which has been creamed. Cut off as thin a slice as possible. Repeat until the number of slices required are prepared. Remove crusts, put together in pairs, cut in squares, oblongs, or triangles. Use white, entire wheat, Graham, or brown bread.

In early 1900s cookbooks, sandwich spreads run to dried fruit pastes with date and fig being particular favorites. There is plenty of Neufchâtel (cream cheese), no shortage of minced nuts and olives. For the most part, early-twentieth-century sandwiches were dainty, one favorite being a buttered thin slice of bread twirled up around a canned asparagus spear tied with a strip of canned pimiento.

For me, one of the more interesting early sandwich

chapters is that in *Mrs. Allen's Cook Book* (1917). Ida Bailey Allen begins by saying:

Sandwiches deserve to be more generally used than as mere adjuncts to the luncheon or picnic basket or accessories to afternoon tea. Made of wholesome bread, spread with delicious butter, and filled with savory meat, cheese or nuts, the sandwich affords a perfectly balanced meal in itself.

To this end sandwiches may be divided into four classes:

First: The open sandwich or canapé, which has been treated in the chapter on Appetizers.

Second: Substantial luncheon or supper sandwiches, such as Club Sandwiches.

Third: A dainty sandwich, containing only a bite or two, used at teas and receptions.

Fourth: The sweet sandwich, which is sometimes used as a dessert substitute.

Although sweet sandwiches and fancy tea sandwiches (checkerboards, pinwheels, ribbons, etc.) became the pride of hostesses during the first third of this century (and remain so in some quarters today), more robust sandwiches began to earn equal time in the second and third decades of this century. By the late 1930s, lunch counters were offering "Dagwoods," towering affairs named after Chic Young's cartoon character, Dagwood Bumstead, who loved to raid the refrigerator and concoct just such sandwiches.

But I'm getting ahead of myself. The list of sand-

wiches in the 1923 edition of "Fannie Farmer" includes club sandwiches, just then going mainstream. In *The Food Chronology* (1995), James Trager says the club sandwich may have been created in 1894 at the Saratoga Club in Saratoga Springs, New York, or perhaps "in the club car of a U.S. passenger train."

In this same 1923 edition, Fannie Farmer also offers Toasted Mushroom Sandwiches, Dream Sandwiches (a clear precursor of Cheese Dreams), Chicken Cream Sandwiches (a cold chicken mousse sandwich), Royal Sandwiches (filled with a forcemeat of shrimp, chicken livers, and onion), Penobscot Sandwiches (salmon salad), even Jelly Sandwiches, which get a topping of finely chopped English walnuts.

Are they the forerunners of today's peanut butter and jelly sandwiches? Perhaps, only Fannie specifies quince jelly in one recipe and currant jelly in another. As any 1990s connoisseur of peanut butter and jelly sandwiches knows, the only acceptable jelly is grape (the persnickety insist upon Welch's).

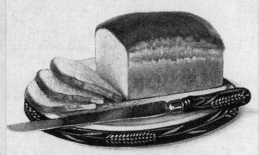

BREADS

WHOLE WHEAT BREAD

1 cupful Borden's Evaporated Milk	2 teaspoonfuls salt
1 cupful hot water	½ compressed yeast cake
2 tablespoonfuls sugar, or	¾ cupful tepid water
1½ tablespoonfuls molasses	2 cupfuls white flour
4 cupfuls entire wheat flour, approximately	

Scald the milk and water together, then cool it till tepid and stir in the sweetening, salt and yeast dissolved in the tepid water. Beat in the white flour and then the entire wheat flour to knead, about four cupfuls. Knead until elastic then set to rise, first brushing the mixture over with tepid water, and taking care to cover it well so that it will be kept at room heat. When double in bulk, cut down and shape into two loaves and transfer to oiled pans. Again set to rise and when nearly double in bulk bake in a moderately hot oven, allowing the temperature to increase gradually until the bread is brown, and then finish baking with the heat reduced. When done brush over with butter.

6

Unfortunately, there is not space in a book of this size to include every twentieth-century sandwich known to man. I have focused upon the classics, then chosen others to round out the mix. Whenever a sandwich has an interesting history, I include it, together with the classic recipe. If a special favorite of yours is missing, I apologize, and can only say that I'd need another hundred pages to include them all.

Reuben Sandwich

Makes 1 Sandwich

❋

TO OMAHANS, this is the one, the only, the original Reuben. The recipe comes from Bernard Schimmel (son of Charles Schimmel who owned the Blackstone Hotel when the sandwich was created). *Omaha World-Herald* Food Editor Jane Palmer included it in her profile of the Reuben, which appeared in the paper on June 9, 1976.

NOTE: There's more dressing here than you'll need for the sandwich. Use the extra to dress salads.

THOUSAND ISLAND DRESSING

> *1 cup mayonnaise*
> *1 tablespoon chili sauce (or more to taste)*
> *½ cup sour cream*
> *1 teaspoon minced pimiento*
> *1 teaspoon minced scallion*
> *2 tablespoons minced green bell pepper*
> *2 hard-cooked eggs, peeled and chopped (optional)*

REUBEN

NOTHING MAKES an Omahan madder than to hear that the Reuben sandwich was invented in New York City. As every good Nebraskan knows, Reuben Kulakofsky, an owner of Omaha's late, lamented Central Market, created the Reuben back in the 1920s.

Here's the story: Reuben and his buddies used to meet regularly to play poker at Omaha's grand old hotel, the Blackstone. According to *Omaha World-Herald* Food Editor Jane Palmer, "Out of each pot, they'd save a nickel or a dime and, later in the day, they'd phone for a cold midnight lunch." What came were cold cuts, bread, condiments, etc., from which the players concocted their own sandwiches. The favorite, hands down, was Reuben Kulakofsky's creation. Blackstone owner Charles Schimmel, one of the "regulars," thought so much of this sandwich he put it on the hotel menu and called it a "Reuben."

So what's this about a New York Reuben? According to Michael and Ariane Batterberry (*On the Town in New York,* 1973), the Reuben was created by Arnold Reuben, owner of Reuben's, a deli that opened on East Fifty-eighth Street between Fifth and Madison in 1928. They add that Reuben's had begun eleven years

earlier "as a sandwich stand in Atlantic City." Even after its move to a posh New York location, the Batterberrys say "Reuben's laid no claim to being more than a delicatessen, and always had a sandwich counter at its entrance." For decades, it was where the theater crowd retreated late at night. Walter Winchell was a regular, Judy Garland, Ginger Rogers, Jackie Gleason, ZsaZsa Gabor.

To the infuriation of the citizens of Omaha, the myth of the New York Reuben persists—in newspaper columns, in books. For example, Craig Claiborne writes in *Craig Claiborne's The New York Times Food Encyclopedia* (1985) that Arnold Reuben's daughter Patricia R. Taylor says her father created the Reuben in 1914 for actress Annette

Seelos. If Claiborne's and the Batterberrys' dates are correct, that would mean that he concocted the sandwich *before* he set up shop in Atlantic City.

There's more to the Omaha Reuben story, too. In 1956, Fern Snider, a cook at the Blackstone, entered a quantity recipe for the Reuben in the first National Sandwich Idea Contest sponsored by the Wheat Flour Institute. It served forty-eight, took top honors, and won her a trip to New York. Did Mrs. Snider try the New York Reuben while she was in the Big Apple? If so, there's no record of it.

In 1976, twenty years after Fern Snider won the sandwich contest, *Omaha World-Herald* Food Editor Jane Palmer profiled the Reuben, interviewing Bernard Schimmel, son of the man who'd put the sandwich on the Blackstone Hotel menu in the late 1920s. She also included Schimmel's tips for making a perfect Reuben:

FOR THE DRESSING: Use homemade mayonnaise or buy Hellmann's and add one fresh egg yolk to each pint. It makes the mayonnaise silkier and cuts the oil.

ON THE SAUERKRAUT: Take out all the moisture you can and chill it. It should be nice and crisp. I have a paper towel under it to absorb moisture. I want it to be flavorful but not watered down.

THE CHEESE: The cheese is the genuine Emmenthaler, not because I was trained in Switzerland but because it has the flavor . . . You can use Wisconsin Swiss. I'm American and I love American products but when you want certain flavors, you want them.

ON THE CORNED BEEF: Buy kosher-style corned beef brisket as sold in Omaha. It has the right amount of fat to give the sandwich the flavor you want. It should be sliced thin and piled high. The thicker you slice this type of meat, the bulkier it gets and you lose the flavor.

BUTTER FOR GRILLING: Use melted butter and put it on with a brush. No matter how well you spread it (soft butter), it's going to be uneven.

ON GRILLING: An electric sandwich grill is preferred because it works like a waffle iron to provide equal heat and pressure to both sides. If a sandwich grill is not available, grill the sandwiches in a hot cast iron skillet, placing an empty saucepan atop the sandwich to retain the heat.

GARNISHES: Alongside the Reuben, Schimmel places a red cabbage leaf and tops it with radish roses that have the leaves attached, carrot curls and kosher dill pickles.

SANDWICH

2 slices dark rye bread
1 tablespoon butter, melted
2 thin slices Emmenthaler cheese
4 (or more) thin slices Kosher-style corned beef brisket
¼ cup chilled, drained sauerkraut
2 tablespoons Thousand Island Dressing (page 342)

1. DRESSING: Mix all ingredients in small bowl; set aside.

2. SANDWICH: Brush one side of each slice of bread with melted butter. Lay, unbuttered-sides-up, side by side on counter. Top each slice with cheese, then pile corned beef on one slice only.

3. Mix sauerkraut with dressing and spread on corned beef.

4. Put sandwich together and grill on both sides, pressing together with spatula, until cheese melts and sandwich is brown, about 2 minutes on each side. Serve at once.

UNDERWOOD DEVILED HAM

THE ORIGINAL Eggs Benedict dates back to 1894 when, it's said, a hungover Wall Streeter named Lemuel Benedict made his way along the buffet table at the newly opened Waldorf-Astoria (Fifth Avenue and Thirty-fourth Street), slapping bacon and poached eggs on buttered toast, then topping the lot with Hollandaise. Later, the Waldorf's formidable maître d'hôtel, Oscar Tschirky, fine-tuned the recipe, substituting English muffins for toast and Canadian bacon for ham.

A second legend attributes Eggs Benedict to Delmonico's and Ms. LeGrand Benedict, a regular there. Finding nothing to her liking one day, Mrs. Benedict huddled with the maître d'hôtel, who concocted the combo now known as Eggs Benedict.

Which story is true? No one knows. But by 1912 Eggs Benedict had become so famous Underwood Deviled Ham built an ad campaign around its own unorthodox version.

Tuna Melt

Makes 6 Sandwiches

✳

WHO CAME up with this broiled, cheese-topped open-face tuna salad sandwich? And when? The first recipe I could find for anything similar appears in Ida Bailey Allen's *Best Loved Recipes of the American People* (1973). "Tuna-Cheese Grilled Open Sandwich," she calls it. The catch here is that Ida Bailey Allen died in 1973. *Best Loved Recipes* is clearly a compilation of recipes gathered throughout her long career, which began early in the twentieth century. There are no dates on any of the recipes, or for that matter, any historical notes. My good friend cookbook author Sandy Gluck thinks Tuna Melt is a '60s or '70s creation and that the creator may have been a dormitory coed with a toaster-oven. Sandy says the first time she was asked to make a Tuna Melt was in the early 1980s when she was the chef at a restaurant in New York's Chelsea district. Tuna Melt recipes differ from cook to cook because tuna salad recipes, themselves, vary. This one is fairly classic.

> 1 (10-ounce) can solid white tuna, drained and flaked
> ½ cup finely diced celery
> ¼ cup finely diced green bell pepper
> 2 tablespoons minced yellow onion
> 1 tablespoon small capers (optional)
> ½ cup mayonnaise

1 tablespoon fresh lemon juice
¼ teaspoon black pepper
6 slices toast
6 sandwich slices American
cheese

1. Preheat broiler. Mix together tuna, celery, green pepper, onion, capers, if desired, mayonnaise, lemon juice, and black pepper.

2. Spread smoothly on toast, dividing total amount evenly.

3. Top each sandwich with cheese slice, set about 5 inches from the heat, and broil 2 to 3 minutes, until cheese melts. Serve hot.

Lobster Rolls

Makes 6 Sandwiches

✻

BECAUSE THESE are made with hamburger buns, they are definitely twentieth century (soft, hamburger-size yeast buns were first manufactured in 1912). This recipe was given to me by a terrific Maine cook named Brownie Schrumpf.

3 cups cubed, cooked lobster
meat
2 tablespoons fresh lemon juice
½ cup finely diced celery
2 tablespoons finely grated
yellow onion
1 teaspoon salt
⅛ teaspoon ground hot red
pepper (cayenne)
½ cup mayonnaise
6 hamburger buns
6 tablespoons unsalted butter
6 crisp lettuce leaves

1. Mix lobster and lemon juice, cover, and refrigerate overnight.

2. Next day add celery, onion, salt, cayenne, and mayonnaise and toss well to mix; cover, and marinate several hours in refrigerator.

3. Spread hamburger buns well with butter, lay lettuce leaves on bottom halves, mound with chilled lobster salad, set bun tops in place, and serve.

Baked Bean Sandwich

Makes 6 Sandwiches

✻

CYNTHIA KELLOGG, with whom I worked at *The Ladies' Home Journal,* then again later at *Venture, The Traveler's World,* told me that these were the "Saturday night special" when she was growing up in Boston in the 1930s. In her words, "they were the traditional way to use up Friday's baked beans." Strange to say, there is no mention of baked bean

sandwiches in any edition I own of *The Boston Cooking-School Cook Book*—from the 1896 original right through 1946. Perhaps Fannie Farmer considered them too commonplace. Ida Bailey Allen didn't and includes this recipe for Baked-Bean Club Sandwich in *Mrs. Allen's Cook Book* (1917):

Toast and butter two slices of entire wheat, or white, bread, and on one of them place a lettuce leaf, covered with boiled salad dressing. Above the dressing spread a generous filling of cold baked beans, cover with a slice of tomato with boiled dressing; add another lettuce leaf, and replace the second slice of toast. Garnish with a bit of bacon and a lettuce leaf.

The recipe here is more classic.

12 thin slices Boston brown
bread
3 tablespoons butter,
margarine, or cream cheese,
softened
1 cup cold leftover (or canned)
baked beans, mashed
½ teaspoon salt
¼ teaspoon black pepper
Water or broth, as needed for
good spreading consistency

1. Spread brown bread slices on one side with butter; set aside.

2. Mix beans with salt, pepper, and enough water for good spreading consistency in small bowl.

3. Spread buttered sides of 6 slices brown bread with bean mixture, cover with remaining slices, spread sides down, and serve.

Louisville Hot Brown

Makes 4 Sandwiches

✳

In 1984, the Newspaper Food Editors and Writers Association, Inc. published a wonderful cookbook called *Food Editors' Hometown Favorites.* In it, Elaine Corn of *The Courier-Journal* of Louisville, Kentucky, writes about that city's most famous sandwich, the "Hot Brown." Legend has it, she says, that it was created in the 1920s by a chef at the Brown Hotel as a way to recycle roast turkey. "It was dubbed a Hot Brown. Today, there are many versions of the recipe. This one is the Brown's original, from the files of *The Courier-Journal*'s late food editor, Cissy Gregg." Unitalicized notations are Corn's.

4 tablespoons butter
1 small yellow onion, chopped
4 tablespoons all-purpose flour
2 cups milk
½ teaspoon salt
¼ teaspoon white pepper
¼ cup shredded Cheddar cheese
¼ cup grated Parmesan cheese
8 slices trimmed toast

Cooked turkey or chicken breast, thinly sliced (8 slices)
Crisp-fried bacon, crumbled (about 4 slices)
Mushroom slices, sautéed (about ¼ pound mushrooms)

1. Preheat broiler.

2. Melt butter in medium heavy saucepan over moderate heat; add onion and sauté about 3 minutes, until glassy. Blend in flour. Add milk, salt, and pepper and cook, whisking constantly, until thickened and smooth. Add Cheddar and Parmesan, remove from heat, and stir until melted.

3. Place one slice toast in each of four ovenproof individual serving dishes. Top each with two slices turkey. Halve remaining toast slices diagonally and bracket each sandwich with two halves.

4. Ladle cheese sauce over sandwiches, dividing equally, set 4 to 5 inches from the heat, and broil quickly until sauce begins to bubble and brown—2 to 3 minutes.

5. Garnish each portion with bacon crumbles and mushroom slices. Serve at once.

The California Club

Makes 4 Sandwiches

✳

The classic club belongs to the nineteenth century (in *The Food Chronology* [1995], James Trager sug-

PHILADELPHIA CHEESE-STEAK

IT BEGAN in the depths of the Depression, maybe 1930, maybe 1932. No one can say for sure. Pasquale ("Pat") Olivieri wasn't doing so well, not selling as many hot dogs as he'd like from his South Philadelphia pushcart.

Just when it seemed things couldn't get worse, they did. Pat's supplier goofed, sent him a chunk of beef one day instead of the usual order of hot dogs.

Pat sliced the beef thin, tossed it on his grill with some sliced onions, then piled the lot into a bun, intending to lunch on it himself.

But before he could take a bite, a cabbie stopped, lured by the smell of freshly browned beef and onions, and asked, "How much?"

"A nickel," Pat replied.

The next thing Pat knew, another cabbie came along and ordered the same thing. Word of Pat's terrific new steak-and-onion sandwich soon spread among Philadelphia cabbies, many of whom drove down to South Philly just to try it.

So where's the cheese? Some say it was added in the early '50s. It seems that Joe Lorenzo, who'd been working for Pat a lot of years, got bored with the same old routine and plunked a slice of American cheese on top of the frizzled steak and onions. It melted on impact, sending rivulets of gold into every nook and cranny.

From that day forward, Pat's sandwich became known as the Philadelphia Cheese-Steak, and everyone from Louis Armstrong to Humphrey Bogart came to try it.

You can get Philadelphia Cheese-Steaks nearly anywhere these days, but for the original, you must go to Pat's King of Steaks in South Philadelphia.

gests that it was created in 1894 at the Saratoga Club in Saratoga Springs, New York, although the first printed recipe I could find for it [*Woman's Favorite Cook Book,* 1902] attributes it to Gunther's in Chicago). But the *avocado* club *is* twentieth century. Some say it originated at the Monkey Bar in New York City. Others point to California. Its debut year is not known, although the fact that a Bacon and Avocado Sandwich appears in a 1932 Kitchen Cabinet reader's column in *Sunset* magazine may provide a clue (this one contains no turkey). An avocado club (*with* turkey) took top honors in the National Sandwich Idea Contest, launched in 1956, and is included in *Winning Sandwiches for Menu Makers* (1976). This recipe is from *Avocado Bravo* (1975), published by the California Avocado Advisory Board (now the California Avocado Commission).

½ cup mayonnaise
2 tablespoons chili sauce
12 slices toast
12 lettuce leaves
2 ripe medium California avocados, pitted, peeled, and sliced
1 large ripe tomato, thinly sliced
4 thin slices cooked turkey
½ pound bacon, crisply cooked
Salt and black pepper

1. Blend mayonnaise and chili sauce; spread on toast, one side only.

2. Top four toast slices with lettuce leaf and avocado, dividing amounts evenly. Add second toast slice and lettuce leaf, tomato, and turkey, then bacon, dividing amounts equally. Sprinkle lightly with salt and pepper.

3. Top with remaining lettuce and toast, arranging spread sides down.

4. Quarter each sandwich corner to corner; secure quarters with cocktail picks and serve.

HAMBURGERS

THEIR HISTORY is as controversial as it is long. The forerunner is believed to be Steak Tartare, which German sailors discovered while on leave in Russian ports in centuries past. They liked this Tartar raw beef specialty and carried the idea home to Hamburg where some enterprising chef shaped the minced beef into patties and grilled them. They soon became known as "Hamburg steak."

By most accounts, a turn-of-the-century American cook was the first to slap the grilled beef patties between two slices of bread. But opinions differ as to who that chef was. According to James Trager (*The Food Chronology*, 1995), the momentous event took place in New Haven, Connecticut, in 1900. He writes: "Louis Lassen grinds 7 cents/pound beef, broils it, and serves it between two slices of toast (no catsup or relish) to customers at his five-year-old, three-seat Louis Lunch."

Jane and Michael Stern expand upon Louis Lunch and its hamburger in *Roadfood* (1977): "The original hamburger 'à la Louis' is a patty of coarsely ground steak, broiled vertically in the ancient stoves ('So the grease drips away,' Louis III explains), and served on toast, with options of cheese, Bermuda onion, and tomato." The Sterns seem to agree that Louis Lassen originated the hamburger-as-sandwich.

Jeffrey Tennyson, however, cites two other possible beginnings in *Hamburger Heaven* (1993). The first takes place in 1885 at the Ouagamie County Fair in Wisconsin at a booth manned by teenager Charles Nagreen. According to Tennyson, fair-goers like his butter-fried ground beef patties but don't want to stand about eating. Nagreen slips the meat between two slices of bread so they can eat on the run and calls his new sandwich a "hamburger."

Tennyson introduces "the second coming" with an obit from the *Los Angeles Times* datelined Akron, Ohio, October 5, 1951. The headline: HAMBURGER INVENTOR DIES. That inventor was Frank Menches, who is said to have concocted the burger at the Summit County Fair in Akron in 1892. To quote the obit: "Menches nearly ran out of sausage. In an effort to please his customers, he ground up a sausage and sold it as a cooked, meat patty." The item goes on to say that "it was unexplainably named 'hamburger' about two years later."

In researching *Hamburger Heaven*, Tennyson apparently talked to Menches's great-granddaughter, Judy Kismits, who corrected the obit thus: "Frank and his brother Charles were well known for their popular pork sausage sandwiches, but the butcher had been unable to provide them with sausage that day, so he substituted ground beef as a last resort."

The obvious conclusion: No one can say for sure exactly when or where the first hamburger sandwich was served. Or by whom.

What nearly all food historians do agree upon, however, is that it was introduced to America at large at the St. Louis World's Fair in 1904. Judy Kismits says the vendor may have been her great-grandfather Frank Menches. But she gets a Texas-size "No way!" from the the great-grandchildren of Fletcher "Old Dave" Davis of Athens, Texas, who operated a sandwich stand on the fair's midway. His specialty: Mustard-swabbed, browned beef patties tucked into homemade bread with a slice of Bermuda onion.

By 1912 hamburgers had become so popular, hamburger buns were being baked on a commercial scale. And in 1921, White Castle opened its first stand in Wichita, Kansas, and began selling hamburgers at five cents apiece.

The rest, as they say, is history.

Sloppy Joes

Makes 4 Servings

✳

I REMEMBER eating these in the 1940s and suspect they may have been a way of stretching precious ground beef during World War II. Apparently not. My friend and colleague Jim Fobel tells me that in his own quest to trace the origin of the Sloppy Joe, he talked to Marilyn Brown, Director of the Consumer Test Kitchens at H.J. Heinz in Pittsburgh (the Heinz "Joe," not surprisingly, is reddened with ketchup). Brown says their research at the Carnegie Library suggests that the Sloppy Joe began in a Sioux City, Iowa, cafe as a "loose meat sandwich" in 1930, the creation of a cook named Joe. It may be so. Unfortunately, I have no idea where my mother got her recipe. The 1943 and 1946 editions of *Joy of Cooking* make no mention of Sloppy Joes, but a 1964 one does. And as far as I can tell, "Fannie Farmer" never acknowledges them. Jane and Michael Stern include Sloppy Joes in The Cuisine of Suburbia chapter of *Square Meals* (1984), which they, in turn, have adapted from a recipe in *The New Hamburger Cookbook* (1965). That book's headnote introduces Sloppy Joes by saying: "Being a mother who knows what to serve while the Beatles are bleating will mark you as 'cool' forever." These are the Sloppy Joes of my own not-so-cool youth.

1 pound ground beef chuck
1 medium yellow onion, peeled and chopped
1 clove garlic, peeled and crushed
1 (6-ounce) can tomato paste
1½ cups water or beef broth
¼ cup ketchup
1 tablespoon Worcestershire sauce
1 teaspoon salt
2 hamburger buns, split and toasted

1. Brown beef in large heavy skillet over moderate heat 2 to 3 minutes, breaking up clumps.

2. Add onion and garlic and cook, stirring often, about 5 minutes until limp. Mix in tomato paste, water, ketchup, Worcestershire sauce, and salt. Reduce heat to low and cook, stirring now and then, about 40 minutes until flavors mingle.

3. Place ½ hamburger bun on each of four plates and ladle meat sauce generously on top. Serve at once.

Western Sandwich

Makes 6 Sandwiches

✳

THE AMERICAN *Heritage Cookbook and Illustrated History of American Eating & Drinking* (1964) fixes the origin of this sandwich in Westward Ho days when pioneer women masked the flavor of over-the-hill eggs by mixing in plenty of onions. Of course those frontier women lacked some of the principal ingredients of the classic Western Sandwich—green and/or red bell peppers. Other food historians believe the sandwich may have originated with chuckwagon cooks, then been refined and embellished over the years. Whatever its origins, the Western Sandwich seems not to have made it into the pages of cookbooks—or onto the menus of restaurants—until well into the twentieth century. In the West, it's often called a "Denver."

6 eggs
⅓ cup milk
1½ cups finely diced boiled or baked ham
2 tablespoons minced yellow onion
2 tablespoons minced green bell pepper
2 tablespoons minced red bell pepper or pimiento
¾ teaspoon salt
¼ teaspoon ground hot red pepper (cayenne)
2 tablespoons butter or margarine
12 slices hot buttered toast

1. Beat eggs and milk until frothy; mix in ham, onion, green pepper, red pepper, salt, and cayenne.

2. Heat butter in heavy nonstick 9-inch square griddle over moderate heat until bubbly; add egg mixture, and fry about 2 minutes until set underneath.

3. Cut egg mixture into 6 pieces of uniform size, turn each over, and cook flip sides 1 to 2 minutes longer.

4. Slip each piece between 2 slices toast, halve diagonally, and serve.

Corn Dogs

Makes 10

✳

MY FIRST encounter with a corn dog occurred in the 1970s and was secondhand at that. Arthur Hettich, then editor-in-chief of *Family Circle,* came home from a trip out West and couldn't stop talking about this wonderful "new" food—a hot dog on a stick wrapped in corn bread. Art asked me if I had any idea how to make it. I didn't because corn dogs were new to me, too. What I didn't know was that they'd been popular west of the Mississippi for some time. According to a resource I find endlessly fascinating—John Mariani's *Dictionary of American Food and Drink,* Revised Edition (1994)—corn dogs were "perfected in 1942 by vaudevillians Neil and Carl Fletcher of Dallas." Mariani goes on to say that they were first sold at the State Fair of Texas as "Fletcher's Original State Fair Corny Dog." Today corn dogs are available everywhere, either straight from the deep-fat fryer of a fast-food franchise or in the frozen foods section of the supermarket. This recipe is adapted from one provided by The Quaker Oats Company.

> Vegetable oil (for deep frying)
> ½ cup unsifted all-purpose flour (for dredging)
> ⅔ cup yellow cornmeal
> ⅓ cup unsifted all-purpose flour
> 1 teaspoon salt
> ½ cup milk

1 egg, well beaten
2 tablespoons vegetable oil
10 ready-to-eat frankfurters (1 pound)
10 wooden skewers

1. Place oil in deep-fat fryer, insert deep-fat thermometer, and begin heating to 375° F. Place ½ cup dredging flour in pie pan; set aside.

2. Mix cornmeal, ⅓ cup flour, and salt in 2-cup glass measure. Add milk, egg, and 2 tablespoons vegetable oil. Mix well and set aside.

3. Thread frankfurters onto wooden skewers. Roll in dredging flour to coat, shaking off excess.

4. Dip frankfurters, one at a time, in cornmeal batter, then fry in 375° F oil until golden brown—about 2 to 3 minutes. Serve warm.

Cheese Dreams

Makes 6 Sandwiches

✳

THEIR ORIGIN, I feel fairly certain, is rooted in the cheese canapés of the late nineteenth and early twentieth centuries—grated cheese and cayenne pepper sprinkled on zephyrettes (thin, crisp crackers) or small rounds of bread, then run in and out of the oven just until bubbly. Cheese Dreams do not seem to have emerged full-blown, however, until the 1920s (the 1923 edition of *The Boston Cooking-School Cook Book* offers Dream Sandwiches—cheese sandwiches browned in butter). Cheese Dream recipes vary noticeably. Some call for shredding or creaming a good sharp Cheddar, mixing it with a spicy mustard and well-beaten egg, spreading on toast, then baking until puffed and brown. Sometimes strips of bacon are added. Although not called Cheese Dreams, this recipe from *Meals Tested, Tasted, and Approved* published by the Good Housekeeping Institute in 1930 is typical of that type:

> OPEN CHEESE
> SANDWICHES
> 1 roll snappy cheese
> ¼ teaspoonful salt
> 1 egg, well-beaten
> ¼ teaspoonful dry mustard
> 1 tablespoonful Worcestershire Sauce
> 12 slices bacon
> 12 rounds bread

Cream the cheese, add the egg and seasonings and spread on the bread which should be cut about ½ in. thick. Place a slice of bacon on each round and bake a few min. in a quick oven of 450°F till the bacon is done. Serve with a green salad.

For me, however, the only Cheese Dream will be the one my mother prepared for me whenever I'd been extra-good. This is her recipe.

> 6 slices bacon, halved crosswise
> 6 slices toast (white or whole-wheat)
> 2 tablespoons butter or margarine, softened
> 6 sandwich slices American cheese

1. Preheat broiler.

2. Sauté bacon in medium heavy skillet until limp, translucent, and some fat has cooked out—2 to 3 minutes. Pour off drippings; drain bacon on paper towels.

3. Spread toast with butter, dividing amount evenly. Top with cheese, then bacon strips laid crisscross fashion.

4. Broil 5 to 6 inches from heat 2 to 3 minutes, until bacon crisps and cheese melts. Serve at once.

HOT DOGS

EVEN THOUGH frankfurters were known in this country's German communities as early as the Civil War and being served on buns in St. Louis in the 1880s, they did not become a national obsession until this century (in 1957, July was declared "National Hot Dog Month").

In the beginning, no one called them "hot dogs." They were *wienerwurst* (Vienna sausage) or, for short, wieners or "weenies." Then, in 1906 Tad Dorgan, a cartoonist working for Hearst, began depicting Germans as dachshunds. People saw the resemblance between the German dog and the German sausage almost immediately and began calling frankfurters "hot dogs."

Frankfurters "all the way"—in buns with assorted trimmings—are said to have been served for the first time at the New York Polo Grounds in 1901. But the man to popularize them was Nathan Handwerker, a Polish shoemaker who opened a hot dog stand at Coney Island in 1916. Before long, Nathan's hot dogs were as essential to a day at Coney Island as a ride on the Cyclone (roller coaster).

What goes on a hot dog varies from one part of the country to another, and regional allegiances run deep. In Kansas, they like their "dogs" with melted cheese and mustard; in Chicago they're served in poppyseed buns; in Texas, the Corn Dog (page 350) is the thing. And in Raleigh, North Carolina, where I grew up, the Chili Dog is the dog of choice: a steaming-hot frankfurter in a steaming-hot bun smothered with chili (ground beef, no beans).

Today, with people counting calories and grams of fat, there are turkey hot dogs, even vegetarian franks fabricated out of wheat gluten and soy protein.

WONDER BREAD

I N 1921, the Taggart Baking Company of Indianapolis, Indiana, came out with a one-and-a-half-pound loaf of white bread and named it "Wonder" because of its bigger size.

But the real wonder of Wonder Bread was that, with the help of the newly invented bread-wrapping machine, the judicious use of preservatives, and motorized delivery, a loaf could be kept fresh long enough for company admen to offer customers a $1,000 freshness guarantee. Within a decade, this increasingly popular bread was the very first to be sold presliced, giving rise to the expression, "the greatest thing since sliced bread." People from other countries—and especially Europe where chewy breads are the norm—often find it hard to understand why Americans are so loyal to Wonder Bread: soft, white, bland, uniformly sliced, nestled in its gay cellophane wrapper decorated with red, yellow, and blue balls (inspired, it's said, by a hot-air balloon race). But even gourmets have to admit that no other bread works quite so well for peanut-butter-and-jelly sandwiches.

Pimiento Cheese Spread

Makes about 2¼ Cups

❋

T HE BEST description I've read of this popular Southern spread comes from North Carolina novelist Reynolds Price, with whom I had the good fortune to attend high school in Raleigh. This is what Price has to say on the subject of pimiento cheese in *The Great American Writers' Cookbook* (1981), which John Egerton reprints in *Southern Food* (1987): "I've failed in a long effort to trace the origins of pimiento cheese, but it was the peanut butter of my childhood—homemade by my mother. I suspect it's a Southern invention (I've seldom met a non-Southerner who knew what it was, though they take to it on contact); in any case, prepared versions can be bought to this day in Southern supermarkets—most of them apparently made from congealed insecticides." The lesson here: Make your own. The pimiento cheese in question is made with sharp Cheddar, *not* with cream cheese, as has long been done in other parts of the country. I was fascinated to learn that Price has worked out a processor version that contains "one or two cloves garlic" (not traditional but terrific), also that he may add "a little lemon juice or a very little wine vinegar or Tabasco—nothing to disguise the bare cheese and peppers and good mayonnaise." Price confesses to "eating a pound [of pimiento cheese] in two days." I'm guilty of that, too, I'm afraid. This recipe is my own.

1 pound sharp Cheddar cheese, coarsely shredded (4 cups)

3 tablespoons minced yellow onion

1 (4-ounce) can pimientos, drained well and finely chopped

⅔ cup mayonnaise or salad dressing

1½ teaspoons spicy brown mustard

4 teaspoons milk or light cream (about)

¼ teaspoon black pepper

¼ teaspoon hot red pepper sauce

1. Beat together all ingredients in large electric mixer bowl at moderate speed just until mixed or pulse quickly in a food processor fitted with metal chopping blade just enough to combine; mixture should be lumpy. If it seems too stiff to spread easily, add a little extra milk or light cream.

2. Transfer cheese mixture to bowl, cover tight, and "ripen" in refrigerator overnight.

3. Use as a spread for bread.

NOTE: The old-fashioned Southern way is to spread two slices of white bread with mayonnaise, then to spread one slice lavishly with pimiento cheese mixture and clap the two together.

FOREIGN INFLUENCE

BREADS, SPREADS & SANDWICHES, ETC.

that Entered the American Mainstream During the Twentieth Century with Their Source

(*Recipe Included)

FRANCE
Baguettes
Brioche
Crêpes
Croissants
*Pissaladière
(Provençal Pizza)

GERMANY
Pumpernickel
Rye Bread

SCANDINAVIA
Danish Pastry

RUSSIA/ MIDDLE EUROPE
Bagels
Blintzes
Boreks
Lavash
*Chopped Chicken Livers

ITALY
Bruschetta
Calzone
*Caponata
*Focaccia
*Pizza

SPAIN AND PORTUGAL
*Portuguese Sweet Bread

EASTERN MEDITERRANEAN (GREECE, TURKEY, MIDDLE EAST)
*Baba Ganouj
(see Appetizers & Snacks)
Gyros (Greek "Heros")
Felafel
*Hummus
(see Appetizers & Snacks)
Pita Bread

CHINA
Egg Rolls
Spring Rolls

INDIA
Nan
Papadams
Paratha
Poori

MEXICO AND LATIN AMERICA
Burritos
*Chimichangas
Enchiladas
*Fajitas
Quesadillas
Sopaipillas
Tacos
Tamales
Tortillas

Caponata (Sicilian Eggplant Spread)

Makes about 3 Cups

✳

JUST THE thing for a hero sand-wich—or a cocktail spread as many with-it hostesses discovered in the '60s. This recipe is adapted from *The New Doubleday Cookbook,* which I coauthored with Elaine Hanna.

NOTE: If stored tightly covered in the refrigerator, caponata keeps well about a week.

¼ cup fruity olive oil
1 small, unpeeled eggplant, cut into 1-inch cubes
1 medium yellow onion, peeled and chopped
1 large rib celery, finely diced
1 cup tomato sauce
½ cup coarsely chopped pitted olives (ripe and/or green)
4 anchovy fillets, minced
2 tablespoons drained small capers
2 tablespoons red wine vinegar
1 tablespoon sugar
½ teaspoon salt (or to taste)
¼ teaspoon black pepper (or to taste)
2 tablespoons minced fresh parsley

1. Heat 3 tablespoons oil in large heavy saucepan over moderate heat 1 minute. Add eggplant and stir-fry 8 to 10 minutes until golden. Add remaining 1 tablespoon oil, onion, and celery; sauté 6 to 8 minutes until glassy.

2. Add tomato sauce, olives, an-chovies, capers, vinegar, sugar, salt, and pepper, cover, and cook slowly, stirring now and then, about 1½ hours until quite thick and flavors meld.

3. Stir in parsley; taste for salt and pepper and adjust as needed. Trans-fer to bowl, cover, and refrigerate until about 1 hour before serving.

Portuguese Sweet Bread

Makes Two 7-inch Round Loaves

✳

THE PORTUGUESE, I've always thought, bake the best bread in the world. The one that's the best known—and loved—in this coun-try is *Pão-Doce,* or sweet bread—rich, golden, and buttery. This recipe is adapted from my cookbook, *The Food of Portugal.*

NOTE: Because this bread is so ten-der, cut it with a sharp serrated knife.

¼ teaspoon saffron threads
1 cup very warm water (110° to 115°F)
2 envelopes active dry yeast
½ cup sugar
5¾ cups sifted all-purpose flour
5 tablespoons butter, at room temperature
1 egg, at room temperature
4 egg yolks, at room temperature

1. Crumble saffron into water and let stand 15 minutes.

2. Mix yeast, 1 tablespoon sugar, and 1 cup flour in large warm bowl, pressing out lumps. Whisk in ⅔ cup saffron mixture, beating until smooth. Cover with cloth and set in warm spot, away from drafts, until doubled in bulk—about 30 minutes.

3. Stir yeast sponge down. Beat in remaining sugar, remaining saffron mixture, butter, and whole egg. One by one, beat in egg yolks. Add remaining flour, cup by cup, to form soft, sticky dough.

4. Scoop into buttered, warm, large bowl, cover with cloth, and let rise in warm, dry spot, away from drafts, 45 to 50 minutes, until doubled in bulk.

5. Toward end of rising, preheat oven to 425° F. Generously butter two (7-inch) charlotte molds or deep metal pans (1-pound coffee tins, if necessary); set aside.

6. Punch dough down, divide in half, and knead each on lightly floured pastry cloth 35 to 40 times until elastic.

7. Shape into balls and place in molds. Cover with cloth and let rise in warm, dry spot, away from drafts, about 20 minutes, until doubled in bulk.

8. Bake on middle oven rack about 25 minutes until puffed, richly browned, and hollow-sounding when thumped.

9. Turn loaves onto wire racks and cool to room temperature before cutting.

Focaccia

Makes 3 (9- or 10-inch) Round Loaves

❋

THESE FLAT rounds of yeast bread are to Genoa what pizza is to Naples. So says Carol Field, a hugely respected cookbook author and one of the first Americans to write in depth about Italian bread. Many northern Italian restaurants in this country now pride themselves on their focaccia and often send baskets of it—warm from the wood oven—to table as soon as you're seated. This recipe is Carol Field's. I've adapted it from her important book, *The Italian Baker* (1985).

NOTE: For spritzing the loaves with water as they bake, use a pristine plant mister.

1 envelope active dry yeast
¼ cup very warm water (110° to 115°F)
2¼ cups plus 1 to 2 tablespoons room-temperature water
2 tablespoons olive oil
7½ cups unsifted, unbleached all-purpose flour (about) or half all-purpose and half bread flour
1 tablespoon fine sea salt or table salt

TOPPING
2 tablespoons fruity olive oil
1½ tablespoons fine sea salt or table salt

1. Mix yeast and very warm water in large mixing bowl; let stand until creamy—about 10 minutes.

2. Stir in 2¼ cups plus 1 tablespoon room-temperature water and the olive oil. Add 2 cups flour and the salt and whisk until smooth. Add remaining flour, 1 cup at a time, beating after each addition, until dough comes together, adding remaining 1 tablespoon water, if needed.

3. Turn onto floured surface and knead 8 to 10 minutes until smooth and elastic.

4. Shape dough into ball, place in lightly oiled, warm, large bowl, turn in bowl to oil all sides. Cover with plastic wrap and let rise in warm, dry spot, away from drafts, about 1½ hours, until doubled in bulk.

5. Punch dough down and divide into 3 equal parts on lightly floured surface. Roll each piece into 9- or 10-inch circle and place in oiled 9- or 10-inch pie pan. Cover with cloth and let rise 30 minutes.

6. Dimple loaves deeply with fingertips; brush generously with olive oil and sprinkle with salt, dividing topping amounts evenly.

7. Cover with moist, clean towels and let rise in warm spot, away from draft, until doubled in bulk, about 2 hours.

8. After 1½ hours of rising, place baking stones (if you have them) on oven rack and preheat oven to 400°F.

9. Bake fully risen loaves 20 to 25 minutes, spritzing three times with water during first 10 minutes.

10. Invert loaves on racks as soon as they come from oven. Serve warm or at room temperature.

——— VARIATION ———
ROSEMARY FOCACCIA: Prepare as directed but knead 1½ tablespoons chopped fresh rosemary or 2 teaspoons crumbled dried leaf rosemary into dough before first rising. Makes 3 (9- or 10-inch) round loaves.

Wolfgang Puck's Pizza with Shrimp and Dried Tomatoes

Makes 4 (8-inch) Pizzas

❋

NO ONE has done more to lift pizza from humble to haute than Wolfgang Puck, an Austrian-born chef who has made his mark in the U.S. Witty and wildly talented, Puck began reinventing pizza at Spago, the star-studded restaurant he opened on Sunset Boulevard in West Hollywood in 1982. A regular on ABC-TV's *Good Morning America,* Puck is now as celebrated as his customers. You no longer have to go to Los Angeles to taste Puck's pizzas. You'll find them—frozen—at your local supermarket. My own favorite is this one, adapted from *The Wolfgang Puck Cookbook* (1986). Note that the dough is made by food processor.

DOUGH

3 cups unsifted all-purpose flour
1 teaspoon salt
1 tablespoon honey
2 tablespoons fruity olive oil
¾ cup cool water
1 package active dry yeast
¼ cup very warm water (110° to 115°F)

CHILI OIL

2 tablespoons peanut, light sesame, or olive oil
1½ teaspoons red pepper flakes

SHRIMP AND DRIED TOMATO FILLING

2 tablespoons chili oil (above)
1 cup grated fontina cheese
2 cups grated mozzarella cheese
¼ cup chopped, blanched, peeled garlic (4 to 5 large cloves)
1 medium red onion, peeled and thinly sliced
¼ cup chopped fresh basil
20 to 24 medium raw shrimp, shelled and deveined
¼ cup thinly sliced dried tomatoes
4 sprigs fresh basil (garnish)

1. DOUGH: Place flour in food processor fitted with metal chopping blade.

2. Blend salt, honey, olive oil, and cool water in small bowl; set aside.

3. Dissolve yeast in warm water and let proof 10 minutes.

4. With processor running, drizzle honey mixture down feed tube into flour, then proofed yeast. Churn 20 to 30 seconds until dough pulls from sides of work bowl and forms

a ball; if dough seems sticky, add a little extra flour and continue processing several seconds, until dough forms ball.

5. Transfer dough to lightly floured board and knead 3 to 5 minutes, until smooth. Shape into ball, place in greased large bowl, turning to grease all round; cover with cloth and let rise 30 minutes.

6. Punch dough down and divide into 4 equal parts. Roll each piece into smooth, firm ball. Place on greased baking sheet, cover with damp towel, and refrigerate until 1 hour before baking.

7. CHILI OIL: Heat oil in butter warmer over moderate heat until very hot but not smoking. Add red pepper flakes, remove from heat, and cool.

8. When ready to proceed, slide large pizza stone onto middle oven rack and preheat oven to 500°F for 30 minutes.

9. TO SHAPE AND FILL PIZZA: On floured board with floured hands, flatten a ball of dough into circle 6 inches across, making outer edge thicker than center. Lift dough and moving fingers clockwise around edge, gently stretch dough into 8-inch circle and place on well-floured baking sheet. Repeat with three remaining balls of dough.

10. Brush dough circle with chili oil. Dividing amounts evenly, top each with fontina and mozzarella cheeses, leaving ½-inch border all round. Top cheeses with garlic, red

onion, chopped basil, shrimp, and dried tomatoes, dividing evenly.

11. Ease pizzas onto preheated stone and bake 10 to 12 minutes until bubbling. Garnish each with basil sprig and serve.

Pissaladière

Makes 6 Servings

✳

NOT THE classic, long-winded recipe for the Provençal "pizza" but a shortcut version I worked out some years ago.

NOTE: Still quicker, a 12-inch prepared pizza crust instead of crescent dinner rolls.

- 1½ (8-ounce) packages refrigerated crescent dinner rolls
- 1 medium red or green bell pepper, cored, and sliced into thin rings
- 2 medium Spanish onions, peeled and sliced thin
- 1 clove garlic, peeled and minced
- 3 tablespoons fruity olive oil
- ¼ teaspoon dried leaf rosemary, crumbled
- ½ cup freshly grated Parmesan cheese
- ¼ pound mozzarella cheese, shredded
- 2 cups marinara sauce
- 2 (2-ounce) tins flat anchovy fillets
- Pitted ripe olives (preferably oil-cured), halved lengthwise

1. Preheat oven to 425° F.

2. Separate rolls into 12 triangles. Arrange in 12-inch pizza pan, overlapping slightly, with points toward center. Press firmly to form thin "crust" over bottom of pan; pinch seams together and press to seal. Trim off ragged edges, then roll overhang under, even with rim, and press firmly to secure.

3. Prick crust well with fork and bake 10 minutes until golden brown.

4. Sauté pepper, onions, and garlic in oil in large heavy skillet over moderate heat 5 minutes until soft; mix in rosemary.

5. Sprinkle baked crust with Parmesan, top with skillet mixture, spreading to edges. Sprinkle with mozzarella, then smooth sauce evenly over all. Arrange anchovies in lattice design on top of sauce and stud with olives.

6. Bake 10 minutes until bubbly. Let stand 4 to 5 minutes, cut into wedges, and serve.

TIMELINE

1964

Nachos are introduced at the Dallas State Fair.

The New York World's Fair opens, with food pavilions from around the world.

Sales of chicken parts soar, thanks to Holly-Pak poultry, chilled, quality-controlled packages introduced by Holly Farms, a North Wilkesboro, North Carolina, poultry processor.

Buffalo chicken wings created at the Anchor Bar in Buffalo, New York.

1965

Gatorade, a flavored thirst quencher, appears.

General Foods launches Tang, a powdered orange juice concentrate.

The giggly, pudgy "Poppin' Fresh" Dough Boy bounces into the national psyche as the new pitchman for Pillsbury.

Beef Chimichangas

Makes 8 Servings

✳

THIS IS a recipe I developed for a *Family Circle* article back in 1979 showing how to stretch a pound of meat over eight mouths or more. I was just back from Santa Fe where I'd eaten chimichangas for the first time. While this may not be an absolutely authentic recipe—it varies from cook to cook anyhow—it *is* good. It is also lower in calories than some chimichangas because these are baked, not deep-fat fried.

FILLING

1 large yellow onion, peeled and coarsely chopped
1 clove garlic, peeled and crushed
2 tablespoons vegetable oil
1 pound ground beef chuck
2 (8-ounce) cans tomato sauce
1 tablespoon India relish
2 canned jalapeño peppers, cored, seeded, and minced
¼ teaspoon ground cinnamon
¼ teaspoon dried leaf oregano, crumbled
¼ teaspoon dried leaf basil, crumbled
¼ teaspoon salt (or to taste)

PASTRY

2¾ cups sifted all-purpose flour
¾ teaspoon salt
⅓ cup lard (hog lard)
⅓ cup vegetable shortening
2 egg yolks, lightly beaten
½ cup water
1 tablespoon fresh lemon juice

ACCOMPANIMENTS

4 cups coarsely shredded iceberg lettuce
2 cups coarsely shredded sharp Cheddar or Monterey Jack cheese

1. FILLING: Fry onion and garlic in oil in large heavy skillet over moderate heat until glassy—about 5 minutes. Mix in beef, tomato sauce, relish, jalapeños, cinnamon, oregano, basil, and salt to taste. Cover, and simmer 30 minutes, breaking up beef clumps from time to time. Uncover, and simmer 10 minutes more, stirring occasionally, until a little thicker than pasta sauce; cool slightly.

2. PASTRY: Preheat oven to 375°F. Mix flour and salt in large bowl; cut in lard and shortening with pastry blender until texture of coarse meal. Mix egg yolks, water, and lemon juice; pour over flour mixture, tossing with fork, just until pastry holds together. Shape into ball and divide in half.

3. On lightly floured cloth, roll pastry, half at a time, into circle slightly thicker than pie crust. Cut each into four 6-inch circles, using saucer, if needed, as pattern.

4. Spoon ⅓ cup filling across center of each circle, leaving wide margin all around. Moisten pastry edges with water, fold in half to enclose filling, and crimp firmly with floured tines of fork. Prick top of each chimichanga with fork.

5. Bake 35 minutes until filling is bubbly and pastry lightly browned.

6. Serve hot on bed of shredded lettuce. Pass Cheddar.

Grilled Beef Fajitas

Makes 6 to 8 Servings

✳

JANE BUTEL, a cookbook author/cooking school teacher I admire, has made a specialty of Tex-Mex cooking. This fajita recipe is adapted from her cookbook *Fiesta!* (1987), published soon after America discovered these hearty steak-stuffed tortillas. Jane makes hers with Pico de Gallo, a peppery red sauce with plenty of fresh tomato, garlic, and cilantro (coriander).

FAJITAS

3 pounds skirt steak or very lean scaloppine-cut bottom round, trimmed of fat and sinew
Juice of 2 limes
6 cloves garlic, peeled and minced
1 teaspoon salt
Black pepper to taste
Pico de Gallo (page 359)
6 to 8 (12-inch) wheat flour tortillas

12 to 16 romaine leaves
1 cup sour cream

PICO DE GALLO

  ½ cup minced fresh jalapeños,
    (about 3 medium)
  ½ cup coarsely chopped,
    unpeeled vine-ripe tomato
    (about 1 medium)
  ½ cup coarsely chopped sweet
    white onion (about
    ½ medium Vidalia or
    Bermuda onion)
  2 cloves garlic, peeled and
    minced
  ½ teaspoon salt
  ½ teaspoon crushed chili
    pequins
  3 tablespoons coarsely chopped
    fresh coriander (cilantro)

1. FAJITAS: Pound steak as thin as possible; cut into strips 4 to 6 inches long and 2 inches wide. Mix lime juice, garlic, salt, and generous amount of black pepper (8 to 10 grindings of mill) in large, shallow glass bowl. Toss beef strips in mixture; let stand at room temperature about 1 hour.

2. PICO DE GALLO: Mix all ingredients in nonreactive bowl and let stand at room temperature about 1 hour.

3. Build charcoal fire and adjust grill 3 to 4 inches from coals. Also preheat oven to 350° F. Bundle tortillas in foil and warm 15 minutes in oven.

4. Grill beef strips until charred on each side but still pink in center.

5. TO SERVE: Lay steak strip in center of each tortilla, bracketing with romaine; top with spoonful of Pico de Gallo. Roll each tortilla, enclosing filling, drift with sour cream, then more Pico de Gallo.

Jewish-Style Chopped Chicken Livers

Makes about 2½ Cups

✳

A WONDERFUL spread unknown to most Americans until after World War II. It was introduced by the "deli culture" of New York and other big cities where immigrants from Eastern Europe began settling early this century. This particular recipe from the late Paula Peck, one of America's most distinguished food writers and cooking school teachers, was included in *Craig Claiborne's Favorites from The New York Times, Volume 4* (1978). Ms. Peck called for putting everything through a meat grinder. I've updated the recipe for the food processor. The bread to use for a chopped chicken liver sandwich? Rye.

  ½ pound fresh, solid,
    unrendered chicken fat, diced
  3 medium yellow onions, peeled
    and chunked
  ½ pound chicken livers
  ½ teaspoon salt (or to taste)
  ½ teaspoon black pepper (or to
    taste)
  4 hard-cooked eggs, peeled and
    quartered

1. Place chicken fat in large heavy skillet, set over low heat, and allow to melt.

2. Meanwhile, pulse onions in food processor fitted with metal chopping blade briskly 6 to 8 times until coarsely chopped.

3. Add ½ cup onions to chicken fat and continue rendering until onion and bits of fat brown.

4. Strain melted chicken fat, reserving both fat and browned bits.

5. Add remaining onions to pan, cover, and steam over low heat until almost dry and sticking to pan—about 30 minutes. Add ⅓ cup melted fat and stir-fry onions until golden brown—5 to 8 minutes; with slotted spoon transfer to food processor work bowl.

6. Add chicken livers to fat in pan and stir-fry over moderately low heat until brown in center and juices run clear when pierced with fork—5 to 8 minutes. Sprinkle with salt and pepper.

7. Add to food processor along with pan drippings, reserved brown bits, and hard-cooked eggs; pulse 12 to 15 times. Scrape work bowl sides down and pulse 12 to 15 times more until good spreading consistency. Taste for salt and pepper and adjust as needed.

8. Transfer to small bowl, seal, if desired, with thin layer of melted chicken fat, and store in refrigerator. Use within a week.

PUDDINGS, PIES, OTHER DESSERTS

FROM COLONIAL days on, Americans have doted on sweets. While researching this chapter, I would begin with cookbooks dating back to the 1820s, then proceed through the decades right up to the 1900s, building a timeline of pies, puddings, ice creams, and sauces. By the time I'd finished scribbling down the dessert titles, I'd covered more than sixty legal-size sheets, which surely says something about our obsession with desserts.

Custards, steamed puddings, and whips predominated during the nineteenth century. And to my great surprise, ice cream recipes appeared in startling variety (even Baked Alaska belongs to the nineteenth century). Fruit desserts were popular—particularly apple, pineapple, whortleberry, gooseberry, raspberry, strawberry and, of course, lemon and orange. Candied fruits were much in favor, too. And rose water as a flavoring.

Chocolate didn't gain ground until the turn of the twentieth century. Certainly not in baked goods. But once it became widely available and reasonably priced, we couldn't get enough of it, which explains the preponderance of chocolate recipes in this chapter.

Strangely, as our kitchens grew sleeker, as thermostated gas and electric ranges replaced stoke-and-pray woodstoves; as electric mixers, blenders, and food processors phased out cantankerous egg beaters, we abandoned some of the quainter recipes in Grandmother's repertoire.

Fools, slumps, and grunts, dowdies and roly-polies virtually disappeared from twentieth-century cookbooks, certainly those published after World War II.

Jell-O went big time, revolutionizing desserts as dramatically as it did salads. I remember Southern ladies, mostly my mother's friends or fellow clubwomen, layering chopped red and green gelatins into parfait glasses, trickling heavy cream over all, and presenting them as

the pièce de résistance of a Christmas dinner. This, mind you, was the '40s and '50s.

Package puddings came along, too, to shortcut kitchen time—vanilla, butterscotch, tapioca, chocolate. Just add milk, heat and stir until thick, ladle into dessert dishes, and chill until ready to serve. What could be easier?

The whole repertoire of whipped-topping desserts, for one thing, which arrived a couple of decades later, and were often folded into partially set Jell-O or melted chocolate chips. These fluffy puddings and pie fillings remain hugely popular to this day out across the land. If you doubt this, you've only to thumb through the nearest community cookbook.

After World War II (make that after jet travel—the late '50s), many of us began to grow more sophisticated about dessert, learning to settle, as Europeans had long done, for a bowl of fruit and a chunk of cheese.

We dined in the best restaurants Paris, Vienna, and Rome had to offer. We discovered the pastry shop, the pastry *cart*. We couldn't get enough Dacquoise and Tarte Tatin. We wolfed down

PUDDINGS, PIES, OTHER DESSERTS

Napoleons and éclairs and Sarah Bernhardts. And those of us who traveled farther east—to Greece and beyond—fell for wispy phyllo pastries.

Discerning a trend here, food manufacturers began packaging frozen puff pastry and phyllo leaves so we could make our own Tarte Tatin and baklava back home. No fuss, no muss.

At first—in the late '70s and early '80s—only big-city specialty food shops carried them. Now they can be found at nearly every supermarket—right there beside the frozen pie crusts and patty shells.

As for this century's quintessential desserts, chiffon pies, angel pies, pudding-cakes, and New York-style cream-cheese cheesecakes win hands down. You will find these—and much, much more—in the pages that follow.

CHIFFON PIES

MY RESEARCH tells me that these fluffy unbaked pies debuted in the early 1920s as "soufflé" or "gelatin" pies. A headnote to the Eggnog Chiffon Pie recipe in *Woman's Day Old-Fashioned Desserts* (1978) says that "Chiffon pies were invented in 1921 by a professional baker who lived in Iowa. By beating egg whites with a fruit-flavored syrup until the mixture was light and fluffy, he achieved a filling that his mother said 'looked like a pile of chiffon.'"

It's a story I've been unable to substantiate. Besides, Knox Gelatine's 1915 booklet, *Dainty Desserts for Dainty People,* features gelatin "sponges," "marshmallow puddings," and "marshmallow creams"—the airy mixes that would one day emerge as chiffon fillings. It only took a few more years for someone to pile them into pie shells.

Searches of several dozen early-twentieth-century cookbooks turned up a few "soufflé" and "sponge" pies, but these contained no gelatin and/or whipped cream. They were baked pies with stiffly beaten egg whites folded in just before they went into the oven.

According to John Mariani (*The Dictionary of American Food and Drink,* Revised Edition, 1994), "Chiffon pie is first mentioned in American print in 1929 as a 'chiffon pumpkin pie' in the *Beverly Hills Women's Club Fashions in Foods.*" He adds that Irma Rombauer's self-published *Joy of Cooking* (1931) included a recipe for lemon chiffon pie. And so did a 1930s Knox Gelatine recipe booklet called *Food Economy.*

The earliest fluffy gelatin pies that I was able to locate both appeared in *Good Housekeeping's Book of Menus, Recipes and Household Discoveries.* The date: 1922. The first, Coffee Soufflé Pie, qualifies on all counts as a chiffon pie. It begins with a coffee gelatin that is chilled until viscous, then beaten until frothy. Next stiffly beaten egg whites are folded in and, finally, stiffly whipped cream, providing extra richness. As for the crust, it's a standard pastry shell, baked and cooled before the filling goes into it.

The second *Good Housekeeping* recipe, Pineapple Gelatin Pie, contains gelatin and heavy cream (two cups of it beaten to stiff peaks) but no egg whites. Still, it is very chiffonlike.

Leafing through 1930s cookbooks, I find four chiffon pies in *My Better Homes & Gardens Cook Book* (1939): lemon, chocolate, pineapple, and pumpkin. All begin with a gelatin "custard," are fluffed with stiffly peaking egg whites, and, in the case of the pineapple, with whipped cream as well. Here, too, the crusts are the standard pastry, baked and cooled (crumb-crusted chiffon pies come later—with pies such as Grasshopper [page 372] and Black Bottom [page 370]).

Two 1940 cookbooks featured a great variety of chiffon pies: *Woman's Home Companion Cook Book* (with nineteen) and *The Good Housekeeping Cook Book* (with thirteen). Despite World War II sugar shortages, chiffon pies surged in popularity during the '40s, driven perhaps by *The Joy of Cooking,* which devoted a special section to them.

Chiffon pies remained popular right through the '70s. Then in the 1980s when salmonella began compromising the wholesomeness of our eggs, they fell from favor. But only briefly. Savvy food manufacturers discovered that powdered egg whites, cream cheese, whipped toppings, and marshmallow cream could double nicely for raw egg whites.

Thus, '90s chiffon pies are likely to contain no eggs at all. And sometimes no gelatin. There's usually no stinting, however, on whipped cream.

Pumpkin Chiffon Pie

Makes a 9-inch Pie, 8 Servings

✳

AMERICAN WOMEN have been baking pumpkin pies for ages, but pumpkin chiffon pies are strictly twentieth century. This recipe, adapted from *Farm Journal's Best-Ever Pies* (1981), may lack the added richness of whipped cream but you won't find a better pumpkin chiffon pie.

NOTE: See Caution about using raw egg whites on page 5.

> 2 envelopes unflavored
>   gelatin
> ½ cup cold water
> 1½ cups cooked, mashed
>   pumpkin (fresh or canned)
> 1 cup dark corn syrup
> ⅓ cup firmly packed brown
>   sugar (dark or light)
> 1 teaspoon ground cinnamon
> ½ teaspoon ground ginger
> ⅛ teaspoon ground cloves
> ½ teaspoon salt
> 3 eggs, separated
> 1½ cups evaporated milk
> 1 (9-inch) graham cracker
>   crust (page 398)

1. Soften gelatin in cold water.

2. Mix pumpkin, ½ cup corn syrup, brown sugar, cinnamon, ginger, cloves, salt, slightly beaten egg yolks, and milk in medium heavy saucepan. Set over moderate heat and cook, stirring constantly, until mixture comes to a boil. Off heat, add softened gelatin and stir until dissolved.

3. Cover pumpkin mixture and chill until consistency of unbeaten egg white—about 2½ hours.

4. Whip egg whites to soft peaks, then beat in remaining ½ cup corn syrup, 1 tablespoon at a time. Continue beating to stiff, glossy peaks. Fold into pumpkin mixture.

5. Return to refrigerator and chill until mixture mounds softly—about 20 to 30 minutes. Turn into pie crust and chill until set—about 2 hours.

Lemon Chiffon Pie

Makes a 9-inch Pie, 8 Servings

✳

ANOTHER CHIFFON pie made without heavy cream, this one adapted from a recipe that appears in *Betty Crocker's Picture Cookbook* (1950). It calls for regular pie crust.

NOTE: See Caution about using raw egg whites on page 5.

> 4 tablespoons lemon-flavored
>   gelatin
> ½ cup boiling water
> 1 tablespoon finely grated
>   lemon zest
> 3 eggs, separated
> ¾ cup sugar
> ¼ teaspoon salt
> ¼ cup fresh lemon juice
> ¼ teaspoon cream of tartar
> 1 (9-inch) baked pie shell
>   (page 399)

1. Soften gelatin in boiling water; stir in lemon zest and set aside.

2. Whisk egg yolks, 6 tablespoons sugar, salt, and lemon juice in medium nonreactive saucepan until nicely blended. Set over low heat and cook, stirring constantly, until mixture almost boils.

3. Off heat, add gelatin mixture, stirring until dissolved. Chill about 30 minutes, until mixture is consistency of unbeaten egg white, then beat until smooth.

4. Beat egg whites and cream of tartar to soft peaks, then add remaining 6 tablespoons sugar gradually and continue beating to stiff peaks. Fold into gelatin mixture.

5. Turn into pie shell and chill until set—about 2 hours.

——— VARIATION ———

LIME CHIFFON PIE: Prepare as directed, substituting lime juice and zest for lemon. Tint pale green, if desired. Makes a 9-inch pie, 8 servings.

Strawberry Chiffon Pie

Makes a 9-inch Pie, 8 Servings

✳

THIS BASIC recipe, my own, can be used to make almost any berry chiffon pie, but blackberries, raspberries, and other berries with large seeds should be sieved after they are crushed.

NOTE: See Caution about using raw egg whites on page 5.

> 1 envelope unflavored gelatin
> ½ cup cold water
> 3 eggs, separated
> ⅔ cup sugar
> 1 teaspoon fresh lemon juice
> 1 teaspoon finely grated orange zest
> Pinch salt
> 1 pint fresh strawberries, hulled and finely crushed or pureed
> 1 tablespoon Grand Marnier
> 1 (9-inch) graham cracker crust (page 398)

1. Soften gelatin in cold water.

2. Whisk egg yolks in double boiler top with ⅓ cup sugar, lemon juice, orange zest, and salt until frothy. Set over simmering water and cook, stirring constantly, until thickened, 7 to 8 minutes.

3. Off heat, add softened gelatin and stir until dissolved. Transfer to large bowl and fold in strawberries.

4. Cover, and refrigerate until consistency of unbeaten egg white, about 30 minutes.

5. Beat egg whites in large electric mixer bowl at high speed to soft peaks; add remaining ⅓ cup sugar gradually and continue beating at high speed to stiff peaks.

6. Gently fold in strawberry mixture and Grand Marnier. Return to refrigerator until mixture mounds softly, 30 minutes.

7. Turn into pie crust and chill several hours or overnight, until set.

Eggnog Chiffon Pie

Makes a 9-inch Pie, 8 Servings

✳

THIS RECIPE is adapted from one in *Woman's Day Old-Fashioned Desserts* (1978).

NOTE: See Caution about using raw egg whites on page 5.

> 1 envelope unflavored gelatin
> ¼ cup cold water

> 3 eggs, separated
> 1 cup sugar
> ¼ teaspoon freshly grated nutmeg
> ¼ teaspoon salt
> 1 cup light cream
> ¼ cup light rum
> ½ teaspoon fresh lemon juice
> ½ cup heavy cream, stiffly whipped
> 1 (9-inch) baked pie shell (page 399)
> Freshly grated nutmeg (garnish)

1. Soften gelatin in water; set aside.

2. Beat egg yolks with ½ cup sugar, ¼ teaspoon nutmeg, and salt; set aside.

3. Bring light cream to simmer in small heavy saucepan. Gradually stir into egg yolk mixture, return to pan, and cook, stirring constantly, over low heat, until mixture coats spoon, 3 to 5 minutes.

4. Off heat, add softened gelatin and stir until dissolved.

5. Chill mixture, stirring occasionally, until consistency of unbeaten egg white, about 30 minutes. Mix in rum and lemon juice, beating until smooth. Fold in whipped cream.

6. Beat egg whites to soft peaks, gradually add remaining ½ cup sugar, and continue beating until stiff and glossy. Fold into gelatin mixture.

7. Pour into pie shell, sprinkle with grated nutmeg, and chill several hours until firm. Let stand at room temperature 20 minutes before cutting.

Chocolate Chiffon Pie

Makes a 9-inch Pie, 8 Servings

✳

AN OLD recipe of my mother's that I've reworked for the '90s. Her original called for raw egg whites, stiffly beaten—risky today because of the danger of salmonella food poisoning. Without compromising the airness of the filling, I've substituted a safe alternative—egg white powder. It's sold in the baking section of many supermarkets (*Just Whites* is one popular brand).

1 envelope unflavored gelatin
¼ cup cold water
6 ounces semisweet or bittersweet chocolate, coarsely chopped
¾ cup milk or evaporated milk
3 egg yolks, lightly beaten
1 teaspoon vanilla extract
¼ teaspoon salt
2 tablespoons egg white powder
6 tablespoons warm water
¼ cup sugar
½ cup heavy cream
1 (9-inch) baked pie shell (page 399)

1. Soften gelatin in cold water 5 minutes.

2. Meanwhile, heat chocolate and milk in medium heavy saucepan over low heat, stirring constantly, until chocolate melts and mixture is smooth.

3. Off heat, mix in softened gelatin and beaten egg yolks. Return to low heat and cook, stirring constantly, until mixture thickens slightly—about 5 minutes. Do not boil or mixture may curdle. Remove from heat and stir in vanilla and salt.

4. Press wax paper flat on surface of mixture and chill until consistency of unbeaten egg whites, about 40 minutes.

5. Combine egg white powder and warm water in medium bowl. Let stand 2 minutes, then beat to soft peaks with mixer set at medium speed. Add 2 tablespoons sugar gradually and continue beating to stiff peaks. Fold into chocolate mixture.

6. Beat cream and remaining 2 tablespoons sugar in small bowl until stiff peaks form. Gently but thoroughly fold into chocolate mixture.

7. Turn into pie shell and chill until firm, about 3 hours.

TIMELINE

1966

R.T. French establishes "The Tastemaker Awards" to honor excellence in cookbooks.

1968

Keebler introduces its new spokesman, "Ernie, the Keebler Elf," who so enchants children that President Ronald Reagan will later use him in his anti-drugs campaign.

1969

"Hippie" health foods and vegetarianism seep into the mainstream.

Whirlpool unveils the trash compactor.

1971

America goes Crock Pot crazy.

Mocha Cloud Pie

Makes an 8-inch Pie, 6 to 8 Servings

✳

I DUG this "eggless" chiffon pie out of a friend's recipe file and gave it a try. It's light and rich at the same time. And couldn't be easier to make. But, alas, it's not for calorie-counters.

> 1 (8-ounce) package cream
>   cheese (at room temperature)
> ½ cup superfine sugar
> ½ cup confectioners' (10X)
>   sugar
> 2 tablespoons instant espresso
>   crystals
> 1½ teaspoons vanilla extract
> ½ cup Dutch process cocoa
>   powder
> ⅓ cup evaporated milk, well
>   chilled
> 2 cups ice-cold heavy cream
> 1 (8-inch) chocolate crumb
>   crust (page 399)

1. Beat cream cheese, the two sugars, espresso crystals, and vanilla in large electric mixer bowl at high speed until fluffy.

2. At low speed, add cocoa alternately with milk. Raise speed to medium and beat until smooth.

3. Gradually add cream, and continue beating at medium speed until stiff.

4. Turn mixture into crumb crust and chill until firm, about 3 hours. Better yet, refrigerate overnight before serving.

White Chocolate Mousse Tart

Makes a 9-inch Tart, 8 Servings

✳

WHITE CHOCOLATE was an '80s obsession, especially white chocolate mousse. This one, adapted from Barbara Myers's *Chocolate, Chocolate, Chocolate* (1983) is cradled in a dark chocolate crust.

NOTE: This mousse contains raw egg, so read Caution on page 5.

CRUST
> ¼ cup (½ stick) unsalted
>   butter
> ½ ounce unsweetened chocolate
> 1½ cups chocolate wafer
>   crumbs (¾ of an 8½-ounce
>   package)

MOUSSE
> 4 ounces white chocolate,
>   coarsely chopped
> ½ cup (1 stick) unsalted butter
>   (no substitute), cut into pats
> 3 eggs, separated, at room
>   temperature
> ⅛ teaspoon salt
> ¼ cup sugar

1. CRUST: Melt butter and chocolate in small heavy saucepan over low heat. Off heat, mix in crumbs; reserve 2 tablespoons for garnish. Press mixture over bottom and up sides of ungreased 9-inch pie plate. Chill well.

2. MOUSSE: Place white chocolate in medium heat-proof bowl and set over (not touching) simmering water. When chocolate begins to melt, add butter. Blend well (butter will separate). Off heat, add egg yolks and whisk until uniformly creamy.

3. Beat egg whites with salt to soft peaks. Add sugar gradually and beat to stiff peaks. Fold about ½ cup beaten whites into chocolate mixture, then fold in balance.

4. Spread evenly in crust, scatter reserved crumbs on top, and freeze until firm. Let stand at room temperature 10 minutes before cutting.

Open Sesame Pie

Makes a 9-inch Pie, 8 Servings

✳

IN 1954, this unusual chiffon pie won the Grand Prize in the Pillsbury Bake-Off Contest for Dorothy Koteen of Washington, D.C. She says what stirred her creative juices was a trip to Charleston, South Carolina, where she bought two pounds of benne (sesame) seeds. Mrs. Koteen's Open Sesame Pie caused a run on sesame seeds across the country, at that time a rarity. Today, sesame seeds are a supermarket staple.

NOTE: Mrs. Koteen's prize-winning recipe calls for a 15-ounce package Pillsbury Refrigerated Pie Crust and for preparing a single pie shell according to package directions. If you use a frozen pie crust, choose the deep-dish variety. To toast sesame seeds, spread in a pie pan and bake 3 to 5 minutes at 375° F.

CRUST

- 2 tablespoons toasted sesame seeds
- 1 (9-inch) unbaked pie shell (page 399)

FILLING

- 1 envelope unflavored gelatin
- ¼ cup cold water
- 1¾ cups chopped, pitted dates
- ¼ cup plus 2 tablespoons sugar
- ¼ teaspoon salt
- 1 cup milk
- 2 egg yolks
- 1 teaspoon vanilla extract
- 1½ cups whipping cream
- ⅛ to ¼ teaspoon ground nutmeg

1. CRUST: Preheat oven to 450° F. Press sesame seeds over bottom of pie shell and bake 9 to 11 minutes until lightly browned; cool thoroughly.

2. FILLING: Soften gelatin in cold water; set aside.

3. Meanwhile, cook dates with ¼ cup sugar, salt, milk, and egg yolks in heavy medium saucepan over moderate heat 10 to 12 minutes, stirring constantly, until mixture thickens slightly.

4. Remove from heat, add softened gelatin and vanilla, and stir until gelatin dissolves; refrigerate until consistency of unbeaten egg white, 30 to 40 minutes.

5. Whip cream with 2 tablespoons sugar in small bowl until stiff. Fold into date mixture and spoon into pie shell. Sprinkle with nutmeg.

6. Refrigerate 2 hours before serving.

Brandy Alexander Pie

Makes a 9-inch Pie, 8 Servings

✳

THIS PIE entered our repertoire at about the same time as Grasshopper Pie (page 372)—sometime in the late '50s or early '60s although some say it dates back to the Prohibition '20s. Before the Age of Salmonella anyway. Like many chiffon pies of that era, this one owes its cumulostratus quality to whipped cream and a stiff uncooked meringue. The best recipe for Brandy Alexander Pie I've found is this one from Craig Claiborne's *New York Times Sunday Magazine* column (January 18, 1970). In his introduction, Claiborne writes, "A chronicler of drinks tells us that brandy Alexander, that smooth combination of cognac, cream, and crème de cacao, came into being during the Prohibition era." He finishes by saying that the ingredients for brandy Alexander "make an equally interesting pie." Indeed.

NOTE: This recipe contains raw egg whites, so read the Caution on page 5.

PIE

- 1 envelope unflavored gelatin
- ½ cup cold water
- ⅔ cup sugar
- ⅛ teaspoon salt
- 3 eggs, separated
- ¼ cup Cognac
- ¼ cup crème de cacao
- 1 cup heavy cream, stiffly whipped
- 1 (9-inch) graham cracker crust (page 398)

TOPPING

- 1 cup heavy cream, stiffly whipped
- ½ ounce semisweet chocolate, shaved into curls

1. PIE: Soften gelatin in cold water in medium heavy saucepan. Add ⅓ cup sugar, salt, and egg yolks; stir to mix.

2. Cook over low heat, stirring constantly, until gelatin dissolves and mixture thickens, about 5 minutes. Do not boil or mixture will curdle.

3. Off heat, stir in Cognac and crème de cacao. Chill until consistency of unbeaten egg white, about 30 minutes.

4. Beat egg whites until stiff. Gradually beat in remaining ⅓ cup sugar; fold meringue into egg yolk mixture. Also fold in whipped cream.

5. Turn into pie crust and refrigerate pie several hours or overnight until firm.

6. TOPPING: Swirl whipped cream over filling and scatter chocolate curls on top.

Classic Black Bottom Pie

Makes a 9-inch Pie, 8 Servings

✳

THIS RECIPE is adapted from one that appears in *Our Best Recipes* (1970), the "First Collector's Volume" of the most popular, the most requested recipes that have appeared in *Southern Living* magazine down the years.

NOTE: Read the Caution about using egg whites on page 5.

CRUST
14 gingersnaps, finely crushed
5 tablespoons butter, melted

BOTTOM LAYER
2 cups scalded milk
4 egg yolks, well beaten
½ cup sugar
1½ tablespoons cornstarch
1½ ounces unsweetened chocolate
1 teaspoon vanilla extract

TOP LAYER
1 tablespoon unflavored gelatin
2 tablespoons cold water
4 egg whites
½ cup sugar
¼ teaspoon cream of tartar
2 tablespoons rum or bourbon

TOPPING
1 cup heavy cream
½ ounce unsweetened chocolate, shaved into curls

Black Bottom Pie

CERTAIN RECIPES are destined to catch the public fancy and become classics, though not necessarily right away. One such recipe is Black Bottom Pie, which James Beard says (in *American Cookery,* 1972), "began appearing in cookbooks around the turn of the century." It appears not to have caught on, however, until the late 1930s when Duncan Hines, author of America's trusted *Adventures in Good Eating,* made note of it.

According to southern food historian John Egerton (*Side Orders,* 1990), Hines "remembered precisely" where he first encountered Black Bottom Pie—"a cozy little diner called Dolores Drive-In at 33 N.E. 23rd Street in Oklahoma City." Later, Hines would recall Black Bottom Pie as "one of those marvelous creations that has somehow managed to keep its light under a bushel."

In 1940 *The Good Housekeeping Cook Book* and *Woman's Home Companion Cook Book* both printed recipes for Black Bottom Pie, only the latter titled it "Two-Tone Chocolate Rum Pie" and called for a crumb shell, "preferably using chocolate wafers," with the standard gingersnap crust as second choice.

One of Black Bottom Pie's biggest fans was Floridian Marjorie Kinnan Rawlings, author of *The Yearling,* who included her version of Black Bottom Pie in her *Cross Creek Cookery* (1942), now a collector's item.

Here it is, exactly as she set it down:

BLACK BOTTOM PIE

I think this is the most delicious pie I have ever eaten. The recipe from which I first made it was sent me by a generous correspondent, and originated at an old hotel in Louisiana. It seemed to me it could be no better. Then another correspondent sent me a recipe for Black Bottom Pie that varied in some details from the first one. Having tried both, I now combine the two to make a pie so delicate, so luscious, that I hope to be propped up on my dying bed and fed a generous portion. Then I think I should refuse outright to die, for life would be too good to relinquish. The pie seems fussy to make, but once the cook gets the hang of it, it goes easily.

CRUST

14 crisp ginger cookies   5 tablespoons melted butter

Roll out the cookies fine. Mix with the melted butter. Line a nine-inch pie tin, sides and bottom, with the buttered crumbs, pressing flat and firm. Bake ten minutes in a slow oven to set.

BASIC FILLING

1¾ cups milk   ½ cup sugar
1 tablespoon cornstarch   4 egg yolks
4 tablespoons cold water   Pinch of salt
1 tablespoon gelatine

FOR CHOCOLATE LAYER

2 squares melted chocolate   1 teaspoon vanilla extract

FOR RUM-FLAVORED LAYER

4 egg whites   ½ cup sugar
⅛ teaspoon cream of tartar   1 tablespoon rum

TOPPING

2 tablespoons confectioners'   1 cup whipping cream
  sugar   Grated chocolate

Soak the gelatine in the cold water. Scald the milk, add one-half cup sugar, mix with the cornstarch, pinch of salt, then beaten egg yolks. Cook in double boiler, stirring constantly, until custard thickens and will coat the back of the spoon. Stir in dissolved gelatine. Divide custard in half.

To one-half add the melted chocolate and the vanilla. Turn while hot into cooled crust, dipping out carefully so as not to disturb crust.

Let the remaining half of the custard cool. Beat the egg whites and cream of tartar, adding one-half cup of sugar slowly. Blend with the cooled custard. Add one tablespoon rum. Spread carefully over the chocolate layer. Place in ice box to chill thoroughly. It may even stand overnight. When ready to serve, whip the heavy cream stiff, adding two tablespoons confectioners' sugar slowly. Pile over the top of the pie. Sprinkle with grated bitter or semi-sweet chocolate.

Caution: This recipe contains raw egg white. To eliminate—or at least minimize—the risk of salmonella food poisoning, know your egg source. Better yet, substitute pasteurized powdered egg whites or meringue powder for raw eggs, following label directions. Bakery supply houses sell both, and so do upscale supermarkets.—J.A.

1. CRUST: Preheat oven to 350° F. Mix gingersnap crumbs and melted butter; pat over bottom and up sides of 9-inch pie pan. Bake 10 minutes; cool.

2. BOTTOM LAYER: Slowly whisk scalded milk into egg yolks and return to pan. Mix sugar and cornstarch and blend into egg mixture. Set over low heat and cook, stirring constantly, until mixture coats back of spoon, about 5 minutes. Scoop out 1 cup custard, blend in chocolate and vanilla, and stir until chocolate melts. Cool, then spread over bottom of crumb crust.

3. TOP LAYER: While chocolate mixture cools, soften gelatin in water and blend into hot custard remaining from bottom layer. Cool. Beat egg whites until stiff, gradually adding sugar and cream of tartar. Fold into custard along with rum. Spread over chocolate layer in crumb crust.

4. TOPPING: Whip cream until stiff, then frost over top of pie. Sprinkle with chocolate curls.

5. Chill pie several hours before serving.

HERE'S ANOTHER novelty chiffon pie that enjoyed more than fifteen minutes of fame during the mid-twentieth century. It clearly descends from the grasshopper cocktail, which, some say, was developed during Prohibition.

Gourmet's Menu Cookbook (1963) prints this recipe for Grasshopper Pie, the earliest I've been able to find in a major cookbook. *This recipe contains raw egg white, so read the Caution on page 5.*

GRASSHOPPER PIE

With a rolling pin crush enough chocolate wafers to make 1½ cups fine crumbs. Mix the crumbs with ¼ cup each of sugar and melted sweet butter. Press the crumbs firmly against the bottom and sides of a well-buttered 9-inch pie plate. Bake the crust in a very hot oven (450°F) for 5 minutes and cool it.

Soften 1½ teaspoons gelatin in ⅓ cup heavy cream and dissolve it over hot water. Beat ¼ cup sugar into 4 beaten egg yolks. Stir in ¼ cup each of crème de cacao and green crème de menthe, and the dissolved gelatin. Chill the mixture until it is slightly thickened. Fold in 1 cup heavy cream, whipped. Pour the filling into the prepared shell and chill the pie until it is firm. Sprinkle the pie with crushed mint-flavored chocolate.

Ten years later, Raymond Sokolov featured another, richer recipe for Grasshopper Pie in *Favorite Recipes from The New York Times*. It calls for 2 cups of heavy cream, also for tinting the pie filling with "6–8 drops green food coloring."

I suspect—but cannot verify—that both recipes descend from one that appeared in *High Spirited Desserts,* a recipe flier published jointly by Knox Unflavored Gelatine and Heublein Cordials.

It begins: "Dinner guests sometimes click their heels with glee over a superb dessert." Then it goes on to urge the reader to be "devil-may-care. Knox Unflavored Gelatine provides a variety of handsome and delectable dishes. Heublein Cordials provide the spirits that give each sweet masterpiece inimitable flavor. Serve with pride. Await applause modestly."

Unfortunately, there's no date on the leaflet. Given its yellowing state, however, its purple prose, and whimsical Jester illustrations, I suspect that it belongs to the late '50s or, possibly, the early '60s.

In *The Dictionary of American Food and Drink* (revised and updated edition, 1994), John Mariani says that Grasshopper Pie "is popular in the South, where it is customarily served with a cookie crust and probably dates from the 1950s."

Grasshopper Pie

Makes a 9-inch Pie, 8 Servings

❋

I'VE TAKEN the liberty of reworking the old Knox Gelatine recipe, substituting egg white powder for raw egg whites. The dried whites whip majestically. Best of all, they're widely available and pose no threat of salmonella food poisoning.

CRUST
  1¼ cups chocolate wafer crumbs
  ¼ cup sugar
  ⅓ cup melted butter or margarine

FILLING
  1 envelope unflavored gelatin
  ½ cup sugar
  ⅛ teaspoon salt
  ½ cup cold water
  3 egg yolks
  ¼ cup green crème de menthe
  ¼ cup white crème de cacao
  2 tablespoons egg white powder
  6 tablespoons warm water
  1 cup heavy cream, stiffly whipped

OPTIONAL TOPPING
  ¾ cup heavy cream, stiffly whipped
  Bittersweet chocolate curls

1. CRUST: Preheat oven to 400°F. Mix crumbs, sugar, and melted butter. Press into 9-inch pie plate, forming crust, and bake 5 minutes; cool.

2. FILLING: Mix gelatin, ¼ cup sugar, and salt in double boiler top. Stir in water, then blend in egg yolks, one at a time.

3. Set over boiling water and cook, stirring constantly, until gelatin dissolves and mixture thickens slightly, about 5 minutes. Off heat, stir in crème de menthe and crème de cacao.

4. Chill filling, stirring occasionally, until consistency of unbeaten egg white—about 40 minutes.

5. Combine egg white powder and warm water in medium bowl and let stand 2 minutes to soften, then with mixer set at medium speed, beat to soft peaks. Add remaining ¼ cup sugar gradually and continue beating to stiff peaks. Fold gelatin mixture into beaten whites, then fold in whipped cream.

6. Turn into prepared crust and chill until firm, about 3 hours. Or better yet, refrigerate overnight. Serve as is, or if desired, top with additional whipped cream and scattering of chocolate curls.

Mile-High Pie

Makes a 9-inch Pie, 6 to 8 Servings

✳

AT A dinner party not so long ago, while I was in the throes of researching this book and talking about it to anyone who would listen, Lou Rena Hammond, a Manhattan public relations executive who reps an impressive list of hotels, restaurants, and cruise ships, said, *"Please* don't forget Mile-High Pie." To be honest, I *had* forgotten Mile-High Pie. The very next day I began polling friends

and colleagues for their recipes and reminiscences about Mile-High Pie. Suzanne Martinson, food editor of the *Pittsburgh Post-Gazette,* surfaced with this recipe and nugget of history. "In 1967," she began, "I was teaching home economics at the North Bend Junior High School in Coos Bay, Oregon. And I remember running across Mile-High Pie in a spiral-bound fund-raiser called *Home Economics Teachers' Favorite Recipes* that was published about that time." The thing about this pie, Suzanne explained, is that you get incredible volume when you beat the sugared, thawed-but-still-icy-cold frozen berries with egg whites. Which is why the pie is called "Mile-High." The name was picked up by cafes, diners, and delis in the '60s and '70s and used to describe pies with meringues of stratospheric height. But those meringue pies weren't true Mile-High Pies, which are nothing more than frozen chiffon pies. Suzanne sent me page 243 of *Home Economics Teachers' Favorite Recipes* (1967), and it contains not one but three different Mile-High Pies, submitted by home economics teachers from all over the country—from Minnesota, Nebraska, Arkansas, North Dakota, Vermont. There's no indication as to who originated the recipe, or, for that matter, when it was dreamed up or where. This is the recipe that Suzanne marked as the best. She makes her Mile-High Strawberry Pie in a nut-crumb crust and she's included that recipe, too.

NOTE: *This recipe contains raw egg white, so read the Caution on page 5.* The home economics teachers who submitted this particular Mile-High Strawberry Pie—Mrs. Ann B. Jones of Mountainburg High School in Mountainburg, Arkansas, and Mrs. Anna Delvo of Carson High School in Carson, North Dakota—say that 1½ cups fresh, sweetened strawberries can be used in place of frozen berries.

CRUST
> ¾ cup (generous) vanilla wafer crumbs (20 vanilla wafers)
> ½ cup finely ground pecans
> ¼ cup (½ stick) butter or margarine, melted

FILLING
> 1 (10-ounce package) frozen unsweetened strawberries, thawed but still ice-cold
> 1 cup sugar
> 1 tablespoon fresh lemon juice
> 2 egg whites
> 1 cup heavy cream, stiffly whipped

1. CRUST: Preheat oven to 350° F. In small bowl, mix crumbs, nuts, and butter. Press over bottom and up sides of ungreased 9-inch pie pan. Bake 12 minutes; cool completely before filling.

2. FILLING: Beat strawberries, sugar, lemon juice, and egg whites in large electric mixer bowl at high speed 15 minutes. Fold in whipped cream.

3. Mound in prepared pie shell and freeze overnight, or until firm.

MERINGUE PIES

Although lemon meringue pies proliferate in late-nineteenth-century cook-books, I find no chocolate or butterscotch meringue pie recipes in print before the 1900s. Or for that matter, chocolate or butterscotch pies, period. *Woman's Favorite Cook Book* (1902), offers a recipe for Chocolate Cream Pie, but the egg whites are folded into the filling instead of being whipped into a meringue and spread on top.

The very next year, however, *A Collection of Choice Recipes* compiled by The Ladies of Des Moines (and later reprinted by Chef Louis Szathmáry in his *Cookery Americana* series), includes a chocolate pie that is "frosted with meringue icing." Three years later (1906), the *Capital City Cook Book,* assembled by the Grace Church Guild of Madison, Wisconsin, offers a chocolate pie that is "covered with meringue."

In *Lowney's Cook Book* by Maria Willet Howard (1907), there is also a chocolate meringue pie although it masquerades as Chocolate Cream Pie. The cornstarch-and-egg-yolk thickened chocolate filling goes into a baked pie shell, then the meringue (two egg whites beaten stiff with two tablespoons sugar) is swirled on top and browned in the oven. The pie is served cold.

Not until 1915 did I find a recipe for Butterscotch Meringue Pie. It appears in the *Larkin Housewives' Cook Book* and was contributed by Mrs. Edgar Gotschall of Jacksonville, Illinois. Here is her recipe:

BUTTER SCOTCH PIE

One cup Larkin Brown Sugar, two eggs, two tablespoons flour, one cup cold water, two tablespoons butter, one teaspoon Larkin Vanilla. Mix sugar and flour together, add the water gradually and stir over the fire until thick. Add the egg yolks and butter, then vanilla. Fill baked crust, beat the whites of eggs to a stiff froth, add two tablespoons sugar. Put this on top and brown in slow oven.

By the 1920s, chocolate and butterscotch pies were becoming commonplace. The Chocolate Custard Pie in the 1924 edition of *The Boston Cooking-School Cook Book* is in fact a meringue pie, as are the two butterscotch pies in the *Library Ann's Cook Book* (1928), put out by the Minneapolis Public Library Staff Association. Not to be left out, Log Cabin Syrup featured Maple Scotch Meringue Pie in *Maple Delicacies,* its 1928 recipe booklet.

As the twentieth century wore on and cooks became more adventurous, other varieties of meringue pie began to appear, too—lime (sometimes wrongly called Key Lime Pie), orange, burnt sugar, even apple.

For a time—mostly in the '60s and '70s—diners and cafes across the country took to piling meringues on their lemon, butterscotch, coconut, and chocolate cream pies to three or four times the usual height and calling them "Mile-High Pies."

True Mile-High Pie, however, is something else again (see page 373).

Marian March Johnson Anderson's Chocolate Meringue Pie

Makes a 9-inch Pie, 8 Servings

✱

WHENEVER I'D gotten a terrific report card or had a really good piano lesson, my mother would bake this pie for me. It's a recipe she worked out in the late '40s and to this day, it's my favorite.

NOTE: To lower fat and calories somewhat, use evaporated skim milk, three egg yolks, and ½ tablespoon butter.

FILLING
1½ cups sugar
3 tablespoons cornstarch
3 cups evaporated milk

3 ounces unsweetened chocolate, coarsely chopped
4 egg yolks, lightly beaten
1 tablespoon butter or margarine
¼ teaspoon salt
2 teaspoons vanilla extract

CRUST
1 (9-inch) baked pie shell (page 399)

MERINGUE
4 egg whites
¼ teaspoon cream of tartar
½ cup sugar

1. Preheat oven to 350° F.

2. FILLING: Mix sugar and cornstarch in medium heavy saucepan. Gradually blend in milk, add chocolate, set over moderate heat, and cook, stirring constantly, until mixture thickens and boils; boil 1 minute longer.

3. Blend half of saucepan mixture into egg yolks, stir back into pan, and cook and stir 3 minutes. Off heat, stir in butter, salt, and vanilla.

4. Quick-chill filling in ice bath, whisking often to keep smooth. Pour filling into pie shell.

5. MERINGUE: Beat egg whites with cream of tartar until foamy. Add sugar gradually and continue beating until stiff and glossy. Swirl meringue over filling, making sure it touches pie shell all around.

6. Bake 15 to 20 minutes until meringue is tipped with brown. Chill pie thoroughly before serving.

1971

Alice Waters opens Chez Panisse in Berkeley, California. Her "California Cuisine" redefines American cooking. Some call her "The Mother of New American Cooking."

The "salad bar" arrives (at R.J. Grunts in Chicago).

The first link in the Starbucks chain of coffeehouses opens in Seattle.

1972

James Beard's massive *American Cookery* is published.

1973

French chefs begin abandoning the classics for Nouvelle Cuisine; American chefs soon follow their lead.

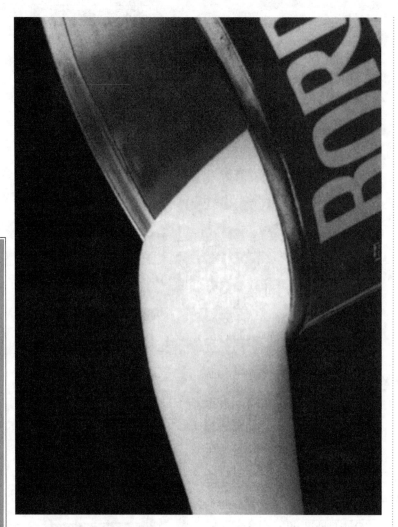

Butterscotch Meringue Pie

Makes a 9-inch Pie, 8 Servings

❋

THIS RECIPE is adapted from my all-time favorite, which appeared in the *American Home All-Purpose Cook Book* (1966). For those who'd prefer an even richer pie, *American Home* suggests a whipped cream topping in lieu of meringue.

FILLING
⅓ cup butter or margarine
1 cup firmly packed light
    brown sugar
1 cup boiling water
5 tablespoons cornstarch
¼ teaspoon salt
1½ cups milk or evaporated
    milk
3 egg yolks, lightly beaten
2 teaspoons vanilla extract

CRUST
1 (9-inch) baked pie shell
    (page 399)

MERINGUE
4 egg whites
¼ teaspoon cream of tartar
½ cup granulated sugar

1. Preheat oven to 350° F.

2. FILLING: Brown butter in medium heavy skillet over low heat. Add brown sugar and cook, stirring constantly, until mixture liquefies slightly and begins to bubble. Add boiling water slowly and carefully. Cook and stir until sugar mixture dissolves.

3. Blend cornstarch, salt, and ¼ cup milk in medium saucepan until smooth. Add remaining milk and brown sugar syrup. Cook over moderate heat, stirring constantly, until mixture thickens and boils; boil 1 minute longer.

4. Blend half of saucepan mixture into egg yolks, stir back into pan, and cook, stirring constantly, 2 minutes. Off heat, stir in vanilla.

5. Quick-chill filling in ice bath, whisking often to keep smooth. Pour filling into CRUST.

6. MERINGUE: Beat egg whites with cream of tartar until foamy. Add sugar gradually and continue beating until stiff and glossy. Swirl meringue over filling, making sure it touches pie shell all around.

7. Bake 15 to 20 minutes, until meringue is tipped with brown. Chill pie thoroughly before serving.

KEY LIME PIE

CCORDING TO John Egerton (*Southern Food*, 1987), Key Lime Pie was known in the Florida Keys "as far back as the 1890s." I don't doubt that one bit because in those prerefrigerator days, fresh milk was a poor keeper. What local cooks had learned to rely on was the sweetened condensed milk Gail Borden had begun canning shortly before the Civil War.

But because Key Lime Pie seems not to have ever reached the rest of America until well into the twentieth century, and because it has become such a favorite, I think it merits inclusion here.

Jeanne Voltz and Caroline Stuart (*The Florida Cookbook*, 1993) call Key Lime Pie "Florida's Ultimate Dessert." They add that "Florida Keys folk are purists about their Key Lime Pie: It must contain Key lime juice, not the Persian limes that are commercially grown; sweetened condensed milk is obligatory, and the filling is never tinted green with green food coloring, but is a natural creamy yellow color." They further say that in the beginning, flaky pastry pie shells were used to cradle the filling, not graham cracker crusts, the choice of many cooks today.

Their Key Lime Pie is swirled about with meringue, but they admit that "there are certain 'legal' variations on the famous delicacy—for example, folding the meringue into the egg-yolk, lime-juice, and condensed-milk mixture for a lighter filling; then topping the pie with whipped cream." They further add that some cooks use only the yolks in the filling, top the pie with whipped cream, and save "the whites for another use."

A word about Key limes: John Egerton says that these small, thin-skinned, mouth-puckeringly-sour yellow limes (also called "golden," "Mexican," or "West Indian" limes) may have been brought to Haiti by Columbus in 1493. Believed to be indigenous to Southeast Asia, Key limes were, according to Egerton, "thriving on the southern tip of Florida well before the Civil War . . . were a thriving commercial crop there until 1926, when a hurricane wiped out the groves."

For Key Lime Pie, freshly squeezed Key lime juice is the purist's preference. But Voltz and Stuart say that bottled Key lime juice makes an acceptable substitute.

They even provide a mail-order source: Florida Key West Inc., 3521 Central Avenue, Fort Myers, FL 33901.

Real Key Lime Pie

Makes a 9-inch Pie, 6 to 8 Servings

✳

I'VE ADAPTED this recipe from one that appears in one of my favorite books, *The Florida Cookbook* (1993) by Jeanne Voltz and Caroline Stuart. They caution that making Key Lime Pie the old-fashioned way is risky today because "uncooked eggs are thought to be a health hazard." They solved the salmonella problem by taking a tip from Jack Donnelly, chef at the St. Petersburg Yacht Club: He bakes his Key lime filling 15 minutes at 350° F, spreads on the meringue, then bakes the pie 15 minutes longer.

FILLING

4 egg yolks, lightly beaten
1 (14-ounce) can sweetened condensed milk (not evaporated milk)
½ cup Key lime juice, preferably fresh

CRUST

1 (9-inch) baked pastry shell or graham cracker crust (pages 398–99)

MERINGUE

4 egg whites
Pinch cream of tartar
½ cup sugar

1. FILLING: Preheat oven to 350° F.

2. Mix egg yolks, condensed milk, and lime juice in large mixing bowl; stir until mixture thickens, 2 to 3 minutes.

NOTE: The intense acidity of the Key limes "cooks" and sets the yolks.

3. Pour filling into CRUST and bake 15 minutes.

4. MERINGUE: Beat egg whites with cream of tartar until foamy; add sugar, 2 tablespoons at a time, and continue beating to stiff peaks. Swirl over hot filling, making sure meringue touches crust all around.

5. Return pie to oven and bake about 15 minutes longer, until meringue is tipped with brown.

6. Cool pie several hours and serve at room temperature.

Sour Cream Raisin Pie

Makes a 9-inch Pie, 8 Servings

✳

LIKE CRANBERRY-RAISIN pie (page 388), Sour Cream Raisin Pie seems to belong to the twentieth century. Joanne Lamb Hayes, food editor of *Country Living*, tells me she found a recipe for it in a booklet published by McNess, a manufacturer of patent medicines and flavorings. "There's no date on the booklet," Joanne lamented, "but there are ads in the back and from the looks of the car the doctor is driving, I'd say this was printed about 1910." My own search turned up a recipe in the *Larkin Housewives' Cook Book* (1915), which calls for one cup each of Larkin Raisins, Larkin Sugar, and sour cream, which Larkin obviously didn't manufacture. For good measure, one teaspoon Larkin Cinnamon is tossed in to flavor the pie. The Larkin pie is topped with meringue. Not so this more modern open-face custard pie. It is adapted from a spicier recipe that appeared in *Betty Crocker's Picture Cookbook* (1950).

NOTE: If you use a frozen pie shell, you will need the deep-dish variety.

3 eggs
1 tablespoon plus 1 teaspoon all-purpose flour
⅔ cup sugar
¼ teaspoon salt
½ teaspoon ground cinnamon
¼ teaspoon freshly grated nutmeg
1⅓ cups sour cream
1⅓ cups seedless raisins
1 (9-inch) unbaked pie shell (page 399)

1. Preheat oven to 350° F.

2. Beat eggs until light and fluffy. Mix flour, sugar, salt, cinnamon, and nutmeg and blend into eggs. Fold in sour cream and raisins.

3. Pour into pie shell and bake 50 to 60 minutes until knife inserted midway between center and rim comes out clean. Cool pie before cutting.

An Exceptionally Serviceable and Most Carefully Built White Porcelain Enameled Sanitary GAS RANGE

Description of Stove on page 1121

View showing big capacity of range with Odor Hood rolled up under Warming Closet; also shows interior of baking and broiling ovens with doors of ovens opened, forming shelves.

☞ If wanted with six cooking holes instead of four, as illustrated, add $3.00 to the price of any size listed below.

View showing closed Ovens and how the Odor Hood when down prevents steam and odor from coming into kitchen. Also shows the Sadiron Heater used as a cake griddle.

☞ Be sure to state whether you use manufactured or natural gas. Cannot be used with acetylene gas or gasoline gas.

PRICES—E-Z-est Way No. 200 White Porcelain Enameled Sanitary Gas Range, made in three sizes, securely crated, ready to set up and use.
☞ If wanted with ovens at left of cooking top to suit the conditions or light in your kitchen, ADD 25 cents to prices below.

Catalog No.	Price for Manufactured Gas	Price for Natural Gas	Baking Oven, Inches	Broiling Oven, Inches	Size Cooking Top, With End Shelf, In.	Floor Space, Inches	Size Pipe, Inches	Shipping Wt., Lbs.
22V786	$35.00	$35.45	16x20x12	16x20x12	30x22¼	46½x26	5	480
22V787	36.49	36.98	18x20x12	18x20x12	30x22¼	48½x26	5	450
22V788	37.96	38.45	20x20x12	20x20x12	30x22¼	50½x26	5	460

We guarantee safe delivery and ship at once from our NEWARK, OHIO, foundry.

It Is Your Duty to Buy as Good a Monument as Your Funds Permit. See Page 1381. SEARS, ROEBUCK AND CO., 474V CHICAGO, ILL. 1119

HÄAGEN-DAZS: WHAT'S IN A NAME?

IN THE late 1920s, a young Polish immigrant named Reuben Mattus hitched up a horse and wagon and set out to peddle ice cream on the streets of the Bronx. After thirty years of moderate success with the old family recipe, Mattus decided to enrich it with egg yolks and a whopping 17 percent butterfat ("I can't be the only one in the world who wants something better," he told his daughter) and at the same time to give it a classier name.

Having astutely observed that Americans were impressed by products with exotic foreign appeal and thus likely to pay more for them, he sat down with his wife, Rose, one evening and together they made up the absolutely meaningless and nearly unpronounceable "Häagen Dazs," which they hoped would sound richly Scandinavian. To further the image, Mattus put a map of Denmark on the package. Then he doubled his price.

"I'll get a few accounts, I'll make a living," he predicted in what proved to be a stunning understatement: the super-rich ice cream was so popular that in 1983 when Mattus eventually sold the company (to Pillsbury) it fetched seventy million. Oddly, a year before his death Mattus did a complete about-face and brought out a 97 percent fat-free ice cream.

French Silk Pie

Makes a 9-inch Pie, 10 Servings

❋

CHOCOLATE PIES were virtually unknown before the twentieth century. But once they began showing up in early 1900s cookbooks, there was no stopping the variations dreamed up by inventive American cooks. This particular recipe—as rich as a French pastry and as smooth as silk—dates to the second half of this century. Adapted from a recipe that first appeared in *Better Homes and Gardens All-Time Favorite Pies* (1978), then reappeared in a salmonella-proof version in the 1996 edition of the *Better Homes and Gardens New Cook Book,* it is as good as they come.

  ¾ cup sugar
  ¾ cup (1½ sticks) butter (no substitute)
  1 (6-ounce) package semisweet chocolate chips, melted and cooled
  1 teaspoon vanilla extract
  ¾ cup frozen egg product, thawed
  1 (9-inch) baked pie shell (page 399)
  1 cup heavy cream, stiffly whipped
  Chocolate curls (optional garnish)

1. Cream sugar and butter in large electric mixer bowl at medium speed 4 minutes, until fluffy. Stir in cooled chocolate and vanilla, then gradually add egg product and beat at high speed, scraping sides of bowl constantly, until light and fluffy.

2. Turn filling into pie shell, cover, and chill overnight or until set.

3. Swirl whipped cream over the top and, if desired, sprinkle with chocolate curls.

Brownie Pie

Makes a 9-inch Pie, 8 Servings

✳

ANOTHER OF the twentieth century's stellar chocolate pies. This one, created in the test kitchens of *Farm Journal* magazine and included in *Farm Journal's Best-Ever Pies* (1981), is a giant fudgy brownie baked in a pie shell. This is my adaptation.

½ cup (1 stick) butter or margarine
4 ounces unsweetened chocolate
¾ cup firmly packed brown sugar (light or dark)
¼ cup water
2 eggs, separated
1 teaspoon vanilla extract
⅓ cup unsifted all-purpose flour
¼ teaspoon salt
¾ cup coarsely chopped walnuts or pecans
1 (9-inch) unbaked pie shell (page 399)
12 walnut or pecan halves

1. Preheat oven to 350°F.

2. Melt butter and chocolate in medium heavy saucepan over low heat. Cool slightly, then beat in sugar, water, egg yolks, and vanilla. Stir in flour and salt; set aside.

3. Beat egg whites to stiff peaks and fold into chocolate mixture. Fold in chopped walnuts.

4. Turn into pie shell and arrange walnut halves around edge of filling.

5. Bake about 40 minutes or until set around edge. Transfer to wire rack and cool to room temperature before cutting. Serve as is or top with a scoop of ice cream.

Mud Pie

Makes a 9-inch Pie, 8 Servings

✳

I REMEMBER distinctly when and where I first tasted this pie, heaven to a chocoholic like me. It was in the mid-'70s at the newly rebuilt Mills House Hotel in Charleston, South Carolina. I was lunching in

the courtyard and at the urging of the waiter, ordered Mud Pie, which I naively believed to be the creation of the chef. Also sometimes called Mississippi Mud Pie, this is a Nabisco recipe, which begins with a pie shell made of finely crushed Oreo cookies. Into it goes a quart of ice cream (the Mills House chef used chocolate; Nabisco calls for coffee). Next come hot fudge sauce and whipped cream. Calorie overload, to be sure, not to mention a glut of saturated fat and cholesterol. But what glorious sin this is.

26 chocolate sandwich cookies, finely crushed
¼ cup margarine, melted
1 quart coffee or chocolate ice cream, softened
1½ cups hot fudge sauce (page 408) or store-bought
1 cup heavy cream, stiffly whipped (flavored, if desired, with sugar and vanilla extract)

1. Mix cookie crumbs and margarine in small bowl; press over bottom and up sides of 9-inch pie plate.

2. Fill crust with ice cream. Top with fudge sauce and freeze until firm—about 6 hours.

3. Cut into wedges and drift each portion with whipped cream.

ANGEL PIE

ONE OF the prettiest and certainly one of the most popular desserts of the Thirties," writes Sylvia Lovegren in *Fashionable Food* (1995), "were meringue tortes (sometimes called meringue cakes, schaum tortes, angel pies, or meringues glacées, if they were filled with ice cream). She adds that these were popular not only "for Ladies' Luncheons, but also for functions when the men were invited." They could, she explains, be baked in rounds and sandwiched together with whipped cream. They could also be shaped into hearts or baskets or pie shells and filled.

In *American Cookery* (1972), James Beard states that Angel Pie was the "most frequently printed of all the pie recipes in sectional cookbooks of the last sixty years," which suggests a date of origin in the early 1900s.

I was unable to find any Angel Pie predating the 1930s, although it's possible that earlier ones exist. The more I searched, the more I began to wonder if perhaps Beard had meringue pie shells in mind, which *are* several decades older than Angel Pie.

I turned up one in *The Settlement Cook Book* (1903). Called "Kiss Torte," it directs the cook to "Beat the whites of six fresh eggs to a stiff dry froth," then to beat in two cups granulated sugar "a little at a time." A teaspoon each of vanilla and vinegar are added for flavor. Two-thirds of the meringue is put into a greased springform pan, and the balance dropped from a teaspoon around the edge in "small kisses" to form the sides of the shell. Once baked and cooled, the shell is filled with whipped cream and berries. Not quite Angel Pie. But a forerunner, surely.

The first Angel Pie I've located dates to 1936 and *Ruth Wakefield's Toll House Tried and True Recipes:* a crispy nine-inch meringue shell mounded with yolk-rich lemon curd, then covered with unsweetened whipped cream. "Put in the ice box until ready to serve," Mrs. Wakefield instructs. "The second day you will still find the pie very good."

The 1943 edition of *Joy of Cooking* (but not the 1931 or 1936 editions) offers a recipe for Angel Pie, and it, like Ruth Wakefield's, consists of a meringue shell, lemon curd, and whipped cream. The Angel Pie in *Fannie Farmer* (1946) is different: A meringue shell filled with crushed fruit swirled about by whipped cream. Fannie Farmer also offers lemon and orange curd variations.

The Good Housekeeping Cook Book (1942) features an Angel Pie of a different sort—Chocolate Nut. Here it is, word for word.

CHOCOLATE NUT ANGEL PIE

1 9-inch Meringue Pie Shell, p. 725	¾ cup semi-sweet chocolate pieces
½ cup chopped filberts, walnuts, or pecans	3 tablesp. hot water
	1 teasp. vanilla flavoring
	1 cup heavy cream, whipped

Prepare Meringue Pie Shell, p. 725. After lining 9-inch pie plate as directed, sprinkle with nuts; bake in slow oven of 275° F about 1 hr. or until delicately browned and crisp to touch. Cool thoroughly. Melt chocolate in double boiler. Stir in water; cook until thickened. Cool slightly, add vanilla; fold in whipped cream. Turn into meringue shell. Chill 2 to 3 hours or until set. Makes 1 9-inch pie.

As lovely as Chocolate Nut Angel Pie may be, the hands-down favorite has to be the classic, lemon-curd-filled Angel Pie. Is any better than this one adapted from James Beard's *American Cookery* (1972)?

James Beard's Angel Pie

Makes a 9-inch Pie, 6 to 8 Servings

✳

FOR THIS Angel Pie, Beard also offers three variations: (1) *Orange Angel Pie* (which substitutes ¼ cup fresh orange juice for the lemon zest and juice in the basic recipe and adds 1 tablespoon each fresh lemon juice and finely grated orange zest); (2) *Lime Angel Pie* (which substitutes 3 tablespoons fresh lime juice, 1 tablespoon lemon juice, and 1 teaspoon finely grated lime zest for the lemon juice and zest called for); and (3) *Berry or Cranberry Angel Pie* (which uses ¾ cup sieved fresh raspberries, strawberries, loganberries, or blackberries [or ¾ cup sieved cranberry sauce or jelly] and 1 teaspoon lemon juice in place of the lemon juice and zest in the basic recipe).

MERINGUE SHELL

2 egg whites
⅛ teaspoon cream of tartar
½ cup sugar

TART LEMON FILLING

4 egg yolks
½ cup sugar
¼ teaspoon salt
¼ cup fresh lemon juice
2 tablespoons finely grated lemon zest
1 cup heavy cream, stiffly whipped

1. MERINGUE SHELL: Preheat oven to 300° F. Slide 9-inch pie pan into oven for a few minutes to heat slightly then, using crumple of paper towel, lightly rub vegetable oil over bottom and sides of hot pan. Blot up excess oil; set pan aside.

2. With electric mixer at medium speed, beat egg whites until foamy. Beat in cream of tartar, then gradually add sugar, beating all the while. Continue beating until meringue peaks stiffly.

3. Spread meringue evenly over bottom and up sides of pan, forming a pie shell, and bake 1 hour. Do not open oven door for the first half hour or shell will not be puffy. When shell is pale yellow, turn off oven, leave door ajar, and cool to room temperature in oven. Shell will sink somewhat in center, but this is as it should be.

4. LEMON FILLING: Beat yolks lightly in top of double boiler. Add sugar, salt, lemon juice and zest, set over slowly boiling water and cook, stirring constantly, until thick. Remove from heat and chill at least 1 hour.

5. Whip cream until stiff and spread half of it over meringue shell, leaving a 1-inch margin all around.

6. Spread lemon filling on top of cream, then frost with remaining whipped cream. Some recipes recommend folding the cream into the filling. In either case, return the pie to the refrigerator and chill 24 hours or overnight before serving.

Pecan Pie

As a good daughter of the South practically weaned on pecan pie, I had always assumed that it dated back to Colonial days. Apparently not. Still, I find it difficult to believe that some good plantation cook didn't stir pecans into her syrup pie or brown sugar pie. Alas, there are no records to prove it. In fact, I could find no cookbooks printing pecan pie recipes before the early twentieth century. And only in the 1940s did "Fannie" and "Joy" begin offering recipes for it.

In *Southern Food: At Home, on the Road, in History* (1987), for me the definitive work on the evolution of Southern cooking, John Egerton writes: "We have heard the claim that Louisianans were eating pecan candies before 1800, and with the sugar and syrup produced from cane at that time, it is conceivable that they were eating pecan pies, too, but there are no recipes or other bits of evidence to prove it."

Food historian Meryle Evans, with whom I discussed the puzzle, says she's been unable to trace pecan pie any further back than 1925. She believes pecan pie may even have been created by Karo home economists. If Karo did not originate pecan pie, it certainly popularized the recipe as a riffle through twentieth-century cookbooks large and small quickly suggests. Nearly all pecan pie recipes call for Karo corn syrup.

The only clue to earlier origins for pecan pie that I've been able to unearth is this syrup pie recipe published in *From North Carolina Kitchens, Favorite Recipes Old and New* published in 1953 by The North Carolina Federation of Home Demonstration Clubs, a network of educational clubs for farm women sponsored by the county, state, and federal governments:

SYRUP PIE

This recipe was taken from the cookbook of the grand-mother of Mrs. C.B. Ross of Tennessee. Another of the Ross standbys in these days of little sugar is the old-fashioned syrup pie. The more pecans you add, the better it is. I believe this must be a really Southern dish, for I never heard of it until I came "down to these parts." But I'll bet it is a dish that we'll be fixing even when we have all the sugar we want.

1 cup syrup
2 eggs
1 tablespoon butter
1 teaspoon vanilla

Pecans—however many you can spare

Beat eggs very hard, add syrup, vanilla and butter. Pour into unbaked pie shell and add nuts. Bake in slow oven (325° F) until set.—Mrs. B.S. Vassar, Durham County

The obvious question here is, How old was Mrs. C.B. Ross of Tennessee in 1953 when this little North Carolina farm women's cookbook was published? If she was an eighteen-year-old bride, her grandmother's syrup pie may belong to the early twentieth century. But if she was up in years herself, that would push the date of this particular "pecan pie" back into the nineteenth century.

So . . . the origin of pecan pie remains a mystery. Not so its popularity. John Egerton elevates it to the status of "national dessert."

Classic Pecan Pie

Makes a 9-inch Pie, 8 Servings

✳

THIS IS the pecan pie that was created using Karo Corn Syrup early this century. It appears, together with three modern variations, in *Karo Sweet & Simple Recipes*, a recipe booklet printed in 1990 by Best Foods, a division of CPC International Inc.

NOTE: If you use a prepared pie shell, choose the deep-dish variety, and bake on a preheated cookie sheet.

3 eggs
1 cup sugar
1 cup corn syrup (light or dark)
2 tablespoons margarine, melted
1 teaspoon vanilla extract
1¼ cups pecan halves
1 unbaked 9-inch pie shell (page 399)

1. Preheat oven to 350°F.

2. Beat eggs slightly in medium bowl. Add sugar, corn syrup, margarine, and vanilla; stir until well blended. Mix in pecans.

3. Set pie shell on heavy-duty baking sheet and pour in filling.

4. Bake 50 to 55 minutes, until knife inserted midway between center and rim comes out clean.

5. Cool pie on wire rack to room temperature before cutting.

---VARIATIONS---

CALIFORNIA PECAN PIE: Prepare as directed, but blend ¼ cup sour cream into eggs before adding other ingredients. Makes a 9-inch pie, 8 servings.

KENTUCKY BOURBON PECAN PIE: Prepare as directed, adding 2 tablespoons bourbon to filling. Makes a 9-inch pie, 8 servings.

CHOCOLATE PECAN PIE: Prepare as directed, but reduce sugar to ⅓ cup. Melt 4 ounces semisweet chocolate along with margarine and blend into filling. Makes a 9-inch pie, 8 servings.

Buttermilk Pecan Pie

Makes a 9-inch Pie, 6 to 8 Servings

✳

THIS RECIPE from *Fiesta: Favorite Recipes of South Texas* (1973), a fundraiser published by the Junior League of Corpus Christi, was sent to me by Lou Hammond, a New York public relations executive, who thinks it's one of the best pecan pies ever. Certainly it's less cloying than most. The recipe came from *Fiesta* coeditor Mrs. Lev H. Prichard III, who offered this bit of history: "This Buttermilk Pecan Pie was a family recipe often prepared by a career U.S. Navy chef for such dignitaries as the late President Harry S. Truman. Through the years of his military career, the chef refused to share his recipe. Finally, when he retired, he allowed it to be published in a navy newspaper."

½ cup (1 stick) butter or margarine
2 cups sugar
2 teaspoons vanilla extract
3 eggs
3 tablespoons all-purpose flour
¼ teaspoon salt
1 cup buttermilk
½ cup coarsely chopped pecans
1 (9-inch) unbaked pie shell (page 399)

1. Preheat oven to 300°F.

2. Cream butter in medium bowl; add sugar, ½ cup at a time, and continue creaming until light. Blend in vanilla. Add eggs, one at a time, beating just to incorporate. Combine flour and salt and blend in. Finally, mix in buttermilk.

3. Sprinkle pecans into pie shell, then pour in buttermilk mixture.

4. Bake about 1½ hours until filling sets like custard. Cool pie on wire rack to room temperature before cutting.

Magnolia Grill Pecan Tart

*Makes an 11-inch Tart,
8 to 10 Servings*

✳

ONE OF the South's outstanding restaurants is Ben and Karen Barker's Magnolia Grill in Durham, North Carolina. Barker, a Tar Heel brought up in the college town of Chapel Hill, graduated in the 1980s from the Culinary Institute of America at Hyde Park, New York. It was there that he met his future wife, Karen, who hails from Brooklyn. Together they now do wondrous things at Magnolia Grill, for the most part reinterpreting "the flavor memories" of Ben's Southern childhood. Karen, the pastry chef, created this stellar variation on pecan pie (what makes it different is that Karen toasts the pecans and browns the butter that go into the filling). She serves it with Bourbon-Vanilla Ice Cream (recipe page 411). Both recipes were printed in the July 1994 issue of *Food & Wine* in a story I wrote on the Barkers.

PASTRY

*1¼ cups plus 2 tablespoons
    unsifted all-purpose flour
1 tablespoon plus 1 teaspoon
    granulated sugar
Pinch salt
½ cup (1 stick) cold butter, cut
    into small pieces*

*1 egg, separated
1 tablespoon milk
1 egg white, lightly beaten*

FILLING

*2½ cups coarsely chopped
    pecans
¼ cup (½ stick) butter
½ cup firmly packed light
    brown sugar
¼ cup granulated sugar
1¼ cups light corn syrup
¼ cup bourbon
1 teaspoon vanilla extract
2 eggs
3 egg yolks
¾ cup pecan halves*

1. PASTRY: Pulse flour, sugar, and salt in food processor fitted with metal chopping blade to blend. Add butter and pulse until texture of coarse meal. In small bowl mix egg yolk and milk. Add to processor and pulse just until dough comes together. Pat dough into disk, wrap in plastic wrap, and chill 1 hour.

2. FILLING: Preheat oven to 350°F. Spread chopped pecans on baking

sheet and toast 5 to 7 minutes, until fragrant. Remove nuts from oven; leave oven on.

3. Brown butter lightly in small skillet over moderate heat, about 3 minutes. Transfer to medium bowl; whisk in the two sugars, corn syrup, bourbon, and vanilla. Whisk in eggs and egg yolks.

4. On lightly floured surface, roll dough into 13-inch circle. Ease into 11 × 1-inch-round tart tin with removable bottom; press dough evenly into pan and up sides. Trim overlap. Prick bottom of tart shell with fork, then set shell in freezer 5 minutes.

5. Line pastry with foil, fill with pie weights or dried beans, and bake 20 minutes. Remove foil and weights and bake 15 minutes, until golden. Brush pastry with egg white and set tart tin on heavy-duty baking sheet.

6. Spread toasted pecan pieces in tart shell. Arrange pecan halves in ring around edge, then gently pour in filling, covering nuts evenly.

7. Bake tart about 45 minutes until filling is set. Cool tart on wire rack to room temperature.

8. Remove pan sides and set tart on large plate. Serve topped, if you like, with Bourbon-Vanilla Ice Cream.

Mock Apple Pie

THIS RECIPE was all the rage when it first appeared in the '30s and remains popular in deepest heartland. To my great surprise, in leafing through late-nineteenth-century cookbooks, I found this Mock Apple Pie in *Mrs. Hill's Southern Practical Cookery and Receipt Book* (1872):

One large grated lemon, three large soda crackers, two even tablespoons of butter, two teacups of sugar, one egg, a wineglass of water poured over the crackers. These will make two pies, baked with two crusts.

All I can say is those nineteenth-century soda crackers must have been as big as pizzas if three of them made two pies.

Mock Apple Pie may not be a wholly twentieth-

century invention. But using Ritz Crackers is, because the National Biscuit Company introduced them only in November 1934. And only in the Philadelphia/Baltimore areas.

They were such a hit, National Biscuit took Ritz national in 1935, priced them at 19 cents a box, and in that one year sold five million crackers.

Because of their "buttery" richness, Ritz Crackers clearly make a finer Mock Apple Pie than ordinary soda crackers. Here, then, is the kitchen-tested recipe for Mock Apple Pie just as it came to me from the Nabisco Consumer Food Center.

Incidental Intelligence: Mock Apple Pie is the most requested Nabisco recipe of all time.

RITZ MOCK APPLE PIE

Makes 10 Servings

Pastry for two-crust 9-inch pie (page 399)
36 RITZ Crackers, coarsely broken (about 1¾ cups crumbs)

1¾ cups water
2 cups sugar
2 teaspoons cream of tartar
2 tablespoons lemon juice

Grated rind of one lemon
2 tablespoons FLEISCHMANN'S 70% Corn Oil Spread
½ teaspoon ground cinnamon

ROLL out half the pastry and line a 9-inch pie plate. Place cracker crumbs in prepared crust. In saucepan, over high heat, heat water, sugar and cream of tartar to a boil; simmer for 15 minutes. Add lemon juice and rind; cool. Pour syrup over cracker crumbs. Dot with spread; sprinkle with cinnamon. Roll out remaining pastry; place over pie. Trim, seal and flute edges. Slit top crust to allow steam to escape.

BAKE at 425°F for 30 to 35 minutes or until crust is crisp and golden. Serve warm.

ESKIMO PIE

O NE AFTERNOON in 1920, as a little boy stood at the counter of his Iowa candy shop agonizing over whether to spend his nickel on ice cream or a chocolate bar, inspiration struck proprietor Christian Nelson: If he could somehow combine the two, he could spare indecisive customers the pain of choosing. After a year of fruitless experiments, he succeeded in coating an ice cream bar with a mix of melted cocoa butter, sugar, and chocolate, then quick-freezing it. Nelson dubbed his invention the I-Scream Bar and gave it a catchy slogan: "I scream, you scream, we all scream for I-Scream." But Russell Stover, Nelson's marketing partner, hated the name. One evening Stover asked his dinner guests to come up with a better one. Someone suggested "Eskimo," someone else added "Pie." And Stover, himself, came up with the idea of wrapping the bars in foil. In a fairy-tale ending, everyone was happy: Eskimo Pies sold like hotcakes, Reynolds Wrap aluminum foil would later become famous, and Russell Stover made it big in the candy business.

Cranberry-Raisin Pie

Makes an 8- or 9-inch Pie,
6 to 8 Servings

❋

ALSO CALLED Mock Cherry Pie, this unusual recipe emerged early in the twentieth century. The 1906 edition of *The Boston Cooking-School Cook Book* includes a recipe for it, as does the 1907 *Lowney's Cook Book* by Maria Willet Howard. From then up until World War II, Cranberry-Raisin Pie was a cookbook staple. Then it fell from favor (except in New England) and has yet to regain its popularity. This particular recipe was given to me by Ruth Buchan, founder of Doubleday's Cook Book Guild. Ruth told me that when she was a girl in North Andover, Massachusetts, this was her favorite pie. It remained so until the day she died in 1995 at the age of eighty.

NOTE: Use a 9-inch frozen pie crust (not deep-dish), or if making pastry from scratch, choose an 8-inch pie pan.

> 2 cups fresh or frozen cranberries
> 1 cup seedless raisins, coarsely chopped
> 1¼ cups sugar
> ½ cup water
> 1 teaspoon vanilla extract
> Pastry for a 2-crust, 8- or 9-inch pie (page 399)

1. Preheat oven to 375°F with heavy-duty baking sheet on middle rack.

2. Mix cranberries, raisins, sugar, water, and vanilla in medium non-reactive pan and cook over moderate heat, stirring often, 10 minutes until cranberries pop and mixture is very thick. Cool 45 minutes.

3. Spoon mixture into unbaked pie shell. Ease top crust into place, roll overhang under and crimp top and bottom crusts together to seal in filling. Make four to six decorative steam vents in top crust.

4. Set pie in oven on baking sheet and bake 10 minutes. Reduce oven temperature to 325°F and bake 40 to 45 minutes longer, until crust is nicely browned and filling bubbly. Cool pie before cutting.

Downright Delicious SUN-MAID Raisin Recipes

CHEESECAKES

"CHEESECAKE," WRITES food historian Meryle Evans (*Fine Dining,* September 1989), "dates back to ancient Greece." She adds that "cakes made with sheep or goat cheese, flour, and honey were fed to runners during the first Olympic games on the island of Delos in 776 B.C."

The Romans, who glorified most things Greek, also glorified cheesecake. "One of the three recipes offered by Cato," Evans says, "called for a topping of pounded poppy seeds and a honey glaze."

Cheesecake went into eclipse during the Dark Ages, but surfaced in France in the eleventh century when monks at Roquefort began making cakes out of their mold-ripened blue cheeses.

Evans also writes that Anne Boleyn, one of Henry VIII's star-crossed wives, had a passion for cheesecake "made with fresh curds." Her recipe, strewn with currants and flavored with sherry, rose water, and cinnamon, remained a favorite in the British royal family, says Evans, for hundreds of years.

In her historical notes to the facsimile edition of Mary Randolph's *The Virginia House-wife* (1824), Karen Hess admits to being puzzled by Mrs. Randolph's omission of a recipe for "cheesecake, which had been popular in England since the early fifteenth century, at least, and remained so in the Colonies."

Many nineteenth-century American cookery books do include recipes for cheesecake, beginning, as often as not, with the curding of the milk with rennet.

But the silky, cream-cheese cheesecake is something else again, a turn-of-the-century arriviste introduced, for the most part, by Jewish delicatessens in New York City.

Evans traces the beginning of "the New York cheesecake saga" to the 1920s and attributes it to "an enterprising delicatessen owner, Arnold Reuben [who] opened a restaurant on 58th Street between Fifth and Madison Avenues" at that time. Soon Reuben had rivals, among them Leonard's on Manhattan's Upper East Side, Junior's in Brooklyn, but maybe most of all, Lindy's, a Broadway restaurant popular with the theater crowd.

According to Molly O'Neill (*New York Cookbook,* 1992), the smooth, rich cheesecake served at Lindy's in the 1940s became the quintessential "New York Cheesecake," the one by which all others are judged. For a time, O'Neill adds, it was baked by A&D Cheesecake of East Brunswick, New Jersey, which dispensed with the thick cookie crust and substituted one made of graham cracker crumbs.

As for the supermarketing of cheesecake, Meryle Evans credits Chicago baker Charles Lubin. "In 1949," she writes, "he founded a new company and named it after his daughter Sara Lee." Lubin's frozen cheesecakes—the classic cream cheese variety with the silky sour cream topping—are now sold by nearly every American grocery. And as the commercials boast—double negatives and all—"Nobody doesn't like Sara Lee."

For some reason, cheesecakes have always tempted the lily-gilder and in this country from the '50s on, there have been cheesecakes of nearly every color, every flavor. Some are glazed with berries or pineapple or marmalades, some are scattered with nuts, some are marbleized. For the nutritionally aware, there are now even tofu cheesecakes.

What follow, beginning with Lindy's New York-Style Cheesecake, are the clear winners.

Lindy's New York-Style Cheesecake

Makes a 9-inch Cheesecake, 10 to 12 Servings

❋

THIS RECIPE was adapted from the one that appears in Molly O'Neill's wonderful *New York Cookbook* (1992).

CRUST

1 cup unsifted all-purpose flour
¼ cup sugar
1 teaspoon finely grated lemon zest
¼ teaspoon vanilla extract
1 egg yolk
½ cup (1 stick) unsalted butter, softened (no substitute)
2 tablespoons water (about)

FILLING

5 (8-ounce) packages cream cheese, softened
1¾ cups sugar
3 tablespoons all-purpose flour
1½ teaspoons finely grated lemon zest
1½ teaspoons finely grated orange zest
5 eggs
2 egg yolks
¼ teaspoon vanilla extract
¼ cup heavy cream

1. CRUST: Mix flour, sugar, and lemon zest in medium bowl; make well in center. Add vanilla, egg yolk, and butter, then with pastry blender or fork, work into dough, adding water as needed so dough holds together. Shape into ball, wrap in plastic wrap, and refrigerate 1 hour.

2. Preheat oven to 400° F. Butter bottom and sides of 9-inch springform pan and set aside.

3. On floured surface, roll one-third of dough into 9-inch round and ease into pan. Dough is fragile; don't worry if it breaks, simply piece together, pressing firmly over bottom of pan. Bake 15 minutes until golden, then cool in pan on wire rack.

4. Roll remaining dough in pieces and fit around sides of pan, one piece at a time, pressing seams all round and keeping edges as neat as possible.

5. FILLING: Raise oven temperature to 550° F. Beat cheese, sugar, flour, and lemon and orange zests in large electric mixer bowl at medium speed until smooth. Beat in eggs and egg yolks, then vanilla and cream.

6. Pour into crust and bake on heavy-duty baking sheet 12 to 15 minutes. Reduce oven temperature to 200° F and bake 1 hour longer.

7. Turn oven off, open door wide and cool cheesecake in oven 30 minutes.

8. Remove from oven and chill before serving.

TIMELINE

1973

Borden retires "Elsie the Cow."

Connecticut engineer Carl G. Sontheimer unveils the Cuisinart Food Processor at the Chicago housewares show.

Mid-'70s

Proliferation of spicy new cuisines in metropolitan America; Hunan and Szechuan restaurants phase out "chop suey" houses.

Yogurt goes mainstream—in a dozen different flavors.

1975

The Doubleday Cookbook appears, providing, for the first time, per-serving calorie counts for each recipe.

1977

"Blush" wines appear.

Cheese Pie

Makes a 9-inch Cheesecake, 10 Servings

✳

TO MY mind, this is the best cheesecake in all creation. The recipe was given to me in the early '50s by a young faculty wife at North Carolina State University in Raleigh who'd gotten it from a New York relative. And I thought so highly of it I included it in *The Doubleday Cookbook* (1975), which I coauthored with Elaine Hanna. Compared to the Lindy's New York-Style Cheesecake (page 391), it's a snap to make.

CRUST

    18 graham crackers, crushed
        (1½ cups crumbs)
    ¼ cup sugar
    5 tablespoons butter or
        margarine, melted

FILLING

    2 (8-ounce) packages cream
        cheese, softened
    2 eggs
    ½ cup sugar
    1 teaspoon vanilla extract

TOPPING

    1 cup sour cream
    ¼ cup sugar
    1 teaspoon vanilla extract

1. CRUST: Preheat oven to 375°F. Mix all ingredients and pat firmly over bottom and halfway up sides of 9-inch springform pan; set aside.

2. FILLING: Beat all ingredients in large electric mixer bowl at medium speed until smooth.

3. Pour into crust and bake 20 minutes. Remove from oven and cool 15 minutes. Raise oven temperature to 475°F.

4. TOPPING: Mix all ingredients and carefully spread over filling. Bake cheesecake 10 minutes longer.

5. Cool cheesecake in pan on wire rack to room temperature, then cover and chill 10 to 12 hours.

Chocolate Marble Cheesecake

*Makes a 9-inch Cheesecake,
16 Servings*

✳

I LOVE cheesecakes and am constantly experimenting with new flavor combinations. This is one of my more recent recipes and it's delicious, if I do say so, myself. A bit of cinnamon in the crust adds mystery.

CRUST

    ⅔ cup graham cracker crumbs
    1½ tablespoons granulated
        sugar

    2½ tablespoons butter or
        margarine, melted
    1 ounce unsweetened chocolate,
        melted
    ⅛ teaspoon ground cinnamon

FILLING

    3 (8-ounce) packages cream
        cheese (at room temperature)
    ½ cup firmly packed light
        brown sugar
    ½ cup granulated sugar
    4 eggs
    4 cups sour cream
    1 tablespoon vanilla extract
    ¼ teaspoon salt
    6 ounces bittersweet chocolate,
        melted

1. CRUST: Combine all ingredients and press firmly over bottom of lightly buttered 9-inch springform pan; refrigerate until ready to bake.

2. FILLING: Preheat the oven to 350°F. Beat cream cheese in large electric mixer bowl at medium speed until smooth. Add the two sugars gradually, beating all the while at low speed. Beat in eggs, one by one, and continue beating until light. Beat in sour cream, vanilla, and salt.

3. Divide filling in half and blend melted bittersweet chocolate into one-half. Scoop alternate cupfuls of plain and chocolate batters into spring-form pan until both are used up. With long, thin-bladed spatula, zigzag through batters to marbleize.

4. Bake in lower third of oven 1 hour until cheesecake jiggles only slightly when nudged. Turn oven off and leave cheesecake in oven 1 hour more.

5. Cool cheesecake in pan on wire rack to room temperature, then cover with large plate or round metal tray and refrigerate overnight before serving.

Welsh Cheddar Cheesecake

Makes a 9-inch Cheesecake, 16 Servings

✳

THIS UNUSUAL cheesecake was developed in the test kitchens of *Family Circle* and appeared not only in the magazine but also in *Family Circle Recipes America Loves Best* (1982).

NOTE: This cheesecake will crack on top, which is as it should be. The cracking will in no way affect the flavor.

CRUST

   1 (6-ounce) package zwieback, crushed (1½ cups crumbs)
   3 tablespoons sugar
   6 tablespoons butter or margarine, melted

FILLING

   4 (8-ounce) packages cream cheese, softened
   2 cups shredded Cheddar cheese
   1¾ cups sugar
   3 tablespoons all-purpose flour
   5 eggs
   3 egg yolks
   ¼ cup beer

SPARE THE SWEETS

DURING WORLD War II, Betty Crocker published *Your Share*, a booklet designed to show women "how to prepare appetizing, healthful meals with foods available today," meaning in the days of sugar, butter, meat, and canned-goods rationing. This advice appeared on page 30:

HERE'S THE WAY WE SAVE OUR SUGAR WHEN WE MUST

Salt brings out sweet flavor of fruits and cooked foods. Add a pinch.
Use BISQUICK for shortcakes, fruit rolls, cobblers. It contains sugar.
Get prepared milk powders. No sugar is needed.
After dinner, serve jam with cheese and crackers.
Reduce tartness of sour fruits by combining with dried fruits.

Serve fruits and vegetables naturally rich in sugar.
Add sugar last when cooking dried fruits. Takes less.
Vary cereals with brown sugar, honey, syrup, dried and sweet fruits.
Include tapioca in fruit pies to cut tartness.
Never throw away canned fruit syrup. Use for beverages, jellies, salads.
Get into the habit of serving coffee cakes and sweet rolls for dessert.

Thoroughly dissolve sugar in beverages. Don't leave in bottom of cup.
Instead of sugar, use corn syrup for beverages, fruits, sugar syrups.
Plan to serve desserts with no sugar (fruit cups, fruit gelatin, etc.).
Serve ripe fruits. They need little or no sugar.

1. CRUST: Mix crumbs, sugar, and butter in small bowl. Press firmly over bottom and halfway up sides of lightly buttered 9-inch springform pan; refrigerate until ready to fill.

2. FILLING: Preheat oven to 475°F. Beat cream cheese with Cheddar in large electric mixer bowl at medium speed just until smooth. Add sugar and flour and beat until fluffy. Add eggs and egg yolks, one at a time, beating well after each addition. Stir in beer.

3. Pour into crust and bake 12 minutes; reduce oven temperature to 250°F and bake 1½ hours longer. Turn oven off and let cake remain in oven 1 hour.

4. Remove cheesecake from oven. Cool in pan on wire rack to room temperature. Loosen cheesecake around edge with knife, release spring, and remove pan sides, leaving pan bottom in place. Refrigerate until ready to serve. Cut the pieces small—this cheesecake is extra-rich.

Chocolate-Glazed Triple-Layer Cheesecake

Makes a 9-inch Cheesecake, 10 to 12 Servings

❋

TO CELEBRATE its twenty-fifth anniversary, *Southern Living* polled its readers to determine which magazine recipes they liked best, then printed the top twenty-five in its December 1990 Silver Jubilee Issue. Among them was this glorious cheesecake. According to the recipe headnote, "When Mrs. Randy Bryant sent this recipe for Chocolate-Glazed Triple-Layer Cheesecake, she had no idea what a hit it would make with our Foods staff. Since it appeared in our December 1986 issue, we've made it in our homes and served it at company-sponsored functions. Many readers have written for reprints of it, too."

CRUST
> 2 cups chocolate wafer crumbs
>   (1 [8½-ounce] package)
> ¼ cup granulated sugar
> 5 tablespoons butter or
>   margarine, melted

FIRST LAYER
> 1 (8-ounce) package cream
>   cheese, softened
> ¼ cup granulated sugar
> 1 egg
> ¼ teaspoon vanilla extract
> 2 ounces semisweet chocolate,
>   melted
> ⅓ cup sour cream

SECOND LAYER
> 1 (8-ounce) package cream
>   cheese, softened
> ⅓ cup firmly packed dark
>   brown sugar
> 1 tablespoon all-purpose flour
> 1 egg
> ½ teaspoon vanilla extract
> ¼ cup finely chopped pecans

THIRD LAYER
> 5 ounces cream cheese, softened
> ¼ cup granulated sugar
> 1 egg
> 1 cup sour cream
> ¼ teaspoon vanilla extract
> ¼ teaspoon almond extract

CHOCOLATE GLAZE
> 6 ounces semisweet chocolate,
>   coarsely chopped
> ¼ cup (½ stick) butter or
>   margarine
> ¾ cup sifted confectioners'
>   (10X) sugar
> 2 tablespoons water
> 1 teaspoon vanilla extract

1. CRUST: Mix crumbs, granulated sugar, and butter. Press over bottom and 2 inches up sides of ungreased 9-inch springform pan; set aside.

2. FIRST LAYER: Preheat oven to 325° F. Beat cheese and granulated sugar in large electric mixer bowl at medium speed until fluffy. Beat in egg and vanilla, then stir in chocolate and sour cream. Spoon over crust; set aside.

3. SECOND LAYER: Beat cheese, brown sugar, and flour in large electric mixer bowl at medium speed until fluffy. Beat in egg and vanilla. Stir in pecans. Spoon over first layer; set aside.

4. THIRD LAYER: Beat cheese and granulated sugar in large electric mixer bowl at medium speed until fluffy. Beat in egg, then stir in sour cream, and vanilla and almond extracts. Smooth over second layer.

5. Bake 1 hour, turn oven off but leave cheesecake in oven 30 minutes with oven door shut. Open door and leave cheesecake in oven 30 minutes more.

6. Remove cheesecake from oven, cool to room temperature, then chill 8 hours or overnight until firm. Carefully loosen and remove springform pan sides. Leave cheesecake on pan bottom.

7. GLAZE: Melt chocolate and butter in double boiler over simmering water, stirring often. Off heat, blend in 10X sugar, water, and vanilla. Smooth warm glaze over cheesecake. Let glaze firm up before serving.

Pumpkin Cheesecake with Caramel Swirl

Makes a 9-inch Cheesecake, 10 Servings

❋

PUMPKIN CHEESECAKE is a twentieth-century—correction, *late*-twentieth-century—variation on our "national pie." This make-ahead recipe adapted from one in *Bon Appétit* (November 1993) is gorgeous.

CRUST

1½ cups fine gingersnap
crumbs (about 40 cookies)
1½ cups finely ground toasted
pecans
¼ cup firmly packed brown
sugar (light or dark)
¼ cup (½ stick) butter, melted

FILLING

4 (8-ounce) packages cream
cheese, softened
1⅔ cups granulated sugar
1½ cups canned solid pack
pumpkin (not pie filling)
¼ cup heavy cream
1 teaspoon ground cinnamon
1 teaspoon ground allspice
4 eggs

TOPPING AND DECORATION

¾ cup cheese-sugar mixture
(above)
5 tablespoons heavy cream
1 tablespoon store-bought
caramel sauce

1. CRUST: Preheat oven to 350° F. Mix all ingredients and pat firmly over bottom and up sides of ungreased 9-inch springform pan; set aside.

2. FILLING: Beat cheese and sugar in large electric mixer bowl at medium speed until light; transfer ¾ cup mixture to small bowl, cover, chill, and save for topping. Add pumpkin, cream, cinnamon, and allspice to mixer bowl and beat well. Beat eggs in, one by one.

3. Pour into crust and bake about 1 hour and 15 minutes, until cheesecake puffs, browns, and jiggles only slightly when pan is nudged.

4. Cool cheesecake on wire rack 10 minutes. Loosen around edge, then cool in pan to room temperature. Cover and chill overnight.

5. TOPPING AND DECORATION: Bring ¾ cup reserved cheese-sugar mixture to room temperature and blend in cream. Press down firmly on edges of cheesecake to even thickness. Spread cheese-sugar mixture smoothly over cheesecake. Spoon caramel sauce in lines over surface, then swirl with knife. Chill well before cutting.

Cranberry Cheesecake

Makes a 9-inch Cheesecake, 10 Servings

✳

ANOTHER THANKSGIVING cheesecake, this one featured in *Yankee* magazine (November 1994). It's the creation of Geraldine Griffith, whose husband owns cranberry bogs near Carver, Massachusetts.

CRUST

1½ cups finely ground
hazelnuts or almonds
2 tablespoons sugar
2 tablespoons butter, softened

FILLING

2 (8-ounce) packages cream
cheese, softened
¼ cup sugar
3 eggs
1 teaspoon vanilla extract
½ teaspoon fresh lemon juice
¼ cup unsifted all-purpose flour
3 cups sour cream

TOPPING

1 cup sugar
1 cup water
1 teaspoon finely grated orange
zest
½ teaspoon ground cloves
2 cups fresh or frozen
cranberries

1. CRUST: Preheat oven to 400° F. Mix all ingredients and pat firmly over bottom and up sides of ungreased 9-inch springform pan. Bake 6 to 8 minutes and cool.

2. FILLING: Reduce oven temperature to 375° F. Churn cheese, sugar, eggs, vanilla, lemon juice, flour, and sour cream in food processor fitted with metal chopping blade 30 seconds. Scrape work bowl sides down and churn 30 to 60 seconds more, until uniformly smooth.

3. Pour filling into cooled crust and bake about 1 hour or until toothpick inserted halfway between crust and center comes out clean.

4. Cool cheesecake in pan on wire rack to room temperature. Cover and refrigerate 3 hours.

5. TOPPING: Cook sugar, water, orange zest, cloves, and cranberries in large nonreactive saucepan, stirring often, about 10 minutes, until cranberries pop. Remove from heat, cool, dump into strainer set over large bowl, and let all excess liquid drip through; discard liquid.

6. Spread cranberry mixture over cold cheesecake, return to refrigerator, and chill at least 4 hours before serving.

CRUMB CRUSTS

"IN THE Keys as far back as the 1890s, a simple pie combining egg yolks, condensed milk, and lime juice in a *graham-cracker crumb crust* [italics mine] was a well-established local favorite." So says John Egerton in his headnote to Key Lime Pie (*Southern Food,* 1987). But Jeanne Voltz and Caroline Stuart (*The Florida Cookbook,* 1993) doubt the use of graham cracker crusts that early.

"Second- and third-generation Key lime pie makers," they write, "say their grandmothers baked a flaky pastry shell for the pie; today many use a graham cracker crust, and prefer it."

My own research suggests that Voltz and Stuart are correct. Graham cracker and cookie crumb crusts appear to be a late-'20s or early-'30s creation, at least I can find no earlier recipes for them. In her essay on New York Cheesecake (*New York Cookbook,* 1992), Molly O'Neill says that Albert Dunayer, owner of

A&D Cheesecake in East Brunswick, New Jersey, which bakes many of New York's "private-label" cheesecakes, claims to have "pioneered the graham cracker crust."

Dunayer, she continued, grew up on the cheesecake made at Junior's, a delicatessen that opened on Brooklyn's Flatbush Avenue in 1929. For its cheesecakes, Junior's buttered springform pans well and coated them with graham cracker crumbs. Dunayer refined the idea by adding other ingredients. He even used a graham cracker crust for his Lindy's cheesecakes because, as he explained to O'Neill, "People didn't eat that heavy cookie crust and I couldn't stand to see the waste."

My own hunch is that crumb crusts, perhaps even Junior's, descended from the zwieback crumb crusts of Eastern Europe that were sometimes used as underliners for cheesecakes.

Cracker and cookie manufacturers, seeing a bonanza here for their crumbled products, surely

must have helped to develop the crumb crusts so popular today. Yet none has stepped forward to take credit. Nabisco, which offers a recipe for Classic Graham Cracker Crust in its booklet, *Honey Maid Graham Crackers: Recipes for You & Your Family,* says nothing about having originated the graham cracker crust. Nor, in its *Nilla Wafers & Fruit Recipes* pamphlet, does it claim to have invented the vanilla wafer crumb crust.

In *Fashionable Food* (1995), Sylvia Lovegren says that the first mention she could find of a graham cracker pie shell was in the 1938 *Watkins Cook Book.* Thanks to some digging on the part of two good friends—Joanne Lamb Hayes, food editor of *Country Living* magazine, and Ella Elvin, formerly food editor of the *New York Daily News*—I've been able to beat that by fifteen years. Both share my passion for old cookbooks and went sleuthing for graham cracker crumb crusts. Joanne located one in *Choice Recipes by Moscow Women,* a cookbook published in 1931 by The Hospitality Committee of the Presbyterian Ladies' Aid of Moscow, Idaho. "It's called Graham Cracker Pie," Joanne said. "But the crust is definitely made of graham crackers."

Then Ella called to say she'd turned up this Graham Cracker Pie in the *Los Angeles Times Prize Cook Book* (1923), which also has a crumb crust:

GRAHAM CRACKER PIE

Roll eighteen square graham crackers, add one egg, well beaten and one-eighth pound of melted butter. Line pie plate by pressing into shape, leaving about three-fourths of a cupful for cover.

Filling: Cook four tart apples, one-half cup seedless raisins, one-half cup sugar, one-half teaspoon of nutmeg or cinnamon. Put in pie plate and sprinkle with chopped walnuts, then cover with remaining cracker crumbs. Put in moderate oven for twenty minutes, let cool and serve with whipped cream.

—MRS. W.E. WOLF, HUNTINGTON PARK

Joanne also unearthed a graham cracker crust recipe in *Delicious New Combinations of Inexpensive Favorites,* a recipe booklet printed in 1934 by the Pet Milk Company. It tells the cook to:

Roll	17 graham crackers
	4 tablespoons butter, melted
Mix together	4 tablespoons Pet Milk

Stir into cracker crumbs. Press mixture over bottom and sides of a 9-inch pie pan, pressing down firmly with the back of a spoon. Bake in a hot oven (450° F) about 7 minutes or until firm.

Strangely, the Pet Milk recipe suggests no filling. I, myself, discovered a graham cracker crust in *Food Economy: Recipes for Left-Overs, Plain Desserts and Salads,* a booklet published in 1936, which does suggest a filling—lemon chiffon. And in *Mrs. William Vaughn Moody's Cookbook* (1931), I found a cheesecake with a zwieback crumb crust. The recipe that follows is just as it appeared in that Depression booklet.

GRAHAM CRACKER CRUST

Roll graham crackers very fine. Mix 1 1/2 cups of the cracker crumbs, 1/2 cup powdered sugar and scant 1/2 cup butter. Press mixture firmly against the bottom and sides of pie pan. Place pie pan in refrigerator or cold place for several hours. Then fill with gelatin pie filling.

Classic Graham Cracker Crust

*Makes a 9-inch Pie Shell,
6 to 8 Servings*

✳

THIS RECIPE (and its three variations) has been adapted from one in a 1984 Nabisco leaflet, *Honey Maid Graham Crackers: Recipes for You & Your Family.*

NOTE: The updated recipe calls for mixing 1¼ cups crumbs with ¼ cup sugar and ⅓ cup *melted* butter or margarine.

> 1⅓ *cups fine graham cracker crumbs (about 16 graham crackers)*
> ⅓ *cup sugar*
> ⅓ *cup butter or margarine, softened*

1. Preheat oven to 375°F.

2. Mix crumbs and sugar in small bowl, then using pastry blender, cut in butter until uniformly fine and crumbly.

3. Press mixture over bottom and up sides of ungreased 9-inch pie plate.

4. Bake 8 to 10 minutes, then cool completely before filling.

──── VARIATIONS ────

FOOD PROCESSOR GRAHAM CRACKER CRUST: Crumble graham crackers into food processor fitted with metal chopping blade and churn 30 seconds. Add sugar and butter and pulse 30 seconds until uniformly fine. Press crumb mixture into pie plate as directed, then bake by conventional oven or microwave. Or chill as directed in unbaked variation below. Makes a 9-inch pie shell, 6 to 8 servings.

UNBAKED GRAHAM CRACKER CRUST: Prepare as directed, then refrigerate 30 minutes before filling. Makes a 9-inch pie shell, 6 to 8 servings.

MICROWAVE GRAHAM CRACKER CRUST: Prepare crumb mixture as directed and press into 9-inch microwave-safe glass pie plate. Microwave, uncovered, on HIGH (100 percent power) 2 to 2½ minutes, rotating pie plate a quarter turn after 1 minute. Makes a 9-inch pie shell, 6 to 8 servings.

Nilla Wafer Crust

*Makes a 9-inch Pie Shell,
6 to 8 Servings*

✳

THIS RECIPE (and the three variations that follow) was adapted from *Nilla Wafers & Fruit Recipes,* a booklet published in 1984 by Nabisco.

> 1⅔ *cups fine vanilla wafer crumbs (42 vanilla wafers)*
> 2 *tablespoons sugar*
> ⅓ *cup butter or margarine, melted*

1. Preheat oven to 375°F.

2. Mix crumbs and sugar in small bowl; add butter and mix well.

3. Press mixture over bottom and up sides of ungreased 9-inch pie plate.

4. Bake 8 to 10 minutes, then cool completely before filling.

──── VARIATIONS ────

FOOD PROCESSOR VANILLA WAFER CRUST: Crumble vanilla wafers into food processor fitted with metal chopping blade and churn 30 seconds. Add sugar and butter and pulse 30 seconds. Press mixture into pie plate as directed, then bake by conventional oven or microwave. Or chill as directed in unbaked variation below. Makes a 9-inch pie shell, 6 to 8 servings.

UNBAKED VANILLA WAFER CRUST: Prepare as directed, then refrigerate 30 minutes before filling. To make serving easier, dip bottom of pie plate in hot water 1 minute before cutting pie. Makes a 9-inch pie shell, 6 to 8 servings.

MICROWAVE VANILLA WAFER CRUST: Prepare crumb mixture as directed and press into 9-inch microwave-safe glass pie plate. Microwave, uncovered, on HIGH (100 percent power) 2 to 2½ minutes, rotating pie plate a quarter turn after 1 minute. Makes a 9-inch pie shell, 6 to 8 servings.

Gingersnap Crumb Crust

Makes a 9-inch Pie Shell,
6 to 8 Servings

✱

THIS RECIPE and the three variations that follow are my own.

1½ cups fine gingersnap
*   crumbs (about 40*
*   gingersnaps)*
⅓ cup butter or margarine,
*   softened*

1. Preheat oven to 350°F.

2. Mix crumbs and butter in small bowl until uniformly crumbly.

3. Press mixture over bottom and up sides of ungreased 9-inch pie plate.

4. Bake 8 to 10 minutes; cool completely before filling.

────── VARIATIONS ──────

CHOCOLATE CRUMB CRUST: Prepare as directed, substituting chocolate wafer crumbs for gingersnap, add 2 tablespoons sugar and reduce butter to ¼ cup (½ stick). Makes a 9-inch pie shell, 6 to 8 servings.

NUT-CRUMB CRUST: Prepare as directed, substituting 1 cup vanilla wafer or graham cracker crumbs and ½ cup finely ground pecans or walnuts for gingersnaps. Also reduce butter to 3 to 4 tablespoons—just enough to hold crumb mixture together. Makes a 9-inch pie shell, 6 to 8 servings.

CORNFLAKE CRUST: Prepare as directed for Gingersnap Crumb Crust, substituting 1½ cups crushed cornflakes for gingersnap crumbs and add 2 tablespoons sugar. NOTE: Any finely crushed crisp cereal flakes (wheat, rice, or oat) can be used in place of cornflakes. Makes a 9-inch pie shell, 6 to 8 servings.

- - - - - - - -

Basic Pie Crust

Makes an 8-, 9-, or 10-inch Pie Shell

✱

I WILL not pretend that this pie crust came into our lives this century. I offer it merely as a convenience so that you needn't riffle through cookbooks to find a good recipe if you don't already have one.

NOTE: For a two-crust pie, double this recipe.

1⅓ cups sifted all-purpose flour
½ teaspoon salt
3 tablespoons ice-cold butter,
*   diced*
3 tablespoons ice-cold lard (hog
*   lard) or vegetable shortening,*
*   diced*
4 to 6 tablespoons ice water

1. Combine flour and salt in large shallow bowl; add butter and lard and cut in with pastry blender until texture of coarse meal.

2. Forking briskly, drizzle 4 tablespoons ice water over surface. If dough does not hold together, fork in 1 to 2 additional tablespoons water. Shape dough into ball, wrap in plastic wrap, and let rest 15 to 20 minutes.

3. Flatten dough into circle 1-inch thick on lightly floured pastry cloth, then with lightly floured, stockinette-covered rolling pin, roll from center outward into circle 3 inches larger all around than the pie pan, giving dough one-eighth turn after every roll (this insures a near-perfect circle).

4. Lop pastry circle over rolling pin, ease into pan, and press lightly to fit to contours of pan. Trim pastry overhang until 1 inch larger all around than pan, fold under on rim, and crimp, making a high fluted edge.

5. Fill pie shell and bake as filling recipe directs.

NOTE: TO "BLIND BAKE" EMPTY PIE SHELL: Preheat oven to 425°F. Prick bottom and sides of pie shell with fork, lay large square of foil, parchment, or wax paper in shell, and fill with pie weights, dried beans, or uncooked rice. Bake, uncovered, 10 to 12 minutes. Lift out foil and weights, return pie shell to oven, and bake 3 to 5 minutes longer until nicely tanned. Cool to room temperature before filling.

PUDDINGS FROZEN DESSERTS

Bananas Foster

Makes 1 Generous Serving

✻

THIS IS one of the recipes that made Brennan's famous. And vice versa. Opened in 1946 and in its present Royal Street location since May 31, 1956, this New Orleans restaurant is as popular as ever. In *Brennan's New Orleans Cookbook* (1961), Hermann B. Deutsch tells how "Breakfast at Brennans" became *de rigueur* for locals and visiting firemen alike. It began not long after *Dinner at Antoine's* (1948), Frances Parkinson Keyes's murder mystery set in New Orleans just before Mardi Gras, seemed permanently stuck on the best-seller lists—and drew droves of customers to Antoine's. "If only something like that could have happened to Brennan's," founding father Owen E. Brennan lamented one day to Lucius Beebe, *Town & Country*'s restaurant columnist. To which Beebe replied, "Why does it have to be a dinner? Why couldn't it be breakfast? What's wrong with Breakfast at Brennan's?" Beebe even had a hand in planning the breakfast menus, one of which included Bananas Foster. According to John Mariani (*The Dictionary of*

American Food and Drink, Revised Edition, 1994), Chef Paul Blangé created Bananas Foster and the Brennans named it in honor of "a regular customer, Richard Foster, owner of the Foster Awning Company in New Orleans." It's a showy dessert, cooked at table in a blaze of glory. This recipe is adapted from the one that appears in *Brennan's New Orleans Cookbook.*

NOTE: Although the recipe serves only one, the ingredients can be doubled to serve two. But don't do more than this amount at one time.

> 2 tablespoons brown sugar
> 1 tablespoon butter (no substitute)
> 1 ripe medium banana, peeled, halved crosswise, then each half sliced lengthwise
> Pinch ground cinnamon
> ½ ounce banana liqueur
> 1 ounce white rum
> 1 large scoop vanilla ice cream

1. Heat brown sugar and butter in flat chafing dish or medium heavy skillet set over moderately high heat until butter melts and mixture is syrupy.

2. Add banana slices and sauté briefly until softened. Sprinkle with cinnamon. Off heat, pour in banana liqueur and rum and blaze with a match. Return to heat and spoon rum mixture over banana slices until flames subside.

3. Spoon banana/rum mixture over and around ice cream and serve.

Lemon Mystery Pudding

Makes 6 Servings

✻

THE "MYSTERY" is that the pudding separates as it bakes, a spongy cake layer floating to the top and a tart lemon curd sinking to the bottom. Where, when did the recipe originate? In *Mrs. Rorer's Philadelphia Cook Book* (1886) I find what may be a forerunner, a sour lemon pudding called *Tout Fait* into which the egg whites "beaten to a stiff froth" are folded in just before baking. Might *Tout Fait,* in turn, have been inspired by the classic Pennsylvania Dutch Lemon Sponge Pie (here, too, the beaten whites go in at the end, causing the filling to separate into sponge and curd)? Following Mrs. Rorer's publication of *Tout Fait,* there seems to be a forty-three-year gap before anything similar surfaces in print, this time as Lemon Cake Pie in the June 1929 issue of *Sunset.* It was sent in by a reader identified only as E.J.S. of Vancouver, Washington, for the magazine's new reader recipe column, "Kitchen Cabinet." Lemon Cake Pie is in fact Lemon Mystery Pudding baked in a pie shell. According to the magazine headnote, "As this dessert bakes, a cake-like topping forms over the sweet-tart lemon filling." Three years later a similar recipe appears—minus the pie shell—in Sheila Hibben's *The National Cookbook* (1932). Lemon

Pudding, she calls it. From the '30s on, the recipe, alternately named Lemon Mystery Pudding, Lemon Pudding-Cake, Lemon Cake-Pudding, or when baked in individual ramekins, Lemon Cups, appears regularly in cookbooks, large and small. The recipe that follows is adapted from the Lemon Cake Top Pudding printed in a Sunkist leaflet, *Luscious Fresh Lemon Desserts*.

4 eggs, separated
1 cup sugar
3 tablespoons butter or
    margarine, softened
3 tablespoons all-purpose flour
¼ teaspoon salt
⅓ cup fresh lemon juice
1 cup milk
Finely grated zest of ½ lemon

1. Preheat oven to 325° F. Butter 1½-quart casserole and set aside.

2. Beat egg whites until foamy in small electric mixer bowl at medium speed; gradually add ¼ cup sugar and beat to soft peaks; set aside.

3. Beat egg yolks and butter well in large mixer bowl at medium speed. Gradually add remaining ¾ cup sugar and beat at medium speed 5 minutes. Add flour, salt, and lemon juice and mix well. Blend in milk and lemon zest.

4. Gently fold in beaten egg whites. Pour into casserole and set in shallow baking pan containing ½-inch hot water.

5. Bake, uncovered, 55 to 60 minutes until lightly browned. Serve warm or cold.

TIMELINE

1978

Food & Wine magazine debuts.

Sphere Magazine reinvents itself as *Cuisine* and devotes itself to food.

The International Association of Culinary Professionals (IACP) is founded.

Ben & Jerry's premium ice creams crank up in Burlington, Vermont. With flavors like Cherry Garcia, Wavy Gravy, and Chubby Hubby, they are soon the coolest ice creams among the hip. Moreover, a percentage of the profits goes to saving the environment.

1979

Bowing to consumer pressure, major baby food manufacturers stop adding sugar and salt to their baby food.

Sarah Tyson Rorer

MRS. HOOVER'S FAVORITE WAR PUDDING (1918)

2½ cups of crumbs
½ teaspoonful of soda
½ cup of chopped suet
1 pinch of salt
1 egg

1 teaspoonful of cinnamon
1 pint of milk
1 cup of raisins
½ cup of molasses
1 pinch of nutmeg

Mix as in making a cake. Steam two hours. Serve with sauce.

From Mrs. Herbert Hoover. *Conservation Recipes,* Compiled by The Mobilized Women's Organizations of Berkeley, California (1918).

Mrs. Herbert Hoover

Swedish Cream

Makes 4 to 6 Servings

✻

IT WAS Margaret Davidson, home-making editor of *The Ladies' Home Journal,* who gave me this recipe back in the '60s. To this day it is one of my favorite desserts. And because I'm constantly struggling with my weight, I've worked out a slimmed-down version.

2⅓ cups heavy cream
1 cup sugar
1 envelope unflavored gelatin
2 cups sour cream
1½ teaspoons vanilla extract
1 quart strawberries, hulled,
    sliced, and sweetened to taste

1. Bring cream, sugar, and gelatin to simmering in medium heavy saucepan over low heat, stirring constantly. Continue cooking and stirring until gelatin and sugar dissolve.

2. Remove from heat and blend in sour cream and vanilla.

3. Transfer to medium bowl and chill 8 hours or overnight, until softly set.

4. To serve, layer into balloon goblets with sliced strawberries.

VARIATION

LOWER-FAT, LOWER-CALORIE SWEDISH CREAM: Prepare as directed, using half-and-half for 2 cups of the heavy cream and substituting low-fat or nonfat plain yogurt or "light" sour cream for regular. Also reduce sugar to ¾ cup. Makes 4 to 6 servings.

Lemon Sponge (Lemon Bisque)

Makes 10 to 12 Servings

❋

CALLED BOTH Lemon Sponge and Lemon Bisque, this was a favorite dessert of mine when I was growing up down South in the '40s. I suspect Mother got the recipe from a Jell-O leaflet or label. Or perhaps a Pet or Carnation milk one. Whoever developed the recipe must have used *blanc mange* as the starting point. Perhaps the lemon-flavored Evaporated Milk Blanc Mange in Knox Gelatine's *Dainty Desserts for Dainty People* (1915). It resembles Lemon Sponge but is not whipped once the gelatin begins to thicken. Or perhaps it descends from the Lemon Snow Pudding in the same booklet, which contains no milk but is beaten until frothy. Or even, perhaps, from "A New Dessert," published in *Woman's Favorite Cook Book* (1902), a fluffy lemon gelatin into which stiffly beaten whites are folded. Whatever Lemon Sponge's original source, Mother added her own fillips during World War II—for starters, substituting honey for sugar, which was rationed.

1 cup vanilla wafer crumbs (about 15 cookies)
1 (3-ounce) package lemon-flavored gelatin
1½ cups boiling water
⅓ cup strained honey
¼ cup fresh lemon juice
2 teaspoons finely grated lemon zest
1 (13-ounce) can evaporated milk, partially frozen

1. Lightly butter 13 × 9 × 2-inch baking pan, add crumbs and tilt pan from side to side to coat evenly. Tap out excess crumbs and reserve.

2. Dissolve gelatin in boiling water. Add honey and cool to room temperature. Stir in lemon juice and zest, then refrigerate until consistency of raw egg white, about 30 minutes.

3. Whip evaporated milk in chilled large electric mixer bowl at high speed until stiff. Reduce speed to medium, add gelatin mixture, then raise speed to high and beat until fluffy.

4. Pour into pan, smoothing to corners and scatter remaining crumbs on top. Chill several hours, until set.

Chocolate Fondue

Makes 6 to 8 Servings

❋

CHOCOLATE FONDUE, unlike cheese fondue, is not Swiss. According to Jane and Michael Stern (*American Gourmet*, 1991), it was dreamed up in the Madison Avenue test kitchens of the Switzerland Association to promote Toblerone Swiss chocolate. The Sterns don't say when the great event took place, but I distinctly remember chocolate fondue being a late-'50s to early-'60s phenomenon. The recipe that follows is adapted from one in *Betty Crocker's Cookbook* (1969), which begins with this headnote: "Guests of all ages will enjoy this unusual dessert—but it's a special favorite of teenagers." For dipping up the chocolate fondue, the recipe suggests everything from apple wedges to cubes of angel cake to maraschino cherries to marshmallows. The idea is to surround the fondue pot with a showy arrangement of "dippers." Topping my own list are fresh strawberries, chunks of fresh pineapple or banana, segments of tangerine or Mandarin orange, seedless grapes. The technique for eating chocolate fondue is the same as for cheese fondue: Spear a piece of food with a fondue fork, dunk into the pot of melted chocolate, and enjoy.

12 ounces milk chocolate, semisweet chocolate pieces, or sweet cooking chocolate, coarsely chopped
¾ cup light cream
2 tablespoons Cointreau, Grand Marnier, kirsch, or brandy
Assorted dippers (chunks of fresh fruit, pound cake, or angel cake)

1. Melt chocolate and cream in heavy saucepan over low heat, stirring until smooth. Off heat, mix in Cointreau.

2. Transfer to fondue pot or chafing dish; serve with assorted dippers.

GRAPE-NUTS PUDDING

EARLY THIS century when cereals were beginning to be mass-produced, manufacturers pumped up sales by developing recipes using their products, especially desserts that salved the national sweet tooth. There were oatmeal puddings, farina puddings, even Shredded Wheat puddings. But none caught the public fancy like GRAPE-NUTS PUFF PUDDING. According to Kraft Foods historians, the recipe appeared in *The Road to Wellville* (1926), a book about C.W. Post, inventor of GRAPE-NUTS and POSTUM, which became the cornerstones of the Post Cereal Company. Although the pudding was popular in the 1930s and 1940s, the recipe didn't land on boxes of GRAPE-NUTS until 1952 and has been on and off the package ever since. This is the official GRAPE-NUTS recipe, one for which Kraft Foods still gets requests:

GRAPE-NUTS PUFF PUDDING

1 teaspoon grated lemon rind	2 egg yolks, well beaten	4 tablespoons GRAPE-NUTS
4 tablespoons butter	3 tablespoons lemon juice	1 cup milk
1/2 cup sugar	2 tablespoons flour	2 egg whites, stiffly beaten

Add lemon rind to butter and cream well; add sugar gradually, blending after each addition. Add egg yolks and beat thoroughly; then add lemon juice. Add flour, GRAPE-NUTS, and milk, mixing well. Fold in egg whites. Turn into greased baking dish and place in pan of hot water. Bake in slow oven (325° F) 1 hour and 15 minutes. When done, this pudding will have a crust on top and jelly below. Serve warm or cold with plain or whipped cream. Makes 6 servings

Strangely, there is another *Grape-Nuts Pudding*, which Kraft Foods seems not to know about, a pudding that uses a full cup of the crunchy cereal. It is particularly popular in the New England states and is a staple in church, club, and community cookbooks, especially those published in the '40s and '50s. This one came from a Colebrook, New Hampshire, fundraiser cookbook that belonged to a Yankee friend's mother. The pages have turned to tan, they flake at the gentlest touch, still I can make out the recipe for Grapenut Pudding. As in most community cookbooks, the recipe appears as *Grapenut Pudding*, not *GRAPE-NUTS*, which is the registered brand name. And it calls for grapenuts, no caps, no hyphens—no *wonder* trademark lawyers go gray.

GRAPENUT PUDDING

Oven-350 deg.	2 qt. casserole	Time-60 min.
1 cup grapenuts	4 eggs	1 tbsp. vanilla
scant 1/2 cup sugar	1 qt. milk, scalded	a dash of salt

Pour scalded milk over grapenuts and let it sit for 5 minutes. Beat eggs, sugar, salt and vanilla. Add to milk and grapenuts. Pour into a greased casserole. Sprinkle very generously with nutmeg. Set in a pan of hot water and bake until a knife inserted 1 inch from center comes out clean.

Chocolate Decadence

Makes 12 to 16 Servings

✳

"LIKE EATING ganache," is the way my friend, Pastry Chef Karen Pickus, described Chocolate Decadence, the 1980s showstopping dessert of trendy chefs and ambitious hostesses. Where did it originate? No one seems to know, although I clearly remember my first bite of it at Hoexter's Market, a restaurant on Manhattan's Upper East Side that is now closed. It was in the late '70s that I went to Hoexter's just to taste the chocolate dessert that had everyone buzzing. As I remember it, Hoexter's Chocolate Decadence—unfrosted, unsauced—was pure sin. The recipe here, adapted from one in Martin Johner and Gary Goldberg's *Mountains of Chocolate* (1981) was brought to them by an assistant at their New York cooking school. She, in turn, got the recipe from Papa Hayden's Restaurant in Portland, Oregon. "The name, Chocolate Decadence," write Johner and Goldberg, "is not hyperbole, so cut this rich dense dessert into small portions. Serve it with raspberry sauce; the color and flavor contrasts are wonderful." I've made the raspberry sauce optional because I prefer chocolate straight.

CAKE

1 pound dark sweet (German's) chocolate, broken into pieces
10 tablespoons unsalted butter (no substitute)
4 eggs
1 tablespoon granulated sugar
1 tablespoon all-purpose flour

FROSTING

2 cups heavy cream
1 tablespoon confectioners' (10X) sugar
1 teaspoon vanilla extract
Semisweet chocolate shavings (decoration)

RASPBERRY SAUCE (OPTIONAL)

1 cup fresh raspberries or 1 (10-ounce) package frozen unsweetened raspberries, thawed
1 tablespoon kirsch
2 tablespoons granulated sugar

1. CAKE: Preheat oven to 425° F. Butter 8-inch springform pan. Line bottom with circle of wax paper, butter paper, then dust paper and pan sides with flour, tapping out excess. Set pan aside.

2. Melt chocolate and butter in medium heavy saucepan over low heat. Blend well and cool.

3. Whisk eggs and sugar in large electric mixer bowl set over (not touching) hot water until sugar dissolves and eggs are warm. Transfer to mixer and beat at high speed until eggs are cool and tripled in volume. Fold in flour.

4. Fold half of egg mixture into melted chocolate mixture, then carefully fold in balance.

5. Scrape batter into pan and bake 15 minutes. Cool in pan on wire rack, then refrigerate several hours or until firm.

6. FROSTING: Whip cream with 10X sugar and vanilla until stiff. Smooth two-thirds over top and sides of cake. Pipe balance through pastry bag fitted with star tip, making decorative rosettes around edge. Mound chocolate shavings in center. Return cake to refrigerator and chill several hours until firm. Cut into slim wedges and serve. For a fancier dessert, proceed.

7. RASPBERRY SAUCE: Mix all ingredients; puree and strain.

8. TO SERVE: Cut into wedges and accompany with raspberry sauce.

THIS RECIPE enjoyed enormous popularity in the '50s and on into the '60s. Essential to its success are Nabisco's Famous Chocolate Wafers, the dark, thin, not-very-sweet cookies that measure about three inches across.

FAMOUS CHOCOLATE WAFER ROLL

1 cup heavy cream
½ cup confectioners' (10X) sugar
1 teaspoon vanilla extract
20 Nabisco Famous Chocolate Wafers

Whip cream, sugar, and vanilla to stiff peaks; measure out and reserve 1 cup. Sandwich wafers together with remaining whipped cream, arranging on sides in 9 × 5 × 3-inch loaf pan to form one long roll. Frost top and sides of roll with reserved whipped cream. Chill several hours or overnight. To serve, slice across roll, diagonally. Makes 4 to 6 servings

Chocolate Pudding Cake

Makes 8 Servings

✷

ONE OF the most interesting cakes to come out of the twentieth century is this one from the makers of Mazola Corn Oil, which separates into layers as it bakes. The top becomes cake, the bottom pudding.

BOTTOM LAYER
1 cup unsifted all-purpose flour
⅔ cup sugar
½ cup coarsely chopped nuts
¼ cup unsweetened cocoa powder
2 teaspoons baking powder
¼ teaspoon salt
½ cup milk
¼ cup corn oil
1 teaspoon vanilla extract

TOP LAYER
⅔ cup sugar
2 tablespoons unsweetened cocoa powder
1 cup boiling water

1. Preheat oven to 350° F. Grease 9 × 9 × 2-inch baking pan; set aside.

2. BOTTOM LAYER: In large bowl, stir together flour, sugar, nuts, cocoa, baking powder, and salt. Mix in milk, corn oil, and vanilla. Spread in pan.

3. TOP LAYER: In small bowl, mix sugar and cocoa and sprinkle over batter. Pour boiling water evenly over mixture in pan.

4. Bake 45 minutes. Serve warm or, if you prefer, cold.

Million-Dollar Macadamia Fudge Torte

Makes 12 Servings

✻

IN 1996, there were two "firsts" in the Pillsbury Bake-Off Contest held in Dallas. It was the first time Pillsbury upped the ante to $1 million. And it was the first time a man won, in this case forty-four-year-old Kurt Wait of Redwood City, California. This single father of an eight-year-old son taught himself to cook in college and entered his first contest only a couple of years ago. Yet in 1995 he concocted a burger that won $10,000 in the Build a Better Burger Recipe Contest sponsored by the Sutter Home Winery. A year later, he picked up a cool million at the Pillsbury Bake-Off Contest. Not bad. *Wait's Tip for Winning:* Use cooking methods you're comfortable with.

⅓ cup low-fat sweetened
  condensed milk
½ cup semisweet chocolate
  chips
1 (1 lb. 2.25 oz.) package
  Pillsbury Moist Supreme
  Devil's Food Cake Mix
1½ teaspoons ground
  cinnamon
⅓ cup vegetable oil
1 (16-ounce) can sliced pears
  in light syrup, drained and
  pureed
2 eggs
⅓ cup chopped macadamia
  nuts or pecans
2 teaspoons water
1 (17-ounce) jar butterscotch-
  caramel-fudge ice cream
  topping
⅓ cup milk

1. Preheat oven to 350° F. Coat bottom and sides of 9- or 10-inch springform pan with nonstick cooking spray and set aside.

2. Cook and stir condensed milk and chocolate chips in small heavy saucepan over moderately low heat until chocolate melts, 3 to 5 minutes; set aside.

3. Beat cake mix, cinnamon, and oil in large electric mixer bowl at low speed until crumbly, 20 to 30 seconds. In second large mixer bowl, beat 2½ cups crumbly cake-mix mixture with pears and eggs at medium speed 2 minutes. Spread in pan.

4. Drop melted chocolate chip mixture by tablespoonsfuls over batter.

5. Stir nuts and water into remaining crumbly cake-mix mixture and sprinkle evenly over torte.

6. Bake, uncovered, until top springs back when lightly touched in center, 45 to 50 minutes. Cool in pan on wire rack 10 minutes. Remove springform pan sides. Cool torte to room temperature.

7. Cook and stir butterscotch topping and milk in small heavy saucepan over moderately low heat until well blended—3 to 4 minutes.

8. To serve, puddle 2 tablespoons warm sauce on each of 12 dessert plates and top with wedge of torte.

TIMELINE

1979

The first Zagat Restaurant Survey appears, a printed sheet of favorite New York restaurants prepared by husband and wife attorneys Tim and Nina Zagat.

**ZAGAT
NEW YORK CITY
RESTAURANT
SURVEY**

1980s

Pressure saucepans enjoy a renaissance.

Tofu comes to the supermarket.

America goes pasta-crazy.

Space shuttle astronauts ask that M&M's Chocolate Candies be included in their rations.

Japan exports *surimi* to the U.S.; this rubbery fish paste masquerades as shrimp, lobster, Alaska king crab legs.

Women chefs—Anne Rosenzweig (New York), Lydia Shire (Boston), Susan Spicer (New Orleans)—make their mark.

Mock Whipped Cream

THE FIRST directions I've been able to find for whipping evaporated milk appear in *One Hundred Tested Recipes* published in 1923 by Carnation Milk Products Company. Here they are, exactly as worded in that '20s booklet:

WHIPPED CARNATION MILK

Place one can Carnation Milk in water and heat to boiling point, remove promptly and thoroughly chill by placing the can on ice or in the refrigerator. When cool, open the can and pour milk (the entire contents of small can or half contents tall can) into chilled bowl (place in another bowl filled with cracked ice). After the milk is thoroughly chilled, whip as usual for about five minutes with an ordinary egg beater. Sweeten and flavor if desired. Keep on ice.

Carnation Milk will whip satisfactorily without heating, but better results are assured when above recipe is followed closely.

TODAY'S METHOD is both safer and simpler. And it should be used instead of the previous recipe, which I include only as an archival curiosity.

WHIPPED CARNATION EVAPORATED MILK

Makes 4½ cups

1 cup CARNATION Evaporated Milk

¼ to ½ cup powdered sugar
1 teaspoon vanilla extract

POUR evaporated milk into small mixer bowl. Chill with beaters in freezer for about 30 minutes or until ice crystals form around edge of bowl.

BEAT on high speed for 1 minute or until very frothy. Gradually add sugar and vanilla; continue beating for 2 minutes or until mixture is stiff. Serve *immediately* spooned over fresh fruit, berries or your favorite dessert.

Grapes with Sour Cream and Brown Sugar

Makes 4 Servings

✳

THIS RECIPE came into *The Ladies' Home Journal* test kitchens in the late '50s or early '60s, a promo, I feel certain, for Thompson seedless green grapes. We liked the recipe so much we began serving it at fancy editorial luncheons in our thirty-first-floor, terraced dining room in Rockefeller Center. Guests often asked for the recipe and when we obliged, they were astonished to discover that it contained only three ingredients.

¾ pound seedless green grapes, stemmed, washed, and patted dry on paper towels (3 cups)
1 cup sour cream
¼ cup brown sugar (light or dark, not firmly packed)

1. Toss grapes with sour cream in large bowl and chill several hours.

2. Toss well again and spoon into stemmed goblets.

3. Sprinkle each portion with 1 tablespoon brown sugar and serve.

Hot Fudge Sauce

Makes about 1½ Cups

✳

THE HOT fudge sundae, it's said, was invented in 1906 at C.C.

Brown's in Los Angeles. Yet I find thick, hot chocolate sauces recommended "especially for vanilla ice cream" as far back as the original *Settlement Cook Book* (1903). As for the soda fountain variety, those who claim to be connoisseurs about such things say that America's very best hot fudge sauce was served at Schrafft's. I agree. When I was younger and thinner—and oblivious to calories—I stopped for a hot fudge sundae at least once a week at Manhattan's West Fifty-first Street Schrafft's. Lucky for me, it no longer exists. Sad to say, I haven't lost my appetite for hot fudge sauce. This one—my own—is one of the best. But I don't dare make it very often.

1½ cups sugar
2 tablespoons flour
¾ cup evaporated milk
¼ cup water
3 ounces unsweetened
   chocolate, coarsely chopped
3 tablespoons butter or
   margarine
1½ teaspoons vanilla extract

1. Mix sugar and flour in medium heavy saucepan. Blend in milk and water. Set over moderate heat and cook, stirring constantly, until mixture boils and thickens.

2. Reduce heat to low, add chocolate, and cook, stirring constantly, until chocolate melts.

3. Off heat, mix in butter and vanilla. Serve hot or warm over vanilla, hazelnut, butter pecan, almond brickle, or chocolate ice cream. Or over any flavor.

A Celestial Dessert

....

THIS IS the sort of dessert that became so popular in the late '40s and early '50s and cropped up in community cookbooks across the country. I reprint it here just as it appeared in *Foods That Rate at N.C. State*, published in the late 1940s by The State College Woman's Club of the North Carolina State College of Agriculture and Engineering, mistakes and all.

FOOD FOR THE GODS

1 pound English walnuts or
   pecans
1 pound dates
2 cups brown sugar

9 tablespoons graham
   cracker crumbs
6 eggs—add whites beaten
   stiff last
2 teaspoons baking powder

Mix half of crumbs with nuts and fruit which have been chopped. Mix the rest with baking powder. Combine and add eggs and sugar. Put in well greased pan and bake in a slow oven. Serve while warm with whipped cream.

Temp: 350°   Time: 1 hour   Serves 6

—MRS. I.O. SCHAUB

POPSICLE

SHEER ACCIDENT led to the creation of one of America's favorite refreshers. One wintry New Jersey night in 1923, Frank Epperson was showing friends how he made "instant" lemonade at a California amusement park by using a special powder. Once the demonstration was over, he left the sludgy mix on the windowsill and there it stayed overnight. Next morning, he found it frozen solid, spoon still stuck in. Epperson gave it a lick, liked it, and patented it a year later as the "Epsicle." Soon his children were calling it "Pop's cycle," which led to Popsicle. Epperson's frozen suckers were immediate crowd-pleasers at baseball games and outdoor concerts, where they were vended through the stands along with popcorn and peanuts. During the Depression, kids pooled their pennies to buy Twin Popsicles at a nickel a pair, broke the halves apart to share, hoping they'd get the stick with "free" printed on it—good for one Popsicle. Today Popsicles are packaged in multiples; they cost about thirteen cents per pair, take eight minutes to make, and five to eight minutes to eat (depending on whether they're bitten or licked). Favorite flavors: cherry, orange, and grape.

Magnolia Grill Bourbon-Vanilla Ice Cream

Makes about 2 Quarts

❋

THE BEST vanilla ice cream you will ever eat. The specialty of Ben and Karen Barker's Magnolia Grill in Durham, North Carolina, it was featured in *Food & Wine* magazine. Serve as is or with Magnolia Grill Pecan Tart (page 386).

3½ cups half-and-half
3 cups heavy cream
1½ large vanilla beans, split
14 egg yolks
1½ cups sugar
Pinch salt
½ cup bourbon

1. Mix half-and-half and cream in large heavy saucepan. Scrape seeds from vanilla beans into cream, then drop in beans. Bring to a boil over moderate heat.

2. Whisk egg yolks with sugar and salt in large bowl. Gradually whisk in hot cream, return mixture to pan, and cook over moderate heat, stirring constantly, until custard reaches 165°F on candy thermometer and coats back of spoon.

3. Strain custard into large bowl, cover, and chill at least 2 hours. Stir bourbon into cold custard.

4. Freeze custard in two batches in ice cream maker according to manufacturer's directions. Transfer to chilled container and store in freezer.

Heavenly Hash

....

ALSO KNOWN in some quarters as Lush Mush, this mélange of fruits, marshmallows, and whipped cream dates back to the early twentieth century. In *Good Housekeeping Everyday Cook Book* (circa 1905), there is a Heavenly Hash. But it resembles today's Heavenly Hash less than this recipe from the same book:

COMPOTE OF MARSHMALLOWS

Preserved peaches (fresh fruit is better if in season), maraschino cherries, oranges, pecan nuts, and fresh marshmallows. Cut in halves, then quarter the peaches and oranges. Mix in the nuts and marshmallows with the fruit juice. Cover all with whipped cream and garnish the top with the cherries. Serve cold.

In *Larkin Housewives' Cook Book* (1915), I find two marshmallow fruit desserts, both clear precursors of Heavenly Hash. The one that follows is reproduced just as it appears in *Bethabara Moravian Cook Book* (1981) compiled by the Women's Fellowship of the Bethabara Moravian Church, Winston-Salem, North Carolina:

HEAVENLY HASH

18 marshmallows, cut into 2 or 3 pieces each
1 No. 2 can pineapple
1 med. size jar maraschino cherries
1 c. cream, before whipping

Put marshmallow, pineapple and juice together and let soak for 3 or more hrs. It's all right to soak overnight. Cut up cherries in several pieces. Add to pineapple and marshmallows. Whip cream and add to other mixture. Good with a few nuts in it and vanilla, but not necessary. Put into freezing tray for at least 6 hours, or can be put in refrigerator instead. Serves 6 to 8.

—Grace Lackey (Mrs. L.W.)

This type of recipe was submitted by many ladies. Use basic idea and add wide variety of fruits.

ICE CREAM CONE

I T HAPPENED at the St. Louis World's Fair of 1904. A vendor of ice cream in assorted flavors was hawking his wares alongside a baker of thin pastry waffles. One customer, more imaginative than most, bought a waffle first, then placed his ice cream on top and ate the two together—like an open-face sandwich.

His companion tried the same trick, only to have his ice cream slide off the flat waffle. They walked off laughing. The waffle merchant thought for a moment, then rolled one of his flat waffles into a cone, and handed it to the ice cream man, who filled it. Thus they invented the ice cream cone—just in time for the next customer.

Many entrepreneurs found the waffle cone promising, but it was eight years more before inventor Frederick A. Bruckman perfected and sold rights to a machine that produced cones quickly and inexpensively. By the 1920s a third of all the ice cream sold in the United States was scooped onto cones, most of them made by McLaren Consolidated Cone Corporation, which soon joined the Nabisco family.

Spicy Pecan Ice Cream

Makes about 1½ Pints

✳

O NE OF North Carolina's most gifted young cooks is Scott Howell, chef-proprietor at Nana's in Durham. This peppery pecan ice cream of his demonstrates how today's chefs are putting a new spin on old favorites. *Food & Wine* magazine thought so highly of it they featured the recipe in their September 1995 issue.

½ vanilla bean, split
1½ cups heavy cream
½ cup half-and-half
5 egg yolks
¾ cup sugar
2 tablespoons dark rum
¼ cup (½ stick) butter
½ cup pecan halves
¼ teaspoon ground hot red
*   pepper (cayenne)*
Pinch salt

1. Scrape vanilla bean seeds into cream and half-and-half in medium heavy saucepan; drop in bean. Bring to simmering over moderately high heat.

2. Meanwhile, whisk egg yolks with ½ cup sugar in medium bowl; gradually whisk in hot cream, return to pan, and cook, stirring constantly, about 5 minutes, until mixture thickens and coats back of spoon. Strain into bowl; cool, then stir in rum.

3. Melt remaining ¼ cup sugar in small heavy skillet over moderately high heat until amber—about 5 minutes. Stir in butter and pecans and cook, stirring constantly, until nuts are well coated. Spread nuts on plate and cool. Sprinkle with cayenne and salt.

4. Break spiced pecans into small pieces and stir into custard.

5. Freeze in ice cream maker according to manufacturer's directions. Transfer to 1-quart container and store in freezer.

Avocado Ice Cream

Makes about 2 Quarts

✳

I N THE 1950s, Americans enjoyed a brief, intense affair with avocado ice cream. Many of the major newspapers and magazines printed recipes for it, sometimes a "quickie" that merely combined pureed avocados with softened vanilla ice cream. Of course the better avocado ice creams were made from scratch—like this one reprinted verbatim from *The Gourmet Cookbook, Volume II* (1957):

With a silver fork mash the flesh of 2 avocados and press through a fine sieve. Stir in ¼ cup lemon or lime juice, ¾ cup sugar, and a pinch of salt and continue to stir until the sugar is dissolved. Stir in 2 cups cream and 1 teaspoon gelatin softened in 1 tablespoon cold water and dissolved over hot water. Mix thoroughly and freeze.

The recipe below is adapted from one in *The Avocado Bravo,* a recipe booklet published by the California Avocado Advisory Board (now the California Avocado Commission).

1 envelope unflavored gelatin
¼ cup cold water
¾ cup milk, scalded
1 cup sugar
2 teaspoons vanilla extract
¼ teaspoon salt
4 ripe medium California
*   avocados, peeled, pitted, and*
*   pureed*
⅓ cup fresh lime juice
⅓ cup light rum
3 cups heavy cream, whipped
1½ cups chopped, toasted
*   hazelnuts or slivered almonds*

1. Soften gelatin in water 5 minutes; mix with milk, sugar, vanilla, and salt in large electric mixer bowl; stir until gelatin and sugar dissolve. Cool, cover, and chill until beginning to set, about 30 minutes.

2. Beat gelatin mixture at high mixer speed until smooth; beat in avocado puree, lime juice, and rum. Fold in whipped cream and hazelnuts.

3. Pour into refrigerator trays or 13 × 9 × 2-inch baking pan, cover with foil, and freeze until firm.

4. Let ice cream soften about 30 minutes at room temperature before serving.

PIES, PASTRIES & OTHER DESSERTS

that Entered the American Mainstream
During the Twentieth Century with Their Source

(* Recipe Included)

FRANCE
Coeur à la Crème, Cream Puffs
Crêpes, Croquembouche
*Dacquoise, Eclairs
Gâteau Saint-Honoré, Mont Blanc
Mousse au Chocolat, Napoleons
Paris Brest, Profiteroles au Chocolat
Strawberries Romanoff
*Tarte Tatin, Vacherin

❀

GERMANY/AUSTRIA/HUNGARY
Linzertorte, *Rote Grütze
Salzburger Nockerl
Apple Strudel
Poppy Seed Strudel

❀

RUSSIA/MIDDLE EUROPE
Paskha

❀

SCANDINAVIA
Danish Pastry, Lingonberry Pancakes

❀

ITALY
Biscuit Tortoni, Cannoli, Gelato, Granita
Panacotta, Spumoni
*Tiramisù, Zabaglione, Zuppa Inglese

❀

GREECE/TURKEY/MIDDLE EAST
Baklava

❀

AUSTRALIA
Pavlova

❀

MEXICO/LATIN AMERICA
*Capirotada

Tarte Tatin

Makes a 9-inch Tart, 8 to 10 Servings

✳

THE UPSIDE-DOWN apple tart that became the '80s "hot" dessert, first in restaurants, then among home cooks. Despite its showiness, Tarte Tatin is easy to make, particularly if you're willing to settle for frozen puff pastry. The recipe here is adapted from *Gourmet's Best Desserts* (1987).

½ cup (1 stick) butter
6 large Golden Delicious apples, peeled, cored, and thinly sliced
1½ cups sugar
½ teaspoon finely grated lemon zest
6 tablespoons water
¼ teaspoon cream of tartar
1 (14-ounce) package frozen puff pastry, thawed by package directions

1. Melt butter in large heavy skillet over moderate heat. Add apples, ½ cup sugar, and lemon zest. Cook, turning apples gently, until translucent, about 5 minutes. Transfer to large shallow baking pan to cool.

2. Cook ½ cup sugar, 3 tablespoons water, and ⅛ teaspoon cream of tartar in well-seasoned 9-inch iron skillet with ovenproof handle over moderately high heat until sugar liquefies and turns amber, about 5 minutes. Watch carefully lest caramel overbrown and turn bitter; also brush down skillet sides with pastry brush dipped in cold water to remove sugar crystals. Remove skillet from heat, tilting so caramel coats bottom evenly; cool until set.

3. Preheat oven to 425° F with heavy-duty baking sheet on middle rack.

4. Arrange prettiest apple slices, overlapping slightly, in concentric rings over caramel in skillet. Top with second layer, overlapping apples in opposite direction. Add remaining apple slices, arranging as compactly as possible.

5. Following package directions, roll puff pastry to thickness of ⅛ inch on floured pastry cloth with floured stockinette-covered rolling pin. Using 9-inch layer cake pan as pattern, cut out 9-inch circle. Ease pastry circle on top of apples, pressing lightly, but do not tuck pastry edges in around sides of skillet.

6. Bake tart on preheated baking sheet until richly browned—40 to 45 minutes.

7. Cool tart to room temperature in skillet on wire rack. Carefully loosen around edge, place large round platter on top of skillet, then invert, giving a quick shake, to unmold tart.

8. About an hour before serving and following directions in Step 2, make a second batch of caramel with remaining ½ cup sugar, 3 tablespoons water, and ⅛ teaspoon cream of tartar.

9. Pour hot caramel over apples; dip metal spatula in hot water, then spreading in one direction, quickly smooth caramel over apples.

10. When caramel firms up, cut tart into wedges and serve. Accompany, if you like, with whipped cream.

Dacquoise

Makes a 10-inch, 3-layer Torte, 12 Servings

✳

OUR AWARENESS of this sublime French torte dates, I believe, to the early '70s. It was the specialty at the now-defunct Coach House Restaurant in Greenwich Village, and that's where I first tried it. The recipe here is adapted from Nick Malgieri's superb *How To Bake* (1995), which is in turn adapted from Gino Cofacci's Hazelnut and Almond Dacquoise originally published in *The Pleasures of Cooking*. Sadly, that magazine no longer exists. Cofacci, a friend of James Beard, had an apartment in Beard's West 12th Street town house, now headquarters for The James Beard Foundation. In his small third-floor flat, Cofacci baked dacquoise for some of New York's finest restaurants. According to Malgieri, it was Cofacci who introduced New Yorkers to dacquoise (he, too, says it was in the 1970s).

NOTE: The easiest way to grind the nuts is to pulse them in a food processor fitted with the metal chopping blade. To toast, spread ground nuts in a large shallow roasting pan and set in a 350°F oven for 10 to 12 minutes until golden. Do not attempt this recipe in rainy or humid weather because the meringues will not stay crisp.

MERINGUE LAYERS

1 cup coarsely ground, toasted, blanched hazelnuts
1 cup coarsely ground, toasted, blanched almonds
1¼ cups sugar
2 tablespoons cornstarch
¾ cup egg whites (about 6 large eggs)
⅛ teaspoon salt
2 teaspoons vanilla extract
¼ teaspoon almond extract

COFFEE BUTTER CREAM

¾ cup milk
½ cup sugar
4 egg yolks
¾ pound (3 sticks) unsalted butter (at room temperature, no substitute)
3 tablespoons instant espresso coffee crystals dissolved in 1 tablespoon warm water

TOPPING

Confectioners' (10X) sugar (for dusting)

1. Slide oven racks into position in upper and lower thirds of oven; preheat oven to 300°F. Line 3 (15½ × 10½ × 1-inch) jelly-roll pans with baking parchment and in center of each, trace 10-inch circle. Set aside.

2. MERINGUE LAYERS: With fork, toss hazelnuts and almonds with 1 cup of sugar and the cornstarch in medium bowl until well combined; set aside.

3. Beat egg whites with salt in large electric mixer bowl at low speed until opaque and snowy, about 2 minutes. Increase speed to high, add remaining ¼ cup sugar in slow stream, then vanilla and almond extracts and continue beating until meringue peaks stiffly but is not dry. With rubber spatula, gently fold in nut mixture until no streaks of white or brown show. Easy does it.

4. Spoon mixture into pastry bag fitted with ½-inch plain tip. Starting in centers of traced circles on parchment-lined pans, pipe mixture round and round in tight coils to form 10-inch meringue circles.

5. Bake until pale tan and firm, 1 to 1¼ hours. Cool meringue layers on parchment and on pans on wire racks.

6. COFFEE BUTTER CREAM: Bring milk and sugar to simmering in medium heavy saucepan over moderate heat. Whisk a little hot milk mixture into egg yolks, stir back into pan, and cook, stirring constantly, until thickened and smooth, 2 to 3 minutes. Do not boil or mixture will curdle. Pour mixture into small electric mixer bowl and beat at high speed until cold. At high speed, add butter, ½ stick at a time, then coffee infusion, and continue beating until fluffy.

7. TO ASSEMBLE DACQUOISE: Center one meringue layer on cake plate and spread with one-third butter cream. Set second layer in place, spread with another one-third butter cream, then top with final meringue layer. Frost sides of dacquoise with remaining butter cream but leave top plain.

8. Refrigerate dacquoise 1 hour or more to firm up butter cream.

9. Just before serving, dust top of dacquoise with 10X sugar.

Tiramisù

Makes 10 to 12 servings

✳

IF MEMORY serves, it was Gael Greene, restaurant reviewer for *New York Magazine,* who first swooned over this rich mocha Italian sweet. I also believe it happened in the early '80s, but perhaps the late '70s. In any event, nearly every Italian restaurant of status scrambled to put *tiramisù* on its menu. Soon, however, *tiramisù* began to suffer from over-exposure and by the '90s, to vanish from menus. Properly made, it is a lovely dessert or, as its name translates, a "pick-me-up." The recipe here—as good as it gets—is adapted from *La Dolce Vita* (1993), written by my friend Michele Scicolone.

1 pound mascarpone cheese
3 tablespoons sugar
2 tablespoons Grand Marnier
2 tablespoons dark rum
1 cup heavy cream, softly whipped
1½ cups cold brewed espresso
24 ladyfingers
½ pound semisweet chocolate, finely chopped

1. Cream mascarpone, sugar, Grand Marnier, and rum in large electric mixer bowl at moderately high speed until smooth. By hand fold in whipped cream.

2. Pour espresso into 2-cup measure and one by one, quickly dip 12 ladyfingers into espresso to moisten slightly; they should not be soggy.

3. Arrange moistened ladyfingers in single layer over bottom of ungreased 8 × 8 × 2-inch baking pan. Spread with half of mascarpone mixture and sprinkle with half of chocolate. Repeat layers.

4. Cover and refrigerate overnight.

5. Spoon onto dessert plates and serve.

Capirotada

Makes 4 to 6 Servings

✳

I PICKED up this recipe for Mexican Bread Pudding in the '70s in Santa Fe. It's spicier—better—than its Anglo counterpart.

8 lightly buttered pieces crisp, dry toast
1 cup sugar
2⅓ cups boiling water
1 teaspoon ground cinnamon
¼ teaspoon ground cloves
1 cup seedless raisins
1½ cups coarsely shredded sharp Longhorn or Cheddar cheese

1. Preheat oven to 350° F. Lightly butter 2-quart casserole; set aside.

2. Break toast into 1-inch pieces and set aside.

3. Melt sugar in medium heavy skillet over moderate heat, without stirring, until color of caramel—3 to 4 minutes.

4. Slowly pour in boiling water—it will sputter and sugar will harden. Cook and stir over moderate heat until brittle dissolves, 8 to 10 minutes. Mix in cinnamon and cloves, reduce heat to lowest point, and keep warm.

5. Build alternate layers in casserole this way: toast, raisins, cheese. Repeat three times. Add hot syrup and toss lightly.

6. Bake, uncovered, until cheese melts and toast absorbs syrup, 20 to 25 minutes.

7. Serve hot, topped, if you like, by trickles of light cream.

Rote Grütze

Makes 6 to 8 Servings

❋

THIS LUXURIOUS red berry pudding seems to have emerged only recently from the parts of the U.S. where Germans and Scandinavians settled in the late-nineteenth- and early-twentieth centuries. I first tasted it in the 1970s at the New York home of Hedy Würz, a Bavarian with whom I subsequently wrote *The New German Cookbook* (1993). This recipe is adapted from that book because Hedy's *Rote Grütze* is the best I ever ate.

NOTE: If fresh, dark, sweet cherries are in season, by all means use them: 1 pound, stemmed, pitted, and quartered.

PUDDING

> 2 (10-ounce) packages raspberries frozen in light syrup, thawed, and drained, with juice reserved
> 1 (16-ounce) package strawberries frozen in light syrup, thawed and pureed with their juice
> 1 (1-pound) can pitted dark, sweet red cherries, drained, with juice reserved
> 1 quart natural red grape juice or cranberry juice (about)
> ¾ cup sugar
> 1 tablespoon finely grated lemon zest
> Juice of 1 large lemon
> ⅔ cup unsifted cornstarch
> 1 cup dry red wine

TOPPING

> 1 cup heavy cream, softly whipped with 1 tablespoon sugar and ½ teaspoon vanilla extract

1. PUDDING: Place raspberry juice, pureed strawberries, and cherry juice in 1-quart measure; add enough grape juice to equal 1 quart.

2. Dump mixture into large, heavy nonreactive saucepan, mix in 2 cups grape juice, sugar, lemon zest, and lemon juice. Bring to boiling over moderate heat, stirring often.

3. Blend cornstarch and wine and whisk into boiling berry mixture. Cook, whisking constantly, until thickened and clear, about 3 minutes. Add raspberries and cherries and cook and stir 1 minute more.

4. Cool to room temperature, transfer to large bowl, cover, and refrigerate 24 hours.

5. To serve, mound in stemmed goblets and crown each portion with generous spoon of TOPPING.

TIMELINE

1980s

Fast-food chains sell 200 hamburgers per second.

The Age of Fitness; spas and "fat farms" proliferate.

Microwave ovens go mainstream.

1980

Wolfgang Puck opens Spago on Sunset Boulevard in Los Angeles.

Cook's joins the field of food magazines.

1981

The Food and Drug Administration approves aspartame for use as an artificial sweetener.

Restaurants begin offering lighter cooking—"Spa Cuisine."

Stouffer's introduces Lean Cuisine dinners and entrées.

CAKES

& FROSTINGS

HOW TO GET THE MOST OUT OF YOUR

Sunbeam
MIXMASTER

LTHOUGH NINETEENTH-CENTURY cookbooks didn't stint on cake recipes, there was precious little variety. Fruitcakes abounded, as did pound cakes, sponge cakes, and jelly rolls. And gingerbreads were so popular whole chapters were at times devoted to them. These were the days of unreliable leavenings, of unregulated wood, coal, or petroleum stoves, so is it any wonder that sturdy brown cakes propped up with fruits and nuts were the cakes of choice?

In her historical notes that accompany the facsimile edition of *The Virginia House-wife* (1824), Karen Hess writes, "I do not find use of chocolate or cocoa in cakes until after mid-nineteenth century in American cookbooks." Quite so. In fact, only in the 1880s did I find chocolate beginning to appear in baked goods. And even then only sparingly.

What some early cookbooks call chocolate cake is nothing more than yellow layer cake filled and frosted with chocolate. These frostings, moreover, were frequently made by adding grated chocolate to white frosting, usually an egg-white-based ornamental icing, which must have given it an unappetizing "tweedy" look. It's curious that few cooks thought to melt the chocolate before blending it in to give the frosting rich brown sheen, or to use cocoa, which had been available for some time. It's also odd that frostings were more likely to be bound with egg whites (or yolks) than with butter.

Marble cakes began appearing after the Civil War, but the dark part was usually colored with spice and/or molasses, rarely with chocolate like the marble cakes of today (the earliest chocolate marble cake I've found appears in *Buckeye Cookery,* published in 1880). Devil's food cake, moreover, seems to be a twentieth-century invention (indeed chocolate is a twentieth-century obsession). Not so angel food, which, according to John Mariani (*The Dictionary of American Food and Drink,* Revised Edition, 1994) dates back to the 1870s. By the

1880s, nearly every cookbook contained at least one recipe for angel food cake, and several offered more than one.

In this century, there were several surges of cake-baking. The 1902 *Woman's Favorite Cook Book* and the 1903 *Settlement Cook Book* both offer cake recipes beyond the usual late-nineteenth-century repertoire: devil's cake, for example, mocha torte, walnut-date torte, poppyseed torte, strawberry cake, tutti-frutti cake, and so on. At about the time of World War I, applesauce cakes began to appear, making it possible to use less sugar and fewer eggs. One applesauce cake in the 1915 *Larkin Housewives' Cook Book* contains no eggs at all.

In the '20s, as gas ranges phased out wood or petroleum stoves and ovens grew more reliable, novelty cakes began to appear, not least of which were upside-down cakes. America's passion for cake-baking continued right through the Depression (fueled by the arrival in the '30s of the electric range and proliferation of the electric mixer), but was stopped cold in the '40s by World War II, butter and sugar rationing. War cakes were, for the most part, leaden loaves chockful of raisins or other dried fruit.

CAKES & FROSTINGS

Some of the war cakes were also of the "dump," or one-bowl, variety that could be mixed in minutes by busy working women. They followed what's known as "the muffin method," meaning all dry ingredients were combined in a bowl, then the combined liquids (including egg) were dumped in and lightly mixed.

These dump cakes led, within a few years, to cake mixes. Between 1947 and 1948, Pillsbury and General Mills (Betty Crocker) both introduced cake mixes. Still, the late '40s craze was the chiffon cake, which General Mills hailed as the "first new cake in a hundred years." Their ads described it as "light as angel food, rich as butter cake." And their test kitchens were kept busy dreaming up new chiffon cake flavors: butterscotch, maple pecan, peppermint chip, holiday fruit, cherry nut, bit o' walnut.

Toward the end of this century, European-style tortes

were de rigueur. Few caught the fancy like Dione Lucas's flourless French chocolate cake, which James Beard gave his own twist and began demonstrating "on the road." Then there was Chocolate Decadence (page 405), really more mousse than cake, which one pastry chef likened to "eating ganache."

In the '90s Age of Fitness, the buzzwords were "fat-free" and "low-fat," and innovative chefs were able to strip cakes of most—even all—of their fat by substituting pureed fruit (usually applesauce) for shortening

and using egg whites in place of whole eggs. And airy, no-fat angel food cakes reemerged in a dozen new shapes and flavors.

In a book of this scope, it is impossible to include every twentieth-century cake, even every popular one. Inevitably, one or more of your particular favorites may be missing.

What I have done is feature those home-grown cakes that caused a stir when they first appeared. And those that have become American classics.

Bake This $25,000.00 Prize-Winning Cake

Lady Baltimore

THE YEAR: 1906. The event: The publication of Owen Wister's romantic novel *Lady Baltimore.* Like his earlier work, *The Virginian,* it became a bestseller. Wister sets *Lady Baltimore* in Charleston, South Carolina, and stages some of the action in the Lady Baltimore Tea Room (Woman's Exchange) there.

Augustus, the book's narrator, lunches at the tearoom and one day sees a young man step up to the counter and order a special cake for a wedding. When the man leaves, Augustus engages the waitress in conversation and orders a piece of the cake for himself.

I returned to the table, Augustus says, *and she brought me the cake, and I had my first felicitous meeting with Lady Baltimore. Oh, my goodness! Did you ever taste it? It's all soft, and it's in layers, and it has nuts—but I can't write any more about it; my mouth waters too much.*

Presently he continues: *Delighted surprise caused me once more to speak aloud, and with my mouth full. But, dear me, this is delicious!*

Wister's raves sent readers scrambling to find the Lady Baltimore recipe, which was "a type well known in the South: a Lady Cake," writes food historian Lee Edwards Benning in *The Cook's Tales* (1992).

"In the 1800s," Benning continues, "cakes had begun to take their names from the person to whom you'd serve it. Expensiveness of the ingredients had everything to do with the ranking of a cake." Thus

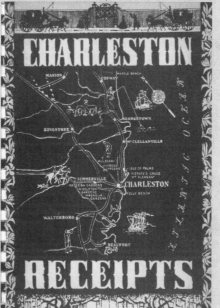

the richest, fussiest cakes, those chockablock with fruits, nuts, and spices were called "King" or "Imperial Cakes."

"Queen" cakes were only slightly less impressive, usually butter-rich affairs flavored with wine, brandy, and rose water plus cinnamon, nutmeg, and mace. "Lady Cakes" were simpler, usually pound or butter cakes, some of them white, some yellow, done in the style of a particular area—North Carolina, for example. Or Tennessee or Baltimore. What usually distinguished one lady cake from another were the fillings and frostings.

"In the case of Lady Baltimore (or Lady Cake, Baltimore-style)," writes Benning, "it was the candylike cooked filling made with walnuts that made it distinctive (Baltimore, at the time, had made itself a reputation for its candy making)." Just how Lady Baltimore became so popular in Charleston, Benning doesn't say. Nor does further digging on my part shed any light.

Strangely, most modern versions of Lady Baltimore, even one printed in *The New York Times* in 1989, are silver cakes devoid of egg yolks. The original, Benning maintains, was made with whole eggs.

Charleston Receipts (1950) offers two recipes for Lady Baltimore. The first is a four-egg, two-layer butter cake measuring eleven inches across. The frosting, which doubles as a filling, is a billowing boiled icing strewn with chopped figs, raisins, and pecans or walnuts. It also contains 2 teaspoons corn syrup, a twentieth-century refinement that keeps the icing from turning gritty as it hardens. The second Lady Baltimore in *Charleston Receipts* is a silver cake —egg whites only.

In *Two Hundred Years of Charleston Cooking*, originally published in 1930 and now available in a paperback facsimile edition from The University of South Carolina Press, two versions of Lady Baltimore are given. Both are yellow cakes and neither one has figs in the frosting. Version one (credited to no one in particular) begins with this headnote:

Each year at Christmas time hundreds of white boxes go out of Charleston to all parts of the country bearing the round, the tall, the light, the fragile, the ineffable Lady Baltimore cakes. There are several ladies of old descent who make an excellent living baking these famous cakes. You have seen Lady Baltimore cakes on many a menu, but it usually means something altogether different from the real Charleston delicacy. By no stretch of the imagination could this cake be called economical, but its goodness makes one willing to forget its eight eggs! Half of the cake, however, will make three medium-sized layers.

The second version (Lady Baltimore Cake II) is attributed to Alicia Rhett Mayberry (Mrs. Ed F.), who may or may not have been the inspiration for Eliza, Wister's *Lady Baltimore* heroine. According to Blanche S. Rhett, a relative of Mrs. Mayberry and the woman who gathered the recipes for *Two Hundred Years of Charleston Cooking*, this is the cake served at the Woman's Exchange where Wister set some of his story. It is also the one I reprint here.

The recipe produces a feathery, three-layer yellow cake that is sandwiched together with two fillings, the second of which, a fluffy white icing strewn with chopped walnuts and raisins, is also used to frost the top and sides of the cake. I tested this recipe, found it wanting on several counts, and offer my corrected version after the original.

LADY BALTIMORE CAKE II

1/2 cup butter	2 cups flour
1 1/2 cups sugar	1 teaspoon baking
2 eggs, separated	powder
1 cup milk	1/2 teaspoon salt

Cream the butter and sugar, add the beaten egg yolks and beat well. Mix and sift the flour and baking powder twice, then sift slowly into the first mixture, adding the milk gradually. Fold in the beaten egg whites last of all. Bake in three well-buttered layer cake pans in a moderately hot oven (375 degrees F) for about twenty-five minutes.

When the layers are baked, pour the soft filling given below on each layer before you put on the hard filling. It is this filling with the indefinite flavor that makes the cake so distinctive.

1 cup sugar	1 teaspoon vanilla
1 cup walnut meats	1 teaspoon almond
1/4 cup water	extract

Put the sugar, walnut meats and water into a saucepan and cook to the very soft ball stage (234 degrees F). Remove from the fire and let cool until lukewarm (110 degrees F). Add the flavorings and beat until slightly thickened before pouring on cake.

For the hard filling use

2 cups sugar	Juice of 1/2 lemon
1/2 cup water	1 cup chopped
2 egg whites	raisins
1 teaspoon vanilla	1 cup chopped
1 teaspoon almond	walnuts
extract	

Bring the sugar and water to the boiling point and cook until it will form a firm ball (246 degrees F). Pour slowly over the stiffly beaten egg whites, beating constantly, and continue beating until cool, adding the raisins, nuts, flavoring and lemon juice as it begins to harden.

—ALICIA RHETT MAYBERRY

CAKES & FROSTINGS

Lady Baltimore Cake II, Updated

Makes an 8-inch, 3-layer Cake, 16 Servings

✻

THIS IS my adaptation of Lady Baltimore Cake II, which appeared in *Two Hundred Years of Charleston Cooking* (1930), a collection of old Charleston recipes assembled by Blanche S. Rhett. You'll find the original on at left.

CAKE

2 cups sifted cake flour
1 teaspoon baking powder
½ cup (1 stick) butter, at room temperature
1½ cups sugar
2 eggs, separated
1 cup milk
¼ teaspoon salt

SOFT FILLING

1 cup sugar
⅓ cup water
1 cup finely chopped walnuts
1 teaspoon vanilla extract
1 teaspoon almond extract

HARD FILLING

2 cups sugar minus 2 tablespoons
2 tablespoons light corn syrup
½ cup water
2 egg whites
1 teaspoon vanilla extract
1 teaspoon almond extract
1 tablespoon fresh lemon juice
1 cup coarsely chopped seedless raisins
1 cup moderately coarsely chopped walnuts

1. CAKE: Preheat oven to 375° F. Lightly coat three 8-inch layer cake pans with nonstick cooking spray, then line bottoms with circles of baking parchment. Set aside.

2. Sift flour with baking powder twice onto wax paper and set aside.

3. Cream butter until light at medium electric mixer speed, then add sugar gradually, creaming all the while (mixture will be crumbly). Beat egg yolks in one at a time.

4. Add flour mixture alternately with milk, beginning and ending with flour mixture and beating after each addition only enough to combine.

5. Beat egg whites with salt to soft peaks and fold into batter.

6. Divide batter equally among three pans (they will be only half full) and bake 20 to 25 minutes until lightly browned and toothpick inserted in center comes out clean.

7. Cool cake layers in pans on wire racks 5 minutes, loosen carefully around edges, and turn out on racks. Peel off baking parchment at once.

8. SOFT FILLING: Mix sugar and water in small heavy saucepan, set lid on askew, and heat 5 minutes over moderate heat. Remove lid, insert candy thermometer, and heat, without stirring, until syrup reaches 220° F. Remove from heat and cool to 120° F. Mix in nuts and vanilla and almond extracts, then spread mixture over top of each cake layer. Do not assemble cake.

9. HARD FILLING: Mix sugar, corn syrup, and water in medium heavy saucepan, set lid on askew, and heat 5 minutes over moderate heat. Remove lid, insert candy thermometer, and heat, without stirring, until syrup reaches 244° F.

10. Meanwhile, beat egg whites until stiff in large electric mixer bowl. With mixer at medium speed, drizzle in hot syrup and continue beating until stiff and glossy. Beat in vanilla and almond extracts and lemon juice, then quickly fold in raisins and walnuts.

11. TO ASSEMBLE CAKE: Center one layer, filling-side-up, on cake plate, and spread with hard filling. Add second layer, filling-side-up, and spread with hard filling. Top with final layer, filling-side-up, pressing gently to anchor. Apply thin layer of hard filling to sides of cake, then a second, thicker coat. Frost top of cake with remaining hard filling, swirling into peaks and valleys. Let cake stand 1 hour before cutting.

Lady Baltimore Cake (Popular Silver Cake Version)

Makes a 9-inch, 3-layer Cake, 16 Servings

❋

DESPITE THE fact that the original Lady Baltimore was a yellow cake, the version most Americans now accept as the classic is a silver cake made with plenty of stiffly beaten whites. Even James Beard, the dean of American cooking, offers the egg-white version in *American Cookery* (1972). *Charleston Receipts* (1950) prints both versions. When did the shift from whole eggs to whites occur? The earliest whites-only Lady Baltimore I could find appears in *Good Housekeeping's Book of Menus, Recipes and Household Discoveries* (1922). It calls for nine egg whites, confectioners' sugar instead of granulated, and rose extract for flavor. Nearer the Lady Baltimores of today is the one in *All About Home Baking,* a slim volume of recipes put out by General Foods in 1933. Here, Lady Baltimore is introduced as a "butter cake which uses egg whites only." My hunch is that General Foods publicized its Lady Baltimore in Swans Down Cake Flour ads, possibly on package labels, too, which would explain why silver cake versions have eclipsed the whole-egg original. That plus the reinforcement six years later by this recipe, which appeared in *My*

Better Homes & Gardens Cook Book (1939). With six stiffly beaten whites, it stands three tiers tall as do many of today's "Lady Bs." The recipe here is my adaptation (language only) of the 1939 *BH & G* recipe.

CAKE

- 3½ cups sifted cake flour
- 2 teaspoons baking powder
- ½ teaspoon salt
- 1 cup vegetable shortening
- 2 cups sugar
- 1 cup milk
- 1 teaspoon vanilla extract
- 6 egg whites, stiffly beaten

FILLING

- 1 cup sugar
- ½ cup water
- ⅟₁₆ teaspoon cream of tartar
- 2 egg whites, stiffly beaten
- 1 cup seedless raisins, cut fine
- 1 cup coarsely chopped nuts
- 1 teaspoon vanilla extract

FROSTING

- 2 cups sugar
- ¾ cup water
- 1 tablespoon light corn syrup
- Pinch salt
- 2 egg whites, stiffly beaten
- 1 teaspoon vanilla extract

1. CAKE: Preheat oven to 350° F. Lightly coat three 9-inch layer cake pans with nonstick cooking spray; set aside.

2. Sift flour, baking powder, and salt together onto wax paper three times; set aside.

3. Cream shortening and sugar until fluffy. Combine milk and vanilla.

4. Add sifted dry ingredients alternately with milk mixture, beginning and ending with the dry and beating well after each addition. Gently fold in egg whites.

5. Divide batter among pans and bake about 30 minutes until springy to touch.

6. Cool cake layers in pans on wire racks 10 minutes, loosen carefully around edges, and turn out on racks. Cool to room temperature.

7. FILLING: Mix sugar, water, and cream of tartar in medium heavy saucepan, set lid on askew, and heat 5 minutes over moderate heat. Remove lid, insert candy thermometer, and heat, without stirring, until syrup reaches 232° F. Drizzle hot syrup into egg whites beating hard all the while. Continue beating until mixture peaks stiffly. Fold in raisins, nuts, and vanilla.

8. TO ASSEMBLE CAKE: Sandwich layers together with filling. Do not spread filling on top of cake. Let cake stand while preparing frosting.

9. FROSTING: Mix sugar, water, corn syrup, and salt in medium heavy saucepan, set lid on askew, and heat 5 minutes over moderate heat. Remove lid, insert candy thermometer, and heat, without stirring, until syrup reaches 238° F. Add hot syrup to egg whites in a fine stream, beating hard all the while. Add vanilla, then continue beating until a good spreading consistency.

10. Frost top and sides of cake, swirling into peaks and valleys.

Lord Baltimore Cake

Makes a 9-inch, 2-layer Cake,
12 Servings

✳

I HAVEN'T been able to pinpoint the arrival of Lord Baltimore Cake; certainly I've found no recipes for it in early-twentieth-century cookbooks. Earlier cookbooks either. Presumably this cake was developed to use up all the yolks left over after making the silver cake version of Lady Baltimore. In *The Chesapeake Bay Cookbook* (1990), John Shields repeats a tale his grandfather told at every July 4 family cookout. It seems that Lord Baltimore, after tasting his wife's egg-whites-only Lady Baltimore cake, huddled with the head cook "into the wee hours of the morning sipping sherry and perfecting a yolk-rich cake. As the sun was rising, and with the sherry nearly gone, Lord Baltimore and Miss Florine, in a fit of culinary ecstasy, threw in everything but the kitchen sink . . . to provide a filling for their masterpiece." Shields admits that he hasn't been able to verify any part of the story. Nor have I.

This good recipe for Lord Baltimore appears in *Betty Crocker's Picture Cookbook* (1950) and begins with a yolks-only gold cake. According to the headnote, this cake was "Named for one of the wealthiest gentlemen who first colonized America . . . George Calvert, Lord Baltimore." Perhaps. But the cake is surely twentieth century.

CAKE
    2½ cups sifted cake flour
    2½ teaspoons baking powder
    1 teaspoon salt
    ¼ cup (½ stick) butter
    ¼ cup vegetable shortening
    1⅔ cups sugar
    5 egg yolks, well beaten
    1 cup milk
    1 teaspoon lemon extract
    ½ teaspoon vanilla extract

FILLING
    ¼ cup dried macaroon crumbs
    ¼ cup coarsely chopped pecans
    ¼ cup coarsely chopped
        blanched almonds
    ¼ cup chopped maraschino
        cherries
    ⅓ cup Frosting (below)

FROSTING
    2½ cups sugar
    1 tablespoon light corn syrup
    ¾ cup water
    ¼ cup maraschino cherry juice
    3 egg whites, stiffly beaten
    ½ teaspoon lemon extract
    ½ teaspoon finely grated orange
        zest

1. CAKE: Preheat oven to 350° F. Grease and flour two 9-inch-round layer cake pans and set aside.

2. Sift flour, baking powder, and salt together onto wax paper; set aside.

3. Cream butter, shortening, and sugar until fluffy; blend in egg yolks. Mix milk and lemon and vanilla extracts.

4. Add sifted dry ingredients alternately with milk mixture, beginning and ending with the dry and beating well after each addition.

5. Divide batter between prepared pans and bake 25 to 30 minutes until springy to touch.

6. Cool cake layers in pans on wire racks 5 minutes, loosen carefully around edges, and turn out on racks. Cool to room temperature.

7. FILLING: Mix crumbs, pecans, and almonds in pie tin and toast several minutes in 350° F oven. Add cherries and set aside; complete after you prepare frosting.

8. FROSTING: Mix sugar, corn syrup, water, and cherry juice in medium heavy saucepan, set lid on askew, and heat 5 minutes over moderate heat. Remove lid, insert candy thermometer and heat, without stirring, until syrup reaches 242° F. Add hot syrup to egg whites in a fine stream, beating hard. Add lemon extract and orange zest and continue beating until mixture peaks stiffly.

9. TO ASSEMBLE CAKE: Mix ⅓ cup frosting into filling mixture and use to sandwich layers together. Swirl frosting over top and sides of cake.

Whipped Cream Cake

*Makes Two 8-inch-round Layers,
8 Servings*

✳

IT WAS Roy Finamore, my editor at Clarkson Potter and a terrific baker himself, who told me about this recipe and sent me a copy. Printed in *Good Things To Cook and How To Cook Them with Your Westinghouse Electric Range* (1940), it substitutes stiffly whipped cream for butter and is essentially a one-bowl mixer cake. I tried the recipe. Roy's right—it *is* terrific and, oh, so easy. The recipe here is adapted from the Westinghouse booklet. I don't include a frosting (nor does Westinghouse), so you can fill and frost as desired. Just be sure to cool the cake thoroughly before you frost it. It's tender.

> *1½ cups sifted cake flour*
> *2 teaspoons baking powder*
> *¼ teaspoon salt*
> *1 cup heavy cream*
> *2 eggs*
> *1 cup sugar*
> *1 teaspoon vanilla extract*

1. Preheat oven to 375° F. Grease two 8-inch round layer cake pans well, line bottoms with wax paper, and grease paper. Set aside.

2. Sift flour, baking powder, and salt onto piece of wax paper; set aside.

3. Whip cream until stiff in large electric mixer bowl. Add eggs and beat until fluffy. Beat in sugar and vanilla.

4. In two additions and by hand, mix in sifted dry ingredients.

5. Divide batter equally between pans, smoothing to edges.

6. Bake until springy to touch and lightly browned—20 to 25 minutes.

7. Cool cakes in pans on wire racks 10 minutes, loosen, then invert on wire racks. Peel off wax paper and cool to room temperature.

8. Serve plain or fill and frost as desired.

Shaker Loaf Cake

Makes a 9 × 5 × 3-inch Loaf, 12 Servings

✳

"SHAKER" DOES not refer to the religious sect but to the jar in which the batter is shaken. I had frankly never heard of this cake until Roy Finamore, my editor on this book, told me about it over lunch one day. He sent me a partial recipe and said I'd find the rest on a box of Presto flour. Alas, no. But I managed to track the recipe through company headquarters in Lakeville, Connecticut. Here a helpful young woman—Marie Bushy—promised to send me the *Presto Recipe Book* in which, she assured me, the recipe appeared. It came within a couple of days and there, on page 21, the Shaker Loaf Cake. While speaking with Bushy, I asked when Presto had come up with this unusual cake. She didn't know but promised to check it out. Two days later she phoned to say that the cake dated to 1961. Here, then, my adaptation of the Presto Shaker Loaf Cake. You can frost the cake if you wish, but it needs no lily-gilding.

NOTE: The best jar to use for shaking the batter is a widemouth, 2-quart (half-gallon) preserving jar with a lid that screws down tight. But you can use any 2-quart jar with a tight-fitting lid. You'll find the ingredients easier to add if you insert a wide-mouth canning funnel into the neck of the jar.

2 eggs
¾ cup sugar
½ teaspoon vanilla extract
1 cup heavy cream
1½ cups unsifted *self-rising cake flour*

1. Preheat oven to 350° F. Grease and flour 9 × 5 × 3-inch loaf pan, tapping out excess flour; set aside.

2. Drop eggs and sugar into widemouth 2-quart (half-gallon) preserving (or similar) jar, screw lid down tight, and shake hard 20 times.

3. Add vanilla and heavy cream, cover, and shake vigorously 20 times.

4. Add flour, cover, and shake 10 times. With long-handled rubber spatula, scrape down sides of jar and along bottom. Cover, and shake batter hard 10 times more.

5. Pour batter into pan, using long-handled rubber spatula to loosen whatever clings to sides and bottom of jar.

6. Bake until springy to touch and lightly browned—45 to 50 minutes.

7. Cool cake in pan on wire rack 15 minutes, loosen around edge, and turn out of pan. Cool thoroughly, then slice about ¾-inch thick, and serve.

Hummingbird Cake

Makes a 9-inch, 3-layer Cake, 16 Servings

✳

FOR ITS Silver Jubilee Issue (December 1990), *Southern Living* reprinted its twenty-five most popular dessert recipes. The number-one, all-time favorite: Hummingbird Cake, a reader recipe submitted by Mrs. L.H. Wiggins of Greensboro, North Carolina, which *Southern Living* first printed in its February 1978 issue. According to the magazine food editors, Hummingbird Cake has subsequently "won blue ribbons at several country fairs across the South."

CAKE
3 cups sifted all-purpose flour
1 teaspoon baking soda
½ teaspoon salt
2 cups sugar
1 teaspoon ground cinnamon
3 eggs, well beaten
¾ cup vegetable oil
1½ teaspoons vanilla extract
1 (8-ounce) can crushed pineapple, with liquid
1 cup coarsely chopped pecans

1¾ cups mashed bananas (about 2 large bananas)

FROSTING
½ cup (1 stick) butter or margarine, softened
1 (8-ounce) package cream cheese, softened
1 (16-ounce) package confectioners' (10X) sugar
1 teaspoon vanilla extract
½ cup coarsely chopped pecans

1. CAKE: Preheat oven to 350° F. Grease and flour three 9-inch-round layer cake pans; set aside.

2. Mix flour, soda, salt, sugar, and cinnamon in large bowl; add eggs and oil and stir only enough to moisten dry ingredients—do not beat. Stir in vanilla, pineapple, pecans, and bananas.

3. Divide batter among pans and bake 23 to 28 minutes, until a toothpick inserted in center comes out clean.

4. Cool cakes in pans on wire racks 10 minutes; loosen around edges, and turn out on racks. Cool completely before frosting.

5. FROSTING: Cream butter and cheese until fluffy. Add 10X sugar and beat until again fluffy. Mix in vanilla and pecans.

6. TO ASSEMBLE CAKE: Sandwich layers together with frosting, then swirl remaining frosting over top and sides of cake.

THE PILLSBURY
BAKE-OFF CONTEST

ONCEIVED IN 1949 as a way for American women to share recipes (and as a promotion for Pillsbury's Best Flour) the Pillsbury Bake-Off Contest has become an American institution—a sort of Miss (or Mrs. or Mr.) America competition for cooks. Today's $1 million top prize is the big lure, but the one hundred finalists all win a free trip to the Bake-Off Contest. Over the years finalists have included everyone from preteens to great-grannies and physicians to bus drivers; recipes have ranged from Cherry Winks (page 480) to Dilly Casserole Bread (page 315). In fact, the recipes clearly trace trends in American cooking.

In the '50s, women's devotion to home and family was reflected in showy recipes requiring painstaking preparation, like Orange Kiss-Me Cake (topped with orange juice and nuts). The '60s showed more interest in convenience foods and mixes that allowed women freedom outside the home: Crafty Crescent Lasagne, a 1968 winner, used refrigerated Crescent Dinner Rolls to save time. The '70s reflected America's concern with nutrition and "natural" whole-grain flours, vegetables, fruits; the '80s and '90s have continued this trend while venturing into ethnic and "family heirloom" recipes.

Contestants today use more fresh and unusual ingredients than they used in 1949, more garnishes, more mixes; more processors, blenders, and small appliances; and less salt. Since 1949, millions of dollars have been awarded to finalists. Sometimes they earn it. One contestant traveled part way to the Bake-Off Contest by dogsled. Another brought eggs from her own hens to make sure her cake would taste fresh. And one poor woman put her pie on a chair to cool, then sat on it.

Who copped the first $1 million top prize in 1996? A man. Kurt Wait of Redwood City, California, whose Macadamia Fudge Torte (page 407)—a return to sweet and gooey—knocked the judges' socks off. Enough said.

Japanese
Fruitcake

*Makes a 9-inch, 3-layer Cake,
16 Servings*

✳

THIS BELOVED Southern fruitcake bears little resemblance to the traditional fruitcake. It begins with a yellow cake, the batter is divided, then two-thirds of it is enriched with raisins and spices. I've never encountered Japanese Fruitcake outside the South, in fact rarely out of the Carolinas. And then mostly at Christmastime in the homes of friends. Nor have I ever heard any explanation of its unusual name; certainly there is nothing Japanese about Japanese Fruitcake. The version below, attributed to Susan A. Houston of Tucker, Georgia, was printed in the November 1990 issue of *Southern Living*. It's not quite the recipe I grew up with; we used dried currants instead of raisins and orange in the frosting instead of lemon (I've taken the liberty of offering these options). And while I can't prove it, I feel certain Japanese Fruitcake belongs to the twentieth century. I have rarely seen recipes for it beyond community fund-raiser cookbooks and in these only from the '30s onward.

A Distinctive Christmas Gift!
A FRUIT CAKE IN A PYREX CASSEROLE

CAKE

3¼ cups sifted all-purpose flour
2 teaspoons baking powder
1 cup (2 sticks) butter or
    margarine, softened
2 cups sugar
4 eggs
1 cup milk
1 teaspoon vanilla extract
1 teaspoon ground cinnamon
1 teaspoon ground allspice
½ teaspoon ground cloves
1 cup seedless raisins or dried
    currants

FROSTING

2 tablespoons cornstarch
1½ cups water
2 cups sugar
1 tablespoon finely grated
    lemon or orange zest
3½ tablespoons fresh lemon
    juice or 2 tablespoons fresh
    orange juice plus 1½
    tablespoons lemon juice
3½ cups grated coconut
    (preferably fresh)

1. CAKE: Preheat oven to 350° F. Grease and flour three 9-inch-round layer cake pans; set aside.

2. Sift flour and baking powder onto wax paper and set aside.

3. Cream butter in large electric mixer bowl at medium speed until light. Add sugar gradually and cream at medium speed until again light. Beat in eggs, one at a time.

4. With mixer at low speed, add flour mixture alternately with milk, beginning and ending with flour

and beating after each addition only enough to combine. Beat in vanilla.

5. Pour one-third of batter into *one* pan. Mix cinnamon, allspice, cloves, and raisins into remaining batter and divide between remaining pans.

6. Bake 20 to 25 minutes until toothpick inserted in middle of layers comes out clean.

7. Cool layers in pans on wire racks 10 minutes. Carefully loosen around edges and turn layers out of pans onto wire racks. Cool to room temperature.

8. FROSTING: Dissolve cornstarch in ½ cup water. Heat remaining 1 cup water to boiling in medium heavy saucepan. Stir in sugar, lemon zest, and juice. Insert candy thermometer and boil 7 minutes, stirring often, until mixture reaches 236° F. Gradually stir in cornstarch mixture and cook, stirring constantly, over moderate heat, until mixture thickens and clears, about 3 minutes. Remove from heat, mix in coconut, and cool to room temperature.

9. TO ASSEMBLE CAKE: Sandwich three layers—spice, plain, spice—together with some of frosting, then spread remaining frosting over top and sides of cake.

NOTE: In North Carolina, we are more generous about what we spread between the layers, then pile the remaining frosting on top of the cake and let it dribble down the sides, making no effort to spread or smooth it.

TIMELINE

1982

The *Zagat New York City Restaurant Survey* emerges as a full-fledged guide.

1984

Cajun chef Paul Prudhomme spreads the gospel of "blackened" cooking.

Cuisine magazine folds.

1985

James Beard dies.

The James Beard Foundation is established and headquarters in Beard's Greenwich Village town house.

The New Doubleday Cookbook appears, providing for the first time per-serving calorie, sodium, and cholesterol counts for each recipe.

1986

Zagat publishes restaurant surveys of Los Angeles, Washington, D.C., and Chicago.

Pineapple
Upside-Down Cake

*Makes a 10-inch-round Cake,
8 Servings*

＊

FOOD HISTORIANS agree that pineapple upside-down cake belongs to the twentieth century but are not so certain about the decade. According to John Mariani (*The Dictionary of American Food and Drink,* Revised Edition, 1994), "the first mention in print of such a cake was in 1930, and was so listed in the 1936 Sears Roebuck catalog, but the cake is somewhat older." In *Fashionable Food: Seven Decades of Food Fads* (1995), Sylvia Lovegren traces pineapple upside-down cake to a 1924 Seattle fund-raising cookbook. Only its contributor, Mrs. Sidney E. Goodwin, titled her cake "Pineapple Glacé." While rooting around old women's magazines, I found a Gold Medal Flour ad with a full-page, four-color picture of Pineapple

Upside-Down Cake—a round cake with six slices of pineapple, candied red cherries, and a brown sugar glaze. The date: November 1925.

In a feature on pineapple (*New York Newsday,* May 9, 1994) staff writer Marie Bianco writes "In 1926 the Hawaiian Pineapple Co., as the Dole Food Co. was called in those days, ran a cooking-with-pineapple contest. The company planned to publish a cookbook titled 'Pineapple as 100 Good Cooks Serve It.' Of the 60,000 pineapple recipes received, 2,500 were for pineapple upside-down cake." The timing makes sense. Perfectly cut canned pineapple rings had only recently become available thanks to James Dole, an entrepreneurial young Harvard graduate who set off for Hawaii in 1899 to make his fortune. Within four years he was canning pineapple; twenty-three years later he bought the island of Lanai and began growing pineapple. He'd already built a cannery in Honolulu and with the help of an inventive

young engineer in his employ, developed a machine that could peel, core, and turn out a hundred whole pineapple cylinders a minute. Today there are scores of recipes for pineapple upside-down cake. This one is adapted from one created by Dole.

TOPPING
- *⅓ cup butter or margarine*
- *⅔ cup firmly packed brown sugar*
- *1 (20-ounce) can pineapple slices (reserve 2 tablespoons juice)*
- *10 maraschino cherries*

CAKE
- *1½ cups sifted all-purpose flour*
- *1¾ teaspoons baking powder*
- *¼ teaspoon salt*
- *⅓ cup butter or margarine*
- *¾ cup granulated sugar*
- *2 eggs, separated*
- *1 teaspoon finely grated lemon zest*
- *1 tablespoon fresh lemon juice*
- *1 teaspoon vanilla extract*
- *½ cup sour cream*
- *2 tablespoons reserved pineapple juice (from pineapple slices above)*

1. TOPPING: Melt butter in 10-inch cast-iron skillet over moderately low heat. Off heat, stir in brown sugar, distributing evenly. Pat pineapple slices dry on paper towels and arrange artfully in brown sugar mixture. Center each pineapple slice with a cherry.

2. CAKE: Preheat oven to 350° F. Sift flour with baking powder and salt onto wax paper; set aside.

3. Cream butter with ½ cup sugar in large electric mixer bowl at high speed until fluffy-light. At medium speed, beat in egg yolks, lemon zest and juice, and vanilla. Combine sour cream and pineapple juice.

4. Add sifted dry ingredients to creamed mixture alternately with sour cream mixture, beginning and ending with the dry and beating after each addition only enough to blend.

5. Whip egg whites with remaining ¼ cup sugar until mixture peaks stiffly. Gently fold into batter.

6. Pour batter into skillet and bake 35 minutes or until springy to touch.

7. Cool cake in skillet on wire rack 10 minutes, then loosen carefully around edge and invert on large cake plate. If any pineapple slices or cherries dislodge, set back into place.

Maraschino Cherry Cake

*Makes a 9-inch, 2-layer Cake,
12 Servings*

✳

MY RESEARCH tells me that this first cousin to Lord Baltimore Cake debuted in the 1930s. General Foods's *All About Home Baking* (1933) recommends it as a "practical treat for picnics." Maraschino Cake was also featured in *Betty Crocker's Picture Cookbook* (1950) and remains popular in the South and heartland (the recipe given below is adapted from Betty Crocker).

NOTE: The word *maraschino* derives, says John Mariani (*The Dictionary of American Food and Drink,* Revised Edition, 1994), from *maresca,* a wild Italian cherry made into a liqueur in which the cherries, themselves, are steeped. Mariani further states that maraschino cherries were made in this country from the turn of the century on and that the process was modified in the 1920s enabling manufacturers to use any kind of cherries for maraschinos. First the cherries were brined, then soaked in a fructose/corn syrup solution, then dyed bright red or green. This cake requires the red.

CAKE
*3 cups sifted cake flour
2½ teaspoons baking powder
1 teaspoon salt
⅓ cup butter
⅓ cup vegetable shortening
1½ cups sugar
¼ cup maraschino cherry juice
¾ cup milk
½ cup coarsely chopped nuts
16 maraschino cherries, cut
    into eighths
5 egg whites, stiffly beaten*

FROSTING
*2½ cups sugar
1 tablespoon light corn syrup
½ cup water
½ cup maraschino cherry juice
3 egg whites, stiffly beaten*

DECORATION
*12 red maraschino cherries,
    stems on*

1. CAKE: Preheat oven to 350° F. Grease and flour two 9-inch-round layer cake pans and set aside.

2. Sift flour, baking powder, and salt together onto wax paper; set aside.

3. Cream butter, shortening, and sugar in large bowl until fluffy; mix cherry juice and milk in small bowl.

4. Add sifted dry ingredients to creamed mixture alternately with milk mixture, beginning and ending with the dry and beating well after each addition. Fold in nuts and cherries, then beaten egg whites.

5. Divide batter between pans and bake 30 to 35 minutes until springy to touch.

6. Cool cake layers in pans on wire racks 5 minutes, loosen carefully around edges, and turn out on racks. Cool to room temperature.

7. FROSTING: Mix sugar, corn syrup, water, and cherry juice in medium heavy saucepan, set lid on askew, and heat 5 minutes over moderate heat. Remove lid, insert candy thermometer, and heat, without stirring, until syrup reaches 242° F. Add hot syrup to egg whites in a fine stream, beating hard. Continue beating until mixture peaks stiffly.

8. TO ASSEMBLE CAKE: Sandwich layers together with frosting, then swirl remaining frosting over top and sides of cake. Arrange cherries in a ring on top of cake.

Amazin' Raisin Cake

Makes a 9-inch, 2-layer Cake, 12 Servings

✳

THE SECRET ingredient in this cake is mayonnaise (as in Hellmann's or Best Foods) and this recipe is one of the more popular to emerge from the test kitchens at Best Foods in Englewood Cliffs, New Jersey. There is no butter or shortening in the batter, only 1 cup mayonnaise, which can be "real mayonnaise" (the old-fashioned variety) or the new "Light" or "Low Fat Mayonnaise Dressing." The Best Foods Creative Kitchen provides no recipe for icing and suggests that you "fill and frost as desired." I favor vanilla butter cream or burnt sugar icing.

3 cups sifted all-purpose flour
2 cups sugar
2 teaspoons baking soda
1½ teaspoons ground cinnamon
½ teaspoon freshly grated nutmeg
¼ teaspoon ground cloves
½ teaspoon salt
1 cup mayonnaise
⅓ cup milk
2 eggs
3 cups coarsely chopped peeled and cored apples (3 to 4 large)
1 cup seedless raisins
1 cup coarsely chopped walnuts

1. Preheat oven to 350° F. Grease and flour two 9-inch-round layer cake pans and set aside.

2. Mix flour, sugar, baking soda, cinnamon, nutmeg, cloves, and salt in large electric mixer bowl.

3. Add mayonnaise, milk, and eggs and beat at low speed 2 minutes, scraping bowl often (batter will be thick). By hand, stir in apples, raisins, and walnuts.

4. Divide batter between pans and bake until springy in center—40 to 45 minutes.

5. Cool layers in pans on wire racks 10 minutes, loosen, and turn out on racks. Cool completely before filling and frosting.

Jim Fobel's Carrot Cake

Makes a 13 × 9 × 2-inch Loaf Cake, about 24 Servings

✳

MY ALL-TIME favorite carrot cake recipe is this one, which my good friend Jim Fobel included in his *Old-Fashioned Baking Book* (1987), a

wonderful collection of recipes and reminiscences that has just been given new life as a paperback. Jim says that this particular recipe was "for a number of years my mother's favorite cake recipe. Needless to say, we contentedly ate carrot cake countless times during a considerable part of my childhood."

CAKE

2½ cups sifted all-purpose flour
1 teaspoon baking powder
1 teaspoon baking soda
1 teaspoon salt
2 teaspoons ground cinnamon
1 cup granulated sugar
½ cup firmly packed light or
*   dark brown sugar*
¼ cup (½ stick) butter,
*   softened*
1 cup vegetable oil
5 eggs
3 cups coarsely shredded, peeled
*   raw carrots (6 medium)*
1½ cups coarsely chopped
*   walnuts*
1 recipe Jim Fobel's Cream
*   Cheese Frosting (page 467)*

1. CAKE: Preheat oven to 350° F. Grease and flour 13 × 9 × 2-inch baking pan; set aside.

2. Sift flour, baking powder, soda, salt, and cinnamon together onto wax paper; set aside also.

3. Beat granulated sugar, brown sugar, and butter in large electric mixer bowl at medium speed until well blended. Add oil and beat until smooth. Beat in eggs, one by one, then continue beating until thick

CARROT CAKE

....

I N HER *New York Cookbook* (1992), Molly O'Neill says that George Washington was served a carrot tea cake at Fraunces Tavern in lower Manhattan. The date: November 25, 1783. The occasion: British Evacuation Day. She offers an adaptation of that early recipe, which was printed in *The Thirteen Colonies Cookbook* (1975) by Mary Donovan, Amy Hatrack, and Frances Shull.

It isn't so very different from the carrot cakes of today. Yet strangely, carrot cakes are noticeably absent from American cookbooks right through the nineteenth century and well into the twentieth.

Before developing its new pudding-included carrot and spice cake mix, Pillsbury researched carrot cake in depth, even staged a nationwide contest to locate America's first-published carrot cake recipe. Their finding: A carrot cake in *The 20th Century Bride's Cookbook* published in 1929 by a Wichita, Kansas, woman's club. Running a close second was a carrot cake printed in a 1930 *Chicago Daily News* cookbook (that paper folded in 1978). Several carrot cake contestants also sent Pillsbury a complicated, two-day affair that Peg Bracken had included in one of her magazine columns sometime in the late '50s or early '60s.

Pillsbury researchers believe that carrot cake may have descended from the *baked* carrot puddings of England. Or perhaps the spicy *steamed* carrot puddings of Europe, which came to this country with the late-nineteenth- and early-twentieth-century wave of immigrants. Whatever its origin, carrot cake didn't enter mainstream America until the second half of this century.

and light, 1 to 2 minutes at medium speed.

4. Add sifted dry ingredients and beat just enough to blend. By hand, mix in carrots and walnuts; batter will be thick.

5. Spoon batter into pan, smoothing to edges. Bake 50 to 60 minutes, until springy to touch and a toothpick inserted in center of cake comes out clean.

6. Cool cake in pan on wire rack to room temperature.

7. Swirl frosting generously over top of cake. Cover pan of cake with plastic wrap and refrigerate. The frosting will firm up. Bring to room temperature before cutting into squares and serving.

APPLESAUCE CAKE

NINETEENTH-CENTURY cookbooks brim with fruitcakes. There's the occasional apple cake, too, usually made with dried apples but sometimes with chopped fresh apples. Yet I find no applesauce cakes. In fact, I've been unable to trace them any further back than 1915. In my battered copy of *Larkin Housewives' Cook Book* (1915), there are two applesauce cakes: Apple Sauce Birthday Cake, which is loaded with chopped citron, candied lemon, and orange rind as well as applesauce, and Eggless Apple Sauce Cake, which contains cocoa in addition to cinnamon and cloves.

During World War I, applesauce cakes became the patriotic way to cut down on eggs, sugar, and butter. The recipe in Mary Swartz Rose's *Everyday Foods in Wartime* (1917) contains no eggs at all and a mere two tablespoons of butter, which are creamed with one cup of applesauce and one cup of sugar.

Applesauce cakes grew in popularity throughout the '20s and '30s, took something of a hiatus, then returned full force in the '60s. In the health-conscious 1990s, Mott's discovered that applesauce could be substituted for shortening in certain sturdy butter cakes without mishap, giving "applesauce cake" whole new meaning. Had Mott's seen Mary Swartz Rose's nearly butterless, World War I applesauce cake, reworked it, and given it a low-fat '90s spin? One wonders.

Still, the applesauce cake most of us know and love is the spicy loaf strewn with raisins and nuts—no stinting on shortening, eggs, or sugar.

Applesauce Cake

Makes a 13 × 9 × 2-inch Loaf Cake, 12 Servings

✳

TO MY mind, the all-time best applesauce cake is this one developed by the *Good Housekeeping* food department. It appeared in *The New Good Housekeeping Cookbook* (1986) in slightly different form.

1½ cups applesauce

2¼ cups sifted all-purpose flour
1¼ cups sugar
⅔ cup vegetable shortening
⅓ cup milk
2 teaspoons baking soda
1 teaspoon ground cinnamon
½ teaspoon salt
½ teaspoon freshly grated nutmeg
½ teaspoon ground cloves
2 eggs

1 cup dark seedless raisins
½ cup chopped walnuts
Confectioners' (10X) sugar (optional) for dusting

1. Preheat oven to 350° F. Grease and flour 13 × 9 × 2-inch baking pan; set aside.

2. Place all but last three ingredients in large electric mixer bowl and beat at low speed until well blended, constantly scraping bowl with rubber spatula. Raise speed to high and beat 2 minutes, occasionally scraping bowl.

3. By hand, mix raisins and walnuts into batter. Pour into pan, smoothing to corners.

4. Bake 40 to 45 minutes, until toothpick inserted in center of cake comes out clean.

5. Cool cake in pan on wire rack to room temperature. Dust top with 10X sugar, if you like, before cutting into squares.

1990s Low-fat Applesauce Ginger Cake

Makes a 13 × 9 × 2-inch Loaf Cake, 12 Servings

✳

THIS IS a recipe I worked out in the early '90s for an article I was writing. I simply took an old family recipe, stripped it of its butter and substituted applesauce. And I have to say I think this "skinny" applesauce cake every bit as good as Grandma's.

Zest of 1 orange, removed in strips
½ cup firmly packed light brown sugar
½ cup granulated sugar
3½ cups sifted all-purpose flour
1 teaspoon baking soda
½ teaspoon baking powder
½ teaspoon ground cinnamon
½ teaspoon ground allspice
¼ teaspoon freshly grated nutmeg
1 cup buttermilk
1 cup applesauce
½ cup molasses
1 tablespoon fresh lemon juice
3 eggs, well beaten
½ cup finely minced fresh ginger

1. Preheat oven to 350° F. Coat 13 × 9 × 2-inch baking pan with nonstick cooking spray; set aside.

2. Buzz orange zest and brown and granulated sugars in food processor fitted with metal blade about 1 minute until zest is finely grated; scrape bowl sides down after 30 seconds.

3. Add flour, soda, baking powder, cinnamon, allspice, and nutmeg and pulse 10 to 12 times. Transfer to large mixing bowl and make well in center.

4. Churn buttermilk, applesauce, molasses, and lemon juice in processor 5 seconds. Add eggs and ginger and pulse 3 to 4 times.

5. Dump applesauce mixture into well in dry ingredients and with large rubber spatula, fold in gently. Batter should be lumpy. Don't overmix or cake will be tough.

6. Spoon batter into pan, smoothing to corners, and bake 35 to 40 minutes, until toothpick inserted in center of gingerbread comes out clean.

7. Cool to room temperature in pan on wire rack before cutting into bars.

Good Things to Eat

MADE WITH

ARM & HAMMER BAKING SODA

Coping with Sugar Rationing

IN 1943 when American women were struggling with the sugar shortages of World War II, General Mills published *Your Share,* a booklet in which Betty Crocker showed women how corn syrup or honey could be substituted wholly or partly for sugar in cakes. Here are the substitution tables "Betty" suggested. Betty Crocker then proceeded, via the chart at right, to show cooks how to make yellow, chocolate, and white cakes using no sugar at all.

WHEN USING SYRUP AND SUGAR

IF CAKE RECIPE CALLS FOR:	AMOUNTS OF SUGAR AND SYRUP TO USE:	TO REDUCE LIQUID: Measure amount of liquid recipe calls for: Then take out:
1 cup sugar	1/2 cup of each	2 tbsp. liquid
1 1/4 cups sugar	5/8 cup of each	2 tbsp. liquid
1 1/3 cups sugar	2/3 cup of each	3 tbsp. liquid
1 1/2 cups sugar	3/4 cup of each	3 tbsp. liquid
1 3/4 cups sugar	7/8 cup of each	3 1/2 tbsp. liquid
2 cups sugar	1 cup of each	4 tbsp. liquid

NOTE: Use syrup or honey at room temperature. In measuring syrup, measure level, not over-full. Syrup rounds up a bit due to surface tension.

Grease pans extra well. Cakes made with syrup are especially moist. Test carefully to be sure cake is thoroughly baked.

WHEN USING ONLY SYRUP

FLUFFY YELLOW CAKE	FLUFFY CHOCOLATE CAKE	FLUFFY WHITE CAKE
1/2 cup shortening	1/2 cup	1/2 cup
2 tsp. orange rind	Omit	1/2 tsp. almond extract
1/2 tsp. lemon extract	Omit	1 tsp. vanilla
1 1/3 cups light corn syrup	1 1/3 cups	1 1/3 cups
2 1/4 cups sifted SOFTASILK	2 cups	2 1/4 cups
1/2 tsp. salt	1/2 tsp.	1/2 tsp.
*2 1/2 or 2 3/4 or 3 1/4 tsp. baking powder	*2 1/2 or 2 3/4 or 3 1/4 tsp.	*2 1/2 or 2 3/4 or 3 1/4 tsp.
2 large eggs	2 large eggs	3 large egg whites
1/2 cup milk	1/2 cup	1/2 cup
	2 sq. choc. (2 oz.) melted	

*Baking Powder . . . smallest amount for double-action type; medium amount for phosphate; largest amount for tartrate type.

THOROUGHLY cream shortening, flavorings, and corn syrup. Sift flour, salt, and baking powder. Stir 1/4 the dry ingredients into creamed mixture. Blend in well beaten egg yolks. Stir in rest of dry ingredients alternately with milk. Fold in stiffly beaten egg whites. Pour into 2 well greased and floured 8-inch round layer pans. Bake 30 to 35 min. in mod. oven (350°).

FLUFFY CHOCOLATE: Same method, except stir melted chocolate into batter just before folding in egg whites.

FLUFFY WHITE CAKE: Same as Fluffy Yellow, but omit egg yolks.

M.F.K. FISHER included this recipe in *How To Cook a Wolf* and even though the book came out during World War II (1942), this War Cake is one she remembers from World War I. "War Cake says nothing to me now," she writes, "but I know that it is an honest cake, and one loved by hungry children. And I'm not ashamed of having loved it . . . merely a little puzzled, and thankful that I am no longer eight." Here, then, is the War Cake recipe exactly as Mrs. Fisher set it down in *How To Cook a Wolf.* It's interesting that she doesn't bother to record ingredients in order of use, which all good cookbook editors insist upon today.

WAR CAKE (WORLD WAR I)

Makes 1 Loaf Cake

½ cup shortening (bacon grease can be used, because of the spices, which hide its taste)

1 teaspoon cinnamon

1 teaspoon other spices . . . cloves, mace, ginger, etc.

1 cup chopped raisins or other dried fruits . . . prunes, figs, etc.

1 cup sugar, brown or white

1 cup water

2 cups flour, white or whole wheat

¼ teaspoon soda

2 teaspoons baking powder

Sift the flour, soda, and baking powder. Put all the other ingredients in a pan, and bring to a boil. Cook five minutes.

Cool thoroughly. Add the sifted dry ingredients and mix well.

Bake 45 minutes or until done in a greased loaf-pan in a 325–350° oven.

Wartime Cake (World War II)

Makes an 8 × 8 × 2-inch Loaf Cake, about 16 Servings

❈

THIS RECIPE is a little richer than M.F.K. Fisher's War Cake, which precedes. It was created by the nutrition committee at General Mills and printed in a 1942 Betty Crocker booklet entitled *Your Share: How To Prepare Appetizing, Healthy Meals with Foods Available Today.* In this little booklet are 52 wartime menus, 226 recipes, and 369 hints including tips for using the government's newly created Basic 7 Food Groups. This particular cake is, as the booklet says, "eggless, milkless, butterless." And "delicious uniced."

1 cup firmly packed brown sugar

1¼ cups water

⅓ cup lard or other shortening

2 cups seedless raisins

½ teaspoon ground nutmeg

2 teaspoons ground cinnamon

½ teaspoon ground cloves

1 teaspoon salt

1 teaspoon baking soda dissolved in 2 tablespoons water

2 cups all-purpose flour mixed with 1 teaspoon baking powder

1. Preheat oven to 325° F. Grease and flour 8 × 8 × 2-inch baking pan; set aside.

2. Mix sugar, water, shortening, raisins, nutmeg, cinnamon, and cloves in large saucepan. Bring to boil over moderate heat, then boil 3 minutes; cool to room temperature.

3. Mix salt and soda solution into pan, then blend in flour mixture.

4. Pour into pan, spreading to corners, and bake about 50 minutes until cake begins to pull from sides of pan and is springy-firm to touch.

5. Cool in pan on wire rack before cutting into squares.

Depression Cake

Makes an 8½ × 4½ × 2¾-inch Loaf Cake, 8 Servings

❋

IN THE March 1989 issue of *Country Living,* Food Editor Joanne Lamb Hayes assembled a fascinating collection of recipes to show "how families coped in the kitchen during the Great Depression and wartime." This sugarless, eggless cake was developed during the First World War. "Sugar, the cheapest and most compact form of energy," Joanne writes, "was saved for our boys overseas, so creative cooks learned to use molasses, honey, or corn syrup instead. For scarce wheat, they substituted barley, oats, or corn; for butter they used vegetable oil." When the Great Depression arrived, just eleven years after the Great War, this frugal cake was renamed Depression Cake.

NOTE: If corn flour is not available, Joanne says "to place ¾ cup cornmeal in food processor with chopping blade and process until finely

SUN-MAID RAISINS THREE VARIETIES

ground. The corn should measure 1 cup."

CAKE

> ¾ cup molasses
> ¼ cup rendered chicken fat or vegetable oil
> 1¼ cups unsifted all-purpose flour
> 1 cup corn flour (see Headnote)
> 1 cup milk
> 4 teaspoons baking powder
> 2 teaspoons ground cinnamon
> ½ teaspoon salt
> ¼ teaspoon ground cloves
> 1 cup dark seedless raisins

SUGARLESS GLAZE (OPTIONAL)

> ¼ cup milk
> 2 tablespoons light corn syrup
> 1 teaspoon cornstarch
> ¼ teaspoon almond extract

1. CAKE: Preheat oven to 350° F. Grease and flour 8½ × 4½ × 2¾-inch loaf pan and set aside.

2. Beat molasses and fat in large electric mixer bowl at high speed until fluffy. Add flour, corn flour, milk, baking powder, cinnamon, salt, and cloves, stirring just until smooth. Mix in raisins.

3. Spoon into pan, smoothing to corners, and bake 60 to 65 minutes, until center springs back when lightly pressed.

4. Cool cake in pan on wire rack 10 minutes. Loosen around edges, turn cake onto wire rack, and cool to room temperature before slicing. Serve as is or top with Glaze.

5. GLAZE: Mix milk, corn syrup, and cornstarch in small saucepan, beating until smooth. Bring to a boil over moderate heat, stir in almond extract, then drizzle over cake.

NOTE: If cake is glazed, it must be refrigerated and served within two days.

Eggless, Butterless, Milkless Cake (Depression Cake II)

Makes a 10-inch Tube Cake, 12 Servings

✳

LIKE THE previous recipe, this one was featured in *Country Living*'s portfolio of "hard times" recipes (March 1989). In her headnote, Food Editor Joanne Lamb Hayes writes, "This cake uses mayonnaise as a source of fat and eggs . . . a clever way to substitute a readily available product for those staples which were needed by the military. A 1918 cookbook warns cooks to reduce their use of fats 'not only that our soldiers and our Allies may have a sufficient supply of this most necessary food, but that fats may be available to furnish the glycerine required in making ammunition'." In 1937, Hellmann's Mayonnaise introduced a chocolate cake not unlike this one (page 444), which substitutes mayonnaise for milk and fat—but not eggs. Did the earlier recipe inspire Hellmann's? Possibly, although I've been unable to verify that. Unfortunately, many food companies have changed hands down the years or merged with others and archives, sad to say, have been lost.

2 cups unsifted self-rising cake flour
1 cup granulated sugar
½ cup unsweetened cocoa powder
1 cup water
1 cup mayonnaise
2 teaspoons vanilla extract
1 teaspoon confectioners' (10X) sugar

1. Preheat oven to 350° F. Grease and flour 10-inch tube pan; set aside.

2. Mix flour, granulated sugar, and cocoa in medium bowl.

3. Gradually whisk water into mayonnaise in small bowl and continue whisking until smooth. Stir in vanilla.

4. Add mayonnaise mixture to flour mixture and stir until well blended.

5. Spoon into pan, spreading to edge, and bake 45 to 50 minutes, until center springs back when lightly pressed.

6. Cool cake in pan on wire rack 10 minutes. Loosen around edge and around central tube, invert on rack, and cool to room temperature.

7. Transfer cake to serving plate and dust top with 10X sugar.

Brown Derby Grapefruit Cake

Makes a 9-inch, 2-layer Cake, 12 Servings

✳

FOR YEARS the recipe for this cake remained a secret. In fact, when I profiled actress Joanne Woodward for *The Ladies' Home Journal* in the '60s, the grapefruit cake recipe we ran was her stab at the Brown Derby original, at that time her favorite cake (recipe follows). This recipe *is* the original, provided by the folks at Walt Disney World, where a replica of the old Hollywood Brown Derby has been built at the Disney-MGM Studios Theme Park. The accents of teak and mahogany are there, the signature brass derby-hat lamps, the tables set aside for gossip queens Louella Parsons and Hedda Hopper. Several original Brown Derby recipes are on the menu, among them this cake. It's a European-style torte, a sturdy yellow cake baked in a springform pan that's split when cool.

NOTE: The frosting is skimpy, little more than a glaze. Pastry chefs will have no problem covering the top and sides of the cake with this amount, but home cooks will be happier if they multiply the frosting ingredients by 1½.

CAKE
1½ cups sifted cake flour
¾ cup granulated sugar
1½ teaspoons baking powder
½ teaspoon salt
¼ cup water
¼ cup vegetable oil
3 eggs, separated
3 tablespoons fresh grapefruit juice
½ teaspoon finely grated lemon zest
¼ teaspoon cream of tartar

FROSTING
2 (3-ounce) packages cream cheese, at room temperature

PHILADELPHIA CREAM CHEESE

BRAND

2 teaspoons fresh lemon juice
1 teaspoon finely grated lemon
   zest
¾ cup confectioners' (10X)
   sugar
2 teaspoons finely minced
   grapefruit (about 1 section)
6 to 8 drops yellow food
   coloring (optional)

FILLING AND DECORATION

1 (1-pound) can grapefruit
   sections, well drained and
   patted dry, or 2 (1-pound)
   grapefruits, peeled, sectioned,
   seeded, and patted dry

1. CAKE: Preheat oven to 350° F.

2. Sift flour, granulated sugar, baking powder, and salt together into mixing bowl; make well in center.

3. Whisk water with oil, egg yolks, grapefruit juice, and lemon zest in small bowl. Dump into well in dry ingredients and beat until smooth.

4. Beat egg whites with cream of tartar in large bowl until stiff but not dry. Gradually add egg yolk mixture to whites, gently folding in with rubber spatula just enough to incorporate. *Do not stir; you'll toughen cake.*

5. Pour batter into *ungreased* 9-inch springform pan and bake 25 to 30 minutes, just until cake springs back lightly when touched.

6. Invert cake on wire rack and cool in upside-down pan to room temperature. Loosen cake around edge; carefully release and remove springform pan sides and bottom.

7. With sharp serrated knife, split cake into two layers and place one cut-side-up on cake plate.

8. FROSTING: Beat cheese, lemon juice and zest, 10X sugar, and minced grapefruit in medium bowl until fluffy. Tint, if desired, with yellow food coloring.

9. TO ASSEMBLE CAKE: Spread thin layer of frosting on bottom layer. Top with half of grapefruit sections (if chunky, halve lengthwise for better fit). Set second layer cutside-down on bottom layer, pressing down lightly. Skim-coat top and sides of cake with remaining frosting. Arrange remaining grapefruit sections in sunburst pattern on top of cake.

NOTE: Store cake in refrigerator; frosting contains cream cheese.

TIMELINE

1987

Cooking Light magazine rolls off the press. By the mid-'90s, it becomes America's most popular food magazine.

Zagat adds restaurant surveys of New Orleans, Boston, and San Francisco.

Nestlé introduces Alpine White, America's first white chocolate bar.

1988

Food Arts magazine debuts.

1989

U.S. pasta consumption soars past four billion pounds or eighteen pounds per man, woman, and child per year.

1990s

The fitness craze continues.

"Oat bran" becomes the mantra of the eat-right-to-keep-fit crowd.

A Milk and Butter Saver

....

HERE'S A Depression chocolate cake that substitutes Hellmann's Mayonnaise for butter and milk. Note that Best Foods Creative Kitchen now gives "light" mayonnaise as an option for "regular."

1937 CHOCOLATE MAYONNAISE CAKE

2 cups flour*
2/3 cup unsweetened cocoa
1 1/4 teaspoons baking soda
1/4 teaspoon baking powder
3 eggs
1 2/3 cups sugar

1 teaspoon vanilla
1 cup HELLMANN'S or
   BEST FOODS real or light
   mayonnaise or low fat
   mayonnaise dressing
1 1/3 cups water

1. Preheat oven to 350°F. Grease and flour bottom of 2 (9 × 1 1/2-inch) round cake pans.

2. In medium bowl, combine flour, cocoa, baking soda, and baking powder; set aside.

3. In large bowl with mixer at high speed, beat eggs, sugar and vanilla 3 minutes or until light and fluffy. Reduce speed to low; beat in mayonnaise until blended. Add flour mixture in 4 additions, alternately with water (begin and end with flour). Pour into prepared pans.

4. Bake 30 to 35 minutes or until toothpick inserted in center comes out clean. Cool in pans on wire racks 10 minutes. Remove; cool completely on racks. Frost as desired. Makes 2 (9-inch) layers.

*Recipe can be prepared with cake flour. Substitute 2 1/4 cups unsifted cake flour for flour.

CAKES & FROSTINGS

Joanne Woodward's "Brown Derby" Grapefruit Cake

Makes a 9-inch, 2-layer Cake, 12 Servings

✳

IN 1960, when I was one of the junior members of *The Ladies' Home Journal* food department, I wrote a feature on Joanne Woodward. Titled "I Love Learning To Cook," the article featured several of the actress's favorite recipes. Among them was this Grapefruit Cake. "I am a great traditionalist about baking cakes," Joanne told me at the time. "One of our favorites is like the famous Brown Derby Grapefruit Cake, a recipe that's a deep, dark secret. But I've worked out something rather similar." Indeed she had. In fact, some people prefer Joanne's light, high-rising cake to the Brown Derby's.

CAKE

    3 cups sifted cake flour
    3 1/2 teaspoons baking powder
    1/4 teaspoon baking soda
    3/4 teaspoon salt
    1 1/2 cups granulated sugar
    1 tablespoon finely grated
       grapefruit zest
    1/2 teaspoon finely grated lemon
       zest
    3/4 cup (1 1/2 sticks) butter
    3 eggs
    1/2 cup fresh grapefruit juice
       mixed with 1/2 cup water

FROSTING AND
DECORATION

3 (3-ounce) packages cream
cheese, softened
1 tablespoon butter, softened
4 teaspoons finely grated
grapefruit zest
1 teaspoon finely grated lemon
zest
1 teaspoon finely grated orange
zest
¼ teaspoon vanilla extract
6 to 6½ cups confectioners'
(10X) sugar
2 medium grapefruits, peeled,
seeded, and sectioned
2 navel oranges, peeled, seeded,
and sectioned

1. CAKE: Preheat oven to 375° F. Grease two 9-inch-round layer cake tins and set aside.

2. Sift flour, baking powder, soda, and salt onto wax paper; set aside.

3. Cream granulated sugar, grapefruit and lemon zests and butter until fluffy-light. Add eggs, one at a time, beating well after each addition.

4. Add sifted dry ingredients in four additions, alternating with grapefruit juice mixture, ending with the dry ingredients and mixing lightly after each addition.

5. Divide batter between pans and bake about 30 minutes until browned and springy to touch.

6. Cool cake layers in pans on wire racks 10 minutes, loosen carefully around edges, and turn out on racks. Cool to room temperature.

7. FROSTING: Cream cheese, butter, grapefruit, lemon, and orange zests, and vanilla in large bowl until fluffy. Beat in 10X sugar, a little at a time, until a good spreading consistency.

8. TO ASSEMBLE CAKE: Sandwich layers together with thin coat of frosting, then swirl remaining frosting over top and sides of cake. Decorate top of cake with sunburst of grapefruit and orange sections, then wreathe remaining sections around base of cake.

NOTE: Because frosting contains cream cheese, store cake in the refrigerator.

Praline Cake

Makes an 8-inch, 1-layer Cake, 8 to 10 Servings

✳

"THIS PRALINE cake has a baked topping and can be reheated in its Pyrex Baking Dish," says the caption for this recipe. It appears in *Pyrex Prize Recipes,* published by Corning in 1953.

CAKE

¼ cup vegetable shortening
¾ cup granulated sugar
1 egg
1½ cups sifted cake flour
¼ teaspoon salt
1½ teaspoons baking powder
⅔ cup milk
1 teaspoon vanilla extract

TOPPING

¼ cup firmly packed brown
sugar
2 teaspoons all-purpose flour
1 tablespoon water
2 tablespoons butter or
margarine, melted
½ cup chopped pecans

1. Preheat oven to 325° F. Grease a 1½-quart (8¼-inch-round) glass ovenware cake dish or 9-inch pie plate well and set aside.

2. CAKE: Cream shortening in large mixing bowl. Add sugar gradually, beating until fluffy. Beat egg in thoroughly.

3. Sift flour with salt and baking powder. Add to creamed mixture alternately with milk, beginning and ending with dry ingredients and beating until smooth after each addition. Stir in vanilla.

4. Spoon batter into cake dish and bake 40 minutes until springy to the touch. Cool slightly, about 10 minutes.

5. TOPPING: Mix all ingredients and spread on warm cake. Return cake to oven and bake 10 minutes more.

Burnt Sugar Cake

Makes a 9-inch, 2-layer Cake,
12 Servings

✳

ALTHOUGH LATE-nineteenth-
and early-twentieth-century cookbooks often feature caramel cakes
(made with brown sugar and butter), Burnt Sugar Cake seems not to
have been popular, or perhaps even
known. I could track it no further
back than 1932. That year it
appeared in Sheila Hibben's *National
Cookbook.* Unfortunately, she credits no one for the recipe, tells nothing about it, doesn't even attribute
it to any specific part of the country, as she does with many of her
other recipes. Today, most comprehensive cookbooks include Burnt
Sugar Cake, among them *The Doubleday Cookbook* (1975), which I coauthored with Elaine Hanna and
from which the following recipe is
adapted.

BURNT SUGAR SYRUP
    ¾ cup granulated sugar
    ¾ cup boiling water

CAKE
    3 cups sifted cake flour
    3 teaspoons baking powder
    ½ teaspoon salt
    ½ cup milk
    1 teaspoon vanilla extract
    ½ cup burnt sugar syrup
        (above)
    ¾ cup (1½ sticks) butter or
        margarine

1⅓ cups granulated sugar
3 eggs

FROSTING
    ⅓ cup butter or margarine
    1 (1-pound) box confectioners'
        (10X) sugar, sifted
    ¼ cup burnt sugar syrup
        (above)
    1 teaspoon vanilla extract
    ¼ teaspoon salt

1. BURNT SUGAR SYRUP: Melt
sugar in heavy skillet over low heat,
shaking skillet frequently. When
amber colored, remove from heat,
add water (it will sputter), return to
low heat, and cook until sugar dissolves, shaking skillet now and then.
Cool syrup to room temperature.

TALES OF TWINKIES

PROBABLY MORE tall tales are told
about Twinkies than any other snack
food. Some of them are even true.
Archie Bunker always carried a
Twinkie in his lunch pail. Baboons,
loose from an Ohio zoo, were lured
back into their cages
with Twinkies. Jimmy Carter was said
to have installed a Twinkies vending
machine in the White House. A bakery
truck in Michigan, hijacked and then
abandoned, was found intact and minus
1,800 Twinkies. But the most famous
story by far (and a true one at that) is
the "Twinkies Defense"—a defense
lawyer's claim that aggressive behavior
triggered by high blood sugar levels made Dan White
murder San Francisco mayor George Moscone.

Twinkies—snack-size creme-filled sponge cakes
—were dreamed up by a Continental Bakeries
plant manager in 1930, their name inspired by a
toe shoe ad (they cost a nickel a pop during the
Depression).

Thanks to television, Twinkies became
a household name in the '50s when Continental's Hostess line cosponsored the
Howdy Doody show.

Today, Twinkies are baked in a 190-
foot-long oven, injected with vanilla
creme at near orbital speed (52,000 units
an hour), and sold at an even faster clip
(more than one billion a year).

2. CAKE: Preheat oven to 350° F. Line two ungreased 9-inch layer cake pans with baking parchment or wax paper; set aside.

3. Sift flour with baking powder and salt onto wax paper; set aside. Mix milk with vanilla and burnt sugar syrup and set aside also.

4. Cream butter in large bowl until light, add sugar gradually, beating all the while; continue creaming until fluffy. Beat eggs in, one by one.

5. Add sifted dry ingredients to creamed mixture alternately with milk mixture, beginning and ending with the dry and beating after each addition just until smooth.

6. Divide batter between pans, spreading to edges, and bake about 30 minutes, until cakes pull from sides of pans and are springy to touch.

7. Cool cakes in pans on wire racks 5 minutes, loosen, and turn out on racks. Peel off parchment, turn layers right-side-up, and cool to room temperature.

8. FROSTING: Cream butter in medium bowl until light, beat in 10X sugar, a little at a time, alternating with burnt sugar syrup. Mix in vanilla and salt and continue beating to good spreading consistency.

9. TO ASSEMBLE CAKE: Sandwich cake layers together with a little of the frosting, then swirl remaining frosting over top and sides.

Poke Cake

....

THE ORIGINAL Poke Cake, a beloved classic in the heartland, seems to have appeared in the early '80s, and this red, white, and green Christmas version in the mid-'90s. Here it is, just as it appeared in a 1994 JELL-O/PILLSBURY ad. "Make a Holiday Classic," it urges.

HOLIDAY POKE CAKE

1 (1 lb. 2.5 oz.) package
  PILLSBURY Moist
  Supreme White Cake Mix
2 cups boiling water
1 package (4-serving size)
  JELL-O Brand Gelatin,
  any red flavor

1 package (4-serving size)
  JELL-O Brand Lime
  Flavor Gelatin
1 can (16 ounces)
  PILLSBURY Creamy
  Supreme Vanilla Frosting

Heat oven to 350° F.

Prepare, bake and cool cake mix as directed on package for 2 (9-inch) cake layers. Place cake layers, top sides up, in 2 clean 9-inch round cake pans. Pierce cake with large fork at ½-inch intervals.

Stir 1 cup of the boiling water into each flavor of gelatin in separate bowls 2 minutes or until dissolved. Carefully pour red gelatin over 1 cake and lime gelatin over second cake. Refrigerate 3 hours.

Dip 1 cake pan in warm water 10 seconds; unmold onto serving plate. Spread with about ¼ cup of the frosting. Unmold second cake layer; carefully place on first layer. Frost top and sides of cake with remaining frosting.

Refrigerate 1 hour or until ready to serve. Decorate as desired.

Makes 12 servings

MYSTERY CAKE
(TOMATO SOUP–SPICE CAKE)

CAKES WITH alien ingredients—sausage meat, an entire bottle of red food coloring—have always intrigued American cooks. But none more so than this "mystery cake," containing a can of Campbell's condensed tomato soup.

Even M.F.K. Fisher, America's poet laureate of the kitchen, liked tomato soup cake. Says she in *How To Cook a Wolf* (1942), "This is a pleasant cake, which keeps well and puzzles people who ask what kind it is. It can be made in a moderate oven while you are cooking other things, which is always sensible and makes you feel rather noble, in itself a small but valuable pleasure."

Fisher's recipe differs from the Campbell's in several respects. For starters, it contains only 3 tablespoons butter and 1 cup sugar (a World War II version that spared precious butter and sugar?). To enrich her cake, Fisher added "1½ cups raisins, nuts, chopped figs, what you will." She baked her cake in a loaf tin— Campbell's is a layer cake.

Even leaner than Fisher's version is cookbook author Jim Fobel's Mystery Cake of 1932 (*Jim Fobel's Old-Fashioned Baking Book,* 1987) which, he says "is one of the few old recipes that can be precisely dated: It was developed in 1932, during the worst of the Depression. In keeping with the rather desperate circumstances of that time, it contains no eggs and very little butter" (2 tablespoons). Fobel's is a cinnamony, soda-leavened sheet cake low on flour (1½ cups) that owes its moist richness to dark brown sugar (¾ cup firmly packed), chopped raisins (1 cup), chopped walnuts (½ cup) and, yes, a can of tomato soup.

Mystery Cake (Tomato Soup– Spice Cake)

Makes an 8-inch, 2-layer Cake, 10 to 12 Servings

✳

ACCORDING TO the headnote accompanying this recipe in *Campbell's Best-Ever Recipes, 125th An-* *niversary Edition* (1994), "This moist spice cake was first made with canned tomatoes, but the tomatoes were replaced by condensed tomato soup in the 1920s. Since then, this basic recipe has changed very little, but it has been transformed into a fruitcake, pineapple upside-down cake, and a microwave cake." The original version here is a layer cake. It calls for cream cheese filling and frosting but doesn't provide the recipe. See Philly Vanilla Frosting (page 468), Jim Fobel's Cream Cheese Frosting (page 467), or use your particular favorite.

> 2 cups sifted all-purpose flour
> 1⅓ cups sugar
> 4 teaspoons baking powder
> 1½ teaspoons ground allspice
> 1 teaspoon baking soda
> 1 teaspoon ground cinnamon
> ½ teaspoon ground cloves
> 1 (10¾-ounce) can condensed
>   tomato soup
> ½ cup vegetable shortening
> 2 eggs
> ¼ cup water
> Cream cheese frosting
>   (optional)

1. Preheat oven to 350° F. Grease and flour two 8-inch-round cake pans and set aside.

2. Place all ingredients except frosting in large electric mixer bowl. With mixer at low speed, beat until well mixed, constantly scraping bowl with a rubber spatula.

3. Raise mixer speed to high and beat 4 minutes, scraping bowl occasionally. Divide batter evenly between pans.

4. Bake 35 to 40 minutes, until a toothpick inserted in center of cakes comes out clean.

5. Cool cake layers in pans on wire racks 10 minutes. Loosen around edges, turn cakes out, and cool completely. Fill and frost, if you like, with cream cheese frosting.

Daffodil Cake

*Makes a 9-inch Tube Cake,
8 to 10 Servings*

✻

THIS UNUSUAL tube cake—a marbleized yellow sponge/angel food—began showing up in cookbooks during the Great Depression. Strange for a cake with so many eggs. But its roots go somewhat deeper. Joanne Lamb Hayes, Food Editor of *Country Living* magazine, says that Daffodil Cake was what her aunt, Mildred Leese Myers of York County, Pennsylvania, always made for family birthdays. Did her aunt know where she got the recipe? Yes, indeed—from *Cake Secrets,* a 48-page booklet published in 1928 by Igleheart Brothers of Evansville, Indiana, producers of Swan's Down Cake Flour (within a few years, Swan's Down would become part of General Mills). Joanne then dug through her own early food company pamphlets and discovered that the Daffodil Cake appeared as "Angel and Sponge Marble" in the smaller 1925 edition of *Cake Secrets* (the later booklet subtitles Daffodil Cake "Angel and Sponge Marble"). From the very beginning, Daffodil Cake was a hit with dieters because it contains no butter or shortening. Joanne's aunt usually served it unfrosted, but for family birthdays she would top it with a butter cream. She also covered the central hole with a cookie so the frosted cake looked like a butter cake three or four layers high. My own search for Daffodil Cake turned up recipes in *All About Home Baking* (1933), *Ruth Wakefield's Toll House Tried and True Recipes* (1936), *My Better Homes & Gardens Cook Book* (1939), then in major cookbooks right through the '40s, '50s, and '60s. The recipe that follows is adapted from that 1925 Swan's Down booklet. I've doubled the amount of vanilla and orange extract originally called for, also beaten the egg whites in an electric mixer instead of "on a large platter."

WHITE BATTER
½ cup sifted cake flour
1¼ cups egg whites (9 to 11)
1 teaspoon cream of tartar
½ teaspoon salt
1 cup + 2 tablespoons sifted sugar
1 teaspoon vanilla extract

YELLOW BATTER
⅔ cup sifted cake flour
4 egg yolks
1 teaspoon orange extract
½ total amount of meringue from White Batter (above)

1. Preheat oven to 325° F.

2. WHITE BATTER: Sift ½ cup flour four times onto wax paper; set aside. Beat egg whites in large electric mixer bowl at moderate speed until foamy. Add cream of tartar and salt and continue beating until silvery. Raise mixer speed to high, add sugar gradually, and continue beating until meringue peaks stiffly. Scoop half of meringue into large bowl and set aside. Fold vanilla and flour into meringue remaining in mixer bowl; set White Batter aside.

3. YELLOW BATTER: Sift ⅔ cup flour four times onto wax paper and set aside. With hand electric mixer, beat egg yolks and orange extract in small bowl at moderate speed until light and lemony. Mix about 1 cup reserved meringue into yolk mixture to lighten it, spoon on top of remaining meringue and fold in gently. Finally, fold in flour.

4. TO ASSEMBLE: Using teaspoon and being generous about amount you scoop up, drop White and Yellow Batters alternately into ungreased 9-inch tube pan. When all batter is in pan, rap pan sharply on counter twice, then with spatula or knife, cut through batter to marbleize, once clockwise about ½ inch from edge of pan, once counterclockwise about ½ inch from central tube.

5. Bake cake until cake tester inserted midway between rim and central tube comes out clean, about 1 hour.

6. If tube pan has "legs" protruding above rim, invert pan and cool cake in upside-down pan 1 hour. If pan has no "legs," insert neck of heavy bottle through tube and cool cake upside-down.

7. With thin-bladed metal spatula, carefully loosen cake around edge and central tube, then turn out on cake plate. Serve plain or, if you prefer, skim-coat with a basic butter frosting, either vanilla or orange.

BETTY CROCKER:
SHE TAUGHT US HOW TO COOK

SORRY, VIRGINIA—there is no *real* Betty Crocker. Although 90 percent of Americans know the name and many believe Betty's a flesh-and-blood woman (they write her letters, send her presents), this spokesperson for Gold Medal Flour was at first nothing more than a name coined by a company adman in 1921. Three years later Betty's "voice" was heard on the "Betty Crocker Cooking School of the Air," and finally in 1936 a face destined to undergo six major changes during the next half century to keep pace with changing styles was seen. The latest "Betty," a computerized composite of seventy-five American women of different ages and ethnic groups, debuted in 1996.

Sheer necessity sparked the creation of America's best-known cooking expert. Faced with a flood of questions about baking spawned by one of their own promotion schemes, executives of the Washburn Crosby Company (now General Mills) decided the replies would inspire more confidence if seemingly written by a woman employee. "Betty" was chosen because of its friendly informality; "Crocker" to honor a retired executive. An immediate hit, Betty Crocker became ever more familiar as her face appeared in magazines and on grocery shelves, as millions joined her radio cooking school, as her advice on rationing and low-cost menus helped families eat well during World War II.

When *Betty Crocker's Picture Cookbook* appeared in 1950, it quickly became a national best-seller, as have all subsequent editions, even though out of 1,240 recipes in the 1991 edition, 60 percent have been published before. So why do today's cooks want a recipe for blueberry muffins that originated at the Illinois State Fair in 1930? "Betty Crocker is not a trendsetter," say her publishers. Young cooks, they claim, buy the books because their own mothers learned to cook from Betty Crocker, and they know they can trust her.

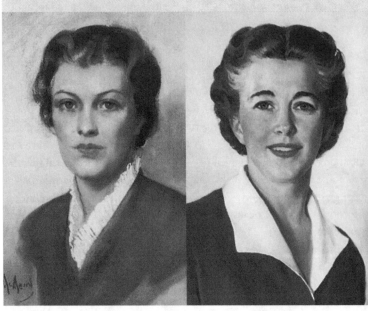

Chiffon Cake

Makes a 10-inch Tube Cake, 10 to 12 Servings

❋

IN THE late '20s, word trickled out of California of a high-rising new cake that melted in your mouth. Its creator, a Los Angeles insurance salesman and hobby cook named Harry Baker, was soon baking his "chiffon cake" for fancy Hollywood functions as well as for the Brown Derby restaurants. But he wouldn't divulge his recipe until General Mills paid him for it in 1947. The "secret ingredient," it turned out, was vegetable oil. General Mills home economists went to work fine-tuning Baker's chiffon cake recipe, experimenting with different flavors. The company printed the basic recipe (plus many variations) in a leaflet in 1948 and again in 1950 in *Betty Crocker's Picture Cookbook,* calling this the "first new cake in a hundred years" and describing it as "light as angel food, rich as butter cake."

> 2¼ cups sifted cake flour
> 1½ cups sugar
> 3 teaspoons baking powder
> 1 teaspoon salt
> ½ cup vegetable oil
> 5 egg yolks
> ¾ cup cold water
> 2 teaspoons vanilla extract
> 2 teaspoons grated lemon
>   zest
> 1 cup egg whites (7 to 8)
> ½ teaspoon cream of tartar

1. Preheat oven to 325° F.

2. Sift flour, sugar, baking powder, and salt into large mixing bowl. Make well in center and add oil, egg yolks, water, vanilla, and lemon zest. Beat until smooth with a spoon.

3. Whip egg whites with cream of tartar to stiff peaks. Pour yolk mixture gradually over beaten whites, gently folding in with rubber spatula just until blended.

4. Pour batter into ungreased 10-inch tube pan and bake 55 minutes. Raise oven temperature to 350° F and bake 10 to 15 minutes longer until surface springs back when lightly touched.

5. Invert pan immediately and cool cake to room temperature.

6. Turn pan right-side-up and rap sharply on counter to loosen cake. Turn cake out and frost, if desired.

─── VARIATIONS ───

BUTTERSCOTCH CHIFFON CAKE: Prepare as directed, substituting 2 cups brown sugar (*not* packed) for granulated sugar and omitting lemon zest. Sift brown sugar with dry ingredients. Makes a 10-inch tube cake.

ORANGE CHIFFON CAKE: Prepare as directed, omitting vanilla and lemon zest and adding 3 tablespoons grated orange zest. Orange juice may be substituted partly or wholly for the water. Makes a 10-inch tube cake.

CHOCOLATE CHIP CHIFFON CAKE: Prepare as directed, increasing sugar to 1¾ cups and omitting lemon zest. Just before pouring batter into pan, fold in 3 ounces semisweet chocolate, grated. Makes a 10-inch tube cake.

DEVIL'S FOOD CAKE

ANGEL FOOD belongs to the nineteenth century but devil's food to the twentieth. How this chocolate cake came to be called devil's food no one knows although it may have been a play on opposites: it was as dark and rich as angel food was light and airy.

My friend and colleague, food historian Meryle Evans, tells me that her research once turned up a nineteenth-century mention of Devil's Food Cake—"in a reminiscence" written in the 1880s or 1890s. Still, the earliest recipes for it I could find were in two 1902 cookbooks.

The first begins with this little headnote—"Fit for angels"—and appears in *Woman's Favorite Cook Book* by Mrs. Gregory and Friends (Chicago). But with only "one-half cake of Baker's chocolate dissolved in one-half cupful of boiling water," it couldn't have been very devilish.

The second, in *Mrs. Rorer's New Cook Book* (Philadelphia, 1902), contains eight times as much chocolate (four ounces)—and a mistake. In the ingredient list, Mrs. Rorer, who was to Philadelphia as Fannie Farmer was to Boston, calls for ½ cup milk. Right away in the first line of the directions, it becomes a half pint. "The success of this cake," Mrs. Rorer instructs her readers, "depends upon the flour used." That and recognizing the obvious typo.

NOTE: The first edition of "Mrs. Rorer" (1886) includes two chocolate cakes—but no devil's food.

The Settlement Cook Book (1903) offers two recipes for Devil's Food Cake, one with "2 squares chocolate (2 oz.)," and the other with "1 cup chocolate." Devil's Food Cake No. 1 is a sour milk-soda cake, and

Classic Devil's Food Cake

Makes a 9-inch, 2-layer Cake, 12 Servings

❋

ALTHOUGH THERE are many different recipes today for devil's food cake—some made with cocoa, some with chocolate, some with buttermilk and soda, some with sweet milk and baking powder—the one that follows is considered the standard. This recipe is adapted from *All About Home Baking* (1933) published by the General Foods Corporation (now Kraft Foods, Inc.). Earlier recipes for devil's food cake called for melting the chocolate in boiling water and adding it toward the end of the recipe. But, promises this 1933 recipe, the best way to make devil's food cake is to add the melted chocolate to the butter, sugar, and egg mixture in the beginning. "This gives an especially light, fine-grained cake."

2 cups sifted cake flour
2¾ teaspoons baking powder
¼ teaspoon salt
⅔ cup butter or vegetable shortening
1½ cups sugar
3 eggs, well beaten
3 ounces unsweetened chocolate, melted
¾ cup milk
1½ teaspoons vanilla extract

1. Preheat oven to 350° F. Coat two 9-inch layer cake pans with nonstick cooking spray and set aside.

2. Sift flour, baking powder, and salt onto wax paper and set aside also.

3. Cream butter in large bowl until light, add sugar gradually, creaming all the while, then continue creaming until fluffy. Beat eggs in, then blend in melted chocolate.

4. Add sifted dry ingredients to creamed mixture alternately with milk, beginning and ending with dry ingredients and beating after each addition only enough to combine. Stir in vanilla.

5. Divide batter between pans, smooth tops, and bake 30 to 35 minutes, until a cake tester inserted in center of layer comes out clean and cake is springy to touch.

6. Cool layers in pans on wire racks 10 minutes, then loosen and turn out on racks.

7. Cool to room temperature, then fill and frost as desired. The classic is Seven-Minute Icing (page 469), but chocoholics may prefer Chocolate Butter Cream Frosting (page 468).

No. 2 a sweet milk-baking powder cake that's further enriched by a pound of brown sugar. For the 1906 edition of *The Boston Cooking-School Cook Book,* Fannie Farmer added Devil's Food Cake I (with two ounces chocolate and four eggs) and Devil's Food Cake II (with twice as much chocolate and half as many eggs).

In the early 1900s, there were a number of bizarre variations on Devil's Food Cake. One called for mashed potatoes and a number for ground cinnamon and cloves in addition to chocolate. A 1920s Rumford Baking Powder cookbook offers a sponge cake type (egg whites only, beaten stiff and folded in at the end) flavored with cloves and nutmeg plus "1 teaspoon each vanilla and lemon extracts." It sounds terrible.

One of the more interesting early recipes, reprinted below, appeared in *A Book for a Cook* published in 1905 by Pillsbury (and reissued in facsimile in 1994). It's interesting on several counts: Measurements are quite precise, yet they are not listed in order of use. No pan sizes are given, no baking times, or temperatures. Strangest of all is the method of mixing: The cake begins with a chocolate custard, which isn't mixed in until just before baking.

DEVIL'S FOOD

(Reprinted from A Book for a Cook, Pillsbury, 1905; facsimile edition, 1994)

MATERIALS:

¼ cup chocolate	1 cup sugar
½ cup sugar	½ cup butter
½ cup milk	1 egg and 1 yolk
1 egg	1 cup milk
2 teaspoonfuls vanilla	1 teaspoonful soda
	2 cups Pillsbury's Best.

WAY OF PREPARING: Put the one-half cup of milk in a double boiler. Melt the chocolate and add it to one-half a cup of sugar, and one egg well beaten. When the milk is boiling hot add it. Put back into the boiler and cook five minutes. Remove and let it cool. Cream together one cup of sugar and a half a cup of butter, add one egg and the yolk of another and beat for five minutes. Then add the cup of milk with the soda dissolved in it, and then the flour. Lastly add the vanilla and combine the two mixtures. Mix thoroughly and bake in layers. Put together with chocolate filling.

QUANTITY: This makes one medium-sized cake.

German Sweet Chocolate Cake

*Makes a 9-inch, 3-layer Cake,
16 Servings*

✳

A WHOLLY twentieth-century cake, a "reader recipe," the story goes, that was printed in a Dallas newspaper in 1957. That Texas food editor, Julie Bennell, clearly had an eye for the unusual (and maybe a craving for chocolate?) for this cake contained a quarter of a pound of *sweet* chocolate. German's Sweet Chocolate was specified, a smooth bittersweet blend named after Samuel German, the Walter Baker & Company employee who'd formulated it in 1852. Though German's sweet chocolate always sold well enough, it didn't take off until 105 years later. And then mostly in Texas. The sudden run on German's mystified the General Foods district manager until he traced it to the newspaper recipe. According to Betty Wason (*Cooks, Gluttons, and Gourmets,* 1962), he asked Julie Bennell, the Dallas food editor, if he might send the recipe to other food editors around the country. And when it appeared elsewhere, reader letters avalanched in. Writes Wason, "A St. Louis homemaker wrote to her paper saying it was like meeting a long-lost friend; her mother-in-law had given her this recipe thirty years before when she was a bride and she had somehow lost it." Before long, home economists at General Foods headquarters in White Plains, New York, refined the recipe, adding another company product: Angel Flake Coconut. Idea men rechristened it German Sweet Chocolate Cake and beginning in 1958, had it printed on the wrapper of every bar of German's Sweet Chocolate. It remains there to this day. Note: General Foods has been absorbed by Kraft Foods, Inc.

CAKE

    2 cups sifted all-purpose flour
    1 teaspoon baking soda
    ¼ teaspoon salt
    1 (4-ounce) package German's
        Sweet Chocolate
    ½ cup boiling water
    1 cup (2 sticks) butter or
        margarine
    2 cups sugar
    4 egg yolks
    1 teaspoon vanilla extract
    1 cup buttermilk
    4 egg whites, stiffly beaten

COCONUT–PECAN FROSTING

    1½ cups evaporated milk
    1½ cups sugar
    4 slightly beaten egg yolks
    ¾ cup (1½ sticks) butter or
        margarine
    1½ teaspoons vanilla extract
    2 cups flaked coconut
    1½ cups chopped pecans

1. CAKE: Preheat oven to 350° F. Line bottoms of three 9-inch layer cake pans with baking parchment or wax paper and set aside.

2. Sift flour, baking soda, and salt onto wax paper and set aside.

3. Melt chocolate in boiling water and cool. *Microwave Method: Place chocolate and cold water in large microwave-safe bowl and microwave on HIGH (100 percent power) 1½ to 2 minutes until chocolate is almost melted. Stir until chocolate is completely melted.*

4. Cream butter and sugar until fluffy. Beat in egg yolks, one at a time. Blend in vanilla and melted chocolate. Add flour mixture alternately with buttermilk, beginning and ending with flour and beating after each addition until smooth. Fold in beaten egg whites.

5. Divide batter among three pans and bake 30 minutes until cakes feel springy to the touch and begin to pull from sides of pans.

6. Cool cake layers in pans on wire racks 15 minutes. Loosen carefully, turn out on racks, peel off baking parchment, and cool to room temperature.

7. COCONUT–PECAN FROSTING: Cook and stir evaporated milk, sugar, egg yolks, butter, and vanilla over moderate heat until thickened and the color of caramel, about 12 minutes. Remove from heat, stir in coconut and pecans, and beat until of spreading consistency.

8. TO ASSEMBLE: Frost top of each cake layer with coconut mixture, then sandwich layers together. Leave cake sides plain.

HERSHEY'S CHOCOLATE

MILTON HERSHEY, whose name will forever be associated with chocolate, got his start selling caramels from a basket carried over his arm. Relatives in Lancaster, Pennsylvania, considered him a failure and were astonished when, in 1900, he sold his caramel business for a cool million and moved into chocolate.

At the turn of the century, chocolate was expensive, often imported, and fancily designed for candy boxes. Hershey, adopting "modern" methods, mass-produced simple chocolate bars and sold them at prices the public could afford. To avoid advertising costs, he embossed the chocolate bars with "Hershey's" in large letters, allowing his candy to advertise itself. (This no-advertising policy continued until 1970.)

The first Hershey's Milk Chocolate Bars went on sale in 1900, and Hershey's Kisses (named for the smacking sound made when the chocolate hit the conveyor belt) in 1907; four years later the company was taking in $5 million annually. A philanthropist as well as an astute businessman, Hershey founded the Milton Hershey School (for orphans), which today owns 42 percent of the company stock. After building his candy factory in his birthplace, Derry Church, Pennsylvania, Hershey added so much to the town (new homes, stores, a bank, trolley system, luxury hotel, golf course, sports arena) that it was renamed "Hershey." Today tourists throng in to tour Chocolate World, to see streetlights shaped like chocolate Kisses, and to tuck into chocolate sundaes at the Hotel Hershey.

Chocolate Fudge Cake

Makes a 9-inch, 2-layer Cake, 12 Servings

✳

THIS RECIPE is so dark, so rich, it can only be considered devil's food. It was published in 1975 in *Family Circle* and is one of the magazine's most requested recipes. According to Food Editor Peggy Katalinich, "Readers who write in for copies of this recipe have called Chocolate Fudge Cake the best chocolate cake ever. We humbly agree."

CAKE

3 ounces unsweetened chocolate
2¼ cups sifted cake flour
2 teaspoons baking soda
½ teaspoon salt
½ cup (1 stick) butter or margarine
2¼ cups firmly packed light brown sugar
3 eggs
1½ teaspoons vanilla extract
1 cup sour cream
1 cup boiling water

FROSTING

4 ounces unsweetened chocolate
½ cup (1 stick) butter or margarine
1 (1-pound) package confectioners' (10X) sugar
½ cup milk
2 teaspoons vanilla extract

NOTE: For richer brown finish, coat pans with unsweetened cocoa powder instead of flour.

1. CAKE: Preheat oven to 350°F. Grease and flour two 9-inch-round layer cake pans, tapping out excess flour; set pans aside.

2. Melt chocolate in small bowl over hot, not boiling, water; cool.

3. Sift flour, baking soda, and salt onto wax paper; set aside.

4. Beat butter in large electric mixer bowl at high speed until soft. Add brown sugar and eggs; beat at high speed until light and fluffy, 5 minutes. Beat in vanilla and cooled, melted chocolate.

5. Stir in dry ingredients alternately with sour cream, beginning and ending with the dry and beating well with a wooden spoon after each addition until batter is smooth. Stir in boiling water (batter will be thin).

6. Divide batter between pans and bake 35 minutes, until centers spring back when lightly pressed with finger.

7. Cool layers in pans on wire racks 10 minutes; loosen around edges with small spatula, turn out onto wire racks, and cool completely.

8. FROSTING: Melt chocolate and butter in small heavy saucepan over low heat; set off heat. Beat 10X sugar, milk, and vanilla in medium bowl until smooth. Add chocolate mixture. Set bowl in pan of ice and water and beat with wooden spoon until good spreading consistency and frosting will hold its shape.

9. TO ASSEMBLE CAKE: Put one layer on serving plate, spread with about one-fourth of frosting. Add second layer, then swirl remaining frosting over top and sides of cake.

Modern Red Devil's Food Cake

Makes a 9-inch, 2-layer Cake, 12 Servings

✳

THE ELECTRIC mixer makes it modern and the cocoa-soda combination makes this devil's food cake redder than those made with solid chocolate. To give the layers a crisp brown finish, the pans are dusted with cocoa instead of flour.

2½ cups sifted cake flour
½ cup cocoa powder
1 teaspoon baking soda
½ teaspoon baking powder
½ teaspoon salt
¾ cup (1½ sticks) butter or vegetable shortening
1⅔ cups sugar
3 eggs
1½ cups water
1½ teaspoons vanilla extract

1. Preheat oven to 350°F. Coat two 9-inch layer cake pans with nonstick cooking spray, dust with cocoa powder, tapping out excess; set aside.

2. Sift flour, cocoa, baking soda, baking powder, and salt onto wax paper and set aside also.

3. Beat butter, sugar, and eggs in large electric mixer bowl at high speed 3 minutes until fluffy-light.

4. Combine water and vanilla, then at low mixer speed add sifted dry ingredients alternately with water mixture, beginning and ending with dry ingredients; scrape bowl often and beat after each addition only enough to combine.

5. Divide batter between pans, smoothing tops, and bake 30 to 35 minutes, until a cake tester inserted in center of layers comes out clean and cakes are springy to touch.

6. Cool layers in pans on wire racks 10 minutes, then loosen and turn out on racks. Cool to room temperature, then fill and frost with Seven-Minute Icing (page 469) or Chocolate Butter Cream Frosting (page 468).

Caramel Devil's Food Cake

Makes a 9-inch, 2-layer Cake, 12 Servings

✳

THIS RECIPE, adapted from *All About Home Baking* (1933), published by the General Foods Corporation (now Kraft Foods, Inc.), more closely parallels those early-twentieth-century devil's food cakes made with brown sugar. To quote the original recipe: "Here soda is used to neutralize the acid in the brown sugar and chocolate, leavening the cake and giving it color. A triple sifting distributes it evenly and removes the tiniest lumps. This is a very simple way of adding soda." This cake gets a caramel frosting and filling.

CAKE
> 2 cups sifted cake flour
> 2 teaspoons baking soda
> ½ cup (1 stick) butter or
>   vegetable shortening, softened
> 1¼ cups firmly packed brown
>   sugar
> 2 eggs
> 3 ounces unsweetened
>   chocolate, melted
> 1 cup milk
> 1½ teaspoons vanilla extract

CARAMEL FROSTING
> 1½ cups firmly packed brown
>   sugar
> 1½ cups granulated sugar
> 1½ cups milk
> 1 tablespoon light corn syrup
> 2 tablespoons butter or
>   margarine

1. CAKE: Preheat oven to 350° F. Grease two 9-inch layer cake pans well and set aside.

2. Sift flour and baking soda together three times on wax paper and set aside also.

3. Cream butter until light, add brown sugar gradually, creaming all the while, then continue creaming until light and fluffy. Beat eggs in, one by one, then blend in melted chocolate.

4. Add sifted dry ingredients to creamed mixture alternately with milk, beginning and ending with dry ingredients and beating after each addition only enough to combine. Stir in vanilla.

5. Divide batter between pans, smoothing tops, and bake 30 to 35 minutes, until a cake tester inserted in center of layers comes out clean and cakes are springy to touch.

6. Cool layers in pans on wire racks 10 minutes, then loosen and turn out on racks. Cool to room temperature.

7. CARAMEL FROSTING: Mix brown sugar, granulated sugar, milk, and corn syrup in large heavy saucepan. Set over moderate heat and bring to a boil, stirring constantly. Insert candy thermometer and continue cooking, without stirring, until mixture reaches very soft ball stage (234° F). Remove from heat, drop in butter, and cool without stirring to lukewarm (110° F). Beat until creamy and thick enough to spread.

8. TO ASSEMBLE CAKE: Center one layer on cake plate and spread with frosting. Add second layer, apply thin layer of frosting to sides of cake, then a second thicker coat. Frost top of cake with remaining frosting, swirling into peaks and valleys. Let cake stand 1 hour before cutting.

THE BUNDT PAN

I N 1950, a group of Minneapolis women, members of Hadassah, approached Nordic Products owner H. David Dalquist and asked him to make an aluminum version of the cast-iron *kugelhupf* pan common in Europe. Obligingly, he made a few for the members and a few extra for the public. Not many of these fluted tube pans sold until ten years later when the new *Good Houskeeeping Cookbook* showed a pound cake that had been baked in one of them. Suddenly every woman wanted a pan just like it.

What really put the Bundt pan on the culinary map of America, however, was the Tunnel of Fudge Cake, which made the finals of the 1966 Pillsbury Bake-Off Contest. Bundt, by the way, is now a registered trademark of Northland Aluminum Products, Inc., Minneapolis. By 1972 the grand prize winner in the Pillsbury Bake-Off Contest was a Bundt Streusel Spice Cake and eleven top winners also called for a Bundt pan; that same year Pillsbury sold $25 million worth of its new Bundt cake mixes.

It's strange to think that fifty years ago there were no Bundt cakes because there were no Bundt cake pans. Today, more than forty million pans exist in America, some still unsold on housewares shelves but most in pantries and many, no doubt, filled with batter and ready to be popped into a hot oven.

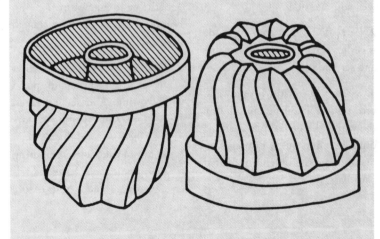

Tunnel of Fudge Cake

Makes a 10-inch Bundt Cake, 16 Servings

✱

T HIS CAKE may not have taken the grand prize in the Pillsbury Bake-Off Contest but it did make the 1966 finals for Texan Ella Helfrich, and it's more beloved than many top winners. According to the headnote that accompanies the Tunnel of Fudge Cake recipe in *The Pillsbury Bake-Off Cookbook* (1990), "the original recipe called for dry frosting mix that is no longer available. Updated and revised, this version still has a soft tunnel of fudge surrounded by delicious chocolate cake."

NOTE: Nuts are essential to the success of this recipe. Because of the cake's soft center, you can't rely on the usual test for doneness—inserting a cake tester and having it come out clean. Instead, make sure your oven temperature is on the mark and bake the cake exactly as directed—for 58 to 62 minutes.

CAKE

1¾ cups granulated sugar
1¾ cups (3½ sticks) butter or margarine, softened
6 eggs
2 cups confectioners' (10X) sugar
2¼ cups sifted all-purpose or unbleached flour (lightly spooned into measure and leveled off)

2 cups chopped walnuts
¾ cup unsweetened cocoa
    powder

GLAZE

¾ cup confectioners' (10X)
    sugar
¼ cup unsweetened cocoa
    powder
1½ to 2 tablespoons milk

1. CAKE: Preheat oven to 350° F. Grease and flour a 10-inch (12-cup) Bundt pan or a 10-inch tube pan and set aside.

2. Beat granulated sugar and butter in large electric mixer bowl at high speed until fluffy-light. Beat eggs in well, one at a time. With mixer at low speed, add 2 cups 10X sugar gradually, blending well after each addition.

3. By hand, stir in flour, then walnuts and ¾ cup cocoa, blending well after each addition.

4. Spoon batter into pan, spreading evenly, and bake 58 to 62 minutes until top feels slightly springy.

5. Cool cake in pan on wire rack 1 hour, then loosen carefully and invert on serving plate. Cool completely before glazing.

6. GLAZE: Mix ¾ cup 10X sugar and ¼ cup cocoa in small bowl, then add just enough milk for good drizzling consistency. Spoon glaze over cake, letting it run down sides.

7. Store cake tightly covered.

Texas Sheet Cake

Makes a 15½ × 10½ × 1-inch Sheet Cake, 24 Servings

ONE OF my all-time favorite cookbooks is a little spiral-bound paperback called *Food Editors' Hometown Favorites* published in 1984 by the Newspaper Food Editors and Writers Association. In it appears this heavenly chocolate cake spread with fudge-pecan icing. It was contributed to the book by Dotty Griffith, food editor of *The Dallas Morning News*. But the accompanying headnote says the recipe was also submitted by food editors all over the country. Some attribute the cake to Lady Bird Johnson. Others say it got its name because it's as big as Texas—well, not *quite*. The cake couldn't be easier to make, it's surprisingly light, but my, is it sweet.

CAKE

2 cups granulated sugar
2 cups sifted all-purpose flour
½ cup (1 stick) butter or
    margarine
½ cup vegetable shortening
¼ cup unsweetened cocoa
    powder
1 cup water
½ cup buttermilk
2 eggs, lightly beaten
1 teaspoon vanilla extract
1 teaspoon baking soda

ICING

½ cup (1 stick) butter or
    margarine
¼ cup unsweetened cocoa
    powder

⅓ cup milk
1 (1-pound) box confectioners'
    (10X) sugar
1 teaspoon vanilla extract
1 cup coarsely chopped pecans

1. CAKE: Preheat oven to 400° F. Coat 15½ × 10½ × 1-inch jelly-roll pan with nonstick cooking spray; set aside.

2. Sift granulated sugar and flour together into large mixing bowl; set aside.

3. Bring butter, shortening, cocoa, and water to rapid boil in medium heavy saucepan, stirring occasionally. Pour over flour mixture and stir well to blend.

4. Mix buttermilk, eggs, vanilla, and soda in large measuring cup. Add to bowl and beat by hand until smooth.

5. Pour into pan, smoothing to corners, and bake 20 minutes, until springy to touch and toothpick inserted in center of cake comes out clean.

6. ICING: Five minutes before cake is done, bring butter, cocoa, and milk to boil in medium heavy saucepan. Add 10X sugar and vanilla and beat with hand electric mixer at high speed until smooth. Stir in pecans.

7. As soon as cake tests done, set on wire rack and immediately spread frosting over top. Cool cake before cutting into bars.

BROWNSTONE FRONT CAKE

T HERE'S PLENTY of controversy about this cake. When and where it originated. What goes into the batter. Whether or not it's frosted.

Much to my surprise, I could find no references to Brownstone Front Cake before 1964, the year the recipe appeared in *The American Heritage Cookbook and Illustrated History of American Eating and Drinking*—alas, without a shred of documentation.

Then I called food historian Meryle Evans, who's spent much of her adult life digging into the origins of recipes. A few days later she called back to say that she'd turned up the recipe in the April 13, 1940, issue of a professional publication called *Baker's Weekly*. This is what it said:

"Another delightful cake is a Plantation Creole Chocolate Cake called Brownstone-Front from the current *Ladies' Home Journal*. This is a feather-fine brown sugar type of chocolate cake that is bound to be a favorite wherever served. It comes from a treasured family cookbook from the legendary city of New Orleans. The recipe for frosting is not given except for the statement that boiled icing is used."

Well, well, well.

That sent me scurrying to my shelf of New Orleans and Creole cookbooks, and once again I came up empty. No Brownstone Front Cake. Having spent nearly ten years in the food department of *The Ladies' Home Journal* (in the late '50s and early '60s), I have to wonder if those *Journal* copywriters might have taken a little poetic license with their documentation of this cake.

Former *New York Times* staffer and food writer Raymond Sokolov gives a recipe for Brownstone Front Cake in *Great Recipes from The New York Times* (1973; a deeply chocolatey version containing ¼ pound of chocolate, and the frosting's chocolate,

too). But once again, there is no trace of origin.

Another former *Times* staffer, Jean Hewitt, offers an entirely different (and paler) Brownstone Front in *The New York Times Heritage Cook Book* (1972) and introduces it by saying, "This is a variety of devil's food cake found in many Western states, but the origin of its name is cloaked in mystery." She attributes it to the state of Idaho.

That same year James Beard's *American Cookery* rolled off the press and here was a Brownstone Front of another color: caramel. Wrote Beard, "This has many more names, some of them very local. All evolved from the fact that the caramelized sugar makes the cake a rich brown." He includes two of those alternate names: "Burnt Leather" and "Caramel Cake."

None of my many editions of *Joy of Cooking* or *The Fannie Farmer Cookbook* offers a recipe for Brownstone Front Cake. But Marion Cunningham's *Fannie Farmer Baking Book* (1984) does. She calls it "A moist and richly flavored caramel cake."

So which is it? Chocolate or caramel? The Brownstone Front Cake I know is chocolate, a loaf cake made with brown sugar and sour cream that's covered with frosting the color of a New York brownstone (the name possibly comes from the fact that many city town houses are faced with sandstone the color of cocoa). I suspect—and Meryle Evans is inclined to agree—that this is a New York City cake. However, neither of us can prove it.

A week or so after this discussion, Meryle called to say she'd located three earlier versions of Brownstone Front Cake, two in community cookbooks dated 1910 (with a caramel icing) and 1903 (with a vanilla cream). The third—and earliest—appeared in the *Atlanta Exposition Cook Book* of 1895. That recipe, submitted by Mrs. Samuel Martin Inman of Atlanta, called for seven squares of Baker's chocolate and was baked in jelly-roll pans. "The thinner the layers the better the cake," Mrs. Inman said. She directed the reader to "Make the frosting first: One and one-half pounds of icing (pulverized sugar), whites of 6 eggs, 1 teaspoon vanilla. Put in a cool place until cake is ready. Do not cook, only beat and spread on while cake is hot."

So maybe Brownstone Front Cake *is* Southern after all. If indeed Mrs. Samuel Martin Inman *was* South-

ern. For all we know, she may have moved to Atlanta from New York. Or have gotten the recipe from a New York friend or relative. It does seem odd that she would call this snowily iced chocolate cake "brownstone."

Does all of this matter? Or that a recipe for Brownstone Front Cake saw print a few years shy of the twentieth century? Not as much as the taste and texture of this American classic.

Brownstone Front Cake

Makes a 9 × 5 × 3-inch Loaf Cake,
12 to 14 Servings

❋

THIS RECIPE was adapted from the one in *The American Heritage Cookbook and Illustrated History of American Eating and Drinking* (1964), which does not differ significantly from the 1940 *Ladies' Home Journal* recipe except that it contains slightly less shortening and brown sugar and only half as much chocolate. Even this makes a firm, dark cake. The original *American Heritage* recipe called for adding 2 cups flour alternately with ½ cup sour cream—difficult. By combining the sour cream with the other liquids, I find the going easier. I have not changed the proportions for the cake, merely the method. I have, however, updated the frosting, which contained a raw egg.

CAKE

2 cups sifted all-purpose flour
1 teaspoon baking soda
¼ teaspoon salt
1 cup boiling water
2 ounces unsweetened chocolate
½ cup sour cream, at room temperature
1 teaspoon vanilla extract
½ cup (1 stick) butter, softened
1¾ cups firmly packed brown sugar
2 eggs, well beaten

FROSTING

1 cup confectioners' (10X) sugar
2 tablespoons butter, softened
1 ounce unsweetened chocolate, melted
Pinch salt
2 to 4 tablespoons milk
½ teaspoon vanilla extract

1. CAKE: Preheat oven to 325° F. Coat 9 × 5 × 3-inch loaf pan with nonstick cooking spray; set aside.

2. Sift flour, soda, and salt onto wax paper; set aside.

3. Pour water into heat-proof 2-cup measure, drop in chocolate, and cool to room temperature. Whisk in sour cream and vanilla; set aside.

4. Cream butter in large electric mixer bowl at high speed until fluffy. At medium speed, beat brown sugar in gradually; continue beating at high speed 3 minutes until light. Beat in eggs.

5. At low speed, add sifted dry ingredients alternately with chocolate mixture, beginning and ending with dry; beat only enough to blend—no more or you'll toughen cake.

6. Pour batter into pan, smoothing to corners, and bake about 1 hour, until springy to touch and toothpick inserted in center of cake comes out clean.

7. Cool cake in pan on wire rack 10 minutes, carefully loosen around edges, and invert on rack. Cool to room temperature.

8. FROSTING: Cream 10X sugar and butter in small bowl, then beat in melted chocolate and salt. Add just enough milk for good spreading consistency; flavor with vanilla. Smooth frosting over top and sides of cake.

Mississippi Mud Cake

Makes a 13 × 9 × 2-inch Loaf Cake,
24 Servings

❋

THIS HAS to be the richest cake in all creation, a chocoholic's idea of bliss. I first encountered Mississippi Mud Cake in the 1970s in Jackson, Mississippi, but I'm told it's popular up and down the Mississippi, particularly from St. Louis south. This recipe is adapted from *Martha White's Southern Sampler* (1989). Southerners all know Martha White, the soft Tennessee flour they've depended on for tender biscuits and cakes for nearly a hundred years (company founder Richard Lindsey named his finest flour after his three-year-old daughter Martha White Lindsey). Founded in Nashville in 1899 as the Royal Flour Mill, the company name officially became Martha White when new owners took over in 1941. Martha White's test kitchens were active almost from the start, developing many of the recipes now considered Southern classics. Note that this cake has no leavening.

CAKE

1½ cups sifted all-purpose flour
⅓ cup unsweetened cocoa powder
½ teaspoon salt
1 cup vegetable shortening
1½ cups granulated sugar
4 eggs
2 teaspoons vanilla extract
1 cup coarsely chopped pecans
2 cups miniature marshmallows

ICING

1 cup (2 sticks) butter or margarine, melted
⅓ cup unsweetened cocoa powder
½ cup evaporated milk
4 cups sifted confectioners' (10X) sugar (about 1 pound)
1 teaspoon vanilla extract
½ cup coarsely chopped pecans

1. CAKE: Preheat oven to 325° F. Grease and flour 13 × 9 × 2-inch baking pan; set aside.

2. Sift flour with cocoa and salt onto wax paper and set aside.

3. Cream shortening and granulated sugar in large mixing bowl at moderate speed until fluffy-light, 6 to 7 minutes. Add eggs, one at a time, beating well after each addition. Beat in vanilla. Mix sifted dry ingredients into batter, then fold in pecans.

4. Scrape into pan, spreading to corners, and bake 30 to 35 minutes, until cake begins to pull from sides of pan and toothpick inserted in center comes out clean.

5. Remove pan from oven and scatter marshmallows evenly over cake. Return to oven and bake 10 minutes more or until marshmallows melt.

6. Cool cake in pan on wire rack. Cake will sink as it cools but this is what gives it its "Mississippi mud" texture.

7. ICING: Blend butter and cocoa in medium mixing bowl. Beat in evaporated milk, then gradually mix in 10X sugar and beat until smooth. Stir in vanilla and pecans. Spread smoothly over cake and let harden before cutting into bars. Make the pieces small; this cake is rich.

Would you like to make ——

GOOD CAKE?

Flourless Chocolate-Cassis Cake with Crème Anglaise

Makes a 9-inch-round Torte,
12 Servings

✳

THE GO-GO '80s seem to have been driven by a national passion for chocolate. According to Gerry Schremp (*Kitchen Culture,* 1991), during that decade "whole cookbooks were written about it [chocolate]—and enthusiasts launched the magazine *Chocolatier.*" Without question, the trendiest chocolate cake of the '80s was the flourless, or almost flourless, chocolate cake, a dense European-style torte about two inches high. This particular recipe is adapted from one that appeared in *Bon Appétit* (January 1994). Unlike many flourless cakes, it is baked and poses no threat of salmonella food poisoning. If you're a devout chocoholic like me, you may want to substitute a chocolate, coffee, or hazelnut liqueur for cassis.

CRÈME ANGLAISE
    2 cups half-and-half
    1 vanilla bean, split
    1/2 cup sugar
    4 egg yolks

CAKE
    10 ounces bittersweet or
      semisweet chocolate, coarsely
      chopped
    3/4 cup (1 1/2 sticks) unsalted
      butter (no substitute)
    1/2 cup unsweetened cocoa
      powder

½ cup crème de cassis liqueur (or chocolate, coffee, or hazelnut liqueur)
5 eggs
1 cup sugar

ICING
¼ cup heavy cream
8 ounces bittersweet or semisweet chocolate, coarsely chopped
6 tablespoons crème de cassis liqueur (or chocolate, coffee, or hazelnut liqueur)

PRESENTATION
Crème Anglaise (above)
¾ cup crème de cassis liqueur (or chocolate, coffee, or hazelnut liqueur)

1. CRÈME ANGLAISE: Bring half-and-half to simmer in medium heavy saucepan. Scrape in seeds from vanilla bean; add bean. Whisk sugar and egg yolks in medium bowl until well blended. Gradually whisk in half-and-half mixture. Stir back into pan and cook about 5 minutes, stirring constantly, over moderately low heat, until custard thickens and coats a metal spoon. Do not boil or mixture may curdle. Strain custard, cover, and refrigerate.

2. CAKE: Preheat oven to 350° F. Butter 2¾-inch-deep, 9-inch springform pan; line bottom with parchment, butter parchment, then dust pan with flour, tapping out excess. Set pan aside.

3. Melt chocolate and butter in medium heavy saucepan over low heat, stirring until smooth; cool slightly. Whisk in cocoa and cassis.

4. Beat eggs and sugar in large electric mixer bowl at high speed until mixture whitens and triples in volume, about 6 minutes. Fold in chocolate mixture.

5. Scrape batter into pan, smoothing to edges. Bake about 40 minutes, until top forms crust and cake tester inserted in center comes out with very moist crumbs attached.

6. Cool cake in pan on wire rack 5 minutes. Press down on crusty portion of cake to even. Release and remove springform pan sides.

7. Invert cake on rack, peel off parchment, and cool completely.

8. ICING: Bring cream to simmer in medium heavy saucepan. Add chocolate and 6 tablespoons cassis; whisk until smooth. Let icing stand until cool but still spreadable, about 15 minutes.

9. Place cake on plate and smooth icing over top and sides. Chill cake 1 hour.

NOTE: Cake can be made a day ahead, covered, and refrigerated until about two hours before serving.

10. PRESENTATION: Simmer ¾ cup cassis in small heavy saucepan about 5 minutes until reduced to generous ½ cup; cool.

11. Pool crème anglaise on plates, spoon reduced cassis decoratively on top of sauce and swirl with knife. Center wedge of cake on each plate. Garnish, if desired, with mint.

TIMELINE

1990

The James Beard Foundation and the International Association of Culinary Professionals (IACP) each establish cookbook awards.

Eating Well magazine appears.

EATINGWELL
THE MAGAZINE OF FOOD & HEALTH

Cook's magazine folds.

Jamba Juice bars serving Powerberry and Raspberry Rush fruit smoothies enriched with "healing" extracts (ginkgo biloba and blue-green algae to name two) debut in health-conscious California.

1991

Horn and Hardart closes its last automat (in New York City).

As an April Fool's stunt, The Smithsonian Institution in Washington, D.C., holds its first annual food conference. Subject: "American History is Jell-O." The symposium also includes a Jell-O cook-off.

The Four Seasons' Chocolate Velvet

*Makes 1 Filled and Frosted
Bowl-shaped Cake, 12 Servings*

✳

WHEN I wrote an article on chocolate desserts for *Family Circle* in 1980, I had to include this ambrosial bowl-shaped chocolate sponge filled with chocolate mousse. It is the creation of Albert Kumin, once master pastry chef at New York's famous Four Seasons Restaurant, which opened more than thirty-five years ago. The cake is fussy to make, yes. But it's guaranteed to wow dinner guests. Besides, it can be made ahead and frozen. The recipe here is adapted from *The Four Seasons Cookbook* (1971).

NOTE: The filling calls for raw eggs, which are sometimes contaminated with salmonella. It pays to know your source; as a rule, conscientious, small local producers are your best bet for wholesome eggs. The recipe also calls for clarified butter, nothing more than melted butter minus the milk solids. These sink to the bottom, making it easy to pour off the liquid butterfat.

CAKE

4 eggs
4 egg yolks
¾ cup granulated sugar
¾ cup sifted cake flour
10 tablespoons (½ cup plus 2 tablespoons) clarified butter
1 teaspoon vanilla extract

CHOCOLATE VELVET FILLING

2 eggs, separated
3 tablespoons firmly packed praline paste (available in specialty food shops)
1½ teaspoons instant coffee powder
2 tablespoons kirsch
2 tablespoons light rum
2 tablespoons crème de cacao liqueur
3 tablespoons unsalted butter, melted
12 ounces semisweet chocolate, melted
Pinch salt
2 tablespoons confectioners' (10X) sugar
1 cup heavy cream, stiffly whipped

SEMISWEET CHOCOLATE ICING

5 ounces semisweet chocolate
½ cup boiling water

THE FOUR SEASONS

The Ultimate Book of Food, Wine and Elegant Dining. 250 Original Recipes from One of the World's Great Restaurants

Tom Margittai and Paul Kovi

1. CAKE: Preheat oven to 350° F. Grease and flour 15½ × 10½ × 1-inch jelly-roll pan; set aside.

2. Place eggs, egg yolks, and granulated sugar in large metal or heat-proof glass bowl; anchor in saucepan over simmering water (bottom of bowl should not touch water). Beat with electric hand mixer at high speed 12 minutes or until mixture triples in volume and is color and consistency of mayonnaise. Remove bowl from pan of water at once and continue beating 15 minutes longer until cool and fairly stiff.

3. Sift flour in 5 or 6 additions over egg mixture, folding in gently each time. Drizzle in clarified butter; fold in gently but completely. Fold in vanilla.

4. Pour mixture into pan, spreading to corners, and bake 25 minutes, until delicately browned and cake springs back when touched.

5. Cool cake 15 minutes in pan on wire rack. Loosen around edges and turn out on wire rack; cool completely.

6. CHOCOLATE VELVET FILLING: Beat egg yolks, praline paste, and coffee powder in small bowl. Add kirsch, rum, and crème de cacao. Beat in melted butter and chocolate. Whip egg whites with salt until frothy, add 10X sugar, and continue beating until stiff. Fold into chocolate mixture, then fold in whipped cream.

7. TO ASSEMBLE CAKE: Lightly butter 2½-quart charlotte mold or bowl (mold should be about 4 inches deep and 7 inches in diameter). Cut a round of cake to fit bottom of mold and set in place; cut 2 strips of cake and line sides of mold; save scraps. Spoon filling into cake-lined mold; cut remaining cake as needed to cover and seal in all filling (it's all right to use bits and pieces).

8. Chill 2 hours or until firm. Loosen mold carefully with thin-bladed spatula and invert on cut-to-fit cardboad circle. Set on cake rack on wax-paper-covered counter.

9. Semisweet Chocolate Icing: Melt chocolate over simmering water; whisk in boiling water and beat until smooth. Cool slightly, then smooth over cake.

10. Refrigerate or freeze cake until shortly before serving.

Wacky Cake or Crazy Cake

Makes an 8 × 8 × 2-inch Loaf Cake, 8 to 10 Servings

✳

In a way, this is a variation of Chocolate Pudding Cake (page 406). But it takes "quick-and-easy" one step further: The cake is mixed in the baking pan. That's part of the wackiness. Another is that the batter contains vinegar and water, but no eggs. Like Chocolate Pudding Cake, this one is shortened with oil instead of butter or margarine. In *Fashionable Food* (1995), Sylvia

Lovegren places the recipe in the '70s. It seems to me I've known Wacky Cake longer than that but can't prove it. The recipe here does come from a '70s cookbook— *Woman's Day Old-Fashioned Desserts* (1978).

Cake

1½ cups sifted all-purpose flour
1 cup granulated sugar
3 tablespoons unsweetened cocoa powder
1 teaspoon baking soda
½ teaspoon salt
6 tablespoons vegetable oil
1 tablespoon vinegar
1 teaspoon vanilla extract
1 cup cold water

Frosting

3 tablespoons butter or margarine
1 cup sifted confectioners' (10X) sugar
3 tablespoons unsweetened cocoa powder
½ teaspoon salt
1 teaspoon vanilla extract

1. Cake: Preheat oven to 350° F.

2. Sift flour, sugar, cocoa, soda, and salt together into ungreased 8 × 8 × 2-inch baking pan.

3. Make three wells in mixture with spoon: one large, one medium, and one small. Into large well pour oil; into medium well, vinegar; into small well, vanilla. Pour water over all and stir with fork until smooth; do not beat.

4. Bake 30 to 35 minutes, until springy to touch.

5. Frosting: Melt butter in saucepan, add 10X sugar, cocoa, salt, and vanilla and beat until smooth. If too stiff to spread, thin with few drops hot water.

6. As soon as cake tests done, transfer to wire rack and spread at once with frosting. Cool cake before cutting.

Jim Fobel's Cream Cheese Frosting

Makes 2⅔ Cups

✳

There are cream cheese frostings and cream cheese frostings. This one from *Jim Fobel's Old-Fashioned Baking Book* (1987, paperback 1996) is marvelous.

1 (8-ounce) package cream cheese, softened
¼ cup (½ stick) butter, softened
3 cups sifted confectioners' (10X) sugar
1 teaspoon vanilla extract

1. Beat cream cheese and butter in large electric mixer bowl at high speed until fluffy, about 1 minute.

2. Beat in 10X sugar, 1 cup at a time, then continue beating until smooth. Beat in vanilla.

3. Chill bowl of frosting in refrigerator, stirring often, until good spreading consistency.

467

Philly Vanilla Frosting

Makes about 2½ Cups

✳

IN THE '30s, Philadelphia Brand Cream Cheese introduced a quick, easy, foolproof frosting that's as popular today as it was sixty years ago. Philly Frosting has become the traditional topper for carrot cake but it's equally good used to fill and frost chocolate, applesauce, and nut cakes.

1 (8-ounce) package cream cheese, softened
3 teaspoons vanilla extract
3 to 3½ cups sifted confectioners' (10X) sugar

1. Beat cream cheese and vanilla in large electric mixer bowl at high speed until fluffy, about 1 minute.

2. At low mixer speed, beat in 10X sugar, ½ cup at a time, then raise speed to high and continue beating until smooth and fluffy-light.

Butter Cream Frostings

STRANGELY, THESE easy icings don't seem to have been in the repertoire of nineteenth-century American cooks, who chose to bind powdered sugar with raw egg white or yolk. Or to cook their frostings.

In searching through several dozen cookbooks dating back to 1880, I found a butter frosting only in the 1915 *Larkin Housewives' Cook Book* (140 pages, twenty-five cents). The Larkin Company, "Pure Food Specialists," sold chocolate, sugar, salt, assorted flavorings, and just about everything else the cook needed. In this little hardcover are "five hundred and forty-eight recipes, of which four hundred and eighty are prize recipes selected from more than three thousand submitted by practical housekeepers in the Larkin Recipe Contests."

One of those "practical housekeepers" was Mrs. Fred W. Gurney of North Attleboro, Massachusetts, who submitted her Mocha Frosting —the first butter cream I've been able to locate. It calls for "one cup powdered sugar, three tablespoons butter, one tablespoon milk, one tablespoon strong coffee, one-fourth teaspoon vanilla extract. Mix well with spoon," she directs, "then beat light with silver fork."

A similar mocha frosting appears in the 1918 edition of "Fannie Farmer," which ups the amount of butter to ⅓ cup, adds "1 tablespoon breakfast cocoa," and instructs the cook to add a "coffee infusion, drop by drop, until of right consistency to spread or force through a pastry bag and tube."

By its 1923 edition, "Fannie" had added four more butter creams. And by the 1930s, these were the frostings cooks had come to rely on. For good reason. They were quick, versatile, and foolproof. Frosting too stiff? Thin with a little milk. Frosting too soft? Work in some extra confectioners' sugar.

Basic Butter Cream Frosting

Makes about 2½ Cups

✳

THIS IS my mother's basic butter cream frosting, the one she taught me to make when I was barely old enough to reach the mixing bowl. To it I've added several of the variations I've developed over the years. In the beginning, Mother made her butter cream by hand, then by electric mixer. Today I use a food processor. The frosting's ready in seconds.

⅓ cup cold butter or margarine, cut into pats
1 (1-pound) box confectioners' (10X) sugar
4 to 6 tablespoons milk or cream
1½ teaspoons vanilla extract
Pinch salt

1. Pulse butter and sugar in food processor fitted with metal chopping blade 8 to 10 times till crumbly.

2. With motor running, drizzle milk down feed tube until good spreading consistency. Beat in vanilla and salt.

——— **VARIATIONS** ———

CHOCOLATE BUTTER CREAM: Prepare Basic Butter Cream as directed, pulsing ⅓ cup unsweet-

ened Dutch process cocoa powder with butter and sugar. Substitute evaporated milk (or evaporated skim milk) for milk or cream and increase vanilla to 2 teaspoons. Makes about 2½ cups.

MOCHA BUTTER CREAM: Prepare Basic Butter Cream as directed, pulsing ¼ cup unsweetened Dutch process cocoa powder and 1 teaspoon instant expresso crystals with butter and sugar. Increase vanilla to 2 teaspoons. Makes about 2½ cups.

CITRUS BUTTER CREAM: Prepare Basic Butter Cream as directed, substituting fresh lemon, lime, orange, or grapefruit juice for milk. Omit vanilla and add 1½ to 2 teaspoons finely grated lemon, lime, orange, or grapefruit zest. Makes about 2½ cups.

MAPLE BUTTER CREAM: Prepare Basic Butter Cream as directed, substituting maple syrup for milk. Flavor with 1 teaspoon each vanilla and maple flavoring. Makes about 2½ cups.

HAZELNUT BUTTER CREAM: Prepare Basic Butter Cream as directed, substituting 1 tablespoon hazelnut oil for 1 tablespoon butter. Beat in ½ cup finely chopped, richly toasted, blanched hazelnuts along with vanilla. Makes about 2½ cups.

BUTTER PECAN CREAM: Prepare Basic Butter Cream as directed. Beat in ½ cup finely chopped, richly toasted pecans along with vanilla. Makes about 2½ cups.

Seven-Minute Icing

Makes about 4 Cups

＊

BOILED ICINGS, in which blistering-hot sugar syrups are drizzled into stiffly whipped egg whites, then beaten until as fluffy as marshmallow cream, were commonplace in late-nineteenth-century cookbooks (and remain so today). Yet Seven-Minute Icing, which puts all ingredients in the top of a double boiler and requires seven minutes of steady beating over boiling water, only entered our lives in 1930. At least that's as far back as I can trace this recipe. A small *Good Housekeeping* cookbook published that year—*Meals, Tested, Tasted and Approved*—includes Seven-Minute Icing. It couldn't have been very easy to make with a rotary beater. I first tasted Seven-Minute Icing in the early '40s and thought it was heaven. My mother always spread her cakes with butter cream, but our new next-door neighbor, a Boston lady, showed me how to make Seven-Minute—with an electric mixer. She even let this still-small child swirl it over a freshly baked devil's food cake. I was hooked, and to this day Seven-Minute Icing remains a favorite. What I didn't realize then —but am delighted to know today —is that this frosting is fat-free. The recipe here is the classic, the one I've used all these years.

NOTE: Powerful electric hand beaters can reduce cooking time to four minutes.

> *2 egg whites*
> *1½ cups sugar*
> *1 tablespoon light corn syrup*
> *⅓ cup cold water*
> *1½ teaspoons vanilla extract*

1. Mix egg whites, sugar, corn syrup, and water in double boiler top.

2. Set over barely boiling water and beat with electric hand mixer 4 to 7 minutes, until mixture peaks stiffly. Begin at low speed, proceed to medium, then high.

3. Add vanilla and continue beating to good spreading consistency.

─── **VARIATIONS** ───

BROWN SUGAR SEVEN-MINUTE ICING: Prepare as directed, substituting 1 cup firmly packed dark brown sugar for 1 cup granulated and dark corn syrup for light. Makes about 4 cups.

CITRUS SEVEN-MINUTE ICING: Prepare as directed, substituting fresh lemon, lime, orange, or grapefruit juice for water. Omit vanilla and add 1 teaspoon finely grated lemon, lime, orange, or grapefruit zest. Makes about 4 cups.

CHOCOLATE SEVEN-MINUTE ICING: Prepare as directed; stir— do not beat—in 2 ounces cooled, melted unsweetened chocolate. Makes about 4 cups.

CAKE RECIPES

*that Entered the American Mainstream
During the Twentieth Century with Their Source*

(*Recipe Included)

FRANCE
Baba au Rhum
Bûche de Noël
*Dacquoise (see Puddings, Pies, & Desserts)
Madeleines
Marjolaine
Pain d'Épice

❉

GERMANY/AUSTRIA/HUNGARY
Black Forest Cake
Doboschtorte
German Prune Cake
Gugelhupf
*Hazelnut Torte
*Poppy Seed Cake
Rigo Jancsi
Sachertorte

❉

ITALY
Panettone
Panforte
Polenta Cake

❉

SPAIN & PORTUGAL
Madeira Cake

Hazelnut Torte

*Makes a 10-inch, 2-layer Cake,
12 Servings*

❋

THIS RECIPE comes from my good friend Hedy Würz, a Bavarian now working in New York. She and I coauthored *The New German Cookbook* from which this recipe is adapted.

NOTE: This recipe contains no flour and no leavening.

TORTE
*10 extra-large eggs,
   separated
1½ cups sugar
4 cups finely ground
   unblanched hazelnuts
¼ teaspoon salt*

FILLING AND FROSTING
*2½ cups ice-cold heavy cream
2 tablespoons sugar
1 teaspoon vanilla extract*

DECORATION
*12 whole blanched and toasted
   hazelnuts*

1. Preheat oven to 350° F. Generously butter and flour two 10-inch springform pans, tapping out excess flour; set aside.

2. TORTE: Beat egg yolks and sugar in large electric mixer bowl at highest speed until mixture "ribbons," about 5 minutes. At low speed, mix in hazelnuts.

3. Whip egg whites and salt until stiff in second large bowl. Fold one-fourth of beaten whites into hazel-

nut mixture, then fold in remainder —easy does it—until no streaks of white or brown show.

4. Divide batter between pans and bake in lower third of oven until springy to touch—about 45 minutes.

5. Cool tortes in pans on wire racks 10 minutes. Loosen, release, and remove springform pan sides, then carefully separate tortes from pan bottoms. Cool on wire racks.

6. FILLING AND FROSTING: Whip cream with sugar and vanilla until very stiff. Sandwich layers together with whipped cream, then frost top of torte with remaining whipped cream. Leave sides bare.

7. TO DECORATE: Arrange a ring of nuts in whipped cream around outer edge of torte.

8. Let torte stand 1 hour before serving.

Poppy Seed Cake

*Makes a 9-inch, 4-layer Cake,
10 Servings*

✳

THIS IS a recipe my mother brought home from Vienna, where she and my father lived shortly after they were married.

NOTE: Freshly ground poppy seeds are sold by many specialty food shops. But you can grind your own in a little electric coffee grinder. Or pulverize them with a mortar and pestle. The seeds must be absolutely fresh, otherwise your cake will be rancid. Vanilla sugar is also available in specialty food shops. But you can also make your own—simply bury a couple of vanilla beans in your sugar canister. Wait a week before using.

CAKE

*2 cups sifted all-purpose flour
3 teaspoons baking powder
¼ cup (½ stick) unsalted butter, softened
¾ cup granulated sugar
1 tablespoon vanilla sugar
1 egg, lightly beaten
2¾ cups finely ground fresh poppy seeds
1 cup milk*

VANILLA BUTTER CREAM

*½ cup (1 stick) unsalted butter, softened
4 cups unsifted confectioners' (10X) sugar
¼ cup vanilla sugar
4 to 6 tablespoons light cream*

1. CAKE: Preheat oven to 325° F. Generously butter and flour two 9-inch springform or layer cake pans, tapping out excess flour; set aside.

2. Sift flour and baking powder together onto wax paper; set aside.

3. Cream butter, granulated sugar, and vanilla sugar in large electric mixer bowl at high speed until smooth; beat in egg. Stir in poppy seeds and ⅓ cup milk.

4. Add sifted dry ingredients alternately to poppy seed mixture with remaining milk, beginning and ending with dry. Batter will be thick.

5. Divide batter between pans and bake until springy to touch—about 40 minutes.

6. Cool cakes in pans on wire racks 10 minutes. Loosen, release and remove springform pan sides, then carefully separate cakes from pan bottoms. Cool on wire racks.

7. VANILLA BUTTER CREAM: Beat butter, 10X sugar, and vanilla sugar until uniformly crumbly, then beat in enough cream for good spreading consistency.

8. TO ASSEMBLE CAKE: Using sharp serrated knife, halve each cake layer horizontally, then sandwich four layers together with butter cream. Swirl remaining butter cream over top of cake but leave sides plain.

9. Let cake stand 30 minutes to 1 hour before serving. Cut into small wedges—the cake is very rich.

COOKIES & CANDIES

OUR ACME ROYAL RANGE,

WITH PORCELAIN LINED RESERVOIR AND HIGH CLOSET.

FOR HARD COAL, SOFT COAL, WOOD OR ANYTHING USED FOR FUEL.

HOW WE TRIM IT

Beautifully nickel plated mountings throughout, including large handsome nickel plated oven door panel, large nickel panel on draft door; very large nickel oven shelf, large, handsome, highly polished nickel bands on main top, hearth and high closet, nickel hinge pins, nickel tea shelves, nickel plated, patent, fancy (always cold) knobs on all doors.

FANCY NICKEL ORNAMENTATION THROUGHOUT....

Highly polished, richly ornamented and decorated, latest Rococo design, and, we believe,

THE HANDSOMEST 1900 RANGE ON THE MARKET.

$25.49 to $30.00 is our price for this, our very finest, completely finished, Acme Royal Range.

This $25.49 Stove is the equal of any range on the market, regardless of price; combines every improvement of every high grade range made, with the defects of none.

Our 20th Century Production. Full Square Oven, Duplex Grate, Cut Tops and Centers, Porcelain lined Reservoir, Oven Door Kicker, Large Fire Box, Large Flues, Balled Ash Pan, Slide Hearth Plate, Latest and Handsomest Rococo Design.

Our Gem Grate furnished FREE, makes it a perfect burner for all kinds of fuel, Coal, Wood or Coke.

Our Binding Guarantee makes you perfectly safe and insures for you such a stove as you could not buy elsewhere.

Our Binding Guarantee.

With every Acme Royal we issue a written, binding guarantee, by the terms of which if any piece or part gives out by reason of defect in material or workmanship, we will replace it free of charge; further, that it must be received by you in perfect condition, found exactly as represented and perfectly satisfactory, or your money will be refunded immediately.

Our New 1900 Line Factory-to-Consumer Prices and Binding Guarantee, commends it above all others.

Most stove dealers would say this oven is three or four inches wider than the size we give.

We furnish this range just as it is shown in the various sizes at prices as listed below.

OVEN MEASUREMENTS DO NOT INCLUDE SWELL OF OVEN DOOR

IF YOU DO NOT USE COAL AT ALL, ORDER FROM CATALOGUE Nos. 75206 TO 75211.

PRICES DO NOT INCLUDE PIPE OR COOKING UTENSILS. SEE PAGES 902 TO 903.

CATALOGUE NUMBER	SIZES	SIZE OF LIDS	SIZE OF OVEN	SIZE OF TOP MEASURING RESERVOIR	SIZE OF FIRE BOX WHEN USED FOR WOOD	HEIGHT TO MAIN TOP	WEIGHT	PRICE
75242	7-18	No. 7	16x17½x11½	42x25	17x8x8	28 inches	455 lbs	$25.49
75243	8-18	No. 8	16x17½x11½	42x25	17x8x8	28 inches	455 lbs	25.54
75244	7-20	No. 8	18x19½x13	45x27	19x9x9	30 inches	495 lbs	27.79
75245	8-20	No. 8	18x19½x13	45x27	19x9x9	30 inches	497 lbs	28.15
75246	8-22	No. 8	20x21½x12½	46x28	21x9x9	31 inches	538 lbs	20.05
75247	9-22	No. 9	20x21½x12½	46x28	21x9x9	31 inches	540 lbs	30.09

IF DESIRED WITHOUT HIGH CLOSET, SEE PRECEDING PAGE.

JUMBLES . . . HERMITS . . . macaroons . . . tea cakes . . . sand tarts . . . sugar cookies . . . molasses cookies . . . ginger cakes, snaps, and drops. These cookies, most of them of the drop or roll-and-cut type, are the ones that show up again and again in late-nineteenth-century cookbooks, notably those by such best-selling authors as Fannie Farmer, Mary J. Lincoln, Maria Parloa, and Sarah Tyson Rorer. But there is little else.

My own theory for the lack of variety is that cookies, even more than cakes, require precise baking times and temperatures. And in days when few ovens were reliable, it stands to reason that many batches came out scorched—or worse. Read, for example, what Mary Lincoln (*The Boston Cook Book,* 1883) has to say on the subject of stoves:

"If you intend to buy a new stove or range, get one simple in construction, that you may quickly learn all its parts and their uses; plain in finish, that you may easily keep it clean; and perfectly fitted part to part, with doors and dampers shutting absolutely close, so that you may control the fire and heat. This latter point is of essential importance in regulating the oven and in preventing a waste of fuel [she might have added 'and food'].

"All stoves," she continues, "have a fire-box, with more or less space underneath for ashes; a slide damper under the fire, letting in the air; an outlet for the smoke; and a damper which regulates the supply of hot air, sending it around and underneath the oven, or letting it escape into the chimney."

Her discussion of stoves goes on for another two pages. One can only wonder what Mrs. Lincoln would think of today's modern gas and electric ranges (to say nothing of halogen burners, convection ovens, and microwaves).

I find cookie repertoires broadening in spurts, paralleling, for the most part, the evolution of the stove. In 1910, for example, gas ranges begin phasing out cumbersome coal, wood, and petroleum stoves. And the 1912 Revised Edition of *Lowney's Cook Book* introduces Creoles (cayenne-spiked brown sugar/pecan cookies baked in small fluted tins), chocolate-walnut wafers, chocolate Swedish meringues (a meringue-frosted brownie), chocolate dominoes, chocolate angelettes, and cocoa/coconut cookies. (Lowney's—it should come as no surprise—was a manufacturer of chocolate.)

Three years later, the *Larkin Housewives' Cook Book* adds jelly cookies, graham cookies, two types of oatmeal cookies, peanut cookies, raisin drops, and eggless date cookies to the usual repertoire. And in the 1918 edition of "Fannie Farmer," I find walnut molasses bars, oatmeal cookies, jelly jumbles, royal fans, peanut cookies, German chocolate cookies, chocolate fruit

cookies, chocolate cakes, Neuremburghs (an almond-orange drop cookie spiced with cinnamon and cloves), Swedish wafers (drop butter cookies sprinkled with almonds), and kornettes (made of popcorn and chopped almonds).

With the arrival of the electric range in many home kitchens in the 1930s, there was no stopping the march of the Cookie Monster until World War II. But at war's end, with butter and sugar no longer rationed, the race was again on to find new and more exotic cookies.

Many of them emerged as mixes, or easier yet, as rolls of refrigerated, ready-to-slice-and-bake cookies in a variety of flavors. Our passion for cookies shows little sign of cooling despite our current preoccupation with fitness. We simply switch to the fat-free variety.

The evolution of candies is less dramatic. Fudges, fondants, caramels, mints, and such were all known well before 1900. But most of these were long-winded recipes requiring plenty of boiling and beating or "pulling" (for taffy and butter mints). What the twentieth century has given us are the instant candies, the no-cook candies.

Plus flavor combinations the nineteenth-century cook would never have dreamed of.

Original Nestlé Toll House Chocolate Chip Cookies

Makes about 5 Dozen Cookies

✳

2¼ cups all-purpose flour
1 teaspoon baking soda
1 teaspoon salt
1 cup (2 sticks) butter, softened
¾ cup granulated sugar
¾ cup packed brown sugar
1 teaspoon vanilla extract
2 eggs
2 cups (12-ounce package)
Nestlé Toll House semi-sweet
chocolate morsels
1 cup chopped nuts

1. Preheat oven to 375° F.

2. Combine flour, baking soda, and salt in small bowl.

3. Beat butter, granulated and brown sugars, and vanilla in large mixer bowl until creamy. Add eggs one at a time, beating well after each addition.

4. Gradually beat in flour mixture. Stir in morsels and nuts.

5. Drop by rounded tablespoon onto ungreased baking sheets, spacing 2 inches apart. Bake for 9 to 11 minutes, or until golden brown.

6. Cool on baking sheets for 2 minutes; transfer to wire racks to cool.

The Origin of the Chocolate Chip Cookie

THE FIRST recipe for chocolate chip cookies appears in Ruth Wakefield's *Toll House Cook Book* (1930), and the ingredients call for two bars of Nestlé Yellow Label Chocolate, Semi-Sweet, which have been "cut into pieces the size of a pea."

All of a sudden, sales of Nestlé Yellow Label Chocolate, Semi-Sweet, soared in the Boston area, then throughout New England, and Nestlé sent a salesman around to see what was up. In suburban Whitman, Massachusetts, he found Ruth Wakefield and the chocolate chip cookie she had invented. Impressed, Nestlé began scoring its bars of semi-sweet chocolate and packaging them with a little chopper, the easier to break them into chips.

Nestlé didn't introduce chocolate morsels until 1939. That same year, Mrs. Wakefield signed a forty-year contract with Nestlé, allowing them to print her recipe on the back of every package of morsels. The contract expired in 1979, and for the first time, Nestlé updated the recipe, shortening baking times, using unsifted flour, and so forth. Still, Nestlé calls it the "Original Toll House Cookie" and has registered the name, meaning no one else can use it without permission. That's why these cookies are better known as chocolate chip cookies.

According to John Thorne, who in 1982 devoted an issue of his culinary broadsheet, *Simple Cooking*, to the chocolate chip cookie, the Original Nestlé Toll House Cookie recipe isn't quite the original. Mrs. Wakefield always dissolved her soda in a teaspoon of water. Nestlé calls for it to be combined with the dry ingredients.

Ruth Wakefield's recipe, created in 1930, contained no nuts. And like so many recipe classics, it was born of a crisis. Mrs. Wakefield, in the midst of making Butter Drop Dos (or Boston Cookies) at her Toll House Inn near Whitman, discovered that she had no nuts. In desperation, she chopped semisweet chocolate and dumped the pieces in in place of nuts. To her surprise, they didn't melt in the oven. Guests loved these "Chocolate Crispies," as Mrs. Wakefield at first called them. Indeed, friend and colleague Mary Lyons remembers going as a small child to the Toll House Inn with her aunt and loving Chocolate Crispies so much her aunt wrapped one in tissue and told her to take it home and ask her mother to duplicate it. The year was 1930.

Soon Mrs. Wakefield was adding chopped chocolate *and* nuts to her beloved Butter Drop Dos and calling them "Toll House Chocolate Crunch Cookies." Today they are America's most popular cookie recipe, accounting for more than half of all cookies baked. The recipe below is printed verbatim from *Ruth Wakefield's Toll House Tried and True Recipes* (1936 edition). At left is the Nestlé modern version.

RUTH WAKEFIELD'S TOLL HOUSE CHOCOLATE CRUNCH COOKIES

Cream
1 cup butter, add
¾ cup brown sugar
¾ cup granulated sugar
   and
2 eggs beaten whole.
   Dissolve
1 tsp. soda in
1 tsp. hot water, and mix
   alternatively with
2¼ cups flour sifted with
1 tsp. salt.

Lastly add
1 cup chopped nuts and
2 bars (7-oz.) Nestlé's
   Yellow Label Chocolate,
   Semi-Sweet, which has
   been cut in pieces the size
   of a pea.
Flavor with 1 tsp. vanilla
   and drop half teaspoons
   on a greased cookie
   sheet.
Bake 10 to 12 minutes in
   375° oven.
Makes 100 cookies.

Reese's Chewy Chocolate Cookies

Makes 4½ Dozen

THIS UPDATE of a recipe in *Hershey's Favorite Recipes* puts Reese's peanut butter chips into what look like chocolate chip cookies in reverse.

   2 cups unsifted all-purpose
      flour
   ¾ cup unsweetened cocoa
      powder
   1 teaspoon baking soda
   ½ teaspoon salt
   1¼ cups (2½ sticks) butter or
      margarine, softened
   2 cups sugar
   2 eggs
   2 teaspoons vanilla extract
   1⅔ cups (a 10-ounce package)
      peanut butter chips

1. Preheat oven to 350° F.

2. Stir flour with cocoa, baking soda, and salt in medium bowl; set aside.

3. Cream butter and sugar in large electric mixer bowl at medium speed until light and fluffy. Add eggs and vanilla and beat well.

4. Gradually add flour mixture, beating well. Stir in peanut butter chips.

5. Drop by rounded teaspoons onto ungreased baking sheets and bake 8 to 9 minutes. (Do not overbake; cookies will be soft. They will puff as they bake but flatten on cooling.)

6. Cool cookies slightly, then remove to wire racks and cool to room temperature.

How Do You Eat an Oreo?

IN 1912, Nabisco introduced three new cookies designed to capitalize on the popularity of British-type sweet biscuits. The three, described by the company as "entirely new varieties of the highest class biscuit," were the Veronese, the Mother Goose, and the Oreo. Today, no one can remember the Veronese or the Mother Goose, but Oreo outsells every other cookie in the world—five billion every year in the United States alone.

"Mainly, little kids eat Animal Crackers," explains one youngster to another in Delia Ephron's revue, *How To Eat like a Child.* * "Pretty much as soon as you know anything, you move right onto Oreos."

But how do you eat an Oreo? Most adults know that most kids twist Oreos apart, then lick the filling off or scrape it off with their teeth; but then, most adults do this, too: 16 percent of men and a whopping 41 percent of women. After eating the filling, most adults eat the chocolate wafers but most kids throw them away.

How did the Oreo get its name? Nobody knows.

---

* *How To Eat Like a Child (and Other Lessons in Not Being a Grown-Up)*. Book by Delia Ephron, John Forster, and Judith Kahan; music and lyrics by John Forster. Based on the book by Delia Ephron. Samuel French, Inc. 1990.

Peanut Butter Cookies

Makes 5 to 6 Dozen

❊

WHEN DID this popular cookie first appear? Who invented it? Peanut butter itself, though developed in the late nineteenth century as a health food, was only introduced to the public at large in 1904 at the the St. Louis World's Fair. The earliest peanut butter cookie recipe I could find was in the *Larkin Housewives' Cook Book* (1915), which called for Larkin vanilla and Larkin peanut butter—but only three tablespoons of it. Perhaps that's why the recipe is titled "Special Peanut Cookies" instead of Peanut Butter Cookies. The dough is rolled thin and cut, not shaped as we shape peanut butter cookies today. Two years later, Janet McKensie Hill published a recipe for peanut butter cookies in *Cakes, Pastry and Dessert Dishes*. It contains ½ cup peanut butter, but these cookies, too, are rolled and cut. In the 1924 edition of *The Beech-Nut Book of Menus & Recipes* by Ida Bailey Allen, the recipe for Beech-Nut Peanut Butter Cookies (which contains ¾ cup Beech-Nut Peanut Butter) offers the cook a choice: rolling and cutting the cookies or shaping them into "jumbles."

Only in *Ruth Wakefield's Toll House Tried and True Recipes* (1936) did I find a recipe that closely parallels the one we use today. It calls for 1 cup peanut butter, for rolling the dough into "balls the size of a nut" and flattening each with a fork, leaving a "crisscross" design on top. The classic recipe that follows isn't so very different, although it gives you the option of using creamy or crunchy peanut butter.

2½ cups sifted all-purpose flour
1 teaspoon baking powder
½ teaspoon salt
½ cup (1 stick) butter
½ cup vegetable shortening
1 cup granulated sugar
1 cup firmly packed light
*   brown sugar*
2 eggs
1 cup creamy or crunchy
*   peanut butter*

1. Sift flour with baking powder and salt onto wax paper; set aside.

2. Cream butter and shortening until light in large electric mixer bowl at moderate speed, add granulated and brown sugars, and cream until fluffy. Beat eggs in one at a time. Add peanut butter and beat at low speed just until blended.

3. Work in dry ingredients, about one-third at a time. Wrap dough and chill at least 2 hours.

4. Preheat oven to 375° F. Grease baking sheets and set aside.

5. Shape dough into 1-inch balls and space 3 inches apart on baking sheets. With a floured fork, flatten cookies crisscross fashion. Bake 10 to 12 minutes, until soft-firm.

6. Transfer at once to wire racks to cool.

Praline Crisps

Makes 4½ to 5 Dozen

I DON'T remember exactly when or where Mother got this recipe—she was always swapping favorites with members of her Book Club and Sewing Circle. But I do remember her making Praline Crisps right after World War II. Searches of '30s, '20s, and earlier cookbooks turn up nothing similar (the two closest are a brown sugar drop in Sheila Hibben's 1932 *National Cookbook,* which contains as many raisins as nuts, and a nutless, rolled-and-cut brown sugar cookie in the 1922 *Good Housekeeping Book of Menus, Recipes and Household Discoveries*). In the 1940s in *The Joy of Cooking,* Irma Rombauer admits to hearing people rave about what she calls Rich Brown Sugar (Butterscotch) Drop Cookies. "A number of cookbooks have much-vaunted recipes for these cookies," she writes. "I have tried many of them and find that they are all practically the same as Butterscotch Brownies on page 587, only they are more troublesome and as they call for more flour are not quite so good as that chewy, flavor-

ful mouthful." She urges readers to try her butterscotch brownies, and then "if you still persist in wanting a drop cookie instead of a bar, just follow the recipe and add 2 tablespoons of flour." Clearly Mrs. Rombauer never tasted my mother's Praline Crisps, which contain more brown sugar, butter, and nuts than her brownies. When I was growing up, I thought Praline Crisps the best cookies ever. I still do.

1 cup (2 sticks) butter
2⅔ cups loosely packed light
*   brown sugar (1 pound)*
2 eggs, lightly beaten
2½ cups unsifted all-purpose
*   flour*
½ teaspoon baking soda
¼ teaspoon baking powder
Pinch salt
1½ teaspoons vanilla extract
1¾ cups coarsely chopped
*   pecans*

1. Preheat oven to 350° F. Lightly grease baking sheets; set aside.

2. Cream butter until light in large electric mixer bowl at medium speed, add sugar, and again cream until light. Beat in eggs.

3. Mix flour, soda, baking powder, and salt in second large bowl, then blend into brown sugar mixture. Stir in vanilla and pecans.

4. Drop by teaspoonful on baking sheets, spacing 2 inches apart. Bake 12 to 15 minutes, until soft-firm and cookies smell irresistible.

5. Transfer immediately to wire racks to cool.

Peanut Blossoms

Makes about 4 Dozen

✳

PEANUT BUTTER cookies with centers of milk chocolate (a Hershey's Kiss is pressed into the center of each cookie as soon as it comes from the oven). The recipe, which uses another Hershey product, Reese's Peanut Butter, was developed in the test kitchens of the Hershey Foods Corporation in Hershey, Pennsylvania, a pin-neat village where streetlamps are shaped like Hershey's Kisses and the very air smells of chocolate.

½ cup vegetable shortening
¾ cup creamy or crunchy peanut butter
⅓ cup granulated sugar
⅓ cup firmly packed light brown sugar
1 egg
2 tablespoons milk
1 teaspoon vanilla extract
1½ cups unsifted all-purpose flour
1 teaspoon baking soda
½ teaspoon salt
Granulated sugar (for coating cookies)
1 (9-ounce) bag milk chocolate kisses, unwrapped

1. Preheat oven to 375° F.

2. Cream shortening and peanut butter in large electric mixer bowl at high speed until well blended. Add ⅓ cup granulated sugar and brown sugar and beat until light and fluffy. Add egg, milk, and vanilla; beat well.

3. Stir together flour, baking soda, and salt; add gradually to peanut butter mixture.

4. Shape dough into 1-inch balls, and roll in granulated sugar.

5. Space cookies 2 inches apart on ungreased baking sheets. Bake 8 to 10 minutes until lightly browned.

6. Immediately place a chocolate kiss on top of each cookie, pressing down so cookie cracks around edges.

7. Remove from baking sheets to wire racks and cool completely.

Cherry Winks

Makes 5 Dozen

✳

SO MANY of the cookies that have entered our repertoire of favorites have done so through the Pillsbury Bake-Off Contest. And not all of them were Grand Prize winners. These cookies, for example, which were entered in the 1950 Bake-Off event by Ruth Derousseau of Wisconsin. They did place, however, and win Ms. Derousseau a trip to the Bake-Off Finals at the Waldorf-Astoria in New York City and a chance to meet such guests of honor as the Duchess of Windsor, Art Linkletter (the host), and Arthur Godfrey. Her win even inspired me, then still a teenager, to enter. But I was soon off to college and too busy to bother. Still, I keep wondering, "What if?"

1 cup sugar
¾ cup vegetable shortening
2 tablespoons milk
1 teaspoon vanilla extract
2 eggs
2¼ cups all-purpose or unbleached flour (lightly spooned into measure and leveled off)
1 teaspoon baking powder
½ teaspoon baking soda
½ teaspoon salt
1 cup chopped pecans
1 cup chopped, pitted dates
⅓ cup chopped, well drained maraschino cherries
1½ cups coarsely crushed cornflake cereal
15 maraschino cherries, well drained and quartered

1. Preheat oven to 375° F. Grease baking sheets and set aside.

2. Beat sugar, shortening, milk, vanilla, and eggs in large mixer bowl at medium speed until light.

3. Mix flour, baking powder, soda, and salt well in small bowl. Add to sugar mixture and beat at low speed until well blended.

4. By hand, stir in pecans, dates, and ⅓ cup chopped cherries.

5. Place cereal in pie tin. Drop in dough by rounded teaspoonfuls and turn to coat. Shape into balls.

6. Arrange balls 2 inches apart on baking sheets and press maraschino cherry piece into top of each. Bake 10 to 15 minutes until pale brown.

7. Transfer at once to wire racks to cool.

Mexican Wedding Cakes

Makes about 4 Dozen

✳

THESE COOKIES masquerade under several names—Butterballs, Russian Tea Cakes, Swedish Tea Cakes, Moldy Mice. "Butterballs" is easy enough to explain—these little balls *are* buttery—but I have no idea how they came by their other pseudonyms. They are also known sometimes as Pecan Sandies, although true sandies are nearer shortbread. Mexican Wedding Cakes were a community cookbook staple throughout the '50s and '60s, and I occasionally see them cropping up in spiral-bound fund-raisers today.

Small wonder they continue to be popular. They are a snap to make, but best of all, they melt in your mouth.

NOTE: Finely ground, toasted blanched almonds can be used in place of pecans.

> 2 cups unsifted all-purpose flour
> ¼ teaspoon salt
> 1 cup (2 sticks) butter
> 1¼ cups confectioners' (10X) sugar
> 2 teaspoons vanilla extract
> ¾ cup finely ground pecans

1. Sift flour and salt onto wax paper; set aside.

2. Cream butter and ½ cup 10X sugar in large electric mixer bowl at medium speed until fluffy; stir in vanilla.

3. Work in flour mixture, ½ cup at a time, stirring only enough to blend. Mix in pecans.

4. Wrap in foil and refrigerate several hours, until stiff enough to shape. When ready to proceed, preheat oven to 325° F.

5. Pinch off bits of dough, roll into 1-inch balls, and space 2 inches apart on ungreased baking sheets. Bake 15 to 20 minutes, until tan.

6. Transfer at once to wire racks to cool, then roll in ¾ cup 10X sugar.

LIONS AND TIGERS AND BEARS, OH MY!

SINCE THEIR debut in 1902, packed in a small box painted to look like a circus cage and provided with its own useful string handle just right for a child's hand, the National Biscuit Company's Animal Crackers—or, more officially, "Barnum's Animals"—have been adored by small children.

Several generations have heard Shirley Temple singing "Animal Crackers in My Soup," and seen the 1930 Marx Brothers movie *Animal Crackers.* Every kid knows how to eat them: back legs first, then front legs, head, body. Many boys and girls can, or

could until recently, name all seventeen animals to be found in the box (bear, bison, camel, cougar, elephant, giraffe, gorilla, hippopotamus, hyena, kangaroo, lion, monkey, rhinoceros, seal, sheep, tiger, and zebra).

In 1997, the Barnum menagerie consists of *endangered* animals, and today's ecologically oriented kids can name them, too, from Chinese Alligator to Mountain Zebra. The carton is made of 100 percent recycled paperboard and each one spotlights a specific animal, with pertinent facts and lifelike drawings. Best of all, five cents from the sale of each packet goes to protect endangered animals and their habitats around the world.

Famous Oatmeal Cookies

Makes about 5 Dozen

❋

THE FIRST recipe I've found for oatmeal cookies appears in the original *Boston Cooking-School Cook Book* by Fannie Merritt Farmer (1896). Nineteenth century, to be sure. But just barely (in fact, they were *barely* oatmeal cookies, containing only half a cup). I include oatmeal cookies here because they did not begin routinely appearing in cookbooks until the twentieth century. Also because they are one of the more nutritious cookies. This particular recipe for crunchy, not-too-sweet cookies was especially developed during World War II by home economists at The Quaker Oats Company to use vegetable shortening in place of precious butter. They've subsequently become a classic.

> ¾ cup vegetable shortening
> 1 cup firmly packed brown sugar
> ½ cup granulated sugar
> 1 egg
> ¼ cup water
> 1 teaspoon vanilla extract
> 3 cups uncooked rolled oats (quick-cooking or old-fashioned)
> 1 cup sifted all-purpose flour
> 1 teaspoon salt (optional)
> ½ teaspoon baking soda

1. Preheat oven to 350°F.

2. Cream shortening with brown and granulated sugars, egg, water, and vanilla in large electric mixer bowl at medium speed until fluffy.

3. Mix oats, flour, salt, and soda in second large bowl; add to creamed mixture and mix well.

4. Drop by rounded teaspoonfuls onto ungreased baking sheets, spacing about 1½ inches apart. Bake 12 to 15 minutes, until soft-firm.

5. Transfer cookies at once to wire racks to cool. Store in airtight container.

Recipe courtesy of The Quaker Oats Company.

Vanishing Oatmeal Raisin Cookies

Makes about 4 Dozen

❋

AND HERE'S the newest oatmeal cookie from the Quaker Kitchens, a spicy brown sugar cookie strewn with raisins. Why "Vanishing?" Because they don't last long.

NOTE: For those who don't like raisins, 1 cup diced, mixed dried fruits can be substituted—or even chocolate chips.

> 1½ cups sifted all-purpose flour
> 1 teaspoon baking soda
> 1 teaspoon ground cinnamon
> ½ teaspoon salt (optional)
> 1 cup (2 sticks) margarine or butter, softened
> 1 cup firmly packed brown sugar
> ½ cup granulated sugar
> 2 eggs
> 1 teaspoon vanilla extract
> 3 cups uncooked rolled oats (quick-cooking or old-fashioned)
> 1 cup dark seedless raisins
> 1 cup coarsely chopped pecans or walnuts (optional)

1. Preheat oven to 350°F.

2. Mix flour, soda, cinnamon and, if desired, salt well in large bowl; set aside.

3. Beat margarine and brown and granulated sugars in large electric mixer bowl at high speed until creamy; beat in eggs and vanilla.

4. Mix dry ingredients in thoroughly by hand, then stir in oats, raisins, and, if desired, pecans.

5. Drop by rounded tablespoonfuls on ungreased baking sheets, spacing 2 inches apart. Bake 10 to 12 minutes, until pale golden brown.

6. Cool 1 minute on baking sheets, then transfer to wire racks to cool. Store airtight.

Recipe courtesy of The Quaker Oats Company.

Pride of Iowa Cookies

Makes about 5½ Dozen

❊

THIS RECIPE was given to me by Alma McGraw of Finney County, Kansas, whom I profiled for *Family Circle* in the 1970s. She told me she had no idea where she got the recipe or how it got its name. What she did know was that these cookies had been a family favorite for years and that when her late son Leland entered a batch of them at the Kansas State Fair, he won the blue ribbon.

1 cup vegetable shortening
1 cup firmly packed light
*   brown sugar*
1 cup granulated sugar
2 eggs, well beaten
2 cups sifted all-purpose flour
1 teaspoon baking soda
1 teaspoon baking powder

¼ teaspoon salt
1 teaspoon vanilla extract
1 cup flaked coconut
½ cup chopped pecans or
*   walnuts*
3 cups uncooked quick-cooking
*   rolled oats*

1. Preheat oven to 375° F. Lightly grease baking sheets and set aside.

2. Cream shortening and brown and granulated sugars in large electric mixer bowl at medium speed until fluffy; beat in eggs.

3. Mix flour with soda, baking powder, and salt in second large bowl, then stir into creamed mixture. Blend in vanilla.

4. Mix in coconut, pecans, and oats; dough will be very stiff.

5. Pinch off bits of dough, shape into 1¼-inch balls, and space 2 inches apart on baking sheets. With fingers, flatten into patties ⅛-inch thick, evening up rough edges. Bake 8 to 10 minutes, until pale brown.

6. While cookies are still warm, transfer to wire racks to cool.

1992

Cook's Illustrated, an ad-free food magazine, appears.

1993

The Food Network, America's first 24-hour television food channel, airs.

Borden brings "Elsie the Cow" out of retirement and gives her a streamlined new look.

The Strong Museum of Rochester, New York, in cooperation with the Historical Society of nearby LeRoy where Jell-O was invented in 1897 by native son Pearl B. Wait, mounts an exhibit of memorabilia generated by the fruit-flavored gelatin. After a slow start, Jello-O emerged this century as "America's Most Famous Dessert." The exhibit runs for eleven months.

Fudgy Bonbons

Makes about 5 Dozen

❋

THESE CANDY-RICH chocolate drops dreamed up by Mary Anne Tyndall of Whiteville, North Carolina, won $50,000 in Pillsbury's 1994 Bake-Off Contest. How did she come to invent the recipe? "I was making fudge balls one day and had some Hershey's Kisses on hand. And I said, 'I b'lieve I'll just put some of these inside and see what happens.'"

NOTE: For 60 bonbons you'll need one and a half (9-ounce) packages of chocolate candy kisses.

*1 (12-ounce) package
    semisweet chocolate chips
¼ cup (½ stick) butter or
    margarine
1 (14-ounce) can sweetened
    condensed milk (not
    evaporated)
2 cups all-purpose or
    unbleached flour (lightly
    spooned into the measure
    and leveled off)
½ cup finely chopped nuts
    (optional)*

*1 teaspoon vanilla extract
60 milk chocolate candy kisses
    or white and chocolate-
    striped candy kisses,
    unwrapped*

DECORATION

*2 ounces white baking bar or
    white candy coating (white
    chocolate)
1 teaspoon vegetable shortening
    or oil*

1. Preheat oven to 350° F.

2. Heat chocolate chips and butter in heavy medium saucepan over very low heat, stirring until chips melt. Add sweetened condensed milk and mix well.

3. Mix flour, nuts, if desired, chocolate mixture, and vanilla well in medium bowl.

4. Shape a level tablespoon dough (use tablespoon of measuring spoon set) around each candy kiss, enclosing completely. Arrange 1 inch apart on ungreased baking sheets. Bake 6 to 8 minutes—no more. Cookies will be soft and look shiny but will firm up as they cool.

5. Transfer to wire racks to cool.

6. DECORATION: Melt white baking bar and shortening in small heavy saucepan over low heat, stirring constantly until smooth. Drizzle over cookies in a zigzag design. Store in airtight container.

Bourbon Balls

Makes about 2½ Dozen

❋

THESE NO-BAKE cookies seem to have surfaced in the '40s, perhaps because they require no butter and very little sugar, both of which were rationed during World War II. They remain popular to this day, particularly down South, where they're likely to show up at teas and open houses. Bourbon balls can be made well ahead of time, in fact they actually improve with age.

*2 cups fine vanilla wafer
    crumbs
1½ cups confectioners' (10X)
    sugar
1 cup finely ground pecans
3 tablespoons unsweetened
    cocoa powder (not a mix)
3 tablespoons dark corn syrup
¼ cup bourbon
¼ teaspoon ground cinnamon*

1. Knead crumbs, 1 cup 10X sugar, pecans, cocoa, corn syrup, bourbon, and cinnamon together in large bowl.

2. Shape into 1-inch balls, then roll in ½ cup sifted 10X sugar.

3. Store cookies in airtight canister and let "season" about a week before serving.

——— VARIATION ———

RUM BALLS: Prepare as directed, substituting light or dark rum for bourbon. Makes about 2½ dozen.

Chinese Chews

Makes about 2 Dozen

✳

THE HEADNOTE to this recipe, published in the *King Arthur Flour 200th Anniversary Cookbook* (1990), says that Lisa Bernard, cocreator of the book, "inherited this recipe from her paternal grandmother, Madeline. The origin of and reason for their name is an enigma, but whatever the answer, these Chinese Chews are truly wonderful." It goes on to say that these are "all-weather" cookies, crisp and chewy at the same time on fair days and on foul. I remember Chinese Chews from the '50s and don't believe they date much further back than that. If so, I haven't been able to find any earlier recipes for them. My '40s editions of "Fannie" and "Joy" and *Better Homes & Gardens* cookbooks don't show them. Chinese Chews do, however, appear in the 1953 *Better Homes & Gardens New Cook Book*—but as bars, not drop cookies like these. The two recipes, however, are virtually identical. The only exception is that the *BH & G* recipe calls for three eggs, this one for two. It also calls for pressing the dough into a greased and floured 15½ × 10½ × 1-inch jelly-roll pan and baking 15 minutes at 350° F. By all means, try the chews this way, too.

¾ cup sifted unbleached all-
*   purpose flour*
1 teaspoon baking powder
1 cup sugar
¼ teaspoon salt

2 eggs, lightly beaten
1 (8-ounce) package pitted
*   dates, chopped*
1 cup coarsely chopped walnuts

1. Preheat oven to 325° F. Lightly grease baking sheets; set aside.

2. Combine flour, baking powder, sugar, and salt in large mixing bowl. Mix in eggs, then stir in dates and walnuts.

3. Drop by teaspoonfuls onto baking sheets, spacing 1½ inches apart. Bake 20 minutes, until pale brown.

4. Transfer at once to wire racks to cool.

Gumdrop Cookies

Makes 5 to 6 Dozen

✳

THIS IS the sort of novelty cookie that caught the fancy of mid-twentieth-century cooks. The recipe appears in most of the major cookbooks from the 1940s on. This version, adapted from the *King Arthur Flour 200th Anniversary Cookbook* (1990) begins with a headnote: "This recipe came out of the original King Arthur Flour Cookbook, *Easy Home Baking,* which appeared almost fifty years ago. In the original recipe, the gumdrops were mixed into the cookie dough. While experimenting, we found that a few gumdrop slices (easily cut with clean, sharp scissors), placed on top of the cookie before it goes into the oven, look more festive . . . The original recipe included a mysterious cup of coconut in the ingredient list, but never mentioned it in the directions. You can include it, adding it in any way you wish, or leave it out altogether."

1 cup (2 sticks) butter
1 cup granulated sugar
1 cup firmly packed brown
*   sugar*
2 eggs
½ teaspoon salt
2 teaspoons vanilla extract
2 cups uncooked rolled oats
*   (quick-cooking or old-*
*   fashioned)*
1 teaspoon baking soda
1 teaspoon baking powder
2 cups sifted unbleached all-
*   purpose flour*
1 cup gumdrops, cut in slices
*   (less if you only decorate tops)*

1. Preheat oven to 375° F. Coat baking sheets with nonstick cooking spray and set aside.

2. Cream butter and two sugars well in large electric mixer bowl at medium speed; beat in eggs, salt, and vanilla. Stir in oats.

3. Stir soda and baking powder into flour, then if adding gumdrops to cookies, add to flour. Mix into dough.

4. Drop by well rounded teaspoonfuls onto baking sheets. If decorating cookies with gumdrops, arrange on top of each cookie randomly or in pattern. Bake 8 to 10 minutes, until lightly browned.

5. Transfer immediately to wire racks to cool.

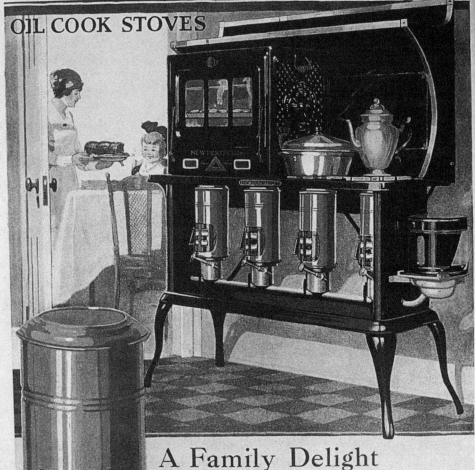

NEW PERFECTION

OIL COOK STOVES

A Family Delight

A tender and juicy roast, sizzling in savory brown gravy—one of mother's delicious dinners cooked on the New Perfection Oil Cook Stove.

No wonder 3,000,000 housewives use the New Perfection Oil Cook Stove! It keeps the kitchen comfortable even in hot weather —gives abundant clean heat for *all* cooking purposes. You, too, should have a dependable New Perfection.

The New Perfection is so satisfactory because of the Long Blue Chimney Burner—it turns every drop of kerosene oil into clean intense cooking heat and drives it full force, directly against the utensil.

And the flame always stays just where you set it, without smoke or odor. No fuel wasted—

it lights and gives full-heat instantly; turns out when you're through. Burners are made of brass and last for years.

There's a New Perfection dealer near you. Be sure to get a New Perfection oven too—it bakes perfectly. *See your dealer or write for New Perfection Booklet. It's free.*

THE CLEVELAND METAL PRODUCTS COMPANY
7541 Platt Avenue   Cleveland, Ohio

Also made in Canada by the Perfection Stove Company, Ltd., Sarnia, Ont.

Ask your dealer to demonstrate this high searing flame

Carrot Cookies

Makes about 5 Dozen

✳

CARROT COOKIES seem to have entered our lives in The Age of Aquarius—the '60s and early '70s —as did Pumpkin Cookies (see variation). Applesauce Cookies (see variation) apparently arrived two to three decades earlier. I traced them back to *Requested Recipes,* a ten-cent paperback of favorite reader recipes published by *The New York News* in 1940. Applesauce Cookies surely existed before 1940—*The News,* itself, must have offered a recipe. Yet several days of sleuthing in cookbooks dating back to 1900 turned up nothing. The three recipes that follow are mine.

> *2 cups sifted all-purpose flour*
> *2 teaspoons baking powder*
> *¼ teaspoon salt*
> *½ cup (1 stick) butter or margarine*
> *½ cup granulated sugar*
> *½ cup firmly packed light brown sugar*
> *1 cup cold, mashed, cooked carrots*
> *1 egg*
> *1 teaspoon vanilla extract*
> *½ teaspoon ground ginger*
> *¼ teaspoon ground cinnamon*
> *¼ teaspoon ground cloves*
> *1 tablespoon finely grated orange zest*

1. Preheat oven to 350° F. Coat baking sheets with nonstick cooking spray and set aside.

2. Sift flour, baking powder, and salt onto wax paper; set aside.

3. Cream butter until fluffy in large electric mixer bowl at moderate speed, add the two sugars gradually, beating well after each addition. Beat in carrots, egg, vanilla, the three spices, and orange zest. Finally, work in flour mixture.

4. Drop by teaspoonfuls onto baking sheets, spacing 2 inches apart. Bake 12 to 15 minutes, until firm to touch.

5. Cool 1 minute on baking sheets, then transfer to wire racks to cool.

——— VARIATIONS ———

APPLESAUCE COOKIES: Prepare as directed, substituting 1 cup good thick applesauce for carrots, and lemon zest for orange. Finally, mix in ¾ cup each seedless raisins and chopped pecans or walnuts. Space cookies 2 inches apart on greased baking sheets. Bake 15 minutes at 375°F, until firm to touch. Transfer at once to wire racks to cool. Makes 6½ to 7 dozen.

PUMPKIN COOKIES: Prepare Applesauce Cookies (above), substituting 1 cup solid pack pumpkin (not pumpkin pie mix) for applesauce and orange zest for lemon. Bake and cool as directed. Makes 6½ to 7 dozen.

TIMELINE

1994

New food labeling laws go into effect.

·············

Saveur magazine debuts.

1995

Betty Crocker enters cyberspace with an on-line hot line to answer cook's questions.

·············

Pillsbury ups the ante, raising the Grand Prize for its Bake-Off Cooking and Baking Contest from $50,000 to $1 million.

·············

M&M's asks fans to pick a new color: pink, purple, or blue. Or to vote "no change." Blue gets 54 percent of the vote and on March 29, the winning color is announced from the top of the Empire State Building, appropriately bathed in the new M&M's "blue." The first "blues" enter the mix in August/September replacing the "tans" introduced in 1949.

REFRIGERATOR COOKIES

EIGHTEENTH- AND early-nineteenth-century cookbooks sometimes called for doughs to be chilled before they were rolled and cut, but slice-and-bake refrigerator cookies arrived about the time electric refrigerators began to replace the old icebox in American kitchens. This means the 1930s, even though Frigidaire introduced a self-contained electric refrigerator in 1915.

The first recipe for refrigerator cookies I could find appears in Sheila Hibben's *National Cookbook* (1932). These are spicy, pecan-studded, brown sugar wafers called St. John Cookies. Ms. Hibben attributes them to my home state of North Carolina and directs the cook to shape the dough "with the hands into a long loaf, and set in the icebox overnight. In the morning," she continues, "cut in slices ¼-inch thick and bake in a good oven."

The very next year, General Foods devoted a section to "Ice box cookies—a modern convenience" in *All About Home Baking*. "No rolling pin—no cooky cutters needed. Just neat rolls of chilled, firm dough from which nicely formed cookies may be sliced and freshly baked whenever they are wanted," the blurb reads. Five refrigerator cookie recipes follow: Vanilla Nut, Peanut Butter, Chocolate Walnut Dollars, Coconut, and Chocolate Pin Wheels.

And in 1936, Ruth Wakefield offered three favorite chill-slice-and-bake cookies in *Toll House Tried and True Recipes*. Nut Tea Wafers, subtitled "Refrigerator Cookies," call for packing the dough in bread tins lined with "paraffin paper" before refrigerating. Mrs. Wakefield adds, however, that "The dough may be formed into a long roll if a round cookie is desired instead of the oblong shape." Her two other "icebox" cookies are Mince Meat and Chocolate Pinwheels, for which white and brown doughs are rolled up in tandem. It's easy to understand why Mrs. Wakefield liked refrigerator cookies. She had an inn to run—and cookie jars to replenish.

Where did slice-and-bake refrigerator cookies originate? I wonder if an appliance company didn't have someone develop the recipe for its owner's manual. Seems logical, although I can't prove it. I do know that refrigerator cookies became a particular favorite of my mother's in the 1930s shortly after her new Westinghouse electric refrigerator was delivered.

As a faculty wife, Mother had to do a lot of entertaining and refrigerator cookies made it easy. She could make the dough well ahead of time, roll it in wax paper, then slice and bake the cookies as needed.

Years later, after she got a modern refrigerator-freezer combination, Mother kept foil-wrapped rolls of cookie dough—several varieties—in the freezer. Frozen assets, you might say. For whenever unexpected guests arrived on our doorstep, she would bring forth a batch of fresh-baked cookies.

My Mother's Orange-Almond Refrigerator Cookies

Makes about 8 Dozen

✳

I LOVED these cookies as a child, and once I learned where Mother stashed her rolls of refrigerator dough, I'd slice off a half-dozen cookies and bake them when she was away. She caught on pretty fast, found a new hiding place in her Westinghouse, then pinned a note to the rolls of dough. "Unh-unh," it said. "Don't touch!" Once World War II was over, Mother let me make my own stash.

2¾ cups sifted all-purpose flour
¼ teaspoon baking soda
½ cup (1 stick) butter
½ cup vegetable shortening
¾ cup granulated sugar
¼ cup firmly packed dark brown sugar
2 tablespoons fresh orange juice
3 teaspoons finely grated orange zest
¼ teaspoon almond extract
1 egg
½ cup blanched slivered almonds

1. Sift flour and soda onto wax paper; set aside.

2. Cream butter and shortening in large electric mixer bowl at medium speed until light; beat in the two sugars, then orange juice and zest, almond extract, and egg.

3. Work in flour mixture, a little at a time, then mix in almonds.

4. Shape into rolls 1½ inches in diameter, wrap in foil, and chill until firm, 12 hours or overnight.

5. When ready to bake, preheat oven to 375° F. Coat baking sheets with nonstick cooking spray.

6. With sharp knife, slice dough in rounds ⅛-inch thick. Arrange 1½ inches apart on baking sheets. Bake 8 to 10 minutes, until pale tan around edge.

7. Transfer at once to wire racks to cool.

Butterscotch Refrigerator Cookies

Makes about 4½ to 5 Dozen

✳

ANOTHER OF my mother's refrigerator cookies. The recipe dates to the 1930s.

2 cups unsifted all-purpose flour
½ teaspoon cream of tartar
½ teaspoon baking soda
Pinch salt
⅜ cup (6 tablespoons) butter
1 cup firmly packed light brown sugar
1 egg
1 teaspoon vanilla extract
½ teaspoon maple flavoring (optional)
½ cup finely chopped pecans

1. Sift flour, cream of tartar, soda, and salt onto wax paper; set aside.

2. Cream butter and sugar in large electric mixer bowl at medium speed until light; beat in egg, vanilla, and if desired, maple flavoring.

3. Work in flour mixture, 1 cup at a time, beating just enough to combine. Mix in nuts.

4. Chill dough about 1 hour or until firm enough to shape. Roll into logs 1¾ to 2 inches in diameter, wrap in foil, and chill until firm, 12 hours or overnight.

5. When ready to bake, preheat oven to 350° F. Coat baking sheets with nonstick cooking spray.

6. With sharp knife, slice dough in rounds ¼-inch thick. Arrange 1½ inches apart on baking sheets. Bake 10 to 12 minutes, until pale tan around edge.

7. Transfer at once to wire racks to cool.

Date Pinwheels

Makes about 8 Dozen

✳

DURING MY tenure at *The Ladies' Home Journal* in the late '50s and early '60s, we kept a supply of these heavenly cookies "on ice" for special occasions. And, of course, we included the recipe in *The Ladies' Home Journal Cook Book* (1960). This is my adaptation.

FILLING

½ pound pitted dates, snipped into small pieces
⅓ cup water
¼ cup granulated sugar
1 teaspoon fresh lemon juice

DOUGH

2 cups sifted all-purpose flour
½ teaspoon baking soda
¼ teaspoon salt
½ cup (1 stick) butter
1½ cups firmly packed light brown sugar
1 egg

1. FILLING: Simmer dates, water, granulated sugar, and lemon juice in small heavy saucepan over moderately low heat 5 minutes, stirring often; cool to room temperature.

2. DOUGH: Sift flour with soda and salt onto wax paper; set aside.

3. Cream butter with brown sugar and egg in large electric mixer bowl at medium speed until light. Stir in flour mixture.

4. Wrap dough in foil and chill until firm enough to roll.

5. Roll dough, half at a time, into 9- × 10-inch rectangles ¼-inch thick. Spread filling on rectangles, not quite to edges, and roll up snugly jelly-roll style. Rolls should be about 1½ inches in diameter.

6. Wrap each roll in foil and refrigerate overnight. Or store in freezer.

7. When ready to proceed, preheat oven to 350° F. Coat baking sheets with nonstick cooking spray; set aside.

8. Slice rolls of dough into rounds ¼-inch thick, arrange on baking sheets 1½ inches apart. Bake 8 minutes, until soft-firm.

9. Transfer at once to wire racks.

Chocolate Pinwheels

Makes about 3 Dozen

✳

THIS RECIPE is adapted from *All About Home Baking,* published in 1933 by General Foods Corporation (today a part of Kraft Foods, Inc.). The battered, splattered copy I now use belonged to my mother. And I'm sure many of the refrigerator cookies she developed (she was forever improvising) began with this slim volume. It was one of her Bibles.

1½ cups sifted all-purpose flour
½ teaspoon baking powder
⅛ teaspoon salt
½ cup (1 stick) butter or vegetable shortening
½ cup sugar
1 egg yolk
3 tablespoons milk
1 ounce unsweetened chocolate, melted

1. Sift flour with baking powder and salt onto wax paper; set aside.

2. Cream butter until light in large electric mixer bowl at medium speed, add sugar gradually, and continue creaming until light. Beat in egg yolk.

3. Add half the flour mixture, then the milk, then remaining flour mixture, beating well after each addition.

4. Divide dough in half and mix chocolate into one half. Wrap each batch of dough in plastic wrap and chill until stiff enough to roll.

5. On lightly floured surface, roll white and brown doughs into 6 × 12-inch rectangles ⅛-inch thick. Lay chocolate rectangle on white one, then roll up snugly, jelly-roll style. Wrap in foil and chill until firm, 12 hours or overnight.

6. When ready to bake, preheat oven to 400° F.

7. With sharp knife, slice dough in pinwheels ⅛-inch thick. Arrange 1½ inches apart on ungreased baking sheets. Bake 5 minutes, until beginning to firm up.

8. Transfer at once to wire racks to cool.

Calumet
Sugar Cookies

Calumet
Nut Cookies

Brownies

BAR COOKIES were apparently unknown until the twentieth century (unless you count shortbread). At least I could find no mention of them until the early 1900s. The original *Boston Cooking-School Cook Book* by Fannie Merritt Farmer (1896) does include a recipe for brownies, but these contain no chocolate; instead, they are "browned" with molasses and baked in fancy individual tins.

The very next year, writes John Mariani in *The Dictionary of American Food and Drink* (revised edition, 1994), "brownie" appeared in print in the 1897 Sears Roebuck catalog. The word, not the recipe, and only in a list of mail-order foods. Moreover, says food historian Meryle Evans, these brownies have nothing to do with the bar cookies we know and love today. They were candies named after J. Palmer Cox's elfin "Brownies," cartoon characters popular at the turn of the century.

The two earliest recipes I could find for *chocolate* brownies appear in the 1906 edition of *The Boston Cooking-School Cook Book* (with "2 squares Baker's Chocolate, melted") and in *Lowney's Cook Book,* written by Maria Willet Howard and published by the Walter M. Lowney Company of Boston in 1907. Lowney's, a manufacturer of chocolate and cocoa, informs readers in the opening pages that "You can eat freely of Lowney's Chocolate Bonbons because they are pure" . . . also that "Lowney's Cocoa is *all cocoa*" . . . and finally that "The Lowney products are *wholesome* as well as delicious."

Two chocolate brownie recipes appear in *Lowney's Cook Book,* and we set them down here exactly as they were written in the 1907 edition.

BANGOR BROWNIES

¼ cup butter	3 squares chocolate
1 cup brown sugar	½ to ¾ cup flour
1 egg	1 cup nut meats
¼ teaspoon salt	

Put all ingredients in bowl and beat until well mixed. Spread evenly in buttered baking pan. Bake and cut in strips.

A note in *Betty Crocker's Baking Classics* (1979) says that Bangor Brownies are probably the *original* chocolate brownies. Legend has it that a Bangor, Maine, housewife was baking chocolate cake one day and it fell. Instead of pitching it out, this frugal cook cut the collapsed cake into bars and served it, apparently with high marks.

Was that the beginning of brownies as we know them today? New York food historian Meryle Evans doubts it, believing this story, like so many others, to be apocryphal.

Some say brownies were invented by a woman named Brownie. Others that brownies are an Americanization of Scottish cocoa scones. Take your pick.

The real story isn't known, although to me the collapsed cake one is the most plausible. Whatever their true origin, brownies didn't become popular until the 1920s.

With twice the amount of butter and eggs, this second brownie recipe from *Lowney's Cook Book* is richer than Bangor Brownies. Again, it is reproduced exactly as it appears in that turn-of-the-century cookbook.

LOWNEY'S BROWNIES

½ cup butter
1 cup sugar
2 squares Lowney's
  Premium
  Chocolate

2 eggs
½ cup nut meats
½ cup flour
¼ teaspoon salt

Cream butter, add remaining ingredients, spread on buttered sheets, and bake ten to fifteen minutes. Cut in squares as soon as taken from the oven.

FUDGE SQUARES

½ cup butter
2 ounces Walter
  Baker & Co.'s
  Premium No. 1
  chocolate
3 eggs
1 cup sugar
¾ cup bread flour

½ teaspoon baking
  powder
½ teaspoon salt
1 cup chopped
  walnuts
1 teaspoon vanilla
  extract

Melt chocolate and add butter. Beat eggs, add sugar gradually and flour mixed and sifted with baking powder and salt, then add chocolate and butter mixture, nut meats and vanilla. Spread evenly in buttered shallow cake tins having mixture ½ inch in thickness. Bake in a moderate oven ten minutes. Remove from pans and cut while warm in two-inch squares.

By 1916, Miss Maria Parloa, a founder of the Boston Cooking-School, developed a number of chocolate recipes for Walter Baker & Company of Dorchester, Massachusetts—with all ingredients worked out by Miss Fannie Merritt Farmer in "Level Measurements to meet the needs of present-day demands." The recipes could not have been brand new because Miss Farmer died in 1915.

Included in this free leaflet of Baker's chocolate recipes were these even richer brownies. Fudge Squares, Miss Parloa calls them. Note that these brownies contain vanilla (as does the recipe in the 1914 "Fannie Farmer"). They also contain baking powder—a first, which produces more cakelike brownies.

Once women learned how easy brownies were to make, they couldn't get enough of them, and food company home economists were quick to oblige with new flavor combinations. Some brownies were frosted, some weren't. Some were layered. Some contained oatmeal, some raisins, some chocolate chips, some coconut, some peppermint instead of vanilla, some molasses in addition to chocolate (a link to the original Fannie Farmer brownies made with molasses?).

Other brownies contained no chocolate at all. The best, to my mind, are Blondies or Butterscotch Brownies. The earliest recipe for them I've found is in *Ruth Wakefield's Toll House Tried and True Recipes* (1936). Only she calls them Butterscotch Pecan Chews. Did she invent these as well as the chocolate chip cookie? I suspect she may have, although I can't verify it.

What follows is a collection of the twentieth century's very best brownie recipes, the chocolate and nonchocolate, the plain and fancy.

Fudge Brownies de Luxe

Makes about 2 Dozen

✳

FROM THE 1920s onward, nearly every general cookbook included at least one brownie recipe and the more recent ones offer several: chewy, gooey brownies for those who like them dark and dense, cakelike ones for those who prefer them lighter. My particular favorite is this recipe, which was tucked into packages of Baker's Unsweetened Chocolate in the 1950s. By then Baker's was part of the General Foods Corporation, a food company known for its busy test kitchens (and today, General Foods belongs to Kraft Foods, Inc.). I've saved this recipe all these years —it's *that* good.

4 ounces unsweetened chocolate
½ cup (1 stick) butter
4 eggs
2 cups sugar
1 cup sifted all-purpose flour
1 teaspoon vanilla extract
1 cup broken walnuts (I prefer pecans)

1. Preheat oven to 325° F. Grease 9 × 9 × 2-inch baking pan; set aside.

2. Melt chocolate and butter together over hot water; cool slightly.

3. Beat eggs until foamy, then gradually add sugar, beating thoroughly after each addition.

4. Blend in chocolate mixture; mix in flour, then vanilla and nuts.

5. Spread in pan, smoothing to corners. Bake about 40 minutes, until brownies begin to pull from sides of pan.

6. Cool to room temperature in pan on wire rack, then cut into squares or bars.

Hershey's Best Brownies

Makes about 3 Dozen

✳

IN *HERSHEY'S Centennial Classics*, a complimentary recipe booklet published by Hershey Foods in 1994 to commemorate the company's 100th birthday, there is a brownie made with cocoa powder. This one has also been updated for the Microwave Age. I've adapted this one also. But only the language.

1 cup (2 sticks) butter or margarine
2 cups sugar
2 teaspoons vanilla extract
4 eggs
¾ cup European-style cocoa powder
1 cup unsifted all-purpose flour
½ teaspoon baking powder
¼ teaspoon salt
1 cup chopped nuts (optional)

1. Preheat oven to 350° F. Grease 13 × 9 × 2-inch baking pan and set aside.

2. Microwave butter in large microwave-safe bowl on HIGH (100 percent power) 2 to 2½ minutes until melted.

3. Stir in sugar and vanilla, then by hand beat in eggs, one at a time.

4. Add cocoa and beat until well blended. Add flour, baking powder, and salt; beat well. Stir in nuts, if desired.

5. Pour batter in pan, smoothing to corners. Bake 30 to 35 minutes or until brownies begin to pull from sides of pan.

6. Cool to room temperature in pan on wire rack, then cut into bars.

Chocolate Syrup Brownies

Makes 16

✳

NOT ALL brownies are made with solid chocolate. In its *1934 Cookbook* (revised and updated in 1971), Hershey's printed this one made with its chocolate-flavored syrup. This is my adaptation.

1 egg
1 cup firmly packed light brown sugar
¾ cup chocolate-flavored syrup
1½ cups sifted all-purpose flour
¼ teaspoon baking soda
Pinch salt
½ cup (1 stick) butter, melted
¾ cup chopped pecans or walnuts

1. Preheat oven to 350° F. Grease 9 × 9 × 2-inch baking pan and set aside.

2. Beat egg in medium bowl until foamy, then mix in sugar and chocolate syrup, beating well to blend.

3. Stir together flour, baking soda, and salt; add to egg mixture, again beating until well blended. Fold in butter and nuts.

4. Spread in pan, smoothing to corners. Bake 35 to 40 minutes, until brownies begin to pull from sides of pan.

5. Cool in pan on wire rack, then cut into squares.

German's Cream Cheese Brownies

Makes about 20

✳

"THE ULTIMATE brownie," reads the Baker's German's Sweet Chocolate ad that appeared in the November 1967 issue of the late lamented *American Home* magazine. "The yummiest thing that's happened to brownies since nuts," boasts another ad of the time. Developed in the General Foods Test Kitchens in White Plains, New York, these marbleized brownies were inspired by that company's famous German Sweet Chocolate Cake (see page 454).

1 (4-ounce) package German's sweet chocolate
5 tablespoons butter
1 (3-ounce) package cream cheese
1 cup sugar
3 eggs
½ cup + 1 tablespoon unsifted all-purpose flour
1½ teaspoons vanilla extract
½ teaspoon baking powder
¼ teaspoon salt
½ cup coarsely chopped nuts
¼ teaspoon almond extract

1. Preheat oven to 350° F. Grease 9 × 9 × 2-inch baking pan and set aside.

2. Melt chocolate and 3 tablespoons butter in small heavy saucepan over very low heat, stirring constantly; cool and set aside.

3. Cream remaining 2 tablespoons butter with cream cheese in medium bowl until soft. Gradually add ¼ cup sugar, creaming until light and fluffy. Blend in 1 egg, 1 tablespoon flour, and ½ teaspoon vanilla; set aside.

4. Beat remaining 2 eggs in second medium bowl until thick and light. Gradually add remaining ¾ cup sugar, beating until thick. Add baking powder, salt, and remaining ½ cup flour. Blend in cooled chocolate mixture, nuts, almond extract, and remaining 1 teaspoon vanilla. Measure 1 cup chocolate batter and reserve.

5. Spread remaining chocolate batter in pan. Top with cheese mixture. Drop reserved chocolate batter from tablespoon onto cheese mixture, then swirl with a spatula to marbleize. Bake 35 to 40 minutes, until brownies begin pulling from sides of pan.

6. Cool to room temperature in pan on wire rack, then cut into bars or squares.

TIMELINE

1995

....

Gourmet launches the *Gourmet Club Network* on the Internet.

....

CondéNet inaugurates *Epicurious* on the Internet with recipes, restaurant reviews, etc., from *Bon Appétit* and *Gourmet*.

1996

....

A hipper Betty Crocker appears, a computer composite of seventy-five women.

....

Girl Scouts begin selling their cookies on the Internet; sixteen varieties are now available, including low-fat and no-fat.

....

For the first time a man wins the Pillsbury Bake-Off Contest and picks up the first $1 million Grand Prize.

Mammy's Chocolate Chip Brownies

Makes 2 Dozen

✻

THIS HEAVENLY recipe appears in *A to Z Bar Cookies* (1994), a splendid collection of brownies and bars written by my friend and colleague Marie Simmons. Marie says these "nothing fussy" bars come from her husband's grandmother, who'd been a dairy farmer's wife in northwestern New Jersey. "These bars have been a favorite treat for four generations of Simmons children."

2¾ cups sifted unbleached all-purpose flour
2½ teaspoons baking powder
½ teaspoon salt
⅔ cup vegetable shortening, melted
2¼ cups firmly packed light brown sugar (1 pound)
3 eggs, beaten
1 cup coarsely chopped walnuts
1½ cups semisweet chocolate chips

1. Preheat oven to 350° F. Lightly butter 13 × 9 × 2-inch baking pan and set aside.

2. Sift flour, baking powder, and salt onto piece of wax paper; set aside.

3. Blend shortening and sugar in large bowl. Gradually mix in beaten eggs, stirring until smooth and lighter in color.

4. Gradually blend in flour mixture; batter will be very stiff. Mix in walnuts and chocolate chips.

5. Spread in pan, smoothing to corners. Bake 25 to 30 minutes, until brownies begin pulling from sides of pan.

6. Cool to room temperature in pan on wire rack, then cut into bars.

Blondies or Butterscotch Brownies

Makes 16

✳

I DIDN'T taste a blondie until after World War II (with butter and sugar both rationed, there was precious little baking). Then one day in the late '40s, our Raleigh next-door neighbor introduced me to them—the best thing I ever ate. At that time, anyway. I believe she cut the recipe off a box of brown sugar, but I can't swear to it. I still have the recipe Eleanor Skaale gave me fifty-something years ago when I was at last old enough to solo in my mother's kitchen.

⅔ cup sifted all-purpose flour
1 teaspoon baking powder
½ teaspoon salt
¼ cup (½ stick) butter or margarine
1 cup firmly packed light brown sugar
1 egg
1½ teaspoons vanilla extract
1 cup coarsely chopped pecans

1. Preheat oven to 350° F. Grease 8 × 8 × 2-inch baking pan and set aside.

2. Sift flour, baking powder, and salt onto piece of wax paper; set aside.

3. Melt butter in saucepan over low heat, blend in sugar, and stir until sugar dissolves; cool 5 minutes.

4. Beat in egg and vanilla until smooth, then stir in flour mixture and pecans.

5. Spread in pan, smoothing to corners. Bake 30 to 35 minutes, until brownies begin pulling from sides of pan.

6. Cool to room temperature in pan on wire rack, then cut into squares.

Butterscotch Oatmeal Bars

Makes 16

✳

THIS BUTTERSCOTCH brownie recipe was printed in a '50s flier to publicize the new "Quickie Mix Cookie Method" developed by Quaker Oats home economists in the company's Chicago test kitchens. "It's sensational and revolutionary!" announces Mary Alden, the "Betty Crocker" of Quaker Oats. "No more creaming of shortening and sugar, and no slow tedious folding in of each separate ingredient. . . . Mixing time is only two minutes as compared to ten to fifteen minutes with the conventional method of mixing." These blondies have plenty of crunch thanks to the raw oatmeal they contain.

¾ cup sifted all-purpose flour
½ teaspoon baking powder
½ teaspoon salt
⅓ cup vegetable shortening (at room temperature)
½ cup firmly packed brown sugar
½ teaspoon vanilla extract
¼ cup milk
¾ cup uncooked rolled oats (quick-cooking or old-fashioned)
¼ cup chopped nuts

1. Preheat oven to 350° F. Grease 8 × 8 × 2-inch baking pan; set aside.

2. Sift flour, baking powder, and salt into a large bowl.

3. Add shortening, sugar, vanilla, and half the milk. By hand, beat until smooth—about 2 minutes.

4. Fold in remaining milk, oats, and nuts.

5. Spread in pan, smoothing to corners. Bake 25 to 30 minutes, until brownies begin pulling from sides of pan.

6. Cut into squares while warm, but cool to room temperature before removing from pan.

Recipe courtesy of The Quaker Oats Company.

Granola Bars

Makes 32

✳

GRANOLA—THE "hippie health food" of the '60s—has gone mass. This 20-minute recipe was developed by my good friend and coauthor Elaine Hanna, for *Micro Ways* (1990), our big, basic microwave cookbook that is now available in paperback.

    1 cup uncooked rolled oats
      (quick-cooking or old-
      fashioned)
    ½ cup wheat germ
    ⅓ cup sifted all-purpose flour
    ¾ cup coarsely chopped pitted
      dates, prunes, seedless raisins,
      dried apples, apricots, and/or
      figs (use any combination)
    ¾ cup unsweetened flaked
      coconut
    ¾ cup moderately finely
      chopped roasted peanuts
    ½ cup firmly packed light
      brown sugar
    ½ cup (1 stick) butter or
      margarine, melted
    2 tablespoons dark molasses
    1 teaspoon vanilla extract

1. Mix oats, wheat germ, flour, dried fruit, coconut, peanuts, and sugar in large bowl.

2. Mix butter, molasses, and vanilla in measuring cup, dump into dry ingredients, and stir well.

3. Spread mixture evenly in well-greased 11 × 7 × 2-inch microwave-safe baking dish, then pat firmly with wet hands.

4. Center on microwave oven rack or elevate on shallow bowl and microwave, uncovered, on HIGH (100 percent power) 5 to 6 minutes, turning dish 180° after 3 minutes, until lightly browned.

5. Let stand in uncovered dish on counter 10 minutes, transfer dish to wire rack, and cool 20 minutes. Score surface, marking off 32 bars, then cool completely in dish before serving.

Dream Bars

Makes about 3 Dozen

✳

YOU MIGHT call these gussied-up blondies. They were developed by home economists at the Pillsbury test kitchens in Minneapolis. The recipe was printed several decades ago in the booklet *Fun-Filled Butter Cookie Cookbook: 50 Recipes from Ann Pillsbury's Recipe Exchange Including Favorite Grand National Prize Winners.* With their toffeelike bottom and crunchy nut/coconut topping, these bars are indeed dreamy. They're easy to make, even easier to eat.

BOTTOM LAYER
    ½ cup (1 stick) butter
    ½ cup firmly packed brown
      sugar
    1½ cups sifted all-purpose flour

TOP LAYER
    3 eggs
    1½ cups firmly packed brown
      sugar

    ¼ cup sifted all-purpose flour
    1 teaspoon baking powder
    ¼ teaspoon salt
    1½ cups finely grated coconut
    1 cup chopped nuts
    1 teaspoon vanilla extract

1. Preheat oven to 350° F.

2. BOTTOM LAYER: Cream butter well in large bowl, then gradually add sugar, creaming all the while.

3. Work in flour until mixture resembles coarse crumbs. Pat firmly over bottom of ungreased 13 × 9 × 2-inch baking pan.

4. Bake 15 minutes, remove from oven, and set aside.

5. TOP LAYER: Beat eggs until foamy in medium bowl, gradually add sugar and beat until thick.

6. Sift flour with baking powder and salt and blend into egg mixture.

7. Stir in coconut, nuts, and vanilla.

8. Spread over baked mixture, return to oven, and bake 25 to 30 minutes.

9. Cool to room temperature in pan on wire rack. Using a wet, sharp knife, cut into bars.

Buttery Lemon Bars

Makes about 20

✳

THE TWO components of these luscious bars—shortbread and lemon curd—are old English favorites. But layering the two in a bar cookie is, I believe, a twentieth-century innovation. My friend and colleague Joanne Hayes, food editor of *Country Living* magazine, remembers lemon bars being tested while she was at *McCall's* magazine back in the '60s. Yet the *McCall's Cook Book* (1963) doesn't include them. Nor do other magazine cookbooks of that time. My hunch is that dessert specialist Maida Heatter popularized lemon bars. Two of her books offer variations on the theme. The more classic—Sour Lemon Squares (a brown sugar shortbread topped by lemon curd)—appears in *Maida Heatter's New Book of Great Desserts* (1982). Maida attributes the recipe to a friend in Scottsdale, Arizona. I wonder if that friend might have added her own touches to the 1970 *Sunset* magazine recipe adapted here, using, for example, brown sugar in the shortbread instead of confectioners'. Or was she the one who sent the recipe in to Sunset's "Kitchen Cabinet" column, a collection of reader recipes?

SHORTBREAD

1 cup (2 sticks) butter or margarine (at room temperature)
½ cup confectioners' (10X) sugar
2 cups sifted all-purpose flour

LEMON CURD

4 eggs
2 cups granulated sugar
1 teaspoon grated lemon zest
6 tablespoons fresh lemon juice
⅓ cup sifted all-purpose flour
1 teaspoon baking powder

FOR DUSTING

Confectioners' (10X) sugar

1. SHORTBREAD: Preheat oven to 350°F. Butter 13 × 9 × 2-inch baking pan and set aside.

2. Cream butter and confectioners' sugar in large electric mixer bowl at medium speed until light. Add flour and beat until well blended.

3. Spread mixture evenly over bottom of pan and bake 20 minutes.

4. LEMON CURD: While shortbread bakes, beat eggs in large electric mixer bowl at medium speed until uniformly liquid; add granulated sugar and beat until the color and consistency of mayonnaise, about 5 minutes. Add lemon zest and juice, flour, and baking powder and beat until smooth.

5. Pour lemon mixture over hot shortbread, return to oven, and bake 15 to 20 minutes, until pale golden.

6. Cool in pan on wire rack 10 to 15 minutes, then sift confectioners' sugar lightly on top. Cool completely before cutting.

Parky Waugh's Toffee Squares

Makes about 40

✻

THERE ARE many variations of these achingly sweet bars, which have been around for several decades. A particular favorite is this one from the Wellesley, Massachusetts, Cookie Exchange, which *Yankee* magazine published in its December 1982 issue. Parky Waugh makes her Toffee Squares with Hershey bars—she's quite specific about that. She's less so about the kind of nuts she prefers. I like pecans best, but think walnuts, lightly toasted, or chopped, blanched almonds or hazelnuts are powerful good, too.

1 cup (2 sticks) butter, softened
1 cup firmly packed light
* brown sugar*
1 egg yolk
2 cups sifted all-purpose flour
1 teaspoon vanilla extract
6 (1.45-ounce) milk chocolate
* bars*
⅔ cup finely chopped nuts

1. Preheat oven to 350° F. Grease 15½ × 10½ × 1-inch jelly-roll pan well; set aside.

2. Cream butter and sugar well in large bowl, then beat in egg yolk. Mix in flour and vanilla.

3. Turn mixture into pan, spreading to corners. Bake 15 to 20 minutes, until set but still soft.

4. Remove from oven, immediately arrange chocolate bars one layer deep on top, and let them melt about 1 minute. Spread melted chocolate evenly, sprinkle with nuts, and press gently into chocolate before it hardens.

5. Cool slightly, cut into 1¾- to 2-inch squares, then cool in pan to room temperature.

Chewy Scotch Squares

Makes 3 Dozen

✻

IN 1949, Pillsbury held a Grand National Recipe and Baking Contest in New York City, the beginning of the biennial Pillsbury Bake-Off Contest, which now offers a $1,000,000 Grand Prize. This recipe, submitted by Mrs. Cecil Ginanni of Carlsbad, New Mexico, and adapted by Ann Pillsbury (the mythical company spokeswoman), was a senior winner in Pillsbury's Fifth Grand National Recipe and Baking Contest in 1953. It was reprinted in a booklet titled *Fun-Filled Butter Cookie Cookbook: 50 Recipes from Ann Pillsbury's Recipe Exchange Including Favorite Grand National Prize Winners.*

¾ cup sifted all-purpose flour
1 teaspoon baking powder
¼ teaspoon salt
½ cup (1 stick) butter
1 cup firmly packed brown sugar

⅓ cup peach or apricot preserves or jam
1½ cups uncooked quick-cooking rolled oats
Confectioners' (10X) sugar (for dusting)

1. Preheat oven to 300° F. Cover baking sheet with aluminum foil, then turn edge up ½ inch all around; set aside.

2. Sift flour, baking powder, and salt onto piece of wax paper; set aside.

3. Melt butter in large saucepan over moderate heat. Add sugar and stir until dissolved.

4. Mix in preserves, then oatmeal, then flour mixture.

5. Spread dough in 6-inch square in middle of foil on baking sheet, then bake 25 to 30 minutes. Dough will spread during baking.

6. Cool 15 minutes, then dust with 10X sugar and cut into squares. Store in tightly covered container.

Pumpkin Bars

Makes about 3 Dozen

✻

I FIRST met pumpkin bars in the 1960s but have yet to find a better recipe for them than this one from White Lily Flour. This is my adaptation of the recipe that appears in *Great Baking Begins with White Lily Flour,* a little book published in 1983 to celebrate this Knoxville, Tennessee, company's centennial anniversary. In it are many of the recipes White Lily made famous throughout the South.

2 cups sifted all-purpose flour
2 teaspoons baking powder
1 teaspoon baking soda
1 teaspoon salt
2 teaspoons ground cinnamon
4 eggs
1 (16-ounce) can solid pack pumpkin (not pumpkin pie mix)
1½ cups sugar
1 cup vegetable oil
½ cup moderately coarsely chopped walnuts or pecans

1. Preheat oven to 350° F.

2. Sift flour, baking powder, soda, salt, and cinnamon onto wax paper; set aside.

3. Mix eggs, pumpkin, sugar, and oil in large bowl, beating well to blend.

4. Add flour mixture to pumpkin mixture, beating well to combine. Stir in walnuts.

5. Turn mixture into ungreased 15½ × 10½ × 1-inch jelly-roll pan and bake 15 to 30 minutes, until springy to touch.

6. Cool in pan on wire rack. Leave plain or, if you like, spread with a cream cheese frosting (pages 467 and 468). Cut into bars.

Apricot Squares

Makes 16

✳

WHAT MAKES these double-decker apricot squares so special is that the apricots are cooked before they go into the topping, which mellows their flavor and bonds them to the other ingredients. The recipe is adapted from *The New Good House-keeping Cookbook: America's Favorite Recipes* (1986), edited by former *GH* Food Editor Mildred Ying.

⅔ cup dried apricots
½ cup (1 stick) butter or margarine, softened
¼ cup granulated sugar
1⅓ cups sifted all-purpose flour
1 cup firmly packed light brown sugar
2 eggs
½ cup chopped walnuts
½ teaspoon baking powder
½ teaspoon vanilla extract
¼ teaspoon salt
Confectioners' (10X) sugar (topping)

1. Preheat oven to 350° F. Grease 8 × 8 × 2-inch baking pan; set aside.

2. Simmer apricots in water to cover in medium heavy saucepan 15 minutes; drain well, chop fine, and set aside.

3. Beat butter, granulated sugar, and 1 cup flour in large electric mixer bowl at medium speed until crumbly.

4. Pat dough evenly over bottom of pan and bake 25 minutes, until golden.

5. Meanwhile, beat apricots, brown sugar, eggs, walnuts, baking powder, vanilla, salt, and remaining ⅓ cup flour in large electric mixer bowl at medium speed until well blended, scraping bowl often.

6. Remove pan from oven, pour apricot mixture evenly over baked layer, and return to oven. Bake 25 minutes until golden.

7. Cool to room temperature in pan on wire rack, cut into 16 squares, and sprinkle with 10X sugar. Store in airtight container.

Date-and-Nut Squares

Makes 16

✳

THIS RECIPE, adapted from *Betty Crocker's Picture Cookbook* (1950), begins with a headnote: "Much like the Bishop's Bread served to circuit-riding preachers in days of Early America." These bars, however, belong to the twentieth century.

½ cup sifted all-purpose flour
½ teaspoon baking powder
½ teaspoon salt
2 eggs
½ cup sugar
½ teaspoon vanilla extract
1 cup coarsely chopped walnuts
2 cups finely cut dates

1. Preheat oven to 325° F. Grease 8 × 8 × 2-inch baking pan and set aside.

2. Sift flour, baking powder, and salt onto wax paper; set aside.

3. Beat eggs until foamy in medium bowl; beat in sugar and vanilla, then stir in flour mixture, then walnuts and dates.

4. Turn into pan, spreading to corners. Bake 25 to 30 minutes, until top has dull crust.

5. Cool in pan on wire rack 5 to 10 minutes, but cut into squares while warm.

6. Cool to room temperature before removing from pan.

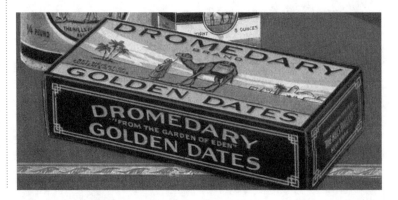

Venetians

Makes about 6 Dozen

✳

ARE THESE bar cookies or little cakes? Probably a bit of both. Whatever they are, *Family Circle* Food Editor Peggy Katalinich says, "They have been so popular with our readers we've had to print the recipe three times." Quite a tribute given the fussiness of the recipe.

NOTE: You must begin this recipe the day before you intend to serve the Venetians.

> 1 (8-ounce) can almond paste (not *marzipan*)
> 1½ cups (3 sticks) butter, softened
> 1 cup sugar
> 4 eggs, separated
> 1 teaspoon almond extract
> 2 cups sifted all-purpose flour
> ¼ teaspoon salt
> 10 drops green food coloring
> 8 drops red food coloring
> 1 (12-ounce) jar apricot preserves
> 5 ounces semisweet chocolate

1. Preheat oven to 350° F. Grease three 13 × 9 × 2-inch pans, line each with wax paper, and grease paper.

2. Break up almond paste in large electric mixer bowl with fork. Add butter, sugar, egg yolks, and almond extract. Beat at high speed until light and fluffy, about 5 minutes. At low speed, beat in flour and salt.

3. Beat egg whites in medium bowl to stiff peaks, then gently but thoroughly fold into almond mixture.

4. Remove 1½ cups batter and spread evenly in one pan.

5. Remove another 1½ cups batter to small bowl and mix in green food coloring. Spread evenly in second pan.

6. Tint remaining batter with red food coloring; spread in third pan.

7. Bake cakes 15 minutes until edges are faintly golden. (NOTE: Each cake will be ¼-inch thick.) Immediately turn cakes from pans onto large wire racks and peel off wax paper. Cool thoroughly.

8. TO ASSEMBLE VENETIANS: Place green layer on upside-down jelly-roll pan. Heat apricot preserves in small saucepan, strain, then spread half over green layer, all the way to edges. Top with yellow layer and spread with remaining preserves. Place pink layer, top-side-up, on yellow layer.

9. Cover with plastic wrap, weight down with large wooden cutting board or heavy flat tray, and refrigerate overnight.

10. Next day, melt chocolate in top of double boiler over hot water.

11. Trim cake edges evenly. Cut cake crosswise in 1-inch-wide strips. Frost top (pink layer) with chocolate. Turn strip on side. Frost bottom (green layer). Let chocolate dry. Cut strip into 1-inch pieces so you have rainbow bars coated with chocolate, top and bottom. Repeat with remaining strips.

TIMELINE

1997

....

C.C. Brown's ice cream parlor, "the home of the hot fudge sundae," which opened in 1906 on Hollywood Boulevard, closes.

....

The Kraft Interactive Kitchen lands on the Internet, bringing with it scores of recipes using such company products as Velveeta, Jello-O, Cool Whip, and Tang.

....

On Easter Sunday, Astronaut Shannon Lucid prepares Jell-O in drinking bags for the Cosmonauts aboard the Russian space station Mir. They like it so much she prepares Jell-O every Sunday thereafter during her 140-day mission.

....

The Food Network, American's first 24-hour television food channel, now reaches 20 million homes.

S'MORES

S'MORE IS a contraction of "some more"—as in "I want some more." Just what Girl Scouts demanded when making these graham cracker/marshmallow/chocolate sweets on cookouts back in the '60s. "They were definitely a Girl Scout thing," says my good friend and neighbor Anne Mead, who was a Girl Scout leader in the '60s and '70s.

In *More Back of the Box Gourmet* (1994), Michael McLaughlin says that since S'Mores "were supposedly invented by Girl Scouts, it seems to me that for proper flavor the marshmallows should be toasted over a smoky, open flame and for proper enjoyment S'Mores should follow a strenuous up-mountain hike and rousing campfire songfest."

Sara Moulton, now executive chef at *Gourmet* magazine, described her own technique for making S'mores. "First you toast the marshmallow, then you sandwich it between two graham crackers with a piece of chocolate. Or sometimes, you might poke a chunk of chocolate inside the marshmallow before you toasted it." Anne Mead adds that among her Girl Scouts, the chocolate "had to be Hershey's Milk Chocolate Bars."

In *More Back of the Box Gourmet*, Michael McLaughlin includes an indoor, open-face version of S'mores, which he says, was developed by Nabisco. It begins with Nabisco Graham Cracker squares. Each cracker is topped with a few semisweet chocolate chips, then a single large marshmallow, then it's popped into the broiler and left just long enough for the marshmallow to brown and melt.

Philly Fudge

*Makes about 5½ Dozen
1¼-inch Squares*

✱

FUDGE IS not a twentieth-century invention, but *fast* fudge is. This recipe, an adaptation of the famous uncooked fudge developed by Philadelphia Brand Cream Cheese, became popular shortly after World War II, is as foolproof as it is fast. And it never turns gritty.

> 1 (6-ounce) package semisweet chocolate chips
> 2 (3-ounce) packages cream cheese, at room temperature
> 2 tablespoons milk or cream
> 4 cups sifted confectioners' (10X) sugar
> 1 teaspoon vanilla extract
> ¼ teaspoon salt
> 1 cup coarsely chopped pecans or walnuts

1. Butter 9 × 9 × 2-inch baking pan well; set aside.

2. Melt chocolate chips in double boiler over hot, not boiling water.

3. Blend cream cheese and milk in large electric mixer bowl, beating at high speed until smooth. Add 10X sugar, ½ cup at a time, and beat at low speed until creamy.

4. Blend in melted chocolate chips, vanilla, and salt, beating until smooth. Stir in pecans.

5. Press mixture into pan, cover with plastic wrap, and chill overnight or until firm.

6. Cut in 1¼-inch squares.

Six-Minute Fudge

Makes about 6½ Dozen 1-inch Squares

✱

THIS ZIP-QUICK fudge from Borden Foods, made with Eagle Brand Sweetened Condensed Milk, is even richer than the cream cheese fudge that precedes. It, too, is velvety-smooth and never turns grainy.

> 3 (6-ounce) packages semisweet chocolate chips
> 1 (14-ounce) can sweetened condensed milk (not evaporated milk)
> ¼ teaspoon salt
> 1 cup coarsely chopped pecans or walnuts
> 1½ teaspoons vanilla extract

1. Line 9 × 9 × 2-inch baking pan with wax paper and butter paper; set aside.

2. Melt chocolate chips with sweetened condensed milk and salt in large heavy saucepan over low heat.

3. Off heat, stir in pecans and vanilla.

4. Turn mixture into pan, spreading to corners. Cover with wax paper and chill several hours or until firm.

5. Invert fudge onto cutting board and peel off wax paper. Cut into 1-inch squares.

6. Arrange on large dessert plate, cover with wax paper, and store at room temperature.

ONCE WORLD War II was over and sugar was plentiful again, cooks wasted no time making candy. The talk of the '50s—the recipe everyone had to have—was this fabulous fudge. Mamie Eisenhower's own recipe. It is printed here just as it appeared in *Who Says We Can't Cook!*, a spiral-bound collection of recipes published in 1955 by the Women's National Press Club of Washington, D.C.

MAMIE EISENHOWER'S MILLION DOLLAR FUDGE

> 4½ cups sugar
> Pinch of salt
> 2 tablespoons butter
> 1 tall can evaporated milk

Boil six minutes.
Put in large bowl:

> 12 ounces semi-sweet chocolate (chocolate bits)
> 12 ounces German sweet chocolate
> 1 pint marshmallow cream (2 jars)
> 2 cups nutmeats

Pour boiling syrup over ingredients in bowl; beat until chocolate is all melted, and pour in pan.

Let stand a few hours before cutting. Store in tin box.

BABY RUTH

THE CURTISS Candy Company, brainchild of Chicagoan Otto Schnering, got off to a shaky start on the eve of World War I with the launching of the Curtiss Milk Nut Loaf, the Curtiss Peter Pan, and Curtiss Ostrich Eggs. Though the candy was delicious, it simply didn't sell. Could it be that the names weren't appealing? After a few years of floundering, Curtiss sales started to rise, apparently all because of a new candy bar made of "roasted, then toasted" peanuts and "the richest chocolate from the East." In a stunning promotion stunt, Schnering hired pilots just home from the war and put them in biplanes to barnstorm America's cities and small towns, "bombing" them with thousands of candy bars that descended by parachute. The name of the candy? Baby Ruth. Most people today assume that the candy was named for baseball superstar "Babe" Ruth. But in 1920 no one would have made that error. Everybody knew, back then, that "Baby Ruth" was the daughter of President Grover Cleveland, beloved by the public and greatly mourned when she died of a fever at age twelve. In 1920 the "other" Babe Ruth had just joined the New York Yankees and had not yet become a celebrity. Whether because of the name, the airdrop, or the ingredients of the candy bar, by 1926 Baby Ruth was "the world's most popular candy," with more than five million sold every day.

California White Chocolate Fudge

Makes about 5½ Dozen
1¼-inch Squares

✳

WHEN WHITE chocolate became the chocolate of choice in the '80s, food companies scrambled to devise new ways of using it in tandem with their own products. One of the most successful recipes is this walnut-and-apricot-studded white fudge from Kraft Foods, Inc., which doesn't stint on sour cream, margarine, or marshmallow cream. White chocolate, for the record, is not chocolate. It's a blend of cocoa butter, sugar, and milk solids.

> *1½ cups sugar*
> *¾ cup sour cream*
> *½ cup (1 stick) margarine*
> *¾ pound white chocolate, coarsely chopped*
> *1 (7-ounce) jar marshmallow cream*
> *¾ cup coarsely chopped walnuts (or pecans, if you prefer)*
> *¾ cup coarsely chopped dried apricots*

1. Butter $9 \times 9 \times 2$-inch baking pan well; set aside.

2. Bring sugar, sour cream, and margarine to rolling boil in large heavy saucepan over moderate heat, stirring all the while. Insert candy thermometer and boil 7 minutes, stirring constantly, until mixture reaches 234° F.

3. Off heat, add white chocolate and stir until melted. Mix in marshmallow cream, walnuts, and apricots.

4. Pour into pan, spreading to corners. Cool several hours or overnight before cutting into squares.

Chocolate-Peanut Butter Fudge

Makes about 3 Dozen 1½-inch Squares

✻

FOR ITS twenty-fifth anniversary issue (December 1990), *Southern Living* printed its twenty-five most popular "sweet-tooth" recipes. Many of them had been submitted over the years by readers, among them this fudge from Carolyn Webb of Jackson, Mississippi. The recipe first appeared in the November 1987 issue. This is not a "fast fudge," but it teams chocolate and peanut butter, a thoroughly twentieth-century combination.

> *2½ cups sugar*
> *¼ cup unsweetened cocoa powder*
> *1 cup milk*
> *1 tablespoon light corn syrup*
> *½ cup (1 stick) butter or margarine*
> *1 cup coarsely chopped pecans*
> *½ cup cream-style peanut butter*
> *2 teaspoons vanilla extract*

1. Butter 9 × 9 × 2-inch pan well; set aside.

2. Mix sugar, cocoa, milk, and corn syrup in very large heavy saucepan and cook over moderate heat, stirring constantly, until sugar dissolves. Add 2 tablespoons butter and stir until butter melts. Cover, and boil 3 minutes.

3. Remove lid and cook without stirring until mixture reaches 234°F on candy thermometer.

4. Off heat, add remaining butter, pecans, peanut butter, and vanilla —do not stir. Cool 10 minutes.

5. Beat mixture until well blended. Pour into pan, spreading to corners.

6. Cool until firm and cut into squares.

Rocky Road Candy

Makes about 2 Dozen 1½-inch Squares

✻

THIS WAS the first candy I ever made. The recipe comes from my very first cookbook, *Young America's Cookbook* (1938), published by The Home Institute of *The New York Herald Tribune*. I was barely old enough to read and had to climb up on a stepstool to see inside the pan on the stove, so I'm surprised Mother let me try a candy that involved melting chocolate in the top of a double boiler. She kept an eagle eye out, to be sure. This was also my first encounter with "rocky road." To tell the truth, I've yet to find an earlier recipe for it, although I did discover, in my mother's 1923

edition of "Fannie Farmer," Chocolate Marshmallow Fudge (a traditional chocolate fudge into which quartered marshmallows are mixed after the fudge has been beaten until creamy). Not quite "rocky road," but a precursor, perhaps.

NOTE: Substitute ½ pound semisweet chocolate chips for the squares of chocolate, if you like, and 1 cup miniature marshmallows for the quartered full-size ones.

> *12 marshmallows, quartered*
> *½ cup coarsely chopped pecans or walnuts*
> *8 ounces semisweet chocolate*

1. Butter 8 × 8 × 2-inch baking pan and scatter marshmallows and nuts evenly over bottom; set aside.

2. Melt chocolate in double boiler over hot, not boiling water, stirring until smooth. Drizzle evenly over nuts and marshmallows.

3. Cool to room temperature and cut into 1½-inch squares.

SNAP! CRACKLE! POP!

T HE WORLD'S only talking cereal" talks, according to Kellogg executives, because when milk is poured on Rice Krispies, air bubbles trapped inside the puffs cause starches to rupture unevenly, producing an audible "snap! crackle! pop!" (but "piff! paff! puff!" in Sweden).

All children know that the sounds are made by the three little elves who appear on the cereal box and have been identified with Rice Krispies for more than a half century. These elves, introduced in the late '30s and redrawn in 1949 with nose and ears bobbed to make them "cuter," have inspired jokes, songs, jingles, and countless imaginary conversations. And even though official credit goes to Kellogg Kitchens for developing Rice Krispie Treats (the rice cereal/marshmallow bars at right), kids believe those elves help stir the pot.

Chocolate Truffles

Makes about 2 Dozen

✳

IN THE opulent '80s, not every chocolate would do. Truffles were the rage and the richer the better. This good basic recipe, my own, is nothing more than a thick ganache (chocolate/cream combo plus a bit of butter and flavoring). When cold, the ganache can be rolled into balls and dredged in anything you fancy: granulated or confectioners sugar, unsweetened cocoa powder, finely ground nuts, lightly toasted finely shredded coconut. Most will stick easily enough to the truffles, but to make sure, confectioners often dip truffles in melted chocolate (usually bittersweet or semisweet) before dredging. Truffles can only be as good as the chocolate that goes into them, so aim for the best. Confectioners favor such imports as Callebaut, Valrhona, and Lindt, all of which are available at high-end groceries.

> 6¼ ounces bittersweet or
> semisweet chocolate, coarsely
> chopped
> ⅓ cup heavy cream or a half-
> and-half mixture of heavy
> cream and evaporated milk
> 1 tablespoon butter
> 1 tablespoon vanilla extract or
> coffee, chocolate, fruit, or nut
> liqueur

1. Place chocolate in medium heat-proof bowl.

2. Heat cream and butter, uncovered, in very small heavy saucepan over moderate heat just until bubbles form around edge.

3. Pour hot cream mixture over chocolate and gently stir until smooth. If all chocolate does not melt, set bowl over—*not in*—boiling water and stir carefully until smooth. Mix in vanilla.

4. Strain mixture into medium bowl, cool to room temperature, then cover and chill until firm enough to shape, at least 4 hours.

5. With teaspoon, scrape up hardened ganache and roll into 1-inch balls. Dredge truffles, if desired, as described in headnote above, then arrange, not touching, on plastic-wrap-lined baking sheet; chill until firm.

6. Store in airtight container, separating layers with wax paper.

Chocolate-Raisin-Nut Bark

Makes 3½ to 4 Dozen Pieces

✳

THIS THREE-MINUTE microwave recipe was developed by Elaine Hanna, my coauthor both for the microwave column we wrote for the Los Angeles Times Syndicate and for our cookbook, *Micro Ways* (1990). It proves how much the microwave can simplify candy making.

> 1 (12-ounce) package
> semisweet chocolate chips

2/3 cup toasted blanched whole
almonds or hazelnuts
1/3 cup dark seedless raisins

1. Line 15½ × 10½ × 1-inch jelly-roll pan with wax paper; set aside.

2. Arrange chocolate chips in doughnut shape in 9-inch microwave-safe pie plate and microwave, uncovered, on MEDIUM (50 percent power) 2½ to 3 minutes, stirring after 2 minutes, until glossy.

3. Stir until smooth, mix in almonds and raisins, and spread thin in pan.

4. Chill until firm, then break into pieces.

Marshmallow Treats

Makes 2 Dozen

✳

ONE OF the most beloved recipes to come out of the Kellogg Kitchens in Battle Creek, Michigan. Kids, especially, dote on these crunchy rice cereal bars and learn to make them early on. With three ingredients only and no baking needed, they're a snap. And here's another plus: These cookies are low in fat (only 2 grams per bar).

¼ cup (½ stick) margarine
1 (10-ounce) package regular
   marshmallows or 4 cups
   miniature marshmallows
6 cups crisp rice cereal (not
   flakes)

M & M ' S

PEOPLE SAY—and believe—all sorts of things about M&M's. That green ones contain a secret aphrodisiac. (Not true.) That the chocolate candies really *won't* melt in your hand. (True.) That in 1995 when Americans were asked to pick a new color—blue, pink, or purple—more than ten million voted, and blue won, capturing 54 percent of the vote. (True.) That if you eat 999 brown ones you will turn into a frog. (Probably not true.) That red ones taste best. (A matter of opinion.)

Few new products capture the public fancy as M&M's did in the '40s. Inspired by a British candy called Smarties, Forrest Mars (son of the inventor of the Milky Way) and Bruce Muries (son of a Hershey's CEO) dreamed up a coated chocolate drop that wouldn't melt in hot weather, used their own initials as a name, and printed it on each candy to discourage imitators. M&M's were a welcome addition to GI rations during World War II, and the soldiers came home with a taste for them.

M&M, which merged with Mars in 1964, keeps tabs on which colors sell best. For M&M's plain chocolate candies, brown wins hands down, with 30 percent of those polled placing it first (yellow and red each get 20 percent, orange and green, each 10 percent, and the new "blues" are selling nicely). For peanut M&M's, added to the line in 1954, percentages are about the same except for green, favored by 20 percent, and tan, which nobody seems to like. Why not is another M&M's mystery.

1. Coat 13 × 9 × 2-inch baking pan with nonstick cooking spray; set aside.

2. Melt margarine in large saucepan over low heat. Add marshmallows and stir until completely melted. Remove from heat.

3. Add rice cereal and stir until well coated.

4. Using a buttered spatula or wax paper, press mixture evenly into pan. Cool before cutting into squares.

MICROWAVE VERSION: Microwave margarine and marshmallows, uncovered, in large microwave-safe mixing bowl on HIGH (100 percent power) 2 minutes. Stir well, add rice creal, and mix until well coated. Press into pan as directed.

COOKIE RECIPES

that Entered the American Mainstream
During the Twentieth Century with Their Source

....

(*Recipe Included)

❋

FRANCE
Palmiers
*Sablés
Tuiles

❋

GERMANY/AUSTRIA/
SWITZERLAND
Lebkuchen
Pfeffernüsse (Pepper Nuts)
Springerle
Spritz
*Vanilla Crescents
*Zimtsterne (Cinnamon Stars)

❋

SCANDINAVIA
Krumkaker
Pepparkakor

❋

RUSSIA/MIDDLE EUROPE
*Ruggelach
*Polish Tea Cakes

❋

ITALY
Amaretti
*Biscotti

❋

GREECE/TURKEY
Kourambiedes

❋

MEXICO/CARIBBEAN/
LATIN AMERICA
*Biscochitos

Ruggelach

Makes about 4 Dozen

❋

WELL KNOWN to those of the Jewish faith, these rolled, nut-filled cookies only became familiar to mass America during the '80s. This recipe is adapted from one I featured in a *Family Circle* article, "Melting Pot Masterpieces," that ran in 1986. The original recipe came from Dr. Gaya Aranoff Bernstein, a New York City pediatrician of Russian descent whom I profiled in the story.

NOTE: The dough must "season" overnight in the refrigerator, so begin the ruggelach the day before you plan to bake them.

DOUGH
   2 cups unsifted all-purpose
      flour
   ½ cup granulated sugar
   1 (8-ounce) package cream
      cheese, well chilled and diced
   1 cup (2 sticks) butter, well
      chilled and diced

WALNUT FILLING
   ¼ cup granulated sugar
   2 teaspoons ground cinnamon
   1 cup finely chopped walnuts or
      pecans

OPTIONAL TOPPING
   2 tablespoons confectioners'
      (10X) sugar

1. **DOUGH:** Mix flour and sugar in large bowl. Scatter bits of cream cheese and butter over mixture and using pastry blender, cut in until fine and crumbly. Gently work with hands just until dough forms; shape into 5 balls of equal size and wrap each in plastic wrap. Refrigerate overnight.

2. **WALNUT FILLING:** Mix all ingredients and set aside.

3. **TO FINISH RUGGELACH:** Preheat oven to 350°F. Roll dough, one ball at a time, on well-floured pastry cloth with well-floured stockinette-covered rolling pan into circle about 8¾ inches across. Using 8½-inch plate or pan lid as template, cut into circle, then with well-floured sharp knife, cut, pie-style, into 8 wedges.

4. Sprinkle 3 tablespoons filling evenly over each wedge, then roll up toward point.

5. Arrange ruggelach, points down, on ungreased baking sheets, spacing about 1 inch apart.

6. Bake 15 to 18 minutes in top third of oven, until uniformly tan.

7. Transfer at once to wire racks and cool. If desired, sift 10X sugar lightly over ruggelach. Store in airtight canister.

Sablés

Makes about 1½ Dozen

✳

AN OLD Norman specialty, these cookie "fans" are glossy but not very sweet.

COOKIES

½ cup (1 stick) butter (at room temperature) (no substitute)
⅓ cup sugar
1½ cups sifted all-purpose flour
¼ teaspoon salt
2 egg yolks, lightly beaten
1 teaspoon vanilla extract

GLAZE

1 egg yolk, beaten with 1 teaspoon cold water
Confectioners' (10X) sugar

1. Cream butter until fluffy in large electric mixer bowl at high speed, then cream in sugar.

2. Mix flour and salt and add to creamed mixture alternately with egg yolks; mix in vanilla.

3. Knead and squeeze dough in bowl about 4 minutes, until no grains of sugar are discernible; dough will be quite soft.

4. Divide dough in half, wrap each half in foil, and chill until firm enough to roll—3 to 4 hours.

5. Preheat oven to 375°F. Grease and flour baking sheets, tapping out excess flour. Set aside.

6. Using floured, stockinette-covered rolling pin, roll dough, a small amount at a time, on lightly floured pastry cloth to thickness of ¼ inch. Using floured, 5- to 6-inch-round cookie cutter, cut dough into circles, then quarter each circle, forming "fans" or wedges.

7. Transfer to baking sheets, spacing cookies 1 inch apart. Prick each cookie well all over with fork, brush with egg glaze, and dust with 10X sugar. Bake until pale tan, about 10 minutes.

8. Transfer at once to wire racks to cool, then store in airtight container.

Vanilla Crescents

Makes about 4 Dozen

✻

NOT SO many years ago I wrote a "Christmas in Munich" story for *Family Circle* magazine and included these melt-in-your-mouth cookies. They also appear in *The New German Cookbook* (1993), which I cowrote with Hedy Würz. The recipe here is an adaptation.

NOTE: To make vanilla-flavored confectioners' sugar, place sugar in airtight jar and in it bury 2 to 3 vanilla beans. Cover tight and let stand one to two weeks before using.

COOKIES

¾ cup plus 2 tablespoons (1¾ sticks) butter (at room temperature)
½ cup granulated sugar
2 egg yolks
3 teaspoons vanilla extract
⅛ teaspoon salt
1 cup finely ground blanched almonds
2⅔ cups sifted all-purpose flour

FOR DREDGING

1 cup vanilla-flavored confectioners' (10 X) sugar

1. COOKIES: Cream butter with granulated sugar, egg yolks, vanilla, and salt in large electric mixer bowl at high speed until light, 2 to 3 minutes. At low speed, beat in almonds and half the flour. Mix in remaining flour by hand.

2. Quarter dough and wrap each in plastic wrap. Refrigerate overnight.

3. Preheat oven to 375° F. Lightly grease baking sheets and set aside.

4. Roll dough, one-fourth at a time, into ropes 12 inches long. Cut each at 1-inch intervals and roll between palms into 3-inch logs, making each end pointed. Bend into crescents and space 1 inch apart on baking sheets.

5. Bake until pale tan, 12 to 15 minutes; lift at once to wire racks.

6. TO DREDGE: While cookies are still warm, roll in vanilla-flavored 10X sugar. Arrange on wire racks set over wax paper and sift remaining dredging sugar over all.

7. Store cookies airtight, separating layers with wax paper.

Zimtsterne (Cinnamon Stars)

Makes about 4 Dozen

✻

THIS RECIPE comes from my Munich friend Gertrud Schaller. The version here is adapted from *The New German Cookbook* (1993), which I coauthored with Hedy Würz.

COOKIES

¾ cup (1½ sticks) butter (at room temperature)
⅔ cup granulated sugar
2 teaspoons finely grated lemon zest
1¼ teaspoons ground cinnamon
¼ teaspoon freshly grated nutmeg
¼ teaspoon salt
2 egg yolks
1 cup finely ground blanched almonds
1 cup finely ground walnuts
1⅔ cups sifted all-purpose flour

ICING

1½ cups confectioners' (10X) sugar
3 tablespoons fresh lemon juice

1. COOKIES: Cream butter, granulated sugar, lemon zest, cinnamon, nutmeg, and salt in large electric mixer bowl at high speed until fluffy. At low speed, beat in egg yolks, then at lowest speed, beat in almonds, walnuts, and flour.

2. Halve dough, wrap in plastic wrap, flatten, and chill overnight.

3. Preheat oven to 350° F. Lightly grease baking sheets and set aside.

4. Working with half of dough at a time, roll between sheets of lightly floured wax paper to thickness of ⅛ inch. Slide dough onto metal tray and set in freezer 5 minutes.

5. Carefully peel off top sheet of wax paper. Using floured 2¾-inch star cutter, cut into cookies with bottom sheet of wax paper still in place.

6. With floured spatula, gently lift cookies from wax paper to baking sheets, spacing 1 inch apart. Bake until lightly browned around edges, 10 to 12 minutes.

7. Cool cookies on baking sheet 3 minutes, then lift to wire racks and cool 5 minutes.

8. ICING: Mix 10X sugar and lemon juice in small bowl, then with pastry brush, skim-coat tops of still-warm cookies with icing. Let icing harden, then apply second thin coat.

9. Once icing has hardened, layer cookies between sheets of wax paper and store airtight.

Polish
Tea Cakes

Makes about 3½ Dozen

✼

ANOTHER WONDERFUL cookie featured in my *Family Circle* "Melting Pot Masterpieces" portfolio in 1986. The recipe—which we know better as Thumbprint Cookies—is adapted both from *Family Circle* and from the original in *The Old Country Cookbook* published by the Iron Range Interpretative Center in Chisholm, Minnesota.

> *½ cup (1 stick) butter*
> *½ cup sugar*
> *1 egg, separated*
> *¾ teaspoon vanilla extract*
> *1 cup sifted all-purpose flour*
> *¼ teaspoon salt*
> *1 cup ground walnuts or pecans*
> *½ cup sieved raspberry or*
>   *strawberry jam*

1. Preheat oven to 325° F.

2. Cream butter and sugar until light and silvery in small electric mixer bowl at high speed; beat in egg yolk and vanilla, then stir in flour and salt.

3. Roll dough into 1-inch balls, dip in unbeaten egg white, then dredge in walnuts.

4. Space 2 inches apart on ungreased baking sheets. Press thumb deep into center of each cookie.

5. Bake 5 minutes. Deepen thumbprints with thimble or broad, rounded spoon handle. Bake cookies 8 to 12 minutes longer, until pale tan and firm.

6. Lift cookies at once to wire racks and when cool, spoon a little jam into each thumbprint. Store cookies in airtight container, separating layers with wax paper.

Biscotti

Makes 5 Dozen

❋

ADELPE VOLPI, a Napa Valley wine-grower's wife of Italian descent who gave me this recipe back in the 1970s, told me the way to eat these cookies was to dip them in wine. "Any kind of wine." In fact, she called them "wine sticks." Today biscotti are the "hot" cookie. They come any flavor—lemon, chocolate, even chocolate chip. And some are crumbly like shortbread. The best, however, are straightforward, crisp, and true to their Italian heritage.

3 cups sifted all-purpose flour
3 teaspoons baking powder
½ teaspoon salt
½ cup (1 stick) butter (at room temperature)
1 cup sugar
3 eggs
1 teaspoon anise extract
1 cup moderately finely chopped unblanched almonds

1. Preheat oven to 350° F. Lightly grease baking sheets; set aside.

2. Sift flour, baking powder, and salt onto wax paper and set aside.

3. Cream butter and sugar in large electric mixer bowl at high speed until fluffy, then beat in eggs, one by one.

4. Mix in dry ingredients, then anise extract and almonds.

5. With floured hands, shape dough into rolls 7 to 8 inches long and 1½ inches in diameter.

6. Arrange crosswise on baking sheets, spacing 2 inches apart, and bake until fairly firm and the color of ivory, about 20 minutes.

7. Remove from oven and while still hot, slice rolls crosswise and on the bias at ½-inch intervals. Raise oven temperature to 400° F.

8. Separate cookies. Arrange upside-down on *ungreased* baking sheets and bake just until crisp and pale tan, 2 to 3 minutes.

9. Remove at once to wire racks to cool. Store in airtight canister.

Biscochitos

Makes 6 to 7 Dozen

❋

THIS RECIPE was given to me by Dolores Gonzales who lived on the San Ildefonso Pueblo just north of Santa Fe. Spicy and crunchy but not too sweet, these were her favorite cookies.

COOKIES
6 cups sifted all-purpose flour
3 teaspoons baking powder
½ teaspoon salt
1½ cups sugar
2 cups vegetable shortening
1 tablespoon whole anise seeds
2 eggs
½ cup water

FOR DREDGING
½ cup sugar mixed with 1 teaspoon ground cinnamon

1. Preheat oven to 400° F.

2. Sift flour, baking powder, and salt onto wax paper and set aside.

3. Cream sugar and shortening in large electric mixer bowl at high speed until fluffy, about 3 minutes. Beat in anise seeds and eggs.

4. By hand mix in dry ingredients, then water. Dough will be stiff.

5. Divide dough in fourths, then roll, one at a time, to thickness of ¼ inch on lightly floured pastry cloth with floured stockinette-covered rolling pin. With floured 2- to 2 ½-inch cookie cutter, cut into rounds.

6. Space 1 inch apart on ungreased baking sheets and bake just until pale tan, about 10 minutes.

7. Remove at once to wire racks and while still warm, dredge in cinnamon-sugar.

8. Cool before eating. Store in airtight canister.

Getting Acquainted With Your G·E Range

GENERAL ELECTRIC

USERS MANUAL

PERMISSIONS

"Sugar Snap Peas with Scallions" from *Cook's Simple and Seasonal Cuisine* by the editors of *Cook's Magazine* (Judith Hill). Copyright © 1988 by *Cook's Magazine*. Reprinted with the permission of Simon & Schuster.

Time-Life Books Inc.: Adaptations of "Cioppino" and "Crab Louis" from *Foods of the World: American Cooking: The Great West* by Jonathan Norton Leonard and the Editors of Time-Life Books. Copyright © 1971 Time-Life Books Inc. Adaptation of "Philadelphia Cinnamon Buns" from *Foods of the World: American Cooking: Eastern Heartland* by Jose Wilson and the Editors of Time-Life Books. Copyright © 1971 Time-Life Books, Inc.

University of South Carolina Press: "Lady Baltimore Cake II" from *Two Hundred Years of Charleston Cooking* by Blanche S. Rhett with Lettie Gay. Published in 1976 by the University of South Carolina Press. Reprinted by permission of the publisher.

Joanne Woodward: Joanne Woodward's "Grapefruit Cake" is based on a recipe given to her by the Brown Derby. This version is reprinted by the kind permission of Joanne Woodward.

Workman Publishing Company, Inc.: "New Potatoes with Black Caviar" adapted from *The Silver Palate Cookbook* by Julee Rosso and Sheila Lukins. Copyright © 1979, 1980, 1981, 1982 by Julee Rosso and Sheila Lukins. "Leek Frittata" adapted from *The Silver Palate Good Times Cookbook* by Julee Rosso and Sheila Lukins. Copyright © 1984, 1985 by Julee Rosso and Sheila Lukins. "Lindy's New York-Style Cheesecake" adapted from *New York Cookbook* by Molly O'Neill. Text copyright © 1982 by Molly O'Neill. Reprinted by permission of Workman Publishing Company, Inc. All rights reserved.

The author and publishers also wish to thank the following for permission to reprint recipes:

American Heritage, The Archibald Candy Corp., The Association of Food Journalists, Sharon Bates, Gaya Arnoff Bernstein, Blue Diamond Growers, *Bon Appétit,* Brennan's Restaurant, California Avocado Commission, California Date Administrative Committee, Campbell Soup Company, Chasen's Restaurant, Conde Nast, Corning Incorporated, *Country Living, Daily News,* Dole Package Foods Co., *Food and Wine,* Frieda's, Inc., Frigidaire Co., *Gourmet,* Gary Goldberg, *Good Housekeeping,* Grant Corner Inn, Geraldine Griffith, Bruner + Jahr USA Publishing, Harry N. Abrams, Heinz USA, Martin Johner, Marjorie Johnson, Junior League of Corpus Christi, TX, Inc., Junior League of Monroe, LA, Inc., King Arthur Flour, Lake Isle Press, Lipton, Inc., *The Los Angeles Times,* Lyons & Burford Publishers, the Magnolia Grill, Martha White Company, McCormick & Company, Inc., Michael McLaughlin, Nabisco, Nana's Restaurant, National Broiler Council, Nestlé USA, North American Blueberry Council, Ocean Spray Cranberries Inc., Oxmoor House, Susan Peery, The Quaker Oats Company, *San Antonio Express News,* Southern Progress, Starkist, Sunkist Growers, Inc., *Sunset,* USA Rice Federation, Westinghouse Electric Corporation, White Lily Foods Company, Wisconsin Milk Marketing Board, and *Woman's Day.*

BIBLIOGRAPHY

BOOKS PUBLISHED BEFORE 1900

Bryan, Lettice. *The Kentucky Housewife* (1839); facsimile of first edition (1839) with an introduction by Bill Neal. Columbia, South Carolina: University of South Carolina Press, 1991.

Buckeye Cookery and Practical Housekeeping, edited by Estelle Woods Wilcox; Borealis Books facsimile of first edition (1880). St. Paul, Minnesota: Minnesota Historical Society Press, 1988.

Burpee's Farm Annual, 1888, Facsimile Edition. Philadelphia: W. Atlee Burpee & Co., 1975.

Cooke, Maud C. *Breakfast, Dinner and Supper.* Self-published, 1897.

Farmer, Fannie Merritt. *The Boston Cooking-School Cook Book.* Boston: Little, Brown & Company, 1896.

Gillette, Mrs. F.L. and Hugo Ziemann, Steward of the White House. *The White House Cook Book.* Chicago: R.S. Peale Company, 1887.

Hill, Annabella P. *Mrs. Hill's Southern Practical Cookery and Receipt Book;* facsimile of the 1872 edition with historical commentary by Damon L. Fowler. Columbia, South Carolina: University of South Carolina Press, 1995.

Lincoln, Mary J. *Mrs. Lincoln's Boston Cook Book.* Boston: Little, Brown & Company, 1883.

Parloa, Maria. *The Appledore Cook Book.* Boston: Graves and Ellis, 1872.

Randolph, Mary. *The Virginia House-wife,* facsimile of first edition (1824), with additional material from the 1825 and 1828 editions; historical notes and commentaries by Karen Hess. Columbia, South Carolina: University of South Carolina Press, 1984.

Ronald, Mary. *Mary Ronald's Century Cook Book.* New York: The Century Company, 1896.

Rorer, Sarah T. *Mrs. Rorer's Philadelphia Cook Book.* Philadelphia: Arnold and Company, 1886.

Rutledge, Sarah. *The Carolina Housewife;* facsimile of first edition (1847) with an introduction by Anna Wells Rutledge. Columbia, South Carolina: University of South Carolina Press, 1979.

BOOKS PUBLISHED 1900–09

A Book for a Cook. Produced by The Pillsbury Company, Minneapolis, 1905. Facsimile Edition. Bedford, Massachusetts: Applewood Books, 1994.

Capital City Cook Book. Published by Grace Church Guild. Madison, Wisconsin, 1906.

Christmas Edition, Gold Medal Flour Cook Book. Facsimile of Original 1904 Edition. Minneapolis: General Mills, Inc., 1977.

A Collection of Choice Recipes. Des Moines: The Ladies of Des Moines for the Benefit of the Des Moines Missionary Sewing School, 1903.

Farmer, Fannie Merritt. *The Boston Cooking-School Cook Book,* Revised Edition. Boston: Little, Brown & Company, 1906.

Good Housekeeping Everyday Cook Book. New York: Good Housekeeping, 1903.

Gregory, Annie R. *Woman's Favorite Cook Book.* Chicago, 1902.

Harland, Marion. *Marion Harland's Complete Cook Book: A Practical and Exhaustive Mannual of Cookery and Housekeeping.* Indianapolis: Bobbs-Merrill, 1903.

Howard, Maria Willett. *Lowney's Cook Book.* Boston: The Walter M. Lowney Co., 1907.

Kander, Mrs. Simon and Mrs. Henry Schoenfeld. *The "Settlement" Cook-Book,* Facsimile Edition of *The Way to a Man's Heart* (1903). New York: New American Library, 1985.

Lemcke, Gesine. *Desserts and Salads.* New York: D. Appleton and Company, 1907.

Rorer, Sarah T. *Mrs. Rorer's New Cook Book.* Philadelphia: Arnold and Company, 1902.

——. *World's Fair Souvenir Cook Book: Louisiana Purchase Exposition, St. Louis.* Philadelphia: Arnold and Company, 1904.

Southern Tier Mills Cook Book. Dedicated to the Users of "Mattie" Flour. Compiled by Mattie, Belle, Maggie, Jessie. Corning, New York, 1902.

Sowle, Henrietta ("Henriette"). *I Go A-Marketing.* Boston: Little, Brown, 1900.

BOOKS PUBLISHED 1910–19

Allen, Ida Bailey. *Mrs. Allen's Cook Book.* Boston: Small, Maynard & Company, 1917.

Campbell's Menu Book. Camden, New Jersey: Joseph Campbell Company, 1910.

Conservation Recipes. Compiled by The Mobilized Women's Organizations of Berkeley, Berkeley Unit, Council of Defence Women's Committee. Berkeley, California: Press of The Courier, 1918.

Dainty Desserts for Dainty People. Produced by Knox Gelatine. Johnstown, New York: Charles B. Knox Company, 1915.

F.W. McNess Cook Book. Freeport, Illinois: Furst-McNess Publishing, circa 1910.

Farmer, Fannie Merritt. *The Boston Cooking-School Cook Book,* Revised Edition. Boston: Little, Brown & Company, 1918.

——. *Catering for Special Occasions with Menus & Recipes.* Philadelphia: David McKay, 1911.

Helps for the Hostess. Camden, New Jersey: Joseph Campbell Company, 1916.

Hill, Janet McKensie. *Cakes, Pastry and Dessert Dishes.* Boston: Little, Brown, 1917.

Hiller, Elizabeth, O. *Fifty-Two Sunday Dinners: A Book of Recipes.* Chicago, New York, St. Louis, New Orleans, Montreal: N.K. Fairbank Company, 1910.

Hirtzler, Victor. *The Hotel St. Francis Cookbook.* Chicago: The Hotel Monthly Press, 1919.

Home Helps, A Pure Food Cook Book: A Useful Collection of Up-to-date, Practical Recipes by Five of the Leading Culinary Experts in the United States: Mrs. Mary J. Lincoln, Lida Ames Willis, Mrs. Sarah Tyson Rorer, Mrs. Helen Armstrong, Marion Harland. Chicago, New York, St. Louis, New Orleans, Montreal: N.K. Fairbank Company, 1910.

Howard, Maria Willet. *Lowney's Cook Book,* Revised Edition. Boston: The Walter M. Lowney Co., 1912.

The Key to The Cupboard. Published by the Ladies' Aid Society of the First Presbyterian Church of Waverly, New York. Waverly, New York: Free Press, 1910.

Larkin Housewives' Cook Book. Chicago: Larkin Company, 1915.

Rose, Mary Swartz. *Everyday Foods in Wartime.* New York: Macmillan, 1917.

BOOKS PUBLISHED 1920–29

Allen, Ida Bailey. *The Modern Method of Preparing Delightful Foods.* New York: Corn Products Refining Co., 1927.

———. *Vital Vegetables.* Garden City, New York: Doubleday, Page & Company, 1927.

Beverly Hills Women's Club Fashions in Foods. Beverly Hills, California: Beverly Hills Women's Club, 1929.

Every Good Cook Knows Another Good Cook. Cincinnati: Procter & Gamble, 1929.

Farmer, Fannie Merritt. *The Boston Cooking-School Cook Book,* Revised Edition. Boston: Little, Brown & Company, 1923.

Good Housekeeping's Book of Menus, Recipes and Household Discoveries. New York: Good Housekeeping, 1922.

Good Meals and How To Prepare Them. By the Good Housekeeping Institute. New York: Good Housekeeping, 1927.

Library Ann's Cook Book. Minneapolis: The Minneapolis Public Library Staff Association, 1928.

Los Angeles Times Prize Cook Book. Los Angeles: *Los Angeles Times,* 1923.

Wallace, Lily Haxworth. *Rumford Complete Cook Book.* Providence, Rhode Island: Rumford Company, 1928.

Ward, Artemas. *The Encyclopedia of Food.* New York: Artemas Ward, 1923.

Y.M.C.A. Cook Book. Grand Forks, North Dakota: Y.M.C.A., 1924.

BOOKS PUBLISHED 1930–39

All About Home Baking. New York: General Foods Corporation, 1933.

Ashley, Diana. *Where to Dine in '39 with 200 Recipes by Famous Chefs: New York Restaurant Guide and Cook Book.* New York: Crown Publishers, 1939.

Charpentier, Henri and Boyden Sparkes. *Those Rich and Great Ones or Life à la Henri being The Memoirs of Henri Charpentier.* London: Victor Gollancz, 1935.

Choice Recipes by Moscow Women. Moscow, Idaho: The Hospitality Committee of the Presbyterian Ladies' Aid, 1931.

Ellsworth, Mary Grosvenor. *Much Depends on Dinner.* New York: Alfred A. Knopf, 1939.

Farmer, Fannie Merritt. *The Boston Cooking-School Cook Book,* Revised Edition. Boston: Little, Brown & Company, 1930.

Food Economy: Recipes for Left-Overs, Plain Desserts and Salads by Mrs. Knox. Johnstown, New York: Charles B. Knox Gelatine Company, 1936.

Hershey's 1934 Cookbook. Produced by Hershey Foods Corporation, Hershey, Pennsylvania. New York: Western Publishing, 1971.

Heseltine, Marjorie. *The Basic Cook Book.* Boston: Houghton Mifflin, 1933, 1936.

Hibben, Sheila. *The National Cookbook.* New York: Harper & Brothers, 1932.

MacPherson, John. *The Mystery Chef's Own Cook Book.* New York: Longmans, Green, 1934.

Magic Chef Cooking. Kingsport, Tennessee: Kingsport Press, 1936.

The Maine Rebekahs Cook Book. Compiled by the Rebekah Assembly. Auburn, Maine: Merrill & Webber Company, 1939.

Meals, Tested, Tasted, and Approved. New York: Good Housekeeping Institute, 1930.

Metzelthin, Pearl. *The World Wide Cook Book and Menus and Recipes of 75 Nations.* New York: Julian Messner, 1939.

Moody, Harriet C. *Mrs. William Vaughn*

Moody's Cook Book. New York: Charles Scribner's Sons, 1931.

My Better Homes & Gardens Lifetime Cook Book. Des Moines: Meredith Publishing Company, 1930.

My Better Homes & Gardens Cook Book. Des Moines: Meredith Publishing Company, 1939.

Platt, June. *June Platt's Party Cook Book.* Boston: Houghton Mifflin, 1936.

Rombauer, Irma S. *The Joy of Cooking.* Indianapolis: Bobbs-Merrill, 1936.

———. *Streamlined Cooking.* Indianapolis: Bobbs-Merrill, 1939.

Waffles: How To Make 'Em and Take 'Em. Meriden, Connecticut: Manning, Bowman & Co., 1938.

Wakefield, Ruth. *Toll House Cook Book.* Boston: Little, Brown & Company, 1930.

———. *Ruth Wakefield's Toll House Tried and True Recipes.* New York: M. Barrows & Company, 1936.

Wallace, Lily Haxworth. *Woman's World Cook Book.* Chicago: The Reilly & Lee Company, 1931.

Watkins Cook Book. Winona, Minnesota: The J.R. Watkins Company, 1938.

Young America's Cook Book. Compiled by The Home Institute of the *New York Herald Tribune.* New York: Charles Scribner's Sons, 1938.

BOOKS PUBLISHED 1940–49

America's Cook Book, New and Revised Edition. Compiled by *New York Herald Tribune* Home Institute. New York: Charles Scribner's Sons, 1942.

Barber, Edith M. *Edith Barber's Cook Book.* New York: G.P. Putnam's Sons, 1940.

Beard, James. *Hors d'Oeuvre and Canapés* (The Classic Edition, 1940). New York: Quill Paperback, William Morrow, 1985.

———. *The Fireside Cook Book.* New York: Simon & Schuster, 1949.

Botkin, B.A. *A Treasury of American Folklore.* New York: Crown, 1944.

Brody, Iles. *The Colony: Portrait of a Restaurant—And Its Famous Recipes.* New York: Greenberg Publisher, 1945.

Cummings, Richard Osborn. *The American and His Food.* Chicago: The University of Chicago Press, 1940.

DeGouy, Louis P. *The Gold Cook Book.* New York: Greenberg Publisher, 1947.

DeWitt County Home Bureau Cook Book. Clinton, Illinois: DeWitt County Home Bureau, 1947.

Diat, Louis. *Cooking à la Ritz.* Philadelphia: J.B. Lippincott, 1941.

———. *French Cooking for Americans.* Philadelphia: J.B. Lippincott, 1946.

Dorris, Nancy. *Requested Recipes* (from *The News,* New York's Picture Newspaper). New York: News Syndicate Company, Inc., 1940.

Easy Ways to Good Meals: 99 Delicious Dishes Made with Campbell's Soups. Camden, New Jersey: Campbell Soup Company, 1949.

Farmer, Fannie Merritt. *The Boston Cooking-School Cook Book,* Eighth Edition, completely revised by Wilma Lord Perkins. Boston: Little, Brown & Company, 1946.

Five Hundred Favorite Recipes. Compiled by the Dorcas Society, Emanuel Evangelical Lutheran Church; Manchester, Connecticut, 1940.

500 Tasty Sandwiches. Edited by Ruth Berolzheimer. Reading, Pennsylvania: Culinary Arts Press, 1941.

Flexner, Marion. *Out of Kentucky Kitchens.* Preface by Duncan Hines. New York: American Legacy Press, 1949.

Foods that Rate at N.C. State. Compiled by The State College Woman's Club of the North Carolina State College of Agriculture and Engineering, 1948.

Fougner, G. Selmer. *Gourmet Dinners.* New York: M. Barrows, 1941.

Given, Meta. *The Modern Family Cook Book.* Chicago: J.G. Ferguson, 1942.

The Good Housekeeping Cook Book. New York: Farrar & Rinehart, 1942.

Good Things To Cook and How To Cook Them with Your Westinghouse Electric Range. Mansfield, Ohio: Westinghouse Electric & Manufacturing Co., 1940.

Herald Tribune Home Institute Cookbook. Compiled by the Food Staff of the *New York Herald Tribune.* New York: Charles Scribner's Sons, 1947.

Heseltine, Marjorie. *The Basic Cook Book.* Boston: Houghton Mifflin, 1947.

Hillstown Grange No. 87 Cook Book. East Hartford, Connecticut: Hillstown Grange No. 87, 1946.

Kirkl and Alexander. *Rector's Naughty '90s*

Cookbook. New York: Doubleday, 1949.

Macaroni Magic. Easton, Pennsylvania: George F. Hellick Coffee Company, 1945.

MacPherson, John. *The Never Fail Cook Book by The Mystery Chef.* New York: The Mystery Chef, 1949.

Platt, June. *June Platt's Plain and Fancy Cook Book.* Boston: Houghton Mifflin, 1941.

Reed, Anna Wetherill. *The Philadelphia Cook Book of Town and Country.* New York: M. Barrows, 1940.

Rombauer, Irma S. *The Joy of Cooking.* Indianapolis: Bobbs-Merrill, 1943.

———. *The Joy of Cooking.* Indianapolis: Bobbs-Merrill, 1946.

Sunset's Kitchen Cabinet Recipes, Volumes One, Two and Three. San Francisco: Lane Publishing Company, 1944.

Tracy, Marian and Nino. *Casserole Cookery.* New York: The Viking Press, 1943.

Wallace, Lily Haxworth. *The Lily Wallace New American Cook Book.* Assisted by fifty-four leading Authorities on Domestic Science and the Art of Modern Cooking. New York: Books, Inc., 1941.

Woman's Home Companion Cook Book. With Introduction by Dorothy Kirk, food editor, *Woman's Home Companion.* New York: P.F. Collier & Son, 1942, 1943, 1944.

BOOKS PUBLISHED 1950–59

Better Homes and Gardens New Cook Book. Des Moines: Meredith Publishing Company, 1953.

Betty Crocker's Picture Cook Book. Produced by General Mills, Inc. New York: McGraw-Hill, 1950.

Brown, Helen Evans. *Helen Brown's West Coast Cook Book.* Boston: Little, Brown, 1952.

Brown, Marion. *The Southern Cook Book.* Chapel Hill: The University of North Carolina Press, 1951.

Cabbage Patch Famous Kentucky Recipes. Compiled by the Cabbage Patch Circle, Louisville, Kentucky, 1952.

Cannon, Poppy. *The Can-Opener Cook Book.* New York: Thomas Y. Crowell, 1951.

Charleston Receipts. Published by The

Junior League of Charleston, Inc. Charleston, South Carolina: Walker, Evans & Cogswell Company, 1950.

Early, Eleanor. *New York Holiday.* New York: Rinehart, 1950.

Farmer, Fannie Merritt. *The Boston Cooking-School Cook Book,* Eleventh Edition, revised by Wilma Lord Perkins. Boston: Little, Brown & Company, 1959.

Fisher, M.F.K. *The Art of Eating: The Collected Gastronomical Works of M.F.K. Fisher* (including *How To Cook a Wolf,* 1942). Cleveland: World Publishing, 1954.

From North Carolina Kitchens, Favorite Recipes Old and New. Compiled by the North Carolina Federation of Home Demonstration Clubs. Raleigh, North Carolina: North Carolina State College Press, 1953.

The General Foods Kitchens Cookbook. Produced by the Women of General Foods Kitchens. New York: Random House, 1959.

The Gourmet Cookbook, Volumes I and II. New York: Gourmet Distributing Corporation, 1950 (Volume I) and 1957 (Volume II).

Harris, Florence LaGanke. *Vegetable Cookery.* New York: A.A. Wyn, 1952.

Hartley, Dorothy. *Food in England.* London: MacDonald, 1954.

Hill, Albert F. *Economic Botany.* New York: McGraw-Hill, 1952.

House & Garden's Cook Book. Contributors: James A. Beard, Helen Evans Brown, Eloise Davison, Ethel M. Keating, Jack King, Dione Lucas, Ruth A. Matson, Ann Roe Robbins, Dharam Jit Singh, Charlotte Turgeon, Myra Waldo. New York: Simon & Schuster, 1958.

Nichols, Nell B. *Good Home Cooking Across the U.S.A.* Ames, Iowa: Iowa State College Press, 1953.

Platt, June. *The June Platt Cook Book.* New York: Alfred A. Knopf, 1958.

Pyrex Prize Recipes. Corning Glass Works, Corning, New York. New York: Greystone Press, 1953.

River Road Recipes. By The Junior League of Baton Rouge, Inc. Baton Rouge, Louisiana, 1959.

Rombauer, Irma S. and Marion Rombauer Becker. *The Joy of Cooking.* Indianapolis: Bobbs-Merrill, 1951.

Rysavy, François and Frances Spatz Leighton. *White House Chef with Favorite Recipes of the President and Mrs. Eisenhower.* New York: Putnam, 1957.

Sardi, Vincent, Jr. and Helen Bryson. Foreword by Victor Borge. *Curtain Up at Sardi's.* New York: Random House, 1957.

Shouer, Louella G. *Quick and Easy Meals for Two.* New York: Henry Holt and Company, 1952.

Showalter, Mary Emma. *Mennonite Community Cookbook.* Scottdale, Pennsylvania: Herald Press, 1950.

The South Carolina Cook Book, Revised Edition. Collected and Edited by the South Carolina Extension Homemakers Council and the Clemson Extension Home Economics Staff. Columbia, South Carolina: University of South Carolina Press, 1953.

Sullivan, Lenore. *What To Cook for Company.* Ames, Iowa: The Iowa State College Press, 1952.

Vehling, Joseph D. *America's Table.* Chicago and Milwaukee: Hostaids, 1950.

Virginia Cookery Past and Present. Compiled by the Woman's Auxiliary of Olivet Episcopal Church, Franconia, Virginia, 1957.

Who Says We Can't Cook! By the Women's National Press Club. Washington, D.C.: Women's National Press Club, 1955.

Winkler, Max. *The Longchamps Cookbook.* New York: Harper & Brothers, 1954.

Zelayeta, Elena. *Elena's Secrets of Mexican Cooking.* Englewood Cliffs, N.J.: Prentice-Hall, 1958.

BOOKS PUBLISHED 1960–69

The American Heritage Cookbook and Illustrated History of American Eating & Drinking. New York: American Heritage Publishing, 1964.

American Home All-Purpose Cookbook. Edited by Virginia T. Habeeb and the Food Staff of *American Home.* New York: M. Evans, 1966.

Anderson, Jean. *Food is More than Cooking.* Philadelphia: Westminster Press, 1968.

Aresty, Esther B. *The Delectable Past.* New York: Simon & Schuster, 1964.

Bailey, Adrian. *The Cooking of the British Isles.* New York: Time-Life Books, 1969.

Beard, James. *Delights and Prejudices.* New York: Atheneum, 1964.

Better Homes and Gardens New Cook Book. Des Moines: Meredith Publishing Company, 1962, 1965.

Betty Crocker's Cookbook. Produced by General Mills, Inc., Minneapolis, Minnesota. New York: Golden Press, 1969.

Bracken, Peg. *The I Hate To Cook Book.* New York: Harcourt Brace & World, 1960.

Brown, Dale and the Editors of Time-Life Books. *American Cooking.* New York: Time-Life Books, 1968.

———. *The Cooking of Scandinavia.* New York: Time-Life Books, 1968.

Cannon, Poppy and Patricia Brooks. *The Presidents' Cookbook: Practical Recipes from George Washington to the Present.* New York: Funk & Wagnalls, 1968.

Child, Julia, Simone Beck, and Louisette Bertholle. *Mastering the Art of French Cooking.* New York: Alfred A. Knopf, 1961.

Claiborne, Craig. *The New York Times Menu Cook Book.* New York: Harper & Row, 1966.

Cook's & Diner's Dictionary with an Introduction by M.F.K. Fisher. New York: Funk & Wagnalls, 1968.

David, Elizabeth. *French Provincial Cooking* with Introduction and Notes by Narcissa G. Chamberlain. New York: Harper & Row, 1960.

Deutsch, Hermann B. *Brennan's New Orleans Cookbook.* New Orleans: Robert L. Crager, 1961.

Dull, Mrs. S.R. *Southern Cooking.* Revision of the original 1928 edition. New York: Grosset & Dunlap, 1968.

Farmer, Fannie Merritt. *The Boston Cooking-School Cook Book,* revised by Wilma Lord Perkins. Boston: Little, Brown & Company, 1965.

The Farmington Cookbook. Published as a fund-raiser for Farmington, an 1810 Federal-style home designed by Thomas Jefferson. Louisville, Kentucky: Courier-Journal Lithographing, 1968.

Favorite Recipes of The Lower Cape Fear. The Ministering Circle, Wilmington, North Carolina, 1964.

The First Ladies Cook Book (New Edition).

Historical Text by Margaret Brown Klapthor, Associate Curator, Division of Political History; Consulting Editor, Helen Duprey Bullock, National Trust for Historic Preservation; Culinary Expert, Dione Lucas. New York: Parents' Magazine Press, 1969.

Gordon, Elizabeth. *House Beautiful's Cuisines of the Western World.* New York: Golden Press, 1965.

Gourmet's Menu Cookbook. New York: Gourmet Books, Inc., 1963.

Hale, William Harlan and the Editors of *Horizon Magazine;* Wendy Buehr, editor; Tatiana McKenna, recipes editor; Mimi Sheraton, historical foods consultant. *The Horizon Cookbook and Illustrated History of Eating and Drinking through the Ages.* New York: American Heritage Publishing Co., distributed by Doubleday, 1968.

Hawkes, Alex D. *A World of Vegetable Cookery.* New York: Simon & Schuster, 1968.

Herter, George Leonard and Berthe Herter. *Bull Cook and Authentic Historical Recipes and Practices.* Hopewell, New Jersey: The Ecco Press, 1969.

Home Economics Teachers Favorite Recipes. Montgomery, Alabama: Favorite Recipes Press, 1967.

House & Garden's New Cook Book. By the Editors of *House & Garden.* New York: Simon & Schuster, 1967.

House Beautiful's Cuisines of the Eastern World. Edited by William Laas. New York: Golden Press, 1967.

James, Ted and Rosalind Cole. *Waldorf-Astoria Cookbook.* Indianapolis: Bobbs-Merrill, 1969.

Kropotkin, Alexandra. *The Best of Russian Cooking.* New York: Charles Scribner's Sons, 1964.

Ladies' Home Journal Cookbook. Carol Truax, editor. New York: Doubleday, 1960.

Larousse Gastronomique. Charlotte Turgeon and Nina Froud, editors. New York: Crown, 1961.

Longstreet, Stephen and Ethel. *A Salute to American Cooking.* New York: Hawthorne Books, 1968.

Maryland's Way: The Hammond-Harwood House Cook Book. Annapolis, Maryland: The Hammond-Harwood House Association, 1963.

McCall's Cook Book. By the Food Editors of *McCall's.* New York: Random House, 1963.

McCully, Helen. *Nobody Ever Tells You These Things about Food and Drink.* New York: Holt, Rinehart and Winston, 1967.

Mead, Anne. *Please Kiss the Cook.* New York: Anne Mead, 1964.

Muscatine, Doris. *A Cook's Tour of San Francisco.* New York: Charles Scribner's Sons, 1963.

The New Good Housekeeping Cookbook. Edited by Dorothy B. Marsh, director of foods and cookery, Good Housekeeping Institute. New York: Harcourt, Brace & World, 1963.

The New York Times Cook Book. Edited by Craig Claiborne. New York: Harper & Row, 1961.

Ortiz, Elisabeth Lambert. *The Complete Book of Mexican Cooking.* New York: M. Evans, 1965.

Paddleford, Clementine. *How America Eats.* New York: Charles Scribner's Sons, 1960.

Patrick, Ted and Silas Spitzer. *Great Restaurants of America.* New York: Bramhall House, 1960.

Peck, Paula. *Paula Peck's Art of Good Cooking.* New York: Simon & Schuster, 1961.

———. *The Art of Fine Baking.* New York: Simon & Schuster, 1961.

Penn Family Recipes: Cooking Recipes of William Penn's Wife Gulielma. Facsimile edition, edited by Evelyn Abraham Benson. York, Pennsylvania: George Shumway, 1966.

Restaurants & Recipes of New York, New Jersey, Connecticut. Produced by Research Unlimited, Inc., Fort Lauderdale, Florida. Edited by Leonce Picot, Text by Kay Daniel Picot. New York: Davis, Delaney, 1964.

Ridley, Helen E. *The Ritz-Carlton Cook Book and Guide to Home Entertaining,* Philadelphia and New York: J.B. Lippincott, 1968.

Rombauer, Irma S. and Marion Rombauer Becker. *Joy of Cooking.* Indianapolis: Bobbs-Merrill, 1963.

Rudkin, Margaret. *The Margaret Rudkin Pepperidge Farm Cookbook.* New York: Grosset & Dunlap, 1963.

The Settlement Cook Book. Revised, newly organized, enlarged edition. New York: Simon & Schuster, 1965.

Spices of the World Cookbook: Recipes from the Simple to the Exotic Tested in the Kitchens of McCormick. New York: McGraw-Hill, 1964.

The Sunset Cook Book. By the Editors of *Sunset* magazine. Menlo Park, California: Lane Book Company, 1960.

Taylor, Clara Mae and Orrea Florence Pye. *Foundations of Nutrition,* Sixth Edition. New York: Macmillan, 1966.

Thomas, Lately. *Delmonico's: A Century of Splendor.* Boston: Houghton Mifflin, 1967.

Wason, Betty. *Cooks, Gluttons, and Gourmets.* Garden City, New York: Doubleday, 1962.

Wolcott, Imogene. *The Yankee Cook Book,* New Edition. New York: Ives, Washburn, 1963.

Woman's Day Encyclopedia of Cookery, Volumes 1 through 12. Nika Standen Hazelton, editor. New York: Fawcett Publications, 1965–66.

BOOKS PUBLISHED 1970–79

A Guide to Creative Gel Cookery. Johnstown, New York: Knox Gelatine, Inc., 1972.

Adams, Charlotte. *The Four Seasons Cookbook;* Special Consultant: James Beard. New York: A Ridge Press Book, Holt, Rinehart and Winston, 1971.

Anderson, Jean. *The Grass Roots Cookbook.* New York: Times Books, 1974.

———, and Elaine Hanna. *The Doubleday Cookbook.* New York: Doubleday, 1975.

Aunt Sammy's Radio Recipes: The Great Depression Cook-book. Edited by Martin Greif. New York: Universe Books, 1975.

Batterberry, Michael and Ariane. *On the Town in New York from 1776 to the Present.* New York: Charles Scribner's Sons, 1973.

Beard, James. *James Beard's American Cookery.* Boston: Little, Brown, 1972.

Better Homes and Gardens All-Time Favorite Pies. Des Moines: Meredith Publishing Company, 1978.

Better Homes and Gardens Heritage Cook Book. Des Moines: Meredith Publishing Company, 1975.

Better Homes and Gardens Mexican Cook Book. Des Moines: Meredith Publishing Company, 1977.

Better Homes and Gardens New Cook Book. Des Moines: Meredith Publishing Company, 1976.

Betty Crocker's Baking Classics. Published by General Mills, Inc. New York: Random House, 1979.

Betty Crocker's Cookbook. Produced by General Mills, Inc. New York: Golden Press, 1971.

Borghese, Anita. *Food from Harvest Festivals and Folk Fairs.* New York: Thomas Y. Crowell, 1977.

The Carolina Collection. Produced by The Junior League of Fayetteville, Inc., Fayetteville, North Carolina, 1978.

The Charlotte Cookbook. Published by the Charlotte Junior League, Inc., Charlotte, North Carolina, 1971.

Child, Julia and Simone Beck. *Mastering the Art of French Cooking, Volume Two.* New York: Alfred A. Knopf, 1970.

Claiborne, Craig. *Craig Claiborne's Favorites from The New York Times, Volume 3.* New York: Times Books, 1977.

———. *Craig Claiborne's Favorites from The New York Times, Volume 4.* New York: Times Books, 1978.

Collin, Rima and Richard. *The New Orleans Cookbook.* New York: Alfred A. Knopf, 1979.

The Cooking Book. Produced by The Junior League of Louisville, Inc., Louisville, Kentucky, 1978.

The Cotton Country Collection. Published by The Junior League of Monroe, Inc., Monroe, Louisiana, 1972.

Darden, Norma Jean and Carole. *Spoonbread and Strawberry Wine.* Garden City, New York: Doubleday, 1978.

David, Elizabeth. *English Bread and Yeast Cookery,* American Edition with notes by Karen Hess. New York: Viking, 1977.

Davidson, Alan. *North Atlantic Seafood.* New York: Viking, 1979.

DeBolt, Margaret Wayt with Emma Rylander Law. *Savannah Sampler Cookbook.* Norfolk, Virginia: Donning, 1978.

The Dessert Collector. Hershey, Pennsylvania: Hershey Foods Corporation, 1978.

Dickson, Paul. *The Great American Ice*

Cream Book. New York: Atheneum, 1972.

DuBose, Sybil. *The Pastors Wives Cookbook.* Memphis, Tennessee: Wimmer Brothers Books, 1978.

The Family Circle Cookbook. By the Food Editors of *Family Circle* magazine and Jean Anderson. New York: The Family Circle, Inc. NYT, 1974.

Favorite American Regional Recipes. Marian Tracy, editor. An unabridged and corrected republication of *Coast to Coast Cookery* published in 1952 by the Indiana University Press, Bloomington, Indiana. New York: Dover Publications, 1976.

Feibleman, Peter S. *American Cooking: Creole and Acadian.* New York: Time-Life Books, 1971.

Field, Michael. *All Manner of Food.* New York: Alfred A. Knopf, 1970.

————. *Cooking Adventures with Michael Field,* Eight-Volume Series: *Breads, Biscuits, and Cakes; Pies, Tarts, and Chou Puffs; Pancakes, Waffles, Omelets, and Crêpes; Fried, Deep-Fried, and Sautéed Dishes; Boiled, Poached, and Steamed Foods; Broiled Meats, Chicken, Fish, and Vegetables; Roasted and Braised Dishes,* by Helen McCully; *Soufflés, Mousses, and Creams* by Helen McCully. Garden City, New York: Nelson Doubleday, 1971, 1972.

Fiesta: Favorite Recipes of South Texas. Published by The Junior League of Corpus Christi, Inc., Corpus Christi, Texas, 1973.

The Good Housekeeping Cook Book. Edited by Zoe Coulson, director of foods and cookery, Good Housekeeping Institute. New York: Good Housekeeping Books, 1973.

Great Recipes from The New York Times. Edited by Raymond Sokolov. New York: Weathervane Books, 1973.

Grigson, Jane. *Jane Grigson's Vegetable Book.* New York: Atheneum, 1979.

Hazan, Marcella. *The Classic Italian Cook Book.* New York: Harper's Magazine Press, 1973.

Hazelton, Nika. *The Unabridged Vegetable Cookbook.* New York: M. Evans & Company, 1976.

Heatter, Maida. *Maida Heatter's Book of Great Cookies.* New York: Alfred A. Knopf, 1977.

Hershey's Cocoa Cookbook. Produced by Hershey Chocolate Company, a Division of Hershey Foods Corporation, Hershey, Pennsylvania. New York: Western Publishing, 1979.

Hess, John L. and Karen. *The Taste of America.* New York: Viking/Grossman, 1977.

Hewitt, Jean. *The New York Times Heritage Cook Book.* New York: Bonanza Books, 1977.

Jones, Evan. *American Food: The Gastronomic Story.* New York: E.P. Dutton, 1975.

————. *A Food Lover's Companion.* New York: Harper & Row, 1979.

Kennedy, Diana. *The Cuisines of Mexico* with a Foreword by Craig Claiborne. New York: Harper & Row, 1972.

The Knox Gelatine Cookbook. Produced by Rutledge Books. New York: The Benjamin Company, 1977.

Kreidberg, Marjorie. *Food on the Frontier: Minnesota Cooking from 1850 to 1900 with Selected Recipes.* St. Paul: Minnesota Historical Press, 1975.

Lang, George. *The Cuisine of Hungary.* New York: Atheneum, 1971.

Leonard, Jonathan Norton and the Editors of Time-Life Books. *American Cooking: The Great West.* New York: Time-Life Books, 1971.

Lewis, Edna. *The Taste of Country Cooking.* New York: Alfred A. Knopf, 1976.

McClane, A.J., photography by Arie de Zanger. *The Encyclopedia of Fish Cookery.* New York: Holt, Rhinehart and Winston, 1977.

Mealtime Mastery. Produced by the American Dairy Association, Rosemont, Illinois, 1976.

Myers, Barbara. *Woman's Day Old-Fashioned Desserts.* Philadelphia and New York: J.B. Lippincott, 1978.

The New Larousse Gastronomique, Charlotte Turgeon, American Editor. New York: Crown, 1977.

New York Entertains. Produced by The Junior League of the City of New York, Inc. Garden City, New York: Doubleday, 1974.

Of Pots and Pipkins: Recipes from The Junior League of Roanoke Valley, Virginia, Inc. Roanoke, Virginia: Stone Printing Company, 1971.

Recipes America Loves Best. By the Food Editors of *Family Circle* magazine. New York: Times Books, 1982.

River Road Recipes II: A Second Helping. By The Junior League of Baton Rouge, Inc., Baton Rouge, Louisiana, 1976.

Rombauer, Irma S. and Marion Rombauer Becker. *Joy of Cooking.* Indianapolis: Bobbs-Merrill, 1975.

Root, Waverley and Richard de Rochemont. *Eating in America.* New York: William Morrow, 1976.

Rosso, Julee and Sheila Lukins with Michael McLaughlin. *The Silver Palate Cookbook.* New York: Workman, 1979.

Sandisfield Cookery: Recipes from a Unique Berkshire County Town. Produced by the Staff of the Sandisfield Historical Society, Sandisfield, Massachusetts. Ellington, Connecticut: K & R Printing, 1976.

Seranne, Ann. *Ann Seranne's Good Food with a Blender.* New York: William Morrow, 1974.

Simon, André L. and Robin Howe. *Dictionary of Gastronomy.* New York: McGraw-Hill, 1970.

The Southern Junior League Cookbook. Edited by Ann Seranne. New York: David McKay, 1977.

Spices of The World Cookbook, Revised Edition. Produced by McCormick and Company. New York: McGraw-Hill, 1979.

Stern, Jane and Michael. *Roadfood.* New York: Random House, 1977.

Sturges, Lena E. *Southern Living: Our Best Recipes.* Birmingham, Alabama: Oxmoor House, 1970.

Trager, James. *Foodbook.* New York: Grossman, 1970.

Two Hundred Years of Charleston Cooking. Recipes gathered by Blanche S. Rhett. Edited by Lettie Gay. Columbia, South Carolina: University of South Carolina Press, 1976.

Voltz, Jeanne A. *The Flavor of the South.* New York: Doubleday, 1977.

Wilson, José and the Editors of Time-Life Books. *American Cooking: The Eastern Heartland.* New York: Time-Life Books, 1971.

Winning Sandwiches for Menu Makers. Produced by the Wheat Flour Institute, edited by Kathleen M. Thomas. Boston: Cahners Books International, 1976.

The World Atlas of Food, Jane Grigson, contributing editor. London: Mitchell Beazley Publishers, and New York: Simon & Schuster, 1974.

Yankee Magazine's Favorite New England Recipes. Compiled by Sara B.B. Stamm and the Lady Editors of *Yankee* magazine. Dublin, New Hampshire: Yankee, Inc., 1972.

BOOKS PUBLISHED 1980–89

Ida Bailey Allen. *Best Loved Recipes of the American People.* New York: Doubleday, 1982.

Anderson, Jean. *Jean Anderson Cooks.* New York: William Morrow, 1982.

————, and Elaine Hanna. *The New Doubleday Cookbook.* New York: Doubleday, 1985.

————. *The Food of Portugal.* New York: William Morrow, 1986.

Anderson, Kenneth. *The Pocket Guide to Coffees & Teas.* New York: Perigee, 1982.

Auburn Entertains. Compiled by Helen Baggett, Jeanne Blackwell, and Lucy Littleton. Nashville, Tennessee: Rutledge Hill Press, 1983.

Bayless, Rick with Deann Groen Bayless. *Authentic Mexican: Regional Cooking from the Heart of Mexico.* New York: William Morrow, 1987.

Beck, Bruce. *The Official Fulton Fish Market Cookbook.* New York: E.P. Dutton, 1989.

Benenson, Sharen. *The New York Botanical Garden Cookbook.* New York: The Council of the New York Botanical Garden, 1981.

Beranbaum, Rose Levy. *The Cake Bible.* New York: William Morrow, 1988.

Berger, Frances de Talavera and John Parke Custis. *Sumptuous Dining in Gaslight San Francisco: 1875–1915.* New York: Doubleday, 1985.

Best of Beef, Volume III: 261 Prize Winning National Beef Cook-Off Recipes. Recipes compiled by American National Cattle-Women, Inc., Englewood, Colorado, 1988 in cooperation with The Beef Industry Council and Cattlemen's Beef Promotion and Research Board.

The Best of Family Circle Cookbook. By the Editors of *Family Circle.* New York: The Family Circle, Inc., 1985.

The Best of Food & Wine: 1985 through 1989 Collections. New York: American Express Publishing.

The Best of Gourmet, Volume IV. Produced by the Editors of *Gourmet.* New York: Condé Nast Books/Random House, 1989.

Bethabara Moravian Cook Book, Seventh Edition. Compiled by Women's Fellowship, Bethabara Moravian Church; Winston-Salem, North Carolina, 1981.

Betty Crocker's Cookbook, New and Revised Edition. Produced by General Mills, Inc., Minneapolis, Minnesota. New York: Golden Press, 1986.

Bon Appétit Recipe Yearbook 1987: Editors' Choice of Recipes from 1986. Los Angeles: The Knapp Press, 1987.

Brennan, Georgeanne, Isaac Cronin, and Charlotte Glenn. *The New American Vegetable Cookbook: The Definitive Guide to America's Exotic & Traditional Vegetables.* Berkeley, California: Aris Books, 1985.

Bryant, Carol A., Anita Courtney, Barbara A. Markesbery, and Kathleen M. DeWalt. *The Cultural Feast.* St. Paul: West Publishing, 1985.

Butel, Jane. *Jane Butel's Tex-Mex Cookbook.* New York: Harmony Books, 1980.

Butter 'n' Love Recipes. Produced by the Crossnore Presbyterian Church, Crossnore, North Carolina. Pleasanton, Kansas: Fundcraft Publishing, 1982.

California Cooking. Produced by The Art Council, Los Angeles County Museum of Art. New York: Clarkson N. Potter, 1986.

Celebrations on the Bayou. Produced by The Junior League of Monroe, Inc. Monroe, Louisiana: Cotton Bayou Publications, 1989.

Charleston Recollections and Receipts: Rose P. Ravenel's Cookbook. Edited by Elizabeth Ravenel Harrigan. Columbia, South Carolina: University of South Carolina Press, 1989.

Charleston Receipts Repeats. Published by The Junior League of Charleston, Inc. Charleston, South Carolina: Walker, Evans & Cogswell Company, 1986.

Claiborne, Craig. *Craig Claiborne's The New York Times Food Encyclopedia.* Compiled by Joan Whitman. New York: Times Books, 1985.

————. *Craig Claiborne's Southern Cooking.* New York: Times Books, 1987.

Classic Desserts from the Dessert Maker: Eagle Brand Sweetened Condensed Milk. Produced by Borden Kitchens. Columbus, Ohio: Borden, Inc., 1984.

Cone, Marcia and Thelma Snyder. *Mastering Microwave Cookery.* New York: Simon & Schuster, 1986.

Cook's Simple and Seasonal Cuisine. Edited by Judith Hill and the Staff of *Cook's* magazine. New York: Simon & Schuster, 1988.

Cooking by the Book: Food in Literature and Culture. Edited by Mary Anne Schofield. Bowling Green, Ohio: Bowling Green State University Popular Press, 1989.

Cooking with Sunshine. Sunkist Kitchens, Sunkist Growers, Inc., B.J. Doerfling, recipe coordinator. New York: Atheneum, 1986.

Corbitt, Helen. *The Corbitt Collection.* Boston: Houghton Mifflin, 1981.

Cost, Bruce. *Bruce Cost's Asian Ingredients,* Foreword by Alice Waters. New York: William Morrow, 1988.

Coyle, L. Patrick. *The World Encyclopedia of Food.* New York: Facts on File, 1982.

Creasy, Rosalind. *Cooking from the Garden.* San Francisco: Sierra Club Books, 1988.

Davidson, Alan. *Seafood, A Connoisseur's Guide and Cookbook.* New York: Simon & Schuster, 1989.

DeBolt, Margaret Wayt with Emma Rylander Law and Carter Olive. *Georgia Entertains.* Nashville: Rutledge Hill Press, 1983.

della Croce, Julia. *Pasta Classica.* San Francisco: Chronicle Books, 1987.

DeMers, John. *Arnaud's Creole Cookbook.* New York: Simon & Schuster, 1988.

Dowell, Philip and Adrian Bailey. *Cooks' Ingredients.* New York: William Morrow, 1980.

Duff, Gail. *A Book of Herbs & Spices: Recipes, Remedies, and Lore.* Topsfield, Massachusetts: Salem House Publishers, 1987.

Egerton, John. *Southern Food.* New York: Alfred A. Knopf, 1987.

Family Circle Recipes America Loves Best. Compiled by Nika Hazelton with the Food Editors of *Family Circle* magazine. New York: Times Books, 1982.

Fast Fabulous Meals. White Plains, New York: Minute Brand Rice, General Foods Corporation, 1989.

Favorite Recipes of The Lower Cape Fear. The Ministering Circle, Wilmington, North Carolina, Revised Edition, 1980.

Fearing, Dean. *The Mansion on Turtle Creek Cookbook.* Edited by Dotty Griffith. New York: Weidenfeld & Nicolson, 1987.

Fobel, Jim. *Jim Fobel's Old-Fashioned Baking Book: Recipes from an American Childhood.* New York: Ballantine Books, 1987; Lake Isle Press paperback, 1995.

Food Editors' Hometown Favorites Cookbook. Edited by Barbara Gibbs Ostmann and Jane Baker for The Newspaper Food Editors and Writers Association, Inc. Maplewood, New Jersey: Hammond, 1984.

Fussell, Betty. *I Hear America Cooking.* New York: Viking, 1986.

Garmey, Jane. *Great British Cooking: A Well Kept Secret.* New York: Random House, 1981.

Goldstein, Joyce. *The Mediterranean Kitchen.* New York: William Morrow, 1989.

The Good Housekeeping All-American Cookbook. New York: Hearst Books, 1987.

Gourmet's Best Desserts. New York: Condé Nast Books, Random House, 1987.

Great Baking Begins with White Lily Flour. Produced by The White Lily Foods Company, Knoxville, Tennessee. Des Moines: Meredith Publishing, 1982.

Greene, Bert. *Greene on Greens.* New York: Workman Publishing, 1984.

———. *The Grains Cookbook.* New York: Workman Publishing, 1988.

Greer, Anne Lindsay. *Cuisine of the American Southwest.* New York: Harper & Row, 1983.

Guste, Roy F., Jr. *Antoine's Restaurant Since 1840 Cookbook.* New York: W.W. Norton, 1980.

———. *The Restaurants of New Orleans.* New York: W.W. Norton, 1982.

Haller, Henry, former White House Chef, with Virginia Aronson, R.D. *The White House Family Cookbook.* New York: Random House, 1987.

Hanley, Rosemary and Peter. *America's Best Recipes: State Fair Blue Ribbon Winners.* Boston: Little, Brown, 1983.

Hardyment, Christina. *From Mangle to Microwave.* Cambridge, England: Polity Press, 1988.

Harris, Marvin. *The Sacred Cow and the Abominable Pig: Riddles of Food and Culture.* New York: Simon & Schuster, A Touchstone Book, 1987.

Hazelton, Nika. *American Home Cooking.* New York: Viking Press, 1980.

———. *Nika Hazelton's Pasta Cookbook.* New York: Ballantine Books, 1984.

Heatter, Maida. *Maida Heatter's New Book of Great Desserts.* New York: Alfred A. Knopf, 1982.

Hershey's Fabulous Desserts. Hershey, Pennsylvania: Hershey Foods Corporation, 1989.

Hooker, Richard J. *A History: Food and Drink in America.* Indianapolis/New York: Bobbs-Merrill, 1981.

Horry, Harriott Pinckney. *A Colonial Plantation Cookbook: The Receipt Book of Harriott Pinckney Horry, 1770.* Facsimile Edition edited by Richard J. Hooker. Columbia, South Carolina: University of South Carolina Press, 1984.

Igoe, Robert S. *Dictionary of Food Ingredients,* Second Edition. New York: Van Nostrand Reinhold, 1989.

Iowa State Fair Blue Ribbon Recipes. Compiled by the Iowa State Fair. Audubon, Iowa: Jumbo Jack's Cookbook Co., 1982.

Ivens, Dorothy. *Main-Course Soups & Stews.* New York: Harper & Row, 1983.

James, Ted and Rosalind Cole. *The Waldorf-Astoria Cookbook,* Golden Anniversary Edition. New York: Bramhall House, 1981.

Johner, Martin and Gary Goldberg. *Mountains of Chocolate.* New York: Irena Chalmers Cookbooks, 1981.

Johnson, Ronald. *The American Table.* New York: William Morrow, 1984.

Jones, Judith and Evan. *The Book of Bread.* New York: HarperPerennial, 1982.

Kafka, Barbara. *The Microwave Gourmet.* New York: William Morrow, 1987.

Kittler, Pamela G. and Kathryn Sucher. *Food and Culture in America.* New York: Van Nostrand Reinhold, 1989.

Krohn, Norman Odya. *Menu Mystique: The Diner's Guide to Fine Food & Drink.* Middle Village, New York: Jonathan David Publishers, 1983.

La Place, Viana and Evan Kleiman. *Cucina Fresca.* New York: Harper & Row, 1985.

Larousse Gastronomique: The New American Edition. Jennifer Harvey Lang, editor. New York: Crown, 1988.

Levenstein, Harvey. *Revolution at the Table: The Transformation of the American Diet.* New York: Oxford University Press, 1988.

Linck, Ernestine Sewell and Joyce Gibson Roach. *Eats: A Folk History of Texas Foods.* Fort Worth: Texas Christian University Press, 1989.

The Los Angeles Times California Cookbook. Compiled and Edited by Betsy Balsley, Food Editor, and the Food Staff of the *Los Angeles Times.* New York: New American Library, 1981.

Luncheonette: Ice-Cream, Beverage, and Sandwich Recipes from the Golden Age of the Soda Fountain. Edited by Patricia M. Kelly. New York: Crown, 1989.

Madison, Deborah. *The Greens Cook Book* with Edward Espe Brown. New York: Bantam Books, 1987.

Martha White's Southern Sampler. Produced by Martha White Foods, Inc., Nashville: Rutledge Hill Press, 1989.

McGee, Harold. *On Food and Cooking: The Science and Lore of the Kitchen.* New York: Scribner's, 1984.

McGrath, Molly Wade. *Top Sellers, USA.* New York: William Morrow, 1983.

Méras, Phyllis with Linda Glick Conway. *The New Carry-Out Cuisine.* Boston: Houghton Mifflin, 1986.

Morash, Marian. *The Victory Garden Cookbook.* New York: Alfred A. Knopf, 1982.

Myers, Barbara. *Chocolate, Chocolate, Chocolate.* New York: Rawson Associates, 1983.

Nathan, Joan. *An American Folklife Cookbook.* New York: Schocken Books, 1984.

Neal, Bill. *Bill Neal's Southern Cooking.* Chapel Hill, North Carolina: University of North Carolina Press, 1985.

The New Good Housekeeping Cookbook. Edited by Mildred Ying, director, food department, Good Housekeeping Institute. New York: Hearst Books, 1986.

The Official 1985 Kentucky State Fair Cookbook. Edited by Deni Hamilton. Louisville, Kentucky: Foodwork, Inc., 1986.

The Old Country Cookbook. Chisholm, Minnesota: The Iron Range Interpretative Center, 1983.

100 Best Recipes for 100 Years from McCormick. John W. Felton, editor. Produced by McCormick & Company, Baltimore. Elmsford, New York: The Benjamin Company, 1988.

The Original Tennessee Homecoming Cookbook. Edited by Daisy King. Nashville, Tennessee: Rutledge Hill Press, 1985.

Panati, Charles. *Panati's Browser's Book of Beginnings.* Boston: Houghton Mifflin, 1984.

———. *Panati's Extraordinary Origins of Everyday Things.* New York: HarperCollins, 1987.

The Picayune's Creole Cook Book. Sesquicentennial Edition. Marcelle Bienvenu, editor. New Orleans: *The Times-Picayune,* 1987.

Prudhomme, Paul. *Chef Paul Prudhomme's Louisiana Kitchen.* New York: William Morrow, 1984.

Puck, Wolfgang. *The Wolfgang Puck Cookbook.* New York: Random House, 1986.

Rice, William. *Feasts of Wine and Food.* New York: William Morrow, 1987.

Root, Waverley. *Food.* New York: Simon & Schuster, 1980.

Rosso, Julee and Sheila Lukins with Sarah Leah Chase. *The Silver Palate Good Times Cookbook.* New York: Workman, 1984.

———. *The New Basics Cookbook.* New York: Workman, 1989.

Sax, Richard with Sandra Gluck. *From The Farmer's Market.* New York: Harper & Row, 1986.

Schneider, Elizabeth. *Uncommon Fruits & Vegetables, A Commonsense Guide.* New York: Harper & Row, 1986.

Shapiro, Laura. *Perfection Salad.* New York: Farrar, Straus and Giroux, 1986.

Simmons, Marie. *365 Ways To Cook Pasta.* A John Boswell Associates Book. New York: Harper & Row, 1988.

Sokolov, Raymond. *Fading Feast.* New York: Farrar, Straus & Giroux, 1982.

The Star of Texas Cookbook. By The Junior League of Houston, Inc. New York: Doubleday, 1983.

Stehle, Audrey P. *Southern Living Microwave Cooking Made Easy.* Birm-

ingham, Alabama: Oxmoor House, 1987.

Stern, Jane and Michael. *Square Meals.* New York: Alfred A. Knopf, 1984.

———. *Real American Food.* New York: Alfred A. Knopf, 1986.

———. *A Taste of America.* Kansas City/New York: Andrews and McMeel, 1988.

Stewart, Louise. *Grant Corner Inn Breakfast & Brunch Cookbook.* Santa Fe, New Mexico: Grant Corner Inn, 1986.

Stewart, Martha. *Entertaining.* New York: Clarkson N. Potter, 1982.

Stobart, Tom. *The Cook's Encyclopedia: Ingredients & Processes.* Edited by Millie Owen. New York: Harper & Row, 1980.

———. *Herbs, Spices and Flavorings.* Woodstock, New York: Overlook Press, 1982.

Storer, Fern. *Recipes Remembered: A Collection of Modernized Nostalgia.* Covington, Kentucky: Highland House Books, 1989.

Szathmáry, Louis. *The Bakery Restaurant Cookbook.* Boston: CBI Publishing Company, 1981.

Tannahill, Reay. *Food in History: The New, Fully Revised, and Updated Edition.* New York: Crown, 1988.

Taste of the South. Compiled by The Symphony League of Jackson, Mississippi, 1984.

Thorne, John. *Simple Cooking.* New York: Viking, 1987.

200 Favorite Brand Name Recipes. By the Editors of Consumer Guide. New York: Prince Paperbacks, Crown Publishing, 1984.

Velveeta Creative Cooking. Glenview, Illinois: Kraft, Inc., 1989.

Vidinghoff, Carol and Patricia Kelly. *Luncheonette: Ice Cream, Beverage and Sandwich Recipes from the Golden Age of the Soda Fountain.* New York: Crown, 1989.

Villas, James. *American Taste.* New York: Arbor House, 1982.

Visser, Margaret. *Much Depends on Dinner.* New York: Macmillan, 1986.

von Welanetz, Diana and Paul. *The von Welanetz Guide to Ethnic Ingredients.* Los Angeles: J.P. Tarcher, 1982.

Walsh, Marie T. *Supermarket Gourmet.* Darien, Connecticut: CCC Publications, 1989.

Ward, Patricia A. *Farm Journal's Best-Ever Cookies.* New York: Doubleday, 1980.

———. *Farm Journal's Best-Ever Pies.* New York: Doubleday, 1981.

Warner, Joie. *The Complete Book of Chicken Wings.* New York: Hearst Books, 1985.

Waters, Alice. *Chez Panisse Menu Cookbook.* New York: Random House, 1982.

Weaver, William Woys. *America Eats.* New York: Harper & Row, 1989.

Wisconsin State Fair Favorites. West Allis/Milwaukee: Wisconsin State Fair, 1981.

Wolfert, Paula. *Paula Wolfert's World of Food.* New York: Harper & Row, 1988.

BOOKS PUBLISHED IN THE 1990s

A Taste of San Francisco. Produced by The San Francisco Symphony. New York: Doubleday, 1990.

Algren, Nelson. *America Eats: The Iowa Szathmáry Culinary Arts Series.* Iowa City: University of Iowa Press, 1992.

America's Favorite Food: The Story of Campbell Soup Company. Historical text by Douglas Collins, foreword by Nathalie Dupree. New York: Harry N. Abrams, 1994.

An American Bounty: Great Contemporary Cooking from the Culinary Institute of America. New York: Rizzoli, 1995.

Anderson, Jean and Elaine Hanna. *Micro Ways.* New York: Doubleday, 1990.

———, and Hedy Würz. *The New German Cookbook.* New York: Harper Collins, 1993.

Anderson, Judith. *Best Recipes of the Great Food Companies.* Berkeley, California: Ten Speed Press, 1992.

Andrews, Glenn. *Food from the Heartland.* New York: Simon & Schuster, 1991.

Behr, Edward. *The Artful Eater.* New York: Atlantic Monthly Press, 1992.

Belk, Sarah. *Around the Southern Table.* New York: Simon & Schuster, 1991.

Benning, Lee Edwards. *The Cook's Tales.* Old Saybrook, Connecticut: Globe Pequot Press, 1992.

———. *Oh, Fudge!* New York: Henry Holt, 1990.

Bennion, Marion. *Introductory Foods, Ninth Edition.* New York: Macmillan, 1990.

Best-Ever Recipes, Volume III, Family Circle. New York: Family Circle Books, 1992.

Best of Beef, 1992 National Beef Cook-Off. Recipes compiled by American National CattleWomen, Inc., Englewood, Colorado, 1992 in cooperation with The Beef Industry Council and the Beef Board, Beef Industry Council and Cattlemen's Beef Promotion and Research Board.

The Best of Food & Wine: Vegetables, Salads & Grains. New York: American Express Publishing, 1993.

The Best of Food & Wine: 1990 through 1995 Collections. New York: American Express Publishing.

Better Homes and Gardens Complete Guide to Food and Cooking. Des Moines: Meredith Corporation, 1991.

Bissell, Frances. *The Book of Food.* Foreword by Alice Waters. New York: Henry Holt, 1994.

Bittman, Mark. *Fish: The Complete Guide to Buying and Cooking.* New York: Macmillan, 1994.

Bloom, Carole. *The International Dictionary of Desserts, Pastries, and Confections.* New York: Hearst Books, 1995.

Borden 135th Anniversary Cookbook. Produced by the Home Economists of the Borden Kitchens. Columbus, Ohio: Borden, Inc., 1992.

Butel, Jane. *Jane Butel's Southwestern Kitchen.* New York: HP Books, 1994.

Campbell's Best-Ever Recipes, 125th Anniversary Edition. Pat Teberg, editor. Camden, New Jersey: Publishing Division of Campbell Soup Company, 1994.

Celebrating 20 Years of the National Beef Cook-Off. Published by American National CattleWomen, Inc. in cooperation with The Beef Industry Council and Beef Board, 1994.

Chalmers, Irena. *The Great Food Almanac.* San Francisco: Collins Publishers, 1994.

The Chicken Cookbook (featuring recipes from the 41st National Chicken Cooking Contest). Produced by the National Broiler Council. New York: Dell, 1995.

Claiborne, Craig. *The New York Times Cook Book,* Revised Edition. New York: Harper & Row, 1990.

Clark, Robert. *James Beard: A Biography.* New York: HarperCollins, 1993.

Clayton, Bernard. *Bernard Clayton's Cooking Across America.* New York: Simon & Schuster, 1993.

Come on In! Produced by The Junior League of Jackson, Inc., Jackson, Mississippi, 1991.

The Complete Book of Baking. Produced by The Pillsbury Company, Minneapolis. New York: Viking, 1993.

Complete Guide to Food and Cooking. Better Homes and Gardens. Des Moines: Meredith, 1991.

Darling, Benjamin. *Helpful Hints for Housewives!* San Francisco: Chronicle Books, 1992.

Davidson, Alan. *Fruit: A Connoisseur's Guide and Cookbook.* New York: Simon & Schuster, 1991.

Davis, James W. *Aristocrat in Burlap: A History of the Potato in Idaho.* Published by the Idaho Potato Commission, 1992.

Designed for Living Corning Cookbook. Edited by Cornelius O'Donnell. Garden City Park, New York: Avery Publishing Group, 1993.

DeWitt, Dave and Nancy Gerlach. *The Whole Chile Pepper Book.* Boston: Little, Brown, 1990.

Downard, Georgia Chan and Jean Galton. *365 Great Soups & Stews.* A John Boswell Associates Book. New York: HarperCollins, 1996.

Egerton, John. *Side Orders.* Atlanta: Peachtree Publishers, 1990.

The Encyclopedia of New York City. Edited by Kenneth T. Jackson. New Haven, Connecticut: Yale University Press in cooperation with The New-York Historical Society, 1995.

The Family Circle Cookbook: New Tastes for New Times. By the Editors of *Family Circle* and David Ricketts. New York: Simon & Schuster, 1992.

The Flavors of Bon Appétit 1995. By the Editors of *Bon Appétit.* New York: Condé Nast Books, Pantheon, 1995.

Fobel, Jim. *The Whole Chicken Cookbook.* New York: Ballantine Books, 1992.

Friedland, Susan R. *The Passover Table.* New York: HarperPerennial, 1994.

Fussell, Betty. *The Story of Corn.* New York: Alfred A. Knopf, 1992.

———. *Crazy for Corn.* New York: HarperPerennial, 1995.

The Good Housekeeping Illustrated Book of Desserts. Edited by Mildred Ying, director, food department, Good Housekeeping Institute. New York: William Morrow, 1991.

Goodwin, Betty. *Hollywood du Jour: Lost Recipes of Legendary Hollywood Haunts.* Santa Monica, California: Angel City Press, 1993.

Gourmet's In Short Order. New York: Condé Nast Books, Random House, 1993.

Great American Brand Name Baking. Produced by Publications International, Ltd. New York: Smithmark, 1992.

Griffith, Dotty. *Gourmet Grains, Beans, & Rice.* Dallas: Taylor Publishing Company, 1992.

Griffith, Linda and Fred. *The New American Farm Cookbook.* New York: Viking Studio Books, 1993.

———. *Onions, Onions, Onions.* Shelburne, Vermont: Chapters, 1994.

Hayes, Joanne Lamb and Bonnie Tandy Leblang. *Grains.* New York: Harmony Books, 1995.

Herbst, Sharon Tyler. *Food Lover's Companion.* Hauppauge, New York: Barron's Educational Series, 1990.

Hess, Karen. *The Carolina Rice Kitchen: The African Connection.* Columbia, South Carolina: University of South Carolina Press, 1992.

Hillburn, Prudence. *A Treasury of Southern Baking.* New York: HarperPerennial, 1993.

Hoffman, Mabel. *Mabel Hoffman's Crockery Cookery,* Revised and Updated Edition. New York: HP Books, 1995.

The James Beard Celebration Cookbook. Edited by Barbara Kafka. Produced by The James Beard Foundation. New York: William Morrow, 1990.

Jamison, Cheryl Alters and Bill. *Texas Home Cooking.* Boston: Harvard Common Press, 1993.

———. *The Border Cookbook: Authentic Home Cooking of the American Southwest and Northwest Mexico.* Boston: Harvard Common Press, 1995.

Kagel, Katharine. *Cafe Pasqual's Cookbook: Spirited Recipes from Santa Fe.* San Francisco: Chronicle Books, 1993.

Kellogg Kitchens Favorite Recipes Cookbook. Battle Creek, Michigan: Kellogg Company, 1991.

Khalsa, Baba S. *Great Vegetables from the Great Chefs.* Introduction by M.F.K. Fisher. San Francisco: Chronicle Books, 1990.

Kimball, Marie. *Thomas Jefferson's Cook Book.* Charlottesville: University Press of Virginia, 1993.

King Arthur Flour 200th Anniversary Cookbook. Published by Sands, Taylor & Wood Company, Norwich, Vermont. Lebanon, New Hampshire: Whitman Press, 1990.

Kirlin, Katherine S. and Thomas M. *Smithsonian Folklife Cookbook.* Washington, D.C.: Smithsonian Institution Press, 1991.

Kochilas, Diane. *The Food and Wine of Greece.* New York: St. Martin's Press, 1990.

Kreag, Judy. *Lake Superior's North Shore in Good Taste.* Kuttawa, Kentucky: McClanahan Publishing House, 1991.

Krondl, Michael. *Around the American Table: Treasured Recipes and Food Traditions from the American Cookery Collections of The New York Public Library.* Holbrook, Massachusetts: Adams Publishing, 1995.

Land O Lakes Treasury of Country Recipes. Produced by the Land O'Lakes Test Kitchens, Minneapolis, with assistance from Robin Krause and Barbara Strand. Montreal, Canada: Tormont Publications, 1992.

Lee, Hilde Gabriel. *Taste of the States: A Food History of America.* Charlottesville, Virginia: Howell Press, 1992.

Lomonaco, Michael with Donna Forsman. *The "21" Cookbook: Recipes and Lore from New York's Fabled Restaurant.* New York: Doubleday, 1995.

Longbotham, Lori and Marie Simmons. *Better by Microwave: Over 250 Recipes for the Foods Microwave Does Best.* New York: Dutton, 1990.

Loomis, Susan Herrmann. *Farm House Cookbook.* New York: Workman Publishing, 1991.

Lovegren, Sylvia. *Fashionable Food.* New York: Macmillan, 1995.

Madison, Deborah. *The Savory Way.* New York: Bantam Books, 1990.

Malgieri, Nick. *How To Bake: The Complete Guide to Perfect Cakes, Cookies, Pies, Tarts, Breads, Pizzas, Muffins,*

Sweet and Savory. New York: HarperCollins, 1995.

Mariani, John F. *America Eats Out: An Illustrated History of Restaurants, Taverns, Coffee Shops, Speakeasies, and Other Establishments That Have Fed Us for 350 Years.* New York: William Morrow, 1991.

———. *The Dictionary of American Food and Drink,* Revised and Updated Edition. New York: Hearst Books, 1994.

Martha Washington's Booke of Cookery and Booke of Sweetmeats. Transcribed by Karen Hess. New York: Columbia University Press, 1995.

McCormick/Schilling's New Spice Cookbook. Produced by McCormick & Company, Baltimore. Edited by Jack Felton. White Plains, New York: The Benjamin Company, 1994.

McKenzie, William A. *Dining Car Line to the Pacific.* St. Paul: Minnesota Historical Society Press, 1990.

McLaughlin, Michael. *The Back of the Box Gourmet.* New York: Simon & Schuster, 1990.

———. *More Back of the Box Gourmet.* New York: Simon & Schuster, 1994.

———. *The New American Kitchen.* New York: Simon & Schuster, 1990.

Medrich, Alice. *Chocolate.* New York: Warner Books, 1990.

Mendelson, Anne. *Stand Facing the Stove: The Story of The Women Who Gave America The Joy of Cooking.* New York: Henry Holt, 1996.

Meyer, Danny and Michael Romano. *The Union Square Cafe Cookbook.* New York: HarperCollins, 1994.

Miller, Mark with John Harrisson, photography by Lois Ellen Frank. *The Great Chile Book.* Berkeley, California: Ten Speed Press, 1991.

Neal, Bill. *Biscuits, Spoonbread, and Sweet Potato Pie.* New York: Alfred A. Knopf, 1990.

O'Neill, Molly. *New York Cookbook.* New York: Workman, 1992.

Over 100 Ways to Bring Out the Best. Englewood Cliffs, New Jersey: Hellmann's Mayonnaise, Best Foods, CPC International, 1990.

Passmore, Jacki. *The Encyclopedia of Asian Food and Cooking.* New York: William Morrow, 1991.

Peterson, James. *Splendid Soups.* New York: Bantam Books, 1993.

The Pillsbury Bake-Off Cookbook. Produced by The Pillsbury Company, Minneapolis; Diane B. Anderson, managing editor. New York: Doubleday, 1990.

Pillsbury Bake-Off Grand Prize Winners. Minneapolis, Minnesota: The Pillsbury Company, 1995.

The Pillsbury Cookbook. Produced by The Pillsbury Company. New York: Bantam Books, 1996.

Pinderhughes, John. *Family of the Spirit Cookbook: Recipes and Remembrances from African-American Kitchens.* New York: Simon & Schuster, 1990.

Porterfield, James D. *Dining by Rail: The History and the Recipes of America's Golden Age of Railroad Cuisine.* New York: St. Martin's Press, 1993.

The Quaker Oats Treasury of Best Recipes. From the kitchens of The Quaker Oats Company. New York: Smithmark, 1992.

Quick & Easy Casseroles. Durkee, Reckitt & Colman, Inc., 1992.

Reader's Digest Down Home Cooking the New, Healthier Way. Gayla Visalli, project editor. Pleasantville, New York: The Reader's Digest Association, Inc., 1994.

Sax, Richard. *Classic Home Desserts.* Shelburne, Vermont: Chapters, 1994.

Schremp, Gerry. *Kitchen Culture: Fifty Years of Food Fads.* New York: Pharos Books, 1991.

Schulz, Phillip Stephen. *Celebrating America.* New York: Simon & Schuster, 1994.

Scicolone, Michele. *La Dolce Vita.* New York: William Morrow, 1993.

Sheraton, Mimi. *From My Mother's Kitchen,* Revised Edition. New York: HarperCollins, 1991.

———. *The Whole World Loves Chicken Soup.* New York: Warner Books, 1995.

Shields, John. *The Chesapeake Bay Cookbook.* Reading, Massachusetts: Aris Books, 1990.

Simmons, Marie. *Rice, The Amazing Grain.* New York: Henry Holt, 1991.

———. *Bar Cookies A to Z.* Shelburne, Vermont: Chapters, 1994.

Smith, Andrew. *The Tomato in America: Early History, Culture and Cookery.* Columbia, South Carolina: University of South Carolina Press, 1994.

Stallworth, Lyn and Rod Kennedy, Jr. *The County Fair Cookbook.* New York: Hyperion, 1994.

Staten, Vince. *Can You Trust a Tomato in January?* New York: Simon & Schuster, 1993.

Stern, Jane and Michael. *American Gourmet.* New York: HarperCollins, 1991.

Sunset All-Time Favorite Recipes. By the Editors of Sunset Books and Sunset Magazine. Menlo Park, California: Sunset Publishing Corporation, 1993.

Sunset Kitchen Cabinet. By the Editors of Sunset Books and Sunset Magazine. Menlo Park, California: Sunset Publishing Corporation, 1995.

Sunset Recipe Annual: 1996 Edition. By the Editors of Sunset Magazine and Sunset Books. Menlo Park, California: Sunset Publishing Corporation, 1995.

Tennyson, Jeffrey. *Hamburger Heaven: The Illustrated History of the Hamburger.* New York: Hyperion, 1993.

Thorne, John with Matt Lewis Thorne. *Outlaw Cook.* New York: Farrar, Straus & Giroux, 1992.

Trager, James. *The Food Chronology.* New York: Henry Holt, 1995.

Uncle Ben's 50th Anniversary Cookbook. Houston, Texas: Uncle Ben's, Inc., 1993.

Unterman, Patricia. *Patricia Unterman's Food Lover's Guide to San Francisco.* San Francisco: Chronicle Books, 1995.

Urvater, Michele. *Monday to Friday Pasta.* New York: Workman, 1995.

Villas, James with Martha Pearl Villas. *My Mother's Southern Kitchen: Recipes and Reminiscences.* New York: Macmillan, 1994.

Voltz, Jeanne and Caroline Stuart. *The Florida Cookbook: From Gulf Coast Gumbo to Key Lime Pie.* New York: Alfred A. Knopf, 1993.

Weaver, William Woys. *Pennsylvania Dutch Country Cooking.* New York: Abbeville Press, 1993.

Wells, Patricia. *Patricia Wells' Trattoria.* New York: William Morrow, 1993.

The Woman's Day Cookbook. Edited by Kathy Farrell-Kingsley and the Editors of *Woman's Day.* New York: Viking, 1995.

Wyman, Carolyn. *I'm a Spam Fan.* Stamford, Connecticut: Longmeadow Press, 1993.

Yankee's Favorite Recipes: Over 100 of the Finest Recipes from Yankee Magazine. Dublin, New Hampshire: Yankee Publishing, 1990.

Ziedrich, Linda. *Cold Soups.* Boston: Harvard Common Press, 1995.

UNDATED BOOKS AND PUBLICATIONS

Child, Lydia Maria. *The American Frugal Housewife.* Boston: Carter, Hendee, and Company, 1833; Facsimile of Twelfth Edition, published in cooperation with Old Sturbridge Village. Bedford, Massachusetts: A George Dawson Book, Applewood Books.

Cook's World Tour Around Elmira. A Collection of Choice Recipes from Many Lands. Contributed by Members and Friends of the International Club of the Elmira Y.W.C.A. Elmira, New York.

Festive Foods for The Holiday Season. Produced by the Home Service Department, Milwaukee Gas Light Company. Milwaukee, Wisconsin.

Wonderful Ways with Soups . . . from Campbell's. Published by Campbell Soup Company, Camden, New Jersey.

INDEX

INDEX

A member of the James Beard Who's Who of Food and Wine in America, JEAN ANDERSON is the author of more than twenty cookbooks, among them the award-winning *Food of Portugal* and the best-selling *Doubleday Cookbook* (with Elaine Hanna), which was named Cookbook of the Year in the R.T. French Tastemaker Awards. She writes regularly for *Gourmet*, *Food & Wine*, *Family Circle*, *Bon Appètit*, and other national magazines. Jean Anderson divides her time between Chapel Hill, North Carolina, and New York City.